Praise for Vince Emery's previous editions of *How to Grow Your Business on the Internet*

"Tops on our list of suggestions is Emery's book. In fact, if you're in business, our advice is to do nothing about the Internet until you've read this book . . . a nuts-and-bolts, tell-it-like-it-is account of business in the real world, which certainly includes the Internet. Having worked for the Net for commercial operations, and having been a consultant for Fortune 500 companies as well as small businesses, Emery has the background to know what he's talking about. For you, the book can be a lifesaver."
    —Earl Selby, *PC Paper*

"I love your book. It has become my 'Internet Bible.' Thank you for writing it."
    —Robert Freeman, Manager, Electronic Commerce, Xerox Corporation

"At last, a book about doing business on the Internet I can endorse wholeheartedly. If you're serious about putting your business or organization on the Internet, Emery's book **will cut months off your learning curve and steer you away from some expensive, easy-to-make mistakes.** Written in a clear style for the non-technical reader and full of practical advice, **this is a breakthrough book, easily worth ten times its cover price.**"
    —Ken McCarthy, *Internet Gazette*/E-Media, ken@e-media.com

"I would like to say the your book is GREAT! I spent 6 hours in the bookstore comparing and reading different Internet business books, but could not find any that came even close to your book."
    —Tony, NetVoyage

"One of the top 10 business builder books."
    —*Ads Plus*

"Because of this show, I get sent literally every single book that's ever published about online computing, and I consider it part of my job to go through and evaluate each one. (This is) **by far the best book I've ever read about business on the Internet.**"
    —Jaclyn Easton, Host, *Log On USA*

"My only problem was that I only brought one 50-sheet pack of little Post-It Notes, and I found so many points I wanted to mark for future reference that I had to start tearing them in half. Whether you're thinking of launching an Internet-based business, plan to use the Internet to enhance your current business, or just want a better understanding of how the Internet is being used for business, then (I *never* say this, but here goes): *How to Grow Your Business on the Internet* is **the only Internet business book you need to buy. Period.**"
    —Art Siegel, *SalesDoctors*

"I've read about ten books on the Internet and must say yours is **by far the most informative** to startup organizations like mine. As a businessperson first, graphic designer second, I really appreciated the case studies and marketing tips. **Thanks for jump-starting my brain!**"

  —Jay Sharpe

"Just read your *How to Grow Your Business on the Internet* and I liked it very much. You're the only one (out of the 12 other marketing Internet books I've read) that **shows a genuine expertise. Definitely the best book out there:** In my bibliography I rate it a 96."

  —Dan Dunne, Ph.D., Torrance, California

"Vince Emery's book is a welcome source of information, inspiration, and support. This book has something for everyone who wants to mix business with the Internet. Whether you are an independent contractor, a sole proprietor of a home-based business, the owner of a small establishment, or an executive in a large company, **this book can help you make more money.**"

  —Ray Lischner, *Computer Bits*

"I had to write to tell you how fantastic your book is. I consider it **the 'Bible' of real business facts relating to the Internet.** Thank you, thank you, thank you for writing a book **for business people rather than techies.**"

  —Shari Peterson, WEBster Group International, St. Louis, Missouri

"Vince Emery's *How to Grow Your Business on the Internet* **gives tested, practical answers** to business questions about the Internet, from assessing the system's potentials for a particular business pursuit to using digital cash on the information superhighway. There are plenty of theories out there on how to use Internet services to advance business pursuits; this is **one of the few to provide practical applications.**"

  —*Bookwatch*

"My overall impression of your book *How to Grow Your Business on the Internet* is WOW ! ! ! ! ! ! ! ! ! ! and WOW ! ! ! ! ! ! ! ! !"

  —Michael Truitt

"Vince Emery's *How to Grow Your Business on the Internet* is a thorough introduction to the value of the Internet as a business tool. The book is well-written, often quite funny, and **focuses on the needs and concerns of non-technical business users.** Emery's attitude throughout the book is that 'The computers aren't important. They are only the tools,' a perspective that results in a rich discussion of how to apply Internet tools to business strategy rather than how to use or install particular tools."

  —Jacqueline Justice, *Internet Bulletin for CPAs*

"I read it cover to cover twice. I think it is a great book and it will help our directory on the Internet succeed. Your book is the **single most important tool I have used** to begin this project"
—John Kerzman, Joss Worldwide

"A **great job of addressing the issues** that will confront anyone who tries and gets his/her company online. The book is organized and very well-written, and it's **packed with information**. While many business-on-the-Internet books are just get-rich-quick schemes, this one is **a great, practical guide** through an issue that's facing more and more corporations. **A** (highest rating)"
—WKC, *The Net* magazine

"Many thanks for your excellent book. We have our site going now and I'm sure the immense amount of clear and specific information will help use our pages effectively. An exceptional book, **by far the most useful**."
—Michael Linehan, Model Mugging of BC

"**Everything you need to know to understand this new medium** is explained in layman's terms. Yes, Emery uses plenty of Net-specific terminology, but he explains each term first. He also goes into **more detail than any other book I've seen on how to deal with financial transactions on the Net**. If you have any interest in making the Internet/World Wide Web work for you, **this is the guide you should read** before trying."
—J.R. Wilson, *Computer Edge*

"The book is an absolute and total peach. We are in the planning stages of setting up our Web presence, and it is if God heard what we needed and dropped your book in my hands. It is **the most down-to-earth, practical guide there is**."
—Larry Rood, Gryphon House, Inc.

"This book takes an honest look at the potential for businesses to use and benefit from the Internet . . . There is a checklist of what you'll need and information on how much it will cost. Emery has done **a better job than other Internet business authors on coverage of the day-to-day details** of running an Internet-connected business, and he deals with issues like credit card billings and billed accounts in a straightforward manner."
—*Database* magazine

"Three cheers! Three cheers! *How to Grow Your Business on the Internet* is absolutely wonderful! I have been writing my own curricula for several years, and yours is so good, I want to burn all of mine! Thanks again for a wonderful resource."
—Wendy Hooks Bannon, University of Pittsburgh

"This is **an extremely practical book**, chock-full of tips, anecdotes, statistics, and case studies. Devoid of much of the hype which characterises many other Internet business books, the well-written chapters provide an excellent overview of business issues ranging from Internet connectivity and reference material to market research and EDI. In sum, this is **an excellent guide for businesses venturing onto the Internet**. The information is concise and comprehensive. The presence of an online companion is also a welcome addition."
   —Madanmohan Rao, United Nations Communications Director, in *I-World*

"I just bought your book and I was extremely pleased with it. I have been Internet marketing since April and had to laugh at some of the mistakes I could have avoided if I had read the book first."
   —T.J. Quesnel, Due North Marketing

"This book provides much more than another review of basic Net terminology or tips on creating an attractive WWW home page. Vince Emery addresses cost considerations, questions to ask of your service provider or consultant, how to get top management involved, and ways to use the Internet to generate strategic marketing information for your firm."
   —*GATF World*

"What a terrific book you've written. It really focuses on the business issues, and it **makes what is highly complex easy to understand**. Lots and lots of common sense."
   —Dodge Johnson, Educational Consultant

"The only Internet book by someone actually involved in business and sympathetic to business concerns—such as losing money."
   —Michael Finley, *St. Paul Pioneer Press*

"It is written clearly, interspersed with practical examples and suggestions . . . This is a worthwhile publication which actually makes (readers) think and understand the underlying motives of Net marketing and Internet technology without treating them like morons. This should be considered as a highly desirable read for anyone considering moving into Net marketing. **Treat it as one of the ten Internet commandments.**"
   —*Internet Business News*

"Before you empty your savings account and sign yourself onto the uncharted waters, definitely pick up this book for some advice."
   —Judith Zausner, *Mauger*

"Vince Emery is one of the more enlightened of the people writing about business use of the Net."
   —Prof. Bob O'Keefe, *Net Value*

"Vince Emery is one of the 25 most influential people in Internet marketing."
 —Mark Grimes, Grimes Communications

"Thanks for your incredible book. I started trying to market on the Net a year ago. After trying several advertising options, I dismissed the Internet as a marketing medium. Basically, I failed miserably in my marketing/advertising on the Internet. About six months ago I picked up your book on a recommendation from a friend. I read it and started applying your tips and strategies to my Internet marketing. That started an upward journey and I've never looked back. **Thank you for changing the course of my business and my life.**"
 —Scott Haines, Haines Publishing Company

Subject: Complaint Department
To: vince@emery.com

TO: VINCE EMERY

RE: HOW TO GROW YOUR BUSINESS ON THE INTERNET

Dear Mr. Emery:

I am very sorry to have to register this complaint about your book.
I was halfway through reading it when I suddenly realized the book
was such a valuable asset that I could no longer keep it in my house.

I now keep the book at my bank in a safe deposit box. Unfortunately,
this means I can only access the book during banking hours. This is
really frustrating because your book is the most fact-filled and
comprehensive source of doing business on the Internet I have been
able to find (and believe me I've been looking!).

Please do not write any more books as I only have a very small safe
deposit box (besides the people in my bank are starting to look at me
suspiciously because of my frequent visits to the vault).

Yours in humor,

Dan Hayner
hayner@computek.net

How to Grow Your
Business
on the
Internet
3rd Edition

Vince Emery

CORIOLIS GROUP BOOKS

an International Thomson Publishing company I(T)P®

Albany, NY ▪ Belmont, CA ▪ Bonn ▪ Boston ▪ Cincinnati ▪ Detroit ▪ Johannesburg ▪ London ▪ Madrid ▪
Melbourne ▪ Mexico City ▪ New York ▪ Paris ▪ Singapore ▪ Tokyo ▪ Toronto ▪ Washington

PUBLISHER	**KEITH WEISKAMP**
PROJECT EDITOR	**ANN WAGGONER AKEN**
COPYEDITOR	**ANN WAGGONER AKEN**
COVER ARTIST	**GARY SMITH/PERFORMANCE DESIGN**
COVER DESIGN	**ANTHONY STOCK**
INTERIOR DESIGN	**MICHELLE STROUP**
LAYOUT PRODUCTION	**CHRIS ROGERS/NOMI SCHALIT**
PROOFREADER	**DENISE CONSTANTINE**
INDEXER	**VINCE EMERY**

How to Grow Your Business on the Internet, 3rd Edition
Copyright © 1997 by The Coriolis Group, Inc.

Limits of Liability and Disclaimer of Warranty

The author and publisher of this book have used their best efforts in preparing the book and the programs contained in it. These efforts include the development, research, and testing of the theories and programs to determine their effectiveness. The author and publisher make no warranty of any kind, expressed or implied, with regard to these programs or the documentation contained in this book.

The author and publisher shall not be liable in the event of incidental or consequential damages in connection with, or arising out of, the furnishing, performance, or use of the programs, associated instructions, and/or claims of productivity gains.

Trademarks

Trademarked names appear throughout this book. Rather than list the names and entities that own the trademarks or insert a trademark symbol with each mention of the trademarked name, the publisher states that it is using the names for editorial purposes only and to the benefit of the trademark owner, with no intention of infringing upon that trademark.

The Coriolis Group, Inc.
An International Thomson Publishing Company
14455 N. Hayden Road, Suite 220
Scottsdale, Arizona 85260
602/483-0192
FAX 602/483-0193
http://www.coriolis.com

Printed in the United States of America
10 9 8 7 6 5 4 3 2

To my grandmother, Alice Emery, who I am always glad to see.

And to the memory of my late grandfather, Emmett Emery, who once observed that I love to read so much that if I were running out of a burning house and saw a newspaper, I'd stop to read it.

He was right.

Contents

Introduction

"If you don't know where you're going, you probably won't get there."

—Yogi Berra

Let's bust two myths about Internet business.

The first myth is "Nobody buys anything on the Internet." To lay that lie to rest, I propose a club: **Emery's Hundred Million Dollar Club**. Members must sell at least $100 million on the Internet in a year:

- **Digital Equipment Corp.** has sold more than $150 million online every year since 1995.

- **3Com**'s Web site sells "several hundred million dollars" per year, according to chairman Eric Benhamou.

- **Amazon.com**'s Web site sells more than $25 million worth of books per quarter.

- The **Fort Worth Department of Housing and Urban Development** sells more than $2 million worth of real estate every week in Web-based auctions.

- Broker **Charles Schwab & Co.** makes more than $234,000,000 per year in commissions on trades from all online sources (Internet, America Online, etc.) If even 43 percent of its online transactions come from the Internet, Schwab makes the club.

The inner circle is **Emery's Million Dollar A Day Club**, companies that sell $365 million per year on the Net or more:

- **Cisco Systems** claims that much or close.

- **Dell Computer** says it will sell $500 million this year from its Web site.

- **Auto-By-Tel** sold over $700 million worth of cars and trucks on the Internet last year, plus more on America Online, Prodigy, and CompuServe.

- The champ, **OASIS**, sells electric power from 172 providers on the Web. It rang up several billion dollars of sales in its first six months.

Those are the big bruisers. Thousands more companies generate lesser (but still healthy) amounts from the Net. If these businesses make money on the Net, *so can you.*

Now the second myth: "*Everybody* makes money on the Internet."

This lie is fostered by shysters who rip off the unwary. It's true that most companies that use the Internet to *save* money succeed. But most companies that *market* on the Net lose money. The first surveys on this topic showed that about 75 percent of the businesses marketing on the Internet lose money. That figure has improved. New surveys say 70 percent lose money. Yikes! If those businesses *lose* money on the Net, *so can you.*

Most losers make certain common mistakes. *My purpose is to help you avoid those mistakes, and to give you tips and techniques from the winners,* from businesses that succeed using the Internet to cut costs and make money.

This guide provides immediately usable information, techniques, and tools so your business can join the winning 30 percent. It explains what works on the Net, what doesn't, and why. Its goal is to provide realistic advice you can use right now.

This book is for businesspeople

First and foremost, this book is not for computer wizards. It's for *businesspeople.* It focuses on business insights and gives true stories of the successes and mistakes of actual companies. These examples were chosen to help you put ideas into practice in your own business.

Instead of technical tips on how to *use* Internet tools, this book shows you how to *apply* them. Rather than memorize commands, I want to show you how to make and save money.

You will get more out of the guidelines here if you have at least a little hands-on experience on the Internet. If you haven't, not to worry—most topics have brief descriptions to clue you in. There is some technical material, but only what you need for *business* decisions.

Opportunities for businesses on the Internet are very different from those faced by individual people. Most people want to *take* information from the Internet. Businesses must *provide* information as well. The actions of a private individual on the Net have consequences mostly for that one person. The actions of a businessperson impact *many* people: co-workers, employees, stockholders, suppliers, and customers.

No two businesses have the same needs. One guy selling cockatoos out of his garage in Toledo, Ohio, has Internet requirements very different from those of the manager of a large department of the Mitsubishi office in Rangoon.

In this book, I try to bridge the gap by presenting information about Internet business for all sizes of businesses in all kinds of industries. If you're a one-person startup, when I recommend that a certain task be assigned, say, to your inventory manager, don't scowl. Just put on your "Inventory Manager" cap and keep reading. The same holds true for any small company. When I come up with more job titles than there are people in your whole business, just realize that I'm talking about different *roles* to play. You can act in many parts, even if the job title I give isn't an exact match with yours.

You'll find hundreds of sales-building, cost-cutting techniques here. They were tested the hard way—by the real-world Internet experiences of other businesspeople and myself. You can profit from the painful lessons we've learned. As Mark Twain said, "Learn from the mistakes of others. You can never live long enough to make them all yourself."

I had the great fortune to be marketing manager of Computer Literacy Bookshops Inc., which pioneered using the Internet for business. I learned from my own successes and mistakes, first with Computer Literacy, then with other companies. I learned more from the advice of other businesspeople, from technical specialists, from hundreds of suggestions from my readers (thank you!), and from audiences at my lectures and seminars.

 I warn you about what can go wrong. If you manage an Internet project and want a pat on your back instead of egg on your face, keep your eye out for Mr. Doom, the bony guy on the left. Throughout this book, he warns you of serious hazards—show-stoppers—that can kill your Internet business.

As the Net has grown, businesses have dreamt up a tremendous number of great new ideas (and new scams). I have to scramble to keep up. This third edition is greatly expanded—more pages, new chapters. About half the book is new material. All the rest is reorganized and updated.

Still, I can't claim this new edition is the last word on its subject. Internet business is still in diapers. Considering what it does as an infant, imagine what marvels it will accomplish once it learns to walk. This volume is just a starting point. If you don't find enough info inside its covers, you'll find more outside.

Put this expandable book to work

Expandable book? Yes, the book you hold in your hand is only part of *How to Grow Your Business on the Internet*. You can review dozens more pages of information, case histories, interviews, and resources.

Point your Web browser to **http://www.emery.com** for a free information resource for readers of this book. My Web site gives you 24-hour access to additional techniques, late-breaking news, and (sigh) corrections.

If you look on my Web site and still can't find what you need, you have one more resource. Send me email at **vince@emery.com**. I can't promise an instant response, but I will answer all questions I can.

Short on time?

Few businesspeople can spare enough time to read this entire book. If that's you, don't despair. Most chapters stand on their own to a degree. In fact, if you do read this book cover to cover, you'll notice a few redundancies when I cover subjects from different angles.

What chapter should you read if you have time for only one? I vote for Chapter 2, "Twelve Reasons Internet Projects Fail—and How to Make Sure Yours Don't." This chapter is drawn from the experiences—good and bad—of dozens of companies. It busts common myths and concludes with a tested set of eleven steps every successful project should take.

The second most essential chapter will depend on your own needs, but look at Chapter 7 if you can: "How to Prevent Break-Ins and Fraud."

Thanks for the memories

This book would be much thinner if you had only my brain to pick. Businesspeople from dozens of companies made room in their overcrowded Daytimers for me. Their memories provided valuable techniques, and I'm grateful.

The biggest lesson I learned writing this new edition is never to have major surgery in the middle of writing a book. Post-op recovery does not induce the mental clarity needed to bang out coherent chapters. Plainly put, after surgery

I was a mental crouton. I'm grateful to my editors Sandra Lassiter and Ann Waggoner Aken for putting up with me. Without their encouragement and patience, you would hold no third edition in your hands. And without the support of my aunt Rosemary Auer, I don't know how I would have survived either the book or the surgery. Thank you, Rosie!

Since the first edition, Deanna McHugh of the University of California, San Francisco and Professor William Murray of the University of San Francisco have given me good input. That first edition's success was due to the efforts of publisher Keith Weiskamp and editor Ron Pronk.

The core background around which everything else in this book is wrapped comes from my experience with Computer Literacy Bookshops, a pioneer in Internet commerce. Tips from many CLB people made their way into this book, especially from Penny Wendland, Robert Mudry, Cherrie Chiu, and Tracy Russ. Most of all, this book wouldn't be here if not for Dan Doernberg and Rachel Unkefer, the two Internet-savvy businesspeople who brought me into Computer Literacy and on the Net in the first place. Thank you both very much.

How to read Internet addresses

All through this book you will see boldface strands of type like this one from a few paragraphs back: **http://www.emery.com**. These are Internet addresses. Here's a quick explanation, in case you're new to the Net.

Internet addresses look like meaningless nonsense at first, but there is actually a simple logic to them.

First, any address with an "@" sign in it is an Internet *email* address. My email address is **vince@emery.com**. When I give my email address over the phone, I pronounce it as "vince at emery dot com." Periods in email addresses are always called "dot." If you say "period" when you give someone an email address on the phone, you expose yourself as a clueless newbie.

The **vince** part of my email address is called my *user name*. A user name is always on the left, before the "@" symbol. After the "@" can come several words or abbreviations, each separated by a dot. The user name is the "who" of an email address, and the rest of the address is the "where." For instance, a message to **fred@ marketing.emery.com** goes to Fred in the marketing department of a company or organization called "emery," which is a "commercial" organization, or **.com**. This last term is called a *top-level domain*. The company name part of the address is called a *domain name*, or just *domain*. Instead of a **.com** domain, my business could chose an address ending in **.us** to indicate that it is an American company. Other domain names, like **.uk, .ca,** or **.jp,** are addresses from other countries (the United Kingdom, Canada, and Japan in these examples). My address could end in **.edu** if I were an educational institution, **.net** if I were a networking organization, **.org** for a non-commercial organization, or **.gov** if I were the government. (Now there's a nightmare . . .)

That address **http://www.emery.com**, you may notice, has no "@" symbol. It is a different kind of Internet address. It is formatted in a standard way called a *URL*, which stands for Uniform Resource Locator, a fancy name for Internet address. In the URL format, the first part of the address tells what Internet tool you use to reach the address.

So **http://** tells you that this is a World Wide Web address. (HTTP stands for *HyperText Transfer Protocol*, the software that moves Web pages. You won't need to remember that, but I thought I'd tell you in case somebody puts you on the spot.) Most software for surfing the Web assumes that any URL you give it is a Web address unless you tell it otherwise. This means that you probably don't need to type that ugly **http://** before Web addresses. (Try typing a Web address without **http://** on your Web browser to see if this works.) Most any Internet address beginning with **www.** is a Web address, even if it doesn't start with **http://**.

To reach an Internet FTP site, the address would be something like **ftp://emery.com/main**, which tells you to use FTP to go to the address **emery.com** and look in a file or directory called **main**. Anything separated from the end of an Internet address with slashes is either a file or a directory.

In the same way, **telnet://emery.com** would take you to my Telnet site, if I had one. You'd type **gopher://emery.com** to reach my Gopher server. If I had a newsgroup, you'd reach it with **news:biz.emery.com** or something similar. You can also use the URL format for email addresses. Try **mailto:vince@emery.com** to reach me from your Web browser software. (Note that you still use the "@" sign.)

Some software chokes on spaces between words, so Internet addresses never contain spaces, with one exception. Telnet addresses optionally use spaces to specify a computer port number in the form of an address followed by a space and a number: **telnet:// emery.com 591**. Otherwise, no spaces are allowed.

One final thing. For some bizarre reason, many Web page addresses contain a funny punctuation symbol "~" called a *tilde*. Pronounce it "till-duh," just like the end of Waltzing Matilda. When you get your own Web address, avoid tildes. Every time you tell your address to someone over the phone, when you come to the tilde the other person will say "What?" and you'll have to explain, "You know, that squiggly punctuation probably on the upper left corner of your keyboard." I hate tildes in addresses.

Business at the Speed of Light

"In earlier history, wealth was measured in land, in gold, in oil, in machines. Today, the principal measure of our wealth is our information: its quality, its quantity, and the speed with which we acquire it and adapt it."

—Richard C. Beaird, U.S. Department of State

The football stadium was packed. Ninety thousand excited fans watched the Rose Bowl, a tight game between California and Georgia Tech on New Year's Day, 1929.

Near the end of the game, with California ahead by one slim point, Georgia Tech fumbled the ball deep inside its own territory. A California player, Roy Riegles, grabbed the ball and took off like a charging rhino. But, confused by the wild scramble, he took off in the wrong direction!

Ninety thousand men and women jumped to their feet and screamed, "You're going the wrong way!" The mighty roar of the crowd only put wings on his feet, and Riegles outran his own team members, who desperately raced to tackle him. He shook off a final tackler near the goal line and scored, winning the game—for his opponents! The nickname "Wrong-Way" Riegles must have stuck with the poor sap for the rest of his life.

Don't laugh. On the Internet, the same thing can happen to you. You can get all the details right on your Internet project. You can have beautiful graphics, clear copy, and the latest, greatest high-tech gadgets. Your details can be perfect, but if your overall direction is wrong—if you pick up the dingus and run the wrong way—it won't matter how fast you run, or how well. What matters most is that you start the right way in the first place. You don't want the nickname "Wrong Way" any more than Riegles did.

The Internet, you see, is not just boxes and wires. The Internet is the promise of wealth beyond the dreams of avarice. That blinds some people, and they make mistakes they would otherwise never have made.

An Internet business project lives or dies by the same rules that govern any other business project. Internet success just moves faster, that's all. That's why I call this chapter "Business at the Speed of Light." Sure, electrons zip through wires pretty swiftly, but that's not what's so great about the Net. What's great is how quickly *you* can move when you use it.

Would you like to reach your customers more quickly? To hear from them more quickly? To make changes and distribute improved results more quickly? Even better, to get paid more quickly?

Businesses do all of that—and more—on the Internet. But put down that football. Before you grab it and run off, it's nice to get an idea where the goal posts are. For your own Internet efforts, a good thing to do first is to look at what other businesses have already done. If you review others' activities, you can see what might work for your own company.

The Internet can help you market and sell

Marketing and sales on the Internet have received more press coverage than any other networked business activities. Businesses love to publicize sales success stories, and there have been many.

More than a thousand companies have made sales over the Internet this year in excess of $1 million apiece. Thousands more have generated lesser amounts. Most Internet sales are *business-to-business* sales, where one company sells to another company, not to an individual consumer. The next-highest amount of sales are to *government agencies*. The third-largest group of customers are *educational institutions*.

In dollar amounts, sales to *individual consumers* fall below those three groups. If you plan to market to consumers on the Internet, be aware that consumer sales were healthy mostly in specific categories. I'll describe them later in this chapter.

Marketing departments pull many companies onto the Internet. This has been especially true since 1992, when the *World Wide Web* appeared. The Internet used to be just walls of type and boring file lists. The World Wide Web has added descriptions, color pictures, and point-and-click navigation, making it easier to get around. Now you'll find more than 100 million Web "pages" on the Internet.

More than 100,000 companies have opened virtual storefronts using the World Wide Web. (For an example, see Figure 1.1.) Some generate millions in sales. However, most Web stores—surveys estimate 70 to 75 percent of them—*lose* money.

Other companies don't actually make sales online, but instead use the Web as a promotional tool, providing information and advertising. Some Web marketing sites are dry and serious. Others are entertaining and humorous, such as Web sites by CBS (David Letterman's lists), by Paramount for *Star Trek*, and by a business called the Museum of Bad Art.

Figure 1.1 The World Wide Web adds color and graphics to the Internet. This is the home page of Software.net's Web store. Because its overhead is much lower than a physical store or a printed catalog, Software.net sells at lower prices than traditional software retailers. It provides 50,000 pages of reviews and information on 16,000 products on the Web. It sells almost 10,000 software packages each week. Note the co-op ads on the right. Manufacturers pay to rent those ad spaces.

The Internet is marketing heaven. It's dirt cheap compared with other media—a lower cost-per-impression than fliers. Response is instant. Reach is worldwide. Visitors to Internet sites leave a trail of statistics that marketers can apply to increase response. Many businesses on the Internet use it mostly for marketing activities.

Companies use the Internet to distribute electronic mass mailings to customers and prospects. The expense for an electronic mailing list is small, the amount of work is minimal, and 1,000 or more of your best prospects can receive a personal electronic mail message from you in a few hours. You can write an electronic mail press release and send it to a list of reporters. Most large printed publications are on the Internet, so email is the fastest way to reach them.

The Internet itself is host to thousands of electronic publications, providing hundreds of publicity opportunities for your business. Electronic newsletters, magazines, and Web sites attract large readerships. Several have readerships of more than one million. If you find electronic publications that your customers and prospects read, they can make excellent targets for your publicity. If you can't find one, you can start an electronic publication of your own.

Many companies, especially high-tech firms, use the Internet for customer support, customer service, and customer retention programs. The programs that succeed all have one ingredient in common: customers who are *already* on the Internet in large numbers.

The Internet is a useful tool for marketing research. Usage statistics from your company's site can generate valuable information. Vast quantities of private and government business and demographic data are available on the Net. Companies research prospects, customers, and potential new markets. Because the Internet is such a fast delivery medium and because it is inexpensive, it is an ideal way to conduct marketing surveys, and specialized software products make this easier.

Question:
What is this Internet thing, anyhow?

If you ask a technical person what the Internet actually is, he'll rattle off a barrage of acronyms and computer arcana until your eyeballs glaze and you enter a deep trance. Then he'll ask you for a raise.

For a less mind-numbing experience, the *Wall Street Journal* described the Internet in a Nov. 14, 1994, story as "...the chain of networks that is generally the easiest and cheapest way for businesses to communicate electronically with the outside world."

The *Journal* definition describes the Internet from a *corporation's* point of view. I prefer to look at the Internet from the point of view of a nontechnical *user*.

Answer:
The Internet lets you scoop up anything in the world and bring it back to your desktop.

From a user's point of view, that's what the Internet is. You can reach anywhere without paying extra for distance. You can search for and find an incredible variety of things. ("Anything" is a slight exaggeration.) And you can bring what you find back to your desktop, whether your desk is at work or at home.

Note that this definition does not even *mention* computers or technology. The computers aren't important; they're only the tools. What's important is the end result: The power to reach and deliver stuff all over the world.

The Internet as a management tool

Management has been defined as consisting of five actions: planning, directing (leadership), staffing, organizing, and controlling. All management tasks require you to collect, evaluate, and distribute information. The Internet is best as a tool for collecting and distributing management information.

Managers dragged kicking and screaming onto the Net never leave once they discover how well the Internet helps them keep tabs on their business, and how it empowers them to spread their views.

The Internet spreads business information both within a networked enterprise, and between the company and the outside world. Companies that make extensive use of the Internet see their world expand. It is easy to cross countries' borders, and there are no "long-distance charges" on the Internet. Companies with international aspirations move quickly. Companies without international plans soon make them. When interviewing companies for this book, again and again I heard managers say they didn't expect international customers or suppliers, but found that the Net quickly made overseas activities a big part of their business. Now they type locally, act globally.

The tool that makes this possible is electronic mail, called email for short. Even in businesses where senior managers don't use email themselves, the closer contact with customers, suppliers, and employees generates valuable feedback not possible in other ways.

Additional benefits are yielded when your company has remote locations (which the Internet can link) or staff members who spend time on the road. With email and other Internet tools, anything you can do at the computer on your desk, you can do on the road.

Special note must be given to the resources on the Net for financial and accounting managers. Accounting associations worldwide have built resources to rapidly spread new changes in accounting regulations and government tax policies. Some governments accept filing of tax forms electronically. If your company is larger than a "mom & pop" firm, your controller and CFO will appreciate entry into the large and rapidly growing body of Internet financial, accounting, and tax resources. I'll talk more about those later.

The Internet can help you with logistics and cost-cutting

The main reason investment giant J.P. Morgan & Co. linked to the Internet was to dramatically improve support from its computer hardware and software vendors. Difficulties that used to take days to repair are now fixed in hours or just minutes. Success in dramatically improving support from its computer hardware and software vendors led Morgan to expand Internet use into other areas.

Better technical support is one of the most common benefits of linking to the Internet. Thousands of high-tech companies from IBM on down offer support, bug fixes, and software upgrades on the Internet. There are tens of thousands of free computer programs on the Internet no matter what your brand of computer. Several companies claim that free software from the Internet has by itself paid for their Internet connection.

In addition, more than 2,000 computer-related discussion groups on the Internet let users ask each other questions. These discussions are wonderful places to evaluate technical products before you buy them. You can question people who actually use the products under consideration—and receive uncensored answers. This is a much more straightforward way to find the good and bad points of, say, an accounting software program, than asking a sales representative who is paid to tell you only the sunny side. "Bugs? No! Our software doesn't have bugs." Sure, buddy. That's not what your users say.

Advice from Internet discussion groups can help you make other kinds of purchases as well. You'll find discussions of security devices (news: **alt.locksmithing**), trucks, and autos. You'll find about 200 discussion groups covering products that aren't computer-related, and the number is growing.

Your company's purchasing agents may be more interested in the National Association for Purchasing Management resources. They'll also like sending request for quotes (RFQs) and purchase orders electronically through the Internet, without having to pay through the nose to join a proprietary network. A General Electric test project to post bid requests publicly on the Net saved the company more than $700,000.

Until recently, the expense of using a proprietary network kept all but the largest companies from using Electronic Data Interchange, called EDI for short. EDI lets companies electronically exchange inventory, purchasing, billing, and shipping information. EDI used to require a mainframe or a minicomputer and 8 to 18 months of work by a dedicated project team. Efforts by an organization called CommerceNet and new software products let companies do EDI on a PC now via the Internet.

The ultimate logistics boon, though, is for companies that not only sell their products online, but actually *deliver* their products over the Internet. I have had books, graphic art, games, and newsletters delivered directly to my computer. More than 200 software companies actually deliver their software programs over the Internet, including documentation. Not every company can deliver electronically, but if yours can, you'll find it to be a dramatic advantage.

The Internet can help your R&D

The Internet was originally built to be a network for research. It still excels at its original purpose. The Net delivers thousands of databases and archives of research data on everything: plastics, explosives, geology, medicine, vehicles, food preparation, electric power, chemistry, manufacturing techniques, even specifications for the ideal baby diaper.

Specialist discussion groups cover hundreds of R&D topics. More than 2,000 research journals maintain back issues on the Internet. Researchers perform automated searches of articles and abstracts, finding information in minutes that would otherwise take days of digging in a library. Software archives provide tens of thousands of usable programs.

An important ingredient in research is what you can learn from your customers. Companies use the Net for trials of concepts and specifications for product improvements and new products. You can try out proposed product features with the people who will actually use them.

The R&D assets of the Internet are so vast and well-known that it's no exaggeration to say that companies without the Internet cripple their product development.

Is the Internet right for your company?

The Internet brings many benefits to businesses, but not every business needs it. Before you jump into the game, make sure you can use what the Internet offers. Here are some questions to help you decide if you should hook up your company to the Internet, and if so, whether you should market online or not.

 Mr. Doom warns you that the Internet has been oversold. Many businesses opened elaborate Internet sites when they would have been better off just sticking to email or not even getting on the Internet in the first place. Many have left the Net, poorer but wiser. You can be very successful on the Net, but you must learn the Internet's rules of the road and follow them. You dramatically increase your chances of winning if you start with something simple and do a little homework first.

1. Who are your customers and prospects?

Who on the Internet would use your product or service, and in what ways? If your customers are on the Internet, then your company should be there. As I mentioned before, you can categorize Internet customers into four groups.

Group 1: Do you sell to other businesses? Most sales on the Internet are business-to-business sales. These usually involve fewer transactions but higher dollar amounts than consumer sales. Many business-to-business sales are conducted entirely via email and not through the World Wide Web.

On the Internet, sales to businesses include both *quantity* sales, such as wholesale transactions or bulk sales of manufacturing commodities, and *one-at-a-time* sales of single items, like a calendar or a software program, to an individual person in a company.

Your chances of finding business customers and prospects depend on what *kind* of businesses buy your products. You won't reach a heck of a lot of vegetarian restaurants on the Net. On the other hand, if you sell to technical companies, you'd better be online. Besides high tech, other industries with high and growing Net participation are: the entertainment industry, publishing (books, magazines, and newspapers), booksellers, accounting firms, investment firms, petroleum-related industries, utility companies, and travel-related businesses.

If you sell to businesses, it matters *who* buys your products. For instance, more publicists are on the Net than janitors. People in technical positions are most likely to be on the Internet. Recruitment and personnel managers are often on the Internet due to the large number of online job banks. Investors are online, so Fidelity Investments gets one out of every 20 new customers from the Net. As a rule of thumb:

- If your customers are white-collar workers below the senior executive level, they are likely to be online.

- Pink-collar clerical workers might be online, depending on the industry in which they work.

- Your customers are least likely to be online if you make business-to-business sales to blue-collar workers.

Group 2: Do you sell to government agencies? In many countries (especially English-speaking ones), the Internet is a fast and economical way to reach government buyers. I heard of a tiny engineering firm in Atlanta that landed a $1.5 million contract with the government of Indonesia from the Net. Many U.S. government purchases are *required* to be made online, so if your company isn't connected, you can't make the sale.

Group 3: Do you sell to colleges and universities? Almost all North American, European, and Australian institutes of higher education are on the Internet, as well as many in Asia and South America, and some in Africa. Whether you want to sell to students, professors, administrators, or maintenance supervisors, if they are at a university they probably have an Internet address.

Group 4: Do you sell directly to consumers? As I pointed out a few pages ago, consumer sales generate the smallest sales volume of the four customer groups, but you can still make a profit on the Net selling to consumers. I know of one business with $500,000 in online sales of grocery products. If you sell to consumers, you must be more aware of how effectively you use the Internet as a marketing tool, and you must work harder to promote your Internet *site* than you do to promote your products.

The newest surveys show that more than half of Internet users are well-educated males age 25 through 45 with above-average incomes. North American users are as likely to be married as single, but Europeans are mostly single. The fastest-growing demographic group on the Internet is women—also affluent and well-educated.

It is cheap and easy to *promote* your product on the Net, but be aware that it takes a larger investment of time and money to *make a sale* online.

How do your customers buy?

There is a high correlation between customers who buy via postal mail and respond to printed advertisements, and those who buy or search for product information on the Internet. This holds true for both consumers and business customers. If you have customers who buy by mail, look more closely at the Net. This match does not carry over to other media. Those who buy via direct response television are unlikely Internet prospects.

Payment method is another indicator. If your business does mostly cash sales, the Internet may not be to your liking. Credit cards and billed accounts are the most popular collection methods on the Net.

2. What kinds of products and services do you offer?

My previous descriptions of uses of the Internet and my list of Internet consumers should give you an idea of the types of offerings you can profitably market online. There have been successes—and failures—in many different product lines, but little predictability exists on Internet buying habits. Projecting how well your company will do on the Net is still a judgment call.

Note that several surveys have indicated that people use the Internet to *find information* about prospective purchases more often than they actually *purchase* online. If you can't decide whether or not you want to *sell* online, you might try the simpler, lower-cost first step of just *marketing* online and providing information about your company and what you offer. If that works for you, you can always add sales capabilities later.

THE SEVEN BEST-SELLING INTERNET PRODUCT CATEGORIES
Some types of products and services sell better online than others. I've arranged them into seven categories, roughly arranged with the categories that are easiest to sell listed first.

Although I use the word "products" here, everything in this list also holds true for businesses that sell services and combinations of products and services.

Note that some products (such as books and travel tickets) appear in more than one category. These categories are not mutually exclusive. In fact, if your product spans multiple categories, that's good. The more categories your product spans, the more your product will appeal to more Internet buyers for more reasons.

Here's the list, best categories first:

1. **Technical products**—The one factor that *everyone* on the Internet has in common is an interest in gadgets. (I used to be able to say that everyone had a *computer*, but WebTV ruined my line. Still, *almost* everyone on the Net has a computer.) The easiest-to-sell products and services on the Net are those having to do with computers and gadgets. In fact, the Net is the best way to sell most technical products: computers, software, computer books, home electronics, video games, battery-operated swizzle sticks, you name it. If you sell gadgets and you can't sell them on the Net, it might be time to look for another line of work.

2. **Information products**—People on the Net are passionate about information, and they buy lots of it: books, videos, CD-ROMs, online courses, subscriptions to email newsletters, and more. Information products sell well and are easy to market online, but competition in this area has heated up as the field has grown more crowded.

3. **Considered purchases**—Some people call these by another name, **informed purchases**, but the two terms mean the same. These purchases are products or services for which the buyer gathers information as part of the buying process and usually compares offerings from different vendors to help make a wise choice. If purchased by a business, the buying decision might be made by a committee. If purchased by a married person, often the husband and wife are both involved in the decision to buy. Travel falls into this category, as do investments and computers. The massive success of Auto-By-Tel proves that consumers will buy considered purchases as costly as new cars over the Net. Business, government, and educational buyers commonly buy considered purchases with even bigger price tags.

4. **"Search-for" products**—These are products that people know they want and actively search for because they are hard to find. The Internet makes it easier for buyers to locate such specialized products as antiques, out-of-print books, or unusual machine tools. In consumer marketing, this especially applies to collectable items. For example, out of the 20,000 Usenet newsgroups, each discussing a different topic, the one with the highest volume of messages posted is devoted to trading cards (such as baseball cards). If you sell to collectors who feel passionate about their collections, try Internet marketing.

5. **Entertainment and travel**—Books, videos, music CDs, video games, concert tickets, and sports events all sell online. Travel sells so well as to earn a category of its own; anything travel-related can be sold on the Internet.

6. **Time bargains** and **cost bargains**—The Internet costs less and is faster than traditional marketing and distribution channels. Internet people are proven bargain hunters. If you can save them time or money, you've got a customer for life. Once again, Auto-By-Tel is a great example. It gives customers a much faster way to buy cars than by driving to auto dealers. It also saves them money. To top it off, many people find Auto-By-Tel less emotionally exhausting than haggling with car sales reps. Another success story in this category is Onsale. I bought my computer on the Internet because Onsale took less time, gave me the information I needed, and charged me half the price of a retail store.

7. **Impulse items**—HotHotHot makes good money on the Net selling nothing but bottled hot sauce. Some companies have done well with novelty T-shirts. Impulse items are hit-or-miss; some do well, many flop. It's hard to predict what will happen. Impulse items take more marketing effort. When they cost less than $10, you have to sell a significant volume to pay back your operational costs.

Note that I did *not* list advertisements as one of the successful categories, even though well over 100,000 Internet businesses sell advertisements. The reason is that pathetically few make any money at it. If you want to know more about Internet ads, I cover them in depth in a later chapter.

If you plan to go online to sell only one product, be extra cautious. It is harder to make a profit from a one-product Internet store. In the real world, it would be like opening a bookstore that sold only one book. It can be done, but not often. You dramatically increase your odds of marketing success if you have a *line* of products to offer.

3. Can you apply the Internet to improve your operations or to cut costs?

I spoke with a manufacturer of custom-built robot submersibles, who was considering an Internet connection. His company was located in Northern California and at the time was working on a remote-controlled craft with a video camera, searchlight, and robot arm to swim against the current up a $4\frac{1}{2}$-mile water pipeline in the Middle East. The company had customers all over world and a sales agent in Brazil. The week before, an emergency had forced an engineer to come to the office in the middle of the night to send a software fix to a customer in Sweden via modem. Normally, it sent software bug fixes by Federal Express.

What could this manufacturer do on the Internet? Instead of modem-dialing long distance to Sweden, it could store software fixes on an FTP site. That way, customers could download software whenever they wished, and the manufacturer would pay no long-distance or Federal Express charges. The company could save phone and fax costs by using email to reach its sales agent and its customers. Instead of sending bids, proposals, and specifications via fax or courier, employees could email them. The design staff could save money and time by using the Net for research. Savings opportunities like these are the ones to find for your own business. Here are some questions to ask:

- Email is cheaper than postal mail, faxes, or phone calls, and is faster than a courier service. How much would you save if you cut fax, phone, and courier bills by 20 percent?

- Ask your technical staff how much you would save if you could use the Internet to receive customer support from software and computer vendors.

- How much would you save downloading free software programs?

- Ask your marketing people how much you would save by sending and receiving graphics files over the Net, by using email for publicity mailings, and by using the Internet for marketing research.

- See if online forms and Internet customer support would reduce your 800 number costs.

- If your company sends out standardized marketing materials to customers, see if you would save printing and postage costs by making electronic versions available.

- Ask your purchasing staff if sending electronic RFQs and purchase orders would generate any savings. (A later chapter covers purchasing savings in detail.)

- Check with your controller to see if there is any advantage to filing government forms electronically.

Cost savings often pay for a company's Internet connection. Sometimes they do not. But cost and work savings do contribute and are worth considering when you decide whether to connect to the Internet.

4. Will your competitors beat you if you don't?

Who are your competitors on the Internet? How do your competitors sell offerings that are similar to yours? What are their strengths and weaknesses?

If you see one of your competitors on the Internet, monitor its site every week or two. If a competitor adds new features, it may be onto a good thing. You won't want to be left out.

5. Can you afford the expense and the work?

I've read a lot of baloney about how it costs companies at least $15,000 or even $20,000 to get on the Internet. Rubbish! Sure, giant corporations spend millions of dollars on their Internet sites, but I've known many companies that spent $1,000 or even $500. I put the first version of my own Web site up in one day for $100.

What will it cost your business? It depends. That subject is so big it needs an entire chapter to explain. In fact, that's what Chapter 3 does.

But before we count nickels and dimes, take a look at the most common causes of Internet business disasters. Then, to avoid them (and that "Wrong-Way" nickname), I'll give you the steps you can take to make sure your Net project is a success.

Who runs the Internet?

Some people glibly say that no one runs the Internet, but that's not true. No one *owns* the Internet. Each company on the Internet owns its own network, and the links between the companies and the Internet are owned by the phone companies and access providers.

But there is a difference between ownership and control. To find who *governs* the Internet you need to look in several places, because different functions are coordinated by different international organizations.

The most prominent organization is the Internet Society. Vinton Cerf, former president of the Internet Society, described its role: "The Internet Society does not operate any of the thousands of networks that make up the Internet, but it assists service providers by providing information to prospective users and involves product developers and research in the evolution of Internet standards. Corporate and individual professional support for this organization is widespread and international."

One important part of the Internet Society, the Internet Architecture Board, is a beehive of research groups, working groups, and task forces. The Architecture Board organizes management, engineering, and design issues, paying close attention to TCP/IP and other protocols. Two of its subsidiary task forces are Internet Research Task Force (IRTF), dealing with R&D for future growth, and Internet Engineering Task Force (IETF), which handles technical issues and everyday operational aspects.

Other organizations have responsibilities within individual countries or for groups of countries, such as Réseaux IP Européens (RIPE), which coordinates internetworking in Europe.

12 Reasons Internet Projects Fail— and How to Make Sure Yours Don't

"Don't assume compatibility. This is how most systems integrators get rich."

—Karen Watterson, Client/Server Technology for Managers

Businesses and the Internet are like teenagers and sex. Everyone's obsessed with it. Everyone thinks everyone else does it. Everyone wants everyone else to think they do it, too. But hardly anyone does it as much as people think, and most of them do it badly.

"Doing it badly" is more common on the Internet than I'd like, especially since a little knowledge can prevent most online failures. Internet flops often run up against one or more of 12 common problems. Internet successes usually avoid them. Here are the chasms and tips to avoid falling into them.

1. They won't come

Suppose you built a Web site and nobody came?

Find People Fast is a business that locates missing friends and relatives, but when the company opened a Web site, the people missing were visitors to the site. Its site averaged five lonely visitors each week—less than one per day!

The single most common reason that Internet projects fail is lack of participants. For email lists, lack of subscribers. For Web sites, lack of visitors. The only research that I've seen indicated that 90 percent of Web site owners were dissatisfied with the amount of traffic they attracted. This is a little higher percentage than my own experience indicates, but the problem is both common and severe.

People often expect that when you open a Web site, visitors show up by magic. A couple of months ago, I spoke with an Australian businessman with a good idea for a project to put on the Web. I asked him, "How are people going to know about this?"

The man replied, "What do you mean? We're going to put it on the Internet."

"Yes, but how will people find it?"

"It'll be on the Web, that's how."

It took several minutes of explanation before the Australian—who is a bright man, just inexperienced in the ways of the Net—realized that prospective visitors have more than half a million Web sites to choose from, and that he would have to work hard to break through the clutter.

Attracting Web visitors by mental telepathy doesn't work. I estimate that 80 percent of the businesspeople on the Net whom I have spoken with are disappointed by the number of visitors their sites attract. This is especially true of consumer retailers on the Internet. People won't magically show up at your Internet site. You need to promote your Internet offerings as vigorously as your toll-free number or your mail-order catalog.

In your budget, allow for promotional costs in order to create awareness of your Internet services. This topic is so important that I devote an entire chapter to it. (Two chapters, if you count the one on banner advertisements.) For now, keep in mind that there are two very different kinds of Web site visitors:

- First-time visitors
- Return visitors

If you want to generate repeat visits, plan to make the *editorial* investment needed to sustain interest in returning. You have the classic retail display window challenge: Put something new and exciting in your front window to get people to come back. It will take staff time to create a steady stream of updated and new information, but it will be worth it.

"If you build it, they will come" is ridiculous on the Web. But if you promote it, they might come...which is a key step in making your site a success.

2. Just because you have a web site doesn't mean it works

Okay, you build your Web site. You get visitors. Then what?

Then (if you're like most businesses) you are disappointed by your results. Either visitors don't do what you want, or not enough of them do what you want. Most companies—especially those that market on the Web—do not generate profits there. Surveys estimate that 70 to 75 percent of Web retailers *lose money*.

How can this be when other companies make millions of dollars on the Net? Let me answer by asking another question: When two Web sites in the same industry sell the same products, what makes one Web site much, much more profitable? Could it be that one business provides a better Web site?

Yes, it could. I'm not saying that the quality of your Web site is the *only* factor that puts potatoes on your table. But once a visitor enters your virtual door, the organization, writing, and design of your site all become extremely important. Unfortunately, most companies' Web sites demonstrate their ignorance of these principles instead of their mastery.

I was once asked to help a company that paid for a Web page that generated *zero* responses. Many people visited, but not one bought the company's product or even asked about it. When I visited the page, the product description was so vague I could not tell what it was. Nothing told me who the product was for. I could not understand if the company wanted to buy a product or sell it. The page lacked any "call to action" to instruct me how to respond.

Pretty basic? I've seen worse. Several sites give no contact information at all. (Do you think that hurts their response rates?) The Golden Turkey Award goes to an elaborate Canadian site with dozens of pages of valuable information, but absolutely no contact information and *not even the name* of any sponsor! And I'll bet that organization—whatever it is—complains about lack of response.

 Most businesses' Web sites are neither written nor designed effectively. If you are not a marketing person, hire somebody who is. Just as the wrong advertising can actually *reduce* the sales of your product, the wrong Web site can chase away your prospects and customers.

The bad news is that you might be disappointed by your initial Internet results. The good news is that you can improve even the worst site and grow your response rate. That approach has worked for thousands of businesses, and it's what this book is all about.

3. Gag 'em with graphics & gizmos

A desperate businesswoman sent a cry for help to an email discussion group on Web site design. She had a terrible problem. Visitors came to her site's home page, but absolutely nobody looked at the pages inside. What was wrong?

A member of the discussion group inspected her site. For starters, he reported, she could redesign her home page. It consisted of a modem-gagging 350,000 bytes of graphics files and had no text links. That meant that any visitor had to wait an excruciatingly long time to view her home page. Home pages are usually fast and efficient. Since hers wasn't, it implied that the rest of her site would be even worse. After such a long wait, who would want to see inside at the cost of even longer waits?

Your site may not charge admission, but visitors still pay a price. Internet users are impatient; the price they pay is suffering for your files while they slowly arrive. Bigger files cause more suffering. Lots of files per page cause more suffering per page.

This is why visitors hate inefficient sites. "Let's cram so many graphics files down their little modems' gullets that they choke" is *not* a strategy for success. Even on my Web site, which has hardly any graphics and is designed for quick access, about 20 percent of the visitors kill the graphics.

Graphics files aren't the only offenders. Needless animation, entry tunnels, frames, and Java applets also drag your site down. These can all be valuable. Many sites have good reasons to use them. The key is not to use them unless you need them to communicate.

Yahoo is the busiest site on the Internet. Part of the reason is its fast-loading pages. Yahoo's goal is page loads of three seconds or less, *including* graphics (which it keeps to 8K maximum per page). Yahoo builds its traffic with neither frames nor animation. It simply delivers what its customers want, with a minimum of fuss, and as fast as possible.

You don't need to "keep up with the Joneses" by adding every flashy new enhancement, whether your visitors want it or not. I'll cover this subject in detail in later chapters. For now, just remember that for Web sites, faster pages grow your wages.

4. "What's that? I can't hear you, my fingers are in my ears"

One of the great things about the Internet is that you get instant, unvarnished feedback directly from your customers and prospects.

One of the stupid things about some companies is that they ignore it.

Your network is only as good as your users say it is. If they say it stinks, it stinks. If they like most of it but harshly criticize some parts, don't take it as a personal attack. Stash your fight-or-flight response in your bottom desk drawer, and change what has been criticized. Then give them more of what they like.

Companies that ignore their customers' wants soon get into trouble. The Internet gives you insights for free that you'd have to pay a market research company big money to uncover. It delivers them faster and without the prefatory psychobabble that researchers use to justify their fees.

Expect criticism, and *welcome* it. You won't get criticism from someone who doesn't give a damn about you. You'll get criticism from people who want you to *improve*—even when their language would incite a saint to attack.

Feedback will come in several ways. Some will come by email. Some from phone calls or conversations between Web visitors and your employees. Some from your sales figures. Some of the most useful feedback will come from the statistics your Web site generates.

Treat responses from your customers as valuable research, and put them to work. As the founder of the great advertising agency Ogilvy & Mather said in his book *The Unpublished David Ogilvy,* "...There is no great trick to *doing* research. The problem is to get people to *use* it—particularly when the research reveals that you have been making mistakes."

Another kind of Internet business ignorance is when businesses do something that reveals they don't know how to act on the Net. Winners learn the rules of the Net, use them, and profit. Losers break the rules and suffer the consequences.

The Internet has been around long enough—more than 25 years— and has enough millions of people onboard to have developed its own rules. No matter how large your company may be, the Net is a redwood to your sapling. You must bend to its rules rather than the other way around.

This doesn't mean that every raving flamer can tell you how to run your business. But if you hear the same accusation from 3 or 4—or 20—people, you know that you have violated Internet rules in *principle,* even if you feel you haven't. As in any court of law, your perception of whether you obeyed the law is irrelevant; it is the judge and jury who make the decision. You have broken a rule when *other people* decide you have broken it.

For example, a manager with the publisher of the *NetGuide* series of books carried on a valiant but hopeless discourse on newsgroups for months. The company promoted a new book by posting announcements in dozens of newsgroups. The newsgroups regarded the announcements as spamming and banned any postings from the publisher's Internet address. The manager argued that since each announcement was slightly different, it was not spamming. The rebuttal was that it was *too* spamming. This manager missed the point. It doesn't matter whether his announcement was *technically* a spam, nor does it matter whether his company *intended* it to be a spam. If it is *perceived* as a spam, he should beat his breast in repentance, say *mea culpa,* and promise never to do it again.

Pay attention to the code of the Internet. You can break some rules in the short term and make a profit, but if you want to build an ongoing business with a repeat clientele (and avoid the Net's own frontier justice), you have to learn how the Internet works and play by its rules.

5. Doing everything on the web

The World Wide Web is *not* the Internet. It is only *part* of the Internet. But when you have a hammer, everything looks like a nail. So if you only know the Web, any idea you have gets hammered into Web pages. The sad results: doomed projects created by people hammering good ideas into deformed Web things.

I've heard many conversations start like this: "I know how we'll get people to come back to our Web site. We'll put a weekly newsletter on our site, so people will visit every week to read it."

If you hear an idea like that, I hope a warning buzzer sounds loudly in your head. Very few Web newsletters or magazines have succeeded in getting regular Web readership. On the other hand, several thousand email newsletters are successful. Some even charge thousands of dollars for advertising. If you have a newsletter idea, 99 times out of 100 you'll increase your odds of success if you start with email delivery.

The same holds for using Web-based discussion groups to draw folks to your site. Even for big companies with expensive, well-promoted Web sites, most Web chat areas are ghost towns. I estimate that you'll need at least 1,000 Web visitors a week (not *hits*, but *people*) to sustain a Web chat area. Five thousand visitors per week is a more realistic figure, but you can have an active and valuable email discussion group with only 50 to 60 subscribers. Then you can use your Web site as a place to subscribe and to search archives of past messages.

Remember to think about email newsletters and email discussion groups. They are faster and easier to set up than Web sites and can generate successful results more quickly and with fewer participants.

6. The ongoing MUS Monster

People—especially managers—often expect the biggest effort and greatest expense of an Internet project to occur *before* it opens. They are wrong. That is when the work and expense *begin*.

It's like you brought a new life into the world. Now you must feed it.

This upsets people who don't expect it. The result is a horrible creature I call the MUS Monster. It eats careers and lays whole Web sites to waste.

The M in MUS stands for "Maintenance." If you don't want your Web site to die after birth, you must plan for someone's time to maintain it. Most of the time won't be technical time, but editorial time creating new content.

U stands for "Update." Your existing content must be kept up-to-date, or your whole company will look out-of-touch, and your Web site will be useless. It is especially important to update the hyperlinks on your pages, a job that nobody likes.

S stands for "Support." The emphasis here is not on *technical* support (though you will need it). You will invest much more time in *customer* support if your Internet project is a success.

If you open a Web site and walk away, you will be ambushed by the MUS Monster. But if you expect the MUS Monster and prepare for it, it cannot hurt you.

You might draw comfort from a line in Walt Disney's speech the day he opened Disneyland: "As long as there is imagination left in the world, Disneyland will never be completed." Neither will your Internet site.

 Some managers assume that once they get their Web pages up, the work ends. They're wrong. That is when the real work begins. One of two calamities happens to these managers. Some panic ("When will it be done?" thundered an angry v.p.) and believe that they did something wrong because they can't get finished. Others never add anything to their sites. They end up watching them wither and die.

Your Net site will require *active* management. It's like a garden. You invest a huge effort in soil cultivation and planting. But unless you take care of bugs, prune dead wood, and plant new growth, you won't harvest much. For your Internet site, you'll also need to take care of bugs, prune dead wood, and especially plant new growth. Your staff will need to add new files, update information, and add new Internet services as they emerge. This becomes an even more urgent priority when any part of your Internet effort touches your customers.

The ongoing costs of maintenance, updates, and support—*especially customer support,* if you sell on the Net—will be your largest expenses. You'll get a good payback by investing extra time and money up front, designing your system to be as easy to use and update as possible.

HOW MUCH TIME DO INTERNET PROJECTS TAKE?

Here are some rough estimates. For a small company, answering email from customers and prospects can take from 5 to 30 hours a week if sales aren't online, from 20 to 80 hours if they are. Large companies have from dozens to a couple hundred full-time employees handling email customer support and email sales.

Filling orders is not as time-consuming as answering questions from customers and prospects. Email makes it easier for them to ask questions, so you'll get more of them. Questions often take time to investigate. The research time usually takes longer than writing the actual answer.

Each email press release and mailing list announcement can take one nontechnical employee from 4 to 6 hours to do. An email newsletter can take from 8 hours per issue to 80, depending on the length and complexity of the newsletter and how many people contribute articles.

Since the uproar over its Pentium chip, Intel reportedly has four full-time employees who monitor Internet newsgroups (these are discussion groups arranged by topic) and post carefully composed responses to Intel-related items. For smaller companies, newsgroups (valuable resources for both research and publicity) can occupy between 5 to 30 hours of netlurking.

In addition to this, employees throughout the company might spend time on newsgroups related to their specific jobs, such as accounting and taxation newsgroups for accountants. This normally takes less than an hour per person per week. Much more time can be spent surfing the Web. The huge potential for wasting time is one reason many companies restrict Web access, allowing it only for specific people who need it.

An FTP server will need 4 to 8 hours per week to maintain, depending on how many changes you add each week to your server. This includes time to reformat documents, create new files, and remove old files.

Maintenance time for a World Wide Web server can range from 4 hours per week to hundreds, again depending on how active you make your site. Note that most of this time is *editorial* time. Once your Web site is up and working, technical maintenance can be as little as an hour or two per week. Your Web site will also generate additional email for your Webmaster and anyone else whose Internet address is listed on your Web pages. Allow another 4 to 30 hours per week to process these email messages.

These times do not include any overall management time. If your company is big enough and your Internet activities are important enough, you may want a part-time or full-time manager of online communications—usually a non-technical person with excellent communications skills. Look for someone who can quench flames and not start them, and who is sensitive to the needs of your customers.

7. The wrong publisher

What's the difference between "dead chicken parts" and "finger-lickin' good"?

That's the difference between technical accuracy and marketing savvy. Most managers would never dream of forcing a computer programmer to write their advertisements. They'd never tell a network administrator to create their customer service procedures, yet that's exactly what thousands of companies do on their intranets and Web sites.

Marketing and technical support require two very different sets of skills. Would you ask your telephone repairman to dictate what you say on the phone to customers? In the same way, you should not ask your computer technicians to tell you what to say to customers on the Internet.

First of all, it isn't fair to your technical staff. They don't need the extra work-load, especially when it's work that should be done by another department.

Second, you get more effective content for your Web site or intranet if your content is created by the people who are accountable for its results. For example, your intranet's personnel policies will be presented most effectively by your human resources department. Your marketing Web pages' contents should be created by your marketing team.

Let your technical people deal with the technical aspects of your Internet project. Give other appropriate departments responsibility for Internet content.

 Make sure your technical staff does not end up in the publishing business.

8. Trying to build Rome in a day

In some ways, this is the most important advice I can give you: *Start simple!*

A team at one large company took more than a year to open its Web site because it planned a project that was too complex. This is ridiculous. For your first Internet project, or your first World Wide Web site, plan the most basic, stripped-down, bare bones minimum possible. Then simplify *that*, and put it online. Start small and grow.

 Don't aim for perfection—your Net site will evolve constantly and will never be perfect. Don't wait until you get things finished—they never will be. Just get something 80 percent done and launch it. Write EXPERIMENTAL and UNDER CONSTRUCTION all over it if you like, but put it out there. No matter how rough and crude your first effort may be, get it up quickly.

Why start simple? First of all, when you have a nasty surprise, you're a damn sight better off if you have only a 3-page Web site instead of a 30-page site, or a handful of FTP files instead of 600. "What? You mean we have to re-input all 600 files!" You don't want that. Second, the more complex you make your Internet site, the more likely you are to have bugs, *and the longer it will take you to find them*. There is mathematical proof of that, but I won't get into that here. It's common sense.

Besides, the more quickly you open your virtual doors, the more quickly you can learn from your visitors. They will tell you what works and what doesn't work with more insight than your product team could possibly muster, no matter how good your people may be.

Put a small piece of your Internet site up first. Tweak it and polish it, and you will always have that functional core in place. If problems develop while adding to your site, you'll know any problems come from the stuff that is new, not from your old reliable core. Then you can build your Net site gradually by adding graphics or text. The Net makes it easy for you to change things and add stuff.

Besides, when you have one small piece up and running, you have a visible sign that your entire project may work. It creates a feeling of momentum, and it boosts morale for your project team.

9. Doing it all yourself

Trying to do everything in-house increases the odds that your Internet project will be an unusable dud.

Sure, it might be more fun to write your own HTML files and CGI scripts. You might feel more in control if you have your own server computer on your premises connected to the Net on your own communications line. But look at the numbers for a minute.

If you host your Web server on your own in-house computer, you must pay for the computer, for Web server and communications software programs, for a person to support the computer, for Internet access, and for your own digital phone line to connect to the outside world. If you host your Web site on a Web host's computer, you might pay $100 to $200 a month or so. But you don't have to buy your own computer. You don't buy your own software. You don't pay for a support person. Your Web host connects you to the Net with faster lines than you could afford on your own. In fact, all the charges put together from a Web site host cost less than an in-house server's high-speed lines by themselves. Look at renting Web space before you do everything on your own computer.

The same holds true for designing and writing your Web pages. When you compare the price of "store-bought" with homemade, the roll-your-own version may *seem* cheaper. The cost soars when you add in training, human resource, and maintenance costs. Purchased services and products cause less drag on your company's other computer-related projects. They save time, so your project comes to life more quickly. And you'll probably gain a more polished, professional Internet presence than you could build on your own.

Besides, creating all this stuff yourself distracts you from your *real* business, from whatever it is you do that your customers pay you for.

Farm Internet projects out whenever you can. Hire temporary programmers and consultants to build your Internet presence. Put your mailing list server and Web pages on your access provider's computer instead of your own.

There are two exceptions to this rule. First, if you plan a Web site with content derived from a large, frequently-updated database, you might want to keep your Web server in-house to manage your database-server connection. Second, it usually makes sense to keep hardware and creation in-house for your intranet.

10. Ripped off by providers and consultants

When Coriolis Group Books, my publisher, first linked to the Internet, its access provider wanted to charge $200 per person for each worker's email address! My publisher quickly found another provider.

 I've seen more companies get ripped off by access providers and consultants than by hackers, industrial spies, and credit card scams combined. Some access providers pull off amazing swindles and charge outrageous prices for negligible services.

Chapters 3 and 4 cover this topic in detail. The most important thing to remember is: Always, always, *always* get three price quotes before you make a commitment. Don't be surprised if you get a 10-to-1 difference between your highest and lowest quote. Also, the cheapest price may not be your safest bet—the quality of work may be slipshod. You may want to choose a price in the middle. If you get three or more quotes, you'll at least have an idea of the going rate.

Beware of self-proclaimed Internet "experts" whose business cards have no email address, or whose addresses end in **@aol.com**. Real Internet experts have their own domain names. In addition to checking references, see if prospective helpers have earned any recognition within their industries. Have they published any articles or books? Do they speak at conferences or teach seminars?

Watch out for people who have *technical* expertise (such as Internet access providers), but suddenly make the great leap over to marketing or Web page design. As I explained in reason no. 7, "The Wrong Publisher," those two areas require very different skill sets. Grill any potential Net marketing consultant on the differences between Internet marketing and traditional channels. A good marketer will understand both and know how to make both work together for you.

And watch out for artist-wannabes who show you their work and expect you to "ooh" and "aah" over how pretty the sites are and what clever people they are. Ask any potential consultant for *results* their work generated. You don't care if they create great art. You want to see your sales curve go up.

11. Ripped off by security breaches

In 1988, the infamous Internet Worm caused hundreds of thousands of dollars of damage to Internet-linked computers. That damage was accidental. What's worse is when a business lets itself get damaged by deliberate attackers.

A lock on your door and other precautions won't stop a crook with an army tank, but they dramatically reduce your chances of being robbed. If a thief has enough resources, anything can be stolen. Just as in the real world, it is impossible to protect anything from all threats; the same holds true on the Internet. If you know the most common security threats, you can take logical steps to protect yourself from them.

Internet security and break-ins are important topics. You'll find a businessperson's guide in Chapters 7 and 8.

12. No management support

You'll need to justify pursuit of your project to managers by using *business* terms and reasons, not technical reasons. Build your case with striking, easy-to-remember words and images. It never hurts to mention specific examples from your competitors.

 Projects without management support risk the perils of reallocated resources, cancellation, postponement, and budget reductions. Due to lack of support from senior managers, new Net projects have been killed or chopped back to the point where they were no longer effective. If you want your project to prosper—and you want credit for its success—you need a visible and vocal champion among higher management.

Most senior managers will want answers to questions like these:

- Wouldn't America Online cost less, be easier, and/or do all the same things?

- How much will starting this project cost? How much per month to run?

- How long will it take to get this project up and running?

- How much in *savings* will this project generate? Where did you get your figures?

- How much in *revenue* will this project generate? How did you arrive at those figures?

- Will this project slow down any urgent MIS projects?

- Can hackers break into our computers through the Internet?

- How do you know our customers use the Internet?

- Won't the Internet bring workers erotica and video games? (I'm not sure which category managers worry about the most.)

- How can we measure whether this works or not?

And, for sales-related Internet projects, they might ask:

- What's the minimum monthly sales volume for your Internet project to break even?

- Will this *increase* revenue or only *shift* it from one channel to another?

- How will you sustain unit margins over time if competitors come in with lower prices?

- Can we offer lower prices on the Internet and higher prices elsewhere?

- How will you manage pricing conflicts with your other sales channels?

- How can you measure the impact of your Net projects on your existing distributors or resellers?

This book gives you much of the ammo you'll need to answer those questions. Make sure your projections are realistic and on the conservative side. Remember: It is always better to underpromise and overdeliver than the other way around.

Besides pointing out what your competitors do on the Net, it can be helpful to enlist support from equal-level managers from other companies. If you know a peer of your managers who has profited by the Internet, ask the peer manager to call your managers and talk with them. It helps to know what your management's hot buttons are.

Internet traffic (especially the World Wide Web) can produce a great deal of statistics for analyses and reports. This can be valuable to top managers. Instead of depending on warm fuzzy feelings to satisfy them, you can actually show how many messages, file downloads, and sales leads the Internet has generated.

The reporting capabilities of the Net can also show managers exactly why you've done things and who your Internet visitors are. Chris Gulker found this helpful when his editors at the *Electric Examiner* (now called *The Gate* at **www.sfgate.com**) questioned his choice of Web page material.

"Editors said, 'You don't have enough stories about city council meetings,' " reported Gulker. "I told them, 'We tried running city council meetings. No one looked at them,' and showed them exactly how many readers read other stories and how few read city council stories." He also showed them *where* visitors to the *Electric Examiner* originate. Based in San Francisco, the *Electric Examiner* has more readers in the U.K. than in nearby Berkeley.

This level of accountability is hard to beat. You can use it to produce reports and especially to track sales sources. You'll find more about this subject in a later chapter. For many senior managers, reports equal results. Producing detailed, informative reports assures continuing support for your Internet project.

Eleven steps to internet success

You've read about the awful things that can go wrong and how to avoid them, but you can't succeed on the Net by avoidance alone. You need to know what steps your business should take to implement a triumphant Internet project—"steps" rather than leaps. For something as potentially complex as a Net project, a step-by-step approach is the best plan.

Step 1.   Decide who you want to reach.

What you say and *how* you can say it will be determined by *who* you want to communicate with. Are your targets employees, customers, or suppliers? Are they first-time buyers or repeat customers? Will they have Web access, or can you reach more of them by email? What connection speeds do they use? Do they want flashy graphics, or do they prefer "just the facts"?

Answer questions like these first, and let your target audience's habits and preferences guide you in shaping a project that reaches them most effectively.

Step 2.   Pick a project manager to assign tasks, monitor the schedule, maintain a budget, and oversee testing.

Choose wisely. As in most business situations, a great manager will increase your chances of success more than any other factor. And it won't hurt if your team leader has actually been on the Internet for a few months and has read this book.

Depending on your project's needs, your budget, and your schedule, you may want to hire an outside expert to manage your project. If you are understaffed or you want to get your Net project up and running as quickly as possible, hire a consultant as project manager. If you cannot afford a consultant, or if detailed understanding of your customers' needs or your company's internal resources is essential to your project, use an in-house person as project manager. Someone who does well at managing non-Internet projects will often be a better choice than someone who knows the Internet but is a poor project manager.

Step 3.   Evaluate your existing needs and resources, including hardware and software, and the availability and skills of your people.

Begin by finding out what you need and what you have. Talk with your staff; you may find an employee or co-worker who surfs the Net at home and can give advice. Involve people across departmental boundaries; the more departments with even a little involvement in your ideas, the more they will support your finished result. As every successful politician since Julius Caesar has known, broad-based support is essential to final success. Make an effort to involve nontechnical people from the very start.

If you want to use the Net for marketing, shop your competition. If you plan to actually sell online, buy something from at least three different Web sites so you can study sales procedures.

Do an information survey of your business. Find out what information your customers, suppliers, and staff will want to access on the Net and then find out where in your company that information lives.

Step 4.   Select a simple, visible pilot project. Define its scope. Set a target timeline with deliverable steps and required compatibilities.

Budgeting is tough, especially when you budget for something you've never done before. Don't think you can budget to the exact dollar or even the exact hundred dollars. The unexpected will crop up. The most important part of your timeline will be the definitions of your deliverables and the milestones you set for them, not any projected dates. Be flexible with delivery dates. Expect your project to be late and overbudget, and reserve 10 percent or more of your budget for unforeseen contingencies.

Remember to start small, as small as you possibly can. A small project is much easier to control. You're traveling in uncharted waters, where a canoe slips through tight spots easier than the *Queen Mary.*

Step 5. Get support from your management—both financial support in the form of budgeted funds and endorsement of deliverables.

Ask for support based on business reasons, not technical reasons. Tie your project into the big picture. How will it support your company's long-term goals? Conservatively, what quantifiable benefits can managers expect after using the Internet for one year? Evaluate your company's culture. If it's a rigid hierarchy (a 'command and control' model), expect resistance.

Step 6. Gather a small project team willing to work hard and produce quickly.

Committees take time. Unless you have a very small company, your first Internet project is no time to build a company-wide consensus. Hand-pick a tight crew who can get along together and who will thrive on pressure.

When appropriate, recruit your elite commandos from different departments. Your Net project may have work that requires different kinds of expertise: technical, marketing, operations, accounting, or sales. A diversity of skills—if they are the particular skills you need—will make it easier to assign specific tasks.

Step 7. Evaluate and select consultants, an Internet access provider, software, and hardware.

Before you carve your specs in stone, it will be easier (and less costly) to hire consultants to help you plan and to do tasks that your team lacks the expertise or time to handle. At this stage you should still be flexible. A consultant or your access provider may suggest alternate ways to meet your objectives that streamline your workload or save money.

Step 8. Create detailed specifications.

Working from your list of deliverables, your manager and team should create detailed specifications. Depending on your project, these may require research by the team. One of the decisions to make at this point is how much, if any, of this project should run on your own computer and how much should run on a computer managed by your Internet access provider. Other important issues at this stage are security measures and the types of reporting to implement. You should have reached the stage of *feature lock* before you complete Step 7.

Be iron-willed about refusing to add feature after feature, no matter how appealing they seem or how easy your staff says they will be to add. Save them for your next project.

Step 9. Develop your prototype and put it online.
After all those steps, finally you get to do something! By this point, you've done your homework and you have chosen advisors for when you need help. If you use your own technical staffers, prototype development will be their busiest stage. Development is where things get exciting and intense. To keep your Internet project team energetic and to build momentum, celebrate each milestone as you reach it. And watch out for *feature creep,* the innate urge to add just one more thing. It seems harmless but is deadlier than any ghoul dreamed up by Stephen King.

Then comes the magic moment when your experimental version first goes online. Let pioneers within your company try to break it first, before you expose it to the outside world. It will help if you can roll a Web site out gradually. When your project goes live on the Net, let a few people know. Quiz them closely about their experiences on your site. Incorporate improvements based on their reactions before announcing your site to the world. Expect problems—there always are some at first.

And expect to conduct training for whomever your Internet project will touch, within your company or customers outside. When training, give people information they can use *immediately*. Let them understand that the Internet is not something to fear. The Net is useful and it's fun. Make sure your own people receive education in netiquette, and that they are capable of internationally acceptable manners, not just U.S. brusqueness.

Step 10. Promote your site.
It is often a mistake to promote your Internet site before you have it up and running. Too many problems can happen. Too much can change. But as soon as your site goes live, pull out the bells and whistles, and honk all the horns! Make as much noise as you possibly can.

Promote your site both inside and outside your company. Make sure your employees know about it. Make sure that any staff members who deal with your customers can answer questions about it. Set up "guided tours" for staffers and senior managers who lack their own Internet access. Start an employee suggestion contest with prizes for those who come up with ways to improve your site.

Outside your company, promote your Net site in as many ways as possible. You'll find lots of ways to do that in the marketing chapters of this book.

Step 11.   Learn from your visitors and grow your site.

The Internet is interactive. You will get feedback. Some will be direct, such as email messages from people who have used your site. Some will be indirect, such as statistics on file download rates or number of visitors to your site. Some may be sales figures or cost savings as your Federal Express bill goes down.

Plan from the beginning to collect that feedback, to analyze it, and to apply it. From your seed project, you can grow your Internet business to serve your company and your customers in many ways. The feedback you receive will be your surest guide.

CHAPTER 3

What Do I Need and How Much Will It Cost?

"A computer does not substitute for judgment any more then a pencil substitutes for literacy. But writing without a pencil is no particular advantage."

—Robert McNamara

When I worked at Computer Literacy Bookshops, Mary Cronin, author of *Doing Business on the Internet*, gave a presentation at one of our stores on the many advantages of the Net for business. After her talk, I saw one man with a puzzled expression, searching through Internet books. "I'm a software consultant," he explained, "and in my business, I certainly could use some of the information in all those databases and archives she talked about. What kind of book could get me started on this Internet thing?"

I showed him some introductory books and directories of Internet resources. "The best book for you depends on what kind of computer and operating system you use," I said.

"I use a Pentium PC with Windows," he replied. "Do you have books for that?"

I showed him a good do-it-yourself book that came with a disk of Windows software to connect to the Net. "Everything is on that one disk?" he asked with suspicion. "All those databases and archives she talked about fit on just one disk?"

"No," I explained, "they're on the Internet. The software here lets you connect to the Net so you can download those databases on your modem."

He stepped back from me in horror. "You mean I have to buy *a modem?*"

Needless to say, he bought no book that night. Most businesspeople's reactions are not that extreme, but that man's situation parallels that of thousands of businesses, large and small. From the outside, the Internet looks simple. But pull off its lid and the Net turns into Pandora's Box, stuffed with phone lines, computers, software, and enough ugly abbreviations to give nightmares to Noah Webster. The benefits of the Internet are enormous, and the costs seem very small. But when you get into it, you find it's more complicated than you first thought. Especially when you try to plan how much it will cost.

The Internet for business is not a one-size-fits-all kind of thing. You can pay less than $50 for the Internet or you can pay millions. That's actually a good thing; the Net is so flexible you can wrestle it more or less into the size and shape you need. But that flexibility makes it tough to budget, because you must choose between hundreds of possible combinations of products and services. This chapter and the one following are here to help.

I'll try to break down your options and explain your choices so you can generate figures for budgeting and estimating profits and losses. Now don't step back like the guy in the bookstore, but to make cost projections and manage your Internet project, you'll have to learn a little bit about the Internet's technical issues. I'll make it as painless as I can.

David Angell and Brent Heslop, in their book *The Internet Business Companion*, clearly explain the dangers of technical ignorance: "As a business decision-maker, you need to understand the issues, even if you plan to have others do the work for you. If you don't understand the tools and options of the Internet, then technical people (consultants, server services, service providers) will decide your business objectives, which can be costly. Keep the technical people where they belong—advising and applying your Internet business strategy, not deciding it."

Seven building blocks

To understand the potential gains and associated costs the Internet can bring to your business, you need to know the seven major tools of the Internet: email, the World Wide Web, intranets, FTP, Gopher, mailing lists, and newsgroups.

Email, which is short for electronic mail, is something you probably already know about. It's easier, faster, and cheaper to send someone an email message than it is to phone, fax, or send a postcard. Email is becoming the dominant way businesses communicate. The simplest form of Internet access is email only.

The *World Wide Web* provides an easy point-and-click way to find information on the tens of thousands of computers on the Net. On the Web, you can reach documents and data stored on computers all over the world without it mattering where they are. The Web displays information on your computer screen as pages of text and pictures. It can also include sound and moving images. Businesses also use the World Wide Web to *collect* information. Web software can provide electronic forms into which a person can enter data, such as credit card information to make a purchase. To find information on the Web, a person needs software called a *Web client* or *Web browser,* such as Netscape Navigator or Microsoft Internet Explorer. Many browsers will let you use the Net to make free long-distance phone calls. To provide information to the millions of people who use Web

Important Note: This concept of two kinds of software—a server to provide information and a client to read it—is the heart of all Internet services. It is important to understand this client/server concept, because every Internet management decision will revolve around clients and servers. Any Internet transaction has three parts: 1) the client, which asks for information; 2) the server, which provides the information; and 3) the Internet itself, which passes the client's request to the server and carries requested information back to the client.

Client *means the client software, the actual program that an individual Internet user runs to use services on the Net. The client is what asks for data and reads it. To read an email message, for example, you must have email client software.*

Server *can have three different meanings. It can be 1) the server software program that provides data, 2) the computer hardware where the server software lives, or it can refer to 3) both the computer and its software program together.*

Your business can use dozens of different kinds of clients and servers.

browsers, your business will need software called a *Web server*. The runaway successes of Web servers are responsible for the wild-eyed media coverage about the Internet.

Intranets apply the advantages of the World Wide Web to reach and distribute information within your business. You don't have to worry about where the information is actually stored, and because the Web is easy to understand, employees don't need training to use your intranets. Intranets make your company's internal documents, software, training programs, and databases accessible to employees worldwide, no matter what kind of computer they use. Because they distribute information over the networks your business already has, intranets are fast to set up. A 1996 study by Forrester Research claimed that two-thirds of U.S. companies have or plan to have intranets in the future.

FTP servers store and provide documents, graphics, software programs—anything that you can turn into a computer file. These servers are cheap to run, easy to set up, and provide a cost-effective way to make large amounts of information available. FTP, which stands for *File Transfer Protocol*, is not quite as easy to use as Web software, and lacks the glamour of graphical design on the Web.

Gopher servers are almost as easy to set up as FTP servers and can provide anything that an FTP server can, with two additional advantages: Gopher software presents a clear menu of choices, making it easier for nontechnical people to use, and Gopher files are easier to find because they are searchable by subject and can be linked to Web pages and to other Gophers. Gopher is efficient, but is rarely used by businesspeople, who prefer using the Web because Gopher is harder to navigate and use. Because of that, Gopher is obsolete.

Mailing list servers are extremely valuable tools for businesses on the Net. There are obvious uses, such as sending mass mailings of a message or newsletter to your customers or to your employees. But you can also use a mailing list server to create discussion groups, in which every message from any member of a list is distributed to all other members. And you can use a mailing list server to automatically send information to answer inquiries from people.

Newsgroups are also used to conduct discussions. When you enter a newsgroup, you read a menu of the subjects of messages posted to that group, each with the name of the person who posted it. You can click on any message you want to read. You can reply by posting your own message, either publicly by posting your reply to the newsgroup for anyone to read, or privately, by sending your reply directly to the person who posted the original message. If you post your reply publicly, or post an original message or question of your own, your reply or question will be seen (and may be commented upon) by all the readers of that group worldwide. Some individual groups have more than 100,000 regular readers. Newsgroups are extremely valuable sources of information. There are more than 20,000 public newsgroups, called *Usenet.* You can also create your own private newsgroups. Some people call newsgroups by another name, *netnews.*

Your company can use and provide dozens of additional Internet services in addition to these, from videoconferencing to network management tools. However, most businesses find that (except for Gopher, which is obsolete) the ones described above are the most useful Internet services.

Obvious costs and submerged reefs

Anytime you're involved in a high-tech project, you know you must budget for hardware (like computers and cables) and software. For Internet projects, you must also add two more certain costs: payment for a *telephone line* (or lines) to connect with the Internet and payment for your *Internet access* itself.

You may purchase both your line and your Internet access from your local telephone company. Or you may purchase the line from your phone company and your Internet access from another company. This second company is called an *Internet access provider* or Internet service provider. The word "service" takes on many meanings when discussing the Internet, so to avoid confusion this book uses the term *Internet access provider* throughout. Keep in mind that an access provider and a service provider are the same thing. The charges from your phone company and your access provider involve many factors: the speed of your connection, your distance from the telephone switching station, the types of services you have, and many more considerations. Your connection and your access provider are so important and so complicated that they get their own chapter (the next one).

When you calculate your Internet expenses, be ready to do some number crunching. Most Internet services are priced separately, forcing you to compare several alternative sets of costs.

In addition to those obvious costs—hardware, software, your connection, and your access provider—you'll find other expenses that may not come to mind as quickly. Training, for instance, often costs more than hardware and software put together. Your technical people will need education in their new environment, and your end-users will need training as well.

The firm of Ernst & Young estimates that for networked systems, 20 percent of your cost will be buying hardware and software, and 80 percent of your cost will be maintenance and additional expenses. The biggest expenses in doing business on the Internet may not be your costs to deliver and present information, but the labor costs of interacting with your customers and updating your information. Don't forget to allow for end-user support and lost productivity during the ramp-up and learning stages. *Training and personnel costs will often be more than half of your expenses.*

Since the Internet is a public network, you will need to invest more in security than you would for a stand-alone computer or a project restricted to your own internal network. Budget for sufficient security, including purchases, installation, and maintenance. If you can't afford security, don't implement your project until your next budget cycle, or change the design of your Internet project to eliminate the dangers. *Security is extremely important on the Internet.* Failure to understand the significance of this statement can damage your business.

Five big influences on Internet costs

For many businesses, five factors have the biggest influences on Internet project costs:

1. *How many people within your company will use the Internet?* You will need to buy client software for each of these people. You will need to train them. You may need to buy networking cards for all of their computers. You may need to run cabling to their desks.

2. *How many Internet services (email, Web, intranet, etc.) will you offer?* The more services you offer, the more hardware and software you will have to buy, the more training your staff will need, the more time it will take to update your information, and the more promotion you will need. Whew!

3. *What type of computer and operating system will you use?* You can run Internet software on every kind of computer from a mainframe to a laptop, but different computers generate different costs. Software for mainframes and midrange computers has higher initial costs, but can support more people, so if you have hundreds of users your cost per person is lower. Unix computers give you lots of free software, but due to the labor involved in system setup and ongoing maintenance, Unix systems cost more to run than other operating systems. Windows NT and 95 systems are also time-consuming to set up and maintain. Macintosh Internet applications are the easiest to set up and maintain, and the most secure, but many system administrators are unfamiliar with Macs. Be aware of the tradeoffs between one platform and another.

4. *What speed of connection will you buy?* A faster connection means higher phone company charges, higher access provider fees, and more expensive hardware and maintenance. A slow 28.8 Kbps modem connection can cost less than $30 per month, but a superfast 155 megabits-per-second ATM OC3 connection will cost more than $10,000 per month.

5. *How much work will you do in-house and how much will you farm out?* Your project will go faster with less bumps in the road if you buy instead of build whenever you can. This also makes costs much more predictable; you can hold an outside vendor to a fixed price agreement, but if your own programmers go way over budget, you have no recourse but to pay. Use the services offered by your Internet access provider as much as possible, and whenever possible hire consultants to reduce your own staff's workload.

Reducing cost uncertainties

To reduce the impact of uncertainties on your own staff, before you sign a purchase order with a vendor, you need to predict the *quality of support* you will receive. Make sure you understand the vendor's pricing structure, especially for licensing, upgrades, and support. Compatibility often affects support. Find out if the vendor's product will work with other software, both software that you use in-house as well as the software your access provider uses. Find out how much training and implementation will cost.

Does your prospective vendor provide estimated or guaranteed turnaround times and response times for support? How does a tech-support question escalate through the vendor's chain of command? How many support technicians does your vendor have? Does your vendor have support technicians for your specific operating system? *An extremely important issue with Internet support is that your vendor offers 24-hour support.* The Internet runs 24 hours every day, and it is impossible to predict when you will need emergency support. If your Internet vendor agreements cover support issues adequately, it will do a great deal toward helping you keep within your budget predictions.

When gathering information for an Internet project's budget, be on the lookout for four types of expenses:

1. Fixed
2. Period-based
3. Project-based
4. Transaction-based

Assuming that all costs will be *fixed* will cause you grief. Some costs are fixed. You buy a cable, it costs a set amount. Other costs will be *period-based*, such as a monthly charge or annual software support agreement. Some will be *project-based*. Hire a consultant to do a project. When it's done, your expenses stop. The costs to watch out for are *transaction-based*.

 Transaction-based costs on an Internet project are less predictable than other types of costs. For example, if you pay a nine-cent fee for every credit card transaction you process, a surge in credit card orders will cause more nine-cent fees. You can get into trouble if you pay your Internet access provider a transaction-based fee tied to the number of email messages that you send or receive, or to the number of hits your Web site generates.

Some types of transaction-based fees are reasonable. But per-message charges for email penalize you when you succeed, and they discourage you from using mailing lists. Besides, per-message charges for email are a scam. It costs your access provider no more to send out 100 email messages than one. Per-message charges for email not only cripple your ability to make accurate cost projections, but they should also be a red flag when you evaluate a possible provider.

Also beware of transaction-based fees for your Web site. If you put your home page on your provider's computer, it is reasonable to pay for the disk real estate you use and an amount for maintenance. But your provider pays a flat monthly rate for its Internet access, and it is unreasonable for you to be charged each time someone visits your page. You should smile when someone reads your Web page, not cringe at the additional expense. When you budget for a Web site, watch out for charges that are per hit, per access, or per megabyte transferred.

Different strokes for different folks

Now you've got the background on important terms and concepts. And you know what expense areas to keep your eye on. (See? I told you that wouldn't hurt.)

With our vocabularies in sync, I can give you some sample costs. To get a grip on some of the pieces that make up your budget puzzle, let's start with the smallest possible business.

Internet budget for a one-person startup

If your company is just you, Internet setup will be pretty straightforward. Unless your business is centered around the Internet, you can get by with one modem, one phone line, and some software. (I assume you already have a computer.)

One tip: It's worth paying for another phone line to keep your Net connection separate from your voice line. Three reasons: First, if you cruise the Net for hours, no one can reach you by phone. Second, call waiting will screw up your Net connection. Third, and most important by far, you won't be able to call technical support for your Internet software and ask them to walk you step by step through solving a problem. (If you have a fax line, think about sharing it between your fax and your modem.)

2nd phone line	$100 hookup, $40/month
Internet access provider	$30 setup, $20-$30/month
33.6K modem (or 56K for $300)	$140
Web browser software	$25
Eudora or Pegasus email client software	$80
WinZip + other software (optional)	$150
Your own domain name (optional)	$150 registration, $50/year renewal
Web host (if you have a Web site)	$90/month
Reference books (optional)	$160

You'll need the Web host service only if you plan to have your own Web site. I assume you'd create a simple Web site on your own. If not, plan on spending $400 to $3,500 for a consultant to create your Web site for you. These prices assume you will *not* accept credit cards over the Net. Credit card processing costs more to set up and adds ongoing costs and per-transaction costs.

If you live in an area where your cable TV company provides Internet access, leap on it. You'll have many times the speed for less than $50 per month. You will need to spend $400 to $500 on a cable modem, though.

Internet budgets for bigger businesses

Move up to, say, a 10-person office and your possibilities expand so dramatically they won't fit in a neat little chart. Your possibilities will fall into three main areas: hardware (computers and gadgets), software, and administration. For many companies, World Wide Web sites cost more than everything else put together, so I've provided a section on that.

Computers and gadgets

You can get all kinds of gadgets for the Net: beepers that give you email messages, wireless modems, $99 TV cameras that mount on top of your computer. I'm waiting for a product announced by Philips Electronics, a tiny wireless Web cruiser that you wear on your arm like a wristwatch. For your more everyday business needs, these next pages give you a sense of some of your hardware choices.

If you want to get material from the Net but don't want to provide any, your needs are pretty simple. You just need the one computer you work on, the fastest modem you can buy, and the fastest Net connection you can afford. Even if you want a fast ISDN connection, the same principles apply. Life gets more complex when you want to *provide* information—such as your own World Wide Web home page—or if you want several people on a LAN or other internal network to be connected to the Internet.

Computers for Web publishing

To provide information, you need a computer to act as your server (or more than one computer if you plan a gigantic Web site). A server is where your data lives. Your server can cost less than $100 or more than $100,000. Most companies pay between $1,500 and $9,000 for a computer to act as Web server. This includes operating system software.

You don't necessarily need a computer of your own for your server. You can also rent space on a computer, either from your Internet access provider or from companies that specialize in renting out space for Web sites. These other companies are formally called *Web hosts* and informally called *Web farms*. You can rent space from a Web host for $20 to $500 per month, depending on your needs.

If you are new to the Internet, or if you are a Net veteran but have never created a server before, you can save time, money, and Tylenol by borrowing expertise from a Web host. Rent space on a Web host's computer. Your host may also allow you to supply a computer kept on the host's premises, which the host's technical staff will manage. If you do this, in addition to $4,000 to $8,000 for your computer, expect to pay your host $200 to $400 per month.

Server computers

There's a lot of talk about how fast and big your server computer has to be to offer services on the Net. In real life, you don't necessarily need a $6,000 high-powered Unix workstation. You might, but the computer is not what slows most sites down. The slowest thing in most Internet sites is the *connection* between the company and its Internet access provider. Even an old 386-based computer is faster than a 28.8 Kbps connection. (*Kbps* stands for kilobits-per-second, a measurement of network speed or *bandwidth*. A *kilobit* is 1,000 bits of data.)

Does your server need to support 10 users concurrently? 200? 1,000? Are your computers linked on a single LAN, or are they dispersed over many buildings, or even throughout different countries? Are visitors to your Internet site downloading huge files of graphics, or just text? Part of your need for speed depends on what Internet services your server supports. A Web server must be fast. An email server can be slow.

To get an idea of how much computer power you need, take a look at what other businesses use:

- *Boardwatch* magazine (**www.boardwatch.com**) ran its first Web server on a 386SX 20 MHz PC "machine that lays on its side and we can't find the cover or most of the pieces for it." On *Boardwatch*'s 56 Kbps connection, the 386 server handled 7,000 hits/day from 1,000 visitors/day.

- Software seller The Corner Store used two PCs running Windows NT to handle incoming email. The two PCs alternated on receiving email. "We have two SMTP servers. One picks up (the modem line) after three rings and one after four rings."

- Aspen Media (**www.aspenmedia.com**) uses a high-speed T1 line to provide a place for designers to display hundreds of huge graphics files. For its server, Aspen uses a $24,000 Silicon Graphics Indy 128 computer with 128 megabytes of memory and 3 gigabytes of disk space.

There is no one answer to the question of what kind of computer you need. The computer that handles your Web site will need to perform *multitasking*—doing several things at once. Web servers need multitasking to handle something called CGI (Common Gateway Interface). To store the information from CGI transactions, you need at least 8 megabytes of memory—16 megabytes would be better. If you plan on 2,500 hits per day on a Unix machine, you'll need that memory to run two to four Unix processes at once. Of course, your Web server could also run under OS/2, Windows NT, Macintosh, AS/400, or other operating systems that do multitasking.

Hardware to link several people to the Net

If you want to link several people in your business to the Internet, you will need a different kind of server, a *gateway server* to process your company's inflow and outflow of information. Your provider may help you with your gateway, but you will probably want to run it on your own computer. You will also need a router. A *router* is a box that takes Internet signals and feeds them to your LAN, and vice versa. Most routers cost between $1,000 and $3,000. If your needs are small enough, you can add *router software* to your server computer to avoid buying a separate router box.

If you lease a high-speed line, you may need another $700-$2,800 box called a *CSU/DSU*. It takes the signal from your leased phone line and converts it so your router can read the signal. These will be the central parts of your Internet connection. You may need other hardware as well. Cables, perhaps, and a firewall to keep out hackers. You also might need a costly box called a *switch* to translate between software formats.

Modems and their ilk

To connect to the Internet, you will need either a phone line and a modem, or another kind of connection and its hardware. I cover these options in depth in the next chapter. For now, I'll just make a few basic points.

First, you really don't want to do business on the Internet with anything slower than 33.6 Kbps speed. A 14.4 Kbps connection may be acceptable if you just provide an email server, but it's unacceptable if you provide a Web site. Even a 33.6 Kbps modem can support only a bare-bones, no-frills low-use Web site without clogging. (By the way, if you use a 28.8 Kbps modem (or faster) on a PC, your system must have a serial card with a UART chip N16550AF to support this data transfer rate.)

If you provide a World Wide Web site on your own computer, you'll need at least an ISDN-level connection. (ISDN stands for Integrated Services Digital Network; its basic level of service, called BRI, provides data transfer rates from 56 Kbps to 128 Kbps.) If you want ISDN speed, you'll need special hardware, and you'll find that different vendors offer widely different prices and services. For instance, Adtran, Inc. (**www.adtran.com**) provides two ISDN "modems." Its ISU Express ISDN box handles both voice and data over one ISDN phone line—voice and data at 64 Kbps and data at 128 Kbps. It supports multiple connections, so you need only one phone line to handle voice, fax, and Internet. The ISU Express costs $900 for voice and data and $700 for data only. Adtran's ISU 2x64 model can cost more than $1,000 and supports up to two computers.

When shopping for other ISDN communication (essentially a modem, but technically not the same) products, look for one that has a built-in NT1 adapter (this device provides the communication interface between your telephone line and your computer). You can purchase ISDN cards and modems from AccessWorks, Fujitsu, Hayes, ISDN-Tek, Motorola, and ZyXel as for as little as $300. Get one that doesn't need an external NT1, unless you want to connect other ISDN phones and gadgets to the same device.

Ascend Communications (**www.ascend.com**) makes solid ISDN routers for home and small office use. The IBM WaveRunner Digital Modem for ISDN is highly rated. This model includes built-in Windows and OS/2 support, and will cost you only about $600.

Connecting to your LAN

To reach the Internet, your computer must have software called TCP/IP. The main personal computer and workstation operating systems—NetWare, OS/2, Mac OS, and the latest Microsoft Windows variations—come with built-in TCP/IP software. With TCP/IP already included, your computers speak the *lingua franca* of the Internet. You can also find Internet client software packages available for every operating system.

That's the good news. The bad news is that you will still need a way to move data between your LAN and the Internet. Even worse, it is extremely difficult to make some popular LAN software packages work well with the Internet, especially Microsoft Mail and cc:Mail.

First, to direct incoming Internet traffic to your LAN computers, you will need either a gateway computer, a router, or a switch. If you have a small-bandwidth Internet connection (56 Kbps or slower), you can buy router software and install it on your LAN server computer. It's generally cheaper to run router software than to buy a hardware version. (At your business, security concerns may rule out running router software on your computer.)

If your connection speed is ISDN (56 Kbps or higher), you will need to buy a router. This will handle your Ethernet-to-Internet connection, and will set you back $800 to $3,000, depending on your Internet connection speed and the number of computers on your LAN. If you have an ISDN Internet connection, look for an ISDN router that costs less and is easier to run than a conventional router. Ascend Communications, for example, makes a well-regarded $1,800 ISDN router that supports up to eight computers.

Your LAN's needs will play an important role in determining which Internet access provider you chose. Some charge much more for supporting different email addresses for your employees on a LAN, for example. Many providers charge $150 to $300 more per month for a LAN ISDN account than for a single-user account at the same speed.

Web site costs

You may have heard about the IDC/Link study claiming that the average cost for a company to create a Web site is $840,000 to $1.25 million. That may be so, but I put the first version of my Web site up in one afternoon for less than $100.

My costs were $35 for one month's rent at a Web farm, $28 to use a scanner at Kinko's Copies to make graphics files, and $25 for a book on writing Web documents. (I already had a copy of Robert Mudry's book *Serving the Web*, but I bought the second one for its quick-reference command guide.) Since I have a background in advertising, I hired myself as a copywriter for nothing (a fraction of my usual fee).

You might not be able to create your own Web site as quickly or as cheaply, but tens of thousands of businesses have opened Web sites for less than IDC's overinflated $840,000. For example, GE Plastics launched its 1,500-page site for under $100,000. Federal Express created its site—including realtime package tracking—for less than $100,000. IBM's Web site cost $30,000 to set up and $300,000 to run its first year.

If you want a simple Web site kept on a Web host and not on your own computer, you may be able to create it yourself for under $1,000 or hire consultants to do it for less than $2,000. A more effective Web site can cost $5,000 to $10,000 if you keep it offsite. You can build an elaborate one for $50,000 or less if you plan carefully.

You have many ways to cut costs. First, if you can, keep your Web site on a computer at an outside company's facilities rather than your own. Rented Web space means you can keep a low-budget Internet connection for the rest of your company, because it won't get swamped by Web traffic. Your Web farm probably has a fast T1 or a faster T3 connection, so your Web pages will fly to the Net at swifter speeds than you would want to pay for.

Second, farm out as much of the work as possible. Hire consultants; they cost more per hour than your employees, but when your project is done, you don't have to feed them. (And an average webmaster earns $45,000 or more per year.) Figure on paying design and copy consultants $40 to $200 per hour, and $10 to $40 per hour for someone to write HTML code. If you need a project manager, expect to pay $1,000 to $2,500 per week for someone to oversee your site development. The more elaborate you make your site, the more you'll pay per hour and in total.

You can outsource almost every part of Web site creation. For instance, if you have hundreds of pages of documents to turn into HTML code, go to a company like Innodata (**www.inod.com**), which hires English-speaking college graduates in foreign countries to convert documents to electronic formats at a fraction of U.S. prices.

You can spend many times more money on your Web site than on all the rest of your Internet activity put together. You can buy more different kinds of software to add to your Web site than for any other part of the Internet. Remember that developing a Web site is the cheapest part. Updating and supporting your site will be the most expensive part. Budget at least 10 percent of development costs per month for ongoing costs.

Internet email considerations

If you have only one person to connect to the Internet or a small number of people, you don't need an Internet email server. If your business is big enough to have its own LAN, you will need your own email server. Setting up an Internet email server can be complicated because you have several decisions to make. Will you use Internet email software to connect to your company's computers, or will you link your existing email software to the Internet?

In other words, will you use mainframe or LAN email client software (Lotus cc:Mail, Microsoft Mail, Lotus Notes, QuickMail, OfficeVision, All-in-1, etc.), or do you want to go for "pure" Internet mail all the way to the desktop?

This is not a seat-of-your-pants decision. There is a lot involved here, so you may want to investigate your options thoroughly.

Because email is vital for your business, I've devoted an entire chapter to the subject. Here, I'd just like to start you thinking about your options. Table 3.1 shows the pros and cons of the various email approaches available to you. It also provides you with criteria for choosing which kind of mail client software you want your users to use to send and read email. If you are a one- or two-person business, your decision is easy: Use an Internet email client. It's the simplest, easiest, and most functional solution. You can get excellent Internet email client software for Windows, Unix, OS/2, Macs, and all other platforms.

With a larger business, you have more factors to consider. The resources of the Internet itself add significant value to Internet email clients, so you may want to replace LAN email software with Internet email software, unless it is cost-prohibitive or you are using Lotus Notes. Notes adds so many capabilities that removing it might not be productive.

In addition to client software, any company larger than a couple of people will need one more software program to use Internet email. Whether you use LAN client software or not, you will need software to pass email back and forth between your clients and the Internet. You must choose between either a UUCP server or an SMTP server. With either of these servers, you can replace your LAN email gateway with the much-easier-to-administer (and much cheaper) Internet email server.

Each of these alternatives creates a different set of tasks for your network administrator, but your users won't be affected.

Table 3.1   Your email options and how they compare.

Mainframe or LAN email software clients

Pro:
Many products available for most operating systems

Use same operating system as other business applications

Integrate with mail-enabled applications

Feature-rich

Con:
Require application gateways or switches

Expensive—gateways cost $2,000 to $5,000 apiece, and you need one for each brand of client; switches are hardware that handle many brands, but cost $20,000 to $300,000

Difficult to install

Time-consuming to maintain

Buggy

Users on the Net must have two addresses, one for the email client and one for the Internet

Most mainframe and LAN mail clients cost more than Internet email software

Internet email software clients

Pro:
Many available for most operating systems

Use same operating system as other business applications

Integrate with Internet services

Good software available free or inexpensively

Users need to learn only one email address

No application gateways or switches required

Con:
Not integrated with mail-enabled applications

Require user retraining if replacing existing email client

Exceptions:
If you use Unix, Internet email is already integrated, so you don't need a gateway unless you use Lotus Notes.

If you use Macs, you have a much easier and cheaper gateway than other platforms: Mail*Link Remote.

If you use OS/2 Warp, you need to know that the Internet Access Kit included provides email for one user, but can have problems when used on your LAN.

UUCP is simpler

UUCP is the simpler of the two. It stands for Unix-to-Unix Copy Protocol, but don't bother to remember that since nobody ever uses its full name. The magic of UUCP is that you can use Internet email, but you don't need to have your computer permanently connected to the Net 24 hours a day.

Instead, your computer uses a modem to periodically call your Internet access provider's computer, which *is* permanently connected to the Net. Your computer sends your outgoing email messages to the access provider's computer, receives any incoming email that has accumulated, and then hangs up. It is simple to completely automate this process of calling and passing messages so your computer sends and receives your messages every 15 minutes, or in any time interval you specify. This does add a delay time to your email correspondence, which is the main drawback of using a UUCP connection for your email.

The advantages of UUCP are low cost and high security. UUCP is much cheaper than a direct connection, is easier to maintain, and is harder for a hacker to break into your computer since it is frequently disconnected from the Internet.

For costs of UUCP, just ask your access provider the fees for a UUCP account.

SMTP is bigger

As Robert Mudry, author of *Serving the Web,* put it, "SMTP is 24-hour instant gratification compared to UUCP."

SMTP (short for Simple Mail Transfer Protocol) requires your mail computer to be up, running, and connected to the Internet all the time. If you are going to turn off and on the computer that is your email server, use UUCP. With SMTP, if you are not connected at the instant an incoming message arrives, the message goes away and comes back later for another try. If you have a leased line to your access provider or a 24-hour SLIP or PPP connection, you might want to use SMTP.

The way SMTP delivers mail makes little sense to the average nontechnical person. SMTP doesn't actually deliver mail itself. It passes mail to another program, such as Sendmail. To send or receive mail, Sendmail (or any SMTP program you use) must run continuously as a server. Your internal SMTP server will be complicated to set up and maintain, but not as complicated as a LAN email gateway.

Sendmail comes in many versions. If you use a commercial version of Unix, throw away the version of Sendmail that comes with it and replace it with the free version. The free one probably has better documentation and more recent bug fixes. Sendmail is included with OS/2 and Windows 95. Sendmail is a kind of software called a Mail Transport Agent (MTA) program. You can use other MTA programs instead of Sendmail. Smail is a drop-in replacement for Sendmail that is easier to set up; it handles both UUCP and SMTP. One called MMDF (Multichannel Memorandum Distribution Facility) is older than Sendmail and still in use.

As I mentioned earlier, with a small business, your choice is easy—Internet email. If, however, you have a medium- to large-sized business with a number of computers, your work is cut out for you. You will want to send and receive email into a gateway computer system that will feed it through a router to a LAN into the email software on everybody's computers. Many LAN email gateways for Windows are expensive, hard to manage, and notoriously buggy. For example, the gateways from both Microsoft and Lotus for their Windows email packages cost more than $3,000 and drop file attachments. John Dvorak pointed out that Lotus Notes has difficulty when it leaves "its own little world," and the $2,500 Notes gateway is part of the reason why.

For the Macintosh platform, on the other hand, you can buy gateways for Microsoft Mail, QuickMail, PowerShare, and Lotus Notes that are not only inexpensive (under $500), but more stable.

Other Internet software

I've mentioned Internet email software and briefly described the World Wide Web, FTP, Gopher, mailing lists, and newsgroups. There are many more Internet software tools to cover. I'm only going to touch on these because they're covered well in many other Internet books.

If your business will have a full-time Internet connection (24-hour ISDN or faster), you will need a computer acting as a server. Your Internet server computer must at least handle email with a SMTP or UUCP server and a post office server running POP (Post Office Protocol) or IMAP (Internet Mail Access Protocol), and it must run DNS (Domain Name System). Let's start our look at other software with DNS.

- **Domain Name System (DNS):** DNS is the navigation system that Internet computers use to find each other. The Unix software program BIND is the most common DNS program. It is included with Unix, but must be added to other operating systems. If you run only one computer on the Net, you don't need your own DNS server. Your Internet access provider's server will carry DNS for you. If your network has a firewall, you may want to run DNS on your firewall computer. The main advantage of having your own DNS server is that you can add and change user names and subdomain names without paying a fortune to your access provider. You won't need DNS until you have multiple users on the Net with different email addresses. You can get DNS server software for all operating systems.

- **Telnet:** Telnet software lets you use the Internet to remotely access another computer and run programs on it. You will find this useful for field staff or customers who need to run software programs on your computer.

- **WAIS (Wide Area Information Server):** WAIS is an extremely useful software product, available in both free and commercial versions. It makes it possible for your business to present large numbers of documents or large amounts of data so users can easily search from the Web and find what they need.

- **Network administration tools:** Your system administrator will need Ping, NSLookup, and Whois for DNS troubleshooting. Ping, Traceroute, Ifconfig, Netstat, and Route are key software tools used to administer your system.

- **IRC (Internet Relay Chat):** IRC lets people anywhere on the Net have typed real-time conversations, like the chat rooms of America Online. You can use IRC for live conferences, with a couple of dozen people typing in different cities, all able to see everything that anyone types.

- **DHCP (Dynamic Host Configuration Protocol):** DHCP gives computers on your LAN temporary Internet addresses. If your LAN uses NetWare, you might want to take a look at Novix from Firefox, Inc. This money-saver for NetWare users operates as a NetWare NLM (Network Loadable Module) and dynamically assigns IP addresses to computers. This means you don't need to load TCP/IP software on each computer—you only have to load it once on your NetWare Server as an NLM. Novix increases security, saves work in configuring PCs, and uses less memory than TCP/IP would use if stored locally on each system. It is also easy to install and fairly easy to maintain. Keep in mind, however, that DHCP servers need the protection of a firewall. A five-user starter kit is available for $1,400 from Firefox, Inc. at **www.firefox.com**. Novix is also available for Macs.

- **Voice Over Network:** VON is short for free long-distance phone calls over the Internet. This is supported by CoolTalk in Netscape Navigator and many other products. If you have a sound card in your computer, and a microphone and earphone, VON lets you use the Net to call any other person who is on the Net. The sound quality isn't as good as a regular phone call, but you can't beat the price.

- **Web Toys:** You can buy more kinds of software to create and add to your World Wide Web site than for any other activity in your company. Some of these will greatly enhance the functionality or marketing strength of your Web site, but many of them are just toys for Webmasters. The costs of these bells and whistles and the time spent playing with them can devour your budget in nothing flat. Don't let your Web team build a toy box on your time.

When choosing software, in addition to your up-front costs, find out about the annual support costs and software upgrade fees. Estimate what the training costs will be on a per-user basis (or per developer, if this is a development tool). Too many companies purchase multiple-user site licenses for software packages, then ignore the need to train people in the use of the software. The result? The software is ignored or misused by employees, and money and time are wasted.

You'll need to determine if a particular software package is designed for programmers, power users, or regular end-users. (Don't believe the brochure.) What operating system(s) does it support? (The more, the merrier.) Does it run on multiple brands of hardware? Look closely at its hardware requirements (disk space, memory, CPU speed). This is an area where software companies often understate true needs, especially for memory. If a software program forces you to add new hardware such as memory chips, the hardware additions can cost more than the software. Pay attention to the vendor's reputation and to the market momentum for this product. Don't get stuck with dying products.

A very important question to ask: *Does the vendor provide online support via the Internet?* Online Internet-based support reduces the time your own technical people will need to spend and it's cheaper too.

An Internet software checklist

Here are the major kinds of software used on the Internet. You won't need all of these. Some (like TCP/IP) are required but are probably built into your computer's operating system. Others are optional; you may need them, depending on which Internet services you want to bring into your company and which ones you want to offer to the world. Use this as a shopping list when choosing an operating system:

Client software (one copy for each person on the Net)

❏ An integrated Internet client package (Netscape Navigator or Microsoft Explorer)

❏ TIA (The Internet Adapter) software if you use a dial-up shell account

❏ Encryption software, if legal in your country

Email software

❏ An email client for each user (either an Internet email client such as Eudora or Pegasus, or a LAN email client such as Lotus cc:Mail or Microsoft Mail)

❏ Either an SMTP or UUCP email server (to send and deliver email to and from your internal network)

❏ Digital signature software

❏ POP or IMAP to deliver email to each person's email client software (on your internal network)

❏ An MTA program such as SendMail, Smail, or MMDF (to communicate between your email server and POP or IMAP)

❏ Gateway software if you want to link LAN email clients to the Net

❏ Mailing list server (such as Listserv, Liststar, Majordomo, etc., for mass emailings and conducting email discussion groups)

❏ X.400 for TCP/IP software, if you use X.400

❏ Directory synchronization software, if you are a large company (500+ employees) and use different email clients

Server software

❏ TCP/IP server

❏ Web server(s) (if you want to provide a Web site; use separate Web servers for external use and for your intranet)

❏ FTP server(s) (if you want to provide FTP files; you might want separate FTP servers to distribute files externally and on your intranet

❏ WAIS server or other search software (to make your own information searchable)

❏ Firewall software

❏ Credit card processing software, if you make sales on the Net

❏ DNS server

❏ NFS server

❏ DHCP server if you have a LAN (or Novix for NetWare or Macs)

❏ Telnet server (if you want to give outsiders Telnet access to your computers)

❏ NNTP server (if you want your own feed of Usenet newsgroups)

❏ Finger server (if you want outsiders to see your Finger files; not recommended)

❏ IRC server (if you want to provide Internet Relay Chat for employees on your intranet)

❏ NTP (Network Time Protocol) server (to synchronize your computer with the outside world; a valuable security tool)

TCP/IP network administration tools (For a catalog of TCP/IP network maintenance software tools, have your system administrator check RFC 1470.)

Special-purpose software

❏ Videoconferencing software

❏ Voice Over Network telephone software

❏ Site-licensed software distribution managers (to automatically distribute new software releases to your employees)

❏ EDI software

❏ Interfaces from Internet sales order systems and EDI to your accounting and inventory systems

❏ Remote Access Software for telecommuters

❏ HTML editing and Web site creation software

❏ Web site enhancements and tools (there are jillions of 'em)

How to get your own domain name

In 1994, Mike O'Connor registered the Internet domain **television.com** as his own. Domain names were free back then, and O'Connor had a hunch. He used to work in the radio business, where a station's call letters (like KOOL or WLIV) are one of its most valuable assets. O'Connor figured the same thing would happen to Internet domain names. His hunch paid off in May 1996, when C|net offered him $50,000 for his rights to **television.com**.

To be a major league team in the Internet game, your business will want a domain name of its own, like **ibm.com** or **microsoft.com**. These valuable intellectual assets cost only a couple of hundred dollars, and make the difference in your image between Internet pro and fumbling amateur. Your domain is more than your address. It tells the world who you are and what you are.

In addition to a domain name containing your *company* name, you can register domains for your *products* (Kraft Foods registered 155 domains, one for each of its products), your markets (Proctor and Gamble has dozens of domains, including such unlikely destinations as **underarms.com** and **diarrhea.com**), and even your slogan (Guess which sneaker company has **justdoit.com**?).

Your Internet access provider or your Web site host will register your domain name for you. The base charge is $100 per name (which is valid for two years), plus a $50 annual fee. On top of that, your provider will usually charge a one-time fee of $40 to $100 for the work it does as part of the registration process. If your provider asks you to pay more than $200 for registration, don't just take it—haggle. You shouldn't pay more than $200 without getting extra services.

Your name cannot duplicate any existing domain name. To see if your idea has been taken by someone else, look up your name at InterNIC's "Whois" searcher at **http://rs.internic.net/cgi-bin/whois**.

Most businesses in the United States (as well as thousands in other countries) choose a domain name ending in **.com** (such as **emery.com**), which stands for "commercial." You have other choices as well. You might use **.org** for a nonprofit organization. If your company is in the network business, your domain name can end with **.net**. You can also choose to end your domain name with a country code, such as **.us** for the United States (such as **emery.us**), **.ca** for Canada, or **.au** for Australia. Businesses in countries outside the United States often use a country domain preceded by **.co** for "commercial," such as the U.K. bank **barclays.co.uk**.

Once you have your domain name, you can prefix it by as many *subdomains* as you like, such as **www.** for your Web site (**www.yourco.com**), or **support.** for your customer support department (**support.yourco.com**).

These procedures and prices may change. Moves are afoot to add new top-level domain names to compete with **.com**. (One proposal is **.firm**.) For more information on domain names and registration, set your Web browser to **internic.net/rs-internic.html**.

CHAPTER 4

Access Providers and Fast Connections

"Spend at least 10 percent of your budget on the best professional advice available before you spend a nickel on anything else."

—Harvey Mackay, Beware the Naked Man Who Offers You His Shirt

This chapter covers only two subjects, but they can make or break your Internet business: your Internet access provider and your Internet connection.

Your *connection* is the actual "wire" that physically links your business to the Net. It doesn't have to be a copper phone wire; it could be a cable television line, a fiber-optic cable, or even a satellite dish. Your Internet *access provider* is the company that feeds the Internet traffic into your connection and feeds outbound stuff from your company to the Net.

You'll find no single "right" way to get connected to the Internet, but plenty of "wrong" ways. That's because you deal with many variables when you get connected, and each variable means you have to answer questions:

- Who do you use to get connected?

- What level of service do you need?

- How much should you pay in startup fees?

- How much should you pay for ongoing access?

- Are there hidden costs involved in getting connected? If so, what?

- What hardware will you need?

- What software will you need?

- How fast should your connection be?

- Do you even *need* to be on the Internet, or can you do everything on America Online?

And perhaps the most important question:

- How do you know you're not getting ripped off?

Unfortunately, getting a business connection to the Internet is rarely instant and easy. The truth is, the more knowledge you have about the Internet—including your available hardware and software options—the more likely you will be to find a satisfactory approach to doing business online.

A good first step is to determine if you want to get on the Internet itself, or if you want to approach the Net indirectly through America Online, CompuServe, or another online service.

Using an online service

Traditional online services include Prodigy, America Online, and CompuServe in the U.S., plus NiftyServe in Japan, Minitel in France, and Cix in the U.K.

What about CompuServe, America Online, or Prodigy?

Online services such as these offer some advantages, and for all but the smallest businesses, some disadvantages. They are easier to set up and easier to navigate. Your network connection is a direct line and more secure than the Internet. Inhabitants of the commercial services are more tolerant of advertising and blatant promotions than Internet dwellers. It's easier for you to set up a business site on the commercial services; handholding is provided. On the Internet, you have to pay a service provider or do it on your own.

On the other hand, commercial services cost a lot more, often putting per-message charges on incoming and outgoing mail. Print publications that put an ezine on a commercial service typically get only 10 to 15 percent of the income they generate. On the Internet, you can keep it all. To put up your online store in CompuServe's Electronic Mall, you'll shell out $15,000 to $20,000, plus 2 percent of your sales, plus advertising fees. Prodigy charges $27,500 a month for its Standard Advertising Unit of five screens. America Online has equally steep startup fees and charges content providers (companies whose product is online information) 70 percent or more of their revenues. AOL charges less for merchants who sell services or hard goods.

Some of the commercial services also restrict the kind of information you can provide. Prodigy is the worst. Prodigy employs editors who screen every message before allowing it to post to Prodigy's equivalent of newsgroups. Sometimes delivery is delayed for days. It also uses software to scan messages for what Prodigy deems "unacceptable" language. America Online also censors. AOL once banned the word "breast" as obscene, which angered women who wanted to discuss breast cancer.

If your business is on the Internet, subscribers to all the commercial services except Minitel can reach you via the World Wide Web. If your business is on one of the commercial services, your visitors are restricted to only subscribers of that particular service. Many companies do business successfully on commercial services as well as on the Internet. Preview Travel, for example, generates 75 percent of its sales from America Online and 25 percent from Web sites. There is no one best way for all businesses. You have multiple choices.

Your need for connection speed

Your first step will be to choose a connection speed and type. For the smallest businesses, this is easy: a modem-based connection. Larger connections have a bewildering range of choices.

Internet speeds are expressed in kilobits per second (1,000 bits per second), abbreviated as Kbps or just K, as in "a 56K connection." Faster speeds are megabits per second (1,000,000 bits per second), abbreviated as Mbps. (See Figure 4.1 for a visual comparison of connection speeds.)

Even when you know how fast a connection you want, you may still have several options as to what type you can use. For example, if you determine you need a 56K line, do you want a 56K modem, Switched-56, ISDN, Frame Relay, Fractional T1, or Flexible DS1?

If that is confusing, help is on the way. Crossing ill-suited options off your list can be easy once you compare price tags and look at geographic considerations. Every connection type is not available in every place.

Table 4.1 can help you make sense of your alternatives. For each connection type, you'll see the *theoretical* speed (in real life, throughput will always be much slower), the names of the hardware required, a ballpark estimate of hardware costs (not including installation labor), monthly line costs, typical fees charged by Internet access providers to start your account, and typical access provider monthly fees. We'll cover most of these in more detail in following sections, so don't worry that you have to memorize all this stuff.

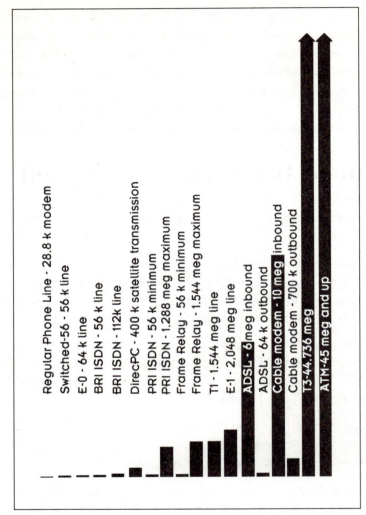

Figure 4.1   This bar chart shows the speeds of different types of connections. This book isn't tall enough to fit T3 and ATM speeds on one page. They are each more than twice as fast as the bars here indicate. ATM can go up to six times as fast as the speed shown in the chart.

Table 4.1 Connection types and their features and speeds.

Connection type	Theoretical speed/sec.	Hardware	Hardware cost	Connection cost/month	Provider setup cost	Provider cost/month
Regular phone line	28.8 Kbps to 33.6/56 Kbps	modem	$100-$400	$25-$40	0-$50	$15-$30
Switched-56	56 Kbps	DSU/CSU	$200-$1,000	$200-$800	$100-$400	$30-$250
BRI ISDN	56 Kbps or 112 Kbps	TA, NT1, router	$300-$2,500	$25-$500 plus metered fees	$50-$500	$25-$400
Frame relay	56 Kbps to 1.544 Mbps	FRAD or DSU/CSU	$600-$5,000	$200-$4,200	$75-$500	$40-$400
Fractional T1	64 Kbps to 1.544 Mbps	DSU/CSU or T1 mux	$600-$12,000	$100-$3,500	$400-$3,000	$150-$1,400
T1, DS1, or PRI ISDN	1.544 Mbps	T1 mux	$4,000-$15,000	$900-$3,500	$500-$3,000	$400-$1,400
DirecPC	400 Kbps	satellite dish, adaptor card	$700	$10-$130 plus metered fees	0-$50	$15-$30
ADSL	6 Mbps inbound, 64 Kbps outbound	ADSL modem	$1,000-$6,000	$20-$30	$50-$250	$35-$400
Cable modems	10-30 Mbps inbound, 700 Kbps outbound	cable modem, adaptor card	$400-$900	$35-$45	varies	zero
T3 or DS3	44.7 Mbps	T3 mux	$20,000 and up	$15,000-$45,000	Here you are usually your own provider.	

Note that Internet access providers always charge more to provide Internet access for LANs than they do for single computers. A single ISDN channel for one computer might cost you $25 to $100 per month for Internet access, but the same Internet access provider will charge $150 to $300 per month more to support a LAN at the same speed.

If you compare these numbers, you'll conclude that cable modem connections are bargains. You'd be right. These connections, provided by cable television operators, are available in only a few dozen U.S. and Canadian locations. More will open this year.

In the meantime, the most common and widely available connection is to use a regular telephone line and a modem.

A phone line and a modem

This is the most basic kind of connection, and for most computer operating systems except for Windows 3.1, it's relatively easy for a businessperson to set up. You need a computer, a modem, communications software, and possibly (depending on what kind of computer you have) a communications card that goes inside your computer.

If you get a modem, get *at least* a 28.8 Kbps modem. Anything slower is obsolete, and will cause pain when you navigate the Web. A 28.8K modem will cost $75 to $125. For $190 to $250, you can get a somewhat faster 33.6K modem. These will work with any phone line with one exception.

 If you use a modem to make your connection to the Internet with standard telephone lines (ISDN is an exception), make sure your phone company has not put you on a Digital Added Main Line (DAML, pronounced "dam-el" to rhyme with "camel"). A DAML is used by local phone companies when they run out of lines in a neighborhood. DAMLs jam two phone lines into the wires of one.

This is not a problem for regular telephone voice transmission. But if you have a DAML and use a modem, it will run only half as fast as normal. Usually, DAMLs are temporary and remain in place only until your phone company can add more physical lines in your neighborhood. This happened to me. If you find out that you are on a DAML, badger your phone company frequently to add a "real" line.

In some places, you can also use a modem that lets you receive data faster, up to 56 Kbps.

No matter what speed your modem is, you have two choices in the type of modem-based Internet accounts you can use. From the names it will seem like four choices, but they can be divided into two camps, with shell accounts on one side of the river, and SLIP, CSLIP, and PPP accounts on the other side.

Shell accounts

The simplest kind of Internet account is a basic dial-up (shell) connection between your computer and your service provider's system. With only a dial-up connection, your computer functions as a terminal. Your system isn't really on the Internet, but your service provider's system is, and it simply passes data between your computer and the Internet server to which your computer is connected.

Under this simple approach, you can only run one network program at a time and, without adding software, you can only send and receive text (no graphics, sound, or other multimedia data). One software program you can add is TIA (The Internet Adapter). It fools your shell connection into thinking it's a SLIP connection, so you can run most SLIP software. A simple dial-up shell connection won't work for most companies serious about business on the Internet.

SLIP, CSLIP, and PPP

The first question that you're going to want me to answer is probably: "What's the difference between SLIP, CSLIP, and PPP?"

SLIP stands for Serial Line Internet Protocol and is a standard method for connecting to a service provider via telephone lines. SLIP was one of the first communications packages to provide home and office PCs with a connection to the Internet, but SLIP is neither the best nor the fastest. However, a modified version of SLIP, called CSLIP (Compressed SLIP) offers slight speed advantages.

PPP (Point to Point Protocol) is identical to SLIP, except PPP is slightly more robust—especially in the area of error detection and error handling. For this reason, access providers say PPP connections are 5 to 10 percent faster than SLIP, and transmission errors are fewer.

With most modem connections to the Internet, you are limited to a speed of 33.6 Kbps or less. That speed is useful for transferring email via UUCP, and for one person to surf the Web with Netscape, but it will not support many services that your business can *provide* over the Net. For instance, a Web server would run at a crawl, so slowly that most visitors would be unable to get in. Most Web page servers need at least a 56 Kbps connection. (This is why many small businesses outsource their Web pages to a service bureau called a *Web host*, which serves Web pages with a faster connection than most businesses can afford on their own.)

Arguing performance differences among SLIP, CSLIP, and PPP is splitting hairs. If you'll look at the bar chart on page 74, you'll see that compared to anything else, even a 33.6 Kbps modem connection is relatively slow.

Modems convert your files into noise—audio signals of beeps and hisses—for transmission over phone lines and convert them back again on the receiving end (called *analog* transmission). Not only are modems limited to slower transmission speeds, but you must also wait for something called "a hand-shake" for every file transmitted. This adds one second of delay per file, which sounds like trivia. But as Publilius Syrus said, "Even a single hair still casts a shadow." Those one-second delays add up quickly. One Web page with 9 graphics files adds up to 10 handshakes, or at least 10 seconds on top of the time to actually move the files across the phone lines. Lack of waiting for handshakes makes other connection types seem many times faster than modem connections. They are also much more reliable. Transient errors rarely kick you off the Net with other types of connections, but they commonly interrupt analog modem sessions.

So how important is it to get a PPP connection rather than a SLIP or CSLIP connection? If you find a local access provider who offers PPP connectivity, and the price is right, take advantage of it. If your local provider of choice only offers SLIP or CSLIP connectivity, you're still in about the same shape. For a much faster enhancement to your SLIP or PPP connection, see DirecPC below.

Faster modems: x2 And K56flex

Normally, a modem connection made through standard phone lines is limited to 33.6 Kbps because the noise on phone lines limits reliable transmissions to 35 Kbps or less. Some companies have come up with a faster way, reaching speeds up to 56 Kbps. In fact, they came up with several faster ways, none compatible with the others.

This lack of compatibility means you need to double-check with your Internet access provider before you move to a 56 Kbps modem. Most access providers support only one type.

Another factor to consider is the quality of your phone lines. Not all phone lines are quiet enough to support 56 Kbps speed. Many countries' phone lines introduce so much noise that even a 28.8 Kbps modem is overkill. I've been places where noisy phone lines limited speeds to 19.7 Kbps or even 2.4 Kbps. Unless your phone company uses digital switching equipment, the new 56 Kbps modems won't work.

If you have a 33.6 or slower modem, you can use it to test the quality of your phone line to see if your line can handle 56 Kbps speed. For information on the phone line quality test, visit the U.S. Robotics Web site at **www.usr.com**.

The two leading 56 Kbps contenders are x2 from U.S. Robotics and K56flex from North American Rockwell (**www.rockwell.com**). Both provide the fast 56 Kbps speed *only in one direction*. If phone line quality supports the higher speed, the modems *receive* data at up to 56 Kbps. But they can *send* data only at 33.6 Kbps. In other words, when you look at Web pages, pages come *to* you at up to 56 Kbps. But if you use these new modems to publish pages, you send pages *out* to your visitors at only 33.6 Kbps, the same speed a regular modem provides.

The next step up: An ISDN connection

An old-fashioned kind of 56 Kbps connection is called Switched-56, but other connections using newer technology are usually more cost-effective than Switched-56. (The European equivalent to Switched-56 is E-0.) Switched-56 and E-0 are neither as reliable nor as cost-effective as most other alternatives. So I rarely recommend them. They are useful only in a few parts of the world where your other options are limited.

Instead, if you want or need more speed than a modem connection offers, your next step up is probably an ISDN connection or a frame relay connection. They are not only faster than modem connections but much more reliable. For ISDN, you'll need special phone lines, which cost more (usually not much more) than regular phone lines. Phone companies normally charge by the minute for ISDN sessions. The rate depends on which phone company provides your ISDN lines and what customer category you fall into. For example, Pacific Bell charges me a few cents per minute during business hours, and since I have a home ISDN account, gives me up to 200 hours per month of free use during non-business hours.

If you want an off-and-on connection that disconnects when you finish a session, regular ISDN might fit your needs. If you need a full-time connection running 24 hours a day, look at ISDN Centrex service or frame relay. Both Centrex and frame relay are billed at flat rates, giving you unlimited connect time at flat rates. You pay the same no matter how long you are connected. You can order Centrex in some cities if you are located close to your Internet access provider.

ISDN stands for Integrated Services Digital Network, and it's only slightly less complicated than the federal budget. The basic ISDN connection theoretically provides up to 64 Kbps in bandwidth (in the U.S., extra signals reduce that to 56 Kbps). Standard SLIP and PPP connections require a modem at your end. In the same way, an ISDN connection requires special hardware at your end. Your Internet access provider must also support ISDN (most medium to large providers do). ISDN is becoming a common choice for businesses located in homes, factories, and offices.

How ISDN works

An ISDN connection uses standard telephone lines but provides digital transmission via improved line-switching equipment. That means you can set up an ISDN connection only if your phone company has converted to ISDN switching facilities. (Even then, you might not be able to use ISDN, as I'll explain shortly.) A benefit of ISDN, in addition to faster speed, is its ability to send or receive data and voice transmission simultaneously.

There are actually two main flavors of ISDN, but the least expensive and most widely used is called the Basic Rate Interface (BRI). Before I can explain more about the benefits, problems, and expenses involved with ISDN, I need to explain ISDN itself.

A standard telephone connection consists of two copper wires. An ISDN BRI connection divides these two wires into three "channels." Two channels are called bearer channels (B channels for short). Each B channel has a speed of 64 Kbps. A BRI connection also uses a third channel, the D channel.

Assuming that your phone company supports ISDN, there are still some other requirements that your equipment must satisfy. First, your external phone line must go straight from your ISDN equipment to the phone company's junction box where the line comes into your building from outside. A telephone technician can tell you whether your line meets this requirement.

Also, the external line from the junction box to the phone company's ISDN switching facility should be 18,000 feet or *less*. If your home or office is located three miles or more from this switch, ISDN is literally out of reach—unless the phone company can boost your signal with a repeater (at an additional cost to you, of course).

If you and your phone company meet all the ISDN requirements I've explained so far, you'll then need to purchase a device called an NT1 or NTU1 (NT stands for Network Terminator), which supplies power to your ISDN line. Some ISDN modems have an NT1 built in. If you connect your ISDN line to your PC or Mac, you can purchase a controller card that comes with a built-in NT1. One of the bizarre things about ISDN is the lack of standardization in equipment. All ISDN equipment is not created equal. Your phone company's switches and your Internet access provider's equipment will only work with ISDN equipment from certain manufacturers. Make sure you select your access provider and talk with your provider and your phone company about what hardware they can work with *before* you buy any ISDN gear.

In the U.S., ISDN actually has two 56 Kbps channels bonded together, so you can make two 56 Kbps connections at once, giving you an effective speed, with most computers, of 112 Kbps. (Other countries get 128 Kbps.) If you want to do this, you'll need a *router*, a box that handles the connections from your PC to the phone lines. You can buy ISDN routers as standalone boxes or as add-in cards that plug into PCs and Macintoshes.

That's the easy stuff. Before you decide to purchase ISDN, you should consider these additional questions:

- How many devices do you want to attach to ISDN? A device can be a computer, fax, telephone, or any similar device. The ISDN router you buy can only support a limited number of devices, or "terminals" as they are referred to in the communications industry, no doubt to confuse the rest of us. ("But that's not a terminal, it's a Princess phone!") ISDN routers can connect from one to dozens of devices. The fewer the devices supported, the lower priced your router. You can get routers that convert between ISDN and Ethernet, Appletalk, and other network protocols.

- Do you want to use one B channel as a phone line? You have two 56 (or 64) Kbps B channels available. You can use one for voice and one for data. Be warned, though, that using a B channel for voice means you will have to buy a special ISDN phone ($150 and up) or a converter gadget called a TE1 that lets you plug a regular phone into your ISDN B line.

- Do you want to bond both B channels? *Bonding* gives you a data speed of 112 (or 128) Kbps, twice as fast as a single B channel. Depending on the type of ISDN router you buy, bonding may require a terminal adapter (TA). The formal high-tech term for bonding is "inverse multiplexing."

- Do you need X.25 packet networking? Probably not. X.25 is slow (2.4 to 9.6 Kbps) and obsolete. If for some odd reason you want to do X.25 networking, you need to buy a separate terminal adapter (TA) for X.25.

- Do you need a repeater? If your home is too far away from your phone company's switching office, your phone company will sock you with an extra monthly charge for a repeater, a device that boosts the signal strength so that it will reach the extra distance.

- Have you had a Loop Quality test performed? This is a test your phone company can do to determine whether your phone lines can actually carry ISDN. Ask for this to be done first. You don't want to find out after your ISDN installation that your line doesn't support it.

- What kind of ISDN switch is used by your phone company's switching office? Your equipment must be compatible with that switch. Some switches have a reputation for being easier to connect with than others. For example, Pacific Bell uses both AT&T and Nortel switches. If you are in a neighborhood served by the AT&T switches, ISDN will be easier to install and will be less troublesome to use than if you were in a neighborhood serviced by the Nortel switches.

How much does ISDN cost?

If you decide you want the benefits that an ISDN connection brings, your next order of business is to tally up the potential costs—before you actually make any purchases. In an illuminating article in the February 1995 issue of *LAN Magazine*, Internet veteran Karl Auerbach gave a detailed account of his tasks in setting up an ISDN connection for his home-based business. He listed these one-time setup costs:

Internet access provider fee	$ 500
Phone company line installation	$ 140
Two ISDN Ethernet bridges	$1,850
Router	$1,500
10BaseT hub	$ 200
Network software for each PC	$ 400
Telephone company ISDN charge	$ 72

Auerbach used a recycled 386 PC as his router to direct Internet traffic to the other computers his business uses. These costs don't include computer maintenance, which Auerbach, a technical expert, says took a few hours per week.

When I had a two-line 112 Kbps home ISDN installed, I had an advantage over Auerbach. He wanted to link the Internet to his multi-computer LAN. I had only *one* computer to link. My costs were much lower.

I spent $850 for an Ascend 25 router rather than $350 for an internal "ISDN modem" card, because I was told that an external router was easier to set up and run than a plug-in router card. I spent $75 for an Ethernet card, $50 for access provider setup, $85 for phone wiring in my house and an ISDN phone jack, $150 for software, and $125 for Pacific Bell setup charges. I also spent more than $300 on support calls to get everything set up and working. Now I pay $30 to $45 a month to Pacific Bell for my two extra phone lines and $35 to $45 per month to my access provider. In spite of long hours on the Net, my total monthly bill for everything is always less than $90.

Of course, you won't incur the same charges as Auerbach or me—you might spend more or you might spend less, depending on your requirements. In general, an ISDN connection, including installation and equipment (not counting your computer) can run from $300 to $2,500. Always plan to spend at least $200 for consultants and support. Most phone companies will charge $80 to $150 extra for installation if you need to add inside wiring and a jack, which is almost the same as a regular telephone jack.

Your phone company will also charge you a monthly charge for your ISDN line, typically between $20 to $30 per month, plus a metered usage charge. Metered usage is why most businesses *don't* use ISDN connections to host Web sites. Web sites must connect to the Net 24 hours a day, and when your phone company charges *per minute*, fees add up quickly. This metered charge can be significant, and it can be multiplied by two if you use two ISDN channels. (Normally, your second channel doesn't stay open all the time. When a big file comes through on your first channel, your second channel pops open while it's needed and then closes.)

Charges get steeper if your ISDN connection is remote enough to incur distance charges. A Pacific Bell representative told me that one poor soul left both channels up 24 hours and had 12 miles of distance surcharges. When he saw his first bill, he called in shock and said, "I have an ISDN line, and my bill was $20,000!"

Internet access provider fees for ISDN service range from about $25 to $400 per month, and more in some areas. If you use an Internet access provider that provides a kind of flat-rate access called ISDN Centrex, your monthly phone company cost is about $23 with no usage fees, and you pay about $400 per month to the Internet access provider. That makes it practical to host your Web site on an ISDN connection. Flat rates can be better than fluctuating fees because you can more easily plan your business expenses.

For example, flat-rate ISDN Centrex is offered in California by access provider GeoNet (**www.geo.net**). GeoNet also has a $70 try-out offer. It lends you the necessary equipment until you decide whether to keep its service. GeoNet rates are higher than some other Internet access providers, but its customer service has earned GeoNet more praise from my readers than any other provider.

Where to find more ISDN info

At present, telephone companies in North America, Europe, and Japan are pushing to make ISDN as accessible and as popular as possible. The greatest penetration is in Germany, where Deutsche Telekom put in place blanket coverage. ISDN is also extremely popular in the U.K., where British Telecom installs more ISDN connections in a week in greater London than Pacific Bell installs in a month in the entire state of California.

In the U.S., Pacific Bell and Bell Atlantic aggressively install ISDN equipment and encourage its use. In fact, Pacific Bell provides a very well written document that explains ISDN. This information is available on its Web site at: **www.pacbell.com/Products/SDS-ISDN/Book**.

Except for Pacific Bell and Bell Atlantic, most U.S. phone companies seem to be in the dark about ISDN. Phone company sales reps will describe services that are not available, and they'll often give you inaccurate price quotes, and the technicians will often screw up your installation.

The best place on the planet to find ISDN information is a site on the Web. If you are even *thinking* of installing ISDN, visit Dan Kegel's ISDN Page first at **http://alumni.caltech.edu/~dank/isdn**. You'll find a list of ISDN dial-tone providers worldwide, and information from the basics ("What Is ISDN?") on up, including ISDN user groups. A user group in your area can be a big help.

I also recommend the book *ISDN Clearly Explained,* by Ed Tittel, Steve James, David Piscatello, and Lisa Phifer. (1997, AP Professional, ISBN 0-12-691412-5). I wish I would have read this book *before* I installed ISDN in my home. It would have saved days of agony. It clearly explains how to install ISDN in your home office, small business, or medium-sized business. This book can save you hundreds of dollars.

Other digital connections

If you're used to a 28.8 Kbps modem connection, the 56 Kbps to 128 Kbps potential of ISDN might seem like dream speed. But Internet connections can be much, much faster. An expensive technology called Asynchronous Transfer Mode, or ATM, moves data at 45 megabits per second at its *slowest.* In February 1996, three different companies demonstrated three different versions of equipment that moved data at a speed of one terabit. That's 1 billion kilobits per second. On the chart on page 74, that would equal a bar almost 25 feet tall—more than 7 meters, the height of a two-story building.

Unfortunately, terabits are far in the future. (I hear readers say, "Oh, darn!" around the world.) Today, these are the most widely-used Internet connections:

- Frame Relay
- DirecPC, delivered via satellite dishes
- PRI ISDN (also called E-1)
- IDSL and MultiDSL
- T1 (also called DS1)
- ADSL, HDSL, and SDSL
- Cable television connections, called "cable modems"
- T3

Frame relay connections

In some places, frame relay costs much less than ISDN.

Frame relay gives you a sort of "party line" connection. It links several businesses to the Internet sharing one high-speed line—usually a T1 line, but sometimes an even faster line. This sharing keeps the price down. Each business is guaranteed a minimum speed, for instance 56 Kbps (usually the slowest frame relay speed available) or 128 Kbps.

Some ISDN connections charge you more based on distance, but frame relay rates usually use distance-insensitive pricing. For some businesses, that can mean serious cost savings over ISDN. Frame relay can cost less than ISDN for another reason: flat-rate pricing. Most frame relay accounts are priced at a fixed rate per month, so you pay the same no matter how many hours you remain connected. This makes frame relay cheaper than ISDN for hosting Web servers.

Depending on the speed you want, your phone company's pricing, and your Internet access provider's rates, frame relay can cost between $500 and $2,000 to install and $100 to $500 per month. In addition, you will need hardware. You can use a frame relay access device, called FRAD for short, as your frame relay "modem," or the same DSU/CSU gadgets that more expensive leased-line Internet connections require.

For everything you wanted to know about frame relay but were afraid to ask, visit the Frame Relay Resources page on the Web at **www.mot.com/MIMS/ ISG/tech/frame-relay/resources.html**.

DirecPC satellite connections

For a faster Internet connection, Hughes Network Systems provides a way for you to enhance a SLIP or PPP modem connection to receive data at 400 Kbps over a satellite dish. Note that this is what the techos call an *asymmetrical* connection; speeds for incoming and outbound data are not equal, similar to 56 Kbps modems.

With DirecPC, you use your regular modem over your plain old phone line for outbound messages. But incoming data—such as Web pages and FTP files—come to your PC over a satellite dish at a much faster 400 Kbps. You'll pay $700 for a satellite dish, software, and a PC adapter card. Expect to pay up to $400 for installation labor or do it yourself. Fees range from $10 to $130 per month, depending on combinations of unlimited use and per-megabyte-downloaded surcharges. You must also have a regular SLIP or PPP account with an Internet access provider.

These prices are for single-computer installations. Hughes Network Systems promises that a version that supports LANs will be available Real Soon Now.

DirecPC is available anywhere in the 48 continental states, Canada, Japan, and Western Europe. It is currently available only for Microsoft Windows computers. For more information, visit **www.direcpc.com**.

PRI ISDN connections (E-1)

PRI stands for Primary Rate Interface. I'm only going to touch on PRI ISDN connectivity briefly because it's physically identical to T1 connectivity.

The major difference between PRI ISDN and T1 connections is the type of provider you have to deal with. PRI ISDN is offered by local phone companies, while T1 is offered by leased-line providers.

A PRI connection offers a bandwidth of 1.544 megabits per second. For the arithmetically challenged, that's 27.5 times faster than a 56 Kbps connection. In Europe, PRI ISDN operates at 2.048 megabits per second and is called E-1.

PRI uses 23 B connections and one data connection, and can support up to 64 "terminal" devices at one time and up to 8 separate phone numbers. With all costs included, PRI ISDN connections cost $1,200 to $5,000 per month, plus you'll pay a few thousand dollars in installation fees. For more on PRI ISDN, visit Dan Kegel's ISDN Page at **http://alumni.caltech.edu/~dank/isdn**.

IDSL and MultiDSL

Phone companies complain that ISDN connections lose money for them. ISDN lines keep phone switches busy because ISDN lines often stay connected 24 hours a day. Some bright minds realized that this problem creates an opportunity and invented IDSL (ISDN Digital Subscriber Line), offering ISDN performance but bypassing phone company switches.

Instead of connecting your ISDN gadgets to a voice phone line to carry ISDN's digital signal to your phone company's nearest switch, IDSL runs a line directly from your ISDN gadgets to a router at your Internet access provider. It actually bypasses the voice part of your local phone company's network. For this to work, the distance between you and your Internet access provider must be 18,000 feet or less. (Farther if you boost your signal with pricey loop repeaters.)

You use exactly the same hardware and software you use for a BRI ISDN line. The only drawback (a mere flea speck) is that you cannot run voice phone calls over the same line you use for your Internet connection. The advantage is that you get a 128 Kbps speed for a $750/month flat rate, plus $150 to $255 per month to your phone company.

If that isn't fast enough, you can bond multiple IDSL lines together. This is called MultiDSL and can go up to 6.144 Mbps.

Few providers offer IDSL now. UUNet does in North America. For more info, visit UUNet's site at **www.uu.net** or Dan Kegel's page at **http://alumni.caltech.edu/~dank/isdn**.

Getting a T1 connection: Is it worth the cost?

T1 is an abbreviation of North American T1 Trunk cable, a dedicated physical copper-wire cabling system that has much greater speed than standard phone cables. T1 is also called DS1. As I mentioned in the previous section, if you lease a T1 connection from your local phone company, you'll get PRI ISDN connectivity.

Like PRI ISDN, T1 service operates at 1.544 megabits per second, and you can get a T1 connection from almost anywhere in the U.S. and in many other countries—especially in Europe and the Pacific Rim. (Where it may be called E-2.) Regardless of where you purchase T1 service, your outlay in both startup and ongoing costs will be substantial.

Instead of a modem, for T1 you will need a box called a DSU/CSU, which will move Internet traffic to and from your router. You will also need an FT1 multiplexor, called a T1 mux for short. Your phone company charges for T1 depending on how close you are to your access provider's nearest location (called Point of Presence or POP for short), so it pays to be close.

For a full-speed T1 Internet connection, expect to pay your Internet access provider between $250 and $1,000 for startup costs and $1,000 to $2,800 per month. Add to this the communications line costs from your phone company, which will fluctuate due to the distance factor, with setup between $1,000 and

$4,000 and monthly fees of $200 to $900. You'll also need a DSU/CSU and router for $800 to $2,500.

Cost saving is possible with a T1 connection. Instead of paying fees to an Internet access provider, you'll probably find your costs are lower if you become one yourself and provide your own Internet access. You can join the Commercial Internet Exchange (CIX), a worldwide organization of access providers and large companies, and subcontract your access through CIX.

As a lower-cost alternative to full T1 speed, you can instead get slower-speed, less expensive fractional T1. Expect Internet access provider charges of more than $500 for startup and monthly fees of $250 and up, plus phone company fees of $1,000 and up for startup, and monthly fees of $125 and up for fractional T1.

Do you need T1?

It's a generally recognized axiom that in planning a business you should plan for growth. That statement suggests that you consider purchasing an Internet connection that's larger than you currently need. But for most businesses, T1 connectivity is excessive.

Today, most T1 customers are major businesses running LANs or WANS that support hundreds, or even thousands of terminals. For these customers, T1 is not so much an Internet solution as it is part of a broader networking solution. Some T1 customers are corporate Web sites (cybermalls) that also lease Web space to other businesses. Some T1 users are businesses with busy Web sites— more than 20,000 pages accessed per day.

If your business is small- to medium-sized, and you want to conduct all or part of your business on the Internet, you will probably find that 56 Kbps or 128 Kbps provides plenty of speed to support incoming and outgoing Internet traffic, especially if you locate your Web server on a Web host's computer and not on your own premises.

If your business needs a total networking solution that includes but isn't limited to the Internet (for instance, you want to set up a WAN for all local offices and you plan on conducting business on the Internet), you might very well require the kind of bandwidth that T1 can provide.

Videoconferencing and heavy graphics transfers are areas where T1 can be an important consideration. Videoconferencing quality on a 128 Kbps ISDN connection is possible, but graphics and video resolutions will be less than ideal, and video transfer times might be slow.

In fact, any business that regularly transfers video, large audio files, large graphics files, or other extremely load-intensive images should consider T1 as a connection option. For instance, if you run a medical facility and you want to regularly receive medical x-ray images across the Internet, T1 might be your connection of choice. For video and graphics companies, Sprint offers a special T1 solution called Drums (**www.sprint.com/drums**).

Some businesses now shop for office space specifically with an eye toward buildings that have T1 connectivity (the cabling and switch) built in. Commercial developers often use T1 as an incentive to attract companies with heavy networking needs. However, T1 connections can be complex and require dedicated administrative support. Most companies that use T1 have at least one full-time network support employee.

Fractional T1 (also called Flexible DS1)

If you feel that your business might grow beyond the 128 Kbps ceiling, you can still have some of the speed of T1 for only part of the cost. Many T1 providers offer a service called "fractional T1" or "flexible DS1," in which customers purchase portions of a T1 line in 56 Kbps or 64 Kbps increments.

This is possible because a T1 line is actually 23 smaller channels put together. Under this approach, you pay only for the portion of the total bandwidth you use. If you only need 256 Kbps, that's all you pay for. Fractional T1 costs are discussed above.

ADSL, HDSL, and SDSL connections

Phone companies feel threatened by cable modem connections, which we explain on the following page. Their weapons to strike back are three technologies that squeeze more bits faster through regular copper-wire phone lines. They are called Asymmetric Digital Subscriber Line (ADSL), High-bitrate Digital Subscriber Line (HDSL), and Symmetric Digital Subscriber Line (SDSL). Since these names are as snappy as income tax instructions, AT&T calls all three the more glamorous name GlobeSpan.

Of the three, ADSL is the least experimental and the most practical for businesses. The technology for ADSL is not patented, to encourage many modem providers to make equipment for it, and it does not have the compatibility problems that plague ISDN. ADSL is asymmetric, so you can *receive* data at 6 to 8 megabits per second, but can only *send* data at 64 Kbps. SDSL allows T1 speeds in both directions, but it is not available yet.

To use an ADSL connection, your business must be located within 3.1 miles (5 km.) of a phone company switch that provides the technology. For the latest information, visit Dan Kegel's ADSL Page at **www.alumni.caltech.edu/ ~dank/isdn/adsl.html**.

Cable modem connections

Telephone companies are limited in the speed they can deliver to your business because of technical limitations of the copper wires that make up most phone company circuits. Cable television companies, on the other hand, have systems made of coaxial cable and fiber optics. These can support much faster connections at a much lower price.

Like DirecPC, cable-modem connections are asymmetrical, but cable modems are much, much faster. According to Chris Coles, Senior Vice President and Chief Operating Officer of TCI Technology Ventures, Internet surfers now using TCI's at-home cable-modem service (**www.home.net**) *receive* data such as Web pages at between 10 and 30 megabits per second. They *send* data at around 700 Kbps. Like frame-relay connections, cable-modem connections are shared by a pool of users. Most providers of cable-modem connections charge only $40 per month for unlimited use—a true bargain.

Currently, cable-modem access to the Internet is available in about 70 locations in the U.S. and Canada. Access speed depends on your cable company's offerings and on the brand of cable modem you use. Most cable television companies expect you to buy a cable-modem from them for between $300 and $600 or to lease it for a small monthly rate. Cable-modem connections offer an excellent value for most businesses. The main drawback is that these connections are available in so few locations.

To see if your area's cable television company offers this service or plans to in the near future, visit the Web site of the newsletter *Cable Datacom News* at **www.cabledatacomnews.com**. Other info is at David Gingol's Cable Modem Resources at **http://rpcp.mit.edu/~gingold/cable**. Gingol's site is not up-to-date.

T3 connections (also called DS3)

T3 connections provide some of the fastest communication available for the Internet, operating as high as 45 megabits per second. T3 connections use fiber optic cables rather than the copper wires used by ISDN and T1 lines.

T3 or DS3 connections are complex and extremely expensive. Few businesses need T3 performance. I mention T3 chiefly to make you aware of its presence.

Other connectivity options

Other Internet connections are available, but the ones I've mentioned so far account for the great majority of connection options. As technology improves, expect to see new connectivity opportunities appear and existing options disappear.

I thought ATM meant Automatic Teller Machine

One connection type is called Asynchronous Transfer Mode (ATM), which provides 45 to 622 megabits per second of bandwidth. As the demand for speed increases with the increased popularity of the Internet and other online services, ATM performance levels may soon become the norm rather than the exception. In some very large corporations with extensive networking facilities, ATM has already become the standard. One additional cost for ATM is that each desktop computer on an ATM network requires an ATM adapter card that costs about $400 to $1,500 and a switch that costs another $900 to $1,500. If your company wants ATM, expect to spend hundreds of thousands of dollars.

Wireless modem connections

Some mobile professionals prefer to use wireless modems to reach the Net. You can use these to receive your email anywhere within the United States, and in some locations you can get a fast enough connection to make Web surfing viable.

Wireless Internet connections are provided by packet radio companies. While they claim speeds of 4.8 to 19.2 Kbps, half of the speed is eaten by signal overhead. Even worse, some companies force wireless modems to share a single radio channel, reducing actual throughput to 1.2 Kbps or below. In other words, it's the Internet for patient people with long attention spans. Always get a demo with your own data before you buy a wireless modem based on packet radio.

A company called Metricom (**www.metricom.com**) offers a different wireless technology called Ricochet that allows theoretical throughput of 40 Kbps access, but in actual use gives you about 28.8 Kbps. Ricochet charges a $45 setup fee and $45 to $60 per month for Internet access, depending on the features you want. The Ricochet wireless modem costs $300, or you can rent it for $10 per month. Ricochet is available in Silicon Valley, San Francisco, Washington, D.C., Seattle, and a few other areas.

Choosing your Internet access provider

The first part of this chapter talks about the physical stuff you need to actually carry your Internet traffic to and from your business. In the rest of the chapter, we'll discuss the company that will use your connection to actually deliver your payloads.

These companies are often called *Internet service providers*, or ISPs. (They are often called other names that are not as nice, but we won't get into that here.) Some people call them Internet *access* providers, or IAPs. I'll stick with Internet access providers as a label, because there are other kinds of companies with "service" in their names that provide other services. This will reduce confusion on what is already a confusing topic.

To pick your provider, your first task is to define a pool of providers that might meet your needs. You can eliminate providers quickly if they don't serve the type of connection you want, if they don't provide the services you need (such as 24-hour, 7-day support), or if they cost too much. Add geographic considerations to your list of criteria. How close is a potential provider's nearest Point of Presence, or POP?

Watch out for long-distance charges when you select an Internet access provider. With some providers, especially national providers, you will have to pay long-distance charges each time you use the Net. These long-distance charges can wipe out any savings you make from bargain rates for access. This is especially true of modem-based Internet accounts, but distance charges from your phone company's switching center or your Internet access provider's nearest POP (Point of Presence) can also blindside you with extra distance-based costs for other types of accounts.

If you are considering a national or worldwide Internet access provider, good customer service may be hard to find. You are not likely to be considered a preferred customer, just another notch in their sales belt. Your ability to negotiate on contractual terms will be limited.

However, a national provider makes sense if you or others in your company will need Internet access during frequent road travel, or if you have offices in several widespread locations. That's probably the major benefit of a national provider: The ability to use the same Internet provider anywhere in the country, or even in several countries.

For many business purposes, a local or regional provider offers more benefits. A local provider is more willing (or should be) to visit your site to make presentations and to consult with you on your company's needs. Customer service hours will match your time zone and you will (or again, should be) given a personal account representative whom you can call directly to resolve any problems.

By far the most popular approach among the smallest businesses who want to connect to the Internet is a SLIP, CSLIP, or PPP account. Within the U.S., many national access providers offer unlimited-use SLIP and PPP accounts for $20 to $30 per month or less. If you have trouble finding a local company at these rates, try one of the larger companies. You can find the names and numbers of larger companies by visiting your local newsstand. Just pick up a copy of *Internet World* or another magazine that covers the Internet and browse its advertisements.

But whether you need a modem connection or a T1 line, and whether you're looking at local providers or international ones, remember Mr. Doom's rule of threes:

Always get *at least three* price quotes from three different Internet access providers before making any decisions.

Gathering your provider pool

So what's the first step in finding providers? The Yellow Pages? Possibly, but what category do you look under—"Internet Services?" There ain't no such animal. "Communication Services?" Good luck. "Telephone Consultants?" Nope.

Perhaps you could try "Computers—Networking". Actually, it's a good bet that one or more of your available providers will be listed here, or under "Computers—Internet." But for something this important, cold-calling a provider that you randomly select from the Yellow Pages does not make good business sense. You might get lucky, but more likely, you'll waste a tremendous amount of time.

If you have Internet access, or have a friend who does, you can get a list from the World Wide Web:

- The most complete, with more than 5,000 providers worldwide, is called The List: **http://thelist.iworld.com**

- Another list, not as complete, is: **www.netusa.net/ISP**

- POCIA's seems up-to-date: **www.celestin.com/pocia/index.html**

- In addition to Yahoo's own list, look for its "Indices" for other lists: **www. yahoo.com/Business_and_Economy/Companies/Internet_Services/ Internet_Access_Providers**

- Or try Clarinet's list: **www.clari.net/iap**

- The well-known PDIAL list is *not* a good place for businesses to look. It includes many nonprofit and academic providers which require you not to use the Internet for commercial activity.

If you don't yet have an Internet account, how do you reach these lists? There is a very good list and guide in print, *Internet Service Providers,* by the staff of *Boardwatch* magazine, a bargain at $10 plus $4 shipping. It provides contact information and prices for U.S. and Canadian providers, and detailed instructions on selecting a provider and getting connected. Order it by calling (800) 933-6038, or by faxing to (303) 933-2939. You can order it on the Web at **www.boardwatch.com**.

Jeff Duntemann suggests that the best way to get on the Internet is to use good old-fashioned networking skills of your own. Begin by calling every business associate you know and ask for references and advice. Call your local chamber of commerce. If a local Internet provider hasn't registered with your chamber of commerce, you already know it's less than on the ball.

Check with professional organizations and user groups in your area. You'll probably find some savvy businesspeople within these groups, several of whom will be happy to relate their own war stories on finding an Internet access provider.

This is important. Even if you do obtain a list of every Internet access provider in your area, you'll want references from their customers. You can ask the provider's sales reps for references, but you're only going to get references that the company knows will say good things about them. That's not what you want. You want the truth about a provider—*warts and all.* Members of local professional societies and computer users groups provide the best resource pool for getting "real" references about local providers.

Evaluating your provider pool

After you've uncovered all of the Internet access providers in your area and determined through references which ones *aren't* worth calling, you're on your own. At this point, you're basically conducting a series of job interviews. But unlike other job interviews, you're probably not going to be entirely sure of the skill set you should expect from your provider. But it's *critical* that you understand this skill set. Otherwise, you most certainly are either going to get ripped off or disappointed.

The first point of order: *Never call a potential Internet access provider until you're relatively sure about the types and levels of services your business will need.* If you don't do this reality check first, you won't be prepared to ask potential providers the questions that really matter.

Begin by asking those questions of yourself first. Here's a laundry list to help get you started:

- How many of your employees will use Internet email? Email is still the largest category of use for most people who do business on the Internet, so you'll want to know how closely Internet traffic will be tied to email traffic. However, it's also true that email is not resource intensive. If *most* of your employees will use *only* email, you can have a slow connection and still provide your employees with good email service.

- For email, will you use no mail server, or use UUCP, or SMTP? The differences are covered elsewhere in this book. UUCP costs less than SMTP.

- Which of your employees will be resource hogs? For instance, if your company has an art department, they're likely to upload and download large graphic files routinely. They'll need more Internet access time and resources than employees who mainly use the Internet for email.

- Most companies can only reach the Usenet newsgroups supplied by their access providers. Will you use only the newsgroups provided by your Internet access provider, or do you want to install a newsgroup feed to your own computers? Will the newsgroups you want be available from your provider?

- How many people will use FTP to copy files and bring them into your company?

- How many employees will use the Internet to do research?

- Will your company need a server for FTP, Web pages, or mailing lists, and if so, will the server be located on your own computer or on your access provider's system?

- Do you intend to do videoconferencing? Or make phone calls on the Net?

- Will your company use the Internet to link local area networks at different sites into a company-wide network?

- Will you process credit card transactions on the Internet? If so, definitely tell your provider ahead of time. This affects the way it sets up your account. Many small providers won't let you securely process credit card transactions.

Answers to these questions will help you determine both the level of service you require and the type of connection that will be best for your business. After you have a good feel for the level of Internet service your company will require, you can begin to approach individual vendors.

Check the technical capabilities of potential providers

Much of the material I've presented in this chapter so far focuses on the potential technical requirements and issues that you'll need to deal with at your site. But equally important, if not more so, is the need to assess the technical capabilities and limitations of potential providers. Your company might have state-of-the-art equipment, but if your provider doesn't, you're going to lose patience with your provider pretty quickly.

The most important question you can ask an Internet access provider is: "How long have you been in business?" If they hem and haw, run, don't walk, in the other direction. But length of operation is not always indicative of the level of service to expect. Some providers start small, then take on an increasing number of customers to keep their cash flow growing, and eventually reach critical mass. This is what separates business-savvy providers from the fly-by-nighters. A provider that takes on every new customer without assessing its growth strategy and its existing traffic capacities is not going to be around for long.

The best way to analyze a provider's equipment is to visit its offices—preferably unannounced. If the provider's system has banks upon banks of modems, you can suspect that most of its customers are using dial-up shell accounts; they're not business customers, so this provider might not be equipped to handle the level of service your business requires.

The hardware and software that your provider shows you might be a mystery to you, but you can still tell a lot about a provider by making a tour. Does the company seem to have enough employees to handle its customer load? Talk to some of the employees. Do they seem qualified? Are they helpful?

To prevent yourself from being duped or conned, you'll want to ask questions that any provider should be able to answer instantly. Here are some essentials:

- How many connections does your potential provider have with *its* access providers? There is a food chain here. Your provider leases lines (probably T1 or T3) from Sprint, AT&T, MCI, or some other large telecommunications company, then splits that line and sells part of its capacity to you. You want your provider to have multiple connections. For example, say that MCI's line goes down and your provider has only one MCI connection; your entire Internet access goes down. If your provider has one connection with Sprint and one with MCI, you are protected from the failure of a single carrier.

- Does the provider offer training and consulting services to help you get started? Many providers now offer installation packages. You can waste days, if not weeks, trying to install software. If a turnkey approach is available, take advantage of it.

- What percentage of the provider's customers are businesses?

- What percentage of customers have the same speed and connection type as the one you are considering? For instance, just because a provider offers T1 connections, you can't assume they also have extensive experience in helping customers set up and maintain T1 connections. You don't want to be one of your provider's "experiments."

- Where is the provider's closest Point of Presence (POP) to your business?

- If you need a router, who will pay for it—you or your provider? And who maintains it?

- Is there an extra charge for technical support?

- What security precautions are in place? I know of one provider that accidentally gave out one customer's password to a different customer, believing that the second customer had recorded his user ID incorrectly. That's frightening.

Perhaps the single, most frequently heard problem voiced by Internet customers is that their provider cannot handle the customer load. Although there's no way to determine for certain whether a provider has sufficient resources, a site inspection can sometimes be revealing:

- Have the employees you met been with the company long? (You can expect any company to have a certain percentage of new hires; but if *everybody* you meet has just come on board, something's wrong.)

- Do the employees look overworked or stressed out?

- Are the phones ringing off their hooks, unanswered?

Some good old, tried-and-true detective work can sometimes reveal a company that has taken on more than it can handle. If you suspect this, get on the phone to some of the provider's other customers. Ask what kind of service they've received *lately*. If you get answers like, "Well, when we first joined with them, they bent over backwards, but now we can't get technical help," that's a very bad sign.

Try calling tech support yourself, just to see how long it takes you to reach a human.

Also suggest that a potential provider come to *your* site for a visit. By looking at your equipment and your company as a whole, a provider might be able to make helpful suggestions about the line speed, connection type, level of service, and other Internet options for your business.

Locate your Web site on your access provider's system

A good option with a SLIP, CSLIP, or PPP connection is to use your local system for access only, and to put your Web site on your provider's computer. In effect, you'll be leasing hard disk space from your provider.

Locating your Web site on your provider's server also typically offers faster connections for your customers, since your provider's connection to the Internet will almost certainly be faster than your connection to your service provider.

Cost considerations and contractual terms

I've already covered most of the costs you can expect for various Internet configurations, but published fees are not always the same as actual fees. This fact can work both for you and against you.

For instance, some providers offer a bargain-basement per-month charge, along with a low one-time installation charge, but then tack on numerous, "hidden" fees, including per-message charges for email or per-bit charges for FTP, Gopher, or Web downloads. Ask your provider if there is any additional charge for any of these services and if so, find out how much:

- Incoming email

- Outgoing email

- Per-hour usage charges (over the agreed-upon limit)

- Disk space use (over a specific limit)

- A corporate mailbox or node

- Additional hardware

- Installing lines

- Registering a domain name

- Training and technical support

This last item is especially important. Some providers keep costs low by leaving their customers hanging out to dry when they have technical problems—either by providing little, if any, technical support or by charging heavy technical support fees. Make sure your contract with your provider clearly details *all* charges that you can expect to pay.

On the other hand, you can often get a provider to lower its prices by negotiating on various terms. Your best negotiating strategy, though, is to comparison shop. If you know what a provider's competitors charge, you're in a position to haggle.

 Some providers will slash their fees if you agree to sign a six-month or one-year contract. *Don't agree to this* the first time you do business with a provider. If its service doesn't meet your expectations, you'll be stuck for months.

In any case, if a provider offers you a contract with terms that appear fixed, and they are not satisfactory to you, negotiate to have them changed. All but the largest providers are willing to be reasonably flexible—if not about price, then perhaps about conditions. If your provider registers a custom domain name for you, make sure *you* own that domain, not your provider. If you need to cancel your account and move to a different provider, you'll want to take your domain name with you.

Some providers will include a disclaimer in your contract saying that they do not bear the responsibility for providing a functional service. If you sign such a contract and they are incompetent, that leaves you with no legal leg to stand on.

With any connection of ISDN speed or faster, your contract should specify the maximum length of turnaround time your provider has to forward any Internet traffic to or from your business. Otherwise, you are left with no recourse if your email piles up for five days on your provider's system. Depending on your company's needs, you might specify a maximum delay ranging from 15 minutes to 24 hours. Also, termination terms should be as specific as possible. And don't tolerate any clause that limits you to using just one provider for access or for providing information.

Never allow your Internet provider to claim rights to any information, software, or other intellectual property that comes from your company. For instance, when you sign on as a business on America Online, you must grant AOL the "royalty-free perpetual right and license" to publish and use anything you post on AOL. That's bad for publishers, financial services, and many other information services. Don't accept this. In fact, you should insist that your contract specifically *prohibits* your provider from ownership or use of your intellectual property, as well as from disclosing any financial information or trade secrets.

How one business chose its provider

Byron Abels-Smit was vice president of Aspen Media in San Francisco. Aspen needed a high-performance, 24-hour Web site. Speed and reliability were important because the company planned to sell Web space to its clients. To meet these needs, Abels-Smit and other members of the company searched for the best access provider available.

After some preliminary winnowing, which included gathering recommendations and critiques about local providers from customers who were already on the Internet, Aspen narrowed its choices to four providers: SlipNet, Netcom, Exodus, and an unnamed provider based in Berkeley.

The Berkeley provider was initially recommended by advertising agency Foote, Cone and Belding. But when Abels-Smit tried to look at the provider's Web site and the Web sites of its clients, "It was difficult to get through," he said, "and it was slow. And when I talked with someone about what we needed, the service just wasn't there." So the Berkeley provider was the first to be dropped from the list.

At SlipNet, "the people were interested in service," Abels-Smit noted, "but they were overwhelmed. They seemed to be running everything with just 3 people, and that included the staff involved in providing 24-hour, on-call service. When I went in to look at the place, I saw a whole bank of modems. I thought, 'How much of that is just for dial-up lines? What kind of connections are they pushing?' "

Abels-Smit noted that the staff used several Macintoshes and seemed comfortable with them, but even their technical expert didn't seem as familiar with Unix. "We used SlipNet temporarily for a dial-up connection before getting our leased line installed, and even then they were down off and on for a week," he said.

At one point, Aspen employees received a "link dead" error message, which means the service is down. "When SlipNet's lines were up, we got lots of busy signals. One time it took nearly an hour to dial in. What really helped us make our decision was that the people didn't seem to have much *business* experience, either in running a business or in serving businesses."

Aspen also found that their next choice, Netcom, was less than satisfactory. "What turned us off to Netcom happened in December 1994. We had the *San Jose Mercury News* come in to do a presentation." The presentation was about the new *Mercury Center*, the Internet version of the newspaper. Aspen had executives from advertising and publicity companies in several cities come in for the presentation.

The *Mercury Center* people set up a line and a screen to make their presentation. "For two-and-a-half hours," Abels-Smit recalled, "they were unable to get online and, when they did connect, they got disconnected after five minutes!" Obviously, Aspen couldn't afford for that to happen. "That's a killer in business," he said, "especially when you're dealing with professionals who don't know that much about the Web. To them, that's like a lost Federal Express shipment or missing an important phone call."

Finally, Aspen turned to access provider Exodus. "The sales representative did work for *me* instead of the other way around,"

Abels-Smit said. And the company seemed to "understand what you need to do to maintain a business. I could tell this from talking to the sales rep, by the questions he asked, and by his level of technical awareness."

According to Abels-Smit, the rep asked what Aspen's ultimate goals were for its Web site and asked about the kinds of servers the company had already looked at. "The rep brought in Avco [a Silicon Graphics reseller] to do a presentation on SGI. He brought in TCG [a local and long-distance phone company that had laid a fiber optic grid over the entire downtown San Francisco area] to pull our T1 line. They recommended a firewall manufacturer."

A site visit to Exodus confirmed that the company served mostly businesses that had connections other than dial-up. Aspen had made its decision.

CHAPTER 5

How to Get Up to Speed Quickly

"The first man gets the oyster. The second man gets the shell."

—Andrew Carnegie

At this point, you probably feel like a mosquito in a nudist colony. You know what you want to do, but you don't know where to start.

Never fear, help is here. You have one sure way to cut weeks off your Internet project time and save a lot of money, without using magic, without cheating. That one sure way is to do a little homework first.

You need to learn how the Internet works, what you can do on it, and how to find stuff on the Net. And you'll need to monitor a couple of newsletters or magazines to keep up with the new tools you can use.

This chapter saves time by steering you in the right direction, toward proven resources. You don't need to read *all* these books or visit *all* these Internet sites. No business needs all of them. And if you're in management, you can delegate Internet studies to your staff. (After all, you read *this* book. You've suffered enough.) But budget to buy at least six books.

I've tried to describe these resources so you can more easily pick and choose the ones that best fit your needs. Each item was selected for its relevance to *businesses*. To clarify which items I found the most helpful, I've used a five-star rating system. Stars indicate *usefulness* and no other factor—not good design, not easiness, not cute cartoons. I looked strictly for information that would most benefit a business.

Business books are first, followed by business periodicals. These are the tools that can help get your Internet project started, help it run smoothly, and ensure growth. Next come printed directories to help you find stuff.

The second half of this chapter gives you information resources from the Net itself. First, some resources to help you learn about the Internet. Next, some resources to help you find business stuff on the Internet.

I wanted to give a top 10 list of books and periodicals, but I would have had to build a different list for every reader. I recommend *The Cuckoo's Egg* and *Web Week* to everyone, but beyond those two titles, I have a hard time making a blanket recommendation. Get books that meet your company's specific needs. To clue you in on which ones are best for you, I've indicated for whom different resources were written.

If you can't find the books you want, I have five sources to recommend. Both Cbooks.com (**www.cbooks.com**) and Amazon.com (**www.amazon.com**) carry huge selections of English-language books, ship worldwide, and take credit card orders over the Net.

In the U.K, try Computer Manuals Ltd. at **www.compman.co.uk.**

The best selection of Internet books I've found in Japanese is carried by the helpful people at Toshokan Ryutu Center at **www.trc.co.jp.**

For German-language Internet books, try JF-Lehmanns Fachbuchhandlung at **www.Germany.EU.net/shop/JFL.**

Books for businesspeople

Most books covering the Internet are nontechnical books for beginners (*newbies*, in Net lingo) that rehash the same information again and again. Most are competent. However, you won't find those beginner books here.

Even so, when you first start, you will need a beginner's book or two. I recommend buying any two introductory "how-to" books, from two different publishers. Because each publisher uses a somewhat different approach, when you can't find what you need in one book, the other may help. After you have your two introductory how-to books, take a look at the books presented in this chapter.

(Other chapters of this book recommend titles on the specific topics those chapters cover. For example, my first chapter on marketing recommends books useful for Internet marketers.)

Books here deal with specific business aspects of the Internet. I culled through hundreds of books to choose these. Bill Gates' book *The Road Ahead* is not on the list because I assume that you've already heard of it. Since book prices change as often as tax rates, I have not included prices here. Besides, if you *really* want something, price is no object, right?

Your guide to the stars

★★★★★	Highest rating: Extremely valuable for all businesses. Rarely given.
★★★★	Very useful to most businesses.
★★★	The most variable rating, ranging from barely useful to all businesses to quite useful, but only for a specific audience.
★★	May have some use for a limited number of businesses.

Corporate Politics and the Internet, by James Gaskin ★★★ (1997), Prentice Hall, 452 pages. ISBN 0-13-651803-6. If you're a manager who needs to set company policies and procedures for Internet use, this book will help. Covers business issues as well as technical and legal matters.

The Cuckoo's Egg: Tracking a Spy through the Maze of Computer Espionage, by Cliff Stoll ★★★★★ (1989), Pocket Books, 332 pages. ISBN 0-67172-688-9. This terrific book spent five months on the *New York Times'* bestseller list. It's as exciting as a Tom Clancy novel, only funnier and with more romance. And it's all true! The author is sent to find the cause of a 75-cent error in an accounting program. It alerts him to an Internet intruder—an East German spy funded by the KGB—breaking into hundreds of military bases and defense corporations. The FBI and CIA get into the act. As the suspense mounts, you learn important facts about Internet security. I like this book so much I've read it three times.

The Digital Economy, by Don Tapscott ★★★ (1996), McGraw-Hill, 342 pages. ISBN 0-07-062200-0. This best-selling book shows how the Internet and other technologies have already fundamentally changed businesses in ways that many people have not perceived. Tapscott also predicts how businesses will differ in the near future.

The Elements of Email Style, by David Angell and Brent Heslop ★★★ (1994), Addison-Wesley Publishing, 157 pages. ISBN 0-201-62709-4. A book for people who write a lot of email and want to make it effective. This book points out how the most effective writing styles differ between postal letters and email, and tells when to use each. This book is useful for publicity and customer service people.

How to Build an Internet Service Company 2nd edition, by Charles H. Burke ★★ (1997), Social Systems Press, 272 pages. ISBN 0-935563-03-2. Not for most businesses, but if you want to become an Internet access provider, this book tells how.

How to Get Your Dream Job Using the Web, by Shannon Karl and Arthur Karl ★★★★ (1997), Coriolis Group, 420 pages + CD-ROM. ISBN 1-57610-125-8. Eventually, everybody needs to find a job. This book and CD combo gives you the strategies and the tools you need to use the Net to get hired in record time. It's well-organized, a breeze to read, and includes good job sources you'd never think of yourself. The CD provides Windows and Mac software to help in your search, a database of employer contacts, and the tools you need to create a Web page resume.

Internet et l'Entreprise, by Olivier Andrieu and Denis Lafont ★★★ (1995), Editions Eyrolles, 395 pages. ISBN 2-212-08906-6. One of the best Internet business books in any language, this well-organized French book is clear and easy to follow. It provides a thorough background in Internet business strategy and includes sound how-to information.

Investor's Guide to the Internet, by Paul Farrell ★★★★ (1996), Wiley, 386 pages. ISBN 0-471-14444-4. Extremely useful how-to book and directory for investors who want to use the Net as a tool to make better investments. By far the best I've seen on this subject.

Manufacturing and the Internet, by Richard Mathieu ★★★ (1996), Engineering & Management Press, 386 pages. ISBN 0-89806-164-4. Solid guide on how manufacturers use the Net and a good directory of online resources for manufacturers. Includes free email newsletter with updates.

Merriam-Webster's Guide to International Business Communications, by Toby D. Atkinson ★★★★ (1994), Merriam-Webster, 327 pages. ISBN 0-87779-028-0. How do you write email to make it understood by people in other countries? What export documentation do you prepare to ship products overseas? What fields does your customer database need to handle addresses, titles, and names for international customers? This is not an Internet book, but it does have a staggering amount of information for American and Canadian businesses with overseas customers. Most of the book is a country-by-country reference of address formats, phone system information, currency formats, and other information needed daily when doing business internationally.

Webonomics, by Evan Schwartz ★★★★★ (1997), Broadway Books, 244 pages. ISBN 0-553-06172-0. Stimulating, entertaining guide to what makes money on the Web and why. Schwartz's myth-busting strategies are based on real companies' successes and flops. I disagree with a couple of his points, but he offers more productive strategies than 99 percent of the people who cover Internet business.

Newsletters and magazines on Net business

This is not a complete list. It seems like a new periodical on Net business comes out every Tuesday. Most are rehashes of the same old stuff or reprints of press releases from software vendors. The handful I've listed here actually provides useful information. If you only subscribe to one, read *Web Week*. Not only is it the best, it's free!

You won't need all of these, but to keep up with profitable new developments, try *Web Week* plus a couple of additional publications that you think might be helpful.

Interactive Content ★★★ Published monthly by Jupiter Communications. (**www.jup.com**) Pricey newsletter for businesses that provide content on the Net, covering mainstream media new to the Internet and major Internet startups.

Internet Bulletin for CPAs ★★★★ Published monthly by Kent Information Services, ISSN 1078-2176. (**www.kentis.com**) This slickly-designed newsletter covers the American Institute of Certified Public Accountants' (AICPA) online activities, how to use Internet tools, security issues, online resources for accountants, and where to go to get up-to-date tax information online. Focuses on the United States. A good value for accountants.

Internet Business Report ★★★ Published monthly by Jupiter Communications. (**www.jup.com**) Pricey-but-solid newsletter covering players, business technologies, and revenue strategies in "the Internet as a business."

Internet Report ★★★ Published monthly by IWT Magazin Verlag GmbH. (**www.iwtnet.de/inet_report**) German "how-to" newsletter with simple tips for small- and medium-sized businesses.

Online Marketplace ★★★ Published monthly by Jupiter Communications. (**www.jup.com**) Pricey-but-insightful newsletter covering electronic payments and shopping, transaction processing, and home banking.

Web Week ★★★★ Published biweekly by Mecklermedia, ISSN 1081-3071. (**www.iworld.com/ww-online**) *Web Week* is the best periodical covering business use of the Internet and intranets. On top of that, it's free. (At least to qualified U.S. and Canadian subscribers.) If you do business on the Net, you need this magazine. Go to its Web site to subscribe.

Learn about the Internet from the Internet

The Internet is a huge storehouse of all kinds of information, so it's no surprise that the Net has lots of information on how to use itself. Best of all, it's free. One thing to keep in mind is that the Internet is always changing. Don't be surprised if some of these resources shut down or get up and walk away to a new address.

This section lists Internet resources that tell you *how to use* the Net. The next section lists *where to find* resources.

Accessing the Internet by Email ★★★ Very good how-to guide by Bob Rankin telling how to use different Internet tools (like Gopher, the Web, and FTP) if you have only email. **mailto:listserv@ubvm.cc.buffalo.edu** and leave the Subject line of your message blank. In the body of your message, type: **GET INTERNET BY-EMAIL NETTRAIN F=MAIL** and nothing else. Note that the dash in "EMAIL" goes *before* the "E", not after it.

FAQs Archive ★★★★ FAQs are lists of answers to Frequently Asked Questions about a topic. The FAQs tell about the newsgroups themselves, and in many cases provide a good introduction to the topic that a newsgroup discusses. Many newsgroups discuss the Internet, so you'll find a lot of information here about the Net. This site has the FAQs from the most popular newsgroups. **www.cis.ohio-state.edu:80/hypertext/faq/usenet**

Japan Network Information Center (JPNIC) ★★★ Best source I've found for information in Japanese regarding the Internet. Allocates Japanese domain names and acts as international and domestic liaison to the Internet. **www.nic.ad.jp/index.html**

Network/Computer Technology Security Index ★★★★★ This site provides *everything* about security on the Net: FTP, Web and Gopher sites, discussion lists, electronic publications, and security incident bulletins from seven organizations. **www.tezcat.com/web/security/security_top_level.html**

news.announce.newusers ★★★ A newsgroup that provides how-to instructions about the Internet, everything from "A Primer on How to Work with the Usenet Community" to "Hungarian Commercial Online Services." You can't post your own questions here; this is a read-only newsgroup. This newsgroup provides helpful information, especially for marketing via newsgroups. **news:news.announce.newusers**

Windows and TCP/IP for Internet Access ★★★ Harry Kriz explains how to install popular Windows Internet software. **http://learning.lib.vt.edu/wintcpip/wintcpip.html**

Yahoo's Guides ★★★★ Links to dozens of resources with instructions on how to do almost everything possible on the Net. Browse **www.yahoo.com/Computers_and_Internet/Internet/Information_and_Documentation** and find more info at **www.yahoo.com/Computers_and_Internet/Internet/World_Wide_Web/Information_and_Documentation**

Where to find stuff on the Net

The first question businesspeople ask about the Internet is, "How do I get connected?" The second question is, "How do I work this #&*@!! software?!" (Swearing at software helps it work better. This has been proven in laboratory tests.) The third question is, "How do I find anything on the Internet?"

This section makes you a finder. If you use the Internet to gather information, you will return to these search sites again and again.

When your business first connects to the Internet, your staff will need training, some more than others. People who already use the Net at home may need no training. But in addition to classes, plan time for your newbies to just browse the Net to familiarize themselves with its resources and tools. The amount of time you should allow depends on which Internet tools (Web, email, newsgroups, etc.) your people use and their positions. Someone in marketing, for instance, should spend from five to eight hours a week for the first four weeks just poking around and finding surprises.

Time invested in early exploration pays ongoing dividends later, because seasoned explorers learn how to find resources on the Net and how to use them. Encourage your people to try as many of the resources described here as they possibly can. Net users familiar with many alternatives rarely ossify into rigid patterns that limit their research abilities.

Pass this section to your newbies. The directories and lists in this section are not *business-specific* directories, although they list businesses and sometimes list valuable resources for businesses. The directories here are general lists. (You'll find a catalog of business-specific resources in Chapter 25.) The general nature of these lists makes them especially valuable for exploration by new Net users. The treasures they find while probing will build their sense of control over the Net, instead of letting them be overwhelmed by its immensity.

Find lost sites with the URL-stripping trick

When you try an Internet address and it doesn't work, someone may have moved your destination to another spot or given it a new name. Here's a search pro's trick that will often help you find what you're looking for. Imagine that you're searching for the Maltese falcon's Web page at: **www.detect.com/casefiles/spade/falcon**

Instead, you get the "Error 404" message that tells you your file is not there. Just delete everything to the right of the last slash, so your URL looks like this: **www.detect.com/casefiles/spade**

You'll either get another Web page, a directory of files, or another "Error 404." If nothing looks like what you want, once again strip away everything to the right of the last slash: **www.detect.com/casefiles**

Maybe you'll find another file named **blackbird**. That might be your **falcon** file renamed. When I find a URL that won't work, URL-stripping leads me to its replacement more than half the time.

Where I look first to find stuff

Every week I spend hours researching stuff on the Net. For most of my searches, my first step is to go to one or more of four sites. Eightyfive percent of the time, these four link me to the information I need. These four have been so rewarding to me that I want to share some tips so you can find things quickly, too.

Alta Vista ★★★★★ www.altavista.digital.com

Excite ★★★★★ www.excite.com

InfoSeek ★★★★★ www.infoseek.com

Yahoo ★★★★★ www.yahoo.com

First, Yahoo, which is the busiest site on the Net—more than 30 *million* pages served every day. Yahoo gives you different information than the other three. It consists of the names of thousands of Internet sites, each with a short description. The description is written by an actual human (the others all use software), and for accuracy is compared with the site it describes before Yahoo adds the description to its database. Yahoo organizes everything in its database under topic categories. When you use Yahoo, you can search for three things:

1. Yahoo's topic categories
2. The names of sites, companies, and organizations
3. Yahoo's short descriptions of sites and companies

Yahoo is built for speed. Since it is much faster than other sites, when I know the name or category of something I'm searching for, I try Yahoo first. Note that Yahoo does not index the contents of sites; it does not let you search through the actual text of Web pages, only the information it stores about those pages. When Yahoo does not find a match for your topic, it automatically searches Alta Vista and gives you Alta Vista's matches for your search terms. In addition to searching Yahoo by typing in a search term, you can also find resources by browsing through its categorized directories. From Yahoo's home page, just click on the category that interests you.

The other three search engines—Alta Vista, Excite, and InfoSeek—all work similarly. They all build huge databases of the actual contents of Web sites. Each stores a slightly different collection of pages, and each indexes them a little differently. So when you can't find what you want from one, it often pays for you to look in the other two as well.

These databases are so gigantic that it is common for a search to return a result of 100,000 pages that match your search terms. The trick with these three, then, is to be able to narrow the results returned to you so that your results match what you're looking for. All three of these search engines let you apply the same techniques to focus your search.

First, understand how they use *capital* and *lower case letters*. If you search for **LOVE**, you will get every page that has the word **LOVE** in all caps, but you won't receive any pages that contain **Love** or **love**. If you search for **Love** with an initial cap, your results will include neither **LOVE** nor **love**. However, if you search for **love** in all small letters, the search engines will ignore capitalization and bring you back all three: **love**, **LOVE**, and **Love**. I do all my searches using all small letters unless I have a strong reason to do otherwise.

Second, know about *quotation marks*. If you search for **vince emery** you will get all the pages that say **vince** anywhere on them and all the pages that say **emery** anywhere, including thousands of pages that say one or the other, but not both. If you search for "**vince emery**" with quotation marks, you will get *only* pages that list whatever you put between quotes, exactly as you have them. Quotation marks are especially useful for searching for book and movie titles and for company and product names. Whenever you want to find a phrase of more than one word, put your phrase in quotation marks.

Quotes introduce another problem, however. If you search for "**vince emery**" with quotes, you will not find any pages that give my name with my last name first: **Emery, Vince** for example. You can type in "**emery, vince**" and "**vince emery**" both in one search and the search engine would give you all pages with either one or the other. But you won't get any pages with **emery, v.**

So you can use *plus signs*. Plus signs come in handy because the search engines assume that a page with any *one* search term you type in is just as good as a page with both or all of them. But if you put a plus sign in front of any word or phrase in quotation marks, the search engine will give you only pages that contain your plus sign terms. So you can type in:

+emery +"how to grow your business on the internet"

and your results will be only pages that list *both* the name and the phrase.

These three techniques won't work on Yahoo—it ignores both capitalization and punctuation. But most search sites on the Internet apply the three techniques of capitalization, quotation marks, and plus signs. Remember these three and use them, and with a little practice, you'll be able to find what you need on the Net almost every time.

Overall search engines and directories

If you search on Yahoo or Alta Vista and fail to find what you need, don't despair. Instead, look in another place. If you don't get what you want in one place, it pays to try several.

Argus Clearinghouse ★★★★ A directory of Internet directories. Find directories by subject. Check out the excellent "Business and Employment" section for nearly 200 business directories categorized by topic. **www.clearinghouse.net**

Hotbot ★★★★ *Wired* magazine's search engine is useful but so garish it hurts my eyes. **www.hotbot.com**

Internet Sleuth ★★★★ The Internet Sleuth links with more than 600 searchable indeces and databases on a variety of topics. **www.intbc.com/sleuth/ index.html**

Open Text ★★★ Open Text searches a database of Web sites, Gophers, FTP archives, and messages from some newsgroups. Open Text actually searches the *contents* of FTP documents (not just their file names), which few search engines do. **www.opentext.com**

RES-Links All-in-One Resource Page ★★★★ A wonderful Web directory dedicated to one thing: helping you find stuff on the Net. It gives you links to all major finding tools on the Net, and even better, *it explains the differences between them.* The first time you visit this page, be sure to read the instructions and the glossary. **www.cam.org/~intsci/index.html**

WWW Virtual Library ★★★ Lists of Web sites by topic. Different people contribute to each topic list; quality differs. Some topics have awe-inspiring lists; some have little. Good sections on Web development, finance sites, German resources, electronic journals, and newspapers. Usable list of standards bodies. Lame list of commercial services. **www.w3.org/hypertext/ DataSources/bySubject**

Specialized directories and search engines

If you are looking for specific companies by name, note that InterNIC Whois (described below) is a good place to find them.

City.Net ★★★★ By location, you can look up any country, state, province, and most major cities and find links to information about it and Web sites in it. Includes detailed street maps as well as directory listings. **www.city.net**

Fedworld ★★★★ Where to find U.S. federal government resources. Directories help you find more than 140 federal agencies and more than 10,000 files of information and software. **www.fedworld.gov**

Hoover's Company Profiles ★★★★★ Condensed versions of Hoover's Profiles on almost 10,000 U.S. corporations. **www.hoovers.com**

Japan Network Information Center (JPNIC) ★★★★ JPNIC provides Japanese Whois searches to find who Internet domains belong to, plus a searchable database of information. **www.nic.ad.jp/index.html**

Thomas Register of American Manufacturers ★★★★★ This is one of the best business resources on the Net. Use the Thomas Register Supplier Finder to search the gigantic Thomas database of thousands of U.S. and Canadian manufacturers either by name or by product manufactured. You must register, but it's free. **www.thomasregister.com/home.html**

What's New in Japan ★★★★ English and Japanese lists of new Web sites in Japan and sites in other countries operated by Japanese organizations. **www.ntt.co.jp/WHATSNEW/index.html**

Finding people and email addresses

For links to other places to find people, visit the RES-Links People page at **www.cam.org/~intsci/people**

Four11 Online User Directory ★★★★ This search site for email addresses contains only a half-million listings, but is still extremely useful. Gives you data contained in no other site. You can search for someone's current email address by any combination of a person's first name, last name, city, country, company, and—get this—old email address. The basic service is free. The company charges for expanded services, including Pretty Good Privacy encrypted key service. **www.four11.com**

InterNIC Whois ★★★ Enter a name or part of a name, and you'll receive a list of all possible domain names, companies, and personal email addresses that match your search term. **http://rs.internic.net/cgi-bin/whois**

Find people with the postmaster trick

Along with the resources, here's a handy trick: how to find a person's email address when you know only his or her company address. Just send email to **postmaster@address**—insert the company's address in place of "address". For example, you know Effie Perine works for Spade & Archer where her company address is **detect.com**. If you want to find Effie's address, you can send a message to **postmaster@detect.com**. Most sites have someone in charge of mail. In your message, ask for the email address of the person you want. Most postmasters will tell you how to reach the person.

Finding FTP files and software

Note that Open Text (described earlier in the chapter) actually searches the *contents* of FTP documents. The two resources below let you search only for file names.

Archie ★★★ If you know the *name* of an FTP file, but you don't know where to find it, let Archie find it. Type in your filename, and Archie will search most of the FTP sites in the world. Use the Archie Web site closest to you. In the U.S.: **http://hoohoo.ncsa.uiuc.edu/archie.html**. In Ireland: **www.ucc.ie/cgi-bin/archie**

Snoopie ★★★ Searches a database of millions of FTP files to find the one you want. **www.snoopie.com**

Finding email discussion lists

Liszt Directory of Email Discussion Groups HHHH Search a database of 40,000 email discussion groups—not the groups' contents, but their names, addresses, and very short descriptions. **www.liszt.com**

Mailbase ★★★ Search a database of 500 U.K. email discussion lists not included in Liszt or Tile.net. **www.mailbase.ac.uk**

Tile.net Lists ★★★ Tile.net lists fewer lists than Liszt, but lets you find them in many more ways. **www.tile.net/lists**

Finding newsgroups and information from them

Note that Alta Vista and InfoSeek, both described earlier in this chapter, also search through archives of past newsgroup messages. Open Text also has some.

Usenet Newsgroups: Resources ★★★★ This site shows you how to find newsgroups to read and how to create your own. **http://scwww.ucs.indiana.edu/ NetRsc/usenet.html**

DejaNews Research Service ★★★ Search through up to a year of archived newsgroup messages. Does not include all newsgroups. **www.dejanews.com**

Tile.net Index of Newsgroups ★★★ Lists all newsgroups worldwide under their hierarchies, plus a searchable database so you can find information by subject or group name. **www.tile.net/news**

Finding Gopher sites and information

Note that Alta Vista, InfoSeek, Excite, Hotbot, and Open Text, all described earlier, also search Gopher sites.

Veronica ★★★ Here you can search 99 percent of all Gopher menus world-wide. Choose "Simplified Veronica: find ALL gopher types." **gopher:// veronica.scs.unr.edu:70/11/veronica**

Finding libraries and other Telnet sites

Hytelnet ★★★ Database of Telnet sites. Especially useful for finding items in libraries. Most of the major libraries in the world let you search through their catalogs using Telnet, and you can even see if a particular book is available or checked out.

In the United States, **telnet://lawnet.law.columbia.edu** Log in as: **lawnet**
In Europe, **telnet://info.mcc.ac.uk** Log in as: **hytelnet**
On the Web, go to:
       http://library.usask.ca/hytelnet
       http://galaxy.einet.net/hytelnet/START.TXT.html

CHAPTER **6**

Breaking the Law

"Lawyers have been known to wrest from reluctant juries triumphant verdicts of acquittal for their clients, even when those clients, as often happens, were clearly and unmistakably innocent."

—Oscar Wilde

Virgin Airways' World Wide Web site cost it a $14,000 fine. Its Web pages advertised a fare that was no longer available and listed fares without taxes in the prices. The Web pages violated U.S. airline regulations, and the U.S. Department of Transportation socked Virgin with the fine.

When I think of legal threats to Internet businesses, the Department of Transportation isn't the first law enforcement organization that comes to mind. The FBI, the Secret Service, the Federal Trade Commission, and the Federal Communications Commission are all more well known as watchdogs for Internet business fraud. And the U.S. Postal Service monitors the Net for direct marketing scams, especially for contests offering vacations and prizes.

And those are only the U.S. agencies. Law enforcers from Canada, the U.K., and many other countries keep a loosely organized watch over businesses on the Net. Any law that affects your business *off* the Net, also applies when you're *on* it.

Brock Meeks found that out the hard way when he became the first person sued for Internet-based defamation. His newsletter *Cyberwire Dispatch* accused Suarez Corporation Industries of running a "scam" by offering free Internet access through a dummy company called Electronic Postal Service. Respondents wouldn't get free access, but instead a solicitation to pay $159 for a book and some software—a bait-and-switch operation. Suarez had been accused before of perpetrating misleading marketing ploys. Suarez sued Meeks for defamation. In August 1994, Meeks settled out of court by reimbursing Suarez $64 for its court filing fee and agreeing to fax questions to the company if he planned to write more articles about it. That sounds better for Meeks that it was—he had to pay $25,000 to attorneys, effectively wiping him out financially.

A business on the Internet needs to step as carefully as a business in any other medium, avoiding all the usual booby traps plus a few new ones. And since the Internet spreads your business around the world, you won't know which country or state those booby traps will come from.

No one place owns the Net, but all try to control it

Of all Internet legal issues, the least settled is jurisdiction. Whose laws apply in cyberspace? This is not a trivial issue. As I write this, one man is in federal prison as a result. Robert Thomas of Milpitas, California, was sentenced to 37 months in prison for obscenity, convicted by a jury in Memphis, Tennessee. His wife was sentenced to 30 months. Thomas has never been to Memphis, but the "local community standards" of Memphis were applied because a federal investigator retrieved files from Thomas's computer in California to the investigator's computer in Memphis. Thomas broke a law in Memphis *without actually going there*. (Thomas used an electronic bulletin board system and was not on the Internet, but there are legal and technical parallels between bulletin board systems and the Net.)

It is easy for your business to break a law someplace else. In some countries, encrypted files are illegal. If a citizen of one of those countries retrieves an encrypted file from your Web server in Florida, is your company liable for breaking the law? What if your employee sends an encrypted email message to someone in one of those countries? In some nations, insulting politicians and religious leaders is punishable by a prison sentence or death. If a policeman in such a nation retrieves an insulting file from your Web site in New York, should your company suffer the consequences? Copyright and trademark laws differ from country to country. What country's laws apply on the global Internet?

Civil codes that regulate business transactions are another source of concern. This is an especially important issue for multinational corporations. A branch in one country could be liable for an Internet message posted by an office in another country far away.

A 1994 seminar at the Practicing Law Institute in New York concluded that publishing electronically may lead to libel actions far from the publisher's physical location, simply because the Net makes stories available at remote distances.

Cross-border advertising and marketing are two of the most confusing legal areas. Some countries, such as Germany, have laws so restrictive they are almost silly. Some places prohibit comparative advertising. Can your business name a competitor even if you don't make a comparison? Some countries say

"No." If your company sells online and ships products to other countries, you are reasonably safe as long as you have no assets in the country whose regulations you violate. But larger companies must step carefully. Offended governments can get court injunctions to stop you from doing business, can impose fines, and can even seize your assets in their country.

Governments and law enforcement agencies have not yet realized that the Internet is a borderless worldwide phenomenon. Like falling rain, the Internet affects a place without originating in it. We are years away from any kind of definitive legal conclusion on this issue.

What the heck is this "Acceptable Use Policy" stuff?

When investigating the legal issues that govern the Internet, one of the first things you will hear about is "Acceptable Use Policy." This term is batted around enough to be called AUP for short. There are actually two kinds of AUPs.

The first was an Internet-wide policy, a fossil from the pre-commercial era of the Net when the National Science Foundation's NSFNet was the main Internet backbone. It said that NSF's part of the Net—which carried almost everybody's traffic—could not be used for profit. Fortunately, as of May 1995, NSFNet went away. For-profit providers now carry almost all traffic, and the old NSFNet Acceptable Use Policy only applies to companies whose access provider is an educational institution, nonprofit agency, or government entity.

The second kind of AUP is very different and is more important to your business today. This is the Acceptable Use Policy—even if it is called by another name—that your Internet access provider expects you to follow. This AUP is not a law, but as a guideline for your activities, it forms the first level of regulation for the Internet. It is a contractual way to manage your relationship as a user or provider. If you violate it, you can be kicked off the system. By using the access provider's services, you agree to follow the rules set by your provider. Your provider can terminate your relationship if you don't. Read the agreement with your access provider to make sure you know what rules apply.

Your provider's policies may or may not specify that you practice *netiquette*, the Internet's code of conduct, but in either case you should keep in mind the practical consequences of not following these established rules.

The most obvious example of misconduct is conducting a mass email advertising campaign to people who haven't asked to receive your message (known as *spamming*). This violates netiquette. The consequence is that you will receive hate email in such vast quantities that it could crash your system and your provider's system. Your provider could then sue you for negligence toward its system, because you knew that your actions would hurt its business.

Tort law on the Internet

Tort law is a broad area remedying wrongs between parties. Tort law also includes breaches of contract between you and your provider.

What other laws apply to your access provider? Surprisingly, access providers are *not* regulated by any commission.

"Access is not regulated by anybody," points out corporate attorney Thomas Cervantez. He represents startups, especially online businesses, and is with the California firm of Pillsbury, Madison and Sutro (**www.cushman.com**). "That's why you can go to a thousand different providers and for the same thing get a thousand different prices."

Internet law is still an infant, but Net tort cases have already been prosecuted and won against businesses. What you can't do off the Net, you can't do on it. The same laws still apply. False advertising, fraud, negligence, misrepresentation, and trademark infringement are tort-based actions that some companies have committed on the Net. Of course, you'll want to plan your company's activities to avoid engaging in these actions.

False advertising is covered under a mix of federal and state regulations called unfair competition laws. Brian Corzine (also known as Brian Chase) won the dubious distinction of being the first person nailed by the Federal Trade Commission for false advertising on the Internet. A federal judge found him guilty and halted sales of his phony $99 credit repair program.

Just so you know that false advertising penalties can cause more pain than a slap on the wrist, keep in mind that for serious cases of false advertising, judges have ordered entire companies seized and *liquidated* to pay fines. That's gotta hurt.

Your company can also be liable if it engages in *product substitution* (offering one product and palming off another as the offered product), trade name or trademark infringement, *trade dress* infringement (making your product or Net site copy the *look* of another company), and character rights infringement. You violate *character rights* if you use a photo of a famous person to sell your product on your Web page without permission. Even dead people have rights. Companies that used Elvis Presley's picture found this out the hard way when Elvis's estate won huge damages from them.

Fraud is another tort liability that can apply to your Internet business and also to your customers' conduct on the Internet. From a legal standpoint, fraud is deception involving "knowing misrepresentation" of a material fact. In other words, there was an *intent* to deceive.

If your customer gives you a bogus credit card number over the Internet, your customer is liable for fraud. If your Web page claims that your product does something when you know it doesn't, your customer can nail you for fraud. Fraudulent offers on the Net have generated complaints from consumers and businesses around the world. In several countries, national and local consumer watchdog organizations actively search for Internet fraud.

Misrepresentation is a tort area related to fraud. Your company can be liable for misrepresentation if you fail to truthfully represent facts about a product, service, or situation, and if your lack of truthful representation is detrimental to the person or organization that receives your representation.

Misrepresentation covers those hazy areas where a business slathers exaggerations on its product description, and when companies fail to disclose the negative aspects of their offerings. I have seen a lot of this on the Net, often from companies big enough to know better.

Negligence happens in the real world when a person or a company is negatively affected because another person or company failed to take care in an action. The careless company is liable for negligence when its judgment failed to meet a legally recognized norm for such actions. On the Internet, negligence is new legal ground.

If you do something (such as spamming, which might generate 100,000 pieces of hate email) that crashes the system of your access provider, you are damaging your provider's business, and you can be sued for negligence. The consequences may be grave: Your provider's system also supports companies other than your own, so if your actions crash your provider's system, other companies can sue *your provider* for negligence that hurts their businesses.

Here's another hypothetical example of Internet negligence. "What about an Internet product catalog company that sells the products of other companies?" asks attorney Cervantez. "Say that product catalog company fails to make sure it has a backup system and its system crashes right before a key trade show for its customers. If the industry standard was to have a backup system and the Internet product catalog company didn't, it could be sued for negligence."

Product liability laws vary from country to country. In the United States and other countries, you can be liable for *selling* a defective product that harms someone even when your company did not *manufacture* that product. Culpability lies in making the defective product available.

There are gradations in liability, from total (You sold this. It caused harm. This is all your fault.) to partial (How much was the user's fault? How much was the manufacturer's?). For a business on the Internet, product liability issues are the same as they are in the real world.

Intellectual property on the Internet

Probably the richest area of the Internet, from a lawyer's point of view, is intellectual property law. Software, patents, books, videos, music, photographs, trademarks, fictional characters, copyrights, Web pages—all are intellectual property.

Copyright law gives the creator of a *tangible* work the right to exclude others from using the work. Note the word "tangible." Copyrights don't apply to ideas or to ways of doing things. They apply only to the finished, executed product.

Don't assume you can copy something just because it lacks a copyright notice. Whether someone puts a copyright notice on a finished work or not, copyright protection applies immediately upon creation of the work.

Obviously, you should attach a copyright notice to anything you don't want copied. And you can choose from a variety of notices if you want to make something freely available and still retain rights to it.

If your company is on the Internet and displays or offers copyrighted property belonging to someone else, and if you haven't obtained permission to display or distribute that work, you are liable for damages. In a well-publicized case, Playboy Enterprises was awarded $500,000 from a company offering *Playboy* magazine photos online.

This holds true even if you just use a small part of a copyrighted work. A magazine that copied only 300 words of ex-President Gerald Ford's 200,000-word autobiography was found guilty of copyright infringement.

Under copyright law, a catalog, database, or directory (such as a list of vendors from a newsgroup) is considered a *compilation*. This is defined as a selection of facts grouped in an organized order. If a sentence is copyrighted, a new copyright can be available for it when it is included in a new compilation. It's important to note that a compilation's copyright protects *all its components*, including pictures.

The way a compilation's components are arranged is also protected. If your competitor features a product in its catalog or Web page and your business sells the same product, you can advertise it as long as you do not copy the illustration, text, or arrangement that your competitor used. You and your competitor can both use the same pictures or descriptions from your vendor, as these are normally copyrighted by the vendor and made available for reuse.

An original compilation of names and addresses is copyrightable, even when the names and addresses are in the public domain. For this type of compilation, only the arrangement is protected, not the names and addresses themselves. In the same way, your home page arrangement of links is protected, even though the links themselves are in the public domain.

The same holds true for trademarks and logos. If you want to use another company's trademark in your Web page, get written permission first. Trademark law is messy in the United States. There are federal laws that offer nationwide coverage, but there are also individual state laws covering trademarks. Some trademarks are registered only in one state or group of states.

International laws add another layer of trademark confusion. For companies not online, this situation is bad enough. Companies on the Internet are in a swamp. If a trademark is infringed on the Net, nobody knows *where,* physically, the infringement took place, and therefore nobody knows which courts and which laws have jurisdiction. Expect court battles and state and federal legislation over this issue.

Trade secrets are another area of intellectual property law. Your company might protect strategies, future product plans, manufacturing methods, or other processes by keeping knowledge about them within your company. This gives them legal protection as trade secrets. But keep in mind that if someone in your company discusses your trade secrets on the Internet or posts documents about them, they are no longer confidential—and you are no longer protected. Trade secrets are major targets for industrial espionage on the Net.

To protect yourself from legal fistfights over intellectual property, you need to remain alert regarding two quite different issues. First, remember that the Net is a *public* communications network, so you need to keep a tight rein on your own intellectual property so you don't lose your rights by improperly making works public. Second, someone in your company needs to accept formal responsibility for making sure your company and its employees don't infringe on someone else's rights.

Internet copyright and trademark notices

For full protection of anything your business puts on the Internet— whether it's a Web page, a product FAQ, or an email newsletter— you should put a copyright notice on it. To be valid, your copyright notice must have three things:

1. Either the word "Copyright" or the symbol © (the use of both is repetitious)

2. The name of the copyright holder

3. The year the work was first disseminated

It won't hurt to add the phrase "All rights reserved." This protects your rights under the copyright laws of some Latin American countries.

You may have seen some lengthy copyright notices on the Internet that make distinctions between who can and who cannot copy the material and under what circumstances. Here is a sampling of Internet copyright notices. If one of these notices meets your needs except for the company name, feel free to copy it and change the business name to your own. Unless your name is Bob Crachit.

- Copyright 1996 by Scrooge & Marley Ltd. All rights reserved. Federal copyright law prohibits unauthorized reproduction by any means and imposes fines up to $25,000 for violations.

- © 1996 by Scrooge & Marley Ltd. All rights reserved. This material may be copied online but may not be reproduced in print or on a CD-ROM without written permission from Scrooge & Marley Ltd.

- Copyright 1996 by Scrooge & Marley Ltd. All rights reserved. This material may not be duplicated for any profit-driven enterprise.

- © 1996 by Scrooge & Marley Ltd. All rights reserved. Unlimited permission to copy or use is hereby granted subject to inclusion of this copyright notice.

- © 1996 by Scrooge & Marley Ltd. All rights reserved. This material may be freely copied and distributed subject to the inclusion of this copyright notice and our World Wide Web URL: www.scrooge&marley.co.uk

- © 1996 by Scrooge & Marley Ltd. All rights reserved. This page may not be copied, downloaded, stored in machine-readable form, or otherwise reproduced, disseminated, adapted, or used without written permission of Scrooge & Marley Ltd.

For maximum protection, you should register your material. If you sue someone for infringing on your copyright, in many cases it is difficult to collect statutory damages unless you registered your material before the infringement took place. In the U.S., you can get registration information and forms from the Library of Congress at **http://lcweb.loc.gov/copyright**. If your country signed the GATT treaty, any copyright registered in any GATT signatory country is automatically valid in all other GATT countries. You can, if you consider it worthwhile, also register your material individually in dozens of non-GATT countries.

If you have a trademark, your home page should have a trademark notice. Trademark notification is supposed to be applied to the "first and most prominent" use of your mark, and your home page is (theoretically, anyway) your first page.

"Trademark" in a legal sense refers to any design, word, or combination of words and designs used for your products and services. You should use a service mark ([SM]) for services and a trademark ([a]) for goods. You cannot use the ¨ for "registered trademark" until you actually register your mark. In the U.S., it will cost you $345 to register with the Patents and Trademark Office.

I once worked on a project with Lucasfilm and saw a memo that said "If there is room for the mark, there is room for the [a]." I figured if that was good enough for George Lucas, it was good enough for me, and I built a [a] symbol into my own company's logo artwork. Keep that in mind and use it on your own logo.

Clearing copyrights: Who gives permission?

Even when you want to use photos or text on your Web page only for display and not for resale, you still need to obtain permission first. If you want to use a professionally recorded song or a clip from a video or TV show, there can be hidden rights that you need to include. For instance, when you include a music recording, do you need to license rights only for your country or for the whole world? This is a gray area in Internet law.

Another gray area is how much one should pay to use copyrighted material on the Net. So far, there are no standard rates for Internet use, so you may be able to use things cheaply, or you may be quoted a sky-high fee.

When clearing text: You need to obtain clearance from the copyright holder (usually the publisher or the author), possibly from the holder of foreign language or foreign territory rights, and possibly from the author—even if the copyright is in the publisher's name. Situations vary, and you'll have to handle each one on a case-by-case basis.

When clearing still pictures: You need to obtain clearance from the copyright holder, possibly from any people seen in the picture, and from the owners of any logos or trademarks included in the picture.

When clearing recorded music: You need to obtain clearance from the music publishers, the musicians' union, possibly the record company, and possibly the performers. Fees can be higher if you accompany the music with visuals.

When clearing a video or movie clip: You need to obtain clearance not only from the copyright holder or holders, but also the actors' union, the writers, the director, and any people heard or seen (including stunt performers and doubles). If music is heard, you also need the musicians' union and the music publishers' permission.

With any tricky clearance situation (especially a music recording or video clip), you can save money in the long run by hiring a clearance professional. Fees will depend on how many clearances need to be obtained and how tight your deadline is, and will range from $200 to thousands of dollars. This is in addition to the actual fee you will pay the rights holder for a license to reuse the material itself. For a smaller fee, some clearance professionals will advise you on which material in your planned Internet project might run into rights difficulties and if there are alternatives that might cost less.

Licensing music for Web sites has been made easier by the American Society of Composers, Authors, and Publishers (ASCAP, **www.ascap.com**), which will sign annual site licenses for you to use music by all of ASCAP's 68,000 members on your Web site. ASCAP has three different agreements for small, medium, and large sites.

One of the few firms with experience in obtaining Internet rights and clearances is Total Clearance, a company in California (**www.totalclear.com**). The company's founder, Jill Alofs, started out handling clearances for Lucasfilm Ltd. and LucasArts Entertainment. Now her company obtains clearances for the reuse of all types of materials in all media for more than 1,500 clients. Total Clearance cleared more than 3,000 clips for the Parker Brothers CD-ROM version of Trivial Pursuit.

Contracts on the Internet

Historically, business contracts were either written or oral, and implied or explicit. Now contracts are electronic.

In an online contract, it's important to specify which laws govern the contract. Besides defining the physical locality of the laws that govern your contract, in the United States you should add whether the Uniform Commercial Code (UCC) or any other statute or law applies to the contract. UCC regulations cover all contracts relating to goods, but not for services. Services are usually covered by state laws. The UCC defines responsibilities for rejecting or accepting goods and most other areas of commercial transactions, and plays an important role in settling commercial disputes in the United States.

In his book *The Law of Electronic Commerce*, attorney Benjamin Wright points out that the UCC says that an agreement for the sale of goods priced at $500 or more is not binding unless the contract is in writing, and that an email contract should qualify as a written contract. There are two problems. Email contracts have no equivalent of an authorizing signature, and without effective security, email can be altered—making contract enforceability questionable. Wright recommends putting a clause in any electronic contract saying "a properly transmitted message is deemed 'written,' and a designated symbol(s) or code(s) within the message is deemed a 'signature.'"

This could apply to digital signatures. Digital signatures are encrypted by the signer and include a checksum that shows if the electronic contract has been altered, even by as little as a comma.

When you form a contract or process a payment transaction online, you are legally conducting electronic data interchange, called EDI for short. The U.S. law that covers EDI is called the Electronic Funds Transfer Act. It applies to most business transactions conducted over the Net, and it is long and complicated. If you really want to be diligent (after all, this law may apply to your company), go over a copy of this act with your lawyer. Additional state laws cover forged electronic funds transfers.

Many agreements made online are "shrink-wrap" contracts, also called "unconscionable contracts or contracts of adhesion, where you don't have any negotiating going on," explains attorney Cervantez. "Courts don't like this."

There are two potential problems with a shrink-wrap contract. With most other contracts, negotiations happen before an agreement is signed. A shrink-wrap contract is a take-it-or-leave-it deal. No negotiation is involved. A court may view this as unfair. The second issue is one of timing. Does the buyer learn the full terms of the deal only *after* the contract was entered? This is often the case when software is purchased. Courts may view this as not disclosing information to the buyer before the purchase, which may make the transaction unfair.

One way to avoid this is with a two-step approach to cover yourself. You can accept signups online and then confirm the commitment offline via fax or postal mail.

Digital signatures for electronic contracts

Digital signatures are now available. You can include them with digital contracts as proof of the sender's identity and that the contracts are unaltered. They can also be used with other electronic documents such as purchase orders, or on email and newsgroup messages.

The encrypted signatures look different on every message you send, so forgers can't duplicate them. Checksums within the signatures show that your electronic document has not been altered.

The digital signature for each document is generated from a private key code you alone possess combined with the text in your signed document. That way, you are guaranteed that your document has not been changed and exactly matches the document you agreed to. Even the tiniest change—capitalizing one lowercase letter or taking away a single space—will invalidate your digital signature by turning it into gibberish. Other parties to your contract can never claim it was revised after signing, because your digital signature would reveal any modification. Since the content must not change, cutting your digital signature off one message and pasting it on another won't work, because the checksum would change.

Since your digital signature itself can't be cracked, your communication is secure from tampering.

State and provincial laws

The first few state and provincial laws covering Internet commerce have been passed by U.S. states and by provinces in other countries. State attorneys general have also been active. The first warning shot was fired by the Minnesota attorney general's office, which issued a memo (**www.webcom.com/lewrose/article/minn.html**) that claimed jurisdiction over all Internet sales and marketing to Minnesota customers, citing online gambling as an example of a prosecutable offense.

The opinion has one glaring hole: How will the attorney general prosecute a company for these alleged violations when all the company's assets and operations are in another state or even another country?

Taxes are an even more important issue for states and provinces because—let's get real here—we're talking about *money,* and they see themselves losing millions in sales and income tax revenues. Tax collectors salivate at the prospect of taxing the Net. The United States federal government has urged states not to pass state laws taxing Internet transactions until this whole messy jurisdiction issue is more clear.

Of course, where you find *taxes* you also find *tax shelters.* Many Internet-based businesses can be located anywhere in the world where bandwidth is high and taxes are low. The government of Anguilla (**http://online.offshore.com**) invites you to locate your corporation there: No income taxes, no corporate taxes, no sales taxes. What tax collectors think of this, I couldn't print in this book.

United States federal laws

Internet business brings many U.S. companies into the export field for the first time. If this is true of your company, be aware of the Export Administration Act of 1979. It includes lists of products that cannot be exported unless your business has an export license, including some computer products, electronics, and software. Besides telling you *what* you can't export, it also tells you *where.* U.S. businesses can send almost anything to France, England, and Germany, but you can't send much to Libya or Cuba.

Two federal laws covering computer crime may affect your business. The Computer Fraud and Abuse Act prohibits unauthorized use of computers owned by the federal government, computer acts that are detrimental to commerce, and computer acts that reveal information that infringes upon a person's privacy. This law was amended in 1994 to cover access without authorization to any computer used in interstate commerce, which includes all Internet computers. Information theft is a felony.

The penalties for violating this act are serious. You can go to prison if you use a federal computer. Recently, a technician with the Lawrence Livermore Laboratories was arrested under this act for using a government computer to download erotic pictures. The technician was fired, which was just a wrist-slapping—he could have been jailed.

The Electronic Communications Privacy Act prohibits electronic eavesdropping. It forbids unauthorized access of electronic communications facilities and prohibits someone with limited access to electronic communications from intentionally exceeding those limits.

In addition, many states have laws addressing computer crime. If someone uses your computer system to commit a crime, or if you become suspicious that this may have happened, contact your local law enforcement agency. Being aware of a crime and taking no action makes your company liable for criminal charges as an accomplice. In a sole proprietorship or a partnership, this exposes management to personal criminal liability.

Even in a corporation, in rare instances the directors or officers of the corporation may be personally charged with criminal liability if corporate systems are used to commit a crime, even if that use is unauthorized.

You should also be aware of the actions of the Federal Trade Commission. In 1996, the FTC nailed nine companies that marketed on the Internet, and this year it expects to nab more. It shut the nine companies down, charging them with making false or unsubstantiated advertising claims. Notice that pesky word "unsubstantiated." The FTC doesn't care whether your Web page is true or not. You must be able to *substantiate* all claims with some kind of proof.

The FTC charged five companies and their officers with making false claims to "repair" consumers' credit records online. The FTC stated that the companies' instructions could violate criminal law. Four people were charged with making unsubstantiated earnings claims to promote work-at-home businesses that didn't generate the cash flow promised. A rip-off grant-assistance Internet business was shut down, as was a company that sold computer memory chips online and delivered them much later than it promised, not offering customers refunds when the chips were late.

The FTC didn't need any new laws to shut down these Internet businesses. It applied existing laws that cover mail-order fraud. If your company sells on the Internet and is not familiar with the definitions of mail-order fraud (late shipments, for example) and what the penalties are, you may want to read a book covering the subject to keep from getting into very hot water with the FTC.

Laws of other nations

If your company has a substantial presence in any country, you should be aware of legal restrictions in the countries where you are located.

For example, if you have offices in Germany, look out for its marketing laws (the most restrictive in the world), because if you violate them, the German authorities can take action against your assets, operations, and officers in Germany. If you have no operations in Germany, the government has nothing to seize.

Some countries have strict laws covering language. French law specifies that any contest open to French citizens must have rules in French. To avoid language laws and many other international legal nuisances, you can add a line to your Web page saying that this offer applies only to residents of certain countries, or is valid only in the United States and Canada (or anywhere you choose). This sort of disclaimer may not be legally valid, but it at least discourages nuisance legal actions. These are especially common in Germany, where attorneys are actually paid a bounty for spotting violations of advertising laws.

If you get serious about sales in Europe, get a copy of the European International Code of Advertising Practice of the International Chamber of Commerce (**www.iccwbo.org**). Mercifully, this is known as the ICC Code for short. You'll find it more restrictive than U.S. regulations, but still something you can follow with a little effort.

Privacy laws, email messages, and email addresses

Email cost Chevron Corp. $2.2 million. It paid that much to settle a sexual harassment lawsuit by four women. Prime evidence in the suit included email messages that the women found offensive, including one that listed 22 reasons why beer is better than women. Pleading "It was a joke!" is no defense.

Email was evidence in another large case when Siemens sued Arco for fraud. Siemens bought a subsidiary from Arco. The price was based on a promising new technology the subsidiary had developed. After the buyout, Siemens found email saying that the Arco subsidiary's technology was "a pipe dream." Ooops!

The World Wide Web may get more news coverage, but more Internet businesses get into more trouble with email. Cover your ass by giving all your employees a formal company policy *in writing* forbidding the use of email for sexual harassment, racist remarks, personal intimidation, or any illegal purposes. If anything happens, your written policy will be your first line of defense. You'll find more on this in the section on company policy considerations in the chapter "Email: Quickest Bang For Your Buck."

Worker privacy issues

The Electronic Communications Privacy Act forbids eavesdropping, but it does not prohibit employers from monitoring the email messages of employees. At present, a business in the U.S. has the right to inspect the incoming and outgoing email messages of its employees.

This may change in the future. The proposed Privacy for Consumers and Workers Act would require employers to provide workers with notification in writing before monitoring email messages and after reading or removing files on an employee's disk drive.

The key thing here is to avoid lawsuits by warning your employees in writing that their email messages may be read by other people within your company.

Unsolicited mass emailings

Email addresses open another legal can of worms. The specific issue here is whether you can send unsolicited email messages to someone's email address. According to the Telephone Consumer Protection Act of 1991, you may be fined $500 per message for each unsolicited message you send.

Subsection (f)5 of this act prohibits "any material advertising the commercial availability or quality of any property, goods, or services which is transmitted to any person without that person's prior express invitation or permission." The regulation prohibits sending such unsolicited messages to any "equipment which has the capacity to transcribe text or images, or both, from paper into an electronic signal and to transmit that electronic signal over a regular telephone line, or to transcribe text or images or both from an electronic signal received over a regular telephone line onto paper."

That description was intended to cover fax machines, but it also fits any computer with a modem and printer. Robert V. Arkow used the Telephone Consumer Protection Act to file suit against CompuServe and CompuServe Visa for sending two unsolicited email messages to him. The companies settled out of court. A consumer privacy group called Private Citizen Inc. plans to encourage more suits under this act, so think twice before sending unsolicited mass mailings. At $500 per message, it could be the most expensive promotion you ever conduct.

The problem of unwanted, unsolicited mass emailings has grown so large that state lawmakers are getting into the act. Nevada, California, Virginia, and Connecticut are working on laws banning unsolicited email. It is already illegal in several European countries; their laws specify that you must ask a person to "opt in" before you add his or her address to your email list.

Watch out for the email list potato—it's getting hotter!

And just because you obey the law, don't assume that everyone else does. Read the next chapter to protect your business before the sirens and alarms go off.

CHAPTER 7

How to Prevent Break-Ins and Fraud

"In more than 80 percent of the computer crimes investigated by the FBI, unauthorized access was gained through the Internet."

—FBI press release

In talking to businesspeople about Internet security, I usually hear one of two points of view. They either assume that nothing will ever hurt their company, or they worry endlessly that their business will be taken over by pizza-faced teenagers working for Saddam Hussein.

Those are two extremes. Reality lies between them. Any computer linked to the Internet is exposed to millions of other computers. Most of those computers are used by everyday people just getting their work done. But *thousands* of Internet computers are used by Bad Guys. Evildoers. Spies. They are not all-powerful and all-seeing, but they can wreak havoc. Most of them will never visit your site. But, as William Cheswick and Steven Bellovin point out in their book *Firewalls and Internet Security*, "It is this way with computer security: the attacker only has to win once."

So the bad news is that your business can be vulnerable on the Internet, just as your physical business is vulnerable in the real world. On the Net, you might not be perfectly secure, but you'll be a darn sight safer than you would be behind the cash register in a liquor store. Whether you set up shop on Park Place or in cyberspace, people can steal from you. The good news is that, with common sense and a little work, you can block all but the most determined attackers.

 Internet security is not about protecting your computer. It's about protecting your *information*. "Who cares if my computer gets invaded?" one manager asked me. "It only cost a coupla thousand dollars. I can get a new one." He missed the point. More important than securing your computer is securing what's *on* your computer.

Internet security is most important when you have competition that plays rough. If you have any information you don't want a competitor to see, you'd better worry about security. Why? Contrary to what TV shows tell you, most successful computer attacks don't come from bored, brainy kids. *Most computer attacks come from industrial spies out to make money.*

Maybe they'll copy your information and sell it. Maybe they'll just *change* it. Some attackers simply want to annoy you. For example, in one Fortune 500 corporation, attackers changed the computer startup files to display X-rated photos during startup. They also altered the corporation's email system so managers couldn't use it.

Other attackers do serious damage. Intruders broke into a steel plant's network and lowered the quality of the steel it produced by sabotaging its quality-control software. Incidents like these make businesses painfully aware of something called *data integrity*. That's the assurance that your data has not been changed.

Of course, you also want to protect the *confidentiality* of your information. The Internet is a glass network. Everything you do is visible to everyone unless you take deliberate steps to cover your nakedness.

And you need to be sure of the *authenticity* of the traffic you receive from the Net, making sure that messages are from the people they claim to be. Internet forgery is a growth industry.

The shocking thing about Internet security is that most businesses who are broken into *never find out about it*. One government study estimated that 97 percent of computer penetrations remain undetected. Some data disappears, or a program stops, but the victim never realizes that the problems were caused by an Internet break-in. Most companies don't have the proper monitoring software in place. Many companies that monitor for break-ins don't review their security reports and so never know what hits them.

Preventing outsiders from ripping you off

1991: The United States Government Accounting Office reveals that, during the Gulf War, military computers linked to the Internet were broken into by hackers from the Netherlands. They copied U.S. military data about Gulf War soldiers, military equipment, and new weapons under development.

1993: A hacker hides programs in the computer of Internet access provider Panix. For weeks—or perhaps months—the hacker's programs collect the passwords and account names of Panix customers. When the break-in is discovered, Panix has to shut down its computer for three days, closing Internet connections for its customers, who must all change their own passwords and check to see if they, in turn, had been broken into.

1994: Hackers install a sniffer program to watch the Internet links of the University of California at Berkeley. The sniffer collects more than 3,000 passwords and account names in 14 hours.

1995: Twenty percent of companies responding to Ernst & Young's security survey reported that during the past year intruders had broken into or tried to break into their corporate networks via the Internet. Several companies reported computer security losses totaling more than $1 million in the past year due to stolen business information and destroyed data.

1995: Hacker Kevin Mitnick steals 20,000 credit card numbers from Internet access provider Netcom, which made the mistake of storing credit card numbers on the same computers it allowed the public to enter. (Never, ever do that.)

1996: The New York Times Syndicate's *Computer News Daily* Web site shuts down for several days because a hacker uses the site's live chat section to sneak a program onto its computer. The program grows bigger until it brings down the entire Web server.

1997: The Computer Emergency Response Team (CERT, **www.cert.org**), the most well-known computer crime-fighting organization, handles 10 reported Internet security breaches on an average day. Those 10 are just the tip of a much bigger iceberg. Most businesses are afraid to announce a break-in, so it is estimated that only 15 percent of breaches are actually reported. Last year, CERT responded to incidents affecting 10,700 sites.

Is your own business vulnerable? Of course. Your customers' credit card numbers, stored in your computer, can be stolen. Your email may be intercepted and read by your competition. Your inventory database can be scrambled. A competitor can spy on your financial records, or even change or delete them.

Serious damage happens all the time. It can hit your business as easily as the bloke down the block. Crooks feel less remorse selling your customer files than you do re-using a postage stamp.

Why security on the Internet is complex

At this point, you may say, "Hey, wait a minute! I use America Online (or CompuServe, or NiftyServe), and I haven't heard of those kinds of problems there."

You're right. These kinds of problems happen more rarely on those commercial services. Security breaches are less frequent, smaller scale, and less publicized. There are two reasons for this:

The first reason is that the commercial services are *centralized* networks, while the Internet is a *distributed* network. That may sound like a meaningless technical distinction, but it's actually a simple, clear-cut difference and easy to understand. (See Figure 7.1.)

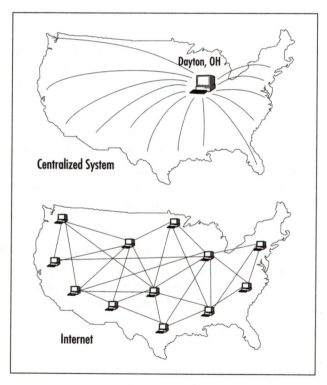

Figure 7.1   In a centralized network like CompuServe or America Online, traffic travels to and from a central site only. However, the Internet is a distributed network. Its traffic travels through several sites to reach its destination.

When you send a message or a credit card number on a commercial service like America Online, your message goes directly from your sending computer to America Online's central computer. It can't go anyplace else, because no other computers are between your computer and AOL's. Then AOL's computer reads the address on your message and sends it out. If the address is another AOL subscriber, your message goes directly from AOL's central computer to your addressee's computer. Again, your message cannot go anyplace else, because no additional computers are between AOL Central and your addressee's computer.

Your message goes right from you to America Online and straight from America Online to its destination. It's tough for anyone else to get ahold of your message, so it's relatively safe.

On the Internet, your message takes a much different route. In fact, several routes. As *San Francisco Chronicle* columnist Robert Rossney described it, "The information sent from one computer to another gets broken up into a zillion pieces, scattered across the network, and then reassembled at the other end, just like the transporter on *Star Trek.*"

When you send an Internet message, your computer breaks it into smaller pieces for efficiency. It sends the pieces to your Internet access provider. Your provider's computer looks at the address on each piece and sends it to whatever available computer is nearest your message's final destination. Depending on which computers and network links are open, that can be a different computer for each piece. Those computers forward your pieces to closer computers. Soon all your pieces reach your destination's computer, which glues them back together.

In short, one Internet message—whether it's an email message or a Web page—goes through several computers and several routes to reach its destination. You can't predict how many computers, which computers, or which routes message pieces will take. *Any of those computers can read your message and change it.* As I said earlier, the Internet is a glass network. People can see everything you send or receive.

The second reason that America Online and its counterparts have fewer security problems is that the commercial services are much smaller than the Internet.

All of the commercial services *put together* are less than one-third the size of the Internet. There are simply fewer people on them and fewer computers to break into. America Online customers are mostly people in their homes. AOL has fewer businesses, so break-ins cause less damage.

A hacker's plan of attack

So what would one of those hackers do after breaking into your computer? A typical hacker has these goals in this order:

1. Break in

2. Hide evidence of the break-in

3. Steal your passwords

4. Take control of your computer

5. Open new doors for re-entry

6. Steal your data

7. Leverage your computer to break into other computers

Field guide to attack types

Call 'em what you want—hackers, crackers, spies, or scum—bad guys are outside your company and looking for trouble. If you manage an Internet project, part of your job is to keep them out. Luckily for you, scum have only a limited number of ways to break in through the Net. Let's take a peek at the doors you need to watch—without technobabble overkill.

Password attacks

Your first line of defense is your software's password protection. Sloppy management of passwords opens doors to far more digital crooks than any other means. Most of the so-called brilliant hackers are actually good at guessing or getting passwords. It doesn't take a giant brain to stop these yeggs. With a couple of hours' planning and never-ending vigilance, you can plug password security holes. Keeping vigilant is the hard part. I provide details on password security later in this chapter.

Software attacks

The second most popular port of entry is your software. You can have more holes than Swiss cheese in your operating system software, communications software, and applications programs—and those holes attract rats. Plug your holes by installing a protective "firewall" between your computers and the Internet, and by deploying your software carefully. You should avoid some programs if possible (Telnet, Sendmail). Others (like Finger), your technical gurus can strip down for safety. Web servers on improperly configured Linux systems are commonly broken into. Your technical staff will need to invest more time securing your software than in any other defense.

Eavesdropping attacks

Passive attacks based on eavesdropping are on the rise. This popularity is fueled by the increase in Internet credit-card traffic—eavesdropping is the easiest way to steal card numbers. Eavesdroppers don't even need to break into your system to access such important information. They sit outside and use software called *packet sniffers* to scan your incoming and outgoing traffic. Packet sniffers recognize patterns like credit card numbers, your product names, and specific people's names. When the sniffer spots a familiar pattern, it copies your message and sends it to the eavesdropper. Packet sniffer attacks have become more common over the last year. Passwords are also targets for sniffers. This year, one government laboratory's network was broken into by an intruder who sniffed out names and passwords. He wiped out the lab's computer data, which cost about $2 million to replace. Non-reusable passwords would have prevented this problem. The reliable way to beat these spies is to encrypt your Internet traffic. Encryption makes your messages look like gibberish. Packet sniffers can't spot patterns because scrambled gibberish has none. Encryption is built into some operating systems such as Macintosh. In others, it's easy enough to add.

Forgery attacks

Forged messages are also on the rise. It is trivial to fake or change an Internet message. Forged Internet messages are called *spoofs*, a deceptively cheerful name. It makes them sound harmless. But some cause serious pain:

- The premier of Ontario, Canada, Bob Rae, was startled to find an explicitly sexual message from his return address posted on a widely read newsgroup. Political opponents used the forged message to embarrass him in the Ontario legislature.

- An evildoer sabotaged more than 30 customers of Internet access provider Net Access in Philadelphia. Apparently an unhappy Net Access customer, the culprit spewed racist forgeries across several Usenet newsgroups, making it look like innocent customers had made racist insults. Responders to the forgeries bombarded each victim with hate email from all over the world. Some lost business as a result.

- The most financially damaging spoof to date accused the Stratton Oakmont firm of investment bankers and its president of fraud and criminal activity in an October 1994 stock offering. The offering's share price dropped 40 percent in less than a month. Stratton Oakmont sued Prodigy for $200 million in damages, since the spoof was mailed from an expired Prodigy address and displayed on Prodigy's "Money Talk" section. The forgery may have been posted by a short-seller to profit from the stock plunge.

Encryption helps defeat spoofing, as do *digital signatures*, which are like high-tech notary public seals, proving that a message came from only one person and that it has not been altered in any way. A digital signature is easy to include with most email. Don't leave home without it.

Virus attacks

Computer viruses have been around long enough so they are no longer big news. You probably already have at least one virus protection software program. If not, get one. Your virus protection vendor will send you updates over the Net to catch and kill new viruses as they emerge. Make sure all upgrades are added quickly, and make sure all software from the Net passes your virus checker before you allow it to touch other programs.

DNS hijacking

This rare new attack redirects all traffic headed for one domain, such as apple.com, and sends it to another, such as playboy.com. If your site is hijacked, it's hard to stop it. If your incoming traffic suddenly drops to almost nothing, try accessing your site from a computer not connected to your internal network.

Web attacks

There are three ways that an intruder can penetrate your intranet and Internet Web servers. The first way is to use Telnet, FTP, Gopher, Finger, or another software program to gain access to your HTTP software. To prevent this, you'll need to eliminate all software from your Web server that isn't absolutely necessary and be careful about other security procedures.

The second way is to leverage bugs in your HTTP software itself to run system management commands. Break-ins rarely happen this way anymore. The latest generation of Web server software makes it extremely unlikely to occur.

The third way, and the biggest Web security hole, is through CGI scripts and other add-on programs. CERT reports CGI-initiated thefts of password files every week and often every day. This is now the most common security hole on the Internet.

CGI makes cool Web tricks possible, such as fill-in-the-blank forms, electronic shopping, and access to databases. A sloppy CGI form can let a hacker fill in the blanks with system management commands. A Web page that generates automatic responses via email might be tricked into emailing your password file. These problems are preventable. Any CGI script you use should be thoroughly inspected and tested for security problems. This is especially true for any free public domain CGI scripts you download from the Net to add to your Web site. Most CGI break-ins exploit the PHF CGI-bin script. The PHF program is installed with many Web servers and contains a flaw that lets intruders run commands and take over your server. Removing the PHF program is the only way to block that door. In addition to CGI scripts, many problems have been reported by Web sites using Java and ActiveX programs. Your technical people should read the overview of CGI security at **www.genome.wi.mit.edu/WWW/faqs/www-security-faq.html**.

Credit card scams

When your company takes credit cards over the Internet, you are vulnerable to all the usual credit card scams plus creative twists unique to the Net. We cover cardsharps in detail in a later chapter.

Denial-of-service attacks

In 1996, instructions and *explosion programs* for executing *denial-of-service attacks* were widely distributed on the Internet. The number of such attacks rose dramatically. Denial-of-service attacks bombard you with hundreds or thousands of messages—sometimes huge ones—that clog your Internet site so nothing can get in or out. Large-scale attacks of this type can shut down your Internet access provider's entire connection. There is no high-tech defense against a denial-of-service attack, but if you read this book carefully you shouldn't need one. Most of these attacks come in response to obnoxious behavior by a person or company. If your people are good neighbors on the Net, you will rarely if ever need to deal with a denial-of-service attack.

Three ounces of prevention

In many ways, the most serious and hardest-to-defend attacks are those based on security holes in your software. Sometimes the most innocent-seeming program is the most dangerous. Who'd ever suspect software as simple-looking as Finger? Yet Finger was the point of entry for the infamous Internet Worm virus that crippled thousands of computers and cost hundreds of thousands of dollars to clean up. Finger remains a favorite target for hackers today.

How about MIME, which lets you send email with pictures? Automatic execution of MIME email can be dangerous. MIME messages can hide commands to take over your computer. Your World Wide Web server software is also vulnerable. Bugs in certain Web servers let outsiders retrieve any file on the Web server's computer. Those files could include your password file or other confidential data.

You'll need to provide your technical staff with books that go into program-by-program detail on software security. We only scratch the surface here. However, keep three rules in mind to minimize software security risks:

1. Keep Internet software away from your other software as much as possible.

When you start on the Internet, it may make sense for you to run as many services as you can on your Internet access provider's computer, or on a separate service bureau or Web host's computer. This is a good idea. If at all possible, you can minimize your risks by keeping your FTP, Gopher, and Web servers on an outside computer.

Instead of using SMTP for email—which requires that your computer is always connected to the Net—use UUCP if your company size justifies doing so. You can set UUCP to connect to your access provider's system every 15 or 30 minutes to send and receive email. This is more secure, and you don't have to run Sendmail, which is famous for security holes. See the index to find more information about UUCP email.

If you are going to run your Web server on your own computer, run it on a standalone computer if possible. This sacrificial computer should not be connected to the rest of your company computers. If it is connected, separate it from your other computers with a firewall. *Whatever you do, make sure not to store any customer information on the same computer as your Web server, especially credit card numbers.* This is very, very, very important and is one of the most basic protection steps you can take. Never store credit card numbers on *any* computer connected to the Internet.

If you offer a Web, FTP, or Gopher site reachable by people outside your company, and you want to connect that site to computers within your company, *separate your open site from the rest of your network with a firewall*. If you can't afford a firewall, you also can't afford to clean up the damage an invader could cause. Keep Internet servers away from your own network unless you have a barrier between your intranet and the Internet.

Think twice before connecting computers that hold your sensitive information, like accounting programs or R & D data. Consider an alternative in departments with secret data. Perhaps you can have your employees walk to an "Internet desk" to use vulnerable connected computers. This may be a little more inconvenient for your employees, but it's a lot less work than cleaning up after a nasty break-in.

2. Keep it simple.

Complex software is more likely to have security bugs. Use simple programs when you can. Use as few programs as you can. As William Cheswick and Steven Bellovin say in *Firewalls and Internet Security*, "Programs that you do not run cannot hurt you."

When analyzing your system, don't trust complicated things. Trust only simple things like files and short programs. When your technical people program security rules into router filters, they should use short rules.

3. Take advantage of security software tools.

Terrific software tools are available to increase your security. Many of them are available for free on the Internet. Check out the Unix software program COPS, which searches your system and finds security flaws. A program called ASET for Sun computers forces users to use hard-to-crack passwords.

One of the most valuable security tools can come to you via email. Your security administrator will want to subscribe to the mailing list from the Computer Emergency Response Team that emails CERT advisories. These advisories warn of all newly discovered software security holes and tell where to get patches to fix them. To subscribe, send email to **cert-advisory-request@cert.org**.

If you follow the guidelines above, you'll reduce your risk of outside invaders from the Internet. The bad news is that those Internet hackers are not your greatest danger. More computer security breaches come from another source, far more hazardous and harder to manage. Your toughest security challenge will come from some other culprits.

They are waiting to break into *your* system. They have passwords and can log on. They know the names of your files and where they are located. According to all studies, they cause thousands of computer security violations each year. Some are minimal. Hundreds do serious damage. Who are they?

Your own employees.

Preventing inside theft and breaches

You've read about hacker Kevin Mitnick stealing the numbers of 20,000 credit cards from Netcom. Fortunately, he was arrested before he did anything with them. Have you heard about Ivy James Lay? He makes Mitnick look like chump change.

In September 1994, the U.S. Secret Service busted Mr. Lay for stealing the numbers of *50,000* credit cards from MCI Communications Corp. and selling the numbers to black market dealers, generating $50 million in bogus charges. How did he do it? Lay was an MCI employee, that's how. He programmed one of MCI's PCs to capture credit card numbers from MCI customers.

 By far the greatest number of computer security incidents are inside jobs caused by employees. This holds true for Internet security violations as well as for non-Internet situations. Many incidents causing data loss are accidental. They can be prevented with more thorough training and better procedures. Deliberately caused computer security violations are harder to prevent, because they can happen for many reasons. Perpetrators can be managers as well as staff.

Some employees violate computer security because they are angry. These violations can be creative and are often difficult to catch. In Chicago, an unhappy *Encyclopedia Britannica* editor took revenge on the book's computer files. He put Mohammed's biography in place of Jesus. Then he wrote unflattering biographies of *Britannica* managers and placed them in the book as regular entries.

Some employees aren't angry. They're just plain sloppy. When I was with Computer Literacy Bookshops, we received a demo disk from a software distribution company. When a manager tried out the software, she got a big surprise. The outside of disk had an elaborately printed label with instructions, but the software inside was no demo. Instead she found a support technician's resume and files of bestiality and homosexual sex material downloaded from the Internet. It looked like the support technician who made the disk had copied his personal directory instead of the demo directory—a careless mistake that reflected poorly on the software distribution company.

Some employees expect to make extra money. I assume that was the motivation of Randall Schwartz, a systems administrator for Intel. Mr. Schwartz used a "Routine Security Check" to introduce a sniffer program to collect Intel passwords. He collected 48 passwords, was caught, and was found guilty of altering computer systems and attempted theft. Insiders commit most funds-transfer frauds, usually working with someone on the outside. Watch carefully over any information that could be leaked for profit, such as customer records or merger and acquisition files, whether computers storing that information are linked to your intranet or not.

Obviously, we can learn a lesson from these examples. Your business is much more vulnerable to computer abuse from employees than from outside invaders. Employees have more opportunities. They know the juiciest targets. They can damage your company in creative ways. And just as the Internet empowers employees to be more productive, it also helps errant employees do worse damage in more ways.

So how do you prevent computer security abuses—especially Internet abuses—by employees? You extend the same guidelines you use for noncomputer security. First of all, limit the information employees can reach to what they need to do their jobs. A manufacturing draftsman doesn't need access to your accounting files. An accounts payable clerk doesn't need your customer list. You would naturally restrict these employees from having complete access to all information from all departments.

When putting limits on the kinds of information employees can reach on the Internet, you have two ways to restrict access. You can limit the types of Internet services a person can reach, and you can limit the sources of data that flow into your company. Internet services are the easier to restrict of these two categories. Perhaps everyone in your company doesn't need Internet access. Those who do may only need email access. You don't have to give FTP, newsgroup, Gopher, Telnet, and World Wide Web tools to all your people. Many companies, for instance, bar access to all newsgroups whose names start with **alt.**. This may be overkill. The **alt.** newsgroups include many valuable business resources, especially for software and hardware technical support. But prohibiting all newsgroups whose names start with **alt.sex.** would probably not harm your business. Blocking **alt.sex.** groups might have prevented that support technician from filling the software demo disk with his private files.

Besides newsgroups, you may want to filter out sites for games, gambling, and other recreational activities. These may be Web pages or FTP sites. You can add their Internet addresses to your router or firewall so it blocks incoming and outgoing traffic to and from those addresses. (On the other hand, if your company hasn't deleted *Solitaire, Hearts,* and *Minesweeper* from Windows 95, why bother?)

A more sophisticated solution is provided by a Windows and Unix software program called Net Access Manager from Sequel Technologies (**www. sequeltech.com**). Managers use it to block employees from reaching forbidden Internet and intranet destinations, and can read reports of every Net destination and file that workers access. Managers can restrict Web, FTP, newsgroup, Telnet, and email use, plus online services such as CompuServe. You can set restrictions for a department overall or differently for each employee within a department. You can change access according to time of day. For instance, employees could use only email during business hours but have unlimited Net access after hours. Prices for Net Access Manager start at $1,000 for a version that handles up to five workers.

To keep your employees away from timewasters such as erotica, games, and online soap operas, the best motivation may be old-fashioned embarrassment. Chances are people won't grab photos from **alt.feelthy.peectures** while other employees look over their shoulders. But at an isolated computer in a private office, your workers have less fear of being caught with their pants down, so to speak. This is another argument in favor of making the Internet available only on a few strategically located communal desks. The higher visibility of a communal computer discourages non-business Internet projects. Expect some personal use of the Internet. That's reasonable, and nothing to make a fuss over. But the possibility of discovery certainly can eliminate the temptation for extreme abuse of Internet privileges.

Another watchful eye on employees should be maintained by your security administrator. Your company may not have a person with that exact job title, but someone needs to audit the log reports created by Internet activity. If that person notices a sudden burst of email and file transfers to one of your competitors, take action. But if no one reviews your reports, you'll miss the most important indicator you have of sudden unexplained activities on the part of one of your employees.

Workers on the Internet have the ability to embarrass your entire company in front of an audience of millions. Be extra careful whom you assign to handle Internet duties.

The cavalry to the rescue

Intranets and the Internet move your business from centralized security to decentralized. This increases your risks. Decentralized security costs more to administer and makes coverage uneven.

To point out security gaps and to find solutions, businesses that can afford the costs hire companies that specialize in security auditing. These specialists can be helpful because they are experts in this field and because they provide another set of eyes to "proofread" your security setup. Some corporations want the reassurance of having their security approved by a disinterested third party.

Costs range from $1,200 to $3,000 per day. IBM, Digital, and AT&T all provide security auditing services for networks. In addition, you can turn to specialist companies like Technologic, Inc. (**www.tlogic.com**), Internet Security Corp. (**www.security.com**), or the National Computer Security Association (**www.ncsa.com**), which provides a service called IS/Recon.

Password protection

The main reason any computer system is broken into—whether on the Internet or off—is because somebody guessed its password. I hate to upset the delicate sensibilities of supermarket tabloid writers, but guessing passwords doesn't make you a mastermind. An eight-year-old child can do it. I'm not exaggerating. I know of one case in which an advertising agency's customer billing database was scrambled by an unknown culprit one night. It turned to be the cleaning woman's eight-year-old daughter. She guessed a password from a Post-It note. You can have a hard time getting employees to treat their passwords seriously. On the Internet, the usual cause of guessing a password is negligence.

The number-one reason hackers can break into computers via the Net is that the computer's owners never bother to change the standard, vendor-supplied passwords that come with software. Software vendors provide a temporary password or two to use during setup, like TEMP, ADMIN, or SETUP. The idea is that you install the software and then replace their passwords with your own. That's the idea, anyhow. Believe it or not, *thousands* of sites never remove the vendor's passwords! Hackers have lists of them. If your system administrators haven't removed them, you might as well give your Internet site a drive-through window.

The number-two way for hackers to penetrate a site is by trying obvious, easily guessed passwords. The first thing a hacker will try is GUEST. Other popular guesses are ROOT, GUARD, ADMIN, ADM, SYSADM, SYSOP, VISITOR, and the ever-popular PASSWORD. Attackers try these guesses because they often work. Next they'll try site-specific guesses: company name, manager names, email addresses, and birthdates.

You want to prevent your people from using such easily guessed passwords. Make sure your Internet users know how to pick safe passwords. Any computer security book can give you guidelines. Here are the basics:

- Short passwords are easy to crack. A password of less than six characters is virtually useless. Eight or more characters is safer.

- Don't use any word from a dictionary. Hackers use dictionary software to crack them.

- Mix numbers with letters.

- Include at least one capital letter and one lowercase letter.

- Make sure your password is not a word or abbreviation associated with you or your company.

- Change your password at least every two months. Every month is safer. One-time passwords are safest.

To enforce selection of safe passwords, your security administrator can get free software that checks proposed passwords and won't let your people use any that are easy to guess. More important is education for all your Internet-using employees on choosing hard-to-guess passwords and keeping them secure.

Part of security is disabling passwords when an employee leaves. At many companies, an employee's password is disabled the instant he or she gives notice or, when an employee is fired, while the manager gives them the news. Check that the employee has only one password. This caused a problem for the Wollongong Group, whose former employee Ming Jyh Hsieh was arrested three months after being fired. She shared a password with five other employees. It wasn't changed when she left, so she dialed in and used it. She was caught in the act of stealing software from the company.

This brings up another important issue about passwords. You should change them often. This is called *password aging*. It prevents incidents like the one the Wollongong Group experienced and limits damage when an attacker or an unauthorized employee captures your passwords. You can have employees choose a new password every 60 days, or even better, every 30 days. This can be done on a volunteer basis, but is more effective if you use software that forces workers to change their passwords when the time limit expires.

The safest passwords are those that change every time you log on. These are called *one-time passwords*, and you have a couple of different ways to implement them. S/Key, software that generates one-time passwords, is highly rated by experts in Net security and encryption. S-Key is relatively easy to install and use. Mac, Unix, and Windows versions are available at **www.bellcore.com/ SECURITY/skey.html**.

Security Dynamics (**www.securid.com**) sells inexpensive SecurID cards ($50 and up) that time-synchronize with its ACE/Server security software ($2,000). The SecurID cards have 6-digit numbers that light up and change every 60 seconds. To log on, you whip out your card and type in the number plus your password. The server software matches your incoming number with its own number, which also changes every 60 seconds. These cards are easy to use.

To keep your passwords from being stolen, don't store your main password file on a vulnerable Internet-accessible computer. Bad Guys use several different Internet tools to steal passwords. FTP, Telnet, and Finger are the worst offenders, but UUCP and other software has also been used. The book *Firewalls and Internet Security* goes into these problems in detail.

Be careful about recording attempted logins. When people accidentally type their passwords on the wrong line—which happens often—it will show passwords. If a hacker grabs your log report file, you are wide open.

Watch out for bogus messages from a system administrator or supposed Internet authority (even your access provider) asking you to set up a guest account or change anything about your password file. If you get a message that sounds even remotely suspicious, get a phone number and call the person back. Make sure that the phone number is that company's normal number.

And remember that people don't need to access your computer or your network to steal your passwords. Passwords have also been stolen from backup tapes and disks.

Encryption

To prevent your information from being read by prying eyes, or even worse, from being altered when it shouldn't be, businesses on the Internet use *encryption*.

In transit on the Net or stored on your computer, encryption transforms your data into an unreadable mass of letters and numbers. This seeming gibberish is easily translated back into readable form, but only by the person (or software program) with the specific software *key* to decrypt that particular chunk of information.

Why encryption?

Since the Internet is a distributed network—that is, open to the public—your messages are exposed while in transit. You can use encryption so that no one except your intended recipient can open your message.

Another threat comes from trespassers into your system. With encryption, you can scramble sensitive files like your password file to make them harder for invaders to use. Encryption is the most practical and safest way to protect your secret information.

Of course, you should not relax just because you have a good encryption program. Your encrypted program is only as safe as your keys. Even when an attacker doesn't have your encryption keys, there are sometimes ways to bust down your encrypted walls. The point to keep in mind is that encryption provides a very high level of security, but don't let that security blind you to possible sneak attacks.

Companies use encryption to secure everything from credit card numbers to legal documents. Encryption lets companies use the Internet as an alternative to a private leased-line network. The Internet alternative, Virtual Private Data Networks (VPDNs), offers security across the shared public networks of the Internet.

Encryption also can be used to create *digital signatures*. You can use your digital signature to authenticate messages when you post them to newsgroups. Digital signatures support *nonrepudiation*, a legal term meaning that the sender of a message with a digital signature cannot later deny having created the message and repudiate any terms or agreements contained in the message.

Another use of encryption is to create *digital certificates*. A digital certificate is like a digital ID card. It proves that you are who you claim to be, and contains the digital signature of a trusted third party to back up your claim. Digital certificates and digital signatures play an important part in secure credit card transactions on the Net. Most digital certificates used in Internet credit card transactions come from a company called Verisign (**www.verisign.com**). A merchant requesting a Verisign certificate must prove its identity and pay $300. The process takes about two weeks.

Note that encryption is not legal in all countries. Encryption is illegal in France unless you give the government a copy of your key and get a written government permit. Other countries forbid encryption, period. The borderless Internet has already spread encryption worldwide, so these government bans are pointless. But if you want to base a bank or a merchant operation outside the U.S., you should check first to see if the country regulates encryption.

A field guide to encryption species and their habitats

Encryption is built into Web browsers and many email systems and some operating systems. Here's an explanation of the different types of encryption systems to help you understand how the technology affects business tasks.

Secret key. In a secret-key system, the same key that encrypts a message is also used to decrypt it. The keys must be exchanged in secrecy, because anyone with the key can read the messages. Some companies use public-key software like PGP to encrypt a secret key before sending it, and then use the secret key for subsequent messages, since secret-key encryption is faster than public-key encryption.

Public key. Several different kinds of encryption are called "public-key systems." This type of system solves the problem of securely distributing decryption keys. A good example is the PGP (Pretty Good Privacy) encryption system. With PGP, it takes about five minutes to first create your two keys (one public key and one secret, private key). Each of your two keys can read a message encrypted by the other key. You will have one public "key ring" to store all your correspondents' public keys, and you will store your own secret key. Next you send your public key to everyone you correspond with. They add your public key to their key rings. When someone wants to send a message to you, he or she encrypts it with your public key. Only your secret key can unlock it. When you send a message, you use your addressee's public key to encrypt your entire message, or your own secret key to sign it with a digital signature. Then your addressee can use your public key to make sure that the message is really from you.

To spread your public key around, you can post it on a Web page. There are also PGP public-key repositories, which hold thousands of public keys so other people can reach them. Once you add a person's public key to your key ring, you can send that person encrypted messages as well as decrypt messages from that person and verify that his or her digital signature really did come from that person. Lotus, Apple, Microsoft, and other companies have settled on public key encryption as a standard solution.

Key escrow. This is not an encryption species, but a habitat where encryption keys live. Trusted Information Systems (TIS, **www.tis.com**), a highly rated provider of firewall and security software, has a key-escrow system that lets businesses store keys in escrow. In this way law enforcement can access keys with a search warrant. The government doesn't escrow keys (preventing governmental abuses) and there are no databases of escrowed keys. The TIS key-escrow system provides a kind of insurance, so if you lose the key to an encrypted file, you can get it back. With key escrow, if an employee forgets a key, or has an accident, your company can still go to a bonded data recovery center and recover its encrypted data.

DES (Data Encryption Standard). DES was invented by IBM in the 1970s and adopted as a U.S. government standard. Any change to a message encrypted with DES turns the message into a mess of random characters. DES is a secret-key system. Although generally secure, DES messages can be decrypted by a huge computer system or thousands of small ones working together. This makes some businesses nervous. Only a large corporation or a national government would have the resources to decrypt a DES encrypted message, but still, if you are competing with a large American, Japanese, or French corporation, you might want to take another approach. Those countries' government espionage departments have "helped" local businesses compete to win international contracts.

Triple DES. This is a heavier-duty, tougher-to-crack version of DES that uses a key three times as long as DES. This secret-key technology can secure your most valuable data, even from a large government.

IDEA (International Data Encryption Algorithm). Invented in Switzerland in the 1980s, IDEA uses a longer key, making it resistant to brute force attacks, and a unique algorithm patented in many countries. For business uses, you must license IDEA from ASCOM Tech AG. Pretty Good Privacy uses IDEA.

RSA (Rivest, Shamir, Adleman). RSA Data Security, Inc.'s namesake technique lets you choose the size of your public key. With a 512-bit key, your messages are secure from all but large corporations or national governments. The 768-bit keys are probably secure from everything but the NSA, and maybe even from them. With a 1,023-bit key, your data is safe from pretty much everyone. It is embedded in Windows, Netscape Navigator, Intuit's Quicken, Lotus Notes, Apple software, and hundreds of other products.

PGP (Pretty Good Privacy). PGP is secure public-key software that is becoming widely used in the United States and Canada and, even though it is theoretically illegal to export, in other countries as well. Governments do not like PGP. It is too hard to crack, which is precisely why businesses want it. It is also easy to use. **www.pgp.com**

Secure Sockets Layer (SSL). This is currently the most widely used method of handling credit card purchases, because Netscape Navigator and Internet Explorer use it. It employs the RSA algorithm to encrypt data. It is approved for export by the U.S. government. There is a U.S.-only version and an exportable version. For credit card sales, expect SSL to be replaced by SET.

HTTPS. A security protocol used by SSL. URLs that use it start with **https://**.

Secure HTTP (SHTTP). SHTTP secures only Web transactions and nothing else. From merchant and customer standpoints, it operates the same as SSL, but is not as widely used. You can use SHTTP with SSL for increased protection. After you receive an encrypted SHTTP transaction, you decrypt it on another computer, separated from your Web server by a firewall.

Secure Electronic Transactions (SET). Developed by Visa and MasterCard, SET is backed by American Express, Microsoft, IBM, Netscape, and other major players. With such strong backing, it will certainly become the major way credit cards are handled on the Internet. SET will be in widespread use this year. Because you are likely to use SET, I describe it in detail in the chapter "Credit Cards and Digital Cash."

Proprietary encryption schemes. Some software applications like Lotus 1-2-3, Microsoft Excel, Microsoft Word, and PKZip come with built-in encryption. These offer only a low level of protection. Hackers consider them encryption for babies. You can even buy (or download from the Net) software tools that decrypt them. They are better than nothing at all, but should not be used for sending valuable data across the Internet.

DSS (Digital Signature Standard). DSS is an encryption scheme invented by the U.S. National Security Agency (NSA) for creating digital signatures to prove that an Internet message was not altered and was sent by the person who claimed to have sent it. DSS won't protect your privacy by encrypting your message. You use DSS only to verify your message by including your DSS signature with it. RSA's encryption technique is more efficient, but recent improvements to DSS took care of many of the objections to DSS from the security community when the NSA first released it.

Audit trails

Even when you protect your computers with firewalls, encryption, and a bullet-proof password system, someone somehow may still break in. Angry employees with passwords may try sabotage, or intruders may fast talk their way in. That's why you need *audit trails*.

Every accountant is familiar with audit reports—or should be. In accounting systems, audit trails let auditors trace the flow of cash through your company and reconstruct the who, what, where, when, and how much of financial transactions. A computerized accounting system audit report is what launched Cliff Stoll on his Internet hunt for a KGB-funded spy ring, as he told in his book, *The Cuckoo's Egg*.

You might not be attacked by international spies, but a competitor or hacker can do just as much damage. That's why any computer you link to the Internet needs to generate its own audit logs. Even the most secure system should record what traffic passes through it and the sources of that traffic. Your audit reports may also be your basis for defense in a lawsuit, or be helpful if your company undergoes an EDI (electronic data interchange) audit or a data processing audit.

Some Internet server software automatically creates activity logs. With most computers, you will need to add software to capture and record Internet transaction information. In an ideal world, your computer's operating system would handle this for you. That is the most reliable way, and the least work to set up. In current computers, this is rare but worth looking for. For instance, Tandem NonStop Computers has a built-in audit function. For any file you choose, the Tandem system can post every completed transaction to an audit file. I wish every system made it that easy.

What will your system need to record? Enough information to let your system administrator reconstruct the who, what, where, and when of Internet trans-actions. Your system needs to record not just unauthorized access attempts, but every login and logout. (A seemingly authorized but forged transaction is what sent Cliff Stoll on his chase.) You'll want the "from" address for each incoming transaction, even though "from" addresses can be forged. And, you'll want to know which files or databases were accessed and especially if they were altered.

Get the date *and* time of each transaction. Timestamps are crucial in reconstructing crimes and catching culprits. Get timestamps for both incoming and outgoing Net traffic. I know of two cases in which businesses used timestamps to nab errant employees. In both cases, data processing managers were able to compare timestamps with payroll timecards to pinpoint the delinquent staffers.

You'll need more detailed audit records if you do sales on the Net or if you make electronic payments. These kinds of transactions affect your cash flow, so you'll need to record transaction amounts, and if you make international sales, currency types. Your accounting department will want specific information to meet your financial software's audit needs. Sales transactions may also need to generate information for inventory audit reports.

Whatever types of audit logs your system creates, look for the ability to pull reports *on demand*. Some systems generate logs only once a month, weekly, or at night after your system has been shut down. Emergencies are not this polite, and audit reports are like hospital emergency rooms. You don't know *when* you'll need them, but when you do, you'll need them *now*. You can't tell when a hacker will hit, or when a virus will take over your disk drive, or when a screaming customer will call you. Chances are bad things will happen when your system is at peak load and the Net is at its busiest.

Just as you can't predict when you'll need audit logs, you can't predict for what time period you'll need them. Perhaps you'll discover a Trojan horse software program in your computer, quietly collecting all your passwords. Its creation date may say it sat there undiscovered for two months. Who put it there? If you save log records for only two weeks, you can't find out. Keep your audit logs for at least three months. Or better yet, for six. In addition, your system administrator can analyze them to spot patterns and trends.

 Beware of systems that won't give you audit reports that are *up to the minute*. Some systems will only give you reports showing yesterday's activity, or worse, last week's. When a problem hits, you'll want to kill it while it's fresh. Yesterday's audit logs won't help you clear out a disaster that erupted in the last 15 minutes. Make sure you can run up-to-the-minute audit reports at any time you want, and without shutting your system down.

Audit logs will help you catch attackers, but even the best logs won't keep Bad Guys out. For that, you need to build a wall. A firewall. I'll explain how to do it in the next chapter.

What to do when trouble strikes

Most computer break-ins are spotted by network administrators and not by business users. Network administrators might see suspicious log reports showing attempts to grab your password files or to log on with top-level security. Or they may see repeated accesses of Finger or many failed attempts to run certain programs. When businesspeople find an intrusion, the symptoms are usually missing or unusable files, or odd error messages. It is rare for a nontechnical person to link these clues to an intrusion without technical help.

Your company should have a short prepared guide outlining how to respond to any suspected computer attack. All employees with Internet access should have a *printed* copy at their desks. (An online version does no good when a virus freezes your computer.) Your attack response guide should have 24-hour phone contact information for all people who need to be notified and quick descriptions of what to do. In general, you should follow these steps:

1. Contact your in-house network administrator. The administrator on duty needs to decide if a break-in has happened, or if your symptom actually is caused by another sort of problem. If you are under attack, the administrator needs to move as fast as possible to prevent damage from spreading and to catch the culprit, in that order of priority. If your company's computers are on the Net 24 hours a day, someone needs to be available 24 hours a day to handle this. Have at least *two* backup people available in case the designated contact is unreachable. An hour's delay can be fatal.

2. If your network administrator thinks that there is even a small chance that an intruder has hit, call technical support at your Internet access provider. Your administrators (including your backup people) should have 24-hour phone numbers for your access provider. Your provider can help with damage control and can also check to make sure that other sites it hosts aren't under attack.

3. As a counterpoint to this, your Internet access provider also needs 24-hour phone numbers for your network administrators. If another business alerts your provider to an attacker in your site, wouldn't you like to know? If your company's Net site only operates during office hours, you might think that your regular phone number will suffice, but that may not be enough. Perhaps your computer is only linked during the daytime, but do you have a home page on your provider's computer? It will run 24 hours a day and will be vulnerable to attack 24 hours a day. Will you use mailing

lists? Lists usually run at night for faster processing. (And, in my experience, only break down in the wee hours. Sigh.) Even when you have only limited Internet access, play it safe by giving your provider 24-hour contact information.

4. If your security has been breached, *immediately call the Computer Emergency Response Team (CERT) at its **24-hour hotline: 412-268-7090**.* CERT staffers can tell you if other sites anywhere in the world have suffered the same problem and are a solid source of advice on how to proceed.

   Your administrator should have this information ready before calling CERT:

   - Internet addresses of your computer or computers compromised

   - Brand name and model of the computer, its operating system, and communications software

   - What security hardware and software you use

   - Any log reports showing evidence of the attack, including timestamps

   - Other computers or sites that may be implicated in the break-in

   - Whether you contacted the other sites, and the contact information if you did

   - Whether you have contacted law enforcement agencies

   - What specific help you would like from CERT

5. If your system administrator decides that a break-in has happened and serious damage has occurred, he or she should contact appropriate non-technical managers to let them know about the situation.

6. If proprietary information has been stolen or damaged, a nontechnical manager should contact your local law enforcement agencies. Don't exaggerate the damage. You will need to describe what has been stolen or damaged in detail. If at all possible, attach a monetary value to your loss, and realistically estimate how much it will cost your business to recover from the attack. Your network administrator should take part in this discussion to address technical issues.

7. Managers need to decide what, if anything, to tell employees about the attack. If employees are suspected, you will want to withhold information until the situation is resolved. Finger-pointing will do no good after an attack, but instructions on how to prevent further break-ins may help you in the future.

8. If you suffered a loss covered by insurance, someone will need to contact your insurance company. Paperwork from the law enforcement agency may be helpful or even required.

Two final tips

Two final tips: Before trouble strikes—ideally, before you even set up your intranet and Internet computers—your security administrator should review the CERT security checklist and security FAQ at **www.cert.org**. While there, he or she can also review past CERT advisories, which describe security holes in popular software and tell how to plug them.

Tip number two is to visit the National Computer Security Association at **www.ncsa.com**. This site will reward both nontechnical people and technoids like your security administrator. You'll find very good tips on security from a business manager's point of view, and clear, non-techie explanations and definitions of high-tech terms. Be sure to visit this Web site if you think you might need a firewall.

CHAPTER 8

How Firewalls Block the Bad Guys

"Information security leaks are like being in a drafty house. If you're sitting in your living room and you suddenly feel cold, it's important to plug the most obvious holes first."

—Dr. Peter Tippett, President, National Computer Security Association

Less than 30 minutes after CheckPoint Software first connected to the Internet, the company's firewall reported an attacker trying to break into CheckPoint's computers. The company's system administrator assumed the firewall had a software bug. How could an attacker find out about CheckPoint's Net connection so quickly?

Then he inspected the log reports. The reports said the attacker was from a university campus. Armed with the logs as evidence, CheckPoint went to the police, who made arrests. The attackers were students who had created a software program that automatically probed all newly connected companies. Police found about 100 megabytes of information the students had stolen from unsuspecting firms.

The firewall in this case did everything a firewall is supposed to do.

- It detected intruders.

- It blocked them from entry.

- It recorded what they did and where they were from.

- It notified the system administrator.

- It produced reports as evidence.

It's easy for you to protect your information from the Internet if your business has just one computer. With more computers, configuring and maintaining security one computer at a time quickly grows impossible. Not only must you patrol all your incoming Internet connections, you must also secure outbound connections. Communications *between* your computers must also be monitored so an intruder can't find a hole in one computer and attack others—and much more importantly, so an employee can only damage (accidentally or on purpose) as few computers as possible. That is where firewalls come in.

What is a firewall?

Simply put, a firewall gives you a single chokepoint through which all incoming and outgoing Internet traffic must pass, allowing you to control traffic. A good firewall prevents Bad Guys from breaking *in* and helps keep confidential data from being sent *out*. (For example, when your employees leave your network to browse the Web, their requests for Web pages can give outsiders IP addresses that can be leveraged to break into your network.) Firewalls also prevent your employees from reaching Net sites you don't want them to see.

You can configure your firewall to allow only email to pass in and out, protecting your internal network against any non-email attacks. Or you can allow other kinds of Internet services under approved conditions. You can use a firewall's audit tools as a wiretap to trace hacker attacks. You can even set a firewall to bar all incoming traffic from the Internet, while still allowing your employees to access the Net without restraint.

In the ideal situation, the Internet and the Bad Guys live outside the firewall. Also outside, on a dedicated sacrificial computer, are the "dirty" network services (hackable and publicly reachable services such as Web and FTP servers) offered by your company. Only authorized users and approved Internet services pass through the firewall, and they are closely and automatically monitored. Your company's computers are inside the barricade, protected.

Although firewalls defend your business, you pay the price of limiting access to some Internet services, or making the Internet less convenient for your workers to use. Other costs include your firewall's purchase price (though you can get some software-only firewalls for free) and its maintenance costs. In addition to dollars, firewalls take time and technical expertise to set up and maintain.

If your company uses a router, you can program it to use *filter* software. Filters spot and discard some types of incoming traffic that you regard as a potential security threat. A really good router will let you filter *outgoing* traffic as well as incoming. You can also use router filters to divide your intranet into subnets and restrict what type of traffic flows between subnets, thus maintaining internal security between company divisions.

A router with filters costs less than a more elaborate firewall and takes less work to maintain, but a router by itself is much easier for Evildoers to penetrate and control.

Who needs a firewall and who doesn't?

Not every Internet site needs a firewall. If your business has only dial-up Internet access via modem, a firewall is probably overkill. You also can get by without a firewall if your Internet activities meet all of the following guidelines:

- If you run any servers that outsiders can reach (such as Web, Gopher, FTP, Telnet, Finger, or email list servers) only: 1) on an outside Web host's computer not on your own premises; or, 2) on your own premises, on a separate standalone computer not connected to any of your other systems.

- If people inside your company can reach the Internet only on standalone computers used for no other purpose, or only using dial-up SLIP, PPP, and ISDN connections that close as soon as an employee exits the Net. A possible exception may be to let only email move between the Internet and your computers, while all other Internet services are blocked.

- If no customer information (especially credit card numbers) or any other confidential data is stored on any of the computers you connect to the Internet.

- If all your employees retrieve email by individually contacting your Internet access provider via dial-up SLIP, PPP, or ISDN, or if you use a UUCP mail server for email and not an SMTP mail server. A UUCP mail server dials up your access provider, exchanges messages, and then hangs up. It leaves no continuous connection between your computers and the Internet. Some Net security experts might disallow this last guideline, because hackers have broken into sites using UUCP. But in general, I find dial-up UUCP safer than its alternative, an SMTP email server open 24 hours.

Life without firewalls

Your firewall-less company can be relatively safe if it meets all four of the conditions. Even so, if you do business on the Internet without a firewall, you'll need to be extra security-conscious. Just because you are firewall-less, don't act clueless. In addition to taking normal precautions to keep your computers and information secure, here are four actions that are especially important if your business has no firewall but is connected to the Internet or to an intranet:

- Watch your passwords. If you can, use a software program like S/Key (described in the previous chapter) to create one-time passwords.

- Always use the latest release of your networking software, because it will have bug fixes of known security holes.

- Turn off and restrict as many Net services as you can.

- Get the list of *dangerous computer ports* from the Computer Emergency Response Team (**www.cert.org**) and block all the "sneak attack" ports that CERT points out.

Pieces of the security puzzle

Which firewall approach is best? You can answer that question several ways. This is not a "one size fits all" situation. Different solutions are appropriate for different businesses. Before you assemble your own security solution, you need to know what pieces will be part of your puzzle:

Filters and routers

Filters are also called *packet filters*. They look at each piece of Internet traffic and check its port number, the service (Telnet, Web, FTP, etc.) it requests, the protocol (TCP, etc.) it wants to use, the sending source, and the destination. After checking this data against rules you have programmed into it, the filter either stops the piece of traffic or lets it pass.

You can set a filter to block all traffic coming *from* a particular destination, all traffic headed *for* a particular destination, or you can choose other parameters.

Filters used by themselves are not a firewall, the same way that Lotus 1-2-3 can't be used to make a spreadsheet if you have only software disks and no computer. You have to run the filter software on a box, either a computer or a router.

A *router* is a piece of hardware that takes incoming data traffic from several places and sends it to other places. For example, a router can take messages coming from all the computers on your LAN and send them out to your Internet access provider, and vice versa. Bay Networks includes CheckPoint firewall software on all its routers, and Cisco and 3Com also include firewall software on their routers. (However, a router used only as a firewall is more secure than adding filters to the same router you use to manage your traffic flow.)

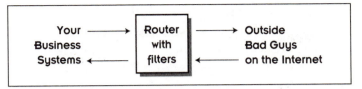

Figure 8.1   Good routers can be set to filter and block unwanted traffic going in two directions, both in and out. The simplest level of protection, this is also the least secure.

You can also run filtering software on a computer instead of a router. Running filter programs on a computer is relatively inexpensive and easy, but newer low-cost routers are just as easy and cost even less. Figure 8.1 illustrates how a router works as a firewall.

What's good about filters is that they are cheap, fast, kind of easy to set up, and are invisible to your employees. What's bad about them is that they don't make traffic easier to monitor, and, since they provide a hard-wired path into and out of your network, they leave your network easy to break into.

Proxy servers

(Proxy servers are also called application gateways, application-level gateways, and gateway proxies.) Proxies are more secure than routers. They isolate your network from the world outside. You can log and control all incoming and outgoing traffic. You can control traffic down to the level of, for instance, restricting outbound World Wide Web access to authorized individuals.

A router by itself still passes traffic directly between your network and the netherworld. A proxy server, on the other hand, actually *stops* all traffic and examines it before forwarding. Here's how proxy servers work:

1. Instead of an employee talking directly to the outside world, his or her Web browser talks to your proxy server.

2. Your proxy server then strips identifying information from your employee's request and forwards it to the remote site.

3. When the remote site responds, the proxy server launders the response and sends it bmack to the original Web browser.

This way, your proxy server is the only user that remote sites see for your network. Since proxies inspect all your incoming and outbound traffic, they create useful log reports of what they see. Another advantage of proxy servers is that they can forward SMTP email, eliminating the need for a separate computer to run email. Proxies also cache the most popular Web sites your employees visit, retrieving them from the internal cache instead of going out to the Web to fetch them. This speeds up Web access for your employees.

Proxies have disadvantages. They are difficult to install, can slow down your incoming and outbound traffic, and they can make Internet use less convenient for your employees by requiring employees to take extra steps to reach the Net.

Type enforcement

Routers and proxy servers filter data based on information in the *header* of the message. This is a major weakness. Even newbie hackers learn to alter a message's header information to give whatever source address the hacker chooses. This is called *identity spoofing*. A hacker can create a fake source, bogus routing information, and a phony ID. Other safeguards provided by firewalls offset this vulnerability to some extent, but firewalls still have no idea what's *inside* an Internet message.

Type enforcement inspects the *content* of messages in addition to the headers. It looks at what is actually inside a message, whether the message is text (such as email) or binary files (such as graphics or a software program).

This approach to content inspection means that customer files and product development files can be restricted from going out on the Net. Viruses are also easier to block with type enforcement. You can use type enforcement to forbid selected activities, no matter what destination was originally on a piece of Net traffic, thus disarming attacks by identity spoofing.

Secure Computing Corp. (**www.sctc.com**) was first (I believe) in this market with its product, Sidewinder. Priced at $7,000 and up, Sidewinder is really a proxy server with type enforcement and extra features to automate intruder detection. It inspects both inbound and outbound traffic, and scans the contents of email, text files (including Web pages), and binary files. Note that Sidewinder cannot scan *encrypted* traffic.

Stateful inspection devices

A stateful inspection firewall not only inspects all traffic headers (and sometimes message contents), but also verifies the applications, users, and transportation methods. Then the firewall builds temporary records of each transmission. It inspects all future transmissions and compares them with records of past transmissions. When the "state" of a transmission and its "context" don't match what's normal, the connection is refused.

Stateful inspection firewalls require significant technical ability to configure and run correctly, but they are quite effective and have earned high marks from security experts.

Sacrificial computers

This lamb sits exposed outside your firewall and runs all services accessible by outside people.

Combination defenses

As a step up from single-router protection, companies use every imaginable combination of routers, proxy servers, and computers. The book *Firewalls and Internet Security* by Cheswick and Bellovin is a good guide to most of these alternatives. It's a technical book. If you'd prefer one that's less technical (and still good), try *Intranet and Internet Firewall Strategies* by Edward Amoroso and Ronald Sharp.

Assembling the pieces

By themselves, filters are comparatively inexpensive. Filter software is included with most router hardware at no extra charge. Filters can be a usable solution, depending on what they are designed to protect. One danger is that when a power failure or other incident shuts down most filters, your company is wide open. When most gateway proxies shut down, your company is still protected.

A twist on the router approach is a strict-but-secure two-router approach. This technique sets up *both* routers to allow outbound traffic only and block all inbound traffic. Your internal network talks only to the inside router, which talks only to the outside router, which talks only to one exposed sacrificial computer outside your network. Even if a trespasser were to take over your exposed computer and use it to breach your outside router, the interloper couldn't break through to your inside router. Your network would be safe.

Another two-router approach puts a gateway computer between two routers, as illustrated in Figure 8.2. Your exposed outside router talks only to a proxy server on the computer in the middle, which talks to both routers. This double defense is more costly to set up than a single router, but it gives you much greater control and more thorough security.

Something similar to this approach is used by Motorola, which has 90,000 employees who use the Internet. For security, it uses a double firewall to put two blocks between the Internet and Motorola's internal network. In addition, Motorola employees must use a special, restricted software application to connect, and they must be listed on an access control list.

One of the best protection tactics is to use an external sacrificial computer to handle mail, newsgroups, Web, Finger, and Gopher services. *Use the address of your sacrificial computer as the one you advertise for outside access.* Any address you advertise will be the one most often probed by attackers, so it makes sense to send them where they can do the least harm.

The vast majority of cases in which an attacker breaches a firewall occur due to one of two reasons. Either the attacker discovers a password, or a router or firewall was improperly set up when it was installed. Configuration errors are the most common problems with routers and firewalls. Some come with all

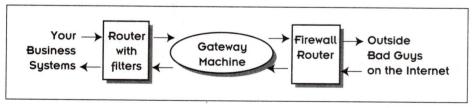

Figure 8.2 This more secure firewall employs two routers with a proxy server on a gateway machine in the middle. The inner router on the left protects your business in case an intruder breaks into your proxy server. The outer router on the right protects your proxy server from outside attack.

options open when you buy them, allowing all traffic in both directions. You must disable unwanted options one step at a time. This requires in-depth knowledge of network protocols and application software. You can also disable your competitors' domains, so they can't enter your site.

Note that you can ask your Internet access provider to install and run a firewall for you, especially if you run your servers on your access provider's computer. There is a charge for this, but it saves you the hassle of firewall maintenance.

Studies have shown that most data loss is caused by employee errors. You can place limits on the damage potential of employee errors by using firewalls or filters to segment your internal intranet into separate sections. Users from one section should not be allowed to enter another unless they have authorization. Usually, an internal barrier is set up to keep people from one department out of another department's files.

In spite of what firewall vendors tell you, firewalls *will* inconvenience your employees to some extent. How much so depends somewhat on which firewall product you buy and how you implement it. This can cause security problems, because if your firewall slows employees down too much or is tricky to use, your own staff will find ways around your firewall, inadvertently opening your gates to the barbarians.

How to buy a firewall

How do you buy a firewall? That reminds me of the old vaudeville joke, "How do porcupines make love?" The answer is the same: "Very carefully."

Watch out for companies that advertise routers with phrases such as "firewall-type features" or "firewall-like capabilities." Both these phrases wave red flags, because they really mean "This product is *not* a firewall." Words like those are used by advertisers with half a conscience who don't want to lie flat-out and maybe get sued. I know a waffle when I see one. Claims like those make me reach for butter and syrup.

The exaggerations in firewall ads would make a politician blush. Almost all firewalls claim to be the most complete, most secure, and highest-performance solution for all businesses. Apparently, God stuffed firewall manufacturers with so many virtues that there was no room left for modesty.

Advertisements for one product, Firewall-1, used to brag that it was completely effective and allowed no leaks, breaches, or compromises. No firewall would be that secure even if it were defended by Klingons. No invention can keep out *all* of the attackers *all* of the time. Be on your guard against such marketing fluff. Never believe a firewall vendor's system is as good as it claims unless you see *unbiased* proof.

One place to look for proof is **www.data.com/lab_tests/firewalls97.html**. You'll find a performance test of 20 leading firewalls, conducted by *Data Comm* magazine. The testers at *Data Comm* launched nearly 100 different attacks against each firewall and stress-tested them by hitting each one with traffic loads equal to hundreds or thousands of simultaneous users. They also checked to see how easy it was to run the darn things.

I don't have space here for reports on all 20 products (and if I did, you probably don't have time to read them), but here's a quick rundown on the top 5, plus a warning about 1 that flunked. (Remember that no matter how highly a test like this ranks a firewall, the product is *no good* for you unless it matches *your specific needs*.)

The top 5

- **Firewall-1** from CheckPoint Software (**www.checkpoint.com**) claims a 40 percent share of the firewall market. Firewall-1 applies stateful inspection and filters. It is not a proxy server, so it's fast, and it is relatively easy to set up. This is a well-planned product. Firewall-1 is available for Unix and Windows NT, and costs $10,000.

- **Cyberguard** uses filters, a proxy server, and "stateful rules" (similar to stateful inspection). Cyberguard costs $10,000 to $20,000. For more information, go to Cyberguard Corp. at **www.cyberguardcorp.com**.

- **Watchguard Security Management System** from Seattle Software Laboratories (**www.sealabs.com**) costs $3,500 and runs under Windows NT or Linux.

- **Solstice EFS Sunscreen** from Sun Microsystems (**www.sun.com**) costs $4,000 and runs under Windows NT and Unix.

- **Alta Vista Firewall 97** from Alta Vista Internet Software (**http://altavista.digital.com/firewall/special/index.htm**) costs $4,000 to $15,000 and runs on Windows NT and Unix. It ranked very high in effectiveness, speed, and ease of use, but got only an honorable mention because it couldn't be configured in as many ways as other products. By the time you read this, Alta Vista may have changed that.

ONE THAT FLUNKED

- Gnat Box from Global Technology Associates flunked *Data Comm*'s tests.

To make sense of the distinctions between firewall products, you need someone who knows this stuff. Purchasing a firewall is a technical job for a technical person. Don't send your purchasing manager out with a shopping cart to buy a firewall unless your purchasing manager has a degree in computer science.

Do some homework before you shop. First you need to answer the question "What information are we protecting?" Figure out how bad it would hurt if that information were lost, copied, or vandalized. Use that as a basis to calculate how much money and time you want to spend on Internet protection. Remember that your upfront costs for firewall hardware and software will be followed by setup costs, training fees, and ongoing expenses for hardware maintenance, software updates, and staff time for somebody to keep the dingus up and running. Different firewall products require different amounts of staff time for upkeep—a potentially decisive cost factor.

Where to find info

With that background in hand, take a look at firewall information on the Net. First, check out the National Computer Security Association at **www.ncsa.com** for the excellent *NCSA Firewall Policy Guide* by Stephen Cobb. (To go directly to the guide, set your browser to **www.ncsa.com/fwpg_p1.html**.) The *Guide* gives you tips on how to buy your firewall, guidelines to create your company policy for Net security, and a good glossary of firewall terms. You can read this guide on the Web, download a Microsoft Word version that you can print at your office, or order a free printed copy. Multiple printed copies are available for $5 each.

He's making a list...

At NCSA's site, you will also find out about something more important: The NCSA certification program for firewalls. A firewall product that is "NCSA Certified" has been tested to protect against a standard range of attacks while still enabling business functions to continue. NCSA tests each certified product quarterly against new threats. If you want a shopping list of firewall manufacturers, NCSA also provides links to all members of the Firewall Product Developers' Consortium. Look for NCSA's list before you shop. In fact, I recommend printing NCSA's list and using it as your shopping list.

A FAQ and frank talk

You can read a good FAQ about firewalls at **www.v-one.com/pubs/fw-faq/faq.htm**.

To find out what users of firewalls say about their products, subscribe to the firewalls mailing list. Email to **majordomo@greatcircle.com** with the body of your email message containing the words **subscribe firewalls** and nothing else. You'll find an archive of past mailing list messages at **ftp://ftp.greatcircle.com/pub/firewalls/Welcome.html**.

What questions to ask

To give you an idea of cost, a basic router can cost $1,300 to $9,000 or more, filters included. Firewalls range in cost from $3,000 for low-volume products with few features to $100,000 for high-end firewalls that can protect 1,000 or more nodes and do everything but bake pizza. Expect to pay at least $3,000 to $10,000 for a serious firewall.

For any Internet security product on your consideration list, ask your potential supplier to describe, with technical detail, how it handles each of the 42 show-stopping bombs listed in *Firewalls and Internet Security*. Brochures for Sidewinder specifically discuss these points. Other vendors will provide the information if asked.

QUESTIONS ABOUT ALL FIREWALLS

Here are important questions to ask about all firewall products:

1. Will it connect to the hardware and software you have, and the Internet access provider you use? Some providers only work with certain firewalls.

2. Will it meet your security needs?

3. Does it have enough throughput so it won't slow down your Internet activities? Many firewall products bog down your Internet access by a considerable amount. (This is especially important when you want to secure your intranet, because your 10-megabit-per-second internal network is likely to be much faster than any access you have to the outside world. Intranets need faster firewalls.)

4. Can it block denial-of-service attacks? (If you'd like a definition of these, see the short section on them in the previous chapter.) Some firewalls can block them. Most can't.

5. Can it be set to block incoming ActiveX traffic? ActiveX has huge security holes, so many business sites do not allow it in inbound traffic. The best firewalls can be configured to block ActiveX.

6. Does it conform to OPSEC, the Open Platform for Secure Enterprise Connectivity? OPSEC is a new standard created by CheckPoint Software and supported by Microsoft, Netscape, Sun, HP, McAfee, Symantec, and more than 60 other vendors. OPSEC makes it easier and more secure for your network administrator to combine security products from different vendors.

QUESTIONS ABOUT FILTERS AND ROUTERS
(AND ONE CRUCIAL DISTINCTION)

When considering a router to use on a firewall to run filter software (or, for that matter, when considering running filter software on a computer), there is a subtle-sounding, but important distinction for your technical people to check. A router can apply filters to:

- *incoming* data when it comes *into* your router
- *incoming* data as it *exits* your router
- *outgoing* data when it comes *into* your router
- *outgoing* data as it *exits* your router

Not all routers can handle all four of these alternatives. Check yours.

Here are questions to ask when looking at filters:

1. Will it filter input, output, or both?
2. Can it inspect packets for source port, destination port, and protocol?
3. Does it let you control the order in which it applies filtering rules?
4. How easy is it to set up and change rules?
5. Does it log rejected packets? What kind of information does it give in log reports?
6. Will it filter established connections?
7. Can it reject source-routed packets?

QUESTIONS ABOUT PROXY SERVERS

If you decide to set up a proxy server, be aware that your proxy machine will need at least 16 megabytes of memory. More is better. For high-volume situations, plan on 128 megabytes of memory. A proxy server will also require lots of fast disk space, and "fast" is the key word here. Get the fastest you can find, because when you have a fast Net connection and plenty of memory, disk access will be the bottleneck that slows down your entire site.

Here are questions to ask potential proxy vendors:

1. Do you need special versions of your application software to work with the proxy server, or will it work with the vanilla versions? If you need special versions, how much work will it take to modify your applications to work with this gateway? (Don't take a vendor's word for this. Get on the firewalls mailing list and get real-life answers from the vendor's customers.)
2. Can you set it to allow only outbound FTP?
3. Ask to see documentation for access control, filtering, and logs. Is it complete and understandable?

4. How understandable is the operator interface? (Most are cryptic.)

5. What kinds of information do the logging reports provide?

6. Does it authenticate both incoming and outgoing traffic?

7. What kinds of traffic will it authenticate? Can you add your own custom authentications?

8. Will it handle your volume of traffic and your type of Internet connection? One size does not fit everyone. For instance, the Microsoft Proxy Server is small and simple, suitable to handle dial-up Internet connections for small companies without 24x7 Net access.

Seven offenders to keep outside your firewall

 You can dramatically decrease your chances of being eaten alive by attacking alligators if you keep certain Internet software programs on a dedicated, sacrificial machine outside your Internet gateway. If your company has no firewall, these processes are prime candidates to run on your Internet access provider's computer instead of your own.

Show this list to your network administrator. Potential offenders include:

1. The *sending* portion of your SMTP email software

2. Any World Wide Web server accessible by non-employees

3. Any FTP server accessible by non-employees

4. Any Gopher servers accessible by non-employees

5. Any mailing list server accessible by non-employees

6. All Finger servers

7. Especially all Telnet servers

Firewalls on the perimeter of your network won't police traffic on your intranet. Any internal-only Web server or other intranet server that contains sales data, customer information, R&D files, or merger and acquisition information should be shielded from unauthorized employee access. Protect sensitive information either by physically isolating the server from the rest of your internal network, or by separating it by an internal firewall.

A word of warning

Once you install a firewall, don't sit back and assume your site is hackerproof. Firewalls don't block viruses. They won't stop attacks in which a program is emailed or copied to a computer inside your firewall and then executed.

A trespasser may still sneak in, so don't rely only on your firewall. You still need to back it up with access log reports and alarms, and you still need to control which people and which programs have access to which files and which other programs.

Break into your own network

For a quick test of your system's security, see if a tiger team of your own technical staffers can break into your site.

You must have your system up and running and plugged into the Net. Ask your technical staffers to enter your system from off-site, perhaps from their homes.

On the day of your test, disable your testers' passwords and accounts so it won't be too easy. Otherwise, keep your network security exactly as it is in real life. Leave other passwords the same. Don't increase defenses just to stump invader wannabes. The whole point is to probe your normal protection.

You want to duplicate the network setting that any stranger would confront. This means that it's okay for your simulators to get help from other people and to use any software tools they can find—just as real hackers do. They can use a free program called Internet Security Scanner (ISS for short) to scan your entire domain or part of it and look for holes. Another free program, Crack, analyzes your encrypted password file to find passwords.

The one restriction to place on your staff before the test is that they refrain from doing anything illegal or anything that's hard to repair.

Your technical staffers may find this a rewarding test of their creative powers, and afterward, they should better understand how to protect your company's systems.

CHAPTER 9

Email:
Quickest Bang for
Your Buck

"You can take out every one of the three hundred to four hundred computer applications that we run our company on and we could continue—but if you took out our email system, Sun would grind to an immediate halt."

—Scott McNealy, Chief Executive Officer, Sun Microsystems Inc.

When you bring the Internet into your company for the first time, you'll want to start with the service offering the lowest risk, the highest visibility, and the quickest return on your investment. That service is email.

- Email is the cheapest way to tighten relations between your company and your customers.

- Email is the fastest way to improve communication among employees within your company.

- Email increases the level of technical support you receive from your computer and software vendors.

- Email makes it easier for your company to collaborate on projects with other companies.

Starting to get the picture?

If your company doesn't use email, you'll find that its money and time savings give you a strong starting point for cost-justifying Internet implementation. Color graphics on a Web page look prettier, but email is a workhorse that will deliver improvements across many areas of your company. Since its benefits are clear-cut and widespread, you should find support from a lot of people who want to get it up and running as soon as possible.

What email can do for you

Let's start with *saving money*. Since you pay a more-or-less flat rate for your Internet account, with email you don't pay extra for each message you send—unlike phone calls or postal letters. (If you're even *thinking* of paying per-message charges, you didn't read Chapters 3 and 4 closely.)

That holds true not just for outgoing messages, but incoming ones as well. Your customers save what they would spend on long-distance phone calls or postage. And you don't pay what you would for incoming calls on your 800 number.

With money saved from converting printed internal and outside newsletters to emailed versions, you can increase their frequency, which will make them more effective.

For some companies, savings from email alone have paid for their Internet connections. Its lower costs drive thousands of organizations away from paper mail. The trend is so widespread that the United States Postal Service estimates that about 30 percent of its business-to-business first class mail has been diverted to fax and email since 1988. The amount diverted to email increases every month.

Can email reduce your staffing needs? Your honor, I display as evidence Rivkin Radler & Kremer, a $42 million law firm with 178 attorneys headquartered in Uniondale, New York, with offices in Illinois and California. The firm used email to cut its paralegal and secretarial staffs by more than 40 percent, while at the same time significantly increasing its billings.

The firm sees email as a money-saver. Its clients see email as a benefit and as a reason to increase their business with Rivkin Radler & Kremer. The firm emails memoranda and legal documents to its clients. Documents go from its document management system PC Docs and cc:Mail out across the Net. Its customers receive the documents with their software (Eudora, cc:Mail, Microsoft Mail, Lotus Notes, and other products). Delivery is faster, plus clients are freed from the useless grind of retyping data into their own computers. Clients no longer have to pay per-page fees for copies of documents, which can be a big expense in a complex case. Also, clients find email a more effective way to communicate with attorneys, who are often hard to reach by phone. (Ever played phone tag with a lawyer?)

If you want the least expensive way to connect electronically with your customers and your suppliers, email is the way to go. The World Wide Web requires more hardware horsepower and a larger network connection because it is interactive—users push a key, then sit and *wait* for your computer to respond. Delays are annoying. People expect your system to respond instantly. With email, on the other hand, no one fires off a message and expects an instant response. You have an hour or more to get back to them. You can use a small, cheap computer for email, as well as a slower and less-expensive network connection.

Companies move to email for reasons that go beyond cutting costs. The greatest advantage of email isn't the savings; it's that email *works better* than phone calls or paper mail. Email increases productivity—dramatically, in some cases. Email is much faster than paper mail. You don't have the delay of printing a copy or copies. Instead of waiting days for delivery, it takes minutes or just seconds, even across long distances. In fact, Internet inhabitants have dubbed postal mail "snail mail," as an indication of its slowness.

Another advantage of email over snail mail comes from the current transformation of the nature of documents themselves. You can pull an email message into your word processor, spreadsheet file, or database more quickly than you can retype it. And it will have fewer errors. This makes a big difference anytime you need to swap documents with another company or a far-flung site of your own company.

One last point of comparison: Email provides more *accountability* than snail mail. Yeah, sure, your postage meter can tell you more or less what your department spends on postage. But with email, you can run analysis reports that give you accountability per person down to the byte. (That's one single English character.) You can break usage down by the day and by the hour. This makes it easier for interdepartmental billing, for client billing (if you charge customers per message or per kilobyte), and for projections.

My favorite email benefits

Now, all of the above reasons are well and good, but as a marketing man, I find that they aren't the most important email benefits to me. There are two marketing reasons to use email that rise above all else.

1. **When companies use email, they multiply the number of customer contact points without additional incremental cost.**

Think about this for a moment. Email spreads direct contact with your customers across your company. The implications are vast. Your customers and prospects gain a depth of service and a tighter interrelationship with your company than you can achieve by any other medium.

And your company gains a depth of insight into what your customers want—and what they don't want—that comes not from guesstimates, but from *first-hand interaction* with your clients.

2. **You can reach large groups as easily as one person.**

This is a slight exaggeration, but not by much. To send your email message to 1,000 people instead of one person takes only a little more work. I've been doing publicity and direct mail advertising for enough years to appreciate how much easier, faster, and cheaper this is than any other alternative. There are caveats about Internet mailing lists, but if you mind the rules, the rewards will surprise you.

Lagniappe: The email pass-around factor

One other thing I like about Internet email is this: Messages are easy to pass around. If you see something you want to share with others, the Net makes it easy for you to copy and forward that message. When somebody likes one of your messages, they can forward it, too.

This is the typed equivalent of good word of mouth on the Net—what some call good "word of fingers." It's a free bonus on the Net. When you send out something successful, it snowballs and generates a greater response than you could have created on your own.

In summary, get email if you want to speed up communication. It reduces decision-making time. You can reach a lot of people quickly—and it's cheap.

The email backlash

Computer Associates International is a $4 billion software company, so you can imagine that its employees used email a lot. In fact, too much. When chairman Charles Wang investigated the actual results of email at his corporation, he found unexpected problems.

One was that his people spent an enormous amount of time on email. Each of his managers received 200 to 300 email messages every day. Another problem: employees didn't talk with each other as much as before, so miscommunication was widespread. Wang took a draconian step. He shut down email from 9:30 a.m. to noon and from 1:30 p.m. to 4 p.m. People must have screamed in pain, but Wang's idea worked. The enforced email-free time allowed people to spend most of their day concentrating on work. People talked with each other instead of sending email, and communication improved.

This story illustrates a growing trend. Email is great, but it's like ice cream: Too much of it will make you sick.

Few businesses go to the extent of shutting down email for most of the day, but the ugly parts of email cause trouble for more and more companies, even for small businesses. I often get 200 email messages a day. Now, I like getting email from my readers—in fact, I *depend* on it, because my readers clue me into new problems and opportunities on the Net faster than anything else. But I have a tough time keeping up with my email, and the same is true with many managers.

Here are common problems that can make your life email hell:

1. Email overwhelm

The Law of Diminishing Utility says that as the quantity of something in-creases, each individual unit is less useful. It's easy to get so many email messages that they grow impossible to keep up with, and therefore become almost useless.

How can you keep this from happening to your business? Maybe by restrict-ing email access as Charles Wang did at Computer Associates International. Definitely by putting in place formal procedures guiding employees about what they should and should not use email to do. It can help if you and your workers know how to use bozo filters and kill files to delete unwanted email before you see it.

To get through your own email messages more quickly, you might adapt the technique used by a friend of mine. He placed his computer on a shelf just high enough so he has to stand up to use it. He figured, and rightfully so, that if he does all his email while standing up, he can get through his email more quickly. It seems to have worked. My friend gets a lot of email and claims that handling it now takes less than 45 minutes a day.

2. Electronic CYA

The letters "cc:" at the bottom of snail mail messages stood for "carbon copies," and told recipients of correspondence who else received a copy. The letters "cc:" survived into the email age, and they still let you know who else received a copy. The letters "CYA" stand for something completely different: Cover Your Anatomy, which is what many businesspeople use "cc:" to do.

The result: Thousands—probably millions—of useless email messages gener-ated by fearful employees carpet-bombing the inboxes of managers and co-workers, usually about minor changes that no one cares about anyway. In response, SmithKline Beecham and many other companies set limits on the number of ccs a worker can send. Some companies permit none. I know one middle manager for a large company whose response was to set the filters on his own email software to automatically delete any message that came to him as a cc. He read only messages that were addressed directly to him. He said that it took a year and a half before someone asked him if he had seen a cc: message.

The ease with which people can contact their supervisors using email creates another CYA problem. Email makes it easy for middle managers to avoid decision-making by shoving decisions up the ladder. This is something to warn managers and supervisors about and can be sharply reduced by training people not to do it.

3. Insert foot in electronic mouth

Two of the advantages of email are that it is easy and informal. Two of the *dis*advantages of email are that it is too easy and too informal.

People get so comfortable with email that they treat it like a conversation. This is a mistake. It is much, much easier to be misunderstood with email. Email takes away your body language, your vocal inflections—the things people use to understand how you feel about what you are saying. Email doesn't have them, so email messages are often misinterpreted.

4. Unleash the terrorist within

If you're a manager, watch out for this one. Bad bosses use email as an instrument of fear to control employees or attack other managers. Sometimes staffers, too, get ugly.

There are two kinds of people who do this. The first group are natural bullies, aggressive in everything they do. It can be in your best interest to keep them away from email. The second group are people who do not like conflict in real life but unleash aggressions in email. These people can lash out and be nasty, and it takes a good manager to keep them under control.

5. The new isolationists

Then we come to people who hide behind email. They can be either managers or employees, but the problem is worse if the person is a manager.

Some managers are uncomfortable talking with employees in person and try to manage via email. This does not work. I've worked with a couple of managers like this, and in both cases the results were out-of-touch managers who were emotionally distant from their underlings and employees with morale problems from working for phantom managers. Watch for symptoms of this in your management. Supervisors who rarely talk to their charges either in person or on the phone sometimes fall into this classification. Nothing replaces managers who make direct contact with the people they manage.

6. The glass network

The Net is as private as a glass shower stall in the middle of Times Square.

 Email is not secure. Unlike postal mail, *other people can read your email.* This can happen by accident or on purpose, and your readers may be people with access authority (like your company's system administrator), or people without authority: hackers, industrial spies, or just a wrong address to whom you accidentally sent secret data.

This is why you are told not to put confidential information in an Internet email message. And why it's not safe to send your credit card numbers in email.

Those are problems with *outgoing* mail. You also need to know a couple of things about *incoming* email. First, email return addresses can be faked. This is called *spoofing.* It sometimes involves forged messages from celebrities, such as a purported message from author Stephen King to the **alt.horror** newsgroup. Spoofed messages have also been created to hurt the reputations of businesspeople and everyday people. The same snooper who can eavesdrop and read your incoming email can also change email messages.

Fortunately, new software will include solutions to email's security loopholes. Most major email packages have optional encryption, either built-in or available as an add-on module. Encryption scrambles your messages so no one can read them except your recipients, who have software keys to unscramble them. And changes can be detected if you add digital signatures to your email messages, which show that the document came from you—it was not spoofed—and has not been altered.

7. Two technical nuisances

In addition to the business issues above, two technical matters infrequently cause problems.

Reliability: Internet email is not 100% reliable

Your Internet messages will usually reach addressees anywhere in the world within minutes, often within seconds. But not always. Since Internet email is passed along from computer to computer to its final destination, if a computer or a network link goes down holding your message, sometimes it can take days to reach its addressee.

You will notice this especially if you often do large (more than 1,000 names), time-sensitive mailings to an email list. Every few mailings, one or two people will complain that you should have sent your message earlier because they didn't receive it in time. Investigation will reveal that the message took a few days or a week to reach the complainers.

Rarely, will an Internet message simply disappear. When you have a complex document to email, make sure you keep a backup copy so your information can't be lost. Email software makes this simple to do. You don't need to copy everything, but ask yourself, "Would I feel pain if this document were lost?" If you would, make a copy. If not, don't bother.

This problem will go away eventually. IBM, Microsoft, Intel, HP, AT&T, and others are developing BQM, Business Quality Messaging. BQM will give Internet email the same 100 percent delivery reliability as banks now use to transfer funds electronically. Expect BQM in a year or two.

COMPATIBILITY: EVERYTHING ON THE NET
WORKS TOGETHER—ALMOST

The Internet was started back in the early 1970s and connects computers from every manufacturer running every operating system imaginable. Some computers on the Net are nearly 20 years old. Everything *almost* works alike. You need to keep this in mind when you send a message to someone. The limits of your recipient's computer and software determine what he or she can read.

If you keep two simple guidelines in mind, your messages should be readable by everyone:

Keep the line length 80 characters per line or shorter. Some networks truncate lines longer than 80 characters. Many email packages automatically limit outgoing line length to fit this limit, or let you choose your message width. If yours doesn't, and you don't want each line of your message chopped off, just hit the return key to end each line before it gets too long. Seventy characters should work. The sample message in "Anatomy of an Email Message" in this chapter is 70 characters wide.

Know how long a message your addressee's system can receive. America Online and the European network EUnet limit incoming message size to 102,400 characters. (That's a lot of characters. To give you a point of comparison, this chapter is less than 50,000 characters.) Several sites limit incoming messages to 65,536 characters (called 64K, for 64,000).

To compensate for these limits, keep messages emailed to AOL and Europe shorter than 100,000 characters unless you know that your recipient's system can handle a longer message. When you mass-mail a message to an email list, keep your message shorter than 65,536 characters—which shouldn't be too difficult.

How to get top management involved

In the early days of the telephone, the chief engineer of the British Postal and Telegraph System (then the world's biggest telecommunications organization) dismissed phones as a needless luxury. He said, "I have one in my office, but mostly for show. If I want to send a message, I employ a boy to take it."

Modern versions of this attitude still exist. If you want to get senior managers to use email, you may have to go to extra lengths to accommodate them. Obviously, it's an advantage when you have managers who are savvy enough to jump right in and send their own email. It's a valuable customer relations tool. Rachel Unkefer, president of Computer Literacy Bookshops Inc., publicizes her email address of **pres@clbooks.com**, and asks customers to contact her directly if they have any problem. That kind of accessibility goes a long way toward making customers trust a company.

For senior execs who refuse to deal with their email first-hand, you can come up with workarounds. Former Apple Computer honcho John Sculley didn't read his own voluminous email. He had two assistants answer it. Hewlett-Packard CEO John Young used a different approach. His assistant printed his email and put copies on Young's desk for Young to read and answer.

The trouble with approaches like these is that the executive who avoids direct involvement with email loses the advantages of immediate, person-to-person contact with employees and customers. A manager with a hands-on approach to email learns a lot more about what really goes on, especially what goes on in the minds of his or her customers.

Writer Sherman Stratfor pointed this out in an article called "The New Computer Revolution" in the June 14, 1993, issue of *Fortune:* "The common ailment of the corporations that got hit on the head by two-by-fours—particularly IBM, Digital, and Compaq—was distance from customers. They ended up making products customers didn't want. The lesson here, which applies to every industry, is that successful companies depend utterly on customer feedback. At winning outfits from GE to Wal-Mart, a primary goal is to create structures—from flattened management to email systems linking employees with customers and suppliers—that increase that closeness."

It might take private training to get your executives to use email. It might take a daily visit from an email "coach" for a few weeks to get a manager up to speed. It might take a secretary to do daily email prescreening, deleting junk email and CYA CCs so the executive only deals with messages from customers and from employees (avoiding the email burnout problem discussed earlier.) But the benefits are worth it, for the manager, for your company, and for the visibility and success of your email project.

There is one type of manager who is better off *not* using email. If you have a top manager who enjoys confrontation and actually *likes* to be obnoxious, that person on email can give your company a bad reputation, generate flames, and get your entire company blacklisted and barred from whole sections of the Internet. You could spend a lot of time cleaning up the damage. Keep bullies away from email.

This is especially true if your company has international customers. Compared to the United States, other countries' manners are more formal and standards of politeness are more important. Someone who just seems rude or impolite in the United States can get you into real trouble internationally.

Anatomy of an email message

To discuss how to apply email in your business, you need to know what the different parts of an email message are called.

All email messages have two parts, the *header* and the message itself, which is called the *body*. Most messages have an optional third part, called the *signature*, or *sig* for short. (See Figure 9.1.)

Fourteen company policy considerations

Email will touch more people in your company than any other Internet service. It is a good idea for you to create formal company policies for employees and email, because it will be widespread, because your employees' email

Header: Tells who sent the message, when it was sent, who it's for, its subject, and how it traveled to its destination.

```
Return-Path: <perine@detect.com>
Received: from moon.earthlink.net by mwmlaw.geonet.com
        (8.6.9/SMI-4.1/Geonet) id VAA20224; Thu, 6 Dec 1928 10:07:51-0800
Received: by mwm.geonet.com (Smail3.1.28.1 #28.2)
        id <m0rUTAI-000LFfC@moon.earthlink.net>; Thu, 6 Dec 28 10:08 PST
Message-Id: <m0rUTAI-000LFfC@moon.earthlink.net>
Content-Type: text
Date: Thu, 6 Dec 28 10:07 PST
X-Sender: perine@detect.com
To: sidney.wise@mwmlaw.com
cc: samuel.spade@detect.com
From: effie.perine@detect.com
Subject: Meeting today with Sam Spade
X-Mailer: <Windows Eudora Version 2.02>
```

Subject: What this message is about. Your subject gets your message read, so it is important. Some email software truncates long subjects, so keep your subjects short.

Body: The message itself.

```
Sid, will you be in your office this afternoon?  Sam would like some
legal advice _before_ the coroner's inquest on Miles' death.
Please have your secretary call me to set up a time.
```

```
Effie Perine, Office Manager                    effie.perine@detect.com
------------------------------------------------------------------
Spade & Archer, Private Investigators                Phone 415-555-2300
Hunter-Dulin Building, 111 Sutter St.                    "Our Specialty:
San Francisco, Calif. USA                       Confidential Investigations"
```

Signature: Automatically added to all Ms. Perine's outgoing messages by her email software. Stored in a file called *sig file*. This sig is five lines tall. Four or five lines tall is a good size for a sig.

Figure 9.1   A typical email message has three major sections—the header, the body, and the signature, along with the important "Subject:" line.

will represent your company to the outside world, and because the ethical and legal aspects of dealing with your employees and email can cost you big bucks.

You benefit from having policies worked out in advance. This makes it easier on your system administrator, who can apply policy guidelines to make the rush decisions that come with email administration. Formal guidelines avoid lawsuits. Your policies will prevent errors by letting employees know what they are expected to do.

Your email policies should become part of your company documentation and your employee training for all who are allowed email access. Your company training needs to cover not just the technical part of how to use email, but also the ethical and liability aspects. Your company documentation should include a set of rules stating clearly what is allowed and what is not when sending email. From a legal standpoint, it may be beneficial to you to clearly state the consequences of failing to follow company email policy guidelines.

1. Make sure your staff understands email is not secure.

First, let your people know that email is *not* private. Email is often copied and reposted, much to the sender's dismay. As Carol Welsh of the Computer Museum says, "Don't say anything in email that you wouldn't want to read on the front page of the *New York Times.*"

Ask Tonya Harding. She made front page news during the 1994 Winter Olympics when reporters snooped in her email. Your employees may not have reporters poking in their mailboxes, but email industrial espionage is on the rise. Maybe your competitors snoop.

Let your workers know that email may be used as legal evidence. The most famous example was during the Iran-Contra hearings, when Oliver North thought he had deleted his email. However, a backup system had saved his messages, and they were used as evidence against him. Email was also used as evidence when Microsoft Corp. was investigated by the federal government. U.S. Justice Department investigators sifted through thousands of email messages from Microsoft employees, dating back years. And email has shown up in court as evidence in divorce cases and sexual harassment lawsuits.

2. Write guidelines on what to include in email and what to exclude.

You need to define what is and what is not permissible for your staff to discuss in email messages. A written policy can protect your company from legal liability due to actions of employees. Hallmark Cards, Inc. gives all email users a written policy that forbids harassment, including any remarks that can be interpreted as sexual harassment; offensive or insulting remarks; emotional responses to business correspondence; and personal information or gossip about the user or someone else.

The most common offense is sexual harassment, which has resulted in many multi-million dollar lawsuits. With printouts of offending email as evidence, most are settled out of court by companies paying huge amounts in damages.

Some companies' policies specifically prohibit "electronic valentines" of any sort and ban any mention of sex or of a person's physique.

Depending on your company's network setup, you may need to differentiate between email sent *inside* your company or site and email sent *outside*. Email is not as open to prying eyes when it stays on your company's internal computer network.

If your company is privately held, you may not want sales figures mentioned in email. Should people mention wage figures in email? How about customer names? Certainly you don't want to leak any of your customers' proprietary data entrusted to you. What about new products and services that your company has under development? Give employees a written guide to what is and what is not emailable, what stays within your company and what can go outside. The more explicit you make your guide, the less chance that someone will unintentionally give away corporate secrets.

3. If your company will monitor employees' email, tell them about it in writing.

Laws differ from country to country, but in the United States, employers do have the right to monitor email sent on company-owned computers. Email is governed by the Electronic Communications Privacy Act of 1986, which recognizes that companies sometimes need to read messages to make sure that no industrial espionage is taking place. The company paid for the email, so it owns the email.

Make employees aware that people *within* your company may have access to their email. A system administrator, for example, normally has access to messages. Other people in your company may have access as well. This needs to be made clear to your employees *in a written notice*. If you tell them about it ahead of time, they'll say, "Yeah, sure, no big deal." But you might encounter some anger if they find out by surprise, even if your monitoring is perfectly legal. A simple phrase will do, such as, "From time to time, your email messages may be read by company managers for various reasons."

As there is no U.S. law preventing an employer from reading an employee's email, there is no law that states an employee must be told when his or her email is inspected. Even so, if there is even the slimmest chance that your company might monitor employee email, you avoid legal brawls and bitter staff confrontations by letting people know about this possibility in advance.

A woman named Alana Shoars who used to work for Epson America sued the company, saying that it violated her privacy by reading her email. She lost. The judge ruled that the company's property rights took precedence over Shoars's privacy rights. Even so, Epson America paid tens of thousands of dollars in legal fees that it might have avoided by giving Shoars a ten-cent written note that someone might read her email. Which would you rather pay for, the lawyers or the note?

4. The legal consequences of reading employees' email differ from those of doing anything with it.

Reading an employee's mail is one thing. Taking action with an employee's mail is very different. When you find a message that you want to copy, forward, or make public, you should discuss it with the employee first, *before* you take any action. There can be severe legal consequences if any of the employee's rights are violated. This varies depending on your local labor laws and union regulations.

5. Decide who in your company will have Internet access and what kind of access they will have.

Who gets email? Who gets the World Wide Web? Some people will forcefully demand complete Internet access. Some will want email as a status symbol. Others will avoid it as a source of more work. Someone in your company will need to create decision-making criteria for who gets what and why.

This doesn't need to be a formal, written document, but put some thought into it. The current trend seems to be that all employees—at least, those with computers—get email access, but only the ones who *need* other Internet tools can use all Net services. As the CFO of one large corporation told me, "Everyone should have email, but only a few get full access. I don't want the guys in the mailroom spending all day playing computer games."

You will find, with rare exceptions, it pays to give email to all your staff who have a computer. Email will be especially important to anyone who has contact with the outside world: sales representatives, purchasing agents, R&D, accounts payable, accounts receivable, customer service, and marketing people. Remember your telecommuters—for them, email is a life-or-death matter.

Then decide which people get access to all the other Internet services. Obviously, your technical staff will need full Internet access to support your own Net efforts. Your marketing people—or whomever will be in charge of maintaining the contents of your Internet presence—will need full Net access to test and monitor your offerings—and your competitors'. You might be surprised to see how much Net activity deals with accounting and finance (maybe that's predictable, given accountants' passion for organized data), so that lets in your number crunchers. A good browse of this book will give you an idea of what the Internet has to offer the different departments in your business. If you're not sure, err on the side of restraint. It will be easier to add more services later than to take them away.

When you give an employee email access to the Internet but restrict access to other Internet services, keep something in mind. Your employee can still reach these services *using only email*: Archie, Veronica, Gopher, FTP, Usenet newsgroups, Finger, Whois, and even the Web. So be aware—restricted access may not be as restricted as you think.

If you want to provide email access for your staff who don't work on computers, you can do this in a limited way. Whether they have a computer or not, all Sprint/United Telephone of Florida employees have an email address. Sprint/UTF sites make terminals available where the computerless can log in, retrieve their email, and log out.

6. Decide who will deal with customer email, then define procedures for them to use.

Who talks with customers in your company now? When your business uses email, the number of customer contact points will multiply quickly. Your clients will touch people in more departments across your company than before, including people who don't otherwise deal with customers. You need to plan for this.

Which email addresses will be publicized to your customers and which will be withheld? Will departments such as customer support and sales make the email addresses of all departmental personnel available to customers? Or will departments give customers a single address as a point of contact? This last approach has advantages.

Define procedures and standards. When you receive an email message from a customer, how long will it be before someone returns a response? Some companies set maximum times, such as a response will go out within 60 minutes or 90 minutes—perhaps not an answer to the customer's question, but at least an acknowledgment that "We have received your question and are working on it." Retailer Hammacher Schlemmer's standard is *5 minutes*.

Let people know about the different tone of voice appropriate for people outside your company's home country. Customers from the United States and Canada usually prefer casual email and are offended by too-formal messages (because formality shows you don't *like* them), but customers from most other countries prefer formal email and are offended by too-casual messages (because informality shows you don't *respect* them).

When a customer emails a complaint, who receives it? Who gets copies of each complaint and its response? (Copies of customer email can be very useful for sales, marketing, and customer service managers.) Someone should prepare statistical reports about emailed complaints. Who will prepare reports? How often? What do you want to track? Who gets the finished reports on complaints? Who decides what actions to take based on your findings?

It is a good idea to store copies of all email from customers. Where do you want to store them? How long do you want to keep them? (Different lengths of time for different types of clients?) How do you want to arrange them—by date, by customer, or by type of message? Email from your customers is the most important kind. Your company's written procedures should answer all these questions about customer messages.

7. Pick a fire fighting team and have it draft procedures for email flames.

 An irrationally intense, angry email message is called a flame. No matter how carefully your company treads, you may be flamed. You need a plan to handle flames.

Designate a fire fighting team that will create procedures and respond to flames. It is important to prevent anyone from responding to a flame with another flame. That will just make things worse. Any employee who receives a flame should contact his or her supervisor or a designated firefighter immediately, and the supervisor should read the flame before a response is made. Keep copies of all flames and responses. After the incident is under control, your team should meet to discuss ways to prevent a recurrence of the situation that triggered the flame.

You might conduct a "flame drill" to test your procedures and find ways to improve them. For a tip on how Intel Corp. deals with newsgroup flamers, see the chapter on publicity.

8. Let your employees know how their email addresses will be assigned.

People get emotional about their names. With email, your address *is* your name. Employees will care about their email addresses. You can prevent outbursts and wasted time answering the same questions over and over by letting everyone know ahead of time the formula by which their addresses will be chosen.

First, decide what combination of domain and subdomain your business will use. What's a *subdomain*? For example, pretend the domain for the detective firm of Spade & Archer was **detect.com**. Your domain name cannot be changed. But you can add a subdomain in front of it, separated from your domain name by a dot. You can assign department names as subdomains. For instance, if Sam Spade worked in the sales department:

sam.spade@sales.detect.com

In a similar way, the people in manufacturing in your company could be assigned email addresses ending in **@mfg.yourco.com**. Some geographically dispersed corporations use cities as subdomains:

sam.spade@san.francisco.detect.com

Next, decide on a standard format for user names. This may sound trivial, but some employees get upset about how their names are handled. Most companies use one of these formats:

1. sspade@detect.com

2. s_spade@detect.com

3. s-spade@detect.com

4. s.spade@detect.com

5. sam.s@detect.com

6. sam_spade@detect.com

7. sam-spade@detect.com

8. sam.spade@detect.com

Names with the first initial and last name (formats 1 through 4) are common. This is preferred by many European companies, where workplace formality leads to co-workers addressing each other only by last names. It is also appreciated by women who feel that they have less likelihood of being treated in a sexist manner by people who can't guess their sex without their first names. If you choose this format, be prepared to make occasional exceptions for duplicates and to prevent saddling someone with a comical, rude, or obscene nickname.

Of formats 1 through 4, the best is number 4. It clearly indicates that the initial is separate from the last name (which format 1 fails to do), but lacks three disadvantages of formats 2 and 3. First, a dot is easier to type than an underscore (which requires a shift) or a dash. This means fewer typing errors in email addresses.

Addresses your business needs

The Internet Engineering Task Force has standardized a short list of email addresses that every business should have. This way, a customer who wants to reach the department or person in charge of a particular activity can do so without the hassle of looking up an individual person's email address.

If your company has its own domain name (which I'll pretend is **yourco.com**), you need to ask your email administrator to set up these addresses and direct email for them to the appropriate people.

Business-related:

> **info@yourco.com**
> **marketing@yourco.com**
> **sales@yourco.com**
> **support@yourco.com** (for customer support)

Computer network operations:

> **abuse@yourco.com** (if someone is bad on the Net)
> **noc@yourco.com** (only if you have a Network Operation
>   Center)
> **security@yourco.com** (to report network intruders)

Internet technical support (only if you have these services):

> **postmaster@yourco.com** (person in charge of email)
> **hostmaster@yourco.com** (if you have your own host computer)
> **usenet@yourco.com** (if you have your own Usenet server)
> **news@yourco.com**
> **webmaster@yourco.com** (person in charge of Web site
>   technical aspects)
> **www@yourco.com** (person in charge of Web site content)
> **uucp@yourco.com** (if you have a UUCP email server)
> **ftp@yourco.com** (if you have an FTP server)

Email list management (if you run an email list)

> **list@yourco.com**
> **list-request@yourco.com**

THE EMAIL ADDRESS TELEPHONE TEST

Second, format 4 passes the telephone test: *Is this email address easy to give over the phone?* Try telling someone an address like format 2 over the phone. You'll appreciate how easily and quickly people understand "dot" compared to other punctuation. (I will admit you could do worse than an underscore. I know someone whose office put a *percentage sign* (%) in everyone's email address!)

Another drawback of adding punctuation is that it makes an email address harder to remember.

Format 5 is mostly used in by less-formal companies that stress customer service. The idea is that customers feel a closer relationship when they know someone's first name.

Formats 6 through 8 give both names. The only difference is what punctuation you use. Once again, the format with the dot creates less screwups.

A "Dilbert" comic strip poked fun at bad email addresses, with Dilbert reading a man's business card and telling him, "You call that an email address? It's 80 characters long and mostly meaningless." Don't make this mistake yourself. People want email addresses that are short, easy to remember, and mean something.

After you have chosen your company's email address format, write some guidelines and distribute them in advance. If carefully written, your policy will eliminate any tantrums over email addresses.

9. Decide whether or not you want standardized signature files.

Some companies let employees write and design their own sig files, so outgoing email messages all are different. Other companies define a style or a few rules that all email signatures must follow, but allow employees creativity within those limits. Other companies make all sig files follow an exact format, with no personalization allowed except the sender's name and phone number.

In most ways, sig file content decisions are marketing decisions. The marketing part of this book covers sig issues in more detail.

There is one legal aspect to consider when you set your policy for email signature files. Employers can be liable when an employee sends abusive or offensive email. As a way of limiting legal liability, some companies require their employees' signature files to say "These opinions are my own, not necessarily the opinion of my employer." Few businesses do this. Whether your business needs to depends on conditions specific to your company.

10. Decide how to handle employees' personal email.

It is silly to pretend that your employees will not send some personal email. That is human nature, and you need to allow for it. As long as it doesn't interfere with their work, be prepared for a reasonable amount to occur.

11. Any person with email should log off a computer before leaving it.

There is a risk in leaving your email program up and running when you're away from your computer. Someone can use your email account to send embarrassing or legally actionable messages. Admittedly, in many companies this is unlikely. But depending on how many people work at your site and what the physical layout is (bullpen vs. private office), you may want to require employees to log off their computers before leaving them unattended.

12. Work with your network administrator to define procedures for shared computers.

As telecommuting grows in popularity, it becomes less cost-effective to have a full-time computer for an employee who is rarely around to use it. There is a growing trend for employees to share computers. Each of these employees will still need a personal email account. Your service administrator can set up multiple mail accounts on a single computer.

13. With your system administrator, set accumulation limits on the age and amount of saved email.

If you let them, some people will never delete any of the email they receive. Old email swallows acres of disk space if you let it. Your system administrator will want to archive messages to a backup disk and delete them from the computer periodically. If done without warning, you'll hear more wailing than two weeks of *All My Children*. Prevent it by telling people ahead of time that they have *x* amount of disk space assigned to them, and that if they go over that limit, their older messages will be removed. People in some positions will need more disk space than others. Allow for that, and plan to give managers more space. But most employees' saved email messages should total 500 kilobytes of disk space or less.

You may think this is irrelevant if you just use a dial-up account with a service provider and store email messages on your service provider's computer instead of your own. You will still need to set limits. If you use too much disk space or leave your messages in your mailbox too long, some providers delete them.

14. Set goals for training to accomplish and remember training in your budget.

When planning Internet projects, people often forget about training. Training is important, time-consuming, and costs money. Without training, your email software will be useless. Plan hands-on training for all people who will use email. Train them either one-on-one or in small groups, with one computer per trainee. In my experience, hands-on training is the only kind that shows results for email software.

Make a list of what specific actions someone needs to know to use your email software. Break those down into a series of step-by-step lessons. Make "cheat sheets" for your employees to use after the classes. After people have used email for four months, give them a second class on more advanced topics.

If your company has people with different amounts of experience with email and the Internet, you might have separate classes for those with little or no background and those with more experience. That way veterans won't make beginners feel slow, and newbies won't hold back your vets.

Personnel management uses

For all the talk about the Internet connecting your business with far-flung places, you will find that many of the most productive uses of email will be for communications *within* your company.

Employee newsletters are a good example. Instead of typesetting, printing, and distributing a newsletter on paper, you can send internal newsletters by email. It is so much easier and cheaper to edit and distribute emailed newsletters that you can send them more frequently. In turn, increased frequency lets your newsletter cover more *immediate* news—which is the single most important key to effectiveness in employee newsletters. Employees must come to rely on your newsletter to break important news *first*. To do that, your internal newsletters must be fast enough to beat the grapevine to the punch. With email, you can.

Email also simplifies *customizing* your newsletter. For instance, you could include core articles that all employees receive, insert technical articles in the versions received by your technicians, add a story about changes in your sales compensation plan for your salespeople, and describe new payroll taxes only to people who work in states that apply the new tax. For employees without computers, supervisors can print the newsletter and distribute it to them. Read the story on the following pages about "Employee News For Less" for an example of how one company spreads the news.

Recruiting is another important management use for email. You can email a job vacancy description to dozens of "Help Wanted" spots on the Net. New ones open every month. Some are general, but the greatest growth is in specialized job banks. For example, mathematicians, economists, and accountants all have specific sites where you can post relevant openings. Some sites charge companies a fee for posting openings, including sites that your recruitment advertising agency will try to sell to you. However, there are so many free sites that you may not need the ones that charge money.

 ## Employee news for less

The most thorough employee propaganda program I've come across has two remarkable aspects:

First, the level to which it saturates managers and employees with needed information on core business issues. Second, the small effort and cost it requires in relation to what it delivers.

Not surprisingly, this program is run by a communications company. Sprint/United Telephone of Florida built the Sprint News Network (SNN) to spread news to its 5,800 people scattered throughout Florida. The Sprint News Network's foundation is email, which delivers five of seven internal SNN media.

The backbone of SNN is an email newsletter, *SNN Today*. It goes to all employees three times a week—more often when hot news breaks. Sprint/UTF employees without email receive *SNN Today* from their supervisors, who distribute paper copies of the newsletter to all email-less subordinates. Some supervisors print multiple copies and hand them out to each employee. Some print a single copy and route it through their department. Others print a single copy and post it on a corkboard that all subordinates check daily. This is a simple and effective distribution plan, and can easily be imitated by your company.

SNN Today is not lengthy. Its goals are frequency and immediacy. Preparing and emailing the newsletter takes about 80 percent of one person's job. Other people contribute some articles.

"Employees appreciate the immediacy of it," says Lloyd Karnes, Sprint/UTF's manager of strategic communications. "That's the key. It used to be that when we'd get an important announcement or a big event and we'd have to notify 5,800 people spread all over the state, it was a big project and took a lot of people a lot of work. With email, it's just a matter of pushing a button. What makes the difference is that we have built a structure to handle news of that kind. Because *SNN Today* comes out so often, people rely on it and expect it to have the important news."

Within the first two hours of each business day, executives receive an additional email newsletter, *SNN Leadership Briefings*. It includes stock market information, industry news, and Sprint-related business news. Also emailed from time to time is *SNN Leadership Letter*, specifically for Sprint supervisors. It covers corporate policies, procedures and news, and contains general articles on management skills.

A fourth email newsletter, *SNN Today and Tomorrow* is delivered weekly to everyone in the company. While the regular *SNN Today* delivers the lowdown on *current* news, this newsletter deals with issues that will affect employees in the *future*: re-engineering, quality improvement, and process improvement.

That's how management gets the word out to staff. But how can Sprint/UTF employees talk back to management? That's where an email free-for-all called "Quanda" steps in. Quanda is the equivalent of 12 private, staff-only newsgroups for Sprint employees. Quanda works like any other Internet discussion group. Employees post questions to anyone in the company, all the way up to top executives. Everyone sees answers to their questions and those from other employees. Karnes's communications department monitors Quanda to make sure that vice presidents and department heads respond to questions asked of them.

"Our goal is not just to say who is Employee of the Month and do that kind of morale-boosting," Karnes explains. "We want everyone to know about the *strategic core issues* of our business." From the perspective of Karnes and his company's executives, their business is so competitive that the only way Sprint/UTF can reach its objectives is if the company presents a unified front of information to all employees. The Sprint News Network is a central piece of that strategy. It has earned high marks from management and staff alike.

What to look for in email software

Which kinds of software will you need? First of all, each person in your company who uses email will need *mail client* software—the program that a person uses to send and read mail. To make things more confusing, email clients are also called *mail user agents*, or MUAs. I'll just stick with mail client.

In addition to mail client programs, you may need: *gateway* software or hardware called *switches,* mail server software, mail transport software (called MTA for Mail Transport Agent), and list server software (if you want to mail to lists of 200 or more names).

Client software is what every emailer in your company will use every day. What should good email client software do? Most email packages cover the basics. Here are extras to look for. Get as many as you can:

- Some people get 500 email messages on a busy day. Yikes! You need software with a *mail handler* or a *mail filter*, two names for the same thing. This option automatically sorts incoming mail according to criteria you define and puts messages in mailbox folders for you to review. That way, you can read your high-priority folders when you don't have enough time to wade through all your email. Most mail filters check sender addresses and subject lines. The best inspect body copy as well. Some call these *bozo filters* because they can automatically send messages from someone you don't want to communicate with to a *kill file* where you can delete it without reading it.

- Part of sorting mail is *message threading*. If you send a message to three people, they reply back to you, you reply to them, and they return another reply, it is useful for you to be able to review that entire correspondence in sequence, separated from your other email. Good message threading does this.

- Does it spell check your outgoing email? Some client programs have a built-in spellchecker. Some let you attach any spellchecker you choose. Some let you attach any *word processor* you choose.

- While you use another program, will your client display an onscreen message telling you that incoming mail has arrived? This is extremely useful, especially for customer service people and people who deal with urgent situations.

- Your client should let you create an *alias* or *nickname* and put mail addressed to it into a designated file or send it to a group list. For instance, could you set up the alias **finance** so any mail sent to that address goes to everyone in your finance department? Can all mail sent to **info@yourcorp.com** go to your customer service manager? Could you create an alias so that **miles.a@detect.com** and **m.archer@detect.com** both go to the same person?

- Are aliases the only way your client software gives you to build a mailing list? Can you build more than one list? What's the maximum number of names you can add to one list?

- Can you send and receive messages using international character sets? This allows messages in languages like Japanese, Arabic, and Russian, which do not use Roman letters.

- *Automatic forwarding* sends email for a vacationing employee to someone else. When an employee leaves your company, you can have his or her email forwarded to someone else. Some email software has a vacation mail feature to accept any incoming messages for a person and send a "Hi, I'm on vacation and won't be back until June 17" reply.

- Some Internet email software lets you request *return receipts* for important messages you send. When your recipient receives and opens your message, you receive an email message telling what day and time your message was opened. Some software can give you a reminder if the message you sent remains unread for a number of days you define. Some vendors call this *certification.*

- You want your mail client to let you attach a file to a message you send. *This is important.* Some programs do it easily. Some not at all. You need this because Internet email can handle only text, not graphics or software programs. To send a nontext file (called a *binary file*), your software must first translate the binary information into text. This is done one of two ways: Uuencode or MIME. The recipient then translates the file back into binary files. Check to make sure your client handles Uuencode, MIME, or both. Then make sure it recognizes and translates them *automatically*. It's a pain in the anatomy to translate files by hand. (Note that some companies don't allow MIME email for security reasons.)

• Will the software encrypt messages? Will it also encrypt *attached files*?

One of the most highly rated email clients is called Eudora Pro. Mac and Microsoft Windows versions are available. Eudora Pro includes mail sorting and management tools, is easy to use, and has links with Microsoft Mail, cc:Mail, and other products. You can get a shareware version of Eudora, but the commercial version costs less than $90 and does much more. Eudora Pro is available at **www.eudora.com**.

Another leading product is free, and also includes sorting and management tools. Called Pegasus Mail, you can download it from most Internet software archives. Versions are available for PC-DOS, Macs, and Windows.

You can also pick up special-purpose Internet email clients. For instance, clients using SNPP, the Simple Network Paging Protocol, let you receive email on pagers.

How to receive email without a computer

Want to communicate with a customer or a supplier who has no email? You may want to let him or her know about services that convert email messages into faxes. You can have an email address and receive email without a computer by using your fax machine.

In the U.S., this service is provided by Powernet for $8 per month plus toll charges when forwarding faxes outside the 310 area code. For information, contact Dirk (**dirk@power.net**) or Ute (**ute@power.net**). You can reach them by phone at 310-643-4908 or by fax at 310-643-4909.

In Europe, a more geographically-widespread email-to-fax solution is available from Digital Mail International. You can call the company at 44-171-231-2929, reach it by email at **info@digitalmail.com**, or visit **www.digitalmail.com/home.htm**.

Flames and mail bombing

One of the more "entertaining" aspects of email is that people using email tend to lose their self-control surprisingly easily. Somehow, email lends a feeling of anonymity and safety. Often email users become more emotional than they would in a face-to-face conversation. People will write things to you that they would never dream of saying to your face.

A good result of this is that people can form close relationships by email without ever meeting each other in person. That's great for customer relations.

The downside is that people become angry easily while reading email and may send you abusive responses. Writing inappropriately angry email is called *flaming*. You can be flamed for something you regard as completely trivial.

Here's an example. After writing an article for *The New Yorker* about Microsoft chairman Bill Gates, writer John Seabrook received this email message:

```
"Crave THIS, asshole:
Listen, you toadying dipshit scumbag . . . remove your head from your
rectum long enough to look around and notice that real reporters don't
fawn over their subjects, pretend that their subjects are making some sort
of special contact with them, or worse, curry favor by TELLING their
subjects how great the ass-licking profile is going to turn out and then
brag in print about doing it. Forward this to Mom. Copy Tina and tell her
the mag is fast turning to compost. One good worm deserves another."
```

Surprisingly, Seabrook said he received this venom from a "technology writer who does a column about personal computers for a major newspaper," according to an informative follow-up story Seabrook wrote for *The New Yorker*, called "My First Flame."

If you or your company are flamed, *don't flame back!* Fighting fire with fire only makes things worse. It generates more flames and can lead to mail bombing or other destructive Net tactics. When you are flamed, the first thing to do is to *cool the situation down* immediately.

The same holds true if someone thinks that you have flamed him or her: Chill out!

Flaming is in the eye of the beholder. If someone feels that a message from you was a flame, it was. Don't try to say, "But I didn't mean it!" That didn't work when you told it to your mom in the second grade, and it won't work in business. If someone accuses you of flaming them, your best response is to apologize, find out *exactly* what trigger made the recipient feel flamed, promise never to do it again, and mean it.

If you get in a flame war or are accused of *spamming* (sending advertisements to inappropriate Internet places), you may be mail bombed. Don't confuse mail bombing with letter bombing. Letter bombs are physical explosives delivered by snail mail. Mail bombs are delivered by email. Sent as revenge, they are designed to overload your system.

Mail bombing is normally done in one of two ways. One tactic is sending the target huge files. For an example, read the sidebar "Mail bombing and its effects.".

The second method is sending thousands of smaller messages. Automated mailing software makes this easy to do, and it is effective. Companies have been mail bombed with more than a hundred thousand messages in a short time. This overloaded the victim's access provider, forcing it to shut down service to *all* companies handled by the provider. Since email can be sent to fax machines, mail bombing has also been done to victim's fax lines, rendering them useless.

Your only defense against mail bombing is to avoid the behavior that triggers it. If you don't send flames and you don't spam, you should be safe.

Mail bombing and its effects

```
From: TerryH@ix.netcom.com (Terry Haggin)
Newsgroups: alt.stop.spamming
Subject: Re: sick of all the long-distance phone price spamming
Date: 18 Jan 1995 19:12:57 GMT
Great group.
What I like to do with the spammers is to put 100 megs in a file
then paste it onto my active system. When I come across a fresh
spam, I open it, then mail them the 100 megs of gobbledegook. I
have OS/2 so I can just go on with what I am doing while the 100
megs of junk is being mailed to them. That should slow them down.
Terry
>
>
Newsgroups: alt.stop.spamming
From: ddern@world.std.com (Daniel P Dern)
Subject: Mail-bombing hurts innocent bystanders (Was: Re: sick of
all the...)
Summary: Crashing systems that other people rely isn't appropriate
Date: Thu, 19 Jan 1995 15:22:00 GMT
In article <3fjp7p$6bd@ixnews2.ix.netcom.com>,
```

```
Terry Haggin <TerryH@ix.netcom.com> wrote:
>What I like to do with the spammers is ...
>... mail them the 100 mgs of gobbledegook,
While this may be gratifying, unless you're certain that the
spammers are the only ones on the target system, what you're
doing may well result impairing the service of other, innocent
users on that system. Coping with mailbombing to preserve service
to non-spamming users can easily require time and effort by
sysadmins there. I don't think this is solving the problem prop-
erly, therefore. The first act should always be complaining to
the postmaster and cc'ing the user (or vice versa). And then we
go sneak up on their homes late at night and blast 'em out of bed
with 10,000 watts of Barry Manilow, or maybe William Shatner
intoning McArther Park. Assuming we're not concerned about both-
ering the neighbors (there goes that pesky problem again...).
DPD
—
Daniel Dern (ddern@world.std.com) Internet analyst, writer,
pundit & gadfly
(617) 969-7947 FAX: (617) 969-7949  Snail: PO Box 309 Newton
Centre MA 02159
Author, The Internet Guide For New Users (McGraw-Hill, 1993) -
info & stuff at URL=gopher://gopher.dern.com:2200 (a.k.a. "Dern"
area on gopher.internet.com)
```

The 10 commandments of email

The Internet has been around more than 25 years and, like any large group, has evolved its own rules of the road. The rules for email are straightforward. After you've been on the Net for two or three months, they make perfect sense.

The rules of behavior on the Internet are called *netiquette*. Make sure that the emailers in your company know these rules and how to apply them. The Net has its own sense of frontier justice. Flames and mail bombs punish businesses that blatantly violate netiquette, and there are other penalties for those that break more subtle rules. These include loss of customers, prospect alienation, removal from mailing lists, active noncooperation in resolving technical problems, and a bad rep on newsgroups.

It makes good business sense to follow the rules of the Internet. Here's a summary of 10 email rules you should know:

I. Thou shalt not spam.

The term "spamming"—sending unwanted advertisements—comes from a Monty Python comedy routine in which every dish on a restaurant's menu includes Spam, no matter how inappropriate. It is similarly inappropriate to email your advertising to people who don't ask for it. Remember, on the Internet, some people *pay* to receive your messages. The recipient of an Internet spam feels as though you interrupted his or her dinner with a *collect* phone call sales pitch.

If you spam, you will receive flames, be mail bombed, have your fax machine jammed with hate faxes, have your phone lines tied up (modems can be programmed to autodial your voice line and jam it), alienate prospects, lose repeat customers, get your entire company permanently cancelled from newsgroups, and possibly get kicked out by your access provider.

If you want to email anything that even *remotely* resembles an advertisement, send it only to people who have *asked* to receive it.

II. Thou shalt not flame.

When sending mail from a business, don't flame. If you are flamed, don't flame back. There are no valid excuses. Period.

III. Thou shalt use the right voice for thy addressee.

On the phone, no one can see your face, but your feelings are still clear. Why? Because the person on the other end hears your tone of voice. Email is the written word, so no one hears your voice. The result is that email misunderstandings are common and often occur when a writer isn't careful with his or her *written* tone of voice.

For example, a knowledgeable computer programmer at Computer Literacy Bookshops often emailed store managers with instructions for software. He thought he was being short and direct. Readers found his instructions brusque and almost rude. One spoke with the programmer about it, and his next emailed instructions were prefaced with the phrase, "Gentle suggestion."

Isn't that a beautiful phrase? It turns a barked command into helpful words from a friend. My gentle suggestion for managers is that they take care with their email, making sure they adopt a supportive tone. Orders seem harsh when emailed, and your employees may resent them. Try phrasing a command as a question and see what results you generate. Or make a "gentle suggestion" of your own.

All emailers need to watch their words—not just managers. Sarcasm doesn't work in email, so avoid it. Avoid vulgarity—it can come back to haunt you. Humor is risky. Match your message's formality to your addressee. You wouldn't speak the same, for instance, with the chairman of the board as you would with your best pal. Don't use the same email voice either.

Don't use email to send bad news. You might do that at home, but sending bad news in business email can have unintended consequences. Your bad news might seem trivial to you, but your recipient can blow it all out of proportion. This is especially true when you are a manager addressing a subordinate. Your message may seem ominous or a threat, creating all kinds of problems.

Try this test: "Will this person feel *good* after reading my message?" If not, don't send it. If you're not sure, talk to the person instead, on the phone or in person. This is especially true when you have to deliver criticism or discuss personnel issues.

What would happen if you thought of each email message you sent as a press release, going out to the media? Would you want to put a positive spin on your personal business activities? To generate favorable coverage (for business email, that means favorable responses), send pleasant messages.

You especially need to tailor your email voice when you correspond with someone from another culture. Sarcasm and humor don't travel well across cultures. Use the other culture's manners. For instance, don't display anger or say "no" directly to a Japanese person—you will seem very rude.

One final gentle suggestion: Reread your message before you send it to catch things that may be misinterpreted. Ask yourself, "Would I say this to this person's face?" I have saved myself a lot of grief by making this a habit.

IV.   Thou shalt not SHOUT.

Typing your message IN ALL CAPITAL LETTERS READS LIKE YOU ARE SHOUTING LOUDLY. So all caps is called *shouting* and people hate it. Besides, as any student of advertising research knows, readability drops sharply when you use all caps for body copy. Want someone to read your message? Avoid all caps.

V. Thou shalt not waste bandwidth.

An Internet saying is, "Talk is cheap. Bandwidth is expensive." Bandwidth—the Internet's carrying capacity—is limited. Sending useless or excessive messages fills the pipeline and slows the Net down for everyone. Useless messages also waste another limited resource—the time required to deal with them. Efficient use of Internet resources is viewed with approval. So don't send unnecessary messages.

VI. Be brief.

Write short messages. Use short sentences. "The most beautiful sentence? The shortest." —Anatole France, as quoted by Dashiell Hammett.

VII. Make thy "Subject:" clear.

In many ways, the Subject of your message is its most important part. A recipient will choose whether to read your message or not based on what your Subject line says.

You should write a Subject line that tells why your addressee should read your message. Make it clear and specific. "Hello" is a bad subject line. "Meeting Saturday about falcon" is a good one.

Keep in mind that many people use software that sorts incoming email automatically based on what's in the Subject line. When you include a project name or other specific name in your Subject line, it increases your chances that your message will be sorted into the proper file and that somebody will actually read it.

VIII. Thou shalt not wash thy linen in public.

Remember that what you write in an email message may be copied and posted to newsgroups, printed in the media, and sent to your worst competitor—or your boss. Keep secrets out of your email.

IX. Honor confidentiality.

Ask for permission before you forward someone else's message to another user, if you think there may be the *slightest* chance they'd be embarrassed or would feel you've violated their confidence.

X. Look twice before thou leapest.

If reading an incoming message makes you see red, reread it carefully *before* you respond. Its sender may not have said what you think. *Don't* assume every message that catches you off-guard is a flame. It might be failed humor or unclear phrasing.

In his book *Navigating the Internet*, Mark Gibbs tells how he became angry when a woman emailed him "I resent your message": "Like a gold-plated, five-star idiot, I phoned and asked her, 'What the hell do you resent?' I then spent the next ten minutes jabbering my apologies. I had mistaken 're-sent' for 'resent'."

IMPORTANT:
Create Email signatures now!

The standard chunk of information at the end of an email message or a newsgroup posting is called a *signature file* or *sig* for short. If your email messages don't end with your sig, every email message you send screams "CLUELESS NEWBIE!" You are also missing out on one of the most potent marketing mechanisms of the Internet.

If you have not yet created your signature file, do it *right now*. Turn on your computer and use this discussion as your guide.

Here's how it works. Your email software and newsreader software lets you create a standard signature file that your software will electronically rubber-stamp at the bottom of every message you send. Sig files will be part of every email message your business sends out and every newsgroup posting made. Any customer or prospect who corresponds electronically with your company will see your people's sig files again and again. They are small-but-potent punches of publicity reaching your best prospects—people you already contact.

You need to decide if you want to create a standardized sig file format for everyone in your business to follow, or if you will allow employees to be creative and come up with their own. Here are a few simple guidelines:

Height: How many lines tall is your sig? Long sigs irk many people, so keep your signature file short. The best height is 6 or fewer lines. Some email lists truncate any sig taller than 8 lines. You can get away with 10.

Width: Some email systems truncate any line wider than 80 characters, and a few chop lines even shorter. Others just jumble wider lines into a mess. Your sig will be safe from cyberscissors if you keep each line 70 characters wide or shorter.

Content: What information should you include in your sig? Four things: 1) Who you are, 2) Your company name, 3) What you do, and 4) How to reach you. The first thing should be your name, and the second most imporant thing—surprisingly—is your email address. Several email systems strip header information off the top of every incoming message, so your recipient may have no way to reply to you if you do not repeat your email address.

Here is a sample sig file from attorney Lewis Rose of the firm of Arent Fox. In only six lines, Rose squeezes in a considerable amount of information. All methods of contact are covered except ESP.

```
Lewis Rose                                  202-857-6012 (voice)
Arent Fox                                     202-857-6395 (fax)
1050 Connecticut Avenue, NW             lewrose@netcom.com (email)
Washington, DC 20036                    Advertising and Marketing Law
Advertising Law Internet Site URL:   http://www.webcom.com/~lewrose/home.html
Moderator of Net-Lawyers Mailing List: net-lawyers-request@webcom.com
```

A less informational but more creative sig was created by movie director (*The Wizard of Speed and Time*), animator, and special effects genius Mike Jittlov, who includes his email address and the name of a newsgroup for his fans, along with a picture—created entirely with normal keyboard punctuation—of a wizard sprinkling pixie dust. Note that Jittlov's sig is only 64 characters wide, so it will fit on the smallest computer screens without getting chopped off. This sig is also six lines tall.

```
                       _____   ___.__‘.*.’_.__ _____
 _____         .   . + * .o  o.* ‘.‘. +.
 Mike Jittlov - Wizard, etc        .   . + * .o  o.* ‘.‘. +.
 Hollywood, California, USA    ‘   *  . ‘ ‘ |\^/|  `. * . *
   jittlov@empire.net        (: May All Your  \V/  Good Dreams
  <& alt.fan.mike-jittlov>    and Fine Wishes  /_\  Come True:)
 ========================================== _/ \_ ===========
```

Jittlov's sig is entirely appropriate for his business, dealing in motion pictures and fantasy. For some professions, you may need a less entertaining sig. Attorneys and bankers, for instance, should avoid art, quotations, and anything that would cause their sig to be labeled "too cute" or "too cartoony."

My own sig is 10 lines tall and 70 characters wide. It includes my name, what I do, the names of two of my books, a testimonial, my company name, and contact information:

```
Vince Emery    Specialist in Internet marketing and electronic commerce
               Public speaker, teacher, and consultant
               Author of "How to Grow Your Business on the Internet"
               Co-author of "Free Business Stuff from the Internet"

"One of the 25 most influential people in Internet marketing"
                                        —Grimes Communications


Vince Emery Productions        Box 460279, San Francisco, CA 94146 USA
www.emery.com      vince@emery.com       415-337-6000   Fax 415-337-6070
```

Your sig will not be chiseled in stone. You can change it whenever you please. Don't worry about being cute or creative. Just be clear. The results your sig generates depend greatly on how well your sig file clearly communicates exactly what your firm offers to your customers.

Intranets and Extranets

"Have you ever noticed how much easier it is to find out about the mating habits of the Gabon viper over the Internet than it is to find last quarter's sales figures for your own business on your own LAN?"

—Vance McCarthy, Datamation

Roche Laboratories, the U.S. arm of the world's second-largest pharmaceuticals company, had a tough but potentially rewarding situation. Product development costs of hundreds of millions of dollars were at stake. It needed to roll out and sell *three* major new products in 1997. Roche's strategy used a coordinated three-pronged approach: Internet, intranet, and extranet.

The Internet part was easiest. On Roche's public Web site, it put information about the products that members of the public might be interested in, including anticipated Frequently Asked Questions.

The second part was delivered on Roche Laboratories' intranet (called RocheNet), accessible only by 2,500 of the company's own employees. Roche's first priority was to support its 2,000 field sales reps. RocheNet supplied them with marketing, sales, and technical information. It also provided government regulations, and automated sales reporting software that cut paperwork and swiftly delivered field sales numbers, letting 200 field sales managers securely import and export Excel spreadsheets.

The third prong was Roche's extranet. In the same way that an *intranet* applies Net and Web tools to communicate within your company, an *extranet* is an intranet with extensions that let a clearly defined group of people (some customers, for instance, or top suppliers) reach and provide information from and to your own internal systems.

In Roche's case, the extranet was accessible to 900,000 physicians. (An enormous percentage of medical doctors are online.) Roche created a password-restricted set of Web pages for physicians, providing journal articles and information about research and product tests. The extranet included educational material and technical marketing information not intended for the public.

Roche's Net-based approach worked. It distributed information more quickly than traditional tactics, coordinated field sales, and returned faster feedback to headquarters.

Your next question is probably, "Yeah, but what kind of resources did Roche Laboratories put into all this?" Not as much as you might think. It took just two full-time employees, plus part-time contributors from several departments. All design and construction was outsourced. The intranet ran on one Web server (a Windows NT Netscape Enterprise Server on a Pentium-powered computer). An Oracle database on an HP Unix computer linked to that

Web server and provided data from corporate research, a data warehouse, and other sources. For extranet security, the Oracle database sat behind a firewall and kept a copy of itself on an identical Oracle database hosted offsite in the offices of Roche's Internet access provider. The provider's computer provided all public and extranet Web pages.

The end result? Roche Laboratories reduced costs, reduced time to market, and increased market penetration. That should translate into hundreds of millions of dollars in increased profits. Not bad for two employees.

Surveys show that two-thirds of all U.S. companies either have their own intranet or have plans for one. You may think the Internet grows quickly, but intranets spread even faster. Netscape says it sells *three times* as many servers for intranets as it does for Internet use.

So what is an intranet anyhow? Most short descriptions sound cute or bland. Some say an intranet is your own private Internet. Amdahl Corp.'s Web pages call an intranet "an Enterprise Wide Web instead of a World Wide Web." The Web site Intranet Journal provides its own dictionary definition: "Intranet— Using Internet technology to meet internal needs."

I like what Michael Millikin, Senior Vice President of Networld + Interop, wrote in *Telecommunications* magazine: "Why are intranets so popular? The simplest answer to this question is that they're fast, they work, and they scale well: basically the same advantages that led to the dominance of TCP/IP. After all, the global network called the World Wide Web is a great deal more complex than that of any single organization, and it seems to satisfy an enormous user base!"

Nontechnical people in your company can use an intranet to produce, distribute, and reach internal information, using the same tools people use to produce, distribute, and reach information on the Internet outside. On your intranet, your employees use a Web browser, email, file transfers, and newsgroups. But instead of reaching Yahoo, they can reach company news, employee phone books, human resources information, product specifications, pricing information, cafeteria menus—any kind of documents, software, or data your managers want to provide. You can run everything over your existing network and still incorporate data from the outside world, such as Reuter's live data feeds of financial information. An intranet is cheaper than print, faster to distribute, easier to update, and can present a uniform face to your employees.

Does your business need an intranet?

Not every business needs an intranet. Obviously, if you're a one-person startup, unless you have a split personality, you can handle intracompany communications in your head.

Some intranet consultants say that the dividing line for intranet payback is when a company has 100 or more employees, although I know one business with 40 employees that regards its intranet (which runs with free software on an old 486 computer) as a life-saver.

That business has a single location, but if your business has more than one site, you're a prime candidate for intranethood. A business distributed over different locations has greater needs for communications and data transfers. An intranet can reduce your bills for phone, fax, and shipping, and will help your locations work more closely together.

As software prices get cheaper and new easy-to-use tools come on the market to manage intranets, it makes sense for a greater range of companies to take advantage of them. My two cents' worth is that if you even think there might be a 50-50 chance that you should use an intranet, you owe it to yourself to take a look. Next to email, intranets are the most consistently profitable use of Internet technology.

What businesses do with intranets

What do businesses do with intranets? That depends on who you ask. Here are the results of three surveys from the second half of 1996. Items on the following page are listed in order of popularity.

Rank	Zona Research	Collaborative Strategies	Web Week
1.	Access manuals	Publish internally	Post pages with corporate & dept. info
2.	Post personal pages	Share info & support	Search corp. databases
3.	Access product & marketing info	Search for info	Collect info from employees
4.	Post job openings	Post calendars & schedules	Collaborate
5.	Revise, approve documents	Access info from a known location	Reach outside databases
6.	Access employee info	Edit documents	Other
7.	Post calendars & schedules	Manage projects in a distributed workgroup	
8.	Access databases	Access remote applications	
9.		Support mobile workers	

You'll notice several similarities between the three sets of results, and some differences. Obviously, which intranet activities are most popular depends a great deal on who you ask and what questions you ask them. My experience confirms *Web Week*'s finding as to the number one use. Corporate and departmental pages are a feature of every intranet I've ever seen. (*Web Week* estimated 96 percent.)

Let's take a look at some of the actual benefits reported by businesses that have put intranets to work.

Human resources managers love intranets

In the same way that many businesses are pulled onto the Internet by marketing people, many businesses set up an intranet due to demand from human resources (HR) managers. The need is immediately apparent. HR pros must frequently distribute updated information to everyone in your company, and they spend much of their time on the phone with employees answering variations on the same questions over and over again. Intranets are the best news to hit the HR profession since help-wanted ads.

Actually, a help-wanted section is one of the features most commonly found on intranets. Web pages that list job openings let employees know about opportunities for themselves and encourage them to act as informal recruiters. Job pages are easy to create and easy to use. Chevron lets employees review openings by experience type, managerial level, and geographical location.

One of the most popular sections of any intranet covers employee benefits. Want to draw heavy visitor traffic? Create a Vacation Policy FAQ. You can also let employees reallocate investments in their 401(k) plans.

One company where I worked gave all managers a set of looseleaf three-ring binders containing benefits, policies, and procedures. It seemed that every week I received updates, corrections, and instructions on what to delete and what to replace. I fought a losing battle to keep the binders up to date and finally gave up. An intranet makes it easier to update employee information than any paper system possibly could. Saves wear and tear on your managers, too.

Your intranet can also process timesheets. Employees can fill out an online form, which can be reviewed and approved by managers before moving to payroll.

You can see why human resource managers love intranets. They save work, and an intranet is much cheaper than paying a person to explain benefits over the phone and less tedious.

Sales and marketing people love intranets

To provide Visa International's employees with contact information on its 19,000 member banks, the company regularly published a 2–volume directory 8 inches thick. Now Visa puts the information on its intranet, saving publishing costs and providing more up-to-date information for Visa's marketing staff.

If you're looking for high visibility and fast payback for your intranet, use it as Roche Laboratories did, to provide data for your marketing, sales, and customer service people. You can store your latest prices, product photographs, and specifications. When sales reps visit customers, they can prepare customized sales literature with your most recent information and prices.

Intranets make it relatively easy to build and reach databases. You can create, for example, a database of status reports on customer problems and make it accessible to all account managers and customer service reps. If your customer service people hear about product defects, they can enter them in a Web form, making them instantly available to your R&D and quality people.

Sales and customer service people are often heavy users of private newsgroups on intranets, using them to conduct ongoing virtual conferences. Sales reps share tips on closing sales. Service people exchange information to quickly answer customer questions. Some businesses host a newsgroup with a single important customer as its topic, making important information about that customer available instantly throughout the company.

If your business sells its own products at a discount to employees, you can set up an online store on your intranet. Nortel markets telecommunications products. It runs a Web store where employees buy telephones to use in their homes.

Intranets benefit your technical staff

Programmers and network administrators at most companies are overloaded and will look askance at any project that promises more work or that might rock their boat (and make them look bad) by blowing up in their faces. An intranet may not be a panacea for them, but it should be relatively painless.

One advantage of intranet technology is that *it's proven*. This stuff works. It has been tested by tens of thousands of businesses. Another advantage is that an intranet is fast to set up and produces results quickly—exactly the kind of project that makes technical people look good.

This is because intranets are *easy to develop*. Web projects are simple client/server applications in which the creator doesn't need to worry about programming the client.

From a technical standpoint, intranets are also *simple to administer.*

Your technical people might also find uses of their own for your intranet. Several companies produce tools that distribute and install software programs through an intranet to employees' computers, eliminating the need for technicians to load disks into one computer at a time. One is InstallFromTheWeb, a $400 Windows program by InstallShield (**www.installshield.com**).

Intranets train workers

One of the fastest-growing areas of intranet use is employee training. At Boeing Co., a staff of more than 20 teachers, subject specialists, and course developers contributed to a Center for Leadership and Learning section within Boeing's intranet. Supervisors, managers, and executives can search a catalog of courses and read synopses. The success of the catalog has led to plans to deliver hundreds of courses over the intranet.

Online training does not take much more work to set up than a procedures manual and is much more effective. Employee orientation can be automated as a self-guided series of Web pages, with interactive tests built in. Businesses use intranets for training manuals and self-paced tutorials on subjects as diverse as how to use a cash register and how to manage people.

Many companies now offer training courses you can buy and drop into place on your intranet, with no programming or lesson-writing of your own. Oracle (**www.oracle.com**) offers more than 100 information technology courses that you can download for $50-$500 per course. Oracle also sells a product that lets you store and customize courses and distribute them on your intranet. Other sellers of intranet courses include AimTech Corp. (**www.aimtech.com**), DigitalThink Inc. (**www.digitalthink.com**), and Street Technologies (**www.streetinc.com**).

Some companies sell tools so you can create intranet courses and tests of your own. Stanford Testing Systems' product IBAuthor (**http://ibt.testprep.com**) creates lessons and tests. IB Author costs $1,000 and up and is available in Windows, Mac, and Unix versions.

Metasys makes a very easy-to-use $500 Mac program called QuizMaker that lets you create, publish, and score Web-based tests. Your tests can include pictures, animation, and audio. It performs statistical analyses of results. You can use QuizMaker to create exams for job seekers and employee assessment as well as training. For a demo, visit **www.metasys.co.jp/software.html**.

Intranets increase teamwork and community

We mentioned that you can use private newsgroups to conduct ongoing virtual conferences about marketing. Your people can also use newsgroups for any other topic. For less formal conferencing, you can also use online *chat*, which gives participants the type-written equivalent of several people speaking at once—kinda like an online cocktail party.

Private newsgroups are popular with most businesses. You can arrange newsgroup discussions according to topic or to the audience you want; a company-wide discussion on quality, for example, or an ongoing forum for manufacturing engineers. By asking a question on your newsgroup, a worker can focus the total IQ of your company on solving a problem. This type of online conferencing can reduce the number of meetings your people hold.

Intranets link distant locations and provide tools enabling dispersed teams to work together. Ford Motor Companies' engineers in Asia, Europe, and the U.S. used its intranet to jointly design the 1996 Taurus.

Distributed work group applications like these increase coordination. You can buy or cheaply build applications such as intranet signup sheets, schedulers, and surveys, as complements or alternatives to traditional groupware.

Replace desktop publishing with desktop information distribution

Picture the paper that floods your in-basket every day: memos, forms, reports, and other paperwork piled high. You have just visualized a key benefit of intranets. When you replace paperwork with intranet publishing, you slash the amount that accumulates in your in-basket, and in everyone else's, too.

Most of that paperwork is sent to you because you might need it sometime. Then again, you might not. But you still have to examine it, classify it, and store it, just in case you need it later. On your intranet, when you need information, you look it up and there it is, waiting for you: information on demand. Want information on personnel policies? Go to your personnel section and get it. You save time wading through the junk information sent to you on the off chance you might need it someday.

That's how an intranet saves people time in storing and retrieving information. You also save time *creating* information. Imagine you need to produce a detailed report. Without your intranet, your finished product might be a 150-page printed copy. Such large business documents are usually not written from scratch. To create that 150-page report, you'd typically spends many hours cutting and pasting, editing material from previous reports. On your intranet, you could present the same information in a couple of hours by creating a few pages of hyperlinks.

Your intranet documents can include online forms for data entry, so they *gather* information as well as provide it. Since there are no printing or distribution costs for adding extra information, you can provide massive amounts of information at little extra expense. Since you have only one master file to update, you can keep your information current. There are no time lags. Information is instantly available throughout your entire company. Eli Lilly & Co. uses its intranet to provide thousands of pages of up-to-date information on pharmaceutical regulations in 120 countries.

Other companies use intranets to store engineering and production documentation so workers at remote facilities can reach technical material. They publish searchable directories of people, products, and suppliers. Of course, they create departmental and personal home pages on their intranets. After time, the information on your intranet will acquire surprising depth and usefulness. With the search tools available for your intranet, you and your co-workers will find that you've grown a rich repository of your collective experiences and expertise; what some people call a corporate knowledge base.

On the other extreme, the cheapness and ease of creating intranet information means you can create temporary documents that are disposable. You can quickly launch an intranet project to handle a short-term opportunity. When you're done, throw it away.

Give presentations over your intranet

Videoconferencing over your intranet is tricky to do and useful for only a few companies. Most businesses, though, give lots of presentations in which one person—or a group of panelists—addresses a larger audience. Software called Auditorium makes that easy to do online (see Figure 10.1).

Your presentation could be an address to employees from your CEO, a training lesson, or a sales presentation to important customers. Auditorium, from PlaceWare, Inc. (**www.placeware.com**), runs on a Netscape, Microsoft, or Apache Web server. Your audience members pull up their Web browsers and go to a special event URL, where they sign in.

Your presenter (or presenters, if this is a group presentation) goes to a special presenter's URL, which shows a seating chart of attendees and has session controls, including a question manager and a tool for

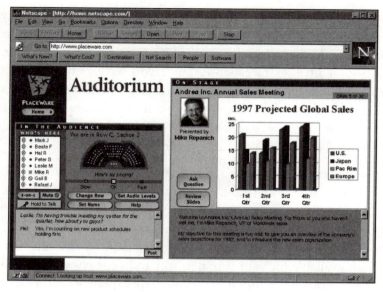

Figure 10.1   Auditorium software lets you conduct presentations to an audience on your intranet and extranet.

annotating "slides" in realtime. The right side of the screen shows a picture of the speaker, displays slides of text and graphics, and provides a spot where audience members can write questions to the presenter.

Audience members hear realtime audio as the presenter speaks and see the slides as they change. They can write questions to the presenter and answer questions as well. They can vote in multiple-choice polls—the virtual equivalent of a show of hands. Audience members can also see who else is in the audience, and send and receive messages from other audience members.

Hewlett-Packard uses Auditorium for meetings with hundreds of customer support engineers around the globe. HP also has created a Desktop Classroom for one-hour brown-bag classes with Auditorium. Other users of the software include Intel, C|net, and the Public Broadcasting System.

Auditorium is efficient enough to link via 28.8 Kbps modems. Web browsers that use it need a special plug-in. Auditorium server software with 100 text-only plug-ins costs $150 per seat. The server software with 100 text and audio plug-ins costs $300 per seat. Plug-ins for additional seats are available at quantity discounts. Auditorium is a bit overpriced, but because it is so efficient and easy to use, it can be very valuable for many businesses.

But wait! There's more!

No, not a Ginsu knife. You probably already know that Microsoft Office 97, Lotus SmartSuite 97, and Corel Office 7 are all tailored for intranet use. Almost every other kind of business function that involves information is also becoming wired to intranets.

Some intranet uses surprise me. For instance, QuickTime is a free Windows, Unix, and Mac software program that I normally associate with presentations of movies, audio, and 3D graphics on Web pages. But QuickTime also provides services for time synchronization and compression management. Manufacturers can use QuickTime for process control, since a QuickTime "movie" is actually a time-based series of instructions, which can run and take input from a milling machine just as easily as a video device.

How about ISO9000 certification? Quality certification normally produces huge masses of paperwork, but companies have been using intranets for ISO9000 since 1994, including Amdahl Corp., Sun Microsystems, and Sybase. The Schlumberger Dowell oilfield services division of Schlumberger Ltd. certified nine locations using an intranet system with more than 4,000 quality management documents. A **mailto:** link at the bottom of each document makes possible the review and approval process that ISO9000 requires for document changes. For more info, email Schlumberger Dowell's quality manager Mike Gibbons at **gibbons@sugar-land.dowell.slb.com**.

Accounting software has become intranetized. Ifas.net by Bi-Tech (www.bi-tech.com) handles fund accounting for governments and schools. It runs on a Microsoft Web server and lets employees use Web browsers to create and view custom reports. As Figure 10.2 shows, information in Ifas.net reports is hyperlinked so you can click on an amount to see detailed data. Great Plains Software (www.gps.com) sells Web-enabled software as well, but it sadly lacks Ifas.net's ability to click for more information.

Many companies submit purchase requests and purchase authorizations on their intranets. Some have employees order supplies from an online catalog maintained by the purchasing department.

Companies use intranets for equipment tracking, and for fixed asset management. Other popular tasks are workflow software for project management, task status reporting, and recording shipping information. (Shipping people record shipments, and customer service reps can retrieve the data to answer

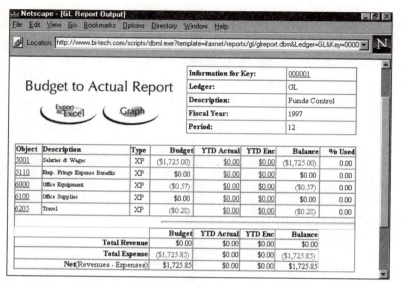

Figure 10.2   Click on a link in this Ifas.net General Ledger report to drill down for more detailed information.

questions. Not as nifty as the Fedex package tracking Web site, but still a great way to cool off customer tempers.)

Some companies place advertising banners on their intranet pages. I've found three kinds of intranet advertisements:

1. Offers from the company itself. These can be as mundane as "Remember to turn in your timesheets today" or as flashy as animated ads for products in an in-house store.

2. Banners for charities that the company endorses.

3. Advertisements for affiliated firms and/or companies that offer discounts to employees, such as local restaurants or travel agencies. Projected revenue from these banners can be used to help managers buy into an intranet project.

If that doesn't give you a few ideas, maybe you'll be more stimulated if we push the Net envelope a little extra.

What's an extranet?

No, an extranet is not a leftover intranet. "Extra" here is used in the sense of "external," or outside. If you had an extranet, you would offer a carefully defined (and tightly secured) subset of the information on your internal network to outsiders. This doesn't mean *all* outsiders, like your company's Web site, but only a chosen group, like frequent customers or established suppliers.

The Roche Laboratories story at the beginning of this chapter told how Roche used its extranet to market to its physician customers.

Another example is electronics parts supplier AMP. Its intranet includes a database with information about more than 70,000 parts. Without access to AMP's database, it took the company's customers about 45 minutes to find and order a part from its catalogs. Now that AMP allows access to its parts database, it takes customers about three minutes. Its customers also get product information and schematic drawings from AMP's database of parts information.

Construction industry supplier Wickes Lumber Co. gives builders extranet access to review account information, receive invoices, pay bills securely with credit cards, and check inventory at 108 Wickes stores. Customers like WickesNet because they no longer have to waste time matching invoices to purchase orders and can place an order, have Wickes' central office process the order, and then send it to the appropriate Wickes yard for fulfillment, all within 15 minutes.

Getting down to nets and bolts, Bell Fasteners used to mail floppy disks every week listing the 25,000 fasteners it carries. With 2,500 customers, that was expensive. Now customers look up information on Web pages that query Bell's internal database and build orders with an electronic shopping cart feature that lets customers see a running total of their purchases.

Twenty Wall Street firms share investment information on an extranet that uses a product called Continuum by PFN (**www.pfn.com**). The system links brokerages like Morgan Stanley with managers of large investment funds, including Fidelity Investments. Continuum is a $1,000 Unix and Windows NT program that lets intranets set up changing, on-demand links with each other.

Extranet means extra problems

Depending on whose survey you read last, between 8 percent and 39 percent of companies with Web sites also have extranets. The percentage with intranets is much higher. Why do fewer firms have extranets?

Security is one reason. You might want a customer to be able to look up information on your products and zap an order directly into your sales order processing system, but you don't want that same customer messing around with your payroll database. Or your top-secret R&D plans for microwave waffle irons.

Technical difficulty is another. Compare extranets to their simpler intranet cousins. The easiest intranet applications let people read Web pages and documents. The harder intranet applications require a new database and software that builds Web pages on the fly to display database content. The hardest intranet applications reach into your legacy systems, those old, huge, and absolutely essential databases that sit at the very heart of your business. Mess with your heart, it stops, and your business stops.

Most extranets *start* with data that's in a legacy system. On top of that, pile the new programming required, and the security worries, and other problems. A Bosnian peace agreement is easier. You can understand why only large companies have the resources to develop an extranet, and why extranet project managers without enough resources develop the emotional stability of a Chihuahua.

Some companies have saved millions of dollars with extranets, and others have generated multimillion-dollar sales increases. Extranets can be very valuable. Just keep in mind that building extranets is for grownups only.

Test drive an intranet

Learning about Web sites is easy. You'll find hundreds of thousands of them clogging the Net that you can visit and study to find what works, what doesn't, and what is just plain weird.

Not so with intranets. They are all neatly tucked away *inside* company networks, safe from the eyes of prying outsiders like you and me. So how can you get ideas? Fortunately, a few companies have opened sample intranets on the Web. Feast your peepers on the five on the following page.

Airius Intranet Center   The folks at Netscape created this fictional company's intranet for you. Netscape suggests that you copy its HTML here and use it to make your own intranet page template. **www.netscape.com/comprod/at_work/vip/index.htm**

Intranet Demo   This Open Text demonstration puts you in the driver's seat of a candy manufacturer's intranet. First you customize your demo by entering your name, your company name, and other data. Then you go through your company's fictional sales, marketing, personnel, and engineering departments. What products are in stock? What price changes are coming up? You can look up phone numbers in your company phone book. **http://salesnet.opentext.com:8080/welcome.html**

Visual Employee Benefits Department   Resource Financial Group assists companies with personnel and benefit needs. If your business uses its services, Resource Financial will provide you with a free human resources site for your intranet. This sample demonstrates the fictional human resources site of Vaporware Inc. **www.benefits.com/vapor/index.htm**

Acme, Inc. Production Summary   An intranet consulting company provides demonstration pages from a fictional manufacturer's intranet. Acme? Isn't that the company that sells defective products to Wile E. Coyote? **www.etechinc.com/acmeinc**

Speedware Calendar Demo   An intranet calendar system by Speedware demonstrates its software tools for building intranet applications. **dallas.speedware.com**

Intranet success stories

I've heard dozens of Webmasters complain about World Wide Web sites that are undervisited on the *outside* Internet. I have never heard anyone say the same about their intranet sites. Success stories are the norm.

Hewlett Packard has one of the most-publicized intranets. HP actually runs hundreds of internal Web servers for everything from accounting to warehousing, but the one that caught the media's eye is called ESP. That stands for Electronic Sales Partner, and it solved a big problem with HP's worldwide sales force. Before ESP, more than half of what HP published for its sales representatives either never reached them or was thrown away. HP created ESP as an intranet for its sales force and used it to serve more than 13,000 documents:

presentation materials, product data sheets, white papers, even interviews with HP executives. Everything is searchable through a search engine from Verity, Inc. HP conducted hour-long presentations on ESP in its larger offices and sent small offices a 25-minute videocassette to introduce it. The end result is that ESP saves each rep an average of five hours per week, and eliminates hundreds of mailings that cost $10,000 each in printing and postage.

Pacific Gas & Electric runs 70 to 80 applications for its 23,000 employees on its intranet. One is a form employees use to send a message to another employee's pager. Another is a custom-built interface to make Lotus Notes accessible from a Web browser. Since many PG&E employees work outdoors, one of its intranet's most popular pages is a weather page with live camera views from three locations and detailed live weather data and forecasts for most of the state of California.

Commercial real estate firm Cushman & Wakefield links 40 locations with a wide area network that runs TCP/IP plus LANs running Novell NetWare. To run its intranet over that existing network, the company bought a Compaq ProSignia 500 to use as its intranet server. (If you're technically inclined, it had 64 megabytes of RAM and a 5-gigabyte hard disk.) The Cushman & Wakefield intranet launched with human resources information and corporate data for a cost under $10,000 and was a hit with employees. The company added data on commercial real estate properties and links to a sales commission system that runs on an IBM AS/400 computer.

To add content to J.P. Morgan's intranet, employees must fill out an online registration form. The form records information for network administrators and helps its Verity and Architext search engines categorize the content. J.P. Morgan uses its intranet to distribute two employee newsletters, an electronic suggestion box called "Ideabox" (the best ideas are posted for all to see), cafeteria menus, worldwide office locations, approved hotels for company travelers, and (no surprise) personnel information. To show Internet-illiterate employees how to use browsers, company trainers conducted events called "Internet Cafe" sessions at all offices, combining browser lessons with coffee and snacks.

One of the advantages an intranet has over the Internet is speed. Most LANs move data faster than the outside Internet. For instance, an Ethernet LAN's speed is 10 megabits per second and a Token-Ring LAN's is 4 megabits per second. The intranet at Lawrence Livermore Laboratory puts that speed to work. It includes videos, sound, and an interactive test as part of intranet-delivered safety training lessons that all new employees take.

To expand use of its intranet, Sandia Laboratories created WebCo, an internal organization that helps employees and departments put up Web pages and intranet applications. Sandia's intranet includes a property management application so an employee can track computers and other items inventoried in his or her name. Another application schedules conference rooms, including whiteboards, overhead projectors, and other equipment and supplies. An archive of internal technical articles is searchable by keywords, and employee manuals and newsletters are on the Sandia intranet. Newsletter publishers provide an online subscription form for signups. When a new issue is put on the Web, subscribers are notified by email.

What can go wrong?

Most intranets succeed, but that doesn't mean that problems don't crop up. Most intranet difficulties that I've run across could have been avoided with planning and careful monitoring on a few key points.

ABANDONED BABIES

Many people in your company will be enthusiastic about creating an intranet project, from complex thousand-page manuals to departmental home pages. The problem begins *after* the project is created and launched.

Until it is launched, most intranet projects are fed and cared for as tenderly as a child, but after the project is launched into the world, many become abandoned babies, dumped on a stranger's doorstep or left to fend for themselves.

Before you start any intranet project, make sure you are clear who will ultimately be responsible for updating and maintaining it. Like a page on your company's outside Web site, intranet projects can take more effort to update than to create. Define specific intervals for updating a project, checking phone numbers in your directory once a month, for example. Unless your intranet pages are accurate, people won't trust them. Make sure you define in writing a seemingly trivial aspect: Who updates links? Somebody needs to check and update hypertext links frequently. This is best done by a person in the department that a particular intranet project serves; someone from HR on a human resources page, for instance.

No schoolin'

Several surveys on intranets revealed a common problem. People who create an intranet usually know how to use it. After all, they planned it. They built it. They know where everything is, and what all those funny little buttons do.

Unfortunately, the rest of the company hasn't a clue. At least, until they've received some training. Training employees how to use an intranet and how to find stuff on it increases your odds of success more often than almost any other single factor.

Lack of employee training in how to use your intranet can increase your chances of failure and lengthen your roll-out time. Either budget time and money for training, or expect apathy, substandard response, and a need to go back and educate employees later.

You'll find it especially rewarding to train employees who don't have computer skills. Don't train until your first-stage intranet is actually up and available. If you train employees before they can get their hands on your intranet and use it, they will forget what you taught them and need to be trained all over again.

The wrong publishers

Would you ask your computer programmers to write your company's advertisements? How about having your technical documentation people create your management strategy? Of course not, but when it comes to their intranets, many companies do just that.

If you build an intranet, make sure your technical staff does not end up in the Web publishing business.

Responsibility for creating and publishing intranet information should rest with the departments who create that same information offline. Let the human resources department publish all HR intranet information. Let your marketing people create tools for marketing and sales people. Your technical staff should be available to help and guide the other departments, and will provide the delivery mechanism, but don't saddle the technical folks with the extra work of creating everybody else's intranet information.

INTRANET KUDZU

Web applications often creep into an intranet without any thought or planning as to how they will fit with other intranet applications, or with your company's strategy and goals. Intranet applications can quickly kudzu into a mess that covers the earth and at the same time provide services that your employees regard as vital to their jobs, making a jungle that is difficult to change. You can prevent this with a minor amount of forethought. If someone doesn't act as an overall coordinator and clearinghouse for all proposed intranet projects, expect to quickly grow an intranet both essential for your business and impossible to manage.

UNFINDABLE INFORMATION

"The Web technology makes the creation and publishing of information easy. It also makes the retrieval and viewing of the information easy. What is not easy is finding the relevant information," writes Steven Telleen (apparently the guy who coined the word *intranet*) in "IntraNet Methodology: Concepts and Rationale," an intelligent analysis of intranets at **www.amdahl.com/doc/ products/bsg/intra/concepts.html.** Don't make your valuable data impossible to find. From the start, plan to make *everything* on your intranet both searchable and also accessible by menus.

HARD TO USE

If your information is harder to reach than an employee thinks it's worth, the employee will either not bother with it, or will find a non-intranet way to get it. The definition of success for intranet data is not when you make information available, but when your staff finds it so easy to read and so reliable that your intranet becomes the *preferred* method of reaching information. If your employees resist your new pages and prefer printed manuals, the problem is not with your employees. They are merely giving you a clue. The problem is with the presentation of your material, and how easy it is to reach.

CGI OVERLOAD

This is a more technical problem, with results visible to even the most non-technical intranet visitor: They can't get in. Each visitor to a page that uses a CGI script—such as an online form—causes a separate copy of that CGI script to be launched, each requiring its own computer resources. CGI does not scale upwards efficiently, so overuse of many CGI pages can become a choke point. If you plan to make many CGI pages for your intranet, pay close attention to your hardware needs so you aren't unexpectedly forced to convert to a faster, more expensive server computer.

SECURITY BREACHES

Security is more important on your intranet than on your outside Web site. Intranet security problems I've seen occurred mostly when network administrators simply assumed that there was no danger from employees. Actually, more computer security problems come from workers (usually accidentally, but not always) than from any other source. Breaches are preventable. An intranet is easier to secure than an outside Internet. If you follow the basic security precautions outlined in Chapters 7 and 8, you can protect employee salaries, meeting minutes, sales forecasts, and other confidential information.

How to grow your intranet

Take a look at 9 steps toward building an effective intranet.

1. Pick a life-saving pilot project.

To start your intranet, you need a champion who wants an intranet and wants it now. Look for someone in pain. Find people who must suffer to distribute information to employees and who think of your intranet as one big aspirin. Many companies begin intranets to help human resources people.

An alternative approach is to find someone who distributes killer data, life-or-death information that must frequently go to many people, the more time-sensitive the better. For Turner Home Entertainment, the killer data that led to the company's intranet was Nielsen television ratings. Every day, ratings had to be distributed to people spread across many locations.

2. Define your pilot's audience.

The number of people served by your first project and their locations will determine how widespread your intranet's first steps must be; what security you will need; and what the technical considerations, budget, and timeframe will be. A human resources intranet project, for instance, will almost always be companywide. An R&D intranet might be confined to a single building or just part of one.

3. Define your pilot's technical and security needs.

First, you'll need a computer to act as a dedicated server to handle your intranet traffic. You might have a small, limited pilot, but plan for extra capacity to handle rapid growth. As soon as you put one piece of information up, others in your company will want to add their own ideas.

Your server doesn't need Unix. You can use a Mac or a PC. What operating system will your server run? Who will install it? You'll need intranet server software, TCP/IP software, and Web browsers for employees. Make sure the Web server software you use on your intranet server has privacy features such as file access control. You'll probably want a firewall. You might need Java, Perl (for CGI scripts and online forms), and Web page creation software. Plan for search engine software and probably software to access your corporate databases.

You might want to tack an Internet email gateway on all your email post offices. You'll have to decide whether to assimilate or eliminate legacy network technologies like SNA and NetWare.

Make sure your security plan includes file management and *backups*.

If your budget and your needs are modest, you can set up a simple intranet without a Web server and without running TCP/IP software. Just put all your HTML files on your Novell server, make sure that everyone's main disk drive contains an identical HTML intranet home page, and give everyone a Netscape browser and a freeware file called **mozilla.dll**. You won't be able to use Java, CGI, or forms, but you'll have a simple and fast intranet. Your employees can use the ability of Netscape to read local files to reach your intranet.

4. Choose who will create your pilot and who will *maintain* it.

Departments that want stuff on your intranet should be responsible for publishing their own documents and data, and for maintaining them. Decide who will create the content for your pilot project. Have that person or persons outline their proposed content and describe who it will affect and how.

Everyone will be eager to create new stuff. Few will be eager to update it. Who will update expired links? Come up with a *written* plan that names peoples' names.

Creating an intranet infrastructure takes three separate development efforts: 1) technical planning, 2) content planning, and 3) intranet management. When you have a plan for all three, a timetable, and a budget in hand, seek approval from your managers.

5. Get management support.

By this point, you have your ducks all lined up in a row. Now it's time to get a blessing from the Pope. Don't try to convince managers that an intranet will *make* money, but document how it will save money and time. Remember to get approval for *ongoing* intranet expenses and not just setup. For most companies this will be minimal, but if you develop a large-scale intranet, maintenance can be substantial. For example, 11 employees work on Turner Home Entertainment's intranet. Most of the ongoing work in any intranet is editorial labor on content. Technical support tends to be minimal.

6. Create publishing guidelines, then build your content.

Plan and storyboard your pilot project. Develop presentation standards and use them from the start to make your intranet look and feel consistent, and to reinforce your company's identity. You can create templates to save time in building your project, reduce repeated effort, and avoid rebuilding oddball pages.

Don't forget that the employees who create—from human resources or any other department—will need a couple of days of training in HTML and Web page creation.

At the same time, your technical people can set up your intranet server, add search engine software, and build hooks to document archives and your corporate databases.

7. Launch and promote your life-saving pilot.

Open your intranet and celebrate. Then, like an outside Internet site, you must *sell* your intranet's contents. Departments must actually *promote* their information to let employees know it's available and where to find it. You can adapt some of the techniques from Chapter 16 to build companywide use of your intranet.

8. Measure your success and report to management.

Measure the use of your intranet—your server statistics, number of newsgroup messages posted, etc.—and measure any savings: HR salaries, printing costs, fax/phone bills, and so forth.

You'll need facts and figures to justify your intranet to top management so you can add new content and features to your intranet, and maybe even get a raise. If employees send you email testimonials, include them with your facts and figures. Support from within always helps.

9. Add more intranet projects and reach more people.

With one success under your belt, it's time to reach for more. Make a plan for future intranet additions of content and applications. Chances are you'll hear suggestions and requests from many people who've used your pilot project.

If your pilot was not implemented companywide, plan to extend your intranet to all employees with computer access. Remember to include remote employees and road warriors. In many companies, remote employees are the heaviest intranet users. You might think of adding DirecPC for faster access (see Chapter 4) or 56 Kbps lines for remote offices.

If your employees use dial-up telephone lines to reach your intranet, get lines that are separate from your voice lines. Call waiting and other voice services create bad side effects on lines used for data communication.

Intranet products and tools

New software products for intranets are launched at a wonderful pace— literally more than one every day. Here are a few to get you started.

Swiss Army knives

These software products offer multiple functions for intranets.

InfoPilot from FirstFloor Inc. is a hot new product that speeds production, management, and distribution of company information over an intranet. It automatically checks for broken links and includes management abilities unavailable on other products. It requires either a Windows NT or Unix server and a plug-in for any Windows or Mac browser to access the data. The price is $3,400 for a server and 25 clients. Check this one out before you look at others. **www.firstfloor.com**

Intranet Genie from Frontier Technologies comes on one CD-ROM for Windows NT. It contains a Web server, applications (conference room management, purchase requisition, expense reports, others), Verity's Topic search engine, Web administration tools (can restrict visitors to specific pages and assign Webmasters to each page), Web authoring tools, secure POP email, security programs, access control, and the CyberSearch search tool. You'll need to add a firewall. **www.frontiertech.com**

Livelink Intranet from Open Text costs $12,500 to $130,000, depending on how many bells and whistles you want. An average configuration runs about $50,000. For Windows NT, Livelink includes Netscape Commerce Server and the Livelink search engine. It can index and search more than 40 file formats (Acrobat, HTML, Word, WordPerfect, PDF, etc.). It includes a document management system. British Petroleum used this product to put millions of pages of technical manuals on its intranet for the engineers maintaining the Alaskan pipeline. **www.openlink.com**

Columbus is Windows software from Hummingbird Inc. It calls Columbus a drop-in intranet server, with document authoring tools and security that lets an administrator restrict or allow user activities by type and time of day. **www.hummingbird.com**

Enterprise/Access is a $20,000 Unix product from Apertus (**www.apertus.com**) that links with your current computer systems—on whatever hardware platform you use—so you can present your data with a Web face. Enterprise/Access communicates across your existing network. For a quick visual demonstration of this valuable tool, check out the before-and-after pictures at **www.apertus.com/prod/access/demo/before.htm**

Action Works Metro costs $40,000 and gives you 22 intranet workflow applications. For another $40,000, you can buy a development system to make your own. A starter kit costs $10,000. This Windows NT software lets customers and employees track progress of projects. The 22 applications include software for human resources, sales, marketing, finance, accounting, and routing documents for approval. The company claims it allows you to build a workflow app in 10 minutes. **www.actiontech.com**

Ultimus is a lower-cost Windows NT intranet workflow solution, costing $3,400 for a starter kit. It uses email to reroute workflow. It's easy to set up and administer Ultimus, but the product doesn't make it as easy for users to track a job as the more expensive Metro. **www.ultimus1.com**

Netscape's Free App Foundry provides free intranet software you can use: two finance forms to reduce paper flow, an employee survey-taker, and a corporate directory with a built-in organization chart. **www.netscape.com/one_stop/ intranet_apps/index.html**

Discussion groups

Adding newsgroup-like discussion groups to your intranet is easy and relatively inexpensive. They often turn out to be extremely popular features.

Collabra Share provides very good discussion group capabilities. **www. collabra.com**

Webboard costs $259 and works with any Win 95 or NT Web server. From O'Reilly & Associates, the product runs up to 255 separate boards with unlimited conferences on each. Webboard also provides automatic message archiving, a valuable feature that not only stores past messages, but provides Web pages where your people can easily reach them. **http://webboard.ora.com**

Web document databases

These handy tools let you take your existing archives of documents and convert them to Web pages. They automatically convert your documents from common formats to HTML-readable files. They provide fast ways for you to present large amounts of information on your intranet with minimal reworking.

DynaText is a $22,500 Unix package from Electronic Book Technologies that converts documents to HTML, but has a reputation as being difficult to administer. **www.inso.com**

Folio InfoBase Web Server is a $7,000 Windows NT package that converts documents to HTML on the fly. This is not a generic Web server (in spite of its misleading name), but only converts documents. It's easy to set up and gives you a searchable database of documents. **www.folio.com**

Web search engines

If your intranet consists of more than a couple hundred documents, a search engine will be a well-appreciated addition to your intranet. Fortunately, you have many to choose from.

Excite for Web Servers is free software that comes in Unix and Windows NT versions, but it can search ASCII and HTML files only. **www.excite.com/ navigate**

Glimpse, Glimpse HTTP, and *WebGlimpse* are three indexing and search tools offered free from the University of Arizona at **http://glimpse.cs. arizona.edu:1994**. They are written for Unix.

Fulcrum Surfboard comes in Unix and Windows NT versions. It costs $6,250 and up, and can search many file formats. **www.fulcrum.com**

InText Retrieval Engine is a $7,500 product for Unix and Windows NT that can search many file formats. **www.intext.com**

PL Web Turbo from Personal Library Software is a $5,000 product for Unix and Windows NT that searches many file formats. **www.pls.com**

Search'97 is a well-regarded $10,000 product from Verity Inc. Available for Unix and Windows NT, it conducts topic searches in several file formats. **www.verity.com**

WAIS Server and *WAIS Toolkit* are available free from the European Microsoft Windows NT Academic Centre. You can guess that this software is for Windows NT. You might like to know that it searches only ASCII and HTML file formats. A free Unix version is available elsewhere on the Net. **http:// emwac.ed.ac.uk**

Web Catalog is a misleadingly-named, inexpensive ($1,000) Windows NT and Mac product from Pacific Coast Software that searches only tab-delimited text. **www.pacific-coast.com**

Web database query software

Seek and ye shall receive, at least if your intranet has a search form hooked up to your company's databases. To do that, you need a software product that can read the CGI input received from your online form and can return something in HTML-able format.

Cold Fusion - This $500 product from Allaire Corp. is available for Windows 95 and NT. It lets HTML pages submit SQL requests to databases and view results. **www.allaire.com**

DB/Text WebServer from Inmagic Inc. converts database files to HTML on demand. It costs $5,000 and creates custom results pages, but it will only link to text and data in its own propriety format. A new variation, *DB/Text Intranet Spider,* uses Lycos's spider technology to search and index all pages (HTML and other formats) on your intranet. **www.inmagic.com**

WebServer from Oracle is a $2,500 package available in Unix and Windows NT versions. **www.oracle.com**

Web.sql from Sybase is a $5,000 Unix product. **www.sybase.com**

Security tools

Internet Monitor from Optimal Networks analyzes intranet and Internet traffic to show who visits **www.nastystuff.com** and who doesn't. This $1,500 Windows product reports, but does not block access, and is available in English, French, and German versions. **www.optimal.com**

Net Access Manager lets you block employee access to undesirable Web, FTP, and Usenet resources. It costs $500-$12,500, depending on your number of users. **www.sequeltech.com**

Webstalker Pro sits behind your firewall to monitor activities that are authorized and those that aren't. It alerts administrators when a potential problem occurs. **www.haystack.com**

WebSense from NetPartner Internet Solutions includes a database (updated daily) of 50,000 sites so you can restrict access. You can restrict by category as well: porn, sports, games, retail shopping, job searching, and more than 20 others. WebSense runs on Windows NT servers and costs $500. **www. netpart.com**

More intranet info

★★★★★ *Intranet Resource Center* - A very good directory of intranet resources on the Net, plus articles on the subject from *CIO* magazine. **www.cio.com/WebMaster/wm_irc.html**

★★★★★ *Intranet Journal* - In spite of its name, this is not a periodical, but an extremely valuable resource spot on intranets. It includes Intranet Soundings, a spam-free moderated discussion group where you can ask questions about intranets and get thoughtful answers from the pros. Follow the links to Netscape for actual screens from the intranets of 3M, Cushman & Wakefield, and National Semiconductor. **www.intranetjournal.com**

★★★★ *Intranet Business Strategies* by Melanie Hill (1996) Wiley, ISBN 0-471-16374-0. If you're going to do a serious intranet project, you need a whole book about it. This one gets my bet as the best intranet strategy book for businesspeople, although I wish it had more depth in a couple of areas.

★★★★ *Intranet Advantage* by Shel Holtz (1996) Ziff-Davis Press, ISBN 1-56276-427-6. Holtz's book provides a slightly different point of view than Hill's, making it a good intranet implementation companion.

★★★ *How to Implement a Successful Intranet Site* is a multimedia course (including free access to a mentor) focused on a specific job category: accountants. This $200 course by the American Institute of Certified Public Accountants helps you make sure accounting and finance needs (such as confidentiality of payroll records) are met by an intranet project. To order, call (800) 862-4272.

CHAPTER **11**

Marketing to Internet Customers

"With the Web, the challenge is not to Tell & Sell, but to Learn & Earn. Information is the communicable form of knowledge. The opportunistic company is at least as interested in knowing as it is in telling, in obtaining information as in disseminating it."

—Doc Searles, president, The Searles Group

Theodore Levitt made the seemingly obvious but pivotal observation that *the purpose of a business is to get and keep customers*. To do that, he continued, you have to do those things that make people want to do business with you. What things make people want to buy on the Internet?

Three things: cost, time, and direct contact. Peter Drucker wrote that a new technology won't be commonly used unless it offers a tenfold advantage in cost. Yes, the Internet reduces costs. But two additional powerful factors are at work here.

In addition to dollars, I believe Drucker's tenfold principle also holds true for *time*. The Internet saves an unbelievable amount of time. David Carlick of Poppe Tyson Advertising said the reason for sales success on the Internet is that "Buyers want instant gratification. It's an undeniable force." The Net offers instant gratification for your customer—and for you, the merchant, as well.

The third advantage of the Net is an emotional bond. The Internet gives your customers *direct contact* with your company. It sweeps middlemen aside. This feeds people's hunger for direct relationships. Internet customers want to be heard and want acknowledgment for what they say. The Net lets you tap your clients' demand for dialog. The relationships you build with customers on the Internet can be closer than anything but in-person sales. This closeness rewards your customers and gives you first-hand insight into what they want and need.

Theodore Levitt also observed that you should recognize *relationships* as the most precious assets your company has and invest in them. Realize that you, the seller, have the responsibility to create and nurture these relationships.

So on the Internet, what's the key to building relationships that are profitable?

Don't fall in love with your Web site. Don't fall in love with your product. *Fall in love with your customer.*

 ## Important: Do this first

Before you begin other steps to market on the Internet, the people in your company should set their email software to automatically add signature files to their email messages. If you don't have a signature file on the bottom of your email, or you are not sure what one is, read pages 224–226 in Chapter 9. You'll be glad you did.

Learn about your customers. Understand them. Find out what they want, and give it to them consistently. If you don't, you'll hear about it. That's one way your Internet customers are different. They don't just ignore disappointments, as the general public seems to. Internet prospects fire back at you.

Their responsiveness is wonderful. It's what makes Internet people such lucrative clients: their thirst for interactivity, their need to respond and be heard. If you don't sell to them the way they want, they'll give you corrections until you get it right.

A Gartner Group study estimated that 90 percent of Web sites are created without asking existing customers what they want. Don't fall into this trap. Listen to your customers, and you won't get bypassed for someone more attentive.

Brave new market and medium

Byron Abels-Smit observed, "The Internet is not just a new medium, but a new *kind* of medium. It's like when television was new, at first advertisers treated it like print or radio. Early TV commercials were just type and a voiceover. That only changed as people learned how to effectively use television for marketing. Newspaper rules didn't apply for TV. In the same way, print media and TV rules don't apply to the Internet."

We learn about something new by comparing it with something we already know. So, let's compare the Internet with more familiar marketing channels:

- **Print media.** *Differences:* After something is printed, it eventually becomes out-of-date. Internet information is easy to change and is more often up-to-date. Print offers a low level of customization to match prospects' individual needs—you can do split-run advertising, but you can only fine-tune a split run into broad general categories. The Internet, on the other hand, lets you tailor exactly what information each individual receives, building custom information on the fly based on that prospect's behavior. Print can only send information, it cannot receive—an Internet server can do both. Print media requires a delay of hours or even days to deliver information. The Internet delivers information almost instantly.

  Similarities: What the Internet and print have in common is that both are *high-density* media (offering a large amount of information), both use the written word, and both require layout and visual design.

- **Broadcast media.** *Differences:* By its nature, broadcast is not customizable; radio and television can't communicate different information to different prospects. The Internet can. Broadcast media cannot *receive* information. The Internet can. Broadcast alone cannot complete a sale. An Internet site can handle the entire sales transaction process. Radio and television are *low-density* media; they cannot communicate a large amount of information, as Internet sites can.

  Similarities: What the Internet and broadcast media have in common is that they both can deliver information instantly over a wide geographic area to many prospects.

- **Direct mail.** *Differences:* Direct mail is somewhat customizable—you can send different letters to different prospects, but the Internet is more customizable. You'll encounter long delays between preparation of a mail campaign, delivery of information, and subsequent response. There is almost no delay between the creation of an Internet marketing campaign, its delivery, and its response. The cost per impression of direct mail is large. The Internet's cost per impression is far less.

  Similarities: What direct mail and the Internet have in common is that both are high-density media, both use the written word, both can be made to deliver only to targeted prospects, both can complete a sales transaction, and both are highly measurable. Also, inappropriately targeted direct mail can be seen as somewhat of an intrusion, and inappropriately targeted Internet marketing even more so.

- **Telemarketing.** *Differences:* A telephone salesperson can sell to only one prospect at a time. An Internet site can sell to hundreds of prospects at once. The cost per impression of telephone sales is higher than Internet marketing. Telemarketing is only a medium-density form of media.

  Similarities: Both telemarketing and the Internet can customize and communicate different information to different prospects, and both can receive information, as well as send. Both can complete a transaction, and both are highly measurable. Telemarketing and the Internet share another characteristic: When inappropriately done, both are perceived as an exasperating intrusion.

The Internet is most like . . .

When comparing differences and similarities between the Internet and older marketing channels, it becomes apparent that the Internet actually has more in common with telemarketing than with any other channel. The second-closest match is direct mail. *Internet marketing is a form of direct marketing.*

What is direct marketing? The Direct Marketing Association defines it as "an interactive system of marketing which uses one or more advertising media to effect a measurable response and/or transaction at any location." The Internet is definitely "interactive," and the transaction tracking possible on the Internet gives you "a measurable response." In the association's definition, the phrase "at any location" means that your customer does not have to travel to a physical store to make a purchase. That is certainly true on the Internet.

This doesn't mean that the *only* type of marketing you can do on the Internet is direct marketing. You can also use the Internet for image advertising, or just to provide background information. But to make full use of the marketing potential of the Net, you need to measure responses and track the sources of your Net-generated sales, just as you would for direct mail, infomercials, or any other form of direct marketing. Mass media marketing is different from direct marketing. If your business has no in-house direct marketing expertise, you may want to hire a consultant or an advertising agency who does. If you plan on hiring marketing staff to work on Internet marketing, look for candidates with direct marketing background.

Net publicity vs. Net advertising

This might seem odd, but on the Internet it's hard to tell publicity from advertising. You'll often find heated arguments over whether a certain thing is or is not an Internet advertisement, so classification becomes a matter of opinion.

In printed magazines, the line of demarcation is simple. If you pay for an insertion, it's an advertisement. If you don't pay, it's publicity. But on the Internet, some types of communication are considered advertisements even though they are free. In fact, Internet people will complain loudly if you violate a non-advertising space with a free advertisement. The very term "free advertisement" suggests that there must be another way to differentiate between Internet publicity and Internet advertising besides the paid/free distinction.

Internet marketing communications are like a famous observation from Montaigne: "A word is half his who speaks it, half his who hears it." In other words, when your reader thinks your communication is an ad, it is one. It pays to be aware of your prospects' opinions on this before you launch a campaign that alienates the very people you want to buy from you.

A medium or a market?

When a business uses both traditional advertisements and salespeople, the two complement each other:

- Mass media advertisements reach a large audience.

- Salespeople customize information and process sales transactions for individual buyers.

Most businesses need a blend of mass media advertising and salespeople to have complete marketing capability. This is not true of Internet-based marketing. The Internet can reach a large audience, provide custom information, and process the sales transaction *all by itself.*

As Figure 11.1 shows, the Bank of Montreal built a Web-based mortgage loan system that automates the entire loan application process and can approve a loan within minutes. The Web loan processor needs human assistance only when it runs into problems.

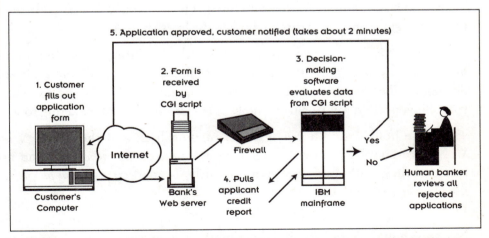

Figure 11.1   The Bank of Montreal's Web loan system approves loans without human intervention.

So the Net gives you different *ways* to reach people. It also gives you different people to reach, prospective buyers with different qualities from your other customers, and different wants.

For these reasons, some say that the Internet is more a *market* than a communications medium. I believe the Net is both. It is a market and a medium, a sea of prospects and a way to reach them. You can improve your business's chance of thriving when you see the Net both ways.

How the Net is different

Let's take a deeper look at how the Internet differs from older marketing approaches.

The Internet is misunderstood because it seems technical

You don't have to learn how to program computers, but to market on the Net, you need to know how to reach and respond to people. That requires learning some technical terms and being comfortable using email, the World Wide Web, and probably newsgroups.

To understand the Net there is no substitute for actually spending hours on it. If you don't have enough hands-on experience actually surfing the Web, finding information, and communicating with Internet people, you will never understand the intense emotional bond that has pushed the Internet to grow so fast so quickly.

Remember, email has become the *preferred* method of business communication of Net users. This is not just a rational, logical decision. It is also an *emotional* decision. What makes people enjoy email so much? If you don't use email yourself, you will never be able to apply email effectively as a marketing tool.

The same holds true for newsgroups, mailing lists, and the World Wide Web. For example, you need to read enough newsgroups to understand not just how they work, but—more importantly for marketers—*how people feel while using newsgroups.*

Solange Van der Moer of Infinity Marketing Group said that to market on the Net you should "Know the terrain. Know the language. Know the customs. Travel and visit often—or better yet, live there. If you only stick a toe in the water, you'll just get a wet toe."

Internet marketing is about *communication* and *interaction*, the foundations of emotional intimacy. If you understand the intimacy of the Net, you can use it to build a stronger emotional bond between you and your customers.

The Internet gives you *two-way* marketing

I mentioned this earlier and will elaborate on it here. For marketers, the Internet's interactivity is both its greatest strength and its biggest puzzle. If you designed print advertisements all your life, it'll take you a while to figure out what to make of this interactivity.

Try thinking of the Net as a *conversation* between you and your prospects and customers. Phineas Gay, of Internet marketing agency Direct Results Group, puts it succinctly: "Internet marketing is *dialogue*—exchanging information— as opposed to *monologue*—which regular advertising is."

In other words, don't talk *at* your Internet customers. Talk *with* them. When you make information available, always provide a way for your readers to respond. Ask how they feel. Ask for responses. Tell how to get more information, and provide your contact information (address, phone, fax, email, Web address). Different prospects want different information, so give them choices. The Net's ability to provide customized information will help you do this. Providing choices will *give your prospects the feeling of control*.

This feeling of control helps your prospects understand your marketing messages. In a recent study by P. L. Wright, subjects who could control the pace of reading and pause to evaluate the information could better explain what they read and could also more clearly define their own points of agreement and disagreement than people who read the same material in a timed video presentation. The more strongly the readers cared about the topic, the more the feeling of control increased comprehension. Wright's findings echo Jean Piaget's and Seymour Papert's theory that the more someone can manipulate and control a presentation, the more that person can internalize it.

The interactivity of information presented on the Internet increases readers' perception of being in control. Anything you do to add to this perception increases a prospect's emotional involvement with your site and your business. Look for opportunities wherever you can to provide your customers with opportunities for control and feedback. Ask for comments about your site. Ask about your service. There are an infinite number of ways to use the

Internet to increase your customers' involvement. Publisher Catbird Press went so far as to put drafts of a novel online so the public could comment and suggest revisions.

In traditional marketing media, prospects don't take your communications as personally as they do on the Net. This intense involvement can lead to intense responses. This can be good, but the emotionality is also what leads to flames and anger as well. Internet customers can be more volatile than your other clients. That's why it's especially important for all your marketing people on the Net to learn about *netiquette*.

"Netiquette is not just about the niceties of behavior or avoiding embarrassment. Netiquette is like the double yellow line in the middle of a highway," said Internet pioneer Howard Rheingold. He's right. Your prospects on the Internet will not tolerate the kind of obtrusive advertising found in other media. Make sure your marketing communications will be welcomed before you post or email them someplace. Always ask permission before emailing advertising or literature to someone. Millions of people pay for each message *received*. They won't be happy to pay for a surprise mailing from your business, and since the Internet makes it easy to respond, they will tell you so. While they're angry, they might also tell thousands of your sales prospects.

SPAM EXPLAINED

You can get short-term sales and tons of hate mail or you can build a loyal, long-lasting base of repeat Internet customers. Which would you rather do?

Fortunately, two pathetic lawyers from Arizona served as global guinea pigs, sparing the rest of us tons of pain. Posting messages to inappropriate places is called a *spam attack*, and the lawyers spammed thousands of Usenet newsgroups with an ad that offered help in getting a U.S. immigration green card. The lawyers made some quick sales, but did nothing to build most prospects' goodwill. They received tens of thousands of hate messages. Upset Internet people used modems to jam the lawyers' phones and fax machine—an example of the backlash made possible by the Net's interactivity.

This sort of newsgroup spamming is harder to do now. Newsgroups are protected by software programs called *cancelbots*. They patrol the groups and remove messages posted on large numbers of newsgroups. Besides cancelbots, the Net offers other punishments for those who abuse its interactivity. Keep in mind that stuff like flames and mail bombs (covered in earlier chapters) can hurt your business.

Wise companies follow the rules of netiquette because it is in their own self-interest to do so. They don't need the pain. ("Gee, I'd wondered why big companies haven't slathered ads all over the newsgroups. I thought it was just because they were polite." Yeah, right. I'm sure Microsoft folds its napkin after every meal.)

SAMPLE SPAM AND ITS AFTERMATH

Here is an example of an actual spammed advertisement and its aftermath. This message appeared on a newsgroup that exists solely to discuss the PageMaker desktop publishing software package.

```
Newsgroups: alt.aldus.pagemaker
Subject: FREE PAGER!
From: (name deleted)@aol.com
Save 10-45% on your long distance service every month.
Attention
Now you can receive big discounts on your long distance calls that other
companies only promise. NTC Dial-1 ressisential and business long distance
services and travel cards offer 6-second billing, prompt payment and
volume discounts combined with great domestec and international rates.
FREE PAGE OFFER LIMITED BY TIME
For more information:
e-Mail
(name deleted)@aol.com
```

"But what's so bad about one little message?" You mean, besides its spelling? This group is about PageMaker. The spammed message is not. It's like a stranger interrupting a Baptist revival meeting with a sermon praising Druids. People read this newsgroup to find out about PageMaker. Some of them pay for each message. They paid to read this commercial. And this spammer is not the only person who does this. Other businesses try, and newsgroup readers feel that to prevent their groups from becoming a sea of advertisements with only occasional islands of news, they must respond forcefully to each and every inappropriate message posted.

Heated responses to an inappropriate newsgroup posting like this are normally emailed directly to the sender of the message, but one person slipped up. He accidentally posted his flame to the entire PageMaker group instead of sending it directly to the person who wrote the above spam.

```
Newsgroups: alt.aldus.pagemaker
Subject: Re: FREE PAGER!
From: (Reply name deleted)
Here's a helpful piece of advice: Get the hell out of our newsgroup with
shit like that before one of us finds out your phone number, ok?
(Reply name deleted)
```

Do you think the person who wrote this was upset? If several people were that angry with your business, how would you feel? This was one of dozens of messages sent to the spammer.

What happened next? My guess is that a reader of the **news:alt.aldus.pagemaker** group noticed that the spam came from an America Online subscriber. AOL puts up with no nonsense. If a subscriber blatantly violates netiquette, AOL kicks the subscriber off its system. The spammer subsequently posted an apology and promised never to spam again.

As a marketer, the thing to remember about this exchange is the flaming, angry message from the offended newsgroup reader. It is a reminder of the interactive, two-way nature of Internet marketing. Your prospects will also get angry if you misuse interactivity.

The Internet markets to different demographics

And who are these people to whom you market interactively? Net folks are upscale, well educated, more highly paid than average, and early technology adapters. Most of them are at work.

A revealing piece of data from *The Gate* (the Web version of the *San Francisco Examiner* at **www.sfgate.com**) is that its busiest Web site traffic times are 6 a.m. to 3 p.m. PST, with an 11 a.m. peak. This means most readers reach this Web site during business hours, either while they are at work or school. *The Gate*'s Web server saves domain names of readers, so its marketers know what kind of people visit. How many are from the business domain **.com**? How many from the academic domain **.edu**? They found the highest percentage of visitors are from companies—two-thirds of its visitors are from **.com**.

Businesstime use of the Internet is confirmed by Barry Parr of *Mercury Center*, the online version of Knight-Ridder's *San Jose Mercury News*. Parr sees the Internet as a distinct market from the commercial services such as America Online. *Mercury Center* has sites both on America Online and on the Internet. *Mercury Center* on America Online is busiest in the evenings, when people reach it from home. However, Internet *Mercury Center* use is busiest in the middle of the day Monday through Friday, when people visit from work.

Companies of all sizes are on the Net, good news if your customers are other businesses. Chiat/Day estimated that the industry groups with the largest number of Web sites are:

1. Computer-related products and services
2. Internet services
3. Financial services
4. Music
5. Travel
6. Automotive

Obviously, if you sell to any of those industries, you can reach your customers on the Net. Here's a slightly different take on the same subject from WebTrack. Its databases measured which industry groups have the largest percentage of U.S. companies with Web sites:

1. Computers and office equipment
2. Electronic entertainment equipment
3. Telecommunications
4. Publishing and media
5. Autos and auto accessories
6. Financial services

For the record, WebTrack also measured which industry groups have the smallest percentage of U.S. companies with Web sites: toiletries and cosmetics, apparel and footwear, drugs and remedies, food products, retailing, and household furniture and supplies.

So if your business sells to other businesses, you know where to look. What if your business sells to individual consumers, regular folks like Joe and Jane Sixpack?

Researchers with The Yankee Group discovered a demographic cluster they called "Technically Advanced Families," or Taffies for short. "They represent about 10 million families who are already putting pieces together," explained Yankee Group managing director Howard Anderson in a December 1994 *Upside* interview. "Any new service or product that succeeds, succeeds with this group first. For example, only 14 percent of American homes now have a modem, but 54 percent of Taffie families not only have a modem, they are bitching and screaming that it's not fast enough. When some families are glued to the radio on snow days to see if school has been cancelled, the Taffie families have already queried the school computer on the Internet and rolled back to sleep."

This smart, affluent, and educated group of customers are the core of Internet consumer sales. In the U.S., the proportion of males to females is approaching 50-50, but most other countries run 65 to 80 percent males. You'll also find more college students on the Internet than in the general population, enough to make sales to students highly profitable for many companies.

A large proportion of Internet users are based in government, non-profit groups, and higher education—organizations whose cultures downgrade commercialism. They distrust businesses to begin with. To win new customers, you have to overcome that attitude first.

Demographics on Internet size and Web use are hotly disputed. One 1997 survey by Nielsen Media Research (**www.nielsenmedia.com**) said that of the 220 million people over the age of 16 in the U.S. and Canada, 23 percent use the Net and 17 percent use the Web. Of those Web users, 39 percent use the Web to find information to help them make purchasing decisions. Nielsen estimates that 15 percent of Web users (5.6 million people) have actually purchased products online. (Remember, those are just buyers in the U.S. and Canada. Internet merchants I've worked with report that about half of their online sales come from customers *outside* the U.S. and Canada.)

Another 1997 survey from Find SVP (**www.findsvp.com**) said 20 million "Americans" (however it defines that term) regard the Internet as "indispensable"—but Find SVP dropped people who use only email, excluding millions of businesspeople who access the Net by email. Find SVP guesses that 27 percent of Internet users buy stuff online.

You'll hear all kinds of demographic claims. My favorite estimated that 44 percent of Internet users identify with Sherlock Holmes.

The Internet is so large, so decentralized, and grows so rapidly that any estimate of its demographics can be nothing more than a calculated guess. For recent figures, visit CyberAtlas (**www.cyberatlas.com**), Network Wizards (**www.nw.com**),

WebTrack (**www.webtrack.com**), ActivMedia (**www.activmedia.com**), and Open Market's Internet Index (**www.openmarket.com/intindex**). For European host statistics, try the RIPE Network Coordination Centre (**www.ripe.net**).

These companies quibble about details, but the consensus is indisputable. Internet users are mostly male. They earn higher-than-average salaries, are better educated than the general public, and almost all use computers. (Some use Web TV.) Most reach the Internet from offices or colleges, not from home. And there are millions of them.

That doesn't mean you have "millions of prospects," as shysters claim. Internet users are a diverse bunch. Just because you have millions of some type of people doesn't mean that all of them are profitable to sell to. Just because millions of people live there, would you sell in the slums of Calcutta?

The Internet has a population larger than any city in the world, and bigger than many countries and states. Its population is so diverse that mass mailings won't work. Thousands of different networks make up the Internet, and the people who use them have little in common except literacy and the use of a keyboard. You've got right wingers, left wingers, and middle-of-the-roaders. You've got Jews, Christians, Moslems, Buddhists, Hindus, and nonbelievers. You've got people who hate animals, professional livestock handlers, and people with 14 cats. Companies often spend a fortune to find the kind of target markets you can pinpoint for free on the Internet.

The most realistic view to remember is that the Internet is really not one big market, but a bunch of markets from large to tiny. A great strength of Net marketing is that you can *narrowcast* and pick exactly the kind of prospects you want for your message. If you offer a World Wide Web site, your prospects will be *self-selecting*. If you promote your site and they are interested in what you offer, they will come to you.

The Internet markets to the world

One of the most difficult Internet concepts to convey to marketers who don't use the Net is its lack of boundaries. Prospects in other countries are not just easier to contact or less expensive to reach on the Net. When you market on the Internet, you quickly discover that borders simply don't matter.

Convincing politicians of this fact is extremely difficult, resulting in some countries passing silly laws that try to restrict cross-border marketing. Some want to regulate Internet marketing, forgetting the difficulties of one country controlling something that does not have borders.

The Federation of European Direct Marketing (FEDIM) works with European governments to guarantee marketers equal access to the Net. As I write this, some bozos in the European Union still propose to apply television regulations to the Internet, claiming that any moving image on a screen is television, including online computers. Like television, the Net would come under restrictive content rules that say a guaranteed percentage of content must be produced locally! This is nuts. What are they going to do, tie up Frenchmen and force them to write more Web pages? This idea was proposed by Net-illiterate politicians once before and defeated, but it has risen from the dead.

This is important, because Europe has proven rewarding for online marketers. Out of the whole world, France is the country with the largest percentage of online sales. This is due to France's Minitel network, a $2 billion business for France Telecom. Some 15 percent of all French direct purchases are made through Minitel, another 25 percent by phone, and the remaining 60 percent by mail. Compare this to the U.S., where sales via the Internet, CompuServe, America Online, and all other online services together add up to less than 1 percent of total direct sales. If 15 percent of all U.S. direct purchases were made online, it would equal $8.7 billion in annual sales. French people have a head start and have grown accustomed to buying online.

Most messages on the Internet are in English, but not all. Estimates of English use among Internet users range from 75 percent to 85 percent. People from many countries speak their mother language plus English. Many Japanese—especially Japanese Internet users—are comfortable with English. Japanese education includes six years of written English, and Japanese people are interested in and likely to buy from other countries, generating average order amounts two to four times higher than U.S. customers.

The number two language on the Net is German. Japanese is number three, and French a distant fourth. As in any other medium, if you really want to reach important prospects, you'll speak their language and not force them to learn yours.

I've helped dozens of companies market on the Internet, from startups to large corporations. The one reaction common to every single one of them was delighted surprise at how many customers they generated from other countries. As I mentioned before, it's common for Net merchants to make 50 percent of sales to customers outside the U.S. and Canada.

When you market on the Net, you instantly go global.

The Internet markets faster

On the Internet, the time span between concept, execution, and customer response is sometimes so short that it's startling. On a busy Web site, you can literally create a new sales piece, post it, and make your first sale, all within hours. No other medium can match this two-way speed.

Internet advertising agency Poppe Tyson's Web page (**www.poppe.com**) puts it this way: "On-line information is all about instant gratification—all the information you want, whenever you want it, in any sequence you like. On-line selling, if properly designed, can be the ultimate in thoroughness and responsiveness. And it can get customers to their decision faster."

Speed matters on the Internet. People get used to fresh information, delivered quickly, and near-instant responses. Word-of-mouth travels with shocking speed. When something hot (or truly awful) is discovered on the Net, an email blizzard alerts people all over the planet. In a matter of days, it's old hat.

This creates an Internet phenomena known as *flash crowds*. The term comes from a story by author Larry Niven. Flash crowds happen when an Internet site receives a sudden, huge surge in visits, followed by an equally sudden dropoff a week or two later. A site's listing on the Yahoo "What's Cool" list, for instance, has sent an extra 40,000 to 50,000 visitors in one week to some Web sites. When new listings bump the Web sites off the list, the visitation rate immediately drops, almost to previous levels.

Novelty and newness have strong drawing power on the Net. This is why most businesses need to constantly update their Web sites. If you want to generate repeat business, you want repeat visitors. To get repeat visitors, you need to feed them a steady stream of new information. Your Web site should be updated often. The more often, the better.

Internet customers will also judge you by the speed of your response. Do you ask for customer feedback? Then you need to respond to it, and quickly. Assign responsibility to someone for maintaining Internet customer dialogue.

This person or people should read and respond to customer email every day—or even better, several times every day. The standard for Intel Corp. is to acknowledge all email within one business day. The customer service department of retailer Hammacher Schlemmer answers all customer email *within five minutes.*

Like so much else on the Internet, responsiveness is a two-way street. If you respond more quickly to your Internet customers, they will be more responsive to you.

The Internet markets inexpensively

Although we covered this before, let's review one more time how the Internet stacks up against other marketing media:

- Relatively low setup cost

- Low cost of updating information

- Low cost of providing customized information

- Low cost of transaction processing

- Extremely low cost of delivering information

- Negligible cost of providing information to additional prospects

- Low cost to increase the *quantity* of information provided

Another low cost is *frequency*. In other media, *reach*—the number of people in your target market that a medium reaches—is the foundation for advertising, because frequency costs too much. On the Internet, frequency is nearly free, but reach is harder and more expensive.

You can use cheap Net frequency to profitably maintain contact with marginal buyers who would otherwise be too costly to keep in your database. For example, Yoyodyne conducted an online promotion to sell magazine subscriptions. To people who didn't subscribe, Yoyodyne extended an offer for a free email newsletter. 80 percent of the nonsubscribers said "yes" to the newsletter, letting the magazine continue to communicate with its prospects and to make new offers in the future.

People who express interest but later say "no" are still good prospects when your cost of keeping in touch is almost nothing. Low costs mean low risks. On the Internet, low risks let you experiment and find new ways to make sales that would otherwise be unprofitable. We cover the possible permutations in the next chapter.

More Net marketing info

More than half of the books about Internet business are marketing books. Many are clueless, or provide little information—the bland leading the blind. Avoid those. Instead, look for these worthwhile books for Internet marketers.

Designing Large-Scale Web Sites, by Darrell Sano ★★★ (1996), Wiley, 288 pages. ISBN 0-471-14276-X. One of the best books on planning and designing a business Web site, this book will be useful to anyone creating a Web site of 30 or more pages. It includes a few pages of technical stuff, but most of the book helps you *organize* your project and its marketing and visual design aspects.

DM News ★★★★ This one isn't a book, but a newspaper, published weekly by Mill Hollow Corporation. (**www.dmnews.com**) It covers direct marketing, including very good reporting on marketing-related Internet news all over the world. It's valuable for advertising, marketing, order desk, and fulfillment managers. Subscriptions are *free* to qualified U.S. subscribers, fee-based to those in other countries.

Guerrilla Marketing Online, by Jay Conrad Levinson and Charles Rubin ★★★ (1995), Houghton Mifflin, 303 pages. ISBN 0-395-72859-2. Good how-to guide for small business marketers. Covers America Online, CompuServe, Prodigy, bulletin board systems, and the Net.

Internet Marketing Plan, by Kim Bayne ★★★ (1997), Wiley, 380 pages + disk. ISBN 0-471-17295-2. Good advice on marketing strategy both on and off the Net, plus 29 checklists and forms you can use. Disk provides software versions of checklists and forms.

Successful Direct Marketing Methods, fifth edition by Bob Stone ★★★★ (1994), NTC Business Books, 654 pages. ISBN 0-8442-3510-5. This book contains absolutely no information about the Internet, but if you do direct marketing, you need this book. And *all* selling over the Net is direct marketing. Stone's tome is the bible of direct marketing. He tells you what kind of research, testing, customer records, and analyses you need, and shows you how to do them.

World Wide Web Marketing, by Jim Sterne ★★★★ (1995), Wiley, 331 pages. ISBN 0-471-12843-0. It's clearly-written, it delivers solid information, and it skips all the useless stuff. (If one more Net business book starts with a history chapter, I'm going to *scream*!) Sterne does not cover credit card or sales issues, but hits the high points of using the Web to achieve marketing goals. One of the best Web strategy guides.

 ## Internet marketing guidelines

These guidelines are suggested by the Interactive Marketing Group of Ogilvy & Mather Direct. "Unbridled commercialization will likely crush what is most precious about the Internet," the group stated. "These guidelines are offered as a starting point towards the responsible participation of marketers on the Internet."

1.   Intrusive email is not welcome.

No one should receive a message they haven't either asked to receive, or more generally, want to receive. If a user requests information from companies that sell ski equipment, companies within this category should be able to send this user relevant information. They may offer to add the user's address to their list server, but under no circumstances should an inquiry result in an automatic subscription.

2.   Internet consumer data is not for resale without the express permission of the user.

Unlike commercial services, where it is clearly understood that data generated through consumer interaction is being sold to marketers, Internet data should remain the private property of the user.

Using the ski example, the fact that I have requested information via the Internet should not de facto allow the ski company to resell my behavioral data to, say, Saab—which may be interested in reaching ski enthusiasts.

3.   Advertising is allowed only in designated newsgroups and list servers.

The most objectionable form of advertising on the Internet comes in the form of off-topic commercial postings to newsgroups and list server conferences, usually cross-posted to dozens or hundreds of groups. These postings generally draw harsh flames from readers, but such feedback may not be sufficient to stop this type of abuse.

Those who post off-topic commercial solicitations should be warned once, then filtered at the source from any commercial postings.

4. Promotions and direct selling are allowed, but only under full disclosure.

Marketers should be free to offer promotions from their own domains, but users should be given an opportunity to clearly review the rules, guidelines, and parameters of the event before they commit. Promotions should be subjected to the same guidelines as above—all promotions should be self-selected.

We suggest the recommendations be consistent with those developed for analog merchants by the Direct Marketing Association and modified or enhanced to reflect the unique attributes of electronic delivery.

5. Consumer research is allowed only with the consumer's full consent.

Marketers should be able to conduct consumer research as long as respondents have ready and easy access to information outlining the uses and implications of participating in the market research survey.

6. Internet communications software must never hide concealed functions.

Several years ago, a commercial online service was accused of using its terminal software to scan users' hard disks for text that appeared to be an address. The program would then allegedly collect this data and, unknown to the user, send it to the service for use in compiling mailing lists.

As client/server applications become more prevalent on the Internet, the opportunity for this type of abuse increases.

CHAPTER 12

Levels of Marketing and Types of Sales

"On the Internet, differentiated, branded assets will drive the market."
—Bill Gates

To old-school marketers, one of the confusing aspects of the Internet is that, unlike traditional media, you have many different things to do and many different ways to do them. If you create a print advertisement, you know it will run in a printed publication. On the Internet, you might use newsgroups or an email list to spread your words, or MIME or the Web to deliver graphics. It might help to think of the Internet as a collection of somewhat different media rather than a single medium.

As far as what you can actually do on the Internet from a marketing point of view, all activities can be roughly grouped into seven levels in order of cost, complexity, and implementation time. It is crucial for you to determine which of the seven levels of marketing is best for you. We'll start with the cheapest and quickest level first, and work our way up to the hardest.

Level 1. Netlurking, posting, and emailing

This method of Internet marketing is relatively easy and can cost the least to do. All you need is email and access to Usenet newsgroups. Monitor newsgroups where your customers hang out. When someone asks a question that you can answer, be helpful and answer it. (Provide real, usable information, not just instructions to buy your product.) Your answers should have your signature file, which will carry your business and name before your prospects. (For more on signature files, see the section in Chapter 9. For more on netlurking and posting, see Chapter 13.) This sounds so simple as to be useless, but I have talked to several businesses selling more than a million dollars a year that use netlurking as their primary—and in some cases, only—method of marketing.

T. R. Sills, operator of The Entrepreneur Connection, says that one newsgroup posting generated twice the response of hundreds of dollars in print advertising. Sills checks business newsgroups daily, looking for business questions to which he can provide an answer, such as telling someone how to perform his own patent search. Sills's answers trade his knowledge for exposure.

If your posted answers provide genuine, useful information, you will not be flamed. You will be welcomed. You can also use the Internet to email electronic press releases to appropriate (that's the key word, *appropriate*) sites, such as print magazines and electronic publications that cover your industry.

Email lists to your customers fall into this cheapest, fastest first level as well. Email newsletters, announcements, and discussion lists cost little and take only a small amount of time to frequently reach a large number of people. If you regularly deliver useful information to a list of prospects and customers, the sales you generate will usually be much higher than your effort and expense. Regularly emailed announcements (*not* advertisements) or newsletters generate a surprisingly good response.

The low costs and quick turnaround time of this first level of Internet marketing make it possible for you to profit from totally new types of sales. A good example is the Internet-spawned phenomena called *house concerts*, a new way the music business sells tickets and CDs. Here's how house concerts work. A performer sets a date to perform in a person's private home. The performer's record label promotes the house concert two ways: 1) by sending email notices to a mailing list of the performer's fans who live near the area where the performance will be held, and 2) by posting notices in appropriate music fan newsgroups. Total marketing costs: nothing, thanks to the Internet. No rent is paid for a concert hall. No sales commissions are charged. From ticket sales and CD sales at the event, the performer makes as much money as from a larger venue, and the intimate concerts generate loyal fans who build careers. Waterbug Records credits house concerts as the major force in establishing the success of folksinger Cosy Sheridan.

Without focused and nearly cost-free marketing communications from newsgroups and email lists, house concerts would be impossibly unprofitable. A little experience with these inexpensive techniques may lead to similar marketing innovations for your business.

Level 2.   Showing your products and services

You may be familiar with "fax on demand" services. This is the Web equivalent, with the added impact that color graphics deliver. It's a low-cost alternative to literature fulfillment; basically, a Web site "billboard" that presents your product information to the world. You can update it instantly and can always add more information.

At this level, your Web site is not interactive. It merely presents your basic information—with little or nothing created especially for the Web—and asks people to write, phone, fax, or email for details.

Most Web billboards fail. Usually either the site fails as a piece of marketing (it's easier to create ineffective Web marketing than ineffective marketing in other media), or few people visit the Web site.

However, in spite of claims to the contrary (I must eat a little crow myself), not *all* Web billboards fail. Some succeed. Read the sidebar about Visual Law for an example. This site (see Figure 12.1) put up a non-interactive billboard (which most people say won't work), hardly promoted it at all (which most people say leads to failure), left it almost unchanged for a year (which everybody warns against), *and generated a profit from it.*

How could Visual Law break so many rules of Internet marketing and succeed? The company is one of a handful of businesses that meet all five qualifications for a successful Web billboard:

I. High-ticket sales. If Visual Law charged $5 per transaction, the 12 projects its site generated would not have paid for its costs. Fortunately, the company earns much more per project, so it makes a profit from its site. Would your company make money from a Web site that brings you only two or three new clients per year? If not, don't try a billboard. Billboards generate few sales, and so work best for expensive products and services.

Figure 12.1   *Visual Law's non-interactive billboard.*

II. Rare products or services. Only a couple dozen companies perform forensic engineering, and few offer Visual Law's level of expertise. Successful Web billboards offer uncommon products that people actively search to find. The best offerings are specialized goods or services that people either greatly need or have a strong emotional attachment to. If your offering is widely available, a Web billboard won't work for you.

III. A small number of offerings. Visual Law essentially offers one service that it can describe on few unchanging Web pages. If your company offers many products in a catalog, you'll have better luck with a Web site that is more interactive. If your products change frequently, you'll need to update your site more often.

IV. Prospects with an urgent need. Time pressure forces prospects to contact you right away. Otherwise, Web visitors take time to comparison-shop, or simply bookmark your site for a return visit later and never get around to later. Are your prospects in a hurry?

V. Prospects who are online. Visual Law helps attorneys win cases. It is usually hired by attorneys. Fortunately, a lot of lawyers are online. If your prospects are professionals, businesspeople, or academics, they are more likely to be online and to respond to your Web billboard. Consumers are less likely billboard prospects. They are more likely to buy from a more complex online site where they can securely give their credit card numbers.

If a Web billboard seems right for your business, you'll need to do three things.

1. Translate your existing literature into HTML Web pages.
2. Monitor customer responses to your site. Learn what works and what doesn't. Then apply that information to fine-tune your content and format to keep your site useful, interesting, and easy to use.
3. Educate your prospects and customers about where they should look and what they should expect. If you don't tell them what you want them to do, they won't do it.

If you use the Internet to showcase your products and services, be prepared to promote your site on a continuing basis.

Visual Law's under $500 Web success

Experts say that Web billboards don't make money, but here's an example that does: Less than a week after choosing a Web space provider, Visual Law landed a new client who more than paid for its Web site.

Visual Law produces computer-animated exhibits used as evidence in court. It re-creates train accidents, automobile accidents, medical malpractice injuries, and other incidents to show jurors in detail what happened step-by-step. This allows jurors to see an incident from the exact point of view of a participant.

Mark Johnson, a principal in the firm, is an attorney and computer graphics artist. He was comfortable with using the Internet, but was puzzled about how to find a company to host Web space for Visual Law. First he spent a couple of days learning about Web sites and Web hosts. "I went out and bought every computer magazine I could lay my hands on," he explained, "and read every article on Web sites and every ad from every Web hosting service."

Johnson compiled a list of Web hosts, their prices, and the differences in what they offered. "I had about 24 potential providers," Johnson said. "They culled out pretty easily. The megabyte limits were about 5 megs in some places. That wouldn't work for us, because we're a graphics company. Many had an upper limit on the number of hits we could receive without extra charges. I wanted to raise that bar as high as I could. The other thing that became important in trying to choose is that I wanted a company that offered a true commercial site."

By "true commercial site," Johnson meant he needed a Web host that would register the **www.visuallaw.com** Internet domain name for Visual Law, would let his company run its site under its own domain name and not the Web host's URL, and would forward the email generated by the Web site. He wanted a price structure that included at least 10 megabytes of disk space and almost unlimited hits, plus support for CGI programs. "I was concerned about hardware and bandwidth," Johnson reported. "The company I selected runs multiple T1 lines with SGI servers (fast, high-end computers) and was adding a T3. I'd read that some Web hosts don't keep their equipment onsite, but subcontract equipment from somebody else. I wanted a Web farm host that did not subcontract. They kept their stuff on site."

He chose Hiway Technologies (**www.hway.net**). They provided everything Visual Law needed for $29 per month, plus a one-time fee of $150 for registering Visual Law's domain name. "We literally had our FTP account and IP number within two hours after I gave them my credit card number," said Johnson. "They gave us a nifty little control panel you access with a password, and you get a library of Perl scripts and a forms generator. What impressed me is email response for tech support was usually within two hours.

"I got my first Web page up within 48 hours of getting our IP number," Johnson continued. "I copied a page from another site and changed it." He spent about eight hours producing his first version of the Visual Law Web site. Then he listed the site with Yahoo. "I clicked its 'List Your Site' button and followed the instructions," he explained. "Within two days, we had a contact. An attorney looked up "forensic engineering" at Yahoo and came up with our site." That contact turned into a sale.

Johnson also went to an autosubmission site and publicized his site by listing it on eight search engines. That and Yahoo are the only promotions he's done for Visual Law. "I get email all the time from places like 'The Experts Page,' saying 'Give us a hundred bucks a month and we'll put your link on our site," he said. "I just laugh and delete 'em."

Johnson explained that his haze of confusion about the Internet magically cleared up once he completed his first project. "There seems to be a bar that once you get over, the Internet becomes understandable. Once you get that door unlocked, then it all becomes clear to you."

Visual Law's site includes a guestbook where visitors can leave their email addresses and comments. For the first 280 hits on the guestbook page, "two dozen people gave their email addresses. Some were from existing clients. One was a potential new employee."

Johnson spends a couple of hours per week following up on the two dozen or so email inquiries per week that the site generates, and an occasional few minutes on its guestbook. "If someone leaves a dirty message in the guestbook, I delete it." In the past year, he's spent only two hours updating his site, and it generated two major new clients and 12 projects—an excellent return on his small investment of time, and proof that for the right business, a billboard site *can* make money.

Level 3.   Processing orders and inquiries

The difference between Levels 2 and 3 is that Level 3 more actively ties into your formal processes for handling sales leads and fulfilling orders, and generates faster response. Part of Level 3 marketing is that you process inquiries and orders several times a day or as soon as they come in.

First Union National Bank's Web site takes credit card applications, which its employees receive and process by hand, contacting credit card applicants offline to give them results. By the end of its first year, First Union's Web site generated more applications than an average branch office.

Another site that does Level 3 marketing is Eastern Mortgage Services at **www.eastmorg.com**, which generates 100 home loan and second mortgage applications per week.

When used for sales-lead fulfillment and human-assisted order processing, the Internet lets you rapidly gather customer feedback about your products, marketing, and customer service. What answers are missing from your literature? You'll quickly find out, because your Internet customers will tell you. Handling orders and inquiries on the Net can be a useful customer service. If done properly, it fosters interest and generates goodwill among your prospects.

You'll need to allow time for customer service reps to answer questions on the Net every day. You'll quickly see the need to develop a library of stock answers and form letters for questions you hear repeatedly. You'll need to set up a mechanism to track sales leads and pass them to your sales or marketing people. When using the Internet for this level of marketing, time will be the crucial ingredient for success—the investment of enough time to support your customers and to update your Internet site.

Level 4.   Processing payment transactions

At this level of marketing, the Net lets you create electronic "mail order." Your customers can place an order *without direct human intervention*. If you want to accept payments on the Net, plan for a significant increase in time and money invested compared to the previous level. And security becomes a much more serious issue.

To succeed at transaction processing, your back-office order fulfillment is extremely important. Besides credit card processing or billing, you also need to plan for sales tax management and the physical shipment of products, including international orders (often more profitable than domestic).

At this stage, the reliability of your Internet access provider becomes mission-critical, because when your provider is down, your cash flow drops dead. Depending on your sales volume, you might look for two or more phone lines to link to your provider, or, use two providers so if one provider goes down, your orders still come in.

Level 5.   Building an online community

Neil Harris is a vice president of Simultronics, a game company he describes as "dedicated to building huge online communities and having them killed by giant robots."

Such dramatic conclusions aren't what most businesses have in mind when they build online communities. Instead, many companies find community-building a powerful and profitable way to build ongoing customer relationships.

The term "online community" loosely covers any and all methods for visitors to contribute to your site. For example, Amazon.com lets visitors post their own reviews—pro or con—of any book in Amazon's catalog. Other common ingredients include chat (people on your site can type and everyone sees what everyone else typed *realtime*), bulletin boards (also called online *forums;* people on your site type a message and see other people's replies to it on their next visit), and simpler efforts such as posting ads on your site for other visitors to see.

The strength of online communities is not just in the additional content visitors provide for your site. The real strengths are the increased loyalty people feel because they have *contributed* to your site (pride of ownership by proxy) and the appeal of social interactions with their peer group.

"People want ratings and recommendations that come from people like them," said Steve Bengston of Travelocity. TV watching is a social substitute. Participating in an online community is also a social substitute, but with a level of involvement that even *Melrose Place* can't match. You get to add your own contribution. And you get to know other people—whether customers or your employees—and build relationships with them. "Consider this the *Cheers* effect. Would you rather try and meet people in Grand Central Terminal or in a bar where everybody knows your name?" asks Unet Vice President Harlan Levinson.

Saturn's Web site asks Saturn owners for their hobbies, spare-time activities, where they drive, and occupations. It makes this information available to all other registered Saturn owners who visit the site, so they can look up other owners in their neighborhoods.

One of best marketing-oriented online communities is on Broderbund Software's Web site for its Family Tree Maker product at **www.familytreemaker.com**. If you buy Broderbund's product, you get your own Web page to post your family tree. Other people can view it and provide missing entries. Customers can place free ads seeking relatives and information. In the first months the site was open, nearly 17,000 upgrade buyers registered to use the site. They created 3,500 home pages, placed 2,400 classified ads, and posted 10,000 messages, and search its data archives 40,000 times a day. The site sells about 100 CD-ROMs daily. The Family Tree Maker site caused a huge jump in the percentage of customers buying upgrades, and the product is repositioned from a report generator to the hub of an online community, a much stronger position.

On a smaller scale, AdvisorWorks (**www.advisorworks.com**) is a more focused site operated by financial planner Peter Johnson. In its first seven months, it attracted more than 300 commission-based investment reps and fee-based investment advisors. Open only to registered professionals, AdvisorWorks's number of members doubles every two to three months. The site's members manage more than $8 billion in assets.

At first, Johnson had an uphill battle to build visitor traffic. "Advertising in trade magazines was very effective at building traffic," said Johnson. He also promoted AdvisorWorks by speaking at conferences of investment pros. He hired a publicist to generate press coverage of his site by investment trade publications. "Exhibits at trade shows were not effective," he commented.

Once visitors joined AdvisorWorks, repeated gentle urgings were necessary to encourage regular use of its forums. "We call people on the phone to give them their passwords," said Johnson, "and encourage them to use the forums. New members get a welcome-to-the-site email message which also mentions the forums." He started with 12 or 13 bulletin board-type "forums," but his visitors were spread out between too many forums to sustain conversations. He reduced the number of forums to three to concentrate visitors and reach the critical mass needed to keep discussions moving. "On any of the forums, people can start discussions under their own topics," he explained. "AdvisorWorks 'Investment Management and Financial Planning Forum' has 17 subtopics. 'Technology and Computers' has 11, and 'Practice Management' has 20. People love being able to talk with other professionals and share ideas."

AdvisorWorks uses the bulletin board software Web Crossing (**http://webx.lundeen.com**), which is available for Mac, Windows, and Unix. Web Crossing also does realtime chat. Johnson said, "The software is easy to run. No maintenance to speak of, except a couple of times we moved a message posted under a wrong heading into the proper one. When people post a message, they can put their photo next to it. We chose it because it's the same software Salon uses, which handles 1.2 million people a month." (For a demo, check out Salon's Table Talk at **www.salon1999.com**.)

You can use realtime chat for customer service. Your clients can ask questions and read the answers to their questions and other people's. Answers can come from each other and from your company's reps. Let customers have their say, even when their comments are negative. What's important is that your customer gets to contribute and feels in control, not that you maintain a monolithic front.

Online communities can be rewarding, but they have drawbacks. First, they take a lot of energy to set up and launch. You must work hard to reach the critical mass of visitors needed to sustain momentum. The quantity you need differs depending on what tools you use.

You might use an email discussion list to start. They are fast and cheap to set up, and you can maintain a viable ongoing discussion with only 30 or 40 participants if they are vitally interested in your topic. (More about email discussions in the next chapter.) You can mirror your email discussions on your Web-based bulletin board to build Web traffic. A standalone Web bulletin board discussion needs at least 500 visitor sessions per week to take off; 1,000 per week is a more realistic minimum. Web-based chat needs even more. Since chat is realtime, someone can communicate only with the other people visiting your site at that same moment. You need at least 5,000 visitors per week to sustain ongoing chat. Periodic short chats of an hour or two can be sustained with much smaller traffic levels if you schedule your chats way in advance and promote the heck out of them.

In addition to hard work to start your online community, plan to work continuously to manage it. Managing the software will be easy. Managing the editorial side is not. Every day, someone must monitor the discussions, answer questions, and fill lulls in conversations.

One more caveat. In fall 1994, Coors launched its Zima site, including online community features targeted at young people. Tens of thousands of visitors registered. The Web site generated international media coverage. It was a success. But the product, which tasted terrible, did not meet sales expectations. Just because you build a healthy online community doesn't mean it will sell your products.

Level 6. Processing database-driven payment transactions

LifeQuote (**www.lifequote.com**) launched its site in April 1996 to give price quotes on life insurance policies from the insurance companies it represents, more than 250 of them. The site lets visitors choose their preferred benefits and terms, and then gives annual premium costs instantly. LifeQuote's site cost less than $50,000 to develop and within a few months generated 60 percent of the company's total sales. Every month, more than 200 people use the site to request quotes. Seventeen percent of requesters convert into paying customers.

How does LifeQuote compute complex pricing and terms from more than 250 suppliers? It stores everything in a database accessible by its Web server. LifeQuote updates its database frequently so its calculation engine doesn't grow out-of-date.

Database-driven commercial Web sites are trickier to set up than other types. They require custom programming before launch and constant technical handholding after. They are more expensive and harder to manage. But the number of them grows exponentially, because they make big bucks.

Not all do, of course. But most Web sites with a large volume of visitors deliver a series of *dynamically generated pages*. These pages are not created in finished form, but are stored in a database (or several linked databases) as bunches of elements. The actual pages are created on the fly by the database, responding to a visitor's request by pulling elements from storage, writing HTML to tie everything together, and shoving completed pages out your Web server's door. (Right, it really goes out a wire, not a door. Just a figure of speech, okay?) Look for more on database-driven sites in the chapter on Web stores.

Figure 12.2   A pioneer in using database contents to generate revenue on the Internet, UnCover's success spawned other profitable innovations.

Databases drive UnCover's success

CARL Systems, Inc. of Denver, Colorado, sells software that automates library catalogs. In 1988, it launched a product called UnCover (see Figure 12.2), a database of the tables of contents from thousands of scholarly journals. The database was available only through the Internet. People in its industry thought CARL Systems was crazy to offer no print equivalent, saying that the Internet wasn't big enough to be a "real" market. Naysayers predicted that UnCover would never break even, let alone generate a profit. The pessimists were wrong. By early 1993, UnCover had grown so profitable that CARL Systems spun it off as a separate company.

Originally, UnCover customers were companies that paid a monthly fee based on the number of people within the client company who had access to UnCover. Customers could only look up information in the database. In early 1990, UnCover added a new service: delivery of articles. Customers could find an article in the UnCover table of contents database, order it online, and pay for it online via credit card, all in one transaction.

The company set up internal systems to process the anticipated order volume and linked with a bank so it could verify credit cards while its customers were still connected online. This added substantial overhead to each UnCover transaction, but let CARL Systems expand its prospect base from educational institutions and corporate libraries (which paid a monthly bill for UnCover use) to millions of small companies and individual researchers. Articles are delivered via fax for about $8.50 each. Since beginning its new service, UnCover has sold and faxed hundreds of thousands of documents.

Document delivery is so profitable that UnCover has made its original product—database lookups—free. Company management reasons correctly that its free table of contents database is now a promotional come-on for buying articles. This matches the experiences of other companies: Giving away free information is one of the most effective lures for Internet customers.

How else does the UnCover Company (**http://uncweb.carl.org**) use the Net as a marketing tool? It provides updates of its new services over the Net to customers. It trains new customers how to use its system. It lets customers check order status, review their account history, and check their current account balance. It maintains a mailing list to answer customer questions and to elicit customer suggestions for improvement. And the company teamed with Journal Graphics to sell an online index of transcripts of television news programs over the Internet. The new service is available only over the Internet, and it, too, is a success.

Level 7. Actually delivering products or services over the Net

Selling clip art online is big business. PhotoDisc sells more than 15,000 images at **www.photodisc.com**. Corel Corp. (**www.corel.com**) sells thousands of clip art images at $7 each. A newer supplier is Publisher's Depot (**www.publishersdepot.com**). Its $20 million Web site sells backgrounds, icons, art, photos, and maps for Web sites and other media. Publisher's Depot's databases offer more than 400,000 items. In its first seven months, it reeled in 10,000 customers, from big guys like Discovery Online, Netscape, and C|net, to one-person startups. Charges range from $30 to $40 for one-time Web or CD-ROM use and $100 for print-quality use.

What do these three online clip art merchants have in common? They all deliver their product over the Internet.

Online delivery is suitable only for certain kinds of businesses. Software, information, reports, consulting, and research of all kinds can actually be delivered over the Net. Several companies deliver online versions of books over the Net. Quote.Com (**www.quote.com**) sells information about stocks, delivered by email and on Web pages.

You don't have to deliver your whole product online. Some companies make money delivering a free taste. Id Software (**www.idsoftware.com**) makes the games Doom and Quake. It gives away millions of online copies of games' first levels. About 1 percent of people who sample the games register and pay $40 for a full game.

Or perhaps you can deliver an add-on offering to enhance an existing product line. Seattle Filmworks (**www.filmworks.com**) develops film. Send in your roll of film. Filmworks will develop it, send you traditional hard copy photos, plus (for $4 extra) digitized photos, with your choice of fast online delivery or snail-mailed floppy disk.

Bank One (**www.bankone.com**) uses Internet delivery to speed a service. It processes millions of checks for its commercial accounts. With this large volume, difficulties arise handling problem checks, or "exception checks" as bankers call them: suspicious recipients, large dollar amounts, or encoding problems. Difficulties come up because of a Federal Reserve rule that says the bank's commercial customers have only until midnight the next day to inspect all exception checks, approve or disapprove them, and return them to the bank. Bank One used to use messenger delivery or fax to deliver exceptions to companies. Now bank customers can receive and process their exception checks on the Web. Companies view an index page listing all their exceptions by problem category. A reviewer can see pictures of the fronts and backs of the actual checks, and use a Web page form to tell Bank One to pay or hold individual checks. Result: faster delivery, lower costs, happier customers.

The challenges of online product delivery are internal and external security, the need for a secure delivery method, and export control. (Export regulations depend on your product or service, the laws of your country, and the laws of your customer's country.) For some products, *copy protection* is also an issue. This prevents your customer from turning around and reselling your product to others without your permission.

So what can your business sell on the Internet? You can sell products. You can sell services—both services that you deliver electronically and services in the real world. You can sell information. You can sell subscriptions to an electronic newsletter, or to a service, or to enter your site. You can sell advertising on your Net projects. You can collect rent and sales commissions from your Net site. You can support your existing sales staff, or direct more customers to your existing distributors and dealers. Let's take a closer look at the four ways you can sell on the Net.

Types of sales on the Internet

For each of the seven levels of marketing you've just read about, you have four ways to make a sale on the Internet. Some of the four are just Internet-ized copies of proven sales models. Some have unique twists without precise counterparts in real life. Before you put your own sales project in motion, decide which of these Net sales models you need. You will need different Internet tools to make different types of sales. It makes sense to know what you need *before* you start, rather than to make a surprise change in the middle of your project.

A word of caution: Don't try to launch a project based just on this book and without any hands-on experience. *Book learning by itself is not enough.* If you are going to sell things on the Net, first go out on the Net and *buy* things. Buy from at least *three* different locations. Keep your eyes open for strengths and weaknesses at the places you buy. Take note of what you like and any good ideas you might see. Also remember things you don't like. As Yogi Berra said, "You can observe a lot just by watching."

Sales support model

The first businesses that used the Internet for marketing applied it to support their existing sales programs. Supporting existing sales efforts is still the most common use of the Net for sales.

Visit the Toyota Web site and you can order a free CD-ROM showing off new Toyotas. Before you get your CD in the mail, your local Toyota dealer will call you, inviting you for a test drive. Toyota successfully uses its site as an educational tool and links Web visitors with its live sales force.

Its competitor Nissan (**www.nissanmotors.com**) brought 230,000 visitors (people, not hits) to its Web site the first 10 months it was open. Seven percent of those visitors requested more information and 4 percent of those information requesters (about 640 people) ultimately purchased a car from a dealer, according to Nissan.

However, most profitable sales support sites are not for consumer sales, but for business-to-business sales. National Semiconductor's Web site (**www.national.com**)

delivers more than 6,000 data sheets a day, as many as its 250-person sales force used to deliver in a year. The site lets 100,000 registered users order free product samples and hard copy data books. National's site is popular because it takes just a few, quick steps to register and even fewer to log on, and provides flexible searching of its database of information on 40,000 parts. Focus groups of National's customers said they wanted fast page delivery, few graphics, and quick follow-up to any requests for human help. National's marketing staff delivered on those customer wants. Its site generates millions in orders for National's account sales reps.

If you plan to do a sales support project, remember that the Net is a two-way street. Your greatest sales leverage will come not from dumping existing sales support materials on the Web (Pete Snell of ad agency CKS Interactive called such Web-ized print brochures "shovelware"). Your highest payoffs will come when you use the Net to reach out to your prospects and customers, and, even better, when you let them reach you.

Remember that *seeing* something in action is more persuasive than just *reading* about it. Like Digital's "Test Drive an Alpha" promotion, you can often use the Web to present remote demonstrations of product capabilities and benefits. On the Web, demos sell. This is especially true for software companies—they've never had such a cheap, effective, and pervasive way to show off their products' strong points.

If your company sells to wholesalers or distributors, you can develop Net projects to support your own sales staff, plus programs to direct consumers to your resellers or retail locations. The Original Cookie Co.'s site (**www.originalcookie.com**) lets you find retail locations and print coupons you can use in its nearly 300 stores.

Remember that although the Web gets the lion's share of the publicity, it may not always be your best option. For instance, if your staff sells to government accounts, your buyers may not have access to the Web. Email is much more common among government buyers. Your staff might generate more sales from frequent email than from a Web site.

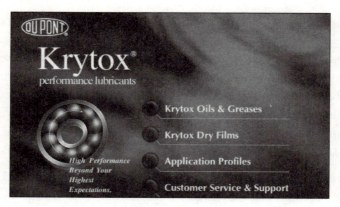

Figure 12.3   DuPont's $15,000 sales support site generated thousands of good email leads.

DuPont's $15,000 Web success

DuPont launched its first Web site on January 31, 1995 (see Figure 12.3). For its pilot site, the corporation chose not to start with a huge corporate umbrella project, but with its smaller Performance Lubricants division (**www.lubricants.dupont.com**). Performance Lubricants sells high-end lubricants that can cost $1,000 per gallon. It has 20,000 customers who "are scientists and chemists who want an enormous amount of information," according to product planner Benjamin du Pont.

Performance Lubricants aimed its site at two target audiences. "One target was to attract college students studying chemistry and engineering," said du Pont. The company believed that some of those students would eventually become customers. They would also provide fertile ground for recruitment. "Our other target was researchers at big and medium companies," added du Pont.

The Web site would satisfy its targets "if we could be *the* resource on lubricants on the Internet," explained du Pont. "We wanted (our prospects) to think, 'DuPont is a place to come to get answers.' "

The Performance Lubricant Web site creation was managed by Benjamin du Pont with Nina Patel of the Corporate Information Science department. They operated under four rules:

1. Only work with existing information.

2. Three clicks or less to meaningful data. (They didn't want visitors to burrow through page after page of menus, explained Patel, "where you click and click and click but don't get anywhere."

3. Easy to navigate.

4. Interactive and fun.

The first rule was a challenge, but it kept du Pont and Patel, who were the only DuPont employees who spent significant time creating the Web site, focused on the most important content. They Web-ized 500 pages of existing technical data. To make the site interactive, they created a way for visitors to ask questions of DuPont's technical staff and receive answers by email. To add an element of fun, they provided information on the Tour DuPont bicycle race sponsored by the corporation. They added photos and information about the racers, and created a way for news on race preparation and the event itself to be updated daily on its Web pages. They publicized the site on Internet directories and search engines, and in print publications covering chemistry, bicycling, or the Internet.

The total cost for the Performance Lubricant site was $15,000 plus the two employees' time. "We spent $10,000 with a contract company for the server. We kept that outside (our company) for security to assure that our internal net wouldn't be changed," commented du Pont, "and we spent $5,000 for graphics."

The company's salespeople were unbelievers "until the leads came in," said du Pont. In eight months, the site "generated 1,000 email messages. One was angry. Half of the email was from real prospects. Half of those came from places like New Zealand, places in the world where we don't have a sales force," expanding DuPont sales into new regions. The company also received a large number of qualified resumes. The site now takes 10 to 15 percent of one person's time to update and administer, and 25 percent of another person's time is spent answering email.

Direct sales model

The Dilbert Store sold $125,000 in Dilbert memorabilia on the Net during its first four months. Not bad for someone who can't even iron his tie.

The dream of every retailer and catalog merchant must be to set up a Web site and watch the sales roll in. Real life is not as effort-free as the dream—direct sales on the Net requires sustained work—but there are plenty of success stories.

One is a retail shop and cataloger that created a Web site that generated worldwide media coverage and sales. Hot Hot Hot sells nothing but bottled hot sauce.

"My husband and I wrote all the text. We made it cartoony and fun and light. With our kind of product, you want it to stay fun," explained Hot Hot Hot's Monica Lopez. "You can't just say, 'Hey, buy from me!' For a Web site to attract people and get them to buy, there has to be information and/or entertainment."

The staff of Web host Presence helped shape the site and handled technical matters, and an artist was hired to create graphics. It took a couple of months of part-time work to create the Web site. Lopez learned as she went along: "We didn't read any books about how to do the Internet until we were already on it." (Words to make an author quake with fear!)

Hot Hot Hot's Web site went online September 29, 1994. "We were surprised at the international orders, that people would actually do that," commented Lopez. She shipped a bottle of "Satan's Revenge" to Tel Aviv, and 10 bottles of sauce to Australia for a wedding. "We had to learn more about international shipping very quickly." Lopez quickly noticed differences between its Internet customers and its catalog customers. "Customers from our catalog order multiple bottles. Internet customers are more likely to order one sauce. They order lots of gift packs at Christmas." Internet orders generated 17 percent of Hot Hot Hot holiday sales.

Hot Hot Hot received coverage in consumer magazines around the world for the fun design of its site. It also drew attention from the Internet community for its technical astuteness. Hot Hot Hot was one of the first sites to include an *electronic shopping cart*. As you go through its site and click on sauces you'd like to buy, Hot Hot Hot keeps track of what you choose. When you go to its order page, your items and their costs are automatically popped into the order form. Hop over to **www.hothothot.com** and try it. You can change your selections or cancel them at any time. Hot Hot Hot accepts credit cards. Its Web pages email the orders and card numbers to Presence, which then faxes the orders to Hot Hot Hot's warehouse.

Lopez continually changes and adds to the Hot Hot Hot site. She compares it to catalog sales: "You keep sending catalogs to the same people; otherwise they forget you exist. But you don't send them the same catalog twice, you move products around and add things and change the art. The Web store is the same. You're constantly looking to improve it, so customers see something new. It really is a work in progress. I don't think it's the type of medium that would support a stagnant thing."

As a test of the medium's marketing effectiveness, Karen Blue of Direct! Direct! (**www.imservice.com/adobe_illustrator/16.html**) ran a five-month comparison, using the same offer to sell the same software product via two media: direct mail and the Web. Her Web campaign cost 30 percent as much as her snail mail campaign (that's 70 percent less!), but the Web generated only half as many leads. The Web's cost per lead, therefore, was 40 percent lower. However, only 18 percent of the direct mail leads were qualified, but a surprising 75 percent of the Web leads were. In addition, Web sales leads were zapped electronically to sales reps, which was faster and cost 70 percent less than processing cumbersome paper leads.

While Hot Hot Hot makes sales like a retail store or catalog business, you can learn from other models for making direct sales on the Net. Accessing a database is possible from a Web site, so some companies charge per lookup for you to use their database. Other companies generate commission-based sales or other transaction fees. The *New York Times* is working on a way for readers of an online *Times'* movie or theater review to buy tickets after reading the review. The *Times* will pocket a fee for each ticket sold. Newspaper publisher Knight-Ridder plans to add a section to its online travel articles so readers can book tickets to destinations mentioned in the articles. Knight-Ridder will receive the travel agent's commission.

Instead of charging per-transaction or per-item, some businesses charge a flat fee per month or per year—a subscription.

CDNow's $20,000 Web success

Twenty-four-year-old brothers Matt and Jason Olim borrowed $20,000 from their parents to open an Internet-only music CD store (see Figure 12.4). CDNow (**www.cdnow.com**) opened its doors in August 1994. CDNow grossed $2 million in sales in 1995, has been profitable since December 1995, and sold $6 million in 1996. Its sales continue to increase 15 percent per month.

The Olim brothers differentiated their business from other Internet CD sellers by offering the largest selection of CDs and related products such as T-shirts. The company claims to offer 150,000 different items. Its online catalog design makes it easy for customers to find

Figure 12.4   Two brothers started CDNow in their parents' basement.

information. CDNow drop-ships most purchases overnight, and accepts returns at no charge to customers. Costs are kept low because few items are physically stocked.

To draw visitors, CDNow ran magazine advertisements, which resulted in little traffic. It hired a PR agency, which generated publicity articles. Articles brought more visitors than ads in the same magazines. Most CDNow visitors come from online marketing. The company is listed in all appropriate search engines (such as Yahoo and Alta Vista) and directories. The listings cost CDNow nothing but the staff time needed to write and submit them, and they send thousands of prospects to CDNow's Web catalog. Jason Olim estimated that 100 prospects a day come from the InfoSeek search engine alone.

Traffic is now so high that other companies pay CDNow more than $10,000 a month to advertise on CDNow's site.

Email to customers is even more productive. Email costs the company nothing to send, so targeted mailings to different classes of its customers (based on customer sales activity) are consistently profitable. CDNow's largest mass mailing went to 15,000 customers offering a 10 percent discount valid only for 2 days. In those 2 days the company grossed more than twice as much as it ever had in any 2-day period. The company's email announcement made some customers angry, a few refusing to buy from the company again. Mindful of the risk of losing customers but still conscious of the value of its email marketing, the Olim brothers are working to refine the effectiveness of their mailings.

Subscription sales model

7,800 people pay Tom Tabor $100 a year to receive his email. Tabor publishes *HPCWire,* a weekly newsletter delivered by email. In addition to revenue from subscribers, Tabor charges up to $4,000 per issue for advertisements. Advertisers pay based on readership; Tabor's advertising readership base is larger than just his paid subscribers because he emails all prospective subscribers who inquire about *HPCWire* the latest table of contents (**www.tgc.com**) plus all advertisements.

ESPN SportsZone also charges subscription fees for its Web site. The site provides plenty of free stuff, which acts as enticements to draw people into paid areas. Subscribers pay $4.95 per month. By mid-1996, SportsZone signed up 140,000 paying members, generating $700,000 per month from subscription fees alone.

These businesses makes straightforward use of the subscription sales model. Many success stories have proven that this model works well on the Net. In subscription sales, you get money from subscribers. You might be paid per year, per month, per week, per hour, or per transaction, but subscribers pay you for content. In the real world, content is usually subsidized by advertising. When people pay for content—whether it is in a book or on a cable TV channel— most of the money pays for the distribution channel, not for the content. This is especially true of mass-market content. Specialized content can claim a higher per-customer price, but that is offset by the fact that specialized content usually sells in much lower quantities than mass-market content.

The interesting thing about the Net is that its technology lets you inexpensively custom-tailor your content, so individual subscribers receive personalized content, highly specialized to meet an individual's precise needs. It's important to note that the final form of the content your subscribers see does not need to resemble any sort of print publication. It can be quite different. Two examples of businesses that do a good job of personalizing content for individual subscribers are Ernst & Young and Quote.com.

Ernst & Young created a service called Ernie (**http://ernie.ey.com**). For a flat fee of $6,000 per year, the Ernie staff will answer your questions about any business topic submitted via email with a guaranteed two-day turnaround. The first 4 hours Ernie was available, 10 companies signed up.

Quote.com (**www.quote.com**) is a classic Internet success story. Chris Cooper started the business with himself, a T1 Internet connection, and a Sun clone computer "because I didn't want to spend enough money to buy a real Sun." Today he has a healthy company with employees, customers worldwide, and several real Sun computers.

Cooper's idea was to receive stock and investment ticker information as it changed, to let subscribers pick exactly the companies and types of quotes they wanted, and to email fresh quotes to them throughout the trading day. He started programming in October 1993 and opened for business July 1994. "I spent zero for advertising," said Cooper. "I did spend money for a PR firm to do traditional publicity for four to five months around the launch. I posted messages in newsgroups occasionally. I received a couple of flames—less than the number of fingers on one hand. When I explained to the flamers what we're doing, I never heard back from them. On newsgroups, I only posted about the free services we offer."

As an appetizer, Quote.com lets prospects subscribe for free to quotes on a small number of stocks, delivered after business hours. To get more information on more stocks delivered during business hours, a subscriber must pay. The company reached its break-even point seven months after its launch. By September 1995, Quote.com had 40,000 subscribers to its free services. The number of paid subscribers averages about 15 percent of the number of freebies. The quantity of both free and paid subscribers grows about 20 percent per month. Customers pay between $10 and hundreds per month to select from an ever-increasing menu of services. One imaginative offering delivers bar charts of IPO prices, updated every five minutes.

Cooper said that Quote.com's main problems were technical ones rising from the company's fast growth. "We had difficulties in scaling up," he reported. "As our number of customers builds, we have to keep increasing our hardware and everything else to keep up. We didn't write our software initially to scale up very well. We thought we did, but when we grew we had software problems that caused problems with customers getting their quotes for a couple of days. Our programmers put in long days and our software is more scalable now." For its Web server, Quote.com uses Netscape's Netsite Commerce Server. "It's great," said Cooper. "It's had no problems at all."

Quote.com takes credit card information on its Web site, and on its 800 telephone number from customers who don't want to send their credit card numbers over the Net. Quote.com is paid with credit cards by about two-thirds of its customers and sends bills to the rest. It emails monthly bills to individuals and sends paper invoices to institutional and corporate customers. Cooper cautions would-be "Interpreneurs," "The problem is that the entry barriers are pretty low. You can get in pretty easily, but so can your next-door neighbor. Anything successful quickly creates competitors."

Quote.com uses the Web for sales and email to distribute to its subscribers, a reminder that the Web is not always the most effective way to distribute to your own subscribers. You can use email like Quote.com and *HPCWire*.

Remember, too, that you can generate other revenue streams in addition to subscriber fees. An Internet-delivered newspaper, *American Reporter*, generates significant revenue through sales of reprint rights to its articles. *Mercury Center* makes 10 years of newspaper stories searchable online for 15 cents per minute, which "generates a heck of a lot of money" according to *Mercury Center*'s Barry Parr. And of course, there is advertising. In fact, some Internet businesses ignore sales to subscribers and prosper on advertising sales alone.

Advertising sales model

According to Robert Young of ProductView, consumers with home computers generate 40 percent of all consumer sales. Several studies show that people with online services watch 25 percent less television than the national average, so TV commercials have less chance of reaching these big spenders. And consumers are only the tip of the iceberg; the real money on the Net is chasing after fat business-to-business and institutional sales prospects.

All of which makes the Net rich turf to sell advertising.

First, you need a strong lure to attract visitors. Owners' Network (**www. owners.com**) lets home owners list homes for sale in its database for free. Add a scanned picture for $10. Sellers save the 6 percent realtors' commission. Owners' Network led to sales of at least 500 homes in its first six months. It took in $200,000 in advertising sales to moving companies, furniture stores, and mortgage companies.

Motorcycle Online (**www.motorcycle.com**) was profitable in less than two years. Created by a small, productive staff of eight people, the site's 140,000 visitors a month brought it a solid core of advertisers on one-year contracts. The site provides more than a thousand stories written by staff and freelancers, a database of motorcycle specs, and videos of racing. Its advertising clients track the visitors they receive from Motorcycle Online advertisements and the orders those visitors generate. The clients know for a fact their advertisements are worthwhile. How profitable is Motorcycle Online? The site's CEO Brent Plummer said, "We're not bragging, but we're not in debt and I'm buying a new house."

Physicians Online (**www.po.com**) has more than 140,000 medical doctors on its private network, which includes access to medical literature and databases, and provides email accounts and specialty-oriented discussion groups. Advertiser-supported, Physicians Online also charges fees to build intranets for physicians' offices. A similar advertiser-supported service for dentists, Dental X Change (**www.dentalonline.com**), is also profitable.

Chances are your Web site won't have the huge audience of Netscape or Yahoo, but you can still make money from advertisers if you have an electronic publication or Web site that delivers the right demographics and numbers. What kind of numbers? If your visitors are another company's perfect sales prospects, you might be able to charge $10 to $40 per thousand impressions for banner ads.

You can sell one of two kinds of advertising: mass market or special interest. In recent years, growth in the traditional advertising industry has been in special interest advertising, and this is the area where the Internet really shines. The Net is not so good at mass market advertising. Instead of broadcasting, the Net does narrowcasting. From your point of view, that's an advantage. You don't have to invest in the heavy-duty hardware and support required by a Net site visited by millions of people. If you deliver a smaller quantity of readers who are more desirable to advertisers, the advertisers will pay you more per person. When you sell space to special-interest advertisers, your revenue per reader will be higher than you'd receive for mass-market advertisements.

As a form of ancillary revenue, you can sell statistical and demographic information based on your readership, although this can be a problem in some countries with strict computer privacy laws.

For a variation on the advertising sales model, you can sell *sponsorships* instead of advertisements. What's the difference between sponsorship and advertising? An advertiser pays to reach your Internet visitors or readers. A sponsor underwrites your operating costs. Sponsorship is better known in the world of nonprofit organizations, but underwriting costs can be beneficial for businesses as well.

For more information on selling banner ads, you'll find a whole chapter on the subject later.

11 steps to Net marketing

You might approach Internet marketing by scanning your existing marketing materials, dumping them on a Web page, and walking away. You might. That will be profitable for some businesses, but not for most. That approach won't reach many prospects, and those few it does reach won't be impressed. Here is an 11-step process to help implement Internet marketing that generates more positive results.

Step 1. Investigate and analyze the Net as a marketing medium.

We're talking hands-on experience here. Reading this book by itself (or any other book, for that matter) will not give you a clear understanding of how the Internet works and how to use it effectively as a marketing tool. Grab a keyboard and jump in.

Step 2. Define your Internet objectives to fit with your other marketing efforts.

Treat Internet marketing as a *supplement* to your existing, traditional marketing methods, not as a *substitute*. Few markets in either the consumer or the business-to-business arenas offer enough Internet penetration for you to go all-Internet and drop other methods of marketing communications.

Don't let the pretty little Web pictures make you lose sight of the more important big picture of your business objectives.

Step 3. Decide who you want to reach.

Everything else in your marketing process revolves around this choice.

Do you want university administrators, businesspeople, or consumers? You'll find all in different places and all have different needs. What age range do you want? Does it make any different where they live? Do you care what language they speak? Do you want a lone individual for an impulse buy or someone part of a committee making a carefully weighed decision? A bargain-hunter or someone who wants the best at any price? What kind of connection speed will they have? (This determines the design direction of Web pages.)

Refine the picture of your ideal target with as much precision as you can. It won't hurt to *ask them* what they want to see.

Step 4. Determine how *specifically* you want your prospect to respond.

We are not talking some generality like "have warm, fuzzy feelings about our company." That is vague and useless. Instead, be specific. Where do you want your prospect to go? What do you want that prospect to do? What steps, in what specific order? How will you measure if your prospect has done this? *Measurability is extremely important.* If your prospect's response isn't measurable in some way, you will never know if your Internet marketing works or not.

Step 5. What is your competitive advantage?

You should already know this. It should be one, short, memorable sentence. Short, because Internet people move quickly. A typical Internet user will not sit still long enough to wade through two screens of boilerplate to find out just what (if anything) makes your company different from its competitors. And, please don't say something vague like "People helping people help people." Yuck! Be specific. Computer Literacy Bookshops Inc. offers "the world's largest selection of computer books." That's short and tells you how that company differs from the rest. Don't worry about being cute. Just be clear.

You need to know your competitive advantage before you plan your Internet marketing so all your Internet projects can reinforce that advantage.

Step 6. What key benefits of your product or service most sharply convey your advantage?

Again, you should already know this. For Internet marketing, you may want to look at your key benefits from a different angle: Which benefits would be most important to *a prospect who uses the Internet*? Internet people might be a bit different from your other prospects. Considering this may cause you to reorder some priorities in a way that will make more impact on the Net.

Step 7. Choose your weapons.

Will you use a Web site? Will you build a customer email list? Do you need a database or a push server? What Internet tools will you use?

Step 8. Decide what information and actions you must present to accomplish Step 4.

You can Internet-ize listings of dealers, contact information for sales reps, data sheets, support information. If you keep up-to-date product information on your Net site, your distributors and resellers have uninterrupted access to the facts they need to promote and sell your products.

Look at the information you already have, and look at what new information you could create. When starting out, don't go overboard. Select only the most important information that would be easiest to deliver on the Net. Look for the information that will generate the biggest results and for what is most "doable." The process of marketing on the Net will change your ideas about how you want to use the Net, so expect to make changes.

IMPORTANT: This step is not complete until you reach a stage of feature lock, as described in Chapter 2.

Step 9. Turn it into digital versions and put it on the Net.

The cost of presenting information on the Internet is influenced by how much information your company already has on disk. If you have the information you need already in electronic format from your catalogs, press releases, product specifications, or newsletters, it's easy to copy the information to your Internet server. Don't get too elaborate. Start simple and watch out for feature creep.

Step 10. Promote, promote, promote.

It is a cruel fact of life that most Web pages are undervisited. If you want yours to be a winner, pull out all the stops. Put your email address and home page address on your business cards, letterhead, advertisements, and brochures. Make your Internet addresses as prominent as your 800 number. Publicize your site to print media and to electronic publications on the Internet. Several companies specialize in promoting Web sites; hire one.

Step 11. Listen to your customers, learn, and improve.

When you open the doors to your Web site, you are not finished. That is the *beginning* of your marketing project. You have created a living, breathing being that is out in the world. Measure your response so you can market better. Welcome comments, even when critical. Seek feedback. Then improve your site. If a bicycle stops moving it will fall over. So will your Internet marketing efforts.

CHAPTER 13

Email Lists and Newsgroups: Fast Sales Boosters

*"When I turn my computer on, money comes out of it.
And I never spent a penny for advertising."*

—Paolo Pignatelli, The Corner Store

The Web gets all the glory, but many companies find that other marketing workhorses on the Net can be faster and more cost-effective: email lists and newsgroups. Both must be used with caution by marketers, but both can be rewarding.

First, what email lists do

Apparel manufacturer Joe Boxer Corp. dropped its 800 number in favor of using its email address **joeboxer@boxer.com** to communicate with customers. In 18 months, Joe Boxer received 20,000 email responses. It then asked everyone who sent it email if they would like to subscribe to its email list. The company uses email to conduct focus group-type research and to email product announcements to its customers. Back in the dark ages when Joe Boxer used an 800 number, the company would hear from customers only on rare occasions when customers wanted to call. With email, Joe Boxer contacts customers when *it wants to reach them*, and it can make contact with them *repeatedly*, unlike an 800 number, which most customers call only once. Joe Boxer uses its email list to build *ongoing* relationships with its customers.

Joe Boxer's tool, a mailing list server, produces the email equivalent of postal mass mailings. Let's say you want to send 2,000 customers a message about your new office in their area, so you send them a notice by email instead of snail mail. How it works: You send one message to your list server. Your server combines your one message with your list of 2,000 email addresses and sends out 2,000 individually-addressed email messages. Faster than postal mail. Takes less work. No stamps required.

This principle of "send one message in, get a bunch of messages out" has other applications as well. For instance, on a collaborative project, a mailing list server can coordinate communications. You can program your server to accept messages from anyone working on a project and to email copies to everyone on your project's list. Thus, everyone on the project sees the same information, and no one gets left "out of the loop."

Or you can create a public discussion group, if you set up your list server so it can receive any sent messages. Your discussion-type lists can be *moderated*—which means that someone inspects and approves every message before it goes out—or *unmoderated*.

A list server also automates signups to your lists. People who want to get your information, or a specific subset of your information, can send email to your list server software and your server will automatically add them to the right list or lists.

Mailing lists are extremely popular. The Internet carries more than 100,000 mailing lists—no one is sure exactly how many. More than 50,000 of them are open to the public.

Second, newsgroups

Newsgroups are like email discussion lists except that instead of coming to you via email, you go to them to read them. You pick and choose the messages you want to read (see Figure 13.1). A newsgroup is an electronic equivalent of a cork bulletin board, where messages are *posted* instead of sent. You don't have to deal with every message, as you do when an email discussion list dumps dozens of messages in your email box. And anything you post to a newsgroup can be read by thousands of people worldwide.

The best thing about newsgroups is that they are *targeted*. About 20,000 Usenet newsgroups exist, each one addressing its own specific topic. The topics neatly classify hundreds of thousands of newsgroup readers into distinct market segments. If you can't find a newsgroup that speaks to your prospects, you can create your own that does. For some companies, marketing on newsgroups generates more sales than any other weapon in their Internet marketing arsenal.

Important first step

Many of the marketing techniques in this chapter assume that you are adding signature files on the bottom of your email messages. If you don't yet have a signature file, or you are not sure what one is, turn now to pages 224–226 in Chapter 9. Chapter 13 will be much more effective for you after you have your own sig file.

Sender		Subject	Date
TexTax	·	Re: Depreciation done...	Thu 18:54
		Help ! Cash gift from a non ...	
TexTax	·	Re: Help ! Cash gift fro...	Thu 18:53
Gill & Co. ...	·	Re: Help ! Cash gift fro...	15:31
Jim G	·	Re: Help ! Cash gift fro...	Thu 18:54
Andy Grossman	·	Re: Help ! Cash gift fro...	15:31
Jusssssstme	·	Re: Health Reimburse...	Thu 18:55
		UGMA Accounts	
HELJAN gal	·	Re: UGMA Accounts	Thu 18:55
Paul Maffia	·	Re: UGMA Accounts	15:30
TaxService...	·	Re: UGMA Accounts	15:30
jonatha@ibm...	·	Re: UGMA Accounts	15:31
TaxService	·	Tax Policy Experts De...	Thu 18:55
Dick	·	Charter of misc.taxes....	14:33
Irek Zawadzki	·	Retirement plan	14:51
Edward Zollars	·	AMT a growing proble...	15:14
Pilsun Bong	·	Question about Tax	15:29
Alan G. Kalman	·	Re: Making a transition	15:30
William Johnson	·	I owe back taxes to th...	15:31
Susan Hinrichs	·	refinancing mortgage	15:31
James H. Fritzs...	·	Taxability of employee ...	15:32

Figure 13.1   In each newsgroup, you pick the messages you want to read by their subject line. These are subjects from the newsgroup **misc.taxes.moderated**.

This chapter tells how businesses use email lists and newsgroups. I'll explain the four uses of email lists, from the easiest to the most complex. Next, I'll cover building your own lists and renting lists, followed by tips for managing your email lists. Then I'll cover posting on newsgroups. The last section, netlurking and posting on email lists and newsgroups, explains a somewhat time-consuming but effective marketing technique.

But first, before all the wonderful things you can do, a few words about a big problem with marketing on email lists and newsgroups.

Don't step in the spam

Why the fuss about spam? As Daniel Janal observed, "Spamming is an ineffective means for producing sales, but a tremendously effective tool to annoy the heck out of your potential market."

Different people have slightly different definitions of Internet spam, but they all boil down to one common thing. Whether you send email or post a message to a newsgroup, if that message is perceived as an unwelcome intrusion, it is spam.

Your prospects on the Net will be offended if you send them unasked-for commercial email or if you post inappropriate commercial messages on newsgroups. As a marketer, be aware that these are the two Net crimes that will cause you to lose the greatest number of prospective customers.

Your role as a marketer is to make any solicitation *effective*. So is unsolicited email effective? In the early days of Net marketing, some companies found that spam was good, claiming response rates of up to three percent. But the Internet has changed, and such response rates for unsolicited email have vanished. Now, one-hundredth of one percent is doing well. I have spoken with some businesses that have rented spam lists that generated no sales at all.

Spamming throws away one of the Internet's greatest strengths for marketers: the ability to target prospects who are interested in what you offer. Instead, spamming spreads a message indiscriminately, addressing more people who don't care than people who do. This is why most spam comes from clue-impaired marketing newbies. More experienced Net marketers talk to people who *want* to hear from them.

How does spam cause problems for you?

Besides annoying potential customers, what other headaches can spam give you?

"When you send unsolicited snail mail, people can throw it away," explained Yoyodyne vice president Jerry Shereshewsky. "When you send unsolicited email, people can retaliate. If they get really crazy, they can download the Library of Congress onto your server."

Remember, the interactivity of the Internet makes it easy for angry people to hit back. If you spam, your 800 number phone bills will soar as angry voices clog your line. Your regular phone line can get clogged, too, and your fax line. Complaints won't hit only you. Your Internet access provider can get so many complaints that it kicks you off the Net. Free software programs automate the process—for example, using InterNIC to look up a spammer's provider and automatically forwarding it a complaint with a sample.

On top of all that, many of your messages *won't get through*. America Online, CompuServe, and Prodigy all block messages from service companies that send unsolicited email. So do many Internet access providers and most large corporations. All top email server software now includes antispam features. Thus, your email will be blocked before anyone ever sees it. And once *some* email from your company is blocked, most blocking software stops *all* email from your company from reaching its destination. Is this a price you're willing to pay?

Spamming is universally despised by consumers. Consumers vote. That is why some nations already have laws on the books prohibiting unsolicited email and why other countries—including the United States—are considering such laws. One now before Congress includes a penalty of $500 *per message*. I expect a federal antispam law to pass within the next year.

"Then, of course, there's Marketing 101: Don't annoy the people you want to sell to," says Jim Sterne, author of *World Wide Web Marketing*. "If only a few people complain, it means that many, many times that number were annoyed and didn't bother. If it's bad manners, then it's bad business. And it *is* bad manners."

SOME SPAM RESOURCES

- For a quick education on what happens to too-blatant advertisers, visit "The Internet Advertisers Blacklist" at **http://math-www.uni-paderborn.de/~axel/BL/blacklist.html**.

- The "Stop Junk Email" Web site (**www.mcs.com/~jcr/junkemail.html**) provides clear, step-by-step instructions on how people get spammers thrown off the Net.

- The FAQ for the newsgroup **news:alt.spam** at **http://digital.net/~gandalf/spamfaq.html** provides additional infomation.

- The "MMF (Make Money Fast) Hall of Humiliation" at **www.clark.net/pub/rolf/mmf** wields a different weapon: humor. It shows examples of stupid spam and pokes fun at them.

- Or you can use free Spam Hater software: **www.compulink.co.uk/~net-services/spam**

Opt-in vs. opt-out

What's the difference between *opt-in* email lists and *opt-out* lists? Does it really matter?

You'll hear these "opt" terms if you work with email lists, especially if you rent lists from other companies to send your own messages to. The difference is important in terms of the response you will generate and because of possible legal repercussions.

Basically, opt-in vs. opt-out means people who have *asked* to be on a list vs. bulk email lists of "non-volunteers." Which is better? You'll get higher responses from good opt-in lists.

Some countries have privacy laws that allow opt-in only. German law, for example, demands prior consent for email marketing messages. These laws apply only to a business that has *not* had a prior relationship with a prospect. For instance, if your Fred Flintstone had not purchased from your quarry before, you could email Fred only from an opt-in list to which Fred had given permission to use his address. But once Fred buys gravel from your quarry, you can email Fred with as many marketing messages as you choose. Just don't make him mad.

For legal reasons and for effectiveness, be cautious about opt-out lists.

Four uses of email lists

Using one software program, you can provide four different kinds of email services. You can run several versions of all four at the same time if you wish. In order of difficulty, from easiest to most time-consuming, the four uses are:

1. Run an email autoresponder or mailbot.
2. Publish email announcements.
3. Publish an email newsletter.
4. Conduct an email discussion group.

Let's look at the pros and cons of each.

1. Run an email autoresponder or mailbot

Your mailing list software can email documents to anyone who requests them. When people say *list server* and *mail archive server*, they are talking about the same software, just configured to handle different duties. When used as an email archive server, the software is often called an *email autoresponder* or *mailbot*.

A mailbot works like a fax-back service: Your customers can send email to automatically receive your brochures, catalogs, and price lists. Because no human intervention is needed, you can offer this as a 24-hour service. Your customers specify what they want in their email, and your server sends it to them.

Here's how it works. You build informational files. Make one a company FAQ list, answering frequently-asked questions—your hours, your location, contact information, information about your products and services—whatever your prospects and customers ask about. Make a file for each of your press releases. Make one for what PR types call a "company backgrounder." You might want another that's a directory of whom to contact in your company for what reasons and how to reach them. You can add files listing dealers who carry your products, product reviews, support notes, and information about add-on products.

Your mailing list server will read incoming messages. An incoming email containing one standard command returns a list of all commands someone can email to your server. Another standard command returns a list of all files that your server can send them. A prospect may ask for, say, your death ray installation instructions, and your list server will send them back. The message that the server returns does not necessarily have to be a pre-existing file. Your server can generate and assemble information on demand.

In other words, a customer could send you an email request for your product catalog, and your list server could pull together your most up-to-date product descriptions and prices, build the catalog file on the fly, and email it to your customer. It could even send back different prices and sales contact information based on your customer's location.

As with other types of Internet services, if you want people to use your mailbot, you must spread the word so they know about it. You can add a line to advertisements, "To learn more, email to productspec2@yourco.com." That address leads to your mailbot, which sends a page describing what sorts of other information the mailbot has available and telling how to reach this information. By using slightly different addresses, one for each source, you can even tally your responses and see which ads or publicity pulled best.

The question is, do you really need this service if you also have a World Wide Web site? In most cases, probably not. A Web page presents information more understandably for consumers and businesspeople than the commands and different email addresses needed to retrieve documents from a mailbot. However, an email archive does offer advantages in some situations. It can present a large quantity of documents inexpensively. It delivers them to people who don't have World Wide Web access, and it doesn't require you to reformat documents into HTML.

You can also use a mailbot together with your Web site. For instance, a Web page could say "If you'd like to receive this 39-page white paper by email, type your email address here and click on the 'Send' button." Your Web page would send the email address to your mailbot, which would automatically forward the white paper. This function is handy to distribute long text documents, which are often easier for people to receive as email than to download in HTML format from the Web.

You don't have to put mailbot software on your own computer. Service bureaus rent space for between $1 and $10 per document per month, usually with a ten to twenty document minimum. This makes it affordable for small companies to make information available by email. *Find a company that does not charge per-request fees* for this service.

2. Publish email announcements

If your business sends announcements by postal mail, you may be able to use the Internet as a replacement. Even better, if a high percentage of your customers use Internet email, you can send regular announcements to remind them about you. An email announcement list is absolutely one of the most powerful marketing tools you can use, and it can be cheaper than dirt. You can use a list to build your Web site traffic, to generate inquiries on new products, to bond to new prospects, and to conduct promotional events.

Computer Literacy Bookshops Inc. holds free lecture events in its stores with top speakers on technical topics. Two weeks before each event, Computer Literacy emails a brief, two-screen announcement of the upcoming free event to its list of subscribers. The result? Hundreds of attendees at a marketing cost of almost zero.

The biggest announcement list I've run across was the one Microsoft created when Windows 95 came out. It attracted more than 750,000 subscribers.

The key to growing a successful announcement list is to get people to *ask* to subscribe. If you add email addresses of your customers who have not requested your mailings, you will get angry customers. People regard unsolicited email as spam, and it makes them flaming mad. If you decide to build an announcement list, plan on constant promotion to add new subscribers. Computer Literacy puts "how to subscribe" instructions on bookmarks, in its catalog, on its Web site, and on flyers. You must be similarly relentless if you want your list to grow.

Your list can be open to the public or by invitation only. If your business has a Web site, you can include a page where Web visitors can enter their email addresses to receive notices of updates to your site. You can send subscribers to your list brief announcements or entire newsletters—anything that is not perceived by your readers as an advertisement. Any message you send should provide a benefit to your subscribers and have real value. If the information you provide has enough value, you might even be able to charge people for subscribing to your list.

You can easily track sources of subscribers. For each new source you use to promote your list, create a unique email address: **news1@yourco.com**, **news2@yourco.com**, etc. If you track and tally how many subscription requests each address receives, you can tell which sources work best at generating new subscribers. You'll learn where to focus your promotional efforts in the future.

Unless you use your list to send a newsletter, keep your announcements short and frequent. If you don't stay in touch at least every two to three months, recipients will forget they gave you their address, and you may get flames asking, "Where the #$! did you get my name?"

An announcement list requires work, but not much. Someone must write and enter the announcements. Keeping the subscriber list up to date is an important chore, and your technical staff will have a small amount of work to perform to send each mailing.

In addition to sending rubber-stamp announcements that are the same for everyone, you can personalize your announcements. For example, if you buy a plane ticket through Microsoft's online travel agency Expedia (**www.expedia.com**), you'll receive an email message describing what you can see and do at your destination during the dates you'll be there.

ZDNet offers an email announcement list called NetBuyer Personal Alert to add value to its NetBuyer shopping Web site. Visitors fill in a Web form describing which products they want, and Personal Alert emails them when those products reach new low price points.

Similarly, the clothing merchant Eddie Bauer offers an E.B. Reminder service that sends email to customers to remind them of important dates, such as birthdays and anniversaries.

To send personalized announcements of your own, you'll need to use an electronic lettershop service, or software such as Alpha Software's NetMailer, or another package that can merge your standard letter templates with the names, addresses, and other data in your customer and prospect files. Your results are individually composed and addressed personal email messages, each one tailored to the needs of its recipient.

Announcements are sent at irregular intervals, whenever the need arises. The next stage up in the email food chain is to send information at regularly scheduled intervals, such as a newsletter.

3. Publish an email newsletter

Scott Adams's *Dilbert Newsletter* goes to more than 40,000 "brighter-than-average and increasingly attractive members of Dogbert's New Ruling Class, poised to take their place at Dogbert's side when he conquers the world and makes everybody else our slaves." Adams reaches his 40,000 fans with email, so his costs of production and distribution are almost nothing. Each issue promotes new Dilbert books and products for true believers to buy.

Adams's business is one of tens of thousands that profitably publishes an email newsletter. Compared to mailbots or email announcement lists, email newsletters take more planning and more sustained work—but their payoffs can be tremendous. I've worked with several businesses that have used email newsletters. Every single one of them saw an increase in sales.

An email newsletter doesn't necessarily need writing as creative as Dilbert. It can be as simple as an automatically-generated file of updated information. For instance, Computer Literacy Bookshops used email to send weekly lists of newly-arrived books on hot topics, such as all new books on C and C++.

Your email newsletter can be much more elaborate, and may even become a profit center. The email newsletter *FlashBack* (**www.flashback.com**) delivers the equivalent of 100 to 300 pages per month to 140,000 subscribers. Subscriptions are free, but owner John McLaughlin is paid thousands of dollars per month by *FlashBack* advertisers.

A good newsletter attracts prospects, helps turn prospects into customers, and keeps customers coming back for more. A newsletter is good for cross-selling or promoting a family of products to a customer who normally buys just one. As people subscribe to your electronic newsletter, you also add names to build your email list, which you can use for other, related purposes.

To succeed, each issue of your electronic publication must deliver news, not fluff and promotions. Don't view it primarily as a selling tool. Research, write, and distribute only articles that deliver genuine benefits to readers. View it as an opportunity to demonstrate that your business delivers value. Don't run self-congratulatory articles or articles based on press releases. They turn off readers.

Tell people about your company's future plans—not promises, but concrete information with figures and facts. You will get good reactions from stories about specific customers and what they have accomplished with your products. Suggestions on how to avoid and handle problems also draw a good response. Include a "Letters to the Editor" section, and encourage your readers to email their ideas to you. Genuinely interesting letters—not empty praise—can interest your readers and reduce the amount of writing for you to do. Another department that has worked well for several of my clients' newsletters is a question-and-answer column.

Frequency is better than length. A newsletter with a little good information that comes out often—once every week or two—will generate more response than a bigger newsletter that appears less often. Besides, a newsletter longer than about ten pages might cause problems for readers whose systems can't handle long messages. If you publish your own electronic newsletter, make it as easy for you to do as possible. Don't get ambitious. Keep it simple and frequent.

Get your own ISSN number

As a finishing touch, you can get an International Standard Serials Number for your newsletter. An ISSN number costs nothing, makes you seem more established, and helps librarians catalog your newsletter. (Yes, libraries do store electronic publications.)

For more information about ISSN numbers and instructions (in English and French) on how to get one for your publication, go to **www.well.com/ www/issnic**.

4. Conduct an email discussion group

The next step up from a newsletter takes a continuing time commitment. In fact, an email discussion group takes a babysitter.

A discussion mailing list is an inexpensive way for your business to provide a place for ongoing online conversations between several people. No central authority polices discussion lists, so you can address whatever topics you choose. You can open your discussion lists to the public or keep them private and by invitation only. You can run discussion lists for your customers and support staff, and other lists for internal use by employees. Discussion lists are a useful way for people on a project to communicate, especially on collaborative projects between your business and other companies.

Before you start your discussion list, plan the type of discussion you want to offer. Who will you target as subscribers? What topics will be discussed? How will you promote your list? Will it be open to the public, open only by invitation, or open only to members of certain companies or organizations?

Do you want to offer subscribers the option of receiving the messages in *digest format*? Digests gather messages and deliver them in bunches, sometimes in condensed form. Digest format offers your recipients a choice between receiving many small messages or a few long ones—an important consideration for people who pay for each message received and people concerned with reducing the volume of email they deal with. Generally, for discussion lists that provide a choice of digest format and non-digest format, about 80 percent of the subscribers will want the digest version. However, chances are that 70 percent or more of the messages will come from non-digest subscribers.

Do you want your list to be *moderated* (someone screens all messages before mailing them to subscribers) or *unmoderated* (senders' messages are emailed directly to everyone on the list without human intervention)? Here's where the babysitter comes in. You don't need a moderator for a 60-person internal discussion list. But if you have a 500-person list with your customers, someone will need to watch over it every day.

Mostly, your moderator will be concerned with rejecting off-topic and inappropriate posts. Reasons to reject posts to your discussion group include:

1. Has nothing to do with your discussion's topic.
2. Lacks any substantive information or is too self-serving.
3. Reiterates a point someone else already made without adding anything new.
4. Covers a topic that has already been discussed in depth and dealt with.
5. Replies to one person and is not valuable to members of your discussion list as a whole. This kind of post is better handled by email.
6. Does not have a proper "Subject:" line.
7. Contains unintelligible writing.
8. Is taken directly from copyrighted material. (You can get into trouble for this.)

Some discussion group software automatically creates an archive of past messages that you can add to your Web site. If you are looking for a way to boost traffic to your site, you can also tie your email discussion list together with a Web site discussion forum. Messages posted to one discussion can be mirrored on the other. Since it takes far fewer participants to sustain an ongoing email discussion (about 50 people) than it does to keep a Web discussion alive (at least 300 regular visitors; more realistically, 500 to 1,000 visitors per week), this email/Web combo is the best way I've found to jump-start a discussion forum on your Web site.

Getting started with email lists

After you decide what uses you want for email lists, explore what you need to run them. Should you hire a third party to process your email lists or should you run them on your own computer? What software do you need? Should you build your own list or rent somebody else's? How and where can you rent email lists to supplement your own?

You can run list software either on your own computer, on a computer run by your Internet access provider, or on a computer provided by a completely separate service company.

Hire an electronic lettershop service, or . . .

Many companies want to create mailing lists for mass mailings or discussions or to provide information from an autoresponder, but do not want to run a server of their own in-house. Never fear, providers are here. You can rent space on a mailing list server from your Internet access provider or from a service bureau. In fact, your access provider and your Web site host are the first places you should check.

They are cheap. Most cost $10 to $15 per month. If you use an outside bureau, check to see if you can use your own domain name as part of the list server's email address. Most often you must pay extra to do so unless you rent list server space from the same company that provides your Internet access.

Unless you have technical staff to monitor your list server software, I recommend farming out mailing list management to another company. Like most other Internet services, prices and quality vary, so shop around. Distance is no factor. Your email list service bureau can be far away. In fact, you may find a better provider in another country.

Most service bureaus provide a basic level of email list processing services. If you do large mass emailings, you may need a company that can do more. These are called *electronic lettershop* services, after the lettershop firms that process large direct marketing campaigns via snail mail.

An important service that electronic lettershops provide is called *merge/purge*. Merge/purge ability is especially important when you rent lists of email addresses from other companies. You'll pay per address to rent outside lists. A lettershop service can cross any list you rent with any other lists so you mail only to unique addresses. For instance, if you rent customer lists from BillyBob's Worm Co. and from Joe's Baitshop, you can first merge/purge BillyBob's list against Joe's, deleting any duplicate addresses from Joe's list so you mail to each one only once (and pay for each one only once!). Then the lettershop merges/purges both lists against your own list of customers, so you don't email to your own clients (this also reduces the number of addresses you pay for).

Two leading electronic lettershops are Netcreations (**www.netcreations.com**) and L-Ease, offered by L-Soft International (**www.lsoft.com**). For a short, incomplete directory of email list providers (but still the best I've found), visit **www.cs.ubc.ca/spider/edmonds/usenet/ml-providers.txt**.

. . . Buy your own list software

What if you want to do everything in-house? You can set up small lists—using Internet addresses—with cc:Mail, Microsoft Mail, or Eudora, but these require you to do a lot of work by hand.

Your can use these software packages and update or edit your list by hand for a singles short list of 200 to 300 addresses. People who want to subscribe to your list, have questions, or want their name removed from your list can send email to the person who manages your list.

It's nice to offer the extra personal touch of processing by hand, but for each address added, deleted, or changed, someone must open a message from that addressee, read it, write down the requested action, type an email reply to the addressee, send it, and type that day's changes to your list. This takes at least a minute per name, often longer. For a thousand-name list with typical churn, you're looking at from two to three hours of tedious work per day.

Automated list management isn't as friendly to subscribers as a live human, but it saves staff time and it's more accurate—no typos when adding an address to your list. For lists longer than 200 or 300 addresses, you'll want automated mailing list software.

Without human assistance, these software programs respond to subscription and cancellation requests, send and retrieve archived messages, and help take care of undeliverable messages that the network bounces back to your list. List servers are efficient; you can run one on a slow old computer and still get fast response time.

Sending to email lists is efficient, but contrary to some hucksters' claims, it is *not* instant. It takes time for your computer to combine your message with your list of addresses and send the finished products. If you have a list of significant length, it can take hours or even days to process your names. The amount of time depends on the message length, your connection speed, and the number of names on your list.

Mailing list management software

Here's a quick guide to the top of the crop in mailing list management programs.

- Listserv (**www.lsoft.com**) is the most popular mailing list management program. Two versions are available: Listerv Lite (for Windows and Unix, $500 to $2,000), and Listserv Classic (For IBM mainframes, Windows, and Unix, $500/year –to $8,000/year).

- Majordomo (**www.math.psu.edu/barr/majordomo-faq.html**) is a free Unix program that is the second most popular mailing list manager.

- ListProcessor (**www.cren.net**) is a popular free Unix program, called ListProc for short.

- A newer free Unix product, SmartList (**www.cpr.com/Documentation/ SmartList**), has earned enthusiastic reviews from its users.

- LWGate (**www.netspace.org/users/dwb/lwgate.html**) is a free Unix add-on for Listserv, ListProcessor, Majordomo, and SmartList that makes the products easier to administer and automatically generates a home page for each list, including automated subscription instructions and Web archives of past messages.

- In spite of its name, the free Mac program Macjordomo (**http:// leuca.med.cornell.edu/Macjordomo**) is *not* related to the Unix Majordomo.

- The best-known Mac program is ListStar (**www.starnine.com/liststar/ liststar.html**), which costs $500 for an SMTP version and $200 for a POP version.

- LetterRip (**www.fogcity.com**) is a fast, incredibly easy-to-use, $300 Mac program.

- eMail Express (**www.iso-ezine.com**) is a $130 to $400 Mac program that integrates with FileMaker Pro databases to generate personalized mass mailings. This program was originally developed to handle subscriptions for electronic magazines and to communicate with registered software users. Add-ons are available for subscription control and subscription tracking.

- GroupMaster (**www.groupmaster.com**) is Windows software with especially good reporting features. You can see who has actually looked at your messages. It costs $500 to $10,000, depending on which version and what add-ons you want.

- SLMail (**www.seattlelab.com**) gets good marks from users I've talked with. This Windows program can work from behind firewalls and costs $200 to $325.

- SVList (**www.cadvision.com/softventures**) is a simple Windows program that costs $30. It can handle only one list at a time.

- EBase/Mailer (**www.braintree.com**) works with a database to send personalized messages. This Windows program costs $30.

- NetMailer (**www.alphasoftware.com**) is a $50 Windows program that also lets you merge your addresses with a database to create personalized messages. It's the best of the low-end Windows mailing list managers.

I do not recommend E-Mail Assistant from Arial Software. I have reports that the $250 to $500 Windows program does not work as claimed, and customer support is negligible.

If you are really serious about your email marketing, you will want to do extensive tracking and reporting. The best software I've found for this is Veranda (**www.tallysys.com**), priced at $3,000 and up for Windows. While intended to monitor internal email use, Veranda can also be useful for mailing list analysis. It uses a Crystal Reports runtime module but could produce many more kinds of reports if the full Crystal Reports program could be integrated with it.

Large companies with tons of incoming email might be interested in another specialized family of software products to automatically respond to customers. Brightware (**www.brightware.com**) makes products that use artificial intelligence to answer email. Brightware reads incoming email messages, analyzes their content, and sends back requested information. When the software can't figure out a piece of email by itself, it forwards the message to a human. It can handle complicated requests; one financial services company uses Brightware to process loan applications, and the software completes 52% of them. Other companies using it for more conventional electronic correspondence report that Brightware takes care of up to 80% of their email. Brightware costs $200,000 and is available for Windows NT, with a Unix version promised Real Soon Now.

QUESTIONS TO ASK

Whether you plan on using your own mailing list server or renting one from a provider, ask these questions before you decide:

- Can this server software handle both moderated and unmoderated lists?

- Can this software check the addresses of incoming software so I can generate private lists?

- Can I split one long list into several shorter ones?

- What kind of error recovery does this software provide? What happens when the power fails or the Net connection goes down in the middle of my mailing?

- How many days or weeks will it take my system administrator to learn how to manage this software?

- Will the software condense messages into digests?

How to run your lists

Okay, so you buy your software and pop it onto your computer, or you hire your Web site host to run your email lists. That's all you need to worry about, right? Can you just kick back and let the techos run everything?

Sorry to pop your balloon, but the answer is "no"! You still need to monitor your lists to make sure everything works—and to head off problems like the following story.

An email list horror story

This is a true story. Names have been changed to protect the guilty.

Joleen Davis, manager of the announcement mailing list for Flavored Colas Inc., opened her email one morning and gasped in shock. The night before,

Flavored Colas had emailed notices to its customers. Joleen expected the usual handful of bounced messages that follow a mass emailing. Instead, she received a flame denouncing the company in vile terms for sending unsolicited email and a demand to remove the recipient from Flavored's mailing list.

Joleen searched through her mailing list, but the address of the flaming writer *did not appear* on it. She wrote a sympathetic reply, telling the flamer that Flavored Colas never put anyone on its list unless that person specifically asked to be added, and that she had searched the email list and not found Mr. Flamer's address. Then she emailed the reply to him.

(Do you see the start of a problem? Flavored Colas had no formal procedure for Joleen to follow when flamed. She should have known to immediately call a technical and management firefighting team.)

Within an hour, Joleen received a second email from Mr. Flamer, more vile than the first. Mr. Flamer accused Flavored Colas of stealing people's email addresses from the Internet and bombarding everyone at Mr. Flamer's company with unsolicited email advertising. Joleen called her supervisor, Sam Bell.

Joleen and Sam searched Flavored's entire email list for Mr. Flamer's address. They couldn't find it. They found three other list subscribers whose email addresses came from Flamer's company, but no address for Flamer himself.

Joleen wrote a polite email explanation of what she had done. Sam reviewed it carefully, and Joleen sent it to Mr. Flamer, hoping it would satisfy him.

That afternoon, Theresa Topnotch, a senior executive at Flavored Colas, opened an email message to read a horrifying attack on Flavored Colas. It was unsigned. Theresa looked at the sender's address at the top of the diatribe and was startled to find it had been sent *from an address within Flavored Colas itself.* Theresa asked Sam Bell to take a look.

Sam noticed that the sender's address was Flavored Colas' announcement mailing list address. Could it be from their own list? He ran to the technical supervisor and asked to check the outgoing email. To his horror, he found hate mail going out to Flavored Colas' entire customer announcement list! *Mr. Flamer had taken over Flavored Colas' mailing list.* The technical supervisor stopped the mailing, but the obscene attack had already gone out to 600 customers.

Here's what happened: To send a message to an email list, you send the text of your message to a program that combines your text with the addresses on your list. The address of that program appears on all outgoing messages. If you don't secure that program so it responds to messages *only* from your authorized control address, *anyone* can reach it.

 Anyone with the address of your email list server can take over your software and send email to your entire list unless you take specific steps to prevent it.

A more technically knowledgeable manager reviewed the addresses in Flavored Colas' list and found what had angered Mr. Flamer. One of the three addresses from Mr. Flamer's company was **all@flameco.com**. Someone at Flameco, probably thinking that everyone at Flameco would want Flavored Colas' announcements, had subscribed to the list using a *group name* that delivered every message it received to *everyone* in Flameco.

 Have your software or an employee inspect new addresses before adding them to your mailing list. Don't accept group names such as **all**, **everyone**, **group**, **co**, **dept**, **everybody**, **company**, or **corp**.

This true story is an example of what can happen if your list server software is not configured correctly. List server software can be tricky to set up and run. There are log files and configuration files to watch, puzzling error messages to decipher, and unhappy subscribers to pacify. Set it up wrong, and instead of sending out 500 messages one at a time, your system will try to send out all 500 at once. If you want to set up a list server in-house, be sure you have a person with the time to configure and maintain your software.

Write a welcome message

When you decide what lists you want and where your list server will be located, and you have put security procedures in place, your next step is to create the information that people who use your list will see. Write a one-paragraph description of your list and instructions on how to subscribe. These will be useful tools when you publicize your list. Write a FAQ about your discussion topic. You will also need to make a subscriber welcome message, with instructions on how to unsubscribe, a description of your list, and the name of whom to contact if there are problems. Here is a good example that I received:

```
Welcome to the adlaw mailing list!

If you ever want to remove yourself from this mailing list, send the
following command in email to "adlaw-request@webcom.com":
     unsubscribe

Or you can send mail to "majordomo@webcom.com" with the following command
in the body of your email message:
     unsubscribe adlaw vince@emery.com

Here's the general information for the list you've subscribed to, in case
you don't already have it:
[Last updated on: Tue Nov 1 13:30-46 PST 1994]

Thank you for joining the Advertising Law Internet Site Mailing List. This
mailing list will be used by the Site's maintainers to send announcements
of new articles, speeches, testimony, regulations, court cases, and
related materials to subscribers. The list may also be used by members of
the list to post questions about advertising and marketing law issues or
related matters. The list is moderated and the moderator retains the sole
discretion to determine whether any particular post should be passed on to
the list.

The list is not intended to create an attorney-client relationship between
the maintainer of the list and subscribers. Information at the Advertising
Law Internet Site and on this list is not intended to be used as legal
advice and is not the substitute for consulting an experienced lawyer with
expertise in the relevant subject matter.

With that out of the way, you can post to the Advertising Law Internet
Site by sending email to the following address: adlaw@webcom.com

Thanks for joining us. If you have any questions, please send me an email
at lewrose@netcom.com
```

Notice that this message is customized for the subscriber. The unsubscribe instructions are personalized with my own email address, and the message tells when it was last updated. It tells where to send a message so everyone on the list can read it, and it tells where to send a private "off-list" message to the moderator. This welcome message makes a good reference for you when you write your own.

Build your list

Your next step is to build your list (or lists) of email addresses. Look upon your list as an intellectual property asset, because it is one. A good list will add value to your business and may become an asset that you can rent or sell.

Collect addresses only from people who either 1) already have a relationship with your company, or 2) are aware of what you are doing with their email address. The best way to make sure of the latter is to actually *ask* beforehand if it is okay with the person for you to use his or her address. As discussed earlier, this practice is called *opt-in*.

To conform with laws in certain countries, you may also need to tell the person what you plan to do with the email address. "The purposes of collecting the person's data must be stated if not already known, and the right to opt out of intended data transfer must be clearly stated when collecting any data," says Alastair Tempest, director general of the Federation of European Direct Marketing (FEDIM), which worked with the European Union to implement the regulations covering customer data collection in Europe. These regulations go into effect in autumn 1998. "For Europeans this is not onerous—and it is a great improvement on some national practices. If a U.S. company collects data—let's say in an Internet site—from a European, it should tell the individual:

- why the data is being collected (usually self-evident);

- how that data will be used ('We may pass this data on to other companies for direct marketing purposes.');

- and promise to block their names if they wish to opt out ('Please let us know if you do not want to be contacted or have your name passed on to others.')."

Many businesses store their email list as text files, but if you have more than one list, you might want to store your lists in databases. Databases let you add additional information to your address: the person's name, a phone number, a postal address, and so on. You can also include the source from which you acquired the address, the date acquired, and information about the person's customer history. Or you can just include the email address as part of your existing databases of customers and prospects.

If you have collected addresses for a specific purpose and would like to convert them to be used for another purpose (such as a list you can rent), here's what to do. Email a message to your existing list members and ask if they'd like to receive mailings about related topics. Move "yeas" in one file and "nays" in another and maintain them separately, only renting out your "yeas." At the same time, change your list signup information to explicitly state that members will receive commercial messages, making clear exactly what kinds. This way new signups to your list already agree to be in your rentable file.

Renting email lists

It can take a few months for you to gather enough names to make your announcement list or email newsletter worthwhile. A shortcut that is growing more and more common is to rent lists from other companies. These are used most often to send out commercial advertisements—the email equivalent of a direct mail letter.

The first rentable email lists appeared in the autumn of 1995. Lists of up to 250,000 names were offered at $50 per thousand, or $12,500 for a one-time use of all 250,000 names. These lists were compiled by a software program that extracted email addresses from newsgroup postings. People whose email addresses were included did *not* know that their addresses had been captured. Reaction among professionals in the direct marketing industry to the rental of such "stolen" names was overwhelmingly negative.

In early 1996, another company offered what it claimed was a list of 27 million email addresses for rent at $99 for each group of 5 million addresses. Again, names were culled from newsgroup postings without notification or permission. One marketer purchased all 27 million addresses, but found after removing duplicates that it contained only 600,000 unique addresses, and half of those were bad and unusable.

Sending a mass emailing to people who don't ask for it seems to suit fly-by-night companies and hit-and-run marketing. The potential legal drawbacks are great, and the angry reactions of customers make it unsuitable for building long-term relationships with customers.

On the other hand, several companies offer lists of *qualified* and *voluntary* opt-in email recipients—people who *want* to receive advertising email on chosen topics. It can be profitable for your business to rent such a list. If the list is good, you can prepare and mail a targeted email advertisement to 1,000 people for less than 25 percent of your cost for sending a flyer by postal mail. You can rent an email list for 5 to 25 cents per name. That is your largest cost. Compare that with snail mail, where you must pay 5 to 15 cents per name, plus printing, plus postage, often totaling more than $1.00 per name.

The drawback of most voluntarily-compiled lists I've seen is that they cover topics that are too broad to interest most marketers. A typical category is "Antiques and Collectibles." Collectible what? Wedgwood? Baseball cards?

Nineteenth century handmade marbles? *Star Trek* memorabilia? All of those things are passionately collected by people who may be completely uninterested in the other items. I am skeptical of the value of vaguely-categorized lists.

Even so, renting opt-in lists can be a fast, cheap way to jumpstart your Internet marketing.

How to rent email lists

As in traditional direct mail, the two most influential factors as to whether your marketing will succeed are your offer and your list.

So take care picking your list. Your best prospects are people who have previously bought online or who have responded to online offers. The best lists are usually customer lists, not subscriber lists. That being said, on the Internet, customer lists are almost impossible to obtain.

Recency matters. How old are these addresses? Are they on a "hit list" of people who've purchased within a specific period of time? Can you rent just the newest addresses added within the last three months? The last six months?

Buyers will be people who want items similar to what you offer. Get as close a match to the characteristics of your existing customers as possible.

Once you've located good lists, negotiate. Don't pay for all the names on the list. Just agree to pay for valid, deliverable addresses that are not duplicated in your other lists.

Don't pay for bad addresses. If you process the list yourself, keep copies of all "bounced messages" that are undeliverable and get a refund for them. If a third party sends out your mailing for you, get a bounce report from the third party and use it to get a refund from your list rental company.

Don't pay for merge/purge duplicates. The process of using merge/purge software to remove *dupes* from lists is called *deduping*. Negotiate so you will not pay for addresses that are dupes with your current customer and prospect lists. A practice that is common in direct mail but is in its infancy with email is deduping from all previous lists that you've rented. This requires use of a bonded lettershop. The lettershop builds a file of all addresses you've already mailed to and dedupes your newly-rented lists against this ever-growing file. You pay only for new, unique addresses. So if you've rented 17 email lists before, when you rent number 18 the list rental company sends list 18 to your lettershop. The lettershop dedupes list 18 and reports to both you and the list rental company how many unique names 18 contained after deduping. You pay for only those unique names. No list rental company in its right mind would trust you, the list renter, to dedupe its list on your own computer, so the only way to do this is by using an electronic lettershop.

Since your profitability in renting a list partially depends on paying for as few non-responding addresses as possible, you can sometimes increase profits using *selections* to more tightly focus the addresses you rent. Selections, called *selects* for short, are identifying characteristics you can use to choose your most likely prospects and eliminate losers. For example, if you sell Unix software and a rentable list lets you select by computer operating system, you can select only Unix addresses and avoid paying for Windows, Mac, and MVS people who wouldn't want your product anyhow.

With email, another reason to use selects is *personalization*. For the extra costs of the selects and a little processing time, you can send custom-tailored messages to your prospects. For example, if I sell software and I can select by operating system, I can change my messages and their subject lines to accurately offer each reader what he or she uses:

```
New Mac software
New Win95 software
New WinNT software
New Unix software
```

At this point, few email lists offer selects. When you choose a select, expect to pay more per name. It is up to you to do some simple math to see if the cost savings of renting fewer names and the increased response makes up for the increased price per name. To see a good example of selects, visit the IDG List Services site described in the next section.

If you rent a large list—10,000 or more addresses—negotiate to rent a test batch first. The typical practice would be to rent between 1,000 and 5,000 addresses as a test. Send those out. Track your response. Based on your results, you can decide whether to rent the remaining names on the list. Of course, with smaller lists, you just have to email them and take your chances.

One question newbies often ask: "Why rent these lists? Why not just buy 'em and use 'em as many times as I like?" Like a snail mail list, your email list will be salted with decoy names. Your list rental company knows every time you use their list and keeps copies of what you send.

When you mail, plan to track your responses by source. Otherwise you won't know if your rental made money or pushed you toward the poorhouse. If you ask for someone to visit a Web page, give it a unique URL (**www.yourco.com/offer2.htm**) so you can track visitors. If you want an email response, use a unique email address and count how many messages it receives. If you ask people to call, give them a "special" phone extension. The whole key to making money with rented email lists is your response tracking. I've known companies to throw away thousands of dollars renting lists without the slightest clue as to whether their money had any effect or not. Don't be a sap. *If you don't track responses, don't bother renting lists.*

If your rental was profitable, rejoice and keep at it. You can try more lists, and you might be surprised at what happens if you reuse a list that was profitable once. You may be able to remail to the same list *with different offers* more than once, tracking your returns until they diminish to the point of unprofitability.

WHERE YOU CAN RENT LISTS

Most email lists available for rent are spam lists, sometimes euphemistically called "opt-out lists" gathered from the unwilling by the uncaring and rented to the unwary. Lists offered by these four companies are all opt-in lists, with a couple of exceptions. Those exceptions avoid the flak and grief of spam because they are specialized opt-out lists that were carefully converted to rental lists.

- NetCreations (**www.netcreations.com**) offers more than 3,000 lists, most consisting of 300 to 600 names each. Lists rent for 10 to 20 cents per name, including list rental, mailing, and merge/purge—a good rate.

- Direct Media: (**www.directmedia.com**) remarkets NetCreations's most popular list, 30,000 Web designers and Internet professionals.

- Worldata (**www.worldata.com**) offers 150,000 E-Shoppers, 88,000 Linkstar Webmasters, and eight other email lists.

IDG List Services (**www.idglist.com**) charges $250 CPM (cost per thousand) for richer lists than those available from other sources, including name, email address, and demographic info. IDG offers 28,000 *JavaWorld Online* readers, 15,000 *SunWorld Online* readers, and 65,000 *PCWorld Online* readers. List selects include job title, job function, industry, products used, operating system, and other selects. To rent an IDG list, you must use the electronic lettershop FDDS, which monitors compliance with IDG contract terms and sends your mailing for $150 CPM. (Ouch! That processing price is too high.)

HOW TO WRITE EFFECTIVE EMAIL ANNOUNCEMENTS FOR RENTED LISTS

Most likely, you'll rent a list to send an email announcement rather than a newsletter or an email discussion. In any email announcement, the "Subject:" line is the most important part. The person who receives your email will make a decision to read your email or delete it based strictly on your subject.

Here is an example of a bad subject line:

```
!!! AMAZING SOFTWARE !!! TERRIFIC DISCOUNT - FOR MACS AND PCS
```

What's wrong with this? First, it uses all caps. ALL CAPS IS CALLED SHOUTING and it makes you look like an idiot. Excessive punctuation looks even dumber.

Second, it is vague. The bad subject doesn't tell what the product does, and it promises no benefit to the reader, other than a discount. But who needs a discount on something they don't want?

Third, it is too long. Most email programs display only the first 30 to 40 characters of a subject. The bad subject is 61 characters long. (Yes, spaces count.) I try to keep my announcement subjects to 35 characters or fewer in length.

Here is a better subject line:

```
New WinNT software moves files faster
```

It is upper and lower case. It is shorter—35 characters long. It tells specifically what the software does. It is personalized to tell the reader that the software runs on his or her operating system. (You can't always personalize your messages and subjects, but do it when you can. Personalization significantly increases your response.) Since email software truncates subjects that are too long, put your most important words first.

Your subject persuades your reader to *open* your announcement. The inside of your message—its body—persuades your reader to *act*.

Some marketers start the body of their announcements with a headline that repeats the subject, but adds a little more detail. Some prefer to start the body straightaway with the announcement text. I know of no test indicating which method draws a higher response, and I've seen both methods work. Do whichever seems best for your particular announcement.

The first sentence of your body text should be your offer. Come to the point right away. If people can't understand your offer in four seconds or less, they will hit the delete key. Use standard journalistic practice. Your first sentence should include all essential information. Put your most important facts in your first paragraph, with less important information toward the bottom.

Make your message as personal as you can. Avoid screaming hype and institutional third-personism. There is no need to overstate or exaggerate the benefits of your offering. Understatement will pull better than overdramatization. Keep your message short; one to three screens of text seems to be the optimum length.

For maximum effectiveness, tailor the content of your announcement to the content of the list you rent. If you rent a list of Mac users, tell in your first paragraph how your offer makes life better for Mac users.

Your message must include a *call to action,* with specific step-by-step instructions telling your readers what you want them to do. Plan on including it twice: a quick version someplace in your first paragraph or two and a detailed version at the end of your announcement. It's important to give your readers a special reason to purchase today. Don't just give your normal prices—add an incentive for them to react now. But before you offer a discount or incentive, establish the value of your offer. Your readers must perceive the benefit of your offering before you discount it, or the worth of the discount will be seen as trivial. First build value. Then offer your discount.

One last point about email announcements: In my experience, email sells more when your message doesn't try to close the sale by itself. In other words, if your email drives people to your Web site (or another source) for more information, and your Web site closes the sale, your total number of sales will be higher.

Tasks for a list owner

When planning your email list activities, remember that you will need to reserve ongoing staff time to update your list, clean up mistakes, and deal with your Internet access provider.

For each of your mailing lists, you must pick one person to be the *list owner.* The owner doesn't have to be a technical person, but if your list is very large, a list owner who is technically astute might save time. Your list owner manages the way your list is organized, controls adding and deleting subscribers, and (for a discussion list) can act as moderator to review and approve each message before it goes out.

The duties of list ownership don't require technical expertise and can be done by a clerical employee with good writing and customer relations skills. You may want to use two people, one as list owner and one as list moderator. A third person can manage the technical aspects of your lists and act as a backup to your list owner. The technical person can answer questions, especially about error messages, and can come to the rescue when problems crop up. (Murphy's law says most list problems erupt when you need to send an urgent mailing. I have scars to verify that.)

Your list owner doesn't need to work on the same computer where the list resides, but can be located anyplace he or she can make email contact with the list server software. The list owner's duties can be handled by remote control via email if your list software is located on your service provider's computer instead of your own.

Depending on how large your lists grow, whether they are moderated or unmoderated, and how often you mail to them, someone will need to spend 2 to 15 hours per list each week, updating and editing the email addresses. If you mail to a list less often than once every two weeks, someone will need to spend two to four hours per mailing to prepare for the mailing, clean up bounced mail, and deal with other situations that pile up after a mailing.

Your list will have several addresses: one for the list owner, one for broadcasting messages to your list (only if your list is a discussion list), one to receive error messages, and one to receive messages about the list. This last one may be the same address as the list owner, or it could be a separate address for a list moderator.

BOUNCED MESSAGES

Make sure bounced messages won't be sent to your list *subscribers* by mistake. Run a test to make sure. Bounced email is most often caused by a simple (and sometimes hard to spot) typo in the address. The second most common cause is that computer systems or the links between systems are temporarily down, blocking the route to your addressee. If your message bounced back to you and you have double checked the address and swear that it's letter-perfect, try resending it in a couple of hours.

The way list server software works, when people send an incorrect command to your server, the list owner will get a *bounced message*, and the person who sent the incorrect message will get an automated rejection notice—an error message. Almost all list software lets the list owner write the text of the error messages it sends. Unless your list is only for computer geniuses, invest the time to make your error messages understandable by the uninformed. The most crucial part is to make the *response* you want absolutely clear. When someone sees a particular error message, exactly what do you want this person to do? If you don't tell people what specific steps you want them to take, chances are they will do something else. Test your error messages on your nontechnical staffers. Ask them, "What would you do if you saw this message on your computer?"

Check your list server's log files often, especially for bounced email from people who tried to subscribe or unsubscribe once, made a mistake, and didn't try again. You can turn angry, silent prospects into contented subscribers by processing those bounced messages by hand and sending them a friendly personal email note to tell them what you've done.

"UNKNOWN HOST" PROBLEMS

Here's a warning about a specific and tricky cause of bounced messages. When you send a mailing, you may get error messages back that say "Unknown host".

This could mean a typographical error happened in which a domain (the part on the right of the "@" sign) in someone's email address was misspelled. But what if you send email to a name ending with an obviously correct address, such as **@ibm.com** and it comes back with the message "Unknown host"? When you get that error message and you know the host name is accurate (especially if you get a whole stack of error messages for several people at different companies), you may have a problem with your Internet access provider or with the service bureau that hosts your list server. If either company configures its software incorrectly or holds on to your message for too long, the message will bounce back to you with the "Unknown host" message. Be skeptical if your provider says this problem was your fault, especially if it happens frequently.

To prove that it was your provider's fault, you will have to document the *exact times* you sent the messages that generated the "Unknown host" error, the *addresses* to which you sent them, and the *exact time* each bounced message was returned to you. Each returned "Unknown host" message automatically includes this data. Collect the information, save it, and present it to your provider for resolution.

MAINTENANCE, STORAGE, AND MAILINGS

People move. People lose interest. Addresses change. Your list of addresses will need constant refreshing to avoid death by old age. Plan to invest time maintaining it. After every large mailing you'll receive bounced messages. Use them as guides to make corrections, and always update your list after every mailing.

Store your mailing list file in-house on your own computer. However, your mailings may go out faster if you copy your list of addresses to your access provider's system so your *provider's computer* (rather than your own) combines your addresses with your message and emails them. Check with your provider to see if this would work for you. For security, maintain your file of addresses on a computer not connected to the Internet. When you mail to a list, move a copy of your list to an Internet-connected computer, then copy it to your service provider. Rather then leaving your list for anyone to read or copy from your provider's computer, delete it after each mailing.

Once you've built a list, send the people on it only information they've asked to receive. For example, if you have a list of people who signed up to find out about your new line of kazoos, don't rent their names to a music stand manufacturer unless you asked your subscribers explicitly for permission to rent their names to other companies. And don't send information on your new line of oboes either.

When you send a mailing, mail to your local addressees first. By *local*, I mean people within your company. They should receive their copies of your mailing before outsiders. This gives you extra eyes to spot a problem. If something bad goes out to your list, your insiders can catch it and stop your mailing before the error reaches the rest of the world.

If you build a large list (1,000 names or more), before you run your list the first time, test it and your software setup by running a small test batch beforehand. When Tripod (**www.tripod.com**) sent its first mass emailing to 30,000 members, 1,000 messages went to one man by mistake. (Luckily for Tripod, he turned out to be understanding of their error.)

Depending on your hardware and software setup, actually processing your list may slow down your computer system. Sending to a long list, or sending long messages, can take hours. You don't want to bog down your system during business hours. Send your emailings at night.

One final tip: If your list deals with customers, archive all messages you receive from subscribers requesting changes and the changes you make in response to those requests. Your archive will give you something to fall back on if you have a problem like Mr. Flamer.

FOUR RESOURCES

For help in selecting a list server or in running one, the newsgroups **news:comp.mail.list-admin.software** and **news:comp.mail.list-admin.policy** are good resources.

Even better are two email discussion groups. They are intended for people who use Listserv software. But they carry more information about mailing list management than any resource I've found, so I recommend them if you're a serious email list provider, no matter what brand of software you use. One group is for technical people, the *list administrators*. The other discussion is less technical and is aimed at list owners. To subscribe to either one, email to **listserv@searn.sunet.se**. Leave your message blank except for a one-line command. To subscribe to the list administrators' discussion, your message should contain only:

SUBSCRIBE LSTSRV-L

If you want to subscribe to the list owners' discussion, your message should be:

SUBSCRIBE LISTOWN-L

Posting on newsgroups

You can place two different kinds of posting on newsgroups. The first is to post an announcement and walk away. The second, which I cover in the next section, is a more interactive method requiring you to study what other people post and to craft your postings in response to them.

The post-and-run technique can generate decent sales if you post the right kind of information on the right newsgroups. By the "right kind of information," I mean making your posting conform to the rules of a specific newsgroup. Many newsgroups have rules specifically prohibiting advertisements, and those bans extend to *any* form of promotion. Almost everything you post on a newsgroup that directly promotes your product or service will be considered an advertisement—any press release, for example. There is no way for an advertiser to fight this perception. "Okay," you respond, "some newsgroups call my information an advertisement and don't want to see it. So where else can I post it?" Fortunately, in several places.

Newsgroups for advertisements

Hundreds of newsgroups are suitable for posting advertisements. They reach different audiences and address different topics. If you find newsgroups that reach your prospects, you can post your promotional information on them in the format appropriate for each specific newsgroup. Some newsgroups accept press releases and announcements. Some accept classified advertisements. Others accept lists of products for sale and their prices.

These can be very effective for some businesses. Joel Chapman of Acorn Books (**www.best.com/~acornbks/acorn.html**) reported that about 15% of his orders for customers seeking a specific title came from postings on newsgroups such as **news:rec.arts.books.marketplace** and **news:alt.marketplace.books**.

To find newsgroups where you can post advertisements, the best place to look is the Web site Tile.net at **www.tile.net**. Search Tile.net under "Newsgroups" for groups with **biz**, **forsale**, **market**, **classified**, **auction**, **advert**, **ads**, or **swap** as part of their names. Real estate listings are in groups with **realtynet.** in their names. From the names of the newsgroups, from the one-line descriptions that Tile.net provides, and from scanning the contents of the newsgroups themselves, you can see if there are groups that your customers might read and that accept advertisements.

If you deal in international sales, you might look at a series of newsgroups that has been created specifically for want-to-buy and for-sale notices for import-export trade:

```
news:alt.business.import-export
news:alt.business.import-export.computer
news:alt.business.import-export.consumables
news:alt.business.import-export.food
news:alt.business.import-export.only
news:alt.business.import-export.raw-material
news:alt.business.import-export.services
news:alt.business.import-export.technology
news:alt.business.import-export.vehicles
The contents of these import-export newsgroups almost totally consist of
buying and selling notices. You'll have to wade through more spam than
you'd like, but you may find worthwhile sales leads here.
```

Newsgroups with **forsale** in their name provide classified advertisements, as do those with **adverts.** The newsgroup **news:misc.forsale** has more than a quarter of a million readers, the highest of any advertisement newsgroup. Some newsgroups cover the world but contain ads only for a specific category of items. Some are specific to a geographic locale, such as **news:bln.forsale** for Berlin, Germany, **news:fj.forsale** for Japan, and **news:uk.adverts.computers** and **news:uk.adverts.others** for the U.K. Some cover a specific topic *and* a specific locale, such as **news:pdaxs.ads.tickets** for selling tickets in the Portland, Oregon area.

Some classified ad newsgroups have a policy that only private individuals, not businesses, can sell items. When you want to post ads from your business, check the group's FAQ first, or if you can't find a FAQ, post a message asking if a business ad is appropriate. (**news:misc.forsale** has a good FAQ that explains how to buy and sell on all newsgroups.)

Some of these newsgroups are very busy. Some have only one ad posted every couple of months. Your message stays on most service providers' computers for a few weeks, so you should not post more often than once every month. Don't cross-post to several groups at once. When you sell a product available only in your local area, target a newsgroup that is local. When a newsgroup's name doesn't start with a geographic prefix, it is worldwide. Use a Subject line that tells what you sell. Provide enough description of your product so someone can tell if he or she wants it. Finally, and most importantly, *post on-topic only*. If you have a lawnmower for sale, be smart enough not to post an ad for it to **news:rec.bicycles.marketplace**. Sending your ad to an unlikely buyer is a waste of your time.

Posting on non-ad newsgroups

New York microbrewery Spring Street Brewery Co. posted information about its $5,000,000 initial public offering of stock on newsgroups and received 20,000 inquiries. It then emailed inquirers an electronic version of its prospectus. Spring Street did not post its prospectus to advertisement newsgroups, but to a small number of carefully selected business and investment newsgroups. As with any announcement of a prospectus, its postings warned that "this is not an offer to sell nor a solicitation."

Posting advertising on other newsgroups is skating on thin ice. If you follow the FAQ rules of your target newsgroup, if you compose your message carefully, and if—and only if—your message ties in closely with that newsgroup's topic, you can post some advertisements to some newsgroups and not anger and drive away your prospects. You must pick and choose your newsgroups carefully.

 If you post off-topic to a newsgroup, you can lose customers, get flamed, and possibly get your message canceled by cancelbot software.

Cancelbots require some explanation. There is no equivalent to them in other media. When you place an ad in several inappropriate newsgroups, you trigger one of several different cancelbots. Cancelbots remove your offending message, warn appropriate system administrators, and post a message like this in the **alt.current-events.net-abuse** newsgroup:

```
From: Cancelmoose[tm]
Subject: Spam Cancelled (cme@io.org (Canadian Music Exchange), **INTERAC-
TIVE MUSIC TALKER/MUCK**)

This 161 message spam has been cancelled from 161 newsgroups. It was not
crossposted. 1 copy and headers follow. Note that this user also has a
different 30 message spam that is not being cancelled at this time (hope-
fully they will clean up some of their own mess, and learn how to
crosspost). This is *NOT* a statement that a 30 message spam is acceptable.

This is not being done because the message is an ad. This is not being
done to censor a critic. This is not being done because I am offended by
the words in his message. To stop a man from speaking his views in the
public square is censorship. To stop a man from speaking his views when he
amplifies his voice 161 times the normal volume is not. Cancelling spam is
not censorship: spamming is disturbing the peace.

*Please* be sure to write to the postmaster at the offending site, and
tell them you do not approve of this behavior. If spam cancelling elimi-
nates the outrage people feel about spam, then it will cease to be a
problem to the uninformed sysadmin. This will cause bigger problems down
the road when they stop educating their users.

Even though this spam is cancelled, please complain *politely* to
postmaster@io.org.

The commercial or noncommercial nature of this spam did not influence its
cancellation. Spam is determined on number of newsgroups posted to, and
not the content of the message. I sincerely hope these people will learn
to crosspost and find a better way to get their message out to the net.
```

(This message has been slightly condensed.) I don't know what happened to the offending advertiser in this case, but many Internet access providers will close your account if you spam. America Online is quite efficient about this. AOL users who spam have their accounts terminated immediately. To avoid mishaps, before posting to any non-advertisement newsgroups, read the rules for posting on Usenet newsgroups: **http://wsspinfo.cern.ch/faq/usenet/posting-rules/part1.**

A handful of other tips on advertisements: Don't post to a general-purpose newsgroup. For maximum effectiveness, tailor the content of your message to the content of the newsgroup. Explain at the beginning of your message how your announcement directly relates to the topic of that group.

My personal experience is that you will get a bigger response if instead of posting press releases or ads, you post the type of messages described as "Netlurking and posting" in the next section. Other businesses report the same.

How to create your own newsgroup

If there is a newsgroup covering your industry, you can use it as a channel for soft-sell publicity. But suppose you find no newsgroups where your prospects hang out. What then?

Start your own, of course. It takes less work to run an unmoderated newsgroup than it does to run an email discussion list. Procedures to create your own newsgroup differ depending on what newsgroup *hierarchy* prefixes the beginning of your group name, such as **comp.** for computer topics or **rec.** for recreation.

Anyone can create a newsgroup under the **biz.** or **alt.** hierarchies. For example, SBT Accounting Systems (**www.sbtcorp.com**) sponsored the formation of the newsgroup **news:biz.comp.accounting** for "discussions between users, developers and recommenders of accounting software," said Diane Causey of SBT. "Our goal is to provide a resource for people who need information about computerized accounting: available software, development trends, technical and implementation issues, and industry news." This lively group offers candid discussions of the strengths and weaknesses of all manufacturers' accounting systems—not just SBT's products. You can go visit to do research before you buy an accounting software program. Because SBT sponsors the group, its prospective customers are more aware of the company and its offerings. SBT also makes an archive of past postings from the group available through its home page, which increases visits by SBT's target market to the SBT Web site.

You can also create a newsgroup to post your press releases or newsletters. Patrick Townson posts two or three digests a day of *Telecom Digest* (**http://hyperarchive.lcs.mit.edu/telecom-archives**) to thousands of email subscribers and also to his own newsgroup **news:comp.dcom.telecom**. Townson's newsgroup is popular with CompuServe and America Online customers. Since newsgroup owners can block their newsgroups from specific domains, Townson is able to charge CompuServe and AOL for monthly access to his newsgroup.

Digital Equipment Corp. sponsors two kinds of newsgroups. Some are discussions to provide customer support for its products. Others are "read-only" newsgroups where Digital posts press releases and newsletters.

Not all newsgroups are accessible by all Internet users. Many Internet access providers carry only a portion of the 16,000 groups available. Many business sites don't allow their staff access to alt. groups, making them less valuable for business-to-business communication. The most widely-distributed newsgroups are the so-called "big eight" hierarchies whose names begin with the prefixes **comp.** (computers), **hum.** (humanities), **misc.**, **news.** (newsgroups about newsgroups), **rec.** (recreational), **sci.** (science), **soc.** (social and cultural), and **talk.** If you start your own newsgroup, extra readership may make it worth your while to start it under one of the big eight, even though they take longer to create. To start a big eight newsgroup, your new group must not duplicate the subject of any existing group, and you must go through a voting procedure before your group is accepted for distribution.

It is simpler to start a newsgroup under one of the less widely-distributed hierarchies, such as those whose names begin with the prefixes **alt.** or **biz.** Anyone can propose such a group. To gain distribution, a new **alt.** or **biz.** group needs only to avoid encountering serious protests to its topic.

Another choice is to start a newsgroup dealing with a topic specific to your geographic location. Some of these are national; their names begin with **us.** for the U.S., **can.** for Canada, **uk.** for the U.K, **aus.** for Australia, etc.. Others cover a state or province. Many cover a single city, such as newsgroups whose names begin with **austin.** for Austin, Texas, **melb.** for Melbourne, Australia, or **pdx.** for Portland, Oregon. If your business deals mostly with local customers, you might want to create a group under your local hierarchy. Most local areas have no local newsgroups, giving you many opportunities to start one as an activity to promote your business in your community.

For specific steps on creating and naming your own newsgroup, read the following guidelines available on the World Wide Web:

Creating New Internet Newsgroups
www.unige.ch/crystal/w3vlc/int.news.crea.html

How to Create a New Usenet Group
http://www.lib.ox.ac.uk/internet/news/faq/
by_category.usenet.creating-newsgroups.html

So You Want to Create an alt. Newsgroup?
www.math.psu.edu/barr/alt-creation-guide.html

biz. Newsgroups FAQ
www.cis.ohio-state.edu/hypertext/faq/usenet/biz-config-faq/faq.html

If you start your own newsgroup, you can run it either as a read-only "news channel" where only you can post or as a discussion group where anyone can post questions, answers, and announcements.

If you start a discussion group, you must choose whether to have someone in your firm moderate your group or not. There are pros and cons to moderation. A moderator tends to inhibit constructive criticism, especially when the moderator is an employee of your company. This defeats one of the main benefits of running your own newsgroup, getting honest criticism quickly. On the other hand, a moderator screens out off-topic emotional outbursts and spam advertisements. Acting as moderator can occupy about five percent of one employee's time. Keeping newsgroups contents on-topic makes your group a more valuable promotional tool, but you must decide if the loss of spontaneity is worth it.

Netlurking and posting

In addition to sending messages from your own email lists and posting advertisements on newsgroups, you can also leverage other people's email discussion lists and post non-advertisement marketing messages on newsgroups that prohibit advertising. These processes are more interactive than discussed in the previous part of this chapter. You read a message from someone and respond to the concerns in that individual message.

You can do variations of this technique on both newsgroups and email lists, but there are some differences between them. First, let's look at newsgroups.

Netlurking and posting on newsgroups

Waterbug Records owner Andrew Calhoun spends time on folk music newsgroups and conducts personal email with folk music lovers—up to 400 messages per day. Folksinger Cosy Sheridan credits this Internet marketing with building her into a rising star. Her fans agree. A T-shirt entrepreneur cashed in by selling a shirt saying, "I heard about Cosy Sheridan on the Internet."

Calhoun noted that the people who use a newsgroup are the most intense, dedicated fans of whatever that newsgroup's topic may be. They spread the word to others, kind of an electronic trickle-down effect. You may catch a newsgroup follower's attention with an advertising message, but you won't generate the same kind of devotion that comes with sustained contact.

It's what Jim Barrick of KeyNote Software calls "The pass-around factor. Good word-of-mouth spreads quickly on the Net. So does bad," he says.

Newsgroup marketing generates significant sales for The Corner Store (**www.ntstore.com**), a retailer of Windows NT software. "When I turn my computer on, money comes out of it," says Corner Store owner Paolo Pignatelli. "And I never spent a penny for advertising."

Publicity on Internet newsgroups and CompuServe forums are the main thrust of marketing for Pignatelli's company. He and his wife look on newsgroups for questions. When Pignatelli cannot answer a question, he delegates the answer to someone else. He finds information-seeking messages from hundreds of people, "talking out loud and hoping somebody will listen to their thoughts." If his company can answer a question or direct someone to useful information, even when the answer or the directions have nothing to do with The Corner Store, his answers—which are read by thousands of people in addition to the specific person addressed—create good will toward Pignatelli's business. Through this approach, he has built a reputation for The Corner Store as a knowledgeable and helpful business. That reputation and the contact information in his sig file has been enough to lead hundreds of paying customers to his business, eager to buy from him.

In spite of all the messages The Corner Store has posted to newsgroups over the years, the company has never been flamed with hate email. Not once.

As far as averages go, this idea—reading newsgroups where your prospects hang out, searching for questions, and posting answers for the world to see—generates the highest percentage of successes of all Internet marketing methods. I have talked with many businesses whose Web pages were unvisited or whose mailing lists had few subscribers. But every single company that invested time to answer questions on newsgroups *and that played by the rules of the newsgroups* reported sales from grateful customers that more than paid for staff time spent in newsgroup marketing. Perhaps you'll find no newsgroups read by your customers, so this strategy might not be for you. But if your customers read Usenet newsgroups, this is a valuable publicity technique.

Do not mistake this discussion as a "thumbs up" for posting press releases on newsgroups. *Press releases are not considered publicity by people who read newsgroups.* They are considered advertisements, and they can cause anger and hostility instead of gratitude.

It is estimated that 16 million people read newsgroups. Of course, not all of them read every group. Most people just read a couple of groups on topics they care about the most. Newsgroups are read by many more people than those who actually post messages. The most-read group is **news:news.announce.newusers** with more than 1,200,000 readers. (For statistics on newsgroup readership, go to **www.tlsoft.com/arbitron** and **www.crl.com/~gherber/ReCount**. Unfortunately, these statistics are not kept up to date, and I have found no replacement.) Don't judge just by numbers. The important thing is to look for a tight match between a newsgroup's readers and your prospects. A group with 500 readers intensely concerned with the product you make will generate more paying customers than 100,000 readers interested in how to kill Barney the dinosaur (**news:alt.barney.die.die.die**).

Which newsgroups should your business use for marketing? To find out, read the instructions on the Web page that tells you how to find the right place to post: **www.landfield.com/faqs/finding-groups/general**. If you are looking for customers, find out what *they* read. Learn what your customers' top ten newsgroups are. Assign staff to read them regularly and contribute to them.

If your business sells to customers in your local area, look for newsgroups that provide information just for your area. Local newsgroups provide a more focused market for some businesses. They start with a prefix to indicate the area they serve. For instance, **news:aus.theatre** covers live theater in Australia, while **news:ba.motorcycles** covers an obvious subject for people in the San Francisco Bay Area.

When you find newsgroups that seem like places you'll want to contact, first do some *netlurking*. This refers to the practice of reading messages without posting anything yourself. Always read enough messages so you get a feeling for the topics discussed and the people discussing them. Are they your customers? If not, try another group. Do your competitors post to this group? How do subscribers of this group treat other companies that post? What kinds of messages generate flames and arguments? If the group fits, you have one more thing to do: Look for the group's FAQ list or lists, and read them. There is no faster way for you to make your company look foolish than to ask or answer a question that is already on the FAQ list. Some groups post their FAQs monthly.

Some people say that you should subscribe to a newsgroup and read all its messages for two weeks before you post anything. There are faster ways to learn about most groups. If a group generates 100 messages in one day and you read all 100, you will have a good idea of the character of that group. You can get a feel for a newsgroup in an hour or less, instead of subscribing for two weeks.

Internet people hate blatant, intrusive advertising, but actively seek information and electronic contact with experts. Your goals should be to establish the people in your company as trusted, helpful experts and to develop name recognition in your target markets.

To build trust, you must follow the newsgroups' rules. Otherwise, with one posted message you can outrage all your prospective buyers and lose your whole target market at once. With newsgroups, you might not get a second chance. As discussed earlier, cancelbot software deletes offending messages and can block offending parties *and their companies* from ever posting on an offended newsgroup again. Individual readers who don't like your messages can list your name or your company name in their kill file. A *kill file* prevents any future messages from a particular person or Internet domain from ever being seen by a user. This is not to mention the fact that posting offending messages on newsgroups can get you flamed and mail bombed with hate mail. Thus, the same wonderful communication speed that spreads good news about your company can also be used to smear your reputation worldwide in a matter of hours.

When you post a business message to a Usenet newsgroup, *stay on topic*. Start your message with a short, to-the-point description of how your message fits the group's main topic. Don't try to cover everything about your product, service, or event. Just give the briefest possible response to the issue that you are posting. Don't post off-topic messages that do not address the specific needs of the group.

Many newsgroups allow no commercial announcements. Don't try to disguise a press release-type of announcement as something else; readers will get angry and may kick you off the group. In some groups, you shouldn't post messages or announcements at all. For instance, **news:alt.binaries.pictures** is reserved just for graphics files, and **news:comp.binaries.ms-windows** is strictly for Windows software programs. Posting your message to a newsgroup not related to your message's topic is spamming.

14 rules for marketing on Internet newsgroups

1. Don't post advertisements or anything that someone might *think* is an advertisement. Ask the test question: "Will a reader feel grateful to receive this information?"

2. Before you first post to a newsgroup, read a group's FAQ and review 100 to 150 messages or so to get a feel for what passionately interests the group. The practice of reading messages without posting your own is called *netlurking*, and is the best way to find out what is really going on.

3. Keep your newsgroup message short—two screens or less (48 lines) and to the point. Shorter messages download more quickly and so get chosen and read more often. Keep it 70 characters wide or less—some software truncates longer lines.

4. Stick to the actual subject of that group—based not on the group's name (newsgroup names are often misleading), but on what you found by netlurking.

5. Remember that thousands of people will read what you post to a newsgroup.

6. When you respond to a message, don't repeat the whole thing. Just quote relevant passages, or summarize it.

7. If someone flames you, don't flame back.

8. Posting articles in more than one newsgroup at the same time is called *cross-posting*. Only cross-post to newsgroups that have something to do with the subject of your message. Keep cross-posting to a minimum. Excessive cross-posting will automatically trigger cancelbot software to remove your message.

9. Don't post the same message twice in the same newsgroup. Post your message once only. Don't email a follow-up note to make sure that readers saw your first one.

10. Don't reprint copyrighted material.

11. Don't copy and reuse posted messages without permission. Remember, under current copyright law, even uncopyrighted text is still owned by its original creator.

12. Don't post messages that say only "I agree," or "Me, too."

13. ALL CAPS IS SHOUTING AND PEOPLE HATE IT.

14. Always end each message with your signature file. That's what spreads the word.

Netlurking and posting on email discussion groups

Some people confuse discussion mailing lists with newsgroups. A newsgroup can be seen as a *place* you visit to read posted messages. A discussion mailing list *delivers* posted messages to you. Messages posted to a newsgroup are seen by the world. Messages posted to a discussion mailing list are seen only by subscribers to that list.

The first part of this chapter covered using *your own* email lists. You can also market on *other peoples'* discussion mailing lists using the same "netlurking and posting" method that I described for newsgroups.

First, find a mailing list that is read by your prospects. Second, you will need to subscribe to a mailing list and read its messages for a while to find out if it has what you are looking for. Some mailing lists have archives where you can review past messages to evaluate a group. Third, after you are familiar with the list, post helpful information when appropriate.

Each email discussion list has its own style and rules, depending on whether the list is moderated or unmoderated, how often its readers post messages, whether they write formally or informally, and whether advertising-type messages are permitted. As with newsgroups, it pays to tailor your communication style to match your readers. Few lists allow advertising or anything resembling an advertisement.

Most mailing list subscribers read only a few of the messages they receive from a list. They decide whether or not to look at your message based on three factors:

- The title of your message as shown in the Subject line
- The name of the person who sent the message
- The length of your message; shorter messages get more readers

To get your message read, your Subject is most important. A Subject like "Message for You" or "Hello" will get you a readership of zero.

It is easier to get kicked off a discussion mailing list than a newsgroup. When you subscribe to some mailing lists, you receive a notice about what kinds of material should be posted and what kinds should not. If you don't know if your posting would be right for a list, you can ask. Just send email to the list moderator and ask for an opinion. (Don't send your query to the list itself, though. Instead of just being a private message for the host, your question will be duplicated and exposed to all readers. Oops!)

Because a list owner can easily throw you out, watch your netiquette when you post to a discussion list. Follow that list's guidelines. Don't make pointless comments about other people's messages like "I agree." (I confess that as a newbie, a list kicked me off for that very sin.) And don't insult your competitors. That's viewed as rude and can get you kicked off a list.

If you are careful to respond to other people's messages with only useful information, and if each of your messages ends with a clear signature file (as explained in Chapter 9), email discussion groups can generate even more sales than newsgroups.

CHAPTER **14**

Your First Web Site

""The outcome of successful planning always looks like luck to saps."

—Dashiell Hammett, The Dain Curse

Some companies are very successful at marketing on the Web. Lew Rose of the law firm of Arent Fox said his firm's Web site (**www.webcom.com/~lewrose/ home.html**) attracted more than 19,000 visitors in its first year and had produced "more than enough business from it to pay for itself for several years. In addition, the publicity from our site generated a tremendous number of very good speaking and writing opportunities." As a promotional item, Rose gives out his Web site on a disk.

Since you're reading this chapter, chances are that you've already heard success stories like that, maybe dozens of them. You've decided to look at using the World Wide Web for your own business.

Why the Web?

What can a Web site do for your business? It can do anything you do with printed matter and then some. It can create awareness for your company and your products or services. It can deliver reference information about what you have to offer. It communicates your "image" more graphically than email. (Let's face it, email looks like a classified ad.) Your Web site is like a 24-hour front desk for your business.

You can put your catalog online on the Web and constantly change it. You can add or remove individual items at any time without having to adjust the rest of your catalog. You can change prices and give different prices for different customers. The ability to update continuously eliminates much of the expense and workload of traditional catalog creation and distribution. Internet catalogers can respond immediately to changes in market demands.

You can find out which information Web readers access most often, an advantage you lack with a printed newsletter. In print, you can never tell what parts people read and what parts leave readers cold. Your Web site can deliver information to your customers that is completely up to date and in turn can deliver instant feedback to you.

Your Web site can actually process a complete sales transaction automatically—without human intervention—and charge the sale to a customer's credit card or billing account. (But making sales on the Web is much more complicated than just advertising.)

Like many advertising people (I do this myself), Poppe Tyson Advertising's David Carlick is fond of numbered lists. When I asked him why a marketer would use the Web, Carlick said, "

1. You can define your own Web space and control it.
2. It's easy to update and keep current.
3. Web technology lets you establish a dialog with your customers.
4. Lowest-cost per visit by prospects—cheaper than flyers.
5. Lets prospects *self-select* the information they need.
6. Reaches influential people.
7. Can generate repeat traffic.
8. A surprisingly cheap way to learn about interactive marketing. If you're in marketing, you *must* learn about interactive technology. There is no way around it.
9. Help lower the cost of selling significantly.
10. You can count the exact number of lookers and the exact number of responses. When many companies compare print cost per inquiry or cost pemr sale with Net costs, their marketing budget will shift to the Net."

Carlick also gave three reasons for an advertiser to prefer the World Wide Web to traditional media: "Interactivity is more involving, deeper material, and richer advertisement content."

This last point, richer advertisement content, is an important difference between the World Wide Web and traditional media. On the Web, there is no limit to the amount of information you provide. You aren't trapped within the confines of a fixed magazine page size or a 60-second spot. You can provide as many thousands of pages of information and illustrations as you need to explain the benefits of your product or service. On the Web, you have the luxury of unlimited length without having to pay substantially more for it.

The Web attracts attention because prospects can view text with pictures. You don't need graphics to have a successful Web page, but illustrations don't cost much and don't hurt as long as they reinforce your selling points and don't distract from them. For some Web advertisers, such as Hot Hot Hot (**www.hothothot.com**), the illustrations establish the selling point.

Choose between two levels of Web marketing. The first level presents simple information (a logo, contact information, overall information about the company, general information about products and services). For most companies, this first level won't generate any business, in spite of hucksters' claims to the contrary. If your company presents only general information on the Web, regard your site as a seed experiment, but don't expect to make money from it.

The second level of Web marketing adds value by presenting more specific information, entertainment, or both. A visitor to this type of site feels *satisfied* in some way for having visited. The visitor has been entertained or has received some type of satisfactory information, perhaps having completed a sales transaction or copied a free software program. Viewer satisfaction with advertising is not an important consideration in traditional media, but it is crucial to Web marketing, especially if you want repeat customers.

The Web as a marketing medium

"Advertising is communications over a medium to reach a target audience," said Carlick. There has been a lot of noise about the Web as a general-purpose medium, which it is not. "The Internet serves *special interest needs*, which publishers have understood for a long time. Over the years, the amount of money advertisers have spent on general media has declined, and special interest (direct mail, special interest magazines) has risen."

The ease and low cost of providing special interest content on the Internet has led the Web to splinter into many micromarkets. Robert Rossney described it in the *San Francisco Chronicle*: "The Web is a lot like that 500-channel television that we hear about from time to time, except that there are more than 25,000 channels, and a significant portion of them seem to be run by undergraduates in the nation's many computer science departments. So there are at least four different sites on the Web where you can get the first 50,000 digits of *pi*. There's a woman at the University of Michigan who has put up a page with a picture of her pet ferret, Potpie, and several examples of his typing. And what are we to make of the unlikely Erik Tjong Kim Sang, who collects and distributes photographs of palindromic Dutch license plates?"

These micromarkets make lies of a lot of claims about Web marketing. An advertisement from one unscrupulous Internet advertising company promises you will "Reach 25,000,000 New Customers!" Not only is that argument a lie, but it also misses the point. All the people on the Internet won't visit your Web site, and you don't want them to. You want only those people interested in what you have to sell. This fundamental difference about the Internet is one that traditional advertising agencies have a tough time comprehending.

Another fundamental distinction of Web marketing is that it is *measurable*. Unfortunately, the *ability* to measure advertising response and the knowledge of what to *do* with measurements are two different things. Most consumer advertising agencies simply lack the know-how for tracking Web visitors and applying the results.

What you need

Once the decision has been made to *do something* on the Web, it seems like more questions arise than can possibly be answered. Do I need to buy a separate computer for a Web server? Should I lease space on a cybermall? How long will it take to open a Web site? How much will it cost to market on the Web?

First, a quick clarification of terms. What's the difference between a *home page* and a *Web site*? Your Web site will probably contain many individual web pages. Although someone can enter your Web site from any page, the front door is your home page. It's like the main lobby of a building, the front page of a newspaper, and the table of contents of a book all rolled into one. Your home page sets the tone for your site, says who you are, excites visitors about your contents, and tells them where to find things.

All the people, services, and things that you need to market on the Web can be grouped into six areas:

1. You need a *Web site*, which will probably consist of multiple *Web pages*. These are made of computer files. The simplest ones are just text files. Most commercial Web sites also have graphics files. Some have sound files, video files, databases, or software programs. They range from simple and cheap to elaborate and expensive.

2. You need someone to write and design your Web pages. You may do this yourself, depending on your available time and marketing and technical knowledge. Creating your first Web pages is the easy part. Maintaining and updating your site after it opens will take the most time and work.

3. You need space on a connected computer to put all the files that make up your Web site. You have four options. You can:

    A. *Rent computer space on a service bureau's computer* for your Web site. This service bureau may either be your Internet access provider or another company, called a *Web host*. To receive sales orders from your service bureau, you will need either email or a fax machine. If you want to correspond with your customers, you will need Internet email. This is your least expensive option.

B. *Rent space on a cybermall.* To receive sales orders, you will need either email or a fax machine. If you want to correspond with your customers, you will need Internet email. Depending on the rates charged by the cybermall, this can be expensive. Cybermalls are covered in Chapter 18.

C. *Buy or lease a server computer and place it at your access provider's site,* where your access provider will run it for you. This is called *co-location.* To receive sales orders, you will need email. With this option, you will need to buy or build all the software needed to run your site. You also need a 56 Kbps ISDN, frame relay, or a faster phone line to go to your computer.

D. *Buy or lease a server computer and place it on your own premises.* In most cases, this is your most expensive option. It is also your most time-consuming option because out of all the alternatives, this is the only one in which you have to worry about running the hardware. You will need at least a 56 Kbps ISDN or frame relay line to your server, and 128 Kbps is better. If you want to link this server computer with any computer you use for your business, you will need a firewall.

4. Sometimes small businesses can get a service bureau or cybermall to fax sales orders to them. But because email is easier for order processing than faxed orders and has many other uses, get email if at all possible. Email requires you to run email software on at least one computer. It also requires you to have an Internet account, which you will get from an Internet access provider. If you want to route your email over a LAN to more than one person in your company, tell your prospective access provider how many people and what kind of LAN before you sign anything.

5. If your business wants to accept credit cards and does not yet have a credit card merchant account, you will need to open one. You will also need an account with a clearinghouse to authorize each credit card purchase. Cards are usually authorized over the phone and may require you to add hardware and a phone line. If you intend to accept credit card orders on your Web page, check with your Internet access provider before you open your account.

6. You will need the support staff and systems to receive orders, process them, and forward the needed information to your inventory and accounting systems. These order fulfillment processes are important. Someone will also need to read and process email messages from your customers and to read activity reports that profile the choices made by your Web site visitors.

Keeping the six needs above in mind, let's look at a twelve-step plan to eliminate confusion and get you up on the Web in an orderly and almost pain-free way.

Building your Web site step by step

The idea of this twelve-step sequence is to get your first Web site up and running. Even if you already have a site of your own, you might find a couple of new tactics here.

For your first Web site, be easy on yourself. What you learn about how the Web works and how to market on it will probably be more important than any results your first site generates. Web sites are changeable, so if you don't like it, reshape it. What you learn stays with you.

What about Gopher?

Before the World Wide Web, Gopher was the fastest-growing method of getting information on the Internet. Now Gopher is fading.

A Gopher server is very efficient and can serve many users at the same time, even with a cheap computer on a slow connection. It is easier to set up a Gopher server than a Web server because you don't have to create HTML files; you can use any kind of files. However, a Web server will attract far more visitors.

From the point of view of a visitor using Gopher, your Gopher site looks like a list of directories and files, with a single-line description of what is in each one. The Gopher presentation of computer file menus is neither as visually exciting as a Web site nor as functional.

Even universities, the last bastions of Gopherdom, are phasing out their Gopher servers for Web servers. In spite of the extra work of creating a Web site, I can think of no compelling reason for your business to invest in a Gopher server.

Help with your first Web site

Could you use free software designed to help you build a Web site? The software "Building Your First Web Site" is based on the step-by-step method presented in this book. You can modify it to meet your own site's specific needs. To get your free copy, download the demo of Project KickStart for Windows from the company Experience in Software at **www.experienceware.com**.

Step 1: Explore other Web sites

Like the saying goes, "ya gotta know your territory." So your first step in creating your own Web site is to study other peoples'—especially your competitors'—sites.

Look up your company, your products, and your competitors in search engines. Visit Alta Vista (**www.altavista.digital.com**), InfoSeek (**www.infoseek.com**), Excite (**www.excite.com**), and Hotbot (**www.hotbot.com**). Type in your business name in all lowercase letters and see what Web pages mention you. (If your name is more than one word, put "quotation marks" around it when you type it in.) Then look up your products and your competitors and their products.

Use your explorations to get ideas of what you like and what you don't like. What sites have functions and features that seem to be popular with your customers? Look for ideas other people had that you can do better.

Part of this exploratory stage is to receive any training you might need. Buy reference materials—books and magazines can help you generate ideas.

If you plan to use the Net for marketing, remember to "shop your competition." Approach your competitors as though you were a prospective customer. If you want to sell online, I recommend that you buy things online from at least three sites. Study how they handle the order process, so you'll know how to stage your own.

Step 2: Decide what you want your site to do

Decide what you want to accomplish. Define your site's purpose and who it needs to reach. Start small. A smaller project with a small goal is much easier to keep under control, especially if it is your company's first Web site. You can start with just a single page of contact information. Then add more pages as you need them. An important question to answer is, "How will I measure my results to determine whether my site is a success?"

Step 2 can be broken into these five substeps:

1. Who is your target audience? Existing customers? New prospects? (People who have never bought from your company require introductions explaining who you are and what your offerings do. They need more persuasion. Existing customers need support and want to be able to get more benefits from their existing relationship with you.) Employees? Distributors? News media? Investors? Focus your first site on one target.

2. Define your goals. Create something as quickly as possible. It is easy to refine it later.

3. Determine if the Web is the most effective medium to reach your goals. The Web is not the best solution for everything. You may be better off using email or a non-Internet way to achieve your goals.

4. Define what action you expect visitors to take as a result of visiting your site. Be specific. Your first site should allow your target audience to do *one thing*. You can add more actions later. Write one "Who will do what" sentence, as in these examples:

    *   Employees worldwide will obtain the latest versions of personnel and insurance forms.
    *   Investors will find all the information they need to invest in our company.
    *   Customers will find enough information in our support database to reduce telephone calls for help.
    *   Prospects and customers will subscribe to our email newsletter.
    *   Customers will find enough information online so they can order offline.
    *   Customers will buy products from our online catalog.

5. Define a "tone" or personality for your Web site. This is an important step. Writing and images in your site can project very different personalities. Will your visitors respond best to a buttoned-down, corporate approach? To one that is fresh and lively? Or to a site that is technical, no-nonsense? Don't choose the tone *you* like; choose the image your visitors expect. You should be able to describe your site's personality in three to five words. Everyone who works on your site should be aware of its tone.

Step 3: Select a site to use as a model

From the sites that you explored in Step 1, choose a site or parts of several sites to use as a model for your own site. Does your model set the tone you want? Does your model perform the actions you want your site to perform?

With your Web browser, you can copy a site to your computer and save its files for study. You can use your browser's "View Source" function to look at your model's HTML text to see how to write your own. Other people's pages are copyrighted—whether they include a copyright notice or not. So I'm not suggesting that you exactly duplicate someone else's site. Just use their pages for inspiration and to gain a little know-how.

Copy relevant pages to your computer. Reduce the number of pages and actions to as few as possible, keeping your starter project to as few pages as you can. It's easy to add more later.

Step 4: Select the information you want to present

What information will your visitors need to complete the actions you want?

Determine what information you already have and what information you will need to create. For your first project, use existing sources as much as you can. You might gather information that you can "repurpose" for your site from brochures, press releases, product specifications, databases, and other sources. A cautionary note: For your first project, letting Web visitors look up information in a large database may be too time-consuming and costly. Save database interfaces for later.

Before moving on to the next step, you should have decided your site's goal, who you want to reach, what actions you want them to do, how you will measure your results to know if your site reaches its goal, and what information you need to present. You now have a basic plan for your Web site.

 Before you actually build your Web site, plan it. Don't run immediately to a Web service bureau. You could wind up with your Web presence shaped to conform to the service bureau's needs. It should be the other way around.

Step 5: Determine what you will do and what you will outsource

At this point you can get cost estimates and decide how much you want to do in-house and how much should be handled by outsiders. Your big decision here is whether your Web site should be on an in-house computer or on rented space on a computer managed by a Web hosting service.

Farm out whenever possible, especially if this is your first Web project. Hiring outsiders lets you focus on your core business and not get sidetracked by Web details. (And there will be lots of 'em!)

With any Web host, consultant, or designer, you should negotiate. Published prices are usually not final. If a price is firm, ask if you can get the vendor to throw in additional services.

For a Web site, outside experts can help you in six areas.

1. IF YOU NEED THEM, HIRE CONSULTANTS

Will you hire a consultant or two to supervise the creation of your site?

Web consultants come in several flavors. Be aware of the differences between marketing expertise, design expertise, and technical expertise. These are three different skill areas. You can add copywriting as a fourth. Deciding *what* your site should do and *who* it should reach is a job that requires strategic analysis, and should be done by a person called a *Web producer* or by an advertising agency that specializes in Web site creation. A Web site *designer* works under the direction of a Web publisher or an agency and establishes the look of your site and the layout of its pages. A designer does not normally decide what your site should do and does not write the text that appears on your pages. A *Webmaster* also works under the direction of the Web publisher or agency and handles the programming and technical aspects of your site.

Before you shop for a design firm, know how much you want to spend and have a clear concept of what you want your site to do. Don't send an email message to every designer you can find. Most won't respond. Send messages to the top four or five, but send *individual* messages. Before you ask for a proposal, meet in person or on the phone with the firm's principals, not a sales rep. Explain your goals and your budget. Don't ask for a price until you've given a detailed description of exactly what you want. Don't expect the company to spend a lot of time responding to a proposal. Don't expect them to create a free demo Web site before you've hired them.

As part of this step, hire any consultants you need. Hire consultants before choosing other helpers because a good consultant may be able to save you time and money on all the following steps, or may have ideas that make your site more productive.

2. Choose your Web site host

Now it's time to choose *where* your Web site will live. (To be picky, where you'll place the computer files that make up your site.) Earlier in this chapter under the section "What You Need," I described the four choices available. Cybermalls are on that list and are covered in the chapter on Web storefronts. Most folks choose one of two other options on the list: either to rent space on a Web host's computer or to locate their site on their own computer.

For your first site, I recommend renting space from a Web host service. Sticking your site on Web host's computer instead of your own will get your site up faster and with a much smaller cash outlay. Besides, a good Web host will also provide hand-holding and support to get you over the rough spots. If you locate your site on your own in-house computer, you have to learn everything on your own.

The demand for renting Web space is so huge that more than 2,000 companies provide Web space for you to lease. If you create your own pages, I've seen service bureau rents start at $20 a month, based on the amount of disk space used. For a detailed guide to renting space from a Web site host, see the separate section later in the chapter.

Your other common alternative, running your Web server on your own computer in your own offices, is the most expensive and time-consuming way to build your Web site. If possible, avoid the hassles of running your own Web server. However, operating your own server does give you more control than a Web host. This can be essential if you plan to link your Web page to an existing internal database, such as your product catalog or inventory. Stay in-house if your site will change many times daily, especially if you will have live links to a database stored on an inside computer.

If you want to build your Web site in-house, you will need Web server software in addition to your own computer. A section below discusses what you'll need.

3. WILL YOU WRITE YOUR HTML PAGES YOURSELF?

Each page of your Web site is actually a page of text with formatting commands inserted. The commands are in *HTML*, which stands for HyperText Markup Language (but no one will ever ask you that).

The basics of HTML are simple. For instance, if you want bold type, you add `<b>` to turn boldface on, and `</b>` to turn if off, like this: `one <b>bold</b>word`. As the Web matures, more and more functions get added to HTML. I used to say that anyone who could use word processing software could write HTML, but that is no longer true.

Fortunately, you can use conversion software to create a page in Microsoft Word, WordPerfect, PageMaker, or several other word processing and layout programs, and convert your document to HTML format. You don't have as much control as you do by writing your page directly in HTML, but for small businesses, these conversion programs give you a way to create simple Web pages yourself.

The question remains, do you want to create your Web pages yourself? Unless your Web site is the core of your business, or unless you can't afford any other alternative, I advise you to hire someone, at least for your site's first version. You spend money, but you save time and can end up with a more productive site. You can also have a more professional-looking site, since *HTML determines the layout and design of your Web pages.*

You can have a single page created for under $500 or even under $50 if you keep it bare-bones simple. If you hire someone to write your Web pages, the fee for HTML coders starts as low as $15 to $35 an hour. Less-experienced graphic designers charge $25 to $50 an hour. You can pay $35 to $100 an hour for programming and complicated techie stuff, $50 to $80 an hour for copywriting, $75 to $100 an hour for "conceptual" work and high-end designers, and $100 to $200 an hour for "strategic" work or for a Web producer who pulls everything together. Standard payment terms are one-third up front, one-third upon delivery of the system, and one-third after it has been running for 30 days so you know everything works.

4. WHO WILL CREATE YOUR GRAPHICS?

HTML determines your layout, but what about logos, graphics, and pictures? You can hire someone to create original artwork for you. Or you can scan your logos, art, and photos to create Web graphics files. The Kinko's Copies chain (**www.kinkos.com**) will do this for you at their locations in the U.S., Canada, and Japan. You can also copy free graphics from Internet archives—see the list below.

5. BUY SITE CREATION SOFTWARE IF YOU NEED IT

If you farm out your site creation and maintenance, you won't need to buy this category of software products. If you create your own site, you will.

Products are available for all computer platforms, at prices ranging from free to tens of thousands of dollars. For a list of site creation software products and descriptions, visit **http://tips.internet.com/_noframes.shtmlHTML_authoring_products.html**.

6. WHO WILL ATTRACT VISITORS TO YOUR SITE?

The number one reason Web sites fail is lack of visitors. Will you attract visitors yourself or hire an agency that specializes in increasing Web site traffic? A promotion to attract visitors to a new site will take about two weeks of full-time work. A traffic-building agency will charge from $600 to $3,000 and will reach more outlets.

Step 6: Build a storyboard and plan

Producers of television commercials know the value of storyboards. In the design of a Web site, storyboards can save your life. They don't have to be fancy. You can build them with a legal pad, using one sheet for each Web page. For each page in your site, a storyboard page should show what graphics are displayed on that page, what kinds of text are presented, what push-buttons there are and what they do, what kind of links are on that page, and what checkboxes or interactive forms there are for your visitors to fill in. Then you can shuffle your paper pages around to determine how you want to connect your Web pages. You may come up with ideas for new pages or ways to combine pages. Your Web pages can have multiple links with each other. You might spot places to add links between pages. When you have an idea of what

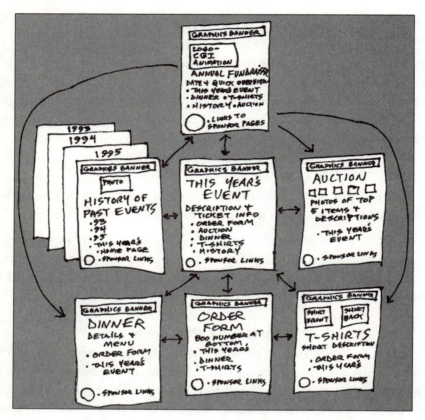

Figure 14.1   In storyboards, neatness doesn't count as long as the concepts are clear. This storyboard shows a Web site for a museum's annual fundraiser. Items with bullets are links to other pages. Arrows are also links. The circle at the bottom left corner of each page represents the museum's logo.

you want, create a smaller-sized version so you can show links between pages. Use arrows to show direction of travel. Figure 14.1 shows a sample storyboard.

You can also use three-by-five cards to create storyboards. Use one card for each page. Write a rough outline of each page's text on its card. You can arrange your cards in different groups to determine which pages should link with other pages and in what order.

Use storyboards to organize your presentation first, then match the contents of your Web site with your concept, not the other way around. The more pages you present, the more expensive your site will be. Pay special attention to your home page. It will be the first impression many Internet users have of your business. Remember that every link can mean a sometimes unendurable wait on hold for your visitor. The more waits, the sooner prospects leave. Plan your pages to cause as few waits as possible. Some Web designers suggest that a visitor should be able to reach any page from any other with no more than *four or five mouse clicks*.

If an advertising agency or marketing consultant is involved in planning your Web site, bring them in early in the storyboarding process. Early involvement (assuming your agency or consultant has Web experience) can cut your planning time by an order of magnitude or more and can give you a better site. When you finish your storyboards, you will know how many graphics files you need, how many text files you need, and other information you need to move to the next step. Create a master list of all the files you will need. Remember to get permission to use any copyrighted material.

When you have a list of all Web pages, files, and features, declare a state of *feature lock*. Resist adding more pages, files, or features, no matter how easy the changes seem. This is the only way to complete your site without going massively over budget and over schedule. Remind people that you can always add more *after* your Web site is up and running. Step 6 is not complete until you decide you have reached the feature lock stage.

Step 7: Create your Web files

Now roll up your sleeves and get to work! Rewrite the text of your pages to produce your final draft. Turn text files into HTML pages.

Find or create all graphics files. If you want advanced functions for your site, buy or write software to perform them. Many Web sites do not need advanced functions such as animation, database access, or multimedia. Your first Web site will be easier to create if you leave advanced functions for later. Software programs to perform advanced functions can include CGI scripts, JavaScript programs, Java software, and interfaces with other software programs.

Step 8: Test files on your own computer

Before adding a new page to the computer that holds your Web site, test your new page first on your own computer. Write down names of files with problems and all error messages. Determine the causes of problems and correct your fields.

You should also test to make sure that your HTML is properly written. Most good Web page authoring tools include built-in HTML testers. If yours doesn't, visit the free HTML testing service at **www.webtechs.com/html-val-svc**. It can't test your entire site at once, but you can use it to test your HTML one page at a time.

In addition to HTML, test for dead links. Test every link on each page. Several software programs automate this task, with different levels of sophistication and reporting:

CyberSpyder Link Test (**www.cyberspyder.com/cslnkts1.html**) Windows; $25
InfoLink (**ftp://ftp.zdnet.com/pccomp/0297/infoeval.2.0**) Windows; $30
Missinglink (**www.rsol.com/ml**) Unix; $20
MOMspider (**www.ics.uci.edu/WebSoft/MOMspider**) Unix; free
SiteAnalyst (**www.microsoft.com**) Windows; bundled with Microsoft
    Site Server
SiteCheck (**www.pacific-coast.com**) Mac, Windows; $80
SiteSweeper (**www.sitetech.com**) Windows; $250
WebAnalyzer (**www.incontext.ca**) Windows; $250
WebMaster (**www.coast.com**) Windows; $250
Webxref (**www.sara.nl/cgi-bin/rick_acc_webexref**) Unix; free

The three $250 Windows products (and Microsoft's bundled software) are by far the best. They produce more reports and charts, and besides finding dead links, they test for duplicated files, missing graphics, and unattached pages. WebMaster even checks dynamically-generated pages.

After you've tested and corrected your files, it's time to move them onto the Web.

Step 9: Copy files to your Web site computer

Your Web site host can tell you how to do this. A good Web site host will provide you with special software to automatically copy your files. Not-quite-so-good hosts provide FTP software and instructions.

Have all files been copied? Use your master list of files as a checklist to be sure.

Step 10: Test your site online

Now that your pages are online, look again at every page. Does each page display? Does every link work? Does every graphic display? Using a 14.4 baud modem, visit each page and time it to see how quickly or slowly your page displays for an average visitor.

If you want industrial-strength testing of your site, you can hire a specialist company to put your site through its paces. Two prominent companies in this field are KeyLabs (**www.keylabs.com**) and Software Testing Laboratories (**www.stlabs.com**). KeyLabs does stress-testing, simulating dozens of simultaneous visitors. Software Testing Labs tests performance as well and also security for transaction systems and password-protected sites. Expect to pay up to $1,100 per day for the kind of heavy-duty testing and thorough reporting these test labs provide.

Don't limit your tests to your site itself. Test off-Web follow-up as well. When a visitor sends an email from your site, does someone receive it? How long does it take? Who gets sales leads and orders from your site? Does the order information reach them in a usable format? Who sends an acknowledgement back to the customer? Make sure the human parts of your Web response work as smoothly as the computerized parts.

Step 11: Attract visitors

Now that your site is online and working, it's time to herd visitors your way. Lack of promotion to attract visitors is the most common cause of Web site failure.

Step 12: Support your site and improve it

Once you have your World Wide Web site up and running, it's time to promote it, learn from the response you generate, and tweak your site to make it more productive. You will need to make the *editorial investment* needed to sustain interest, making frequent changes and additions to attract return visitors. Return visits don't just happen due to random molecular collisions. You need to *motivate* return visits, to provide customers with a reason to come back.

When you budget your staff time, pencil in the 4 to 40+ hours per week that an average business Web site requires for maintenance (mostly editorial time, not technical time), plus 2 to 30+ hours per week to answer email, depending on your email volume.

For many companies, especially smaller ones, the most difficult part of building a Web site comes when they need to hire a competent host. Let's take a detailed look at the process of hiring a good Web host.

Renting space from a Web host

Hundreds of thousands of businesses rent Web space on computers owned by their Internet access providers or by service bureaus called *Web hosts*. Every computer magazine published today carries ads from Web hosts that lease Web space for $20 per month and up.

If you locate your Web server on a Web host's computer, be aware that your host can be *anywhere in the world*. You send all of your files to your Web server over the Net, so distance doesn't matter. Web Communications Corp. (**www.webcom.com**) has attracted businesses from all over the world with low rates. Its fees start at $25 per month for a small business server, and $60 per month for a larger one.

Higher-end Web hosts are sometimes called *virtual servers*, because you get almost as much control and functionality as if you ran your own server in your own office. Distinctions between virtual servers and Web hosts used to be clear-cut. However, intense competition between Web hosts has forced more hosts to add services, so many Web hosts now offer the same level of functionality as virtual servers. The difference between virtual servers and Web hosts has become nearly meaningless.

Most virtual servers charge $50 to $150 per month. One example is Virtual Site at **www.virtualsite.com**. For a $75 setup fee and $75 to $100 per month, you get standard services plus many extra bells and whistles, including an FTP server and an email POP server so you can create an unlimited number of email accounts.

How to select your Web host

Choosing a Web host can seem overwhelming if you're not sure how to go about it. Following this seven-step process will simplify matters. Looking for a role model? You might read the sidebar in Chapter 12; it tells how the firm Visual Law chose its Web host.

Step 1: Identify your needs

If you don't know what you need, you won't be able to find a host that can help you. Will your site have hundreds of files or just a few dozen? Will you have lots of graphics? How often will you update it? Will you use CGI scripts?

Do you want Real Audio to provide live sound? How about video? Will you use Java? Roughly how many visitors per month do you expect?

You especially need to answer the following three questions:

Do you want to use your own domain name? Some hosts force you to use theirs. Many hosts charge extra for you to use your own. (For more about domain names, read the sidebar "How to get your own domain name" at the end of Chapter 3.)

Do you want your Web site to sell to consumers? Eighty percent of Internet consumer sales are made by people typing their credit card numbers into online forms on Web pages. If you want to sell to consumers on the Net, your Web host needs to provide processing for secure credit card transactions. Some don't.

Do you want visitors to your site to be able to use a database? Database hookups are complicated. If you intend to integrate with a database, let a potential host know. Since Web databases can be tricky, I don't recommend one for your first Web project. It's more realistic to start with a simpler site and add a database later.

STEP 2: GATHER A POOL OF WEB HOST CANDIDATES

First, check your own Internet access provider. Most access providers also rent Web space. Next, ask people who you know who already have a Web site. Are they satisfied?

Look at ads in newspapers, computer magazines, and in the Yellow Pages under "Computer." And visit directories on the Internet. Visit the Budget Web Index at **www.budgetweb.com**, Publishing Product Information on the Web at **www.alumni.caltech.edu/~dank/webinfo.html**, and Leasing a Server at **http://union.ncsa.uiuc.edu/HyperNews/get/www/leasing.html**. (On this last one, vendors write their own descriptions, so take 'em with a grain of salt.) If you visit that site, be sure to read its helpful FAQ about Web space leases. If you want virtual Web server providers, go to Yahoo and search for "virtual server".

People sometimes ask who "the best" Web host is. I think that depends on your specific needs. I have heard nothing but good things about GeoNet (**www.geo.net**), but GeoNet is a high-end Web host and provides more than smaller sites need. Each of its clients gets its own Sun computer and a 10-megabit-per-second connection. GeoNet charges $1,000 for installation and monthly fees of $2,000 and up, but provides a higher level of customer support than other Web hosts I've worked with.

For my own Web site, I've been very satisfied with GoSite from Internet Direct (**www.gosite.com**). Businesses using GoSite range from large (Motorola, Phoenix Suns) all the way down to mom and pop startups. GoSite includes a software package program called GoGadget, available in Mac and Windows versions, that copies all your HTML, graphics, and program files from your computer and installs them on your Web site, automatically replacing or deleting any obsolete files. GoSite lets you accept encrypted credit cards. If you don't have your own credit card merchant account, Internet Direct will help you open one. Your site is completely portable and can be moved to another service bureau. GoSite Web servers come with email autoresponders, mailing lists, Real Audio, private FTP dropboxes, and more goodies. The base rate for GoSite is $50 to $300 per month, depending on which options you choose. There are no per-transaction charges. Best of all, GoSite includes 24-hour phone support. I've found its support technicians knowledgeable and extremely helpful.

STEP 3: ELIMINATE HOSTS THAT DON'T MEET YOUR NEEDS

Quickly compare the hosts in your pool of candidates. Some will leap out as obvious mismatches. Knock 'em out of the competition, along with any obvious weaklings that don't stand up to your semifinalists.

STEP 4: GET PRICE QUOTES FROM AT LEAST 3 HOSTS

Estimate how much disk space you will need. If your site will present large graphics, audio, or multimedia, you will need more disk space.

Turn the "Checklist of Questions" section below into your own list of questions to ask each candidate. You can email or fax your questions to each prospective host and ask them to send a price quote back to you.

STEP 5: COMPARE PRICES AND SERVICES

When you get price quotes back from your candidates, it's obvious that you will compare *prices*. (Be suspicious of a price drastically lower than others. A cheap host may be shoddy, with frequent failures and long waits for access. Reliability and access speed can be critical for your site.)

What's not so obvious is that you will also compare *services*. There is no such thing as a standard bundle of Web host services, so each different host does different things. While you're at it, test their support. Call each host's technical support phone number yourself and time it. See how long it takes you to reach a real human being.

Now you can eliminate all but a small number of finalists.

STEP 6: CHECK CLIENT REFERENCES

From each finalist, get at least three client references. Check each reference in at least two ways.

First, call clients and get uncensored opinions. Ask each client what the Web host could have done better. If the client had to do it again, what would the client do differently? What kind of service has the client received *recently*? Would the client use this Web host again?

Next, visit the Web sites of the clients and see if pages are delivered to you quickly. What you look for is an obvious difference in delivery speed between your different host finalists. If client pages from all finalists arrive slowly, the problem might not be with the Web hosts. It might be that your own Internet access provider is overloaded and slow. Also, are the client sites similar to yours, or just easy baby sites?

After checking references and visiting client sites, eliminate Web hosts that are unreliable or are overloaded and provide slow access. Be more lenient with reports of poor support. The Web's fast growth has overwhelmed Web hosts, so poor support is the norm.

STEP 7: MAKE YOUR SELECTION

Avoid getting stuck in a long-term contract. Some Web hosts offer a discount for a one-year or six-month contract. The longer the lease, the lower the price. When you start your first Web site, consider it an experiment and don't sign up for longer than three months. A month-to-month arrangement is even better. If your host is a lemon, you don't want to be trapped for a year.

Finally, if your first Web host does not satisfy you, move your site to another one.

Checklist of questions for Web hosts

Use this list of questions *(with hints in italics)* as a starter kit to create your own list to fax or email to prospective Web site hosts.

FEES

- Is there an initial setup fee, and if so, how much? What does the setup fee cover?

- How much is the charge per month?

- How much disk space does the monthly charge include? What is the rate for extra disk space?

- Is there an access fee for the number of times my site is accessed? If so, how much? *Avoid hosts that charge a per-access fee.*

- Is there a per-megabyte fee for the volume of data transferred? If so, how much is the fee, and how much data per month does it cover? What is the charge for additional data transferred?

- Is there an extra charge when you update your server? *Avoid per-update fees. You will want to update your site as frequently as possible.*

SUPPORT

- Do you provide live 24-hour phone support?

- To get phone support, must I leave a voicemail message or call a pager? *Voicemail and pagers don't count. Valid phone support means you reach a live human being.*

- Is phone support available 7 days a week? *This is crucial. Don't even think of any host that does not provide 24-hour phone support, seven days a week.*

- Does the Web host provide tutorials or classes for new users? *Good training is worth paying extra.*

DOMAIN NAMES

- Can I use my own domain name? *Many service bureaus will not let you use your own domain name. This may force you to use a URL such as www.servicebureau.net/~yourco when you would rather use www.yourco.com. Some will only let you use your domain name with a file name added to the end: www.yourco.com/yourco. Some will force you to have a tilde (~) in your URL. Tildes are hard to type, harder to remember, and impossible to explain to someone over the phone. Don't put up with tildes.*

- Is there an extra fee for this?

Site Management

- Does the Web host provide software I can use to manage my site? If so, what is it and what does it do? *Site management software is worth paying extra for. Make sure that you get more than just HTML editing software. HTML editing software is not worth the extra money. Likewise, many hosts just provide you with FTP software to add and change your files. Better hosts provide software that checks which files you have changed and moves them automatically. Bare-bones FTP software is not worth paying extra for.*

- How often can I change files on my site? *I almost choked and died when I found a Web host that only allowed its clients to change their sites once a month! I've seen a few that allow changes only once a week. Don't put up with this. You should be able to make changes as many times a day as you wish.*

- When I add, delete, or move a file on my site, how long does it take before my change is available to visitors? *Some hosts, including America Online, update changes overnight. Some do not update changes on weekends. The correct answer to this question is that your change is available immediately.*

- Is there a limit to the number of files I can use? *Don't put up with any limits to the quantity of files your site can contain.*

Reports

- Can I get reports showing how often my pages are visited? *This is important. If you cannot measure visitor traffic, you cannot effectively improve the results generated by your Web site.*

- Do reports show hits on my overall site or accesses for each page and file? *Overall reports are worthless. Data must be reported for each individual graphics and text file.*

- Do I get a referer log report? *This extremely valuable report shows where visitors to a page come from, both for traffic within your site and for visitors entering your page from another site. You want this report because it shows where your visitors come from. In addition, for visitors who come to you from search engines like Yahoo and Alta Vista, it shows the actual search terms visitors entered to find you.*

- Are reports generated daily, weekly, monthly, or whenever I want one? *The last answer is the one you want.*

- Is there an extra fee for reports?

- Can I get sample reports or view samples online? *The chapter covering direct web marketing tells you more about what kinds of data you want in Web site reports, what they mean, and what you can do with them.*

PROTECTION

- How fast is the host's connection to the Internet?

- Does the host have two connections, one each from two different phone companies? *This keeps your Web site running if one phone company's line goes down.*

- Does the host have backup power to keep your site running in the event of a power failure? *Only the best hosts provide backup power.*

- Does the host back up and archive Web sites? If so, how often? *A technical failure can wipe out your site if it has not been copied and archived. Few hosts provide this service.*

- What security is used to protect my site?

CREDIT CARDS

- What support is provided for credit card sales?

- Does the Web host support the S.E.T. (Secure Electronic Transactions) standard?

- Will the Web host create a secure order page for me? *An additional fee should be charged for this service.*

- Does the Web host supply a standard CGI script for card processing, so I don't need to hire a programmer to write my own?

- Does the Web host supply an HTML template that I can customize to create my own secure order page? If so, does the order page template include JavaScript validation routines to prevent customer errors when I fill out my order form?

- How will the host send my sales orders (including customer credit card numbers) to me? *Make sure they're encrypted.*

TECHNOLOGY

- Does the host support CGI scripts and Java programs? *You need to ask this question only if you plan for your pages to use CGI or Java, which some providers do not allow. Secure credit card transactions require CGI scripts. You may not need Java; most Web sites don't.*

- Can I run other custom software?

BUSINESS

- How long has the host been in business? *You want one that has been in business for at least six months.*

- How many clients does it host? (This figure should not include access clients who are not hosted.) *Under "Protection" you asked the host for its connection speed to the Internet. Divide that speed (in Kbps) by the number of clients, and you get the average speed per client.*

- *This is not a question you can ask the host, but one you answer yourself: Visit the host's own Web site. Is it slow?*

EXTRA SERVICES

- Can I get an FTP dropbox? If so, is it password-protected? *This lets people drop off files for you and gives you a place to leave files for other people to pick up.*

- Can I get an email autoresponder?

- Can I run an email list from your hosting service?

- Will you do anything to attract visitors to my site? *It may be worth paying extra for this. Some hosts have arrangements with top companies to attract visitors to their hosted sites. If your host does provide this service, check to see how it attracts visitors for you. Does it just use a clunky auto-submit service, or the alternative (which generates more visitors), an agency that submits by hand?*

- What additional services do you provide?

Choosing server software

Okay, but what if you decide not to go with a Web host, but want to run your own Web server on your own computer? Then you will need to buy Web server software.

The six leading Web server software packages are Apache, a hugely popular free software program for Unix and OS/2; Microsoft's Internet Information Server, which is "free" if you buy Windows NT Server; the free NCSA server for Unix; Netscape's $500-and-up servers for Unix and Windows NT; Website, a Windows NT server from O'Reilly & Associates, with versions for $250 and $500; and Starnine's Webstar for Macs and Windows NT, which comes in $500 and $600 versions.

Which should you choose? Well, Webstar for the Mac takes about three hours to get your pages online (no, really), the Windows NT servers take about 40 hours, and Unix servers take between 20 to 60 hours, depending on which version of Unix you use and what brand of computer. But there are more considerations to selecting a platform—many more—than how quickly you can set it up. The most powerful considerations aren't logical, but emotional. People get passionate about their computing platforms. Someone once said that operating systems are religions, and I'm inclined to agree.

My advice is to respect your technical folks' religious preference for an operating system and go with their choice. All six of the packages above are proven, solid performers, so you'll come out okay in the end. You can also choose from about 50 lesser-known Web server products for many brands of computers. To find the latest news about secure servers and their prices, visit ServerWatch at **www.serverwatch.com**. This site features a chart of the leading Web servers for Macs, Unix, and Windows, and their prices, with links to server suppliers.

Note that if you run your own Web server, your server software will be only the tip of the software iceberg. Expect to spend about three to four times the cost of your server software on all the other software doodads you will add on later.

You'll also need to pay for your server's own phone line (which should be 128 Kbps or faster), its own router, and its own human for technical support.

Web design and construction

I don't have enough pages to explain all the details of Web construction or the basics of marketing and how they apply to the Web. Plenty of books give good information on those topics. More important are key concepts about how Web sites work, so you can apply those insights whether you supervise somebody else building Web pages for you or you roll up your sleeves and do it yourself.

First, don't listen to all the fluff that calls Web sites "online billboards." Your Web server can survey your customers, take orders, calculate sales tax and shipping charges, validate a credit card or account name, and even deliver products (consulting reports, software programs, pictures, and so on). Billboards can't do any of that. If you think of your Web site as a billboard, your whole mindset will be wrong when you plan your site. So don't.

Your home page

The most important page for most sites is the home page. (If you take online sales orders, your order entry page is the most important.) Your home page is a limited but valuable piece of screen real estate, and it needs to convey a number of ideas at once. It should show a visitor at a glance what kind of business you are in, what your site has to offer, and why the visitor should explore further.

Many companies have a few lines of description of the company, but most visitors care more about what's available from your site. On your home page, don't sell your company. Don't sell your products. *Sell your site.* Your home page's job is to get eyeballs inside, where other pages can handle persuasion. Your home page is the place to put a table of contents for your Web site. Don't make visitors wade through a page of glib nothingness to reach another page that actually gives information or takes them somewhere. Put a menu right up front, on your home page.

Also, Web visitors want to see things that are new. On your home page, list anything new or changed. People who return to your Web site usually scan your home page menu. If it shows nothing different from their previous visit, they might leave without looking further.

Above the fold

The most important part of your home page—and of every other Web page— is the *top* part of the page. The top displays onscreen first, before a visitor scrolls down. The experience of hundreds of Web publishers verifies that what you put on top of a page will be selected much more often than anything below. (See Figure 14.2.)

The increased potency of the top of Web pages is universally recognized and is called *above the fold*. This is a phrase to remember, and one I should explain. It sounds silly at first. After all, Web pages don't fold.

Figure 14.2   Like its paper counterpart, this USA Today Web page (**www.usatoday.com**) puts its most compelling headlines and pictures above the fold.

But newspaper pages do. The phrase "above the fold" is stolen from the newspaper business, where above the fold means life or death. When you look at a newspaper vending rack and decide whether or not to buy a copy of today's *Daily Planet*, you decide based on the only part of the paper you can see: the top half of the front page. All the burden of persuading a reader to buy the entire paper is carried by the photos, headlines, and teasers above the fold of that front page.

Editors know this. They save their most compelling photos and headlines to place above the fold. Reporters fight to get their stories above the fold because good position gives them more readers. You can pick up any successful paper, study its editorial strategy, and swipe ideas to increase readership of your Web pages.

The bad news is that newspaper pages are much bigger than computer screens. You have only a small amount of space and many elements fighting to squeeze in. Recognizing this, you can make sure that the most important elements on any Web page fit above the fold, and you can avoid making mistakes that squander this precious resource.

On many home pages, companies begin with a huge logo. This wastes space, pushing other elements below the fold. (Besides, big logos look dumb. People don't look at Web pages from across the room, but from only a few inches away. Look at Yahoo's logo for a good size.)

Another way to waste screen real estate is by using frames. Ninety-five percent of the sites that use frames don't need them. They needlessly chop usable above-the-fold space in half. This is a crime. Use frames only when you absolutely have to. (Not that I hate frames. To see my favorite use of frames, visit **www.webpagesthatsuck.com**.)

When you review the design for one of your Web pages, root out spacewasters like these. Make sure your most important links and information always display above the fold.

Icons vs. category headers vs. descriptions

You want your visitors to be able to navigate through your site, to find what they need and not waste time with dead ends or unwanted information. Many sites create icons (Figure 14.3) or category headers (Figure 14.4) to help visitors get around, but recent evidence shows that those may not always be the best way to go.

When RSA Data Security (**www.rsa.com**) added paragraphs to its home page announcing new events, people navigated by the links in those paragraphs and ignored its category headers. More visitors went inside the RSA site. In response, RSA added more descriptive paragraphs. Traffic inside increased further as a higher percentage of home page visitors decided to look more deeply.

Kurt Stammberger of RSA explained the increased results: "For several hundred years, newspapers have perfected the art of informing the reader what an article is about in a paragraph or two, so they decide if they want to read the rest. You can't do that with an icon and a two-word category." In other words, descriptive paragraphs grab more visitors.

Other sites report similar results. After formal research, Excite increased the number of links on its home page. Both the National Computer Security Association (**www.ncsa.com**) and MapQuest reported increased traffic after adding more links to their home pages. The Web version of *USA Today* reports that story descriptions outpull its section headings. Yahoo must be the champ. I counted 112 text links on my last visit to Yahoo's home.

Text links, especially text links with descriptions (Figure 14.5), outdraw icons and graphical category headers. Toolbars providing only keywords draw less traffic inside. Use these tactics to lure more visitors inside your own Web site.

Figure 14.3   Some sites use icons like these to help visitors navigate.

NEWS   PRODUCTS   CONTACTS   SEARCH   FEEDBACK

Figure 14.4   Category headers help visitors navigate a site. When several category headers are combined in one graphic, the result is called a toolbar.

- New product announcements, special bargains, and press releases
- Product information and how to order
- Contact our staff in the U.S., Canada, the U.K., and Australia
- Search our site
- Send email to customer service, or to our Webmaster

Figure 14.5   Some sites use text links with descriptions like these.

Budgeting pages for speed

The biggest arguments among Web page designers involve the amount of graphics. Should you have big, beautiful graphics files that take a long time to download? Or should you have as few graphics as possible so your pages are faster? As far as I know, no one has yet done a split-run test (which could be easily done on the Web) to answer this debate. In my experience, both camps are right. There are times when large graphics files are the better approach. Other times, minimal graphics are preferable. A frequently-used search engine like Yahoo would drive people nuts if they had to wait for a 40 K graphics file before they could use it. Your choice depends on your target visitors, what they expect, and how patient they are.

Some simple math gives you a size budget for Web page files. You can set a goal of a number of seconds for total download time for a page, and size your text and graphic files to fit under that time limit. You need to take into account the kind of connection your customers have. If they use a modem, each download takes one second for the modem to *negotiate* the download with your Web server software. If your customers use ISDN or any faster digital connection, each download's negotiation will take less than one-tenth of a second on average. (How do you know what speeds your customers use to connect? For your first Web page, you'll have to guess.)

Even with a slowpoke 14.4 K modem, Yahoo's home page is designed to load in 13 seconds or less. It always consists of three files: one HTML text file and two graphics files. The total size of all three files together is 18 K (that's 18,000) or less—but wait! File sizes are commonly given in *bytes*, but Internet connection speeds are given in *bits*! How annoying. This means we have to pull out our calculators, because *one* byte equals *eight* bits. All three files together equal 18,000 bytes, so multiplying by eight makes their total size 144,000 bits. Yahoo's target is 13 seconds. Its home page consists of three files, so we must subtract three seconds, one second for the modem negotiations for each file; 13 seconds minus three leaves us with 10 seconds. Since a 14.4 K modem is supposed to move 14,400 bits per second, in 10 seconds how many bits should it move? Let's see here, um, 14,400 times 10 is, um: 144,000. How 'bout that? Yahoo has enough time to move 144,000 bits, so it keeps its files that size or smaller.

What would happen if Yahoo added a tiny 200-bit graphics file—maybe a colored bullet—to its page? Would it still keep close to its 13-second limit? The answer is: no way! Even a tiny file adds another one-second negotiation session. Adding another file, even if the file size were *zero*, still adds another second of time. This math may seem a bit much, but it demonstrates an important but little-known fact about Web graphics.

 Several tiny Web graphics take much longer to download than a couple of medium or large ones. Web browsers have kill buttons, and between 20 and 30 percent of all Web users surf the Web with graphics turned off, or kill large graphics files and never see them. Increase the number of people who actually *see* your graphics by including only a few graphics files on each page.

Even with a 28.8 or 56 K modem, you still add another second in wait time for each file you add to a page. Negotiation time will be shorter only for ISDN, frame relay, and other all-digital connections. And these are theoretical conditions. In real life, everything takes longer. So keep time in mind and budget your pages for speed, especially your home page. If you don't optimize for the 14.4K crowd, you might cut yourself out of the biggest part of your market.

Free art for Web pages

So you're not an artist and you don't have one in house? Try these sites for some art resources you can download or use for free:

- Pixelsight: **www.pixelsight.com**

- The Icon Browser: **www.di.unipi.it/iconbrowser/icons.html**

- Tony's Icons: **www.bsdi.com/icons/tonys.html**

- Textures and Backgrounds Wonderland: **http://cameo.softwarelabs.com/hotlist/hotlist.htm**

- ColorMaker: **www.missouri.edu/wwwtools/colormaker**

A final tip

One final design tip from author Jaclyn Easton: "When you're done designing your Web page, go to Prodigy and look at it." You might design your Web page on a Power Mac or a Sun workstation, but most of your customers view it under far worse conditions. Get a 14.4Kbps modem and review your work the way real people see it.

CHAPTER 15

Writing for the Web

"Words sell. Words get attention, create interest, generate desire, and produce action. Good design presents the words in a visually pleasing way. Don't confuse the two."

—Thom Reece, CEO, Online Marketing Group

This chapter is for people who need to put words on Web pages. It is about writing text—the kind that humans read—rather than about coding HTML. (Though I do cover junctions where HTML overlaps the Queen's English.)

Web copywriting is 10 percent technical tricks and 90 percent marketing savvy. One of the main jobs of writing for the Web is to use information and/ or entertainment to *differentiate* your company from competitors. You *will* have competition on the Web because the barriers to entry are so low. How is your company different? What information (not hype) can you provide that shows that difference clearly?

Let's take a look at two Web sites that succeed in using Web writing to differentiate themselves and drive sales.

A good example: Vicarage Hotel

Imagine you're going to London and want to find a place to stay. You go to Yahoo or Alta Vista and look up "london hotels." One of the links the search engine gives you is the Vicarage Hotel (**www.deadlock.com/hotels/london/ vicarage**). The description sounds promising, so you click on it.

On the Vicarage home page (see Figure 15.1), the first thing you see is a welcome message and a small photo of the hotel along with its address, phone number, and the names of its proprietors. To the left of the photo is a link, "Photo [24K] The Hotel," and to its right "Photo [24K] The Team." You can click on the underlined links to see large photos. Putting the size of the file after each link lets you know how long it will take to bring the photo file to your computer. How thoughtful. The team photo shows real, live people, adding warmth and building trust.

You scroll down to read an introduction: "I wouldn't tell you which under-pants to wear, the same as I won't tell you which browser to use. You can view this site with whatever you please. So there. However, it is highly recom-mended to browse this site to the accompaniment of Aerosmith's 'The Other Side' or Pink Floyd's 'Wish You Were Here' (if it's raining)."

Figure 15.1   *The home page of the Vicarage Hotel.*

You probably think "What?" and read further. This page has a sense of humor. (Or, since it's British, a sense of *humour*.) By extension, so does the product it advertises, the Vicarage Hotel. Your Web site visitors will assume that your product has the same characteristics your site does.

Collect email addresses

Next on the Vicarage site, you come to a tiny cartoon of a robot and this text: "**Jimmy the robot:** *Don't bother* bookmarking this page. You have enough of them already, am I right? Instead, let Jimmy send you a message whenever I update this page. Then you can come back here and check the Recent Updates section. Just **type your address and click**." Immediately below is an online form where you can type your email address, and a "Send It!" button. More humorous copy.

As a Web visitor, you may or may not be impressed by this, but as a Web page writer, you should be. This tactic has worked again and again on Web sites I've been involved with. One of the cheapest, easiest, and most effective ways of getting visitors to return to your site is to ask them to sign up for a email notifications of site updates. The subscribers you get are qualified prospects who've already seen your site, like what you offer, and want to see more. The Vicarage Hotel site asks for subscribers right up front in a prominent position, yet does so in a friendly way that is neither pushy nor intimidating. Neat trick.

First, set the stage

Next, the page introduces the writer: "Hi! I'm Jim and I work in this small hotel with my boss Mandy. In my spare time I like to mess around on this Web thing, so I thought I'd put the two together and write this page to let you know about the best place to stay in London."

This short paragraph *by itself* has more personality than 90% of business Web sites I've seen. How would you describe Jim? Unpretentious? Informal? Do you think he'd be friendly? How does this make you feel about the hotel? Note that you know nothing about the Vicarage Hotel yet, other than that it is small and in London. But you have a feeling for its personality. This is a soft sell. First the Web copy establishes an overall tone, which frames everything else you read. Only *after* discovering its personality do you get specifics.

"The Vicarage is a family run hotel, taking pride in offering its guests a relaxing and charming 'home from home' in London with many guests returning on a regular basis.

"This splendid Victorian house which retains many original features is situated in a quiet residential garden square [Photo - 43K] in a particularly pleasant part of the Royal Borough of Kensington, yet only a stroll away from the exciting shopping in High Street Kensington, Knightsbridge and Portobello Market.

"There are eighteen comfortable, centrally heated bedrooms (see pictures) consisting of single, double/twin and family rooms for up to four people, all are individually decorated in keeping with the period of the house.

"To fortify our guests for the day ahead, we provide a hearty cooked breakfast in a charming dining room [Photo - 28K]."

Lots of photos without clogging modems

Now you have an idea of the hotel, its neighborhood, and what it offers. Although you read the information as text, you can still look at plenty of photos if you want to, since each photo is presented as a link with a file size. (Remember, this site markets to *consumers*, who primarily use modems with

14.4 or 28.8 K speeds. File size matters, because bigger files mean longer waits.) This is much more courteous than forcing many large graphics files down your visitor's throat whether he or she wants them or not.

Most Web sites dump their graphics in your modem, giving you no choice. The Vicarage method of photo presentation makes visitors feel more in control.

Click on the breakfast link and you read a full breakfast menu. Looks good. This little hotel offers a lot and seems very friendly. Only now, after you understand the value that it offers, does the Vicarage give you its room rates. They are low, and include breakfast—what a deal! At this point, if you are going to London and are comfortable that the Vicarage (like most bed and breakfast inns) has shared bathrooms, this hotel has probably made your short list of finalists. You might click on "More info about making reservations," or you might continue down the page.

Once again, the Vicarage site demonstrates proper *sequencing*: Establish value first, then discuss price. First, you became aware of all the hotel's desirable qualities and charm; second, you found out its prices are low. What happens when these two points are made in the opposite order? If you find out the price is low first, you read all remaining copy trying to figure out why. Is this a piece of junk? You hunt for flaws. That's a tough state of mind to overcome. By making the hotel look good first, the low price becomes yet another pleasant surprise instead of a source of anxiety.

You scroll down the page to read more about the hotel's amenities and neighborhood. Next is a section labeled "Pictures," giving you links to more photos, with captions like these:

"The Hotel [24 K] Mandy nagged me to get all her flowers in the shot, so please tell her how much you admire them.

"Dining Room [28 K] Some people having their breakfast interrupted by an annoying photographer."

Again, personality. Then you see a link to "Contact us to make a booking or just to say hi. If you have any questions in the back of your mind about the hotel, travel, or anything else at all, then this is the place to go." What easygoing, helpful people. I'll bet a stay at the Vicarage would be relaxing.

Scrolling down, you see links to reviews by travel guidebooks and "messages from *real people* who have actually stayed here." Establishing credibility is hard to do on the Web, and testimonials help make Web pages believable. The guidebooks and people seem to like this hotel.

At the bottom of the page, you find links to other pages within the site: maps, directions, more information for visitors to London, great instructions on how to get service in a crowded London pub. You'll probably read some of these additional pages, most of which link to each other. What an amusing and useful site. It's quite easy for a London-bound traveler to spend half an hour or 45 minutes at the Vicarage Hotel site. You can't help but feel a warm spot for this little hotel.

The proof is in the pudding

Does that warm glow translate into sales? You bet it does. This London bed and breakfast hotel is always full. More than 50% of its sales are generated by its Web site. The site's emotional pull is so strong that it overcomes a major inconvenience that kills sales on other consumer Web sites: the Vicarage doesn't accept credit cards! Although you can use email to confirm a vacancy, you must use snail mail to send a check to reserve a room. This charming site may seem simple and homemade, but don't let it fool you. It was actually carefully constructed by Jim Rhodes, one of the most clever Web copywriters on the planet.

All well and good, but what if your company can't use charm and humor? What if your customers are the kind who prefer a serious approach—such as business-to-business customers?

A different good example: SoftMail

Pretend you have a software product and you need new ways to market it. Your company is in crisis. (Aren't software companies *always* in crisis?) You are under pressure. Your job is on the line.

Figure 15.2   The first screen you see when you visit SoftMail's Web site.

You visit the home page in Figure 15.2, a company called SoftMail Direct (**www.softmail.com**). Not much here at first: an address (but no phone number), a welcome statement, some text saying that this company is "the leading (if I had my way, any company that used that cliche would be fined) direct response agency (whatever that is) serving the software and new media markets." You guess that means your company. The last line of text says, "A listing of resources available at this site can be found below," so you scroll down.

As Figure 15.3 shows, you see a link, "<u>Direct Response Survival Handbook</u>— Tips and helpful advice for selling software direct." As a software marketer desperate to increase sales, are you interested in this? You bet you are. Below that, you see links for "An archive of critical reviews of recent software offers in the mail," and "Get on the mailing list for our helpful electronic newsletter."

Why should I click on this?

Each heading used by SoftMail promises you a *benefit* for clicking on that link. It gives you a reason to go deeper into the SoftMail site. This is a technique to imitate in your own site. When you provide a link, motivate your visitor to choose it. Don't just give the name of your link, give a reason why. (Imagine how much weaker the appeal of SoftMail's links would be if it just listed names. "Critique Corner" sounds blah unless you know what it is.)

You want helpful advice for selling software direct, so you click on <u>Direct Response Survival Handbook</u>. You see a two-sentence introduction: "We are constantly adding new articles to this book. You can come back to this site periodically to read them, or <u>subscribe</u> to SoftMail Direct, and we'll send you

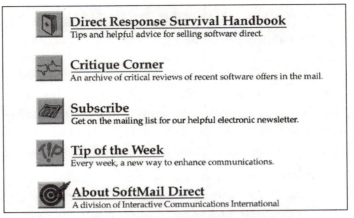

Figure 15.3   Scrolling lower on SoftMail's home page, you discover more options.

articles via email as they are published." How helpful, and what a good way to gather customer email addresses.

Below are links to the chapters that make up the *Direct Response Survival Handbook*: <u>Birth of the Direct Response Web Site</u>, <u>Getting Into Direct Mail: Look Before You Leap</u>, <u>The 20-Second Tour of a Direct Mail Piece</u>, and others. All are targeted toward people who market software. Are you going to be interested? You market software, so of course you are. You read some chapters. You find places you can get free mailing lists. You probably print that page. There are good tips for postcard mailings. You print that page, too. You find a lot of information, all of it interesting and very valuable to you in your job. Before you know it, you've spent half an hour.

These SoftMail people seem to know a lot about this stuff. Which, of course, is the point of all this information. As you, the prospective customer, are impressed by the quality of a lesson, you also acknowledge the expertise of the teacher. SoftMail's useful tips prove that the company knows how to market software.

To visit another section of the site, you click on "<u>Critique Corner</u> - An archive of critical reviews of recent software offers in the mail." The top of the page tells you this is a short version of a service SoftMail provides for its clients. The company cleverly gives away these free tastes to whet your appetite to hire them for an in-depth review of your own direct mail. Below, you find 52 reviews of printed direct mail advertisements for software products and Internet access.

Microsoft goofs and you benefit

You click on <u>Microsoft—Reaching Out With The Mail</u>. The page analyzes a Microsoft postcard mailer (Figure 15.4) that promotes software to build Web sites. It asks, "Why would a company that has one of the most highly-visited sites on the Internet bother to use direct mail to drive people to its site?" Good question. The SoftMail reviewer likes many aspects of the mailer, but isn't shy about pointing out failings. As Phil Scanlan (who first told me about SoftMail) said, "These guys don't pull any punches, do they?"

You already understand some of the points SoftMail makes—so you agree with SoftMail and bond with the company. Other details are new to you. "Gee, I didn't know these little details could affect my sales." SoftMail has especially pointed criticism for errors Microsoft made using its Web site to give away free software—errors that are simple to fix and that you are sure you will never commit on your own Web site, thanks to SoftMail's insight.

After reading critiques, you visit "<u>Tip of the Week</u> - Every week, a new way to enhance communications." You see links to tips on direct mail, Web design, sales order forms, and <u>Top Ten Tips for Direct Email</u>." A treasure trove of information. This stuff is significant and can make a big difference in your job. And they deliver new tips free, once a week.

You decide to subscribe and go to the subscription page. In addition to the free email newsletter, you can subscribe to "SoftMail Direct's *PRIVATE* snail mail list to receive information periodically which cannot be sent elec-

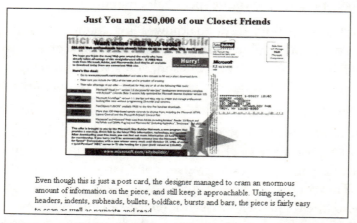

Figure 15.4   SoftMail analyzes a Microsoft postcard mailer and the Web site that provides fulfillment.

tronically (i.e., actual samples of direct mail pieces)." Fresh! So you fill out the online form and get back to work.

Wait a minute—this site never actually *sold* anything! It didn't ask for money, quote prices, or provide lists of products or services. That's right. SoftMail is in the same marketing boat as many other business-to-business marketers. It sells to a small group of potential customers—in SoftMail's case, only a few thousand software companies that conduct significant direct marketing projects. SoftMail has a longer sales cycle than most consumer marketers, with a greater emphasis on qualifying prospects before moving forward in the cycle. The SoftMail site just generates sales leads.

Because its customers have different needs than the Vicarage, SoftMail uses a different style of writing. The software industry is cutthroat. SoftMail's clients fight just to survive and are serious about their businesses. So SoftMail avoids flashiness, clever copy, and especially humor. Would you put the fate of your business in the hands of a clown? Of course not, and neither would SoftMail's clients.

"Correct hitting is invisible"

Instead of entertaining, SoftMail informs. It understands what kinds of information its clients need and provides bucketfuls. To a software marketer, the SoftMail site is more compelling than the Vicarage Hotel's because it addresses marketers' own self-interests. Make no mistake about it. People visit the SoftMail site and subscribe to its email list because they are interested in themselves and in solutions to their own problems.

The clever thing that SoftMail does (except for the first half of its home page) is avoid one of the stupidest mistakes in business-to-business Web writing: the Brag & Boast Syndrome. You must have seen sites like this. They prattle on and on about how they are the leading company in their field, how they are first, how they are the best, how they are dedicated to total customer satisfaction and world-class quality, and other meaningless babble. Instead of bragging about how good it is, SoftMail *shows* you.

Rather than say, "We are experts," SoftMail gives you the information to decide that on your own. (Which are you more likely to believe: somebody else's Web site or your own judgment?) Rather than tell you it understands software marketing, SoftMail leads you to conclude, "Gosh, these people know tons about selling software."

This is done firmly but subtly, by writers who understand the Shansi kung fu proverb that "Correct hitting is invisible. Your enemy should fall without seeing your hands move."

As a direct marketer, SoftMail tracks sales sources, so it knows its Web site works. The site attracts sales leads. SoftMail's sales force qualifies the leads and converts them into customers. Gordon Powell, SoftMail's vice president of operations, told me his site "absolutely has brought in new customers. It also shortens selling cycle. It pre-qualifies new people, so we don't have to work as hard." This site is a breadwinner.

Web writing style

From the preceding two examples, you can see the importance of deciding on your site's personality. Clearly, establishing your site's personality is crucial not only for your Web site, but also for creating a brand for your products. As David Ogilvy observes, "Over time, the brands that succeed are the brands with the most sharply defined personality."

The personality you establish should be defined by *what will most attract your customers*. David Carlick of agency Poppe Tyson Advertising (**www.poppe.com**) explains, "The business of advertising on the Net is more *invitational*. It takes a whole different mindset on the part of the advertiser: Be attractive rather than intrusive. Instead of positioning your Internet advertising around intrusive methods, position it to say, 'If you're interested in this, come and take a look.' In a way, this is database marketing turned inside-out."

A site offering terrific tips on machine tool maintenance will be read only by people who maintain machine tools. People passionate about Barbie dolls won't care about it. On a good Web site, prospects are *self-selecting*. This means you need to understand who your customers are and how to satisfy their needs.

Pay attention to sequence

In the previous chapter, I explained the significance of the phrase *above the fold*. Newspaper front pages are designed so that the most compelling stories are on the top half of the page, above the fold. A story below the fold won't be seen in a newspaper vending machine. In the same way, people look mainly at what is on the top of a Web page. People miss links, graphics, and copy at the bottoms of Web pages. Keep that in mind when writing for the Web, and make sure all of your most essential information is at the top of each page.

As its production manager, Chris Gulker brought the *San Francisco Examiner*'s Web site (**www.sfgate.com**) online. He says, "Your home page is like a newspaper front page, which is a highly refined technology. For best results, arrange your Web page and write your Web stories as journalists write newspaper stories, in descending levels of detail. Start with general information, then more specific information, and finally, yet more specific information. Readership of Web pages drops proportionately from the top to the bottom. When 25 percent of readers read any one story out of all the stories on a newspaper page, that story was a hit. The same holds true with Web pages." As an example, Gulker says that out of 1,000 visitors to the site's San Francisco 49ers Web page, the most popular story on the page is the one selected by about 250 people.

Since Web advertisers can measure how many times a story is chosen, the online newspaper is able to tailor its content to increase visitor satisfaction. Gulker elaborates, "There was no response to stories about President Clinton, but any story with the word 'hacker' in its headline did great."

You and your reader

Every day, tens of millions of people visit Web sites. As a Web writer, you need to answer a key question: How many people does your Web writing speak to?

The answer is: One at a time. No matter how many people read your page, in the mind of each one, he or she is the only person reading your page at that time.

Queen Victoria complained that Prime Minister Gladstone talked to her as if he were addressing a public meeting. She preferred his rival Disraeli, who talked to her like a human being. Follow Disraeli's example. When you write for the Web, pretend you are speaking to one person. Talk person-to-person.

Avoid third person: "There are advantages to this. People often like it." Use second person: "You'll find advantages to this. You'll probably like it." When you can't use second person, use "I" or "we." Remind your reader that you are a person writing, not some cold, soulless Federal Department of Numbness. People are interested in themselves and in other people. The more you humanize your copy, the more your visitors will read.

Another trap to avoid is confusion between what you offer and what people want. For instance, what's the difference between "dead chicken parts" and "finger-lickin' good"? One is a technically accurate description of what Kentucky Fried Chicken sells. The other is the reason that people buy it.

In the same way, many companies make the mistake of providing product features and technical specifications and nothing more on the Web. Now, features and specs matter, and you should provide them. But your job as a Web writer isn't finished until you've explained who your product is for and the benefits of using it.

On the other hand, this doesn't mean you should get carried away with adjectives and adverbs. Going too far with benefits produces Web fluff, and fluff aggravates another problem for Web writers.

Your credibility gap

Credibility is a big problem on the Web. A first-time visitor to your Web site may never have heard of your company before and will doubt your words until proven otherwise. How do you show your believability? First, avoid the Brag and Boast Syndrome. No self-congratulation. It turns people off. Avoid superlatives ("the best," "the biggest"), unless they come in a quotation from somebody else.

Use testimonials. Add case histories; how has somebody actually used your product? True stories interest readers and add credibility at the same time. If you can, give a demonstration on your Web site. Or try the "problem/solution" approach: Here is a problem, here is how our product or service solved it. Show the *end result* of using your company.

And on the Web, always provide as much information as you can. People are on the Internet because they want more information. Unlike TV spots or magazine ads, your Web site lets you provide as much info as you want. Rich information equals greater believability.

Spamdexing and word spamming

The terms *spamdexing* and *word spamming* refer to ways some Web writers try to get better positions on search engines and attract more visitors. Spamdexing and word spamming cause only two problems: They slow down your pages, and they don't work.

The idea in both cases is to add words—in some cases, hundreds of words—to the text of a page, hoping that people will enter those words in a search engine. For example, if your company makes the Acme Death Ray, you might add these words in teeny, tiny type at the bottom of your page:

```
Acme Death Ray, Acme Death Ray, Acme Death Ray, ACME DEATH RAY, ACME DEATH
RAY, death ray, death ray, death ray, disintegration, disintegration,
disintegration, destruction, destruction, annihilation, annihilation
```

and repeat it a hundred times or more. The theory is that when Jill Sixpack goes to Alta Vista and searches for `death AND disintegration`, Alta Vista will look at its index of your page and think, "This Acme page sure has a lot of death and disintegration on it. I'll put it on top of the list and send it to Jill." Some companies add the names of their competitors, or terms that they think will attract visitors but have nothing to do with their products, such as:

```
sex sex sex Pamela Anderson Pamela Anderson Sandra Bullock Sandra Bullock
```

Instead of using tiny type at the bottom of the page, some try concealing the extra words by making the type the same color as the Web page's background color. Others hide the text in the HTML as an undisplayed comment:

```
<!- Acme Death Ray, Acme Death Ray, etc., ad nauseam ->
```

What really happens is that *all* of the major search engines use anti-spamming routines to inspect pages. Pages with obvious word spamming are *penalized*, not rewarded. In some cases, they aren't indexed at all. Some search engines check for type that matches the page background color and then ignore any such words or drop the whole page from their databases. Some search engines ignore any words in "don't display me" brackets `<!- such as this ->`.

There *are* effective ways you can get your pages high up in search engine rankings. I cover them in this chapter and the next one. But don't bother with word spamming. It's a waste of your time.

On each page

Some stuff should be common to each Web page you write. One quality that draws debate is page length. Will you have better results from many short pages, or from fewer Web pages that are longer? The earliest recommendation was made by Tim Berners-Lee, the inventor of the Web, who figured the equivalent of five typewritten pages of text (*not* screens) as max length. Other pundits say the most effective length is two or three screens of text per Web page.

On the other hand, some sites thrive on long pages. The Vicarage Hotel is a good example. Most of the work on its site is done by one extremely long home page. My take on page length is to use moderation unless your situation demands otherwise. If you measure traffic, you have a better option. Try a long version and a short version and test which appeals most to your visitors. When all the smoke clears, what your visitors *do* determines your best approach, not anybody's pet theory.

Each Web page should stand by itself. Don't start your text with a continuation or assume someone has seen another page. People can enter and exit from every page on your site, so starting your copy in the middle of a thought will baffle visitors unless you preface it with a link to the beginning. For the same reason, each page should include a link to your home page. Hunting for a book on Alta Vista once landed me on the book's page in its publisher's site. Great, I'll order it. The problem was the book page contained no link to the publisher's order page or home page. It was a dead end. I couldn't go anywhere from the book page, so I left and went to Amazon.com. Avoid that dilemma by making sure each of your pages includes a link back home.

In most cases, you should make the essential points on a page obvious to a reader who scans your text rather than reads it. Web visitors give a page a quick once-over before deciding whether to read it or to click and move on. You lose those visitors if you don't arrange your text so they pick up your main points without reading the rest. The easiest way to do this is to break up your text with subheads and lists.

Read your Web pages aloud. You'll catch clumsy phrases and repetitive words.

Your text should include, at the bottom of each page, a link to the email address of your Webmaster and perhaps his or her name. (The term *Webmaster* is derived from "postmaster" and is the person in charge of the technical aspects of your Web site.) This is the standard way for visitors to report problems—HTML errors, dead links, broken graphics—with a page. If an email link isn't there, no visitor will report problems, so you will never know your site is broken. Each page also should include your company name and probably a way to contact your order desk or a link to your order page. You also may want to include copyright information on each page.

You put each page on your site for a reason. Usually you want your visitor to do something. Want to increase your response? Ask for action. Tell your visitor what to do. If, like SoftMail Direct's site, your site has one central purpose, use SoftMail's tactic. It wants to capture addresses for its email list, so every page on its site in one way or another asks or reminds you that you can subscribe to its weekly newsletter. What is your offer? Reiterate it on every page.

Each page will also call on your writing skills in another way: for keywords and key phrases. They are significant enough to earn a section of their own.

Keywords and key phrases

You need to know about keywords and key phrases for only one reason: So people find you. If no one ever reads your page and that's okay, skip this section. But if you want people to find your page, read this section extra carefully. You might even want to read it twice.

What are keywords and key phrases? They are the words and phrases that you think people will type into search engines to find your Web pages.

For instance, someone looking for shampoo might search Alta Vista (**www.altavista.digital.com**) by typing the word **shampoo**. Alta Vista then looks for all the pages with the *keyword* **shampoo** in its database. The page of results that Alta Vista returns start with the notice "Word count: shampoo: 30724. Documents 1-10 of about 20000 matching the query, best matches first."

Of course, most people don't have the patience to read 20,000 pages to find shampoo, even if their hair is very dirty. They will search more precisely by adding a word or two: **unscented shampoo**. These two words together are a *key phrase*, and this time Alta Vista returns "Word count: unscented: 1145; shampoo: 30724. Documents 1-10 of about 5000 matching the query, best matches first."

That's better, but 5,000 is still too many pages. An experienced Net searcher will enter the key phrase **"unscented shampoo"** with quotation marks to reduce the number of mismatches. Alta Vista returns "Word count: unscented shampoo: about 9. Documents 1-7 of 7 matching the query, best matches first."

That's more like it. If your company sells shampoo, your job as a Web page writer is obvious: To get on that short list of seven, preferably near the top. This isn't just for Alta Vista. You need results from all major search engines.

This is crucial because most Web sites get half or more of their visitors from search engines.

In other words, you can double the number of visitors you get—and perhaps your Web sales as well—by strategic use of keywords and key phrases.

If this idea isn't clear, spy on real people as they search. Visit **http:// voyeur.mckinley.com/cgi-bin/voyeur.cgi** to see 12 randomly-selected realtime search terms. The page automatically updates every 15 seconds. It leaves me in awe of the range of human curiosity and the popularity of Pamela Anderson.

Choosing your keywords and key phrases

The vital part—and the hard part—of keywords and key phrases is choosing the best ones for your page. Note that I said "page," not "site." *You will almost certainly need a different set of keywords and key phrases for each page on your site.* If the topics of your pages are different, your keywords will be different.

For example, one page on my site markets *The Funniest Computer Songs* and another supports readers of *How to Grow Your Business on the Internet.* People searching for these two pages would use very different search terms, so my keywords and key phrases must be different. One overall, sitewide keyword list would be appropriate for neither page.

To pick your keys, you need to make a list of words and phrases people use when they look for your company or products. Some possible places and ways to find keywords and key phrases:

- Your company name

- Any company nickname or abbreviation

- Your product name

- Product categories

- Your industry

- Your customers' industries

- Your customers' tools, job titles, and concerns

- What people ask you on the phone

- Visit your competitors' sites and "View Source" to see what keywords they use.

- Look at your referer log report. This report is produced by your Web server and tells you what search engines people used to find your site and what search terms they entered.

- Plunk a customer down at the computer. Ask him or her, "Can you find my Web site?" Then clam up and take notes of search terms your customer uses.

You should end up with a list of at least ten and no more than twenty words and phrases for each Web page. If you have more than twenty (excluding names of people and things), cut your list down. Next, arrange your words and phrases in order of priority, beginning with your most important word or phrase first.

For *The Funniest Computer Songs* Web page, my list is: Funniest Computer Songs, computer jokes, computer humor, comedy, parody, parodies, music, funny, humour, Vince Emery Productions, HAL 9000, and the names of the performers.

Now test your keys. Visit major search engines and enter them to see what comes up. You might find new keys.

Testing also eliminates words that are too common. For example, if you visit Alta Vista and enter **software**, you will receive a page saying "Ignored: software: 8492386. No documents match the query." When a word occurs too frequently, instead of serving eight million pages, the search engine ignores it. Some too-popular words are:

business	software	computer	Internet
Web	service	Webmaster	time
FTP	net	program	page

If a potential keyword on your list is so common that it returns the "No documents match the query" message, drop it from your list unless you can incorporate it as part of a key phrase. For example, either **business** or **software** returns "No documents match," but **"business planning software"** returns about 100 pages that match the phrase. If you sell business planning software, you should include the phrase on your list of keys.

Now that you have your list, you need to make a few additions. First, add *plurals*. When people search for something, they often use a plural. Someone looking for a bicycle will often type **bicycles**. If your keyword list says **bicycle**, it is *not* a match and your page will be skipped. But if your keyword is **bicycles**, your page matches both **bicycles** and **bicycle**, since search engines match **bicycle** as part of the longer word. Therefore, make plural all keys that are nouns. For nouns not made plural by just adding **s** or **es** (such as thief and thieves), provide both singular and plural versions.

Next, add variations in capitalization. When you enter your search term in only lowercase letters (**book**), you will retrieve any page with **book, Book**, or **BOOK**. But someone who searches for **Book** will match only pages with **Book** and not the other two variations because using one capital letter makes the entire search term case-sensitive. In the same way, a searcher who types **BOOK** (usually a newbie—experienced people don't search in all caps) will *not* match either **book** or **Book**.

My recommendation is to list your terms with initial caps (**Book**), plus the redundant all caps (**BOOK**) for words you feel are worth it. You don't need to list in all lowercase because a lowercase search term matches the other variations.

Writing with keywords and key phrases

So now you've got a list of keywords and key phrases for each Web page (or at least, each prime page) on your site. What do you do with them?

Leverage your keys in six places:

1. **Body text (near the top).** Work as many of your keys as you can into the text of your Web page. Some search engines read only text at the top of your page—your first 100 or 200 words. Others give words at the top greater weight, so it pays to use your keys up front if you can. Some give the headlines and subheads in your text greater weight. However, don't maim good writing just to squeeze in keywords. Clear, persuasive writing is the primary reason your page exists. Adding keywords is only secondary.

2. **Page titles.** Covered below.

3. **URLs.** When a keyword appears in your URL, search engines move you high on their list. Part of the reason the Vicarage Hotel site draws traffic is that its Web address **www.deadlock.com/hotels/london/vicarage** brings it to the top of any search for **london hotels**. To take advantage of this, use keywords for the actual directory and file names of your site.

4. **Alt tags.** Covered below.

5. **Meta tags.** Covered below.

6. **Signature files for email messages.** (If you don't already use a signature file on your email messages, turn to the discussion in Chapter 9 and create yours now.) Messages your employees post on newsgroups and contribute to email lists become archived and searchable on sites like AltaVista, InfoSeek, and DejaNews. Keywords in signature files draw people who search to your Web address in the signature files and thereby to your site.

Page titles

Web page titles appear in three places: 1) on your visitors' menu bars at the top of their screens, 2) on bookmark lists, and 3) in search engine listings. When a search engine returns your page in a list of matches, it highlights your page's title. Your prospective visitor may choose to visit your page or not largely based on what you name your page title.

Titles are a matter of life and death because almost all search engines weight titles more than any other element. (URLs earn second place.) So if you want your pages to climb on top of a list of 5,000 sites, keywords in page titles are the *only* way you can do it. Your title must have a closer keyword match than everybody else's titles.

Fasten your seatbelts, we're gonna get technical here. A title is part of the HTML code that makes up your Web page. A title does *not* display on your page's text, only on the menu bar. To write a title, you have to do this:

```
<TITLE>The Funniest Computer Songs Collection of Musical Jokes & Humor
  </TITLE>
```

The first bracketed command marks the start of your title. The last bracketed command marks its end. (Think of the slash as an "Off" switch.) Okay, that's the end of the technical part. Wipe the sweat off your forehead.

Every page should have a title. Four suggestions for effective title tags:

• Titles should include three or four keywords and key phrases, especially the names of your company and products. Put your keys near the front of your title.

• When Tim Berners-Lee invented Web pages, he limited titles to 64 characters. (Spaces count. The sample title above is 63 characters long.) Your title can be longer. This is called *title packing*. Some search engines ignore everything after the 64th character. Some browsers truncate longer titles. You don't care. As long as your keys are up front, truncation doesn't hurt.

- Your title should make sense when taken out of context. If someone sees your page title on a bookmark list, will they know what your page contains?

- Each page should have a different title. Try to include a different keyword or phrase in the title of each page. If all your pages are titled "Welcome to Yourco" and some searcher gets a list of 70 of your pages, how will the poor soul know which page to click?

Titles are extremely simple. There's not a heck of a lot I can say about them. But a title is also extremely powerful in luring visitors to your site. Don't leave your home page without it.

Headlines

Legendary advertising writer John Caples wrote the book *How to Make Your Advertising Make Money.* What makes headlines work takes up *half his book.* Why so much emphasis on headlines? As Caples writes, "If you have a good headline, you have a good ad. Any competent writer can write the copy. If you have a poor headline, you are licked before you start. Your copy will not be read."

We know that Web visitors normally scan a page (at least, the part above the fold) for three to five seconds before they decide to stay or move on. Headlines are a proven way of getting visitors to read your page, but many Web writers don't use them. Ignorance, I guess.

A good headline gets your visitor interested in examining your page more carefully. It acts as a condensed version of what your page is about. A headline can make an offer, promise a benefit, or provide helpful information, all good ways of convincing a visitor to stay just a little bit longer.

Pick up any good book on writing advertising. Turn to the section on headlines, then turn on your Web page visitors.

Links

For most writers, a Web site is their first experience with hypertext links. Writing with links is fun, but don't get carried away and make a link every time a word—your company name, for example—appears. Follow the storyboards for your Web site. Link only words needed to take people to and from the places listed on the boards.

Every link should have a description. If your link is in a paragraph of body copy, something in that paragraph should say what that link is. If you have a list of links to sites, add an explanation to each link. The ability to write copy to describe a file or a page is what distinguishes the World Wide Web from Gopher or FTP. Visitors looking for something on your site get frustrated when they click on one of your links and are detoured to an unwanted destination. Author Jaclyn Easton visited more than three thousand sites researching her book *Shopping on the Internet and Beyond.* She wasted hours chasing down vague links. The attitude of your customer, says Easton, is "Don't make me click at three bucks an hour and tap my toes for a full ninety seconds to find out that's not where I want to be."

When you provide a downloadable file and write a link for it, also write the *size of the file* next to your link. (The Vicarage Hotel Web site shows how to do this.) This holds true for all kinds of files, whether they contain software, graphics, or text. The price Web users pay for files lies in their download time. When you give someone a file without the size, it's like trying to sell him or her something without giving a price. Without knowing a file's size, a customer will start to download it, change his or her mind halfway through, and cancel the download. That wastes machine cycles for your Web server and irritates your customer. Just put the size in parentheses after your link:

`Mona Lisa` (56 K)

When you plan where to put links, here's a plea to add frequent routes to your order page. I've gone to Internet sites specifically to buy things but was forced to wade through six (and once, seven) pages of stuff before I could fill out an order form. Any retail store with that many barriers in front of its cash registers would go broke in a week. Make it easy for your customers to buy.

Alt tags

Alt tags are often-overlooked parts of Web writing that greatly influence 20 to 30 percent of your visitors. They are also used by search engines to direct visitors to your site.

What is an Alt tag? An optional part of the HTML code that puts a graphic image on a Web page. Here's sample HTML. The Alt tag is in italic.

```
<IMG SRC="emery.gif" ALT="Welcome to Vince Emery Productions - logo (5K)">
```

What's great about Alt tags (or *Alt statements*, as they are sometimes called) is that they appear on a Web page only when the graphic does *not* display. In the example above, if for any reason the file **emery.gif** does not display, a visitor to my home page sees:

Welcome to Vince Emery Productions - logo (5K)

So if my image file is broken, or gets clogged by a slow connection, my visitor sees a greeting message and my company name instead of blank space. From reviewing my site's log reports, I know that 25% of my visitors do not view graphics. Some use text-only browsers like Lynx, but many people use Netscape Navigator or Microsoft Explorer *with graphics turned off*. (I do this myself. It's the fastest way to surf the Web. If you get impatient waiting for Web pages, read "How to speed up the Web" below and try it yourself.) Your site probably has a similar percentage of visitors who ignore your graphics. If you don't write Alt statements, you miss opportunities to market to these people.

How to speed up the Web

It's easy. Turn off the graphics on your Web browser and see how quickly Web pages appear. It's the technique of choice for busy Web veterans.

If you use Netscape Navigator: On the menu at the top of your screen, choose "Options." Then click on "Auto Load Images."

If you use Microsoft Explorer: On the menu at the top of your screen, choose "View" then "Options." Then select the "General" tab, find "Show Pictures," and click on the check mark.

Now when you visit a Web page you'll see the text with little icons that indicate graphics. If you want to see a graphic image, just click on the icon and the picture will appear. If you use Netscape and want to make all of the graphics on a page appear at once, just click on the "Images" button near the top of your screen. (Microsoft has no equivalent to the "Images" button yet.)

> If you change your mind and want to return to the realm of slow Web graphics, just redo the same steps you used to turn graphics off. I go back and forth between graphics off and on several times in a day.

You, the writer, don't need to program the HTML code, but you should have a list of every major graphical image and write text to take the place of each. (Just significant graphics—I'm not suggesting you write an Alt statement for every bullet or border.) Let whoever writes your HTML combine your text with the actual code.

What should an Alt statement say? It should describe your image. Your graphics-off visitor can read your description and decide whether seeing it is worth the wait. "To see or not to see, that is the question." (That's why I put the file size of 5K on my example above. File sizes help visitors decide.)

There is an exception. If your image is a *link*, your alt statement should not describe what your image shows. It should describe what your image link *points to*—the destination that a visitor will reach if he or she clicks on your image.

Your Alt statements should contain keywords and key phrases. Search engines *cannot* index any type in your graphics files, but they do index Alt statements. So Alt tags help bring new visitors into your site. Considering the small amount of work it takes to write Alt tags, the payback is considerable.

Meta tags

Web pages can include several kinds of Meta tags, but we care about just two: Meta description and Meta keywords. Both types exist solely for one purpose: To help search engines send visitors to your site.

To visitors, Meta tags are invisible, but to search engines, Metas are Ed McMahon waving a red flag, shouting, "Hey, look what I have for you!" Some search engines (including Excite) ignore Meta tags, but most rank their contents highly, especially when your Meta tags are near the top of your page and in front of your body text. If you want your page returned at the top of the search engine heap, Meta tags are a tool you must use.

Like page titles, each of your Web pages can and should have a different pair of Meta tags, and each should use your keywords and key phrases.

Meta description

The meta description tag is a one- or two-sentence description of your page or what it features:

```
<meta name="description" content="The Funniest Computer Songs: 8 perform-
    ers sing 12 humorous songs about computers and users.">
```

When your Web page matches somebody's search terms and a search engine displays your page in its list of results, most search engines show your Meta description in their list. Some search engines truncate descriptions after 15 words. (The example contains 14 words.)

Writing a Meta description is simple. Just write a short description of what your page offers, and use as many keywords as you can.

Meta keywords

Can you believe it? Search engines actually *ask* for your list of keywords and key phrases! Here's a sample:

```
<meta name="keywords" content="Funniest Computer Songs, Computer Jokes,
    Computer Humor, Comedy, Parody, Parodies, Music, Funny, Humour, Vince
    Emery Productions, HAL 9000, Hal 9000, Frank Hayes, Bob Franke, Orrin
    Star, Vinnie Bartilluci, Tom Payne, Steve Savitzky, Engineer's Rap, Bill
    Sutton">
```

Your Meta keywords can contain up to 200 words. List them in order of importance. To avoid getting kicked off a search engine by its anti-spam software, don't repeat any one word more than seven times. (Some say no more than three times.)

Some people write Meta keywords without commas. Commas make keywords easier for *me* to read, and InfoSeek prefers keywords separated by commas, so I use them. Initial caps on each keyword cause a slight difference in results. Someone who searches for **comedy** will get back either **comedy** or **Comedy**. But someone who searches for **Comedy** will hit on my page only if my page says **Comedy** with a capital "C." So to draw as many visitors as possible, I use initial caps for my Meta keywords.

Your home page

I'll wrap up this chapter with a few observations about writing home. Home page, that is. Except for your order page, it's the most important page on your site.

Aim the copy on your home page directly at getting a visitor *into your site*, not at selling your company or its products. It persuades visitors to enter, not to buy. The place to sell products comes later. Your home page needs to tell what is inside, what is new, and how to get there.

Your home page should give contact information for your business: phone, fax, postal address, and an email address. It is amazing how few Web sites provide all this information. Some actually give no contact info at all! Researching this book, I went over every page twice at the site of one company I wanted to contact. The site listed absolutely no contact information, not even the Webmaster's email address. And I bet that company complains it gets no business from its Web site! More and more, people use the Web like a giant Yellow Pages. They want to reach you. Help them with contact info right up front.

What else should you write for your home page? Some people propose that your home page should be a *splash page*, with one dominant graphical image and a single link to go inside. In his highly stimulating book *Creating Killer Web Sites*, David Siegel goes even further, proposing to replace your home page with an *entry tunnel*, a series of cleverly-designed pages that move your visitor through a sequence of images and text that introduce your company and your site.

These seem like good ideas. And for some sites, they are excellent, such as motion picture promo sites or game sites, which need to be highly dramatic. But I haven't seen any split-run tests comparing these theatrical entrances with pages of information and links. Which kind of home page persuades more first-time visitors to enter? Which persuades more visitors to return? Does one kind of entrance cause any difference in the number of pages or length of time a visitor spends at a site? Do entrances make any difference in sales?

I'd love to find answers to these questions from rigorously controlled tests, but for now I rely on anecdotal evidence. Take the Web site of *Upside* magazine at **www.upside.com**. It used to consist of a large picture of the cover of the current issue, plus a few links to top stories. *Upside*'s Webmaster found that pages linked to its home page received *an order of magnitude* more visitors than pages without a home page link. The magazine added more home page links. Readership of pages inside its site went up. It added still more links. Readership went up even more. Whether links were above the fold of its home page or below, and whatever the topic, *Upside* found that the fastest way to increase a page's readership was to give it a link on its home page.

I'm not saying that when you write the text for your home page you need to include a link to every page inside. *Upside*'s visitors may not be at all like yours. I just think you should be prepared to experiment, to watch your readership statistics, and to draw your own conclusions from your own customers. Without testing, don't believe anybody's pet theories, including my own.

To get visitors into your site, you must first lure them to it. This chapter gave you some tools to draw people to you. The next chapter gives you some more and puts those tools to work.

How to Attract Visitors to Your Web Site

"Anyone who puts up a Web site just bought themselves a ticket to anonymity in cyberspace. Nobody is going to find you, nobody is going to have a reason to come to you, and nobody is going to come back."

—William Tobin, President, PC Flowers & Gifts

More computer software is sold on the Internet than any other type of product, so the makers of Planmaker Business Plan Software figured that a Web site was a sure bet. A month and a half after its Web site opened, all bets were off. In all that time **www.planmaker.com** had generated ten visitors and zero sales.

To attempt a turnaround, the company hired Webster Group International, a company that specializes in attracting visitors to Web sites. Webster Group listed Planmaker in directories and search engines, placed links to Planmaker on Web sites that dealt with software or business, and submitted the site to as many reviewers as possible. In four months, Planmaker generated nearly $20,000 in orders from its Web site, averaging one sale for every 13 visitors. Those numbers are even more impressive when you consider that most Internet software buyers look up purchase information online but buy offline. It's impossible to estimate how many sales the Web site generated for Planmaker in retail stores and other offline channels. Planmaker's story is just one of thousands that shows that to make your Web site work, you must lure visitors.

Suppose you built a Web site and nobody came

If your business printed a catalog, you wouldn't expect people to order until you put it in front of them. In the same way, people won't visit your Web site unless you bring them to it. You must let them know about it. That means attract them when you launch. Attract them after you launch. Attract them when you add anything new.

There are two kinds of attraction, and you need to use both. *Pull attraction* is when they find you because they are looking specifically for your company, product, or service. *Push attraction* happens because to generate interest, you push your company or product in their faces.

The leading method of pull attraction is to use search engines and online directories to direct visitors to you. A 1997 Nielsen study reported that 71 percent of people mostly use search engines to find Web sites. Only 8.1 percent find sites by surfing from site to site. Search engines deliver your visitors, so this chapter talks a lot about search engines.

Another study conducted by Viaweb showed that impulse purchases are rare on the Net. Seventy percent of online purchases are made by people *looking to buy* specific merchandise. They use the Web like a giant Yellow Pages. Find that 70 percent, because they generate your sales. People who aren't looking for your product are low-quality visitors who won't make your sales go up.

How can you tell? Track your visitors. It's the only way. The site **www.seeflorida.com** increased traffic 1,300 percent by hiring Webster Group International, but if it didn't measure traffic, its manager wouldn't have known if its investment paid off or threw money down the drain. I cover visitor tracking in another chapter, but remember to put it in place before you begin to attract visitors. Unwatched Web sites bleed dollars.

What else should you do before you start?

Lay your groundwork

You have work to do on your site itself before you start, and you need to make a basic decision about how you will proceed. First, look at your site.

Pre-flight checklist

Is your site ready to attract visitors? Never make the mistake of promoting your site before it is up and running. One firm I know launched a huge promotion for its site, sending T-shirts to customers and advertising in magazines. Its only problem was that technical snafus caused the site to open a month and a half late! The company embarrassed itself in front of its customers and had to repeat its expensive launch when it finally did get online.

Run through this checklist before you start. Hold promotional programs until you can answer a firm "Yes!" to every question on this list, with the possible exception of the last one.

1. Do your employees' email messages include a signature file with your home page URL?

2. Have you put together a list of keywords and key phrases *for each page*?

3. Did you add keywords or key phrases to your page titles whenever possible?

4. Did you use keywords and key phrases in the body text of your Web pages?

   - Whenever possible, are they in the first 200 words of text? Or better yet, the first 100?

   - If possible, are they in the headlines and subheads of your page?

5. If your page has important graphics files, did you create Alt tags with keywords?

6. Does each page have a pair of Meta tags using keywords and key phrases?
   - A description Meta tag that describes your page?
   - A keywords Meta tag that lists your keywords and key phrases?

7. Could you use a keyword or two in your page's URL? (This is not always possible.)

If you need a refresher on email signature files, see the email signature file section at the end of Chapter 9. Instructions on how to complete all the other pre-flight actions are in the previous chapter. Once you pass your pre-flight tests, you have a choice to make.

Money vs. time

When promoting your Internet projects, you will invest either money or time, depending on which of the two is more valuable to you. Which do you have less of, money or time? You can do everything yourself very inexpensively—which will cost a lot of time—or you can save time and pay somebody else. You can also take a middle path between these two extremes.

Compared with traditional advertising agencies, the agencies that promote and publicize Web sites charge very reasonable rates. A bare-bones site promotion costs just a few hundred dollars, and even a large-scale effort can cost only a few thousand.

You can do a mediocre job on your own in a couple of days by following the instructions in this chapter, a good job in a couple of weeks. For less than $200 you can buy software to help.

Skim through this chapter before you make your choice. Then you can draw up your plan of attack—um, I mean attract.

Traffic-building battle plan

The rest of this chapter walks you through seven steps:

Step 1: Identify your target visitors. This should be easy. I hope you did it *before* you built your site. In any case, *who* you want determines *where* you go to reach them.

Step 2: Fix your stealth pages. Pages can be invisible to search engines. You get more visitors when you clean off the camouflage.

Step 3: Leverage your existing marketing channels. The Internet isn't the only medium that can bring visitors to your site.

Step 4: Use email to attract visitors. Email is push attraction. It's cheap and it generates results quickly.

Step 5: Either hire an agency to increase traffic or do it yourself. This step is where the bulk of the work gets done.

Step 6: Decide if you want to pay for banners and links. Your work before this step may bring enough visitors. If you want more visitors, you can pay for more.

Step 7: Monitor your results and maintain ongoing promotion. Measure your traffic flow and you can improve your response.

Step 1: Identify your target visitors

Western Digital manufactures hard disk drives. Its Web site at **www.wdc.com** is aimed at its main customers, quantity buyers for computer manufacturers and OEMs, so its site has a formal, strictly-business personality. To attract more traffic, it added Dr. Download, a playful subsite where visitors could get free software. Dr. Download worked, but not the way Western Digital intended. It attracted thousands of *consumers*—people who don't buy directly from Western Digital. They swamped its Web server, pushing profitable quantity buyers away. A few months later, Western Digital dropped Dr. Download.

The moral of the story is that you don't want to just increase traffic. You want to increase *profitable* traffic. That means you need to know exactly *who* you want to attract.

Who do you most want to visit your Web site? Employees? Investors? Suppliers? Customers? If the answer is customers, what kind of customers: individual retail consumers, wholesale buyers, MRO buyers? Do you want more first-time visitors, or more return visitors? (Methods of attracting the two are quite different.) If your site will attract more than one type of visitor, you might concentrate on the three most important types. Rank them in order of priority, and focus on your top priority first.

Once you define your targets, you need to research places where to find them. Which Web sites do they visit? Which newsgroups do they read? Which email lists? What printed publications?

A little searching on the Net will tell you which specialized search engines and directories to get listed in, like MRO Explorer (**www.mro-explorer.com**) for manufacturers or WWWomen Search Directory (**www.wwwomen.com**) for women who own businesses. Or if you have a Spanish-language site, check out Fantástico (**www.fantastico.com/es**) or CiberCentro (**www.cibercentro.com**).

Next, answer this question: Why would somebody want to visit your site? Compile a list of reasons. Be specific. You'll use your list in subsequent steps.

Step 2: Fix your stealth pages

During the Gulf War, a joke made the rounds about an Iraqi radar technician looking for incoming Stealth Bombers, which are designed to be invisible to radar. The technician's commanding officer called and asked if he saw any planes. "No, sir," replied the technician, "I see a guy sitting down at 20,000 feet, but no planes."

To search engines, some Web pages are like that Stealth Bomber. The search engine's radar looks at a Web site's URL and reports back, "I see a URL, but no pages." When a search engine can't see your page, potential visitors can't find it. From the standpoint of attracting business, your page might as well not exist.

Stealth pages like these have four causes that many search engines can't handle: image maps, frames, password protection, and pages generated on-the-fly from databases. To understand these problems, you have to know a little bit about how search engines work. A few search sites (such as Yahoo) are databases built by human beings, but most are built by software robots called *spiders*. Spiders read Web pages, pull out pertinent information for their search engine's database, and follow links from those pages to other pages that they also read.

Trouble happens when a spider reads a page but can't get to its text, or can't follow the links on it to other pages. If that happens on your site, the text on your page might go unread, and any other pages in your site will be undiscovered.

Image maps

Image maps are graphics that take you to different pages, depending on what your cursor is over when you click your mouse, such as a graphic toolbar listing several destinations.

Image maps (especially a home page that is only an image map or a tunnel) block most spiders. Fortunately, this is easy to fix.

You can provide text links somewhere on your page as an alternative to your image maps. And you can use Alt tags (explained in the previous chapter) to give spiders something they can read and follow. Both alternatives have the added advantage of making your image-based links viewable by the 20 to 30 percent of people who visit your site with graphics turned off.

Frames

Most search engines cannot navigate frames. The solution is to add a Noframes tag to any of your pages that use frames.

Use of the Noframes tag lets spiders index the text on framed pages, including links from that page into other pages in your site. An explanation of Noframes is a bit too technical for this book, but here is an example for the person who writes your HTML code:

```
<HEAD>
<TITLE>Joe's 486 Swap Shop</TITLE>
</HEAD>
<FRAMESET ROWS="8.*">
    <FRAME SRC="joelinks.htm">
    <FRAME SRC="486price.htm">

    <NOFRAMES>
    <BODY>
    <H1>For the lowest prices, shop at Joe's</H1>
    Body text goes here.
    </BODY>
    </NOFRAMES>
</FRAMESET>
```

I have heard that some small, specialized search engines can't read the Noframes tag, but all large search spiders use it. Even so, on your home page I recommend avoiding frames to assure maximum search engine exposure.

Password protection

Password protection keeps unwanted visitors away from restricted materials. Many sites use passwords to restrict their best information to paid subscribers. Unfortunately, spiders can't reach these pages, so *prospective* subscribers will never know that this great data exists. A valuable marketing opportunity is lost.

Only a few search engines (Excite, InfoSeek, and Lycos) can index password-protected pages, and then only when you give them a password ahead of time.

One way around this is to provide some unrestricted pages with good information, visible to all visitors and all spiders.

Another solution is to create *one-way* pages. Your regular pages provide links so your visitors navigate through your site. A one-way page provides the same contents as your password-protected pages, but contains only one link to your home page. One-way pages are designed so a search-engine-directed visitor can find your page and read it, but can reach only your home page and none of the other protected pages on your site. When you submit pages to search engines for indexing, you must individually submit the URL of each one-way page, since there is no way for a visitor to reach a one-way page unless the visitor knows that page's exact URL. This tactic is not useful for all password-protected sites, but can increase traffic substantially for yours if you can apply it.

Database-generated pages

Books Unlimited sells collectable and hard-to-find books. When its Web site opened at **www.booksunlimited.com**, owner Owen Tierney noticed a problem. The site's inventory was invisible to people hunting for books on the Web. Here's what happened.

The Books Unlimited Web site let visitors search its inventory database for authors and titles once they reached its site. But how could a book hunter find the Books Unlimited Web site in the first place? When people search for books (and other products) on the Web, they go to a search engine like Alta Vista or InfoSeek and look for it by entering something like **+"photographs of the southwest" +"adams, ansel"**. However, even if Books Unlimited had *Photographs of the Southwest* in stock, the information was not on an indexable Web page but tucked away in its database.

The solution was simple. Books Unlimited used its database to generate one huge page listing every book it had, and then added a link to that page from its home page. Now when the database is updated, it generates a new inventory page. The URL of the new page can then be submitted to search engines, which will send out their spiders to scan it. Now when Alta Vista visitors search for books, they can find those available at Books Unlimited.

If your site has database-generated pages that are created on the fly for visitors, a similar approach is the only way to make your site findable by people who search for what you sell. This is especially important if you use a database to present a catalog of products. You might not be able to present all your products on regular pages, but at least present your top sellers.

Step 3: Leverage your existing marketing channels

First use the means you already have at hand to promote your Web site. They take the least amount of time to implement, and they build a foundation for your other promotional projects.

(Of course, make sure your Web site is ready to go *before* you announce it to anyone outside your company. If customers visit your Web site and find nothing there, the damage can take considerable effort to repair. Don't pre-announce.)

Start in your own backyard

Think of your home page URL as an equivalent to your 800 telephone number. If you expect anyone to use it, you've got to spread it around.

Your URL should be printed on anything that has your company's phone number. Why? You'd rather have a customer go to your Web site than call you. It costs your Web page less to answer a question than for an employee to do it. This means business cards, checks, product labels, letterheads, print advertisements, catalogs, press releases, fax cover sheets, and brochures—all should provide your URL. Put "Visit us on the Web at…" wherever you can. Clothing manufacturer Joe Boxer weaves its URL into the waistbands of its underwear!

If your business has a customer newsletter, include your URL. Put it in your employee newsletter, too. You'll want all your employees to be familiar with your Internet projects, especially any employee who works with your customers. Ask your customers, dealers, and employees to visit your site or to subscribe. Make sure all of your customer service staff members understand what you offer on the Net and can clearly describe it to your customers and prospects. Your salespeople can tell prospects at trade shows.

A company called WebShirt (**www.webshirt.com**) prints your home page on t-shirts for $12 each plus $3 shipping. Dakota Engraving (**www.uspronet. com/engrave/frame.html**) sells license plate frames with your email address at the top and home page URL at the bottom. Plates cost $11 plus $2 to $4 shipping worldwide.

Can press coverage help your business? Use your Web site to generate coverage in traditional media, especially in trade publications and in your home town newspaper. If your business is in a small town, you might even generate free television coverage of your Web site. All it takes is a press release, photos of your site, and phone calls to editors. For a sample press release that you can copy and change, visit my Web site at **www.emery.com/webpress.htm**. A text version is at **www.emery.com/webpress.txt**.

Direct mail and paid advertisements

Some companies report good results from direct mail and from paying for print and broadcast advertisements. Others don't. For either alternative—ads or direct mail—you *must* use some way of tracking your response (such as a separate URL used only for one list or one ad), or you throw your money down the drain.

Direct mail seems to be most cost-effective when you send something inexpensive—such as a postcard mailing—to a list of names you already have, such as existing customers, prospects, or distributors.

You can also rent lists of names and postal addresses from mailing list brokers. For example, the list CDNow Music Buyers/Inquirers offered by Charles Crane Associates gives you access to people who bought or made inquiries at CDNow's Web store. These buyers spent an average of $50 for CDs and other music items over the Internet from CDNow. From 21st Century Marketing (**www.21stcm.com**) you can rent 500,000 Sierra Online customers who use the Net and 60,000 Claris Software customers who use the Net. Direct Media (**www.directmedia.com**) rents snail mail lists of subscribers to Internet magazines such as 127,000 *Web Week* subscribers and the 750,000 people who read *Internet World*.

By the time you add up name rental, postage, processing, and printing, and subtract the people you mail to who *won't* visit (the majority), you can easily pay $10 or more for each visitor generated. Don't rent lists unless a high cost per prospect is worthwhile to you.

What about paid advertisements? Again, don't do it unless you can track your results. I know one company that spent tens of thousands of dollars on print ads to promote its site. I asked its site producer how well its advertisements had done. He told me, "We think we might have had a lot of visitors from them." *Think? Might?* I pressed him for details and he said that he didn't know. His company had no way to tell who visited its site after reading its ads.

There is no excuse for this. We're not talking rocket science here, but simply making a copy of your home page at **www.yourco.com**, naming it **www. yourco.com/ad1** and putting that URL in your first ad. Put **www.yourco.com/ ad2** in your second ad. Count page accesses and you have a rough idea.

Enough ranting. Anyhow, you can run paid ads for your site. You can buy ads in printed magazines that cover the Internet. You'll find dozens at any good newsstand. You can also advertise your site on radio and television shows that deal with the Internet, such as the radio program *Log On USA* or *C|net* on television. Their ad rates range from refreshingly inexpensive to minor larceny.

Your best bet, though, might be to advertise in publications and on shows that have nothing to do with the Internet but reach the core of your target audience. If you want lawyers, try legal publications. If you want photographers, try photography magazines.

Contests

Contests are a proven way to build site traffic, especially if you have a Web site targeting consumers. Contests encourage repeat traffic and can generate publicity.

One of the most successful users of contests is SportsLine (**www.sportsline.com**), which has an entire department that designs and administers contests. Some SportsLine contests take seconds to play. Others take hours. One big success gave away a football a day signed by Joe Namath. Originally planned to run for three months, the giveaway was so successful that SportsLine extended it, building a database of nearly 100,000 visitors. Although each football has a street value of $400, it cost SportsLine only the price of the football, since Namath has a financial interest in the site.

SportsLine received national publicity from a contest to submit ideas for baseball player Mike Schmidt's Hall of Fame induction speech. The site discovered prizes don't have to be big: Bob Costas asks for readers' comments on topics and generates a big response offering only recognition. Winning readers see their name and remarks posted online.

Legal matters can get sticky for Internet contests. SportsLine has each contest checked by two separate legal firms that specialize in contests and in lawsuits relating to contests. To avoid jurisdictional hassles, it makes its contests available only to people in the U.S. and Canada, except Quebec. (Quebec has a law that requires you to do things in French.)

If you want to run an Internet contest, learn about the legal consequences first. Violations of U.S. contest laws draw huge fines, and in Canada, contest law offenses are punishable by up to two years in prison.

How to create an effective URL

800-FLOWERS became the world's largest florist partly because its phone number is incredibly easy to remember. Businesses pay premium fees for memorable telephone numbers. Your URL is just as important. Increasingly, your Internet address is not just *where* you are, it's *what* you are, and sometimes even *who* you are. Make it understandable. Can you guess that **www.mgdtaproom.com** is Miller Beer? I couldn't.

Many visitors will find your site not by clicking, but either by remembering your URL or by writing it down, and then by typing it. If you want 'em to visit, help 'em out. Give them a URL that's easy to remember, easy to write accurately, easy to type, and easy to say on the phone. This last is important. *Put any proposed URL through the phone test.* If a nontechnical person can't say your URL over the phone to another nontechnical person, you have a bad URL.

Keep it short. Keep it simple. Keep it easy to remember. The most memorable, of course, is like 800-FLOWERS' phone number, where your company name *is* your URL: Quote.com and Industry.Net are just two of dozens of companies that use this trick. The classic URL format of **www.yourco.com** gives another minor advantage: Most visitors have to type only your name. Try this yourself. If you use any version of Netscape Navigator, type only the word **yahoo**. Your software automatically adds the **www.** and the **.com**. Navigation doesn't get easier than that.

Too-long filenames, hieroglyphic-like abbreviations, and weird punctuation marks don't even give your URL a chance. Tildes (~) and underscores are awful. Less obvious is confusion between similar numerals like "o" and "0," or even worse, "1" and "l." (At first glance on this page, could you tell which of those is the number one and which is a letter?) Avoid "=," "$," or "?" They make spiders freak.

Take advantage of aliases to use all the variations your customers might try. For example, you can reach the Bank of America's home page by typing either **www.bofa.com** or **www.bankofamerica.com**. With Web server tricks like redirects, remapping, and aliases, your actual Web server filenames do not have to match the address you give to the outside world. Unless you have an uncooperative service bureau that forces you to use tildes, you can create a catchy URL that anyone can understand.

Step 4: Use email to attract visitors

As I said before, if you want to promote your site to generate repeat visits, the best thing you can do is email people who have already visited your site. Email addresses you acquire by voluntary sign-ups on your Web site are your prime prospects. By signing up for your list, they self-select themselves as wanting to hear more from you. You know they are interested in your message, and adding a page to ask for visitors' email addresses costs you almost nothing.

Russ Jones, manager of Digital Equipment Corporation's Internet project, points out that building an email list from your Web site can be especially profitable if your company markets to other businesses. "Because your amount per transaction is higher," he explained, "one sales lead can pay for your whole Web site, if your sales price is large enough."

Start collecting customer email addresses before you open your site. Provide a place on your Web site where visitors can subscribe to an email list.

Every month or so, email announcements of what is new on your Web site and other useful information to your email list. Sending short announcements frequently will generate more responses than sending long announcements less often. To avoid angry email from people who don't remember subscribing to your email list, start each announcement with a reminder that "You signed up to receive this announcement" and instructions on how to unsubscribe.

Step 5: Hire an agency to increase traffic or do it yourself

Decide whether you want to hire an agency to build your traffic or you want to promote your site yourself. I recommend hiring a traffic-building agency if you can afford one. Good ones are cost-effective.

Do you have enough free time to do it yourself? To effectively launch a new Web site will take one person who is familiar with the Internet two weeks or more of full-time work. Using an automatic traffic-building site or traffic-building software can reduce this figure, but not by much.

Do you want the most effective promotion possible? A good traffic-building agency helps you effectively use keywords and key phrases. A good agency knows many more promotional venues than you can find. A good agency follows up with each promotional venue to make sure your site is listed properly.

Do you need results in a hurry? A traffic-building agency has no learning curve. It can complete your promotion more quickly than you can do on your own. It has ongoing relationships with important search engines so your listings will appear more quickly.

Do you need a one-shot promotion, continuing promotion, or both? Agency fees differ for these alternatives.

Finally, can you afford to pay an agency? A traffic-building agency will charge $600 to several thousand dollars to promote the launch of a new Web site. This is a one-time-only fee. Ongoing promotion is available for an additional fee. If you do it yourself, your main investment is time (lots of it), and perhaps $60 to $150 for software.

Before you make your choice, read both sections that follow. The first describes what agencies do and how to work with them. The second describes what you do if you promote your site on your own.

Work with a traffic-building agency

Find People Fast locates lost and missing friends and relatives. It built a Web site at **www.findpeoplefast.com** that includes online ordering. Managers were dismayed when the site averaged five visitors a week for a three-week period. After site promotion by Webster Group International, Find People Fast's traffic jumped to 2,000 visitors per week. The company's sales nearly tripled.

Why use a traffic-building agency? It's not all that time-consuming to submit your Web site to just one Internet search engine, say Alta Vista. It might take only five minutes. But if you plan to submit to 100 or more search engines and directories, and you customize your description to match each one's format, five minutes each adds up to 8 hours and 20 minutes. And that doesn't include finding those engines and directories, learning their quirky rules, resending submissions that get lost, or taking bathroom breaks.

In real life, it will probably take one person a couple of weeks of full-time work to do a thorough promotional job launching your Web site. I'm a big booster of all the great free stuff on the Net, but this is one area where you might be better off shelling out hard-earned cash. To promote your site on the Net for free you either have to spend many hours of work, or you must restrict yourself to auto-submit sites, which have severe limitations.

If you hire a professional, you keep your workload more bearable and probably wind up with a better end result. A good Web traffic-building agency knows places to promote that mere mortals could never imagine. They know the unpredictable quirks of search engines and directories, and the equally unpredictable people who run them. They'll get you better service from search engines than you could on your own, and they'll get your listings available more quickly across the Web. Where regular folks wait weeks for a Yahoo directory listing, Web promotion pros get you on Yahoo in 48 hours.

A good traffic-building agency will also advise you on how to write your Web pages to increase your locatability by search engines, so people who find your site actually want your product or service and not Pamela Anderson pinups.

Beware of agencies that submit listings automatically. Some just dump your description in a software program and walk away. Listings that are not hand-tailored to the specifications of a search engine are often rejected. WebCrawler often refuses automated submissions, and InfoSeek site says, "InfoSeek reserves the right to restrict automated or robotic submissions." If you want potent results, stick with traffic builders who prepare listings by hand for submission; that is, they customize your information individually for each search engine and its requirements.

STEPS IN HIRING A TRAFFIC-BUILDING AGENCY

When choosing an agency to promote your Web site, don't decide based only on the agency's Web site. Follow this sequence of steps.

1. Identify a group of candidates.

2. Compare services and prices from at least three candidates. Ask these questions:

   - What services does this agency offer? (Take notes—different agencies offer very different services.)

   - Will this agency help me integrate keywords and key phrases in my page titles, page text, meta tags, and site descriptions?

   - Does this agency tailor my site descriptions to meet the requirements of the different search engines and other promotional resources? (Very important.)

- On about how many places will this agency get me listed? (A flat 200-to-500 figure is a bad sign; that's probably automated entries. You want someone to say something like, "Fifty general search engines and directories plus others that are appropriate for your site's topic.")

- Does this agency look for regional and special-interest sites?

- How long will this agency take to list my site on Yahoo? (Good ones take only 48 hours.)

- Does this agency arrange for me to swap links with sites that relate to mine?

- Does this agency list my site only on Web sites, or does it also cover newsgroups and email lists?

- Does this agency give me reports saying where my listing was submitted? Can I see a sample? (Ask to receive a report showing the actual confirmation for each and every submission. If you don't get a copy of each submission or a screen printout of your actual listing, you probably got gypped.)

- Will it follow up to verify my listing has been placed? If after one month it has not, will the agency resubmit for free?

- Does this agency send press releases to print media?

- What fees does this agency charge? (Ask this last, so you know you are comparing apples to apples.)

3. Eliminate obvious losers and get at least three client references from each finalist.

4. Call each client reference. If possible, get specific numbers about how much each client's traffic increased. What would the client do differently next time? Would the client hire this agency again?

5. Hire the agency that will bring you the most *targeted* visitors, not just random bodies.

Avoid a problem

Traffic building agencies' number one problem is that clients take too long to return materials presented for client completion or approval. Avoid this problem by returning materials to your agency within 24 hours.

Where to find a traffic-builder

I've received feedback from my readers about the Web promotion agencies they use. My readers' choices for best Web promotion agencies seem to be I-traffic, NetPost, and Webster Group International. Other agencies may be as good, but I haven't heard about them. All fees mentioned below are, of course, subject to change.

I-traffic (www.i-traffic.com) clients are a handful of large companies with large media budgets. I-traffic works with search engines and uses other methods of generating traffic, but is best known for conducting more offbeat promotions. I-traffic prices its services on a case-by-case basis, charging several thousand dollars a month as its minimum retainer.

NetPost (www.netpost.com) offers two standard services. For a site launch, the firm charges $400 to $1,000. Its site launch promotion includes URL submissions to about 250 places drawn from its database of nearly 4,000 topic-specific sites and email lists. The launch can also include press releases via NetPost's URLWire service. URLWire is available separately for $600. It sends individually targeted press releases to 300 to 350 print and online editors who cover Web content on the same specific interest areas as the client site. NetPost also performs custom projects for extra fees.

Webster Group International (www.wgi.com) offers packages of traffic-building services for $500 and up. The company will improve the "findability" of your pages, submit listings to search engines and other sites, place links on topic-specific directories, and create and place banners. Its packages include site launch services as well as ongoing promotions.

You'll find a couple of hundred more site promoters on the Web—at least, you'll find them if they can competently promote themselves. For a list, visit **www.yahoo.com/Computers_and_Internet/Internet/World_Wide_Web/ Announcement_Services.**

How to do it yourself

If you want to promote your site yourself, your first step is to create a plan. There are tens of thousands of places where you can promote your Net offering. Dozens of them, or perhaps hundreds, will be good places for you to use as promotional tools.

Don't try to lure everyone. Identify your most likely prospects and go after them first. You need to find the places where people are most eager to find what you offer. Go where they go.

1. FIND SITES WHERE YOU CAN SWAP LINKS FOR FREE.

Reciprocal links generate one-third of the visitors to the River Estate Guest House site (**www.mmv.com/riverestate**), according to Webmaster Mark Barbanell. About 20 percent of visitors make a booking—an extraordinary conversion rate.

Personally contacting related sites and exchanging a text link on your site for one on theirs is a proven strategy. If you choose your swap sites carefully, the traffic you get will be valuable because it will be tightly targeted. Look for sites of customers, suppliers, and anyone else who draws the visitors you want and will trade a link to their site for a link to yours. You can swap links or trade a mention of their company or site on your page for a link on their page pointing to yours.

Approach a prospective swap from the other site's point of view. What's in it for them? This tactic works best if you have valuable information or entertainment on your page, not just an ad. What sites offer content that would be enhanced by linking to your site? Some Webmasters won't link to your home page, but they may link to specific information within your site if it relates to their audience.

Link with professional sites that look busy and get a decent amount of traffic. Don't link with kids' pages that list favorite URLs, or the kinds of add-a-URL pages that let anyone dump a link on a pile that nobody reads.

Approach each potential partner individually by sending a short personal email note to its Webmaster:

```
Dear [first name],
I enjoy your [name of their site] very much, so I've added a link to you
on my page at [URL of your page with their link].
My site provides interesting information on [subject matter], which may be
useful to people who visit your site. If you'd like to provide a link to
my site, I'd be grateful. Thank you for providing such a worthwhile site.
[your signature file goes here]
```

You can also swap advertising banners through Internet Link Exchange and other companies; this is covered in the chapter on banner ads.

Who links to your pages?

Who is linked to you now? The major search engines let you find out. Each one gives slightly different results, so look at all of them.

Alta Vista: Enter `link:http://www.yourco.com -url:http://`
`www.yourco.com`

Excite: Select "Power Search." You want to search "the Web," and your search results must contain "the words" http://www.yourco.com. Near the bottom of the page, select "Display the top 40 results grouped by web site" and click on "Search."

HotBot: In the second pop-down menu box, select "links to this URL," type http://www.yourco.com, and click "Search."

InfoSeek: Enter +link:yourco.com -url:yourco.com

WebCrawler: Go to **www.webcrawler.com/WebCrawler/Links.html**

If you want to get sneaky, enter your competitors' URLs. Find out who links with your competitors' Web pages and persuade them to switch their links to your site instead.

2. FIND PLACES WHERE YOU CAN LIST YOUR SITE.

This is the research phase. Before you promote, you need to know *where* you will promote. Don't only promote on general directories and search sites. Find category-specific directories, such as All the Hotels on the Web (**www.all-hotels.com**) if your business is a hotel. These special-interest directories deliver higher-quality sales leads than more generalized ones. Find newsgroups. Find email discussion lists. Find email newsletters.

Much of this chapter talks about search engines and directories, but newsgroups and email lists make excellent places to promote your site. Since newsgroup postings appear almost immediately, they may bring visitors to your site more quickly than search engines, which can take weeks to list you. You can follow the strategy for netlurking and publicity outlined in Chapter 13. For the most effective use of newsgroups and email lists to generate visitors, treat this as an ongoing process, not as a one-shot deal. If you participate regularly in a discussion list or newsgroup, the number of visitors you generate will build over time. Traci Wrenn of AntiquesLink reports quadrupling her Web site traffic by posting different messages to **news:rec.antiques.marketplace**.

In your announcements to newsgroups and email lists, don't stress the commercial aspects of your site. Instead, explain how it makes a contribution to the main topic of that specific newsgroup or discussion list. Don't talk about your products, talk about your site. What do you offer of value? Techniques? Information? Entertainment? And don't commit the sin of repeatedly posting the same announcement to one group unless you like to be flamed.

You'll find a starter list in the "Where To Promote" section below.

3. Decide whether to use site promotion software or automatic promotion sites, or to do it all by hand.

Will you use automatic promotion sites? These Web sites let you submit promotional information about your site to several promotional venues from one place. Most do not properly tailor your submission to meet different sites' requirements, so your listings have a high reject rate. Web sites such as Sub-mit-It *claim* you can create one entry and automatically submit it to several places. The problem with the "one submission fits all" theory is that it blocks you from customizing your description for each engine and for each audience. Some engines will reject your automatically submitted listing for tiny format-ting errors, and you will never know. Other engines will accept your entry but will send few visitors to you because your listing was not optimized for its search mechanism. For these reasons, be cautious of using auto-submission sites. You will receive many more visitors if you custom-tailor your listing to each resource, and only a few auto-submission sites (like Postmaster, below) let you do this.

Will you use automatic promotion software? Several software packages are available. If you use software, the life-or-death distinction is the ability to custom-tailor your listing for each search engine's different needs. If you look at a package that does not let you do this (and ideally, give you guidelines to help you customize your listings), toss it out. Good site promotion software will also help with ongoing promotional efforts, and help you monitor your submissions to make sure they appear correctly and don't mysteriously disap-pear from a search engine. Two good ones are The Promotion Artist (**http://deadlock.com/promote/artist.html**), a $60 Windows program, and the more feature-rich SitePromoter (**www.sitepromoter.com**), available for $100 to $120 for Windows and Macs.

4. Write a two-sentence description of your site.

To save time, create a core listing that you can copy and change. Your core listing should have the name of your resource and a brief two-sentence de-scription. You can expand the one-sentence description you already have for your Meta description tag. Keep it short. Remember to include your keywords and key phrases. Your two-sentence core description might sound great, but it will return zero visitors if you don't include your keys.

5. RESEARCH THE NEEDS OF EACH PROMOTIONAL VENUE.

For the second item in this process, you built a list of promotional venues: Web sites, email lists, etc., where you can announce your site. Now go to each one. Look up its requirements and write them down.

Almost every visitor-generator wants different formats and different information. Some want plain text. Some ask for submission in HTML. You must research the needs of each search engine and directory, decide under which categories your site belongs for each, choose the keywords to index your site, and provide other information to meet their needs.

6. MODIFY YOUR TWO-SENTENCE DESCRIPTION TO MEET THE NEEDS OF EACH VENUE.

Each promotional venue has different requirements. Follow them exactly.

7. SUBMIT YOUR LISTINGS.

Some engines say, "Submit one page from your site, we will follow your links to the others and add them automatically." They will, but one to three months later. If you don't want to wait that long, submit your pages (at least your most important ones) individually.

8. MONITOR EACH SUBMISSION.

Keep track to make sure that your listing is not lost or scrambled. When you find a problem, resubmit your listing until your site is accurately listed.

9. REPEAT THE PROCESS.

Repeat this process whenever you add a major improvement to your site.

MORE ABOUT SEARCH ENGINES AND DIRECTORIES

The biggest sources of visitors to many Web sites are the Internet's hundreds of search engines and directories. If you submit your listings to them yourself, you need to understand a bit about how they work.

Your goal with search engines is not just to have a listing in a database. If a potential customer searches for a detective agency and receives 1,297 listings of agencies with Spade & Archer as number 987, then Sam Spade is out of luck. Nobody in their right mind will wade through hundreds of listings. You need to rank in the first fifty listings returned, or even better, the first 25.

"Rank is everything," said Shari Peterson of Webster Group International. Search engines try to give people the most relevant search results first. This is called *relevance ranking*, and your job in writing listings is to make your listing as relevant as possible for potential visitors looking for your site.

Search engines calculate relevance rankings in seemingly mysterious ways that actually make sense once you look closely. First and foremost, relevance is based on keywords and key phrases. (Aha! That's why I prattled on so long about keys in Chapter 15.)

Each search engine ranks keyword placement a bit differently, but in general, here is where keys have the greatest weight to move your listing to the top of the list, with the most important listed first:

1. Page title (first word weighs most)
2. URL
3. Headlines in body text
4. Body text, especially first 100-200 words
5. Meta tags
6. Alt tags

Engines also examine *search term density*, which is not how many times a term appears on your page, but only its percentage of text. For example, if someone searched for "used textbooks" and the only words on your page were "Used textbooks," your page would have a search term density of 100%. If your page said, "Used textbooks sold here," your search term density would be 50%. (On real pages the actual density is usually a fraction of one percent.) Density ranks both page title and body text.

Engines look for *proximity*: Search terms closer to each other rank higher.

And they look for what they consider spamming, which they penalize. InfoSeek defines spamming as:

- Overuse or repetition of keywords
- Use of Meta refresh faster than the human eye can see
- Use of colored text on same-color background
- Use of keywords that do not relate to the content of the site
- Duplication of pages with different URLs.

Here are some idiosyncrasies of the most important search sites:

Yahoo: Yahoo is the most important general site in terms of the number of visitors it delivers. Some Web sellers report that up to 70 percent of their sales come from Yahoo visitors. Yahoo is not built by an automated spider, but by actual human beings who inspect each listing and site submitted, and edit listings for accuracy and conciseness. This quality control makes Yahoo popular, but it also causes a four- to six-week backlog in adding listings to its database. Yahoo does not index text from your site. It indexes only your page title, your URL, and your description, plus the names of the Yahoo categories under which your site is classified. When a person searches Yahoo, matches of search terms to categories outrank page titles, and matches in page titles outrank matches in descriptions. When you register on Yahoo, *always* fill in Yahoo's "Additional Categories" option, and cut your description to 15 words. Yahoo says you can use 20, but often chops descriptions. Keywords in category names are most important, but Yahoo checks so your categories must match your page's title.

Alta Vista: This search site rejects an identical URL submitted more than once in one day. It also rejects many URLs submitted from one domain in one day. If Alta Vista's "Add URL" form won't process your submission, you know you've submitted too many that day. Keywords unrelated to text bounce your pages to a human inspector.

Excite: This search site ignores Meta tags and hidden comments; instead, Excite applies artificial intelligence to pick the "theme" of your page. Based on its theme, it displays a "summary sentence" instead of your Meta description. If search terms are found in a complete sentence (i.e., one with punctuation at the end), then your page ranks higher. Excite notifies you when your submitted page is actually added to its index, a courtesy that hardly any other site offers.

Lycos: Lycos ranks headlines higher than body text.

Galaxy: Search terms in first line of a page or the first line of a paragraph rank higher with Galaxy.

Table 16.1 compares seven important search sites. (WebCrawler has an almost-useless tiny database, but it is the search site presented to AOL users and so delivers a huge amount of traffic.) "Indexes what?" tells you what parts of your page the site actually copies into its database and indexes. "Meta tags?" tells you if your Metas help move you up the list. "Reads image maps?" tells which spiders aren't locked

Table 16.1 A comparison of seven search sites.

	Yahoo	Alta Vista	Excite	InfoSeek	WebCrawler	Lycos	HotBot
Indexes what?	category, title, URL, description	full text	full text, themes	full text	full text	summary	full text
Meta tags?	no	yes	no	yes	yes	yes	yes
Reads image maps?	n/a	yes	no	yes	no	yes	no
Indexes frames?	n/a	no	no	yes	no	yes	no
Weighs popularity?	yes	no	yes	no	yes	yes	yes
Spam penalty?	yes	yes	yes	yes	yes	yes	yes
Page depth?	n/a	varies	all	all	1	3	all
Entry lag time?	4-6 weeks	submitted page = 1 day, others = 2 weeks	2 weeks	submitted page = 1 day, others = 1 week	1 month	submitted page = 1 day, others = 1 month	1 month

out by image maps. "Indexes frames?" tells the same for frames. If a Web site has many links from other sites pointing to it, some search engines give it a higher ranking. "Weighs popularity?" tells you which ones. You have no control over this. "Spam penalty?" is obvious. "Page depth?" tells how many pages deep in your site a spider will index. "Entry lag time?" tells how long you wait after submitting your listing before it is available for people. Note that pages you submit are added faster than pages that a spider must find by following links from your submitted page.

If you want to know more about search engines, the place to go is Search Engine Watch at **www.searchenginewatch.com.** Danny Sullivan runs this great site, packed with free information, including a valuable free email newsletter. You can get tons more useful info for $20 a year (a bargain).

Where to promote

We've talked about how. So *where* can you promote your Net offerings?

Here's a bunch of places for you to use. I've used a time-saving strategy on this list. Instead of listing a jillion individual directories and search engines, I've mostly given you directories of directories and search engines. In other words for most of these listings, you visit a site and find pointers to many places where you can submit your Web site or your email list or whatever for promotion.

Look especially for email lists and newsgroups. Some of them carry nothing but announcements of new Net stuff. Any newsgroup, for example, with **.announce** in its name will accept announcements—although some have rules about what kind.

Happy submitting!

To publicize any kind of Internet site

- The *Net-Happenings* newsletter covers every kind of resource. To read articles, go to **www.mid.net/NET**. To submit listings, go to **www.mid.net/NET/input.html**.

- Where to Announce Your WWW Pages and Electronic Journals includes eight places to promote Web sites and a few for electronic newsletters: **www.vtt.fi/inf/nordep/projects/webpilot/newjour.htm**

- How to Announce Your New Web Site FAQ at **http://ep.com/faq/webannounce.html** includes places to announce all Net resources, not just

Web sites. Its 35 places to promote include offline places such as books (Hey, I'm listed here!) and print magazines. Not as up-to-date as it could be.

- Most countries have national directories. For instance, to promote Japanese sites, the Japan Network Information Center includes Japanese Whois and other resources: **www.nic.ad.jp/index.html**. Some provinces, states, and cities also have their own directories.

- Go to RES-Links to find more places to publicize: **www.cam.org/~intsci**

- Look in the Liszt Directory of Email Discussion Groups to find email groups where your prospects hang out: **www.liszt.com**. While you're at Liszt, look through its index of newsgroups to find congenial newsgroups. Of course, if you want to promote your own email list, list it on Liszt.

- To find email discussion lists in the U.K., visit Mailbase at **www. mailbase.ac.uk/lists.html**.

TO PUBLICIZE YOUR FTP SITE

- Your Web server should point to your FTP server.

- To publicize your FTP site's offerings on Archie, send email to **info-archie@bunyip.com**.

- Get listed in the Snoopie database at **www.snoopie.com**.

- Try FTP Search at **http://ftpsearch.ntnu.no**.

TO PUBLICIZE YOUR NEWSLETTER

- Never post your full newsletter to a Usenet newsgroup. You can put out a notice that a free new issue is available and briefly summarize its contents.

- Find Internet archives of information for your industry and ask if they'd like to store your newsletter. Most will do so if your newsletter has worthwhile information.

- Gleason Sackman's NEWSLTR will distribute your complete newsletter to hundreds of sites worldwide. For information, email to **newsltr@ vm1.nodak.edu**.

- The Association of Research Libraries will distribute your newsletter through its NEWJOUR-L service. Email to **newjour-l@e-math.ams.com** for information.

- The CICnet Archive of Electronic Journals and Newsletters will archive your newsletter and make it available. For information, Gopher to **gopher.cic.net**. Here are two more archive sites:
  - University of Waterloo **gopher://uwinfo.uwaterloo.ca** Go to: **Electronic Resources Around the World**
  - University of Bath **gopher://ukoln.bath.ac.uk** Go to: **BUBL Information Service**

To publicize your email list

- Get on the directory of Publicly Accessible Mailing Lists: **www.neosoft.com/internet/paml**

- Email a short description of your list to **interest-groups-request@sri.com** and to **newlist@vmi.nodak.edu**.

- Get on Diane Kovacs's Directory of Scholarly and Professional E-Conferences: **www.n2h2.com/KOVACS/**

- Besides Liszt (described above), go to Tile.net at **http://tile.net/lists**.

- The email list NEW-LISTS announces newly-born lists. Email to **listserv@vml.nodak.edu** with your message blank except for the single line **subscribe NEW-List Yourfirstname Yourlastname**.

To publicize your Web site

- Previously one of the best-known places to announce Web sites, the newsgroup **comp.infosystems.www.announce** now may be useless for you. Starting in February 1996, it stopped accepting announcements from businesses.

- **All in 1 Promotion** at **www.erspros.com/internet-promotion** lists 1,600 places to promote to.

- Most countries have national directories. For example, in Japan: **www.ntt.co.jp/SQUARE/www-in-JP.html**. You can also get on "What's New in Japan," at **www.ntt.co.jp/WHATSNEW/index.html**. In France: **http://web.urec.fr./France/web.html**.

- **Apollo Web Referencing Site** at **http://apollo.co.uk/web-kit.html** is a guide to 23 places to register your Web site. It includes instructions.

- **Promote-it (www.itools.com/promote-it/promote-it.html)** lists dozens of spots, including many "Site of the Day" spots. Just links, no instructions or descriptions.

- **A1 Index (www.a1co.com/freeindex.html)** gives you a directory of more than 600 sites where you can publicize your site. You'll also find a very good directory of "Cool Tools" for your Web site, including clip art, CGI scripts, and design tools.

- **Pointers to Pointers (www.homecom.com/global/pointers.html)** will auto-submit your URL to more than 100 spots. It gives you a list of newsgroups to which you can announce your site, and includes a free *Net-News* newsletter for Internet marketers.

- **Postmaster (www.netcreations.com/postmaster)** lets you auto-submit your URL to 415 places for $250. It is the only auto-submission site I've found that lets you customize your submission for the different needs of different search engines. If you are going to use an automatic submission site, PostMaster is probably the way to go.

- **Webstep Top 100 (www.mmgco.com/top100.html)** gives you a list of 100 places where you can publicize your site, with good, short descriptions of each.

- **All-in-One Cool Sites Page** at **www.all-internet.com/coolsite.html** is a directory of sites that review new sites. Dozens of sites are described.

- **WebPost (www.webpost96.com)** provides a directory of sites to promote to, each with a good, clear description, but it has not been updated for more than a year.

- **Web Site Promotion Services (www.meh.com)** gives you a long list of sites where you can publicize your site, and is one of the very few to actually describe the sites so you know what the heck you are promoting to. Not up to date.

Step 6: Decide if you want to pay for banners and links

After completing these promotional activities, you may still be hungry for more visitors. An alternative is to pay for banner advertisements. This is explained in a later chapter.

Step 7: Monitor your results and maintain ongoing promotion

While on a train trip, a friend asked Mr. Wrigley why, with his chewing gum selling so strongly, he continued to advertise. Couldn't he save money by stopping for a while? Wrigley replied, "How fast do you think this train is going?"

The friend answered, "I would say about ninety miles an hour."

"Well," asked Wrigley, "do you suggest we unhitch the engine?"

In the same way, once you have your Web traffic up to speed, you need to maintain your momentum. Your work doesn't end when you submit your listing. You must track each search engine and directory to see that you do get listed and that your description doesn't drop between the cracks. It is common to have to resubmit to make sure you are included.

When you add something new to your site, promote your new jewels. When you find a new search engine or resource has opened, promote to it. Monitor your traffic and response rate. If levels fall, improve your site or add something new and promote again.

Whatever you do, don't unhitch your engine. Your Web site will grind to a stop.

CHAPTER **17**

Credit Cards and Digital Cash

"At first, our customers could only pay online. When we finally included additional payment options via fax, 800 number and postal mail, our sales increased nearly 100 percent . . . I cringe when I think of all the sales we must have lost in the beginning."

—Debra Shatford, President, Focused Presence (as quoted by Jaclyn Easton)

Carlos Salgado Jr. was busted by the FBI for stealing more than 100,000 credit card numbers and selling them for $260,000. He stole the credit card numbers over the Internet from an Internet access provider that foolishly stored the numbers on a computer reachable over the Net.

The first rule of Internet credit cards: Never, never, never store credit card numbers on any computer connected to the Internet.

You are more at risk taking a naked credit card number over the Net than when you take a credit card number over the phone, via fax, or through postal mail. With ordinary Internet email and Web transactions, you can't prove that a customer is who he or she claims to be. You can't prove that the order you received carries the same information your customer originally sent. Someone could have altered it. Your customer's order and credit card number could have been copied on its way to you. If fraud occurs, your customer can deny that he or she sent the order to you and you haven't a leg to stand on.

And that's not to mention card number theft. Your customer is liable for only $50 per card in fraudulent billings, so guess who's stuck holding the bag for the rest? You, the merchant, that's who. The one good thing about MCI's $50 million card theft incident is that it hit a company large enough to stand the pain. A loss that big would close the doors of most businesses.

Getting paid

Credit cards on the Internet garner many CNN headlines, but cards are only one of many ways you can get paid online. In fact, most sales on the Internet are paid for in other ways because most Internet sales are business-to-business sales, not consumer sales. Businesses use many ways to pay.

Your Internet customers might see your Web page and call you on the phone, perhaps with a credit card number or perhaps with a purchase order number. You might receive payment information in a fax, especially for purchases from non-U.S. businesses. You might get a check or payment information via good old postal mail.

Some Web sites bill to 900 telephone numbers. Some take electronic checks. A few take smart cards, which many people say will grow to be the most popular way to pay online over the next couple of years. Some Internet merchants accept digital money, which makes new kinds of transactions possible.

Ninety-nine percent of what you read in the press covers these payment methods from the point of view of a consumer. But you're not a consumer, you're a business. Everything looks different from your end of the telescope, even the simplest ways of getting paid for online sales.

Phone/fax/snail mail

Accepting payment only by online credit cards can be a big mistake, whether you sell to consumers or to businesses, but especially if you sell to businesses. The quotation from Debra Shatford that opens this chapter illustrates that point. Her Web site (**www.comfind.com**) sells advertisements to businesses. When she added additional payment methods to her site, sales nearly doubled. Online credit card payments are used for significantly less than half of Internet sales to businesses. When you sell to businesses online, you need to offer other payment options.

To a lesser extent, the same is true when you sell to Internet consumers. On the average, 80 percent of Internet consumer sales are made via credit card, but that isn't true for all businesses. So offer your Web customers as many ways to buy from you as you can.

If your business sells to consumers in Japan, you might want to accept bank and postal transfers. The Japanese often prefer not to use credit cards, and they have no system of personal checks. Only 16 percent of Japanese consumers pay direct merchants (such as Internet merchants) with credit cards, but 60 percent pay with bank and postal transfers, similar to U.S. money orders. If your business would like to accept Japanese transfers, call Sharon Barnett with Prestige International at (415) 986-7332. Prestige takes orders for American companies in Japan and can accept transfers for you.

Billed accounts

If your business accepts purchase orders, or if your customers are businesses instead of individual consumers, you can bill your accounts. You probably have most of the mechanisms already in place. Perhaps you bill accounts monthly, perhaps weekly, perhaps every time your customer makes a purchase. In any case, your billing procedures can be adapted for Internet purchases with a minimum of fuss and little risk.

That's *little* risk, not *zero* risk. I've seen a case where a business received a large merchandise order to ship to a long-standing institutional client. There was just one tiny difference with this order. It came from an authorized Internet address and carried the name of an authorized buyer, but the ship-to street address was a little different than normal. The order was taken by a new order entry employee who forgot to check the ship-to address and sent the merchandise. It was a forged order and the business was never paid. The slight difference in address was a house down the street from the institutional client. It was rented by a thief for a short time. He received merchandise from several vendors at that address for two to three weeks and then moved. He was caught by the police, but the businesses still lost their merchandise.

To prevent this from happening to you, require that all new billed Internet accounts are opened by a signed document sent to you either by fax or by postal mail. That document should list the names of any authorized buyers, the email addresses of those buyers, all authorized ship-to addresses, and purchase amount limits, if any. Any changes to those initial items should be made by sending you a signed change request via fax or postal mail. *Your order staff should verify with your customer by telephone before making shipments to any changed address.* Send an email confirmation of each order when you receive it and an email shipping notice when you make a shipment to your Internet customer.

To increase security, your customers can use digital signatures, encryption, or a secure method of Electronic Data Interchange (EDI) across the Internet to make their orders.

If your customers are consumers who pay you monthly, you can use Microsoft's MSFDC subsidiary or a similar company to process your payments electronically. This type of payment is actually not a billed account in the sense discussed above, but a variation of online check payment. I discuss online checks below.

900 numbers

You've probably seen TV commercials for outfits like Psychic Friends Network that give you a 900 phone number and then bill your phone number. Microsoft tech support works this way, for a flat fee per call. Other 900 numbers charge a per-minute rate. Some Web merchants use 900 numbers to bill payments for products or services to visitors' phone numbers.

If you use a 900 number for payment, a visitor to your site will fill out an online form that asks the visitor to call your 900 number. On the phone with your sales rep, the visitor okays a dollar amount and receives a redemption code. The visitor enters the redemption code on your Web form for immediate entrance to the fee-based part of your site or to download information.

Logicom (**www.logicom.com**) provides 900 number billing for Web sites as Web900, and Galaxy (**www.galaxy-net.com**) does it as WebCash. Both charge the same rates, a steep 20 percent service fee. If your company already has a 900 number, you can tie it into your site and avoid these charges.

I'm a bit dubious about 900 numbers for consumer sales. A person with only one phone in the house has to unplug the modem, plug in the phone, call your 900 number, unplug the phone, plug in the modem, and return to your Web site. Whew! But who am I to argue with success? Some adult Web sites rake in $20,000 per month from Web visitors who pay via 900 numbers.

NetSpeak (**www.netspeak.com**) makes a more sophisticated version of 900 number billing and credit card billing available for Web merchants and doesn't charge a percentage. NetSpeak's Credit Processing Services Server software costs $10,000 and is part of a system that lets a visitor to your Web site make a Web phone call to your customer service rep. A company called Zodiac Group uses NetSpeak software to bill Web visitors for consultations with online astrologers. A Web visitor selects the astrologer he or she wants from a menu of stargazers and is billed by the minute for two-way audio conversations that also includes live video of the astrologer. Consultations are billed to the customer's choice of credit card or phone bill. NetSpeak's product does *not* require your customer to have two phone lines, since the "call" travels over the Web. Chapter 19 has more on NetSpeak.

Credit card problems and solutions

If someone steals your customer account information, the thief can steal from your business only. Credit card numbers, however, are like money. Not only are there lots of places to use card numbers for purchases, they can be sold on the black market.

"We really don't know how much fraud there is on the Internet," reports Steve Herz, Visa's senior vice president in charge of electronic commerce. "There are three reasons for that. First, today the volume of fraudulent transactions on the Internet is so low that it's hard for us to track. Second, the Internet is such new technology that professional crooks haven't figured it out yet. Third, the hackers who do understand the technology don't do much credit card fraud. We want to get secure procedures in place *before* fraud becomes a problem. Just the perception that there might be a problem is already a damper on electronic commerce."

MasterCard reports that, on the average, it finds one case of customer fraud and three cases of merchant employee fraud out of every 1,000 credit card transactions. These are the fraud rates for real-world sales, and MasterCard reports that card fraud on the Internet runs at slightly lower rates, but with the same one-to-three ratio for outsider vs. insider fraud. In other words, you are three times as likely to get ripped off by your own people.

Card numbers are most often stolen by order department employees. If your business is the likely source of a card theft, the first place any outside detective will look is on your staff logs. What employee was on duty when this credit card came in? Who has access to your credit card information? And the classic question any police detective uses to find suspects: Who had an opportunity, and who had a motive? As a preventive measure, it is in your own interest to limit employee access to your customers' credit card information.

 Don't store credit card numbers or customer account information on any computer connected to the Net. Move your customers' card numbers off your Internet-connected computer as quickly as possible. If you store card numbers even temporarily, it is a good idea to split the numbers and expiration dates into separate files, and to encrypt them.

Software vendor The Corner Store keeps credit card and customer information on a separate computer, completely unconnected to any network. Its orders come in via the Net to one computer and are moved frequently to a floppy disk. An employee transfers the disk with the sensitive data from the Internet-linked computer to the isolated computer.

Daniel White, Ernst & Young's national director of information security effectiveness, reported in the *Wall Street Journal* that an identical procedure is followed by an Ernst & Young client. It receives orders over the Internet from large retail chains. Orders arrive on a stand-alone PC. An employee moves the orders to a disk, scans the disk for viruses, and then takes the disk to another computer not connected to the Internet, protecting the company from both hackers and viruses.

In addition to safely receiving card information via email or the World Wide Web and designing Web forms to collect information from purchasers, you also need to worry about the rest of the transaction. What do you do with that credit card information once you receive it? The best scenario is to validate the cardholder information and pass the transaction data and validated information on to your payment-processing company for payment authorization—ideally doing both while your customer is still online, so you can send your customer an order confirmation and not keep him or her waiting.

If you run your Web site on a Web host's computer instead of your own, you must plan procedures for your host to collect the data and then pass the data to you. Mine receives my orders, encrypts them, and emails them to me. If yours does the same, you can move them to an isolated computer where you can unscramble them safely. Some Web hosts provide the alternative of faxing your orders to you.

The most popular credit cards online, in order of greatest use, are Visa, MasterCard, American Express—though for some business-to-business marketers, AmEx is number one— Japan Credit Bureau (JCB), Discover, Diners Club, and Carte Blanche.

If you accept Visa cards, the VisaNet authorization system must approve each transaction. For each transaction it clears, the company that clears your Visa transactions will require a transaction number (called the *unique transaction identifier*) generated with the VisaNet authorization, the authorized amount, the VisaNet authorization response, and the VisaNet validation code.

Until 1996, Internet sales were lumped by Visa with mail order/telephone order sales (or MOTOs, as Visa employees call them). "When these transactions come through right now, they get labeled as MOTO transactions. We made a field available to banks in 1996 for Internet transactions," says Visa's Herz. "The banks are just starting to use it."

Visa has different reporting requirements for sales depending on whether they are Internet or MOTO sales. It is to your advantage that your bank accurately report your transaction type. Visa's reporting requirements for MOTO transactions differ from country to country. U.S. MOTO merchants, for example, must provide a customer address verification request, with at least the ZIP or postal code for each Visa customer. German MOTO merchants are not required to do this.

But Herz reports that Visa wants "Internet transactions everywhere to be the same. No matter where the customer is and where the merchant is, transactions in France or in the U.S. work the same way." In the future, Visa also may charge different rates for MOTO and Internet transactions.

To make sure your bank properly reports your Internet sales to Visa, you must contact your bank. If all your credit card sales are made over the Internet, ask your bank to tag all of your transactions as Internet transactions. If your card sales are a mix of Web sales, MOTO sales, and/or retail sales, talk with your bank to make sure your bank correctly tags all of your Internet transactions.

If your transactions are tagged as Internet transactions and your Web server software uses the Visa/MasterCard/Amex Secure Electronic Transactions (SET) system, you should be saved from another onerous MOTO task: calling banks to check cardholder addresses. The SET system handles cardholder authentication for you.

With SET, "The cardholder has a digital certificate signed by the cardholder's bank and signed by Visa," explains Visa's Herz. "The software will check the cardholder's digital signature and digital certificate. The merchant won't have to worry about it. The merchant will authorize the transaction, just like any credit card transaction, but will not have to authenticate the cardholder."

Many companies accepting MOTO credit card orders verify cardholder addresses. If you accept credit cards over the Net and don't use SET, address verification reduces risks—and on the Internet, you need the extra protection. Besides, Visa and MasterCard already require it for MOTO orders.

Like any other direct marketer, an Internet merchant can verify addresses and still get ripped off. One scam hit the Leslie Shoe Company twice in one day. Two new customers ordered on two credit cards. One card's order went to an Illinois address, the other to an address in Virginia. Both asked for overnight delivery and provided their own Federal Express account numbers for delivery billing. Both orders were shipped to the correct name and address for their respective credit cards. That night, two phone calls to Federal Express asked to reroute the packages to a third address in Baltimore, Maryland. The orders were fraudulent. Not only was Leslie Shoe liable for the purchase price, but also for the Federal Express charges!

Fed Ex and United Parcel Service both offer this rerouting service. You can guard against such delivery devilry by using *your own* Fed Ex account number for shipment to first-time customers, and by verifying a cardholder's address with the issuing bank and shipping only to that verified address. Again, if your Web server software uses SET, your need for such double-checking is reduced. With each SET credit card sale, you have a doubly-certified record that your customer is who he or she claims to be.

Besides integrating your Web servers with credit card-processing and approval systems, don't forget that you must calculate sales or VAT tax. You will also need a way to pass transaction information—manually or electronically—to your order processing, inventory, and accounting systems. Web server software products vary greatly in their ability to provide these important functions and links. Higher-end servers do everything. Cheapo secure servers force you to do more of the work yourself.

 ## How to start processing credit cards

To accept credit cards, your business needs four things: 1) a merchant account, 2) a modem, 3) a phone line, and 4) either a computer and card authorization software OR a credit card POS terminal.

Open your *merchant account* with a bank. It is hard for any U.S. business to open a credit card merchant account. It is even harder for a direct merchant. Bankers assume that all merchants steal from oppressed people, such as widows, orphans, and of course, bankers. They're even more afraid of Internet merchants. We scare bankers so much their jowls quiver. Web stores deal in *non-swiped transactions,* the kind of sales when credit card numbers are not pulled off physical cards (also called *card-not-present transactions).* When you want to accept credit cards over the Internet, expect interrogation by your bank's version of the Spanish Inquisition. You'll go through a credit check and need to show your business license or articles of incorporation. If your bank approves your account, you'll pay a monthly fee of about $25, plus a *discount rate* (a percentage of each purchase, typically 2.5 to 4 percent for a

Web-only business; retail stores pay less), plus a charge of 10 cents or more per transaction.

If your bank refuses to open a merchant account for your Internet business, you have another option. Banks' antiquated attitudes have created a major opportunity for middlemen who act as match-makers between banks and merchants. These go-betweens are called ISOs (Independent Service Organizations). When you deal with ISOs, it's scam-o-rama time. Some ISOs hire sales agents who get paid when you open your account and will say anything to get you to sign up. After you sign up, they don't care, so be careful what you sign.

You might get thrown to the ISOs although you are applying to your regular bank. Many banks simply broker your merchant account application to an ISO, which in turn brokers it to another bank. Each middleman takes a slice from your pie. Some ISOs even broker other ISOs. For example, credit card companies with "EMS" in their names resell an ISO called EMS that itself resells the services of First Charter Bank of Beverly Hills.

Making your task more tricky is the fact that pricing for credit card services has more varieties than Heinz pickles. When an ISO brags about how low its rates are for certain specific services, take an extra-picky look at the ones it doesn't mention. You'll be charged a discount rate of about 3 to 5 percent for a Web-only business (an ISO promising lower Web-only rates may run a bait-and-switch operation), plus a per-transaction charge (aim for 30 cents or under). There are many additional fees and charges. Look for the lowest monthly billing fee, which might be called something else. The Web page for EMS2000 brags, "We never charge a monthly minimum billing fee," but they charge a monthly "statement fee." Most also charge a "network access fee" as well.

Canadian businesses have an easier time because most Canadian banks will open a merchant account to a small business for a fee of $25 or so.

For a list of merchant account providers, check out **www. yahoo.com/Business_and_Economy/Companies/Financial_ Services/Financing/Credit_Cards/Merchant_Services**. Keep both eyes open and one hand on your wallet. One ISO that I have heard good things about is the National Association of Credit Card Merchants (phone 407-737-7500), which does not require you to sign a lease for equipment.

Once you have your merchant account, you will need to select a firm for payment processing, which is also called *payment enabling*. Banks call credit card processors *service bureaus*. Your bank or ISO will give you a list to choose from, or you can look at **www. yahoo.com/Business_and_Economy/Companies/Financial_ Services/Transaction_Clearing**. Make sure you get a payment processor that offers a toll-free phone number for card authorization.

Your modem and **your phone line** will be used to authorize each credit card purchase. You (or your software) enter the credit card number, expiration date, purchase amount, and other data. Your POS terminal uses your modem to dial your payment processor, which checks the card information and gets back to you with an authorization number, all in 6 to 15 seconds. If you want to have charges authorized while your customer is still online at your Web site, you will need a separate modem and a separate phone line for card authorizations. If your Web site is not in your offices but at your Web host, ask your host about adding a modem and line to verify your transactions.

The fourth thing you need is a **POS terminal** (one of those gadgets that cashiers run your card through at the checkout stand) or its software equivalent running on a computer. Most ISOs twist your arm to get you to *lease* a credit card terminal at an inflated price. Would you lease a telephone? Then don't lease a credit card terminal. You can buy one new for $500 to $600. You can buy one used for $200 to $350. (I've even seen a used one for sale for $50.) Some ISOs want you to buy one for $1,000, or lease one for $40 per month for three years ($1,440!). What if you have your own terminal or software? Then be prepared to get a pitch to shell out $225 to $500 as a bogus "setup fee" or "programming fee." The sales agent needs you to shell out your cash up front because half your deposit and lease is his or her commission. As an Internet merchant, you probably won't need a terminal since you can use authorization software instead. If you sign a contract that says you must use their equipment, protect yourself from getting stuck with it even if you change banks. Specify in your agreement that if the bank refuses to process your charges for *any* reason, the contract is voided and you will return the equipment and owe no further payments.

Unencrypted credit cards via email and the Web

Most of the companies taking naked credit card data over the Net are small companies. Big companies know better. They don't want to expose themselves to the risk. You may think, "Hey, wait a minute—that doesn't make sense. A big corporation could more easily afford to pay the fraud charges from a bad card." That would be true if only one card number were stolen at a time, but that isn't how it works.

Usually a thief collects lots of card numbers from just a few merchants. A large company with many credit card transactions is a much more juicy target, and if hit, would suffer a larger loss than a small company selling, say, only $20,000 over the Net each week. That doesn't mean that if your business is small you won't get hit. That doesn't mean it won't hurt. You're still at risk taking naked numbers, and you still can be wounded.

So what if, for some reason, you can't accept encrypted credit card numbers? Maybe your business is in a country where encryption is illegal. What then?

You could take the credit card numbers off-line on the phone, by fax, or by postal mail. This is the solution preferred by Visa. If you can't encrypt, says Visa's Steve Herz, "we advise our cardholders and our merchants to do alternate methods of handling card numbers. In an Internet transaction, ask your customer to call you with the card number or to send it in the mail, but don't ask to use unencrypted card numbers over the Internet."

If you are absolutely desperate to accept card numbers but can't use encryption, a less-desirable alternative is one used by software retailer The Corner Store. Some of The Corner Store's customers send naked credit card numbers over the Net, *but in pieces*. To reduce the risk of sending naked numbers over the Net, The Corner Store asks its customers to send the credit card number in one email message and to send the card's expiration date in a separate message. The Corner Store's order desk personnel quickly move incoming orders—especially the card numbers and dates—from the merchant's Internet-linked computer to an isolated computer. There, they reunite the card number, expiration date, and customer order by matching the "sent from" email addresses.

Note that this procedure does not eliminate the risk of theft, but merely reduces it. Still, the broken pieces do not match the patterns that packet sniffers normally search for, making ordering more safe. For you, the merchant, having your customers split the card number from the date before sending them gives you the advantage of a very easy-to-implement solution for email customers and for World Wide Web customers as well. Your Web order form can be set to similarly scramble the order of card numbers and expiration dates, providing the same minimal level of protection.

Keep in mind that this is not your only option. There are other, safer Internet order procedures that do not use encryption but avoid sending naked card numbers over the Net.

Credit cards: Avoiding loss without encryption

The safest way to take credit cards without using encryption software and the method that has been used the longest on the Internet is a two-stage order operation. There are many variations on this theme, but they all boil down to the same essentials: Your customer sends you the order over the Net, but sends the credit card information via fax, phone, or snail mail. Although some of the largest Internet merchants use a two-stage order operation, it is so simple it can still be used by the smallest.

For a classic, fine-tuned example of a two-stage operation, take a peek at Computer Literacy Bookshops' Web page, **www.clbooks.com**. Look for instructions on how to order. You'll see carefully worded instructions, letting customers know that the order procedures are in place to protect them. You'll also see a "Preregistration Form" that customers can print and use to send account information by fax or postal mail. Note that the form is designed to be used both by new customers and by existing customers who want to change account information, and that the instructions further down the form state (in a friendly tone of voice) that account changes will not be accepted over the phone or via the Internet. Computer Literacy Bookshops uses an email version of this form to send to email buyers, and a printed version is included in Computer Literacy's catalogs. An advantage of the Computer Literacy system is that it does *not* require the customer to memorize yet another bloody password, as many two-stage order operations do.

A company called First Virtual (**www.fv.com**) offers a different twist. A prospective customer phones First Virtual with credit card information and sends a confirming email message. First Virtual emails the prospective customer a password. The customer uses that password to make purchases from any Internet merchant that accepts First Virtual for payment. When the customer makes a purchase, First Virtual sends him or her an email message listing what was purchased and the price, and asking the customer to confirm the authenticity of each purchase. The customer confirms with an email reply, and First Virtual bills the credit card and pays the merchant.

To accept First Virtual purchases, you, the merchant, pay First Virtual $10 to $350 and go through a simple sign-up procedure. When a customer buys something from you, First Virtual deposits funds directly into your checking account. You pay $.29 per charged transaction, 2 percent of the charged amount, and $1 each time a deposit is made to your account. First Virtual is a technically sound concept and is secure. It is simple for a merchant to sell using the service, but I haven't talked to any merchants who have had more than a few hundred dollars in sales from First Virtual customers.

Two-stage order operations like these are secure. Some, like Computer Literacy Bookshops use no password and so provide nothing for crooks to steal. Two-stage operations that require passwords do not use words that match credit card formats, so the passwords are less likely to be sniffed by hackers. If a merchant-specific password is stolen, it can be used only at that merchant or group of merchants. It can't be used worldwide and can't be sold on the black market. Since a merchant-specific password has no resale value, it is a less inviting target for thieves.

Credit cards: Encrypted transmission

Encrypted Internet orders have become easy and are the way most credit card purchases are handled on the Web.

Using encryption for an Internet sale assures a merchant of three things. First, that the order has reached you without being altered in any way. Second, that any enclosed credit card numbers, customer information, and order data was not copied while the order was en route. Third, if the order includes a digital signature, that the order was sent to you by the person who claims to have sent it and not by some bozo who plucked a card number off carbon forms he found in a trash bin.

An order with a valid digital signature supports *nonrepudiation*. Your customer can't claim that he or she didn't agree to the transaction. A secure sale also protects the customer from merchant fraud. A merchant can't pad the bill with fake charges. Billing twice for the same transaction is prevented by timestamps.

You need two items to process encrypted sales orders from your customers. First, your customers must have software to encrypt their orders. Most Web browsers do this automatically. Second, you need a secure way to receive customer orders and decrypt them.

STEP 1: VALIDATION AND ACCEPTANCE

Secure Web servers are the most common way for businesses to accept credit cards over the Net. If your business uses a secure Web server, almost any customer with a Web browser can establish a secure link with your Web site and send credit card info to you by simply filling in a Web form.

If your business does not run its own server computer but instead rents computer space from a Web host, you may still be able to securely accept credit cards over the Web. Check with your Web host to see if it provides secure card acceptance.

At this stage you can also *validate* your customer's card information. Validation means you inspect the information to make sure that the card number isn't just gobbledygook and that the expiration date hasn't already expired. Either your Web server validates using a Java or CGI routine, or you can validate with JavaScript built into your Web page itself—the simplest and most efficient way. The next chapter has more on order pages and validation.

Secure Web servers are available from several companies. They range from free simple ones to high-end secure servers costing tens of thousands of dollars that do everything but walk your dog. For a comparison of leading Web servers, visit **www.serverwatch.com**.

Whether you have your own Web server or rent space from a Web host, you need one additional item to securely accept credit cards: a certificate. Most servers currently use a security setup called SSL, so you'll need an SSL certificate. If you use the SET process described below, your business will need SET certification as well. The leading certificate provider is VeriSign (**www.verisign.com**), which charges $300 for an SSL certificate. A competitor, Thawte Consulting (**www.thawte.com**) sells SSL certificates for $100. Some Web hosts have a *blanket certificate* that covers all its clients and is included with the Web hosts' regular monthly fees or for a slight additional charge.

STEP 2: VERIFICATION, AUTHORIZATION, AND SETTLEMENT

Okay, now you've *accepted* a credit card number from your customer. How do you turn that into nickels in your piggy bank? Your next step is called *verification*, which returns to you an *authorization*.

Physical stores run credit card sales through a POS terminal or credit card terminal. The terminal calls a toll-free phone number to reach a processing center and receives an authorization or denial within 10 or 15 seconds. The money is deposited in the store's account within two business days.

As an Internet merchant, you don't need a credit card terminal. Instead, you can install credit card processing software on your computer. When you process a credit card sale, you either type in the transaction information or have your software lift it directly from the data your customer enters into your Web order form. Your computer uses a modem to call your processing center and receives an authorization or denial within 10 to 20 seconds. The money is deposited into your account within two business days. This last step is called *settlement*.

The great advantage of credit card processing software is that your computer can obtain authorization *while your customer is still online* at your Web site. It can do this "hands-off," without human help. You still need a bank and a processing network, of course. If you use credit card processing software, run it on a separate computer behind your firewall. Otherwise someone could copy credit card numbers, and they could use software to buy things from you and void the charges.

The four dominant software programs to process credit cards are IC Verify, PC Authorize, Mac Authorize, and CyberCash Cash Register. All four products support all major cards and work with most U.S. banks and processing networks. All can bill recurring transactions (monthly payments, for instance) automatically. All handle authorizations, voids, and returns, plus manual card processing, so they handle all your card-not-present transactions.

IC Verify (**www.icverify.com**) is feature-rich, with modules for specific business types (hotels, restaurants, etc.) and more reports than its competitors. IC Verify's big drawbacks are its ugly interface and that it is hard to use. You can hook up IC Verify to your Web server and other programs to import and export data, but doing so is difficult, requiring a programmer. IC Verify takes a few hours to install, and a couple of days to integrate with your other software. It is available for DOS and Windows starting at about $350, and for Unix starting at $1,000.

PC Authorize and *Mac Authorize* from Tellan Software (**www.tellan.com**) are easy to use and understandable by nontechies. Both Tellan products make it easier than competing products to hook up with Web servers and other software programs. The products take only half an hour to install and about eight hours to integrate with your other software. PC Authorize for Windows and its Mac counterpart start at $350.

CyberCash Cash Register (**www.cybercash.com**) is free and does almost everything a merchant would need. So it should be wildly popular, right? But it isn't, and for two good reasons. First, CyberCash has done a terrible job of marketing it. Most Net merchants don't even know that CyberCash gives away free card processing software. Second, it takes 50 to 100 hours to configure and install it. Ouch! CyberCash Cash Register is available for Windows and Unix.

Additional card authorization programs are *PC Charge* for Windows (**www.gosoftinc.com**), *Credit Card Verification System* for Unix and Windows (**www.hks.net**), and for Canadians, *CreditCHEQ* for Windows (**www.tender-retail.com**). IBM plans one called *eTill*.

A word of caution: I haven't mentioned several card processing software programs that only work with one ISO or one bank. Avoid 'em. They lock you in so you can't switch if you develop problems.

ANOTHER OPTION

If you don't have secure Web server software and you want to accept credit cards, you have another alternative. A company called Versanet (**www. versanet.net**) provides a service called Secure Order for businesses without a secure Web server. Your server must be able to run CGI scripts. Versanet will give you a script that lets your Web server call your own secure order page on Versanet's Web server. From your customer's point of view, your site presents its own secure order form. The customer fills out the form, and the order is securely processed on Versanet's server. The order is authorized while your customer is still online, and confirmations are sent to you and your customer. Secure Order is an ingenious solution to the hassles of doing your own online credit card processing. It also allows you to accept checks online. To use Secure

Order, you must have a credit card merchant account. Setup costs $600, and in addition you will pay fees of $.50 to $.90 per credit card sale, or, for purchases paid for by online checks, the larger of $1.50 or 1.5 percent. You can also use Secure Order if you rent Web space from a Web host.

SET = Secure Electronic Transactions

Secure Electronic Transactions (SET) is promoted by Visa and MasterCard, and backed by American Express, Microsoft, IBM, Netscape, CyberCash, Terisa Systems, and VeriSign. With the clout of its backers, its implementation in leading Internet software, and its success at handling crucial security requirements, SET will become the leading method of credit card processing on the Internet.

Visa plans intensive marketing to consumers to convince them to use SET and nothing else for Internet purchases. Visa also plans for a more focused but equally intense marketing effort to Internet merchants. Visa may use rule changes or prices changes as carrot-and-stick persuaders for merchants. "For Internet transactions that are SET-compliant, compared to non-compliant Internet transactions, or MOTO transactions, or MOTO transactions, or will we adjust rules and/or rates?" rhetorically asks Visa's vice president of electric commerce, Steve Herz. "We don't know yet."

Seven habits of highly successful transactions

SET was planned to accomplish seven goals in Internet credit card sales:

1. *Keep payment information confidential.* Credit card numbers, for instance, are not transferred as part of a payment transaction, so they can never fall into the hands of eavesdroppers or merchant employees.

2. *Maintain data integrity.* All data sent between the customer, the merchant, and the bank(s) cannot be altered.

3. *Provide authentication to the merchant* that the customer is a legitimate user of a valid card.

4. *Provide authentication to the customer* that the merchant is a legitmate credit card acceptor and not a scam artist.

5. *Apply security techniques* to prevent profitable intrusions from outsiders.

6. *Create a protocol that works with more than the Internet*, including America Online, smart cards, and other forms of electronic payment transactions.

7. *Operate on all software platforms and networks.*

As a seller on the Internet, SET takes care of one of your main worries: you know who you are dealing with. Without SET, you can't tell who your customers really are. As Visa's Herz comments, "We have no identification of who they are. They're just blips on a screen."

SET not only identifies your customer, but it lets you know that the credit card used by that customer is a valid card belonging to that specific person. To do this, SET uses a combination of encryption, digital signatures, and digital certificates so the customer and the merchant both know the other is legitimate. The technical innards of SET that pull all this off are staggeringly complex, but that doesn't matter to you and your customer. Software does the dirty work for you.

Anatomy of a SET sale

A SET purchase is simple on the surface. Underneath, all kinds of frantic messages go back and forth with more signatures than the Declaration of Independence. Of course, these signatures are digital. One thing that does *not* go back and forth is your customer's credit card number. All SET's one-time-only authentication routines mean that card numbers are not needed. You'll never see the card number from a SET sale. Visa likes that a lot. It means a merchant can't collect card numbers, eliminating the possibility of massive card theft or large-scale merchant employee abuses.

The customer sends you a digital certificate to prove that he or she is a valid cardholder. You must have a digital certificate from your bank to prove that you are who you claim to be. "The merchant gets a digital certificate from the merchant's bank, just like the merchant now gets a merchant agreement with the bank," explains Herz. You'll be able to use your digital certificate to accept smart card purchases as well as credit cards.

Every silver lining has a cloud. I can see two potential problems with SET. First, SET messages are embedded in MIME messages. MIME itself can be a security breach, as an earlier chapter discussed. Some businesses won't accept MIME messages. SET forces businesses to accept MIME, thus introducing a possible security breach. It may be wise to separate your SET-using computers from other computers to prevent MIME-transmitted contamination.

The second problem isn't security-related, but customer service-related. Research shows that customers will wait for only 20 seconds on average before aborting an order due to impatience. SET requires a lot of behind-the-scenes number-crunching and message-sending. It uses public keys, which take longer to encrypt and decrypt than private keys. Plan to use fast computers for SET processing, and pray your Internet connections don't clog or slow down.

Visa plans to expand its use of SET aggressively into several areas beyond Internet consumer credit cards. Right now, Visa is looking at extending its business-to-business commercial purchasing cards onto the Net.

And, says Visa's Herz, "Somewhere along the line we're going to have to deal with the concept of portable Internet security." He gave the example of a sales kiosk in a mall. If you want to purchase from it, how can you pay if your digital signature is on your computer at home or in the office? Visa is working on transportable solutions and integration with smart cards.

"What we are doing with SET and the Internet now," promises Herz, "is just the beginning."

Smart cards

A smart card looks like a regular credit card, but instead of a magnetic stripe on the back, it's got a chip inside. Smart cards are much bigger in Europe and Japan than in the U.S. Visa has issued nearly 6 million of them worldwide.

A user jams a smart card into a slot on a computer or a bank ATM machine. The user enters a PIN number (just like a debit card) and specifies the amount of cash to be withdrawn from an account and loaded onto the card. The chip on the card keeps track of how much is added, how much is spent, and the remaining balance. At the point of sale, electronic cash is transferred off the smart card and into the merchant's account.

Visa's SET-compliant version is called Visa Cash Card or VisaCash. Visa's tie-in projects are Smart Commerce Japan with Toshiba in Tokyo and Projet e-COMM in France. Its eventual goal is to combine your debit, credit, phone, frequent flyer, and other cards onto one piece of plastic.

Europay, MasterCard, and other companies are creating their own smart cards compatible with Visa's. All follow the same standards, EMV (which lets all smart cards operate on all hardware regardless of location, manufacturer, or financial institution) and Java Card API (so all hardware can accept all smart cards and so card providers can update the programming of the cards remotely).

Where does this smart card stuff tie in with the Internet? Right now VisaCash users can make purchases on the Web from CardMart Greetings, Broderbund Software, Newsletter Technologies, and other test sites. Visa expects its smart card to be widely in use in 1998. The advantage is that smart cards are proven to work on the consumer level because they are mindlessly easy to use. All we need is a way for people to use smart cards on their computers.

VeriFone has come to the rescue with its VeriSmart system (cute name, eh?) that lets users use smart cards with PCs, smart phones, and set-top boxes. Hewlett Packard is releasing PC keyboards with VeriFone's smart card reader built in and the software for Windows to make it work. Many people predict that within two years it will be difficult to buy a computer *without* a smart card reader. Look to see if your business should accept smart cards, especially if you sell to Web consumers. If you already have SET-compliant software to accept credit cards, adding smart cards will be easy.

Online checks

Although not as popular as credit cards, electronic checks are also accepted by hundreds of merchants on the Net. While most electronic check schemes require the merchant to use special software, electronic checks might appeal to you if you do not currently have a credit card merchant account. To accept electronic checks, you don't have to go through merchant account qualification. You just deposit them in your bank account as *pre-authorized drafts*, normal checks that the customer has approved but that do not require a physical signature.

Online check schemes fall into three categories. In the first, a consumer pays you, the merchant, directly.

CUSTOMER PAYS YOU

To do this, you must purchase special software, and provide your customers with a special Web page that acts as an online blank check. The customer enters the information typically found on a paper check: account number, account holder's name, bank, amount, date, etc. Most electronic check systems enable your Web server to accept the information, verify it, obtain authorization, and return approval while your customer waits online.

One company that makes this possible is VersaNet (**www.versanet.com/ so.html**), which sells a service called Secure Orders that you can use with your Web server so you can accept U.S. and Canadian checks on the Web. Secure Orders costs $300, plus a $99 activation fee to process checks and an additional $99 to process credit cards as well. VersaNet charges a $1 to $1.50 processing fee for each VersaNet transaction.

Other simple ways of accepting online checks are Online Check System (**www.onlinecheck.com/how.html**), TurboDraft (**www.sies.com/checks**), InstaCheck (**www.instacheck.com**), and Redi-Check (**www.redi-check.com**). A more sophisticated version is offered by CyberCash: **www.cybercash.com/ cybercash/paynow**.

Customer pays third party that pays you

In this situation, intermediary companies process your online billing and collections for you. Your customers pay the intermediary of your choice, and the intermediary forwards the money to you, less a collection fee.

These alternatives are useful mostly for companies that bill a customer regularly, like once a month. Microsoft calls this Electronic Bill Presentment and Payment. It makes a lot of sense to use the Internet for presenting bills and accepting payments. Just think of all the printing and postage costs that utility companies will save.

The big companies offering this service are CheckFree: (**www.checkfree.com**), Visa ePay (formerly Visa InterActive) (**www.visa.com**), Microsoft subsidiary MSFDC (**www.msfdc.com**), and once again, CyberCash with its PayNow service (**www.cybercash.com/cybercash/paynow**).

Consumer pays consumer; business pays business

CyberCash PayNow (**www.cybercash.com/cybercash/paynow**) lets consumers write checks to each other, so you can give your nephew money for college textbooks. It also lets businesses pay businesses online, without a monthly or periodic invoice. At this time, CyberCash offers the most flexible and advanced online check acceptance for Internet merchants.

Future online checks

Another form of electronic check is under preparation by the Financial Services Technology Consortium (FSTC), an organization of 65 banks, financial services firms, and related companies. The FSTC system will let merchants verify the electronic check at any step. Once issued, the check will be tamper-proof. A merchant or bank can detect immediately if it has been altered. Participants in creating the FSTC system include IBM, Sun, BellCore, and seven of the largest U.S. and Canadian banks. Processing will be provided by members of the same organization that now clears paper checks: the National Automated Clearing House Association (**www.nacha.org**), which has created the Electronic Check Council and a consortium of banks and large businesses called the Internet Council. The FSTC plans to eventually cover smart cards as well. For a progress report, visit **www.fstc.org**.

At present, many more Internet merchants accept credit cards than electronic checks. The extra work of dealing with electronic checks is worthwhile mostly for merchants who deal with a large volume of purchases or merchants who market to low-end consumers who can't obtain credit cards. In the future, *businesses* might use electronic checks to make purchases, especially using the FSTC method above and CyberCash PayNow. If so, business-to-business marketers will want to look at accepting electronic checks.

Digital money

Digital money, virtual currency, ecash—call it whatever you like, it sure receives lots of media hype. Some of it is even accurate. Often, though, systems described as digital money are really secure credit card schemes. The system used by First Virtual, for instance, is really just a secure way to buy on the Net and have it billed to your credit card.

The term "digital money" (and its many equivalents) is loosely applied to five kinds of online payments, each affecting merchants differently:

1. **Credit card billing** - Some people use the term digital money to describe an online payment billed to a credit card, for instance CyberCash's secure card processing (which is actually free to merchants, a very good deal).

2. **Credit card accumulations** - A problem with credit cards is that pesky per-transaction charge. Paying your bank between ten and thirty cents per transaction is okay when your transactions are ten dollars or more, but what if you'd like to charge people twenty-five cents for downloading an electronic booklet, or ten cents per information look-up in your database? These small transactions, called *microtransactions*, have the potential to generate

millions of dollars in sales. But with credit card per-transaction fees, you'd lose money on each sale. *Accumulations* are a way to work around that. Instead of billing each microtransaction individually, a company stores them and bills the accumulated small transactions as one medium-sized transaction. Instead of paying credit card per-transaction charges of $.30 apiece on ten $.25 transactions, you pay one $.30 charge on one $2.50 transaction.

3. **Stored value accounts** - A smart card is an example of a stored value account. You transfer funds electronically from another account to the smart card, which remembers how much you have available and subtracts your remainder after each purchase. Some companies offer the cardless equivalent of a smart card, an online account into which you can transfer funds and make purchases, which then are subtracted from your online account. These were predicted to be huge on the Net, but they have not taken off. There is little demand for smart cardless stored value accounts.

4. **Debit card billing** - Instead of subtracting purchase amounts from online accounts, your customers can choose to transfer them from their existing checking accounts. (In bankers' lingo, a checking account is a *demand deposit account*, or *DDA* for short.) Like a plastic debit card, use of online debit card billing requires the customer to enter a secret PIN number, which must somehow be carried to the customer's bank for processing.

5. **Digital checks** - Like a debit card, digital checks directly transfer money from an existing demand deposit account. The difference is that online checks need no PIN number, making online checking transactions simpler for you to process.

To process some or all of these types of digital money, some companies offer consumers free *wallet software*. This handles security on the purchaser's end of the transactions. Purchasers regard wallet software as a big hassle, and it has failed dismally as an optional plug-in. The only way wallet software will succeed is when Netscape and Microsoft build it into their browsers, which will probably happen in the near future. In the meantime, purchasing technologies requiring wallet software are at a severe disadvantage. Some companies, including CyberCash, offer both wallet and wallet-free payment methods.

Table 17.1 shows seven players in the game of digital money. It tells you what kinds of online transactions each handles, the smallest microtransactions each

Table 17.1 Seven companies offer many flavors of so-called digital money.

	Credit cards?	Accumulations?	Stored value?	Debit cards?	Digital checks?	Smallest transaction	Wallet software?	Where to get merchant software
CyberCash	Yes	No	Yes	No	Yes	$.25US	Yes/No	Free download
VeriFone	Yes	No	No	No	No	n/a yet	Yes	From your bank
GCTech	Yes	No	Yes	Yes	Yes	$.01US	Yes	From your bank
DigiCash	No	No	Yes	No	No	$.01US*	Yes	Download
First Virtual	Yes	Yes	Yes	No	No	$.25US	No	Download
Cybank	Yes	Yes	Yes	Yes	No	$.01US	Yes	Download
DataCash	Yes	Yes	Yes	No	No	$1.00US	No	Westminster Bank

*But DigiCash charges users $1-3 per transaction!

processes, whether the company offers its own wallet software (some require it, some do not), and where you can get the company's merchant software.

CyberCash (**www.cybercash.com/cybercash/merchants/getstarted.html**) is the one company that has everything available now and working. It also offers an important advantage for you: CyberCash software and services are free to merchants except for a per-transaction charge for online check processing. Because of CyberCash's excellent security protection, some banks require merchants to use CyberCash for online credit card processing.

VeriFone (**www.verifone.com**) has a lock on the world of physical POS card swipe terminals, with about 85 percent of the market. Backed by its parent company Hewlett Packard, VeriFone is aggressively pursuing online payments as well. Some VeriFone software is available through Microsoft.

GCTech (**www.gctec.com**) offers a family of GlobalID online payment processing options, including smart cards. It is active mostly in Europe.

DigiCash (**www.digicash.com/ecash/startshop.html**) offers a superior technology for online payment processing but markets it dismally. The company makes money by licensing its technology to others, but it is dead as a digital money contender on its own. There is no reason for your business to accept DigiCash payments.

First Virtual (**www.fv.com**) is discussed in detail earlier in this chapter.

Cybank (**www.cybank.net**) is a smaller player, but offers a wide range of payment options.

DataCash (**www.businessmonitor.co.uk/spicers/datacash.html**) is an example of digital money for a specific niche market. For $1.00 per lookup, you can use DataCash to research the Spicers Centre database of European Union documents. The database goes back to 1952 and adds new commission documents within 48 hours of receipt. It is one of the most complete and up-to-date places in the world for businesses who deal with the European Union to get information on regulations and procedures. DataCash is not for everybody, but you can see the high value it offers for its specific market.

It is too early yet to predict what forms of digital money will succeed. The easiest way for you to decide if you want to accept digital bucks as payment might be to visit your competitors' Web sites. What brands, if any, do they accept? Then ask your customers, "Would you like to pay for your orders using digital money? If so, what kind?" Make your decision based on your findings.

Some resources

Payment on the Net is evolving rapidly. We have workable methods to get paid now, but we aren't even close to the final resolution. For the latest information on credit cards and payments over the Net, here are three good directories:

Payment Mechanisms Designed for the Internet
> **http://ganges.cs.tcd.ie/mepeirce/Project/oninternet.html**

Internet Commerce Resource Center
> **www.verifone.com/products/software/icommerce/html/resources.html**

Electronic Commerce Products
> **http://tips.iworld.com/_noframes.shtml/Electronic_commerce.html**

CHAPTER **18**

Web Storefronts

"When you lose a sale, you lose it twice: you don't get the money, and your competitor does."

—Bill Gates

When Paramount Pictures opened a Web site selling *Star Trek* merchandise, it received 3,600 orders in the first two weeks. At the Internet Shopping Network (**www.internet.net**), 10,000 people visit each day. About 30 percent of its customers are repeat buyers. A typical first-time customer buys a low-ticket item, then comes back and makes a more expensive purchase. Many businesses, large and small, have reported success at Internet retailing. But for every Web store that makes money, many don't. I've discussed many of the reasons why and why not in earlier chapters. This chapter covers direct selling on the Internet, with strategies and tactics to maximize your chances for profits—and a few warnings about what to avoid.

Cybermalls

At first glance, if retail stores work well on the Net, the shopping mall model should be even better. That hasn't proven to be true. The Internet has not been kind to cybermalls. iMall (**www.imall.com**), which is considered a successful cybermall, has 1,600 stores and processes $10,000 to $15,000 worth of transactions a day—a whopping $9.50 or less average per store. I'd call that a success for the mall, but scarcely one for most of its tenants.

MecklerMedia's project to create a mall died after they spent more than a quarter of a million dollars and attracted only one tenant. Slickly-designed Marketplace.com opened January 1994 and closed 16 months later. The original CyberMall closed in May 1995. In spite of hugeTV and print advertising expenses, MCI's MarketplaceMCI disappeared without a trace in mid-1996. Shopping 2000 folded in January 1997.

One of the most loudly-trumpeted cybermalls was IBM's World Avenue. Big Blue charged a $30,000 startup fee, $2,500 a month for a catalog of up to 300 items, plus 5 percent of gross sales. Not cheap. IBM reeled in more than 20 suckers to pay these outrageous fees, but closed World Avenue in fewer than twelve months. All its stores wanted out. On its busiest days, a typical World Avenue Web store got *four* visitors a day (and even fewer buyers!). Most days, *nobody* visited.

The reason these cybermalls died is because they offered nothing to their tenants that their tenants couldn't get on their own for a far lower cost. Some people say that to sell on the Net you need to have a "storefront" on a mall.

Rubbish. This is a common misunderstanding, often compounded by pro-longed exposure to Liquid Paper.

There is no such thing as a "prestigious" location on the Net. There are places with more visibility than others, but that is because they have higher amounts of traffic or good volumes of *appropriate* traffic. On the Internet, customers don't walk through an entry passageway to go to your retail site. They look up your URL on a search engine like Yahoo and go straight to your store, or straight to a page within your store. No Internet customer cares—or even knows—what institution hosts your site as long as you have the product, service, or information he or she wants.

In a real-world shopping mall, the landlord has two revenue streams: rent and a percentage of gross sales. The rent covers fixed expenses. The percent-age of the action is an incentive for the landlord to do everything in its power to pull customers into the mall. Physical retail stores become tenants because the mall brings traffic to their stores. With a cybermall, the "land-lord" collects fees that are fixed (like rent), or possibly per transaction, or on a percentage of sales, or per hit. There may also be additional charges for disk space used and services performed.

What do you, the cyber-retailer, get in exchange for these fees?

- *A listing and hot link on the cybermall's home page.* This is worthless. Internet shoppers will bypass it.

- *Space on the cybermall's computer and technical assistance.* This is better, but the services provided by a cybermall are no different from the same ser-vices provided by any Internet service bureau—and the cybermall services often cost much more. Many cybermalls are really just a collection of links to the clients of one Internet service bureau. Make sure you don't overpay a cybermall for the same services you could get from a Web host at a far lower price. Use Viaweb (described later in this chapter) as a point of comparison. It costs so little to open a Web site that it makes no sense to pay a cybermall $10,000 a year just to be a passive host.

- *Secure credit card processing and an electronic shopping cart.* This is okay. Implementing secure credit card processing on the Net can be a nuisance for a merchant. The price of secure Web servers are falling, and virtual Web servers like GoSite also offer secure card processing, but a cybermall handling secure sales still gives you some value—though not as much as some cybermalls charge. Again, use Viaweb as a point of comparison.

- *Access to customer traffic.* Bingo! On the Internet, this is the only reason that will hold up over time for a merchant to join a cybermall. Cybermalls that bring customers to their tenants' virtual doors are the ones that will succeed.

With the cost of setting up shop on your own going down steadily and more than 2,000 new Internet merchants opening every month, it becomes more and more difficult for you to make yourself heard above the roar. If you are considering signing a lease with a cybermall, look for one that *draws customers*, especially one that brings in exactly your kind of customers.

The Internet Shopping Network (**www.internet.net**) is more a cyberstore than a cybermall, but it does include other merchants on its site. It charges no up-front fee and no monthly rent, but between 10 and 15 percent of sales. Merchants on the site include Lillian Vernon, FTD Florists, Hammacher Schlemmer, Celestial Seasonings teas, Minolta cameras and Radio Shack. The guest merchants are all there to take advantage of the flow of customers to the ISN site, and the Internet Shopping Network promotes its clients heavily throughout its site. Getting paid only by commission must be a strong motivation.

The Electronic Newsstand (**www.enews.com**) sells only magazine subscriptions, and its tenants are all publishers. It charges publishers between $1,000 and $5,000 per year plus a commission of about 10 percent. It has been so successful offering one-stop shopping for hundreds of magazines that it now has a couple of Internet competitors.

The Internet Underground Music Archives (IUMA) at **www.iuma.com** is another specialized mall. IUMA features music from more than 1,000 bands, which it gives away for free. How can IUMA make any money by giving everything away for free? Easy as pie. To enter IUMA, you register. IUMA adds your registration data to a database. It tells potential sponsors how many tens of thousands of registrants it has and what their demographics are. Sponsors such as Intel, Volvo, and Coca Cola pay IUMA for advertising space. Bands and record labels used to give recordings for free to IUMA because people who wouldn't otherwise hear about the bands discover them and buy their CDs. I say "used to" because now IUMA actually *charges* bands a fee. So IUMA has a steady cash flow that grows as it gets more visitors.

Catalogs on the Web

Catalogs on the Web present special challenges and take more work to implement successfully than other online sales projects.

However, an Internet catalog offers significant advantages over a paper one, eliminating printing and mailing costs while being easier to keep up-to-date. Besides, email and Web orders don't rack up charges to your 800 number. If a product sells poorly, you can instantly reduce its price, change its description, or make it more prominent.

If your company has an existing catalog that works well, your first temptation might be to create Web pages that exactly copy your printed pages. Commit this sin and suffer twice: You miss the Web's strong points while being hurt by its weak ones. If your Webalog merely mimics your print book, you'll miss out on the interactivity of the Web. Your site will bore prospects instead of satisfying them. Worse yet, you won't be able to apply online traffic and sales information from your Web site to expand, shrink, and change Web pages according to your customers' behaviors.

You'll need to make changes as you learn what works online and what doesn't. You can't assume that Internet catalog buyers act the same as your print catalog's customers. Give your design team enough leeway to discover the differences and use them.

OBI: Open Buying on the Internet

If your business sells to other businesses, your catalog can dramatically increase your sales by following the OBI standard for Open Buying on the Internet. This standard was created by the nonprofit OBI Consortium, an offshoot of the Internet Purchasing Roundtable. It is supported by many Fortune 500 corporations, financial companies, and high-tech companies, including Netscape and Microsoft. OBI gives purchasers a cheap, fast way of using Web catalogs to buy the high-volume, low-cost items that account for 80 percent of most organizations' purchasing activities. OBI is designed with the understanding that business-to-business marketing is very different from consumer marketing.

OBI uses Web browsers and servers. To sell to OBI purchasers, you maintain a Web catalog that gives accurate product and price information. If you negotiate discounts for buyers in certain companies, then your catalog must present that company's discounts when its buyers use your catalog. This means your catalog must be able to identify a buyer, verify the buyer's identity based on a digital certificate from the buyer, select appropriate prices from your pricing database, and present them on database-generated Web pages. As I'm sure you've guessed, a fair amount of programming work is involved. To receive OBI orders, your Web catalog must be integrated with your inventory and order management systems and with a secure Web server (which acts as your OBI server). Your Web server must be able to authorize certain transaction types with a payment processing company.

OBI might sound like a lot of work, but for some merchants the sales payoff will be enormous. You can get more information on OBI from Supply Works at **www.supplyworks.com/obi/index.html** or from the OBI Consortium at **www.obi.org**.

Before you start your Web catalog

First, get a rough idea of what you want to do with your Web catalog. Nothing fancy, you can scribble it in pencil on the back of an envelope. Jot down:

1. The approximate number of products you want to feature.

2. How will you display products on a page? Many on one page, with few photos? Several products and photos on one page? One product and the product's variations on a page?

3. The approximate number of pages you might need.

4. How will you present specials and limited-time discounts?

5. How will you receive orders? Via FTP from your Web host's secure server? Secure email? From your own in-house server? How many offline (phone, fax, postal mail) methods will you use to accept orders?

6. What payment methods will you accept?

7. How will you calculate shipping charges and sales tax?

8. What special instructions should be on your order form?

With this information in hand, you have points of comparison to look for when you take a look at other catalog sites, which should be your next step.

Allow time for your Web catalog team to invest days poking at other catalogers' sites before they lift a finger to build yours. The amount of rework and agony that exploration can save is considerable. How easy is it to navigate their site? How much time does it take to move from page to page? Do you waste time on pages you don't need, or can you find what you want and go right to it? How does the cataloger use its electronic shopping cart? Does it have any clever order form ideas you can borrow? Even if you don't need to buy anything, visit several sites and go as far through the ordering process as you can without actually giving your credit card number.

One Web catalog site to study is Lands' End (**www.landsend.com**). Note the many differences between its printed and online catalogs. Its in-house copywriters completely rewrote the catalog copy, using a different style for the Web. Lands' End's online copy is written in a chatty first-person style, in keeping with the informality of the Internet. The Web site offers much more information on how to determine your clothing size than would ever fit in the print catalog. This causes lower return rates for Internet customers. Study the order form; it checks inventory, lets the customer know a product is in stock, and provides two different forms for U.S. and international customers, making each easier to fill out.

Another site to study is Viaweb (**www.viaweb.com**), and some of the merchants it supports. Viaweb provides a good way for small businesses to open a low-cost virtual storefront with the least possible technical annoyance. Viaweb charges $100 a month rental for stores selling 12 or fewer items online and $300 a month for stores selling 13 to 1,000 items. Nontechnical merchants can follow Viaweb's instructions and set up a standardized store, including product descriptions and photos, in half a day. Viaweb provides secure credit card processing and well-designed Web pages that walk you through the process of building your store, one step at a time. Good online reports profile your visitor traffic. (Make sure you look at these when you visit the Viaweb site.) Note that Viaweb provides an inexpensive site and the tools to create it quickly, but does not promote your site. That is left for you to do. Viaweb is well thought out. I've recommended it to several companies, and the ones who've used it are satisfied.

ViaWeb is not the ideal solution for every company. You may decide to run your Web store on your own Web server. If so, keep in mind that most Web server software programs for merchants are actually catalog software. If a catalog business is not right for your company's Web site, look for other types of Web servers. Even companies that are catalog-oriented often start with a standard secure Web server and add other commerce-oriented Web software to assemble something that closely meets their needs.

Paper catalogs on the Web

If you are looking for the simplest way to make your original paper catalog available to Web prospects, two companies specialize in that:

CatalogLink (**www.cataloglink.com**) showcases more than 100 catalogs. Visitors to CatalogLink typically order three or four catalogs each time they visit. A visitor can see your catalog's cover, read information about it, order your catalog (at no cost to the visitor), and directly link to your Web site. Visitors cannot order merchandise through CatalogLink, just catalogs. It costs you nothing up front to include your catalog on CatalogLink, but the company charges you $.50 for each U.S. or Canadian name that asks for your catalog, and an amazing $1.50 for each name from other countries. (Why the higher price? It costs CatalogLink nothing extra to collect an international name and send it to you.) Blossom Flower Shops (**www.blossomflwr.com**) reports that CatalogLink generates more than 20 requests a day for its print catalog.

Mall of Catalogs (**www.mallofcatalogs.com**) contains 1,600 catalogs from which visitors can select. Mall of Catalogs sells you the requestor's name and address for 50 cents so you can send the requestor your catalog. You can also pay for a clickable link to your Web site. Thirty-three percent of the visitors to Mall of Catalogs order catalogs. An average visitor orders 20 catalogs! With such a large number of catalogs per visitor, do enough catalog requestors convert to customers to make it profitable for you to send your catalog to prospects from Mall of Catalogs? Or because catalog ordering here is so easy, are these low-quality prospects like most magazines' bingo card leads? Forcing catalog requestors to fill out a simple survey before they click and ask for catalogs might dramatically improve the profitability of leads from this site.

How to build an order form

When you use the Web for sales, the most important page of your entire Web site is your order form. It should be the culmination of your visitors' experience on your site. Everything else on your site should subtly direct your prospect to your order page. Your order page itself needs to be understandable at a glance, and your prospect should feel that completing your form will be simple.

Of course, one person's "Simple!" is another person's "Huh?" To make your order form work, you will need to invest more thought and do more testing of this page than anything else on your site.

Marketing consultant Martin Gross has written about how some people, especially creative types who consider themselves artistic, underappreciate the order form: "After all the glitter, wit, and inventiveness, it stolidly shuffles to the front of the stage with its hand out, asking for money."

Your order page has important work to do. It must keep your customer's interest, reinforce the persuasive efforts of the rest of your site, and collect information from your customer. You don't need to call your order page an "order form." You can label it with a headline that promises a benefit or asks for action. All parts of your order page must be clear, including any legal requirements. Look at your order page from your customer's perspective, not your company's. Does it guide your customer step by step in a logical order? Is it laid out to be understandable at a glance?

If you do not accept credit cards online, design options for your order form are limited. You can list your phone, fax, and snail mail addresses and ask prospects to order by those methods. A step up is to provide text that customers can print out, fill out, and mail or fax to you. This is secure and can be simple for your customer to fill out after it's printed, but many nontechnical people have an extremely difficult time printing a Web text file. In my experience, such "download-and-print" forms are mostly used by programmers and other technical folks. If your customers are among the technically-impaired, you might provide other options.

Fortunately, the World Wide Web makes interactive order forms easy to create. If you (or your service bureau) use secure server software, you'll have a relatively easy task receiving encrypted credit card orders. The key is that you must have software programs that run under CGI, the Common Gateway Interface. (Note that many rent-a-space Web hosts will *not* let you use CGI programs, so you cannot create Web pages with interactive forms.)

CGI lets you do a lot of things on your order page. While your customer waits online, he or she can look things up in your database, use an electronic shopping cart to build a list of purchases that includes a running total of costs, automatically calculate shipping and taxes, check your inventory levels, verify shipping information ("UZ is not a valid state name."), and verify credit card information. Behind the scenes, CGI programs can interface your order entry system to decrease your inventory quantities, authorize credit, enter the order, and pass information on to your accounting department. Not bad for a little ol' order form.

Your business may not want to do all that stuff. But take a look at what a full-blown Web order form can do, and then you can scale it down for your own needs.

Steps in an order form

1. *Build a shopping list.* This optional step requires a CGI electronic shopping cart program. It runs not just on your order form, but is also part of all your Web pages that list products to purchase.

2. *Calculate charges.* Include prices, currency conversion, taxes, shipping, and/or customs duties.

3. *Check stock levels.* An optional step; use if you want to sell only what you have in stock, or if you want to notify your customer when a product is out of stock and may take longer to ship.

4. *Accept credit and shipping information.* The most important step.

5. *Verify credit information.* This is necessary whether you accept credit cards or debit a corporate account.

6. *Return acknowledgment to customer.* The second most important step. If your customer does not immediately receive some kind of acknowledgment that you received the order, the customer will assume that something went wrong and will get angry, will send you the same order again, or both.

7. *Pass information on to fulfillment department.* The third most important step. Get the order to your fulfillment people as quickly as you can so they can act on it.

8. *Pass information on to accounting department.* Don't re-enter the data when you can move it electronically.

9. *Make information available for order status inquiries.* Sounds boring, but gets lively when you've got an angry customer yelling in your ear.

Making your form work

All this is great, but how does all this order information get to you? By email. Any form your customer fills in on your Web page is emailed to you. Or actually, to your Web server. The order form you send to your customer is a standard HTML document like any other Web page, but with one difference: It contains the name and address of a CGI script on your Web server. When your customer completes your order form, your customer's Web browser sends the information to your CGI script. Your CGI script reads the returned information, decides what to do with it and what response is required, and then passes the information on to wherever it needs to go while sending your customer an order acknowledgment, an error message, freshly calculated shipping charges, or whatever else you think your customer should see.

 Make sure your Web server sends your orders to an email address set up just for orders and nothing else. Make sure you send an emailed order confirmation before you ship an order. Send confirmations from an email address used for confirmations and nothing else. If an order confirmation returns to you as bounced mail, you may have received a fraudulent order. Of course, the cause also may be just a typo. But when an order confirmation bounces back to you, give it a high priority. You need to determine why it returned before you ship your product.

The ideal time for your customer to receive a confirmation is while the customer is still online with your Web server. This requires your software to forward the purchase amount and credit card information to your credit card clearinghouse and receive authorization from the clearinghouse while your customer is still online. This is only possible with an automated transaction processing system, but is the safest method for you as the merchant. If you can't do this and your customer is offline before you get authorization, email a confirmation to your customer saying that the transaction was approved.

INTERIM PAGES INCREASE SALES

While your software checks your inventory to make sure the ordered products are in stock and while it sends out your customer's credit card data for authorization, your customer must wait for 20 seconds or so. To an impatient customer, it seems like eternity. Just at the point of closure, you can lose your sale. The solution is to present your customer with *interim pages* to use up the time.

Usually two interim pages are enough. The first can be your acknowledgement page: "You have ordered 1 tribble (purple) and two zygotes (plaid) for a total amount of $87.27 to be shipped Fed Ex overnight to Amy Amiable, 27 Freak Street, Brisbane, Australia. Click here if correct." The second page can be a profuse expression of gratitude: "We appreciate your order and are your slaves for life. Thank you so much. Click here." By that time the credit card is authorized. You can send your acknowledgement page that lets your customer know the credit card was approved, the item was in stock, and it should arrive Tuesday morning.

You can also generate add-on sales with an interim page. This works on the same principle that a good salesperson uses to convince you to buy a couple of ties and a shirt to go with the suit you're buying. Right when you make your decision to buy, you are the most open to suggestions of add-on sales of complimentary products. Your interim page can suggest "A matching plaid tartan to go with your zygotes would be half off with your order, a bargain at $10.00. It would bring your total order to $97.27. Would you like this tartan?" Next to a photo of the tartan are two buttons that say "Yes" and "No." Web catalogers I've worked with who use this technique have increased sales between two and four percent. Your add-on page can be custom-generated to go with a customer's specific order, as in the example above, or it might be a special of the day that's the same for everyone.

ORDER VALIDATION DECREASES PROBLEMS

Validation is the step when the information your customer entered into your order form is inspected to make sure it makes sense. Did the customer enter all 15 digits of his or her American Express card number, or only 14? Was a ship-to name entered? Is the postal code valid?

If your business is small, the information might be validated manually by you when you receive the order. But most Web merchants would rather let their software do the dirty work, especially because software can notify your customer of glaring errors and let the customer correct them while still online.

Automatic validation can be done by a CGI script on your server or by a Java program or a JavaScript routine on your customer's computer. It's faster for your customer if as many corrections as possible are done on the customer's computer. The easiest way to do this (though it still takes a programmer to do it) is to build JavaScript validation routines right into your Web pages. You build the JavaScripts, they go with your Web page to your visitor's computer, and they run on your visitor's computer. An example JavaScript validation page by Alan Simpson is at **www.coolnerds.com/jscript/alanform.htm**. Your programmers can view its HTML and use it as a model to create your own JavaScript order form validation.

Validation can inspect what your customer entered in five ways: 1) disallowing blank items (must enter a customer name, for instance), 2) defining the quantity of allowable characters (AmEx cards must have 15 digits), 3) defining acceptable characters (numerals only for phone numbers), 4) defining formats, and 5) defining permissible numeric values.

Customers often goof up credit card numbers, so they are one of the most important things to validate. Each brand of credit card starts with specific numbers, has its own standard length, and conforms to a standard mathematical format. A free CGI routine by Dave "Spider" Paris verifies the length of all Visa, MasterCard, American Express, and Discover numbers. You'll find his Credit Card Verifier at **http://worldwidemart.com/scripts/readme/ccver.shtml**. An add-on routine by Dave MacRae checks card expiration dates: **http://worldwidemart.com/scripts/faq/ccver.shtml**. For a complete list of major card formats and the check digit formula they use to make sure the right numbers are in the right place, look at **www.beachnet.com/~hstiles/cardtype.html**.

MORE ORDER FORM TIPS

What payment method should your form offer? As many as you can. A good Web order form lets your customer choose which way to pay. Accept encrypted credit card orders. Provide your fax and phone numbers for people who don't want to send credit card data over the Net. For business-to-business customers, you'll profit by accepting purchase orders and by opening corporate accounts that are billed monthly. Give your customers as many ways as possible to buy from you.

Your order form should include your snail mail address. Even in this paperless age, you'll be surprised how many people send you checks and money orders. Specify the currency checks and money orders should use: "In U.S. dollars drawn on a U.S. bank." Most American banks are babies at currency exchange. They can take weeks to clear a foreign check and will hit you with a painful service charge. This is another reason credit cards are popular for international purchases. Card companies convert currencies for you.

When something goes wrong, and the card number does not go through or there are any other problems with the order, you will save yourself time and keep your customers happier if your order page requires your customer to provide a *telephone number* for contact, not just an email address. Some people

don't like to give out their phone number because they hate telephone solici-
tors. To reassure them that you won't do that, your order page can say "Only
used if we have questions about your order" or something similar. You need
this *and* an email address because most Internet people check email only once
a day. If you have a problem, you can respond to impatient customers faster
with a phone number.

When you write and design your order form, make sure your design team
includes someone who has daily *hands-on* experience with your current operation: customer service, order taking, fulfillment. "Hands-on" is the key phrase
here. With all due deference to your highly-paid managers, who I am sure are
very intelligent, you want opinions here from the grunts under fire in your
trenches. If possible, run your order page design by *everyone* in your customer
service department, especially order clerks. Sometimes adding a single question to your form can dramatically reduce your fulfillment error rate, and can
save you hundreds of dollars in long-distance troubleshooting phone calls.

And before you create your Web order form, remember author Douglas
Hofstadter's Law: "It always takes longer than you expect, even when you take
Hofstadter's Law into account."

Electronic shopping carts

If you have more products to sell than can easily fit on a Web order form that's
one page long, an electronic shopping cart might increase your sales by making it easier for your customers to buy. Electronic shopping carts encourage
impulse buying.

We discussed Hot Hot Hot on previous pages. Its order form uses a shopping
cart to create an online invoice for you as you shop. It also gives clear error
messages. If you leave a required line blank in the order form and try to
submit your order, a message pops up saying "Please fill in the critical information you have left blank." Then the message lists what blank or blanks you
need to fill, so you don't have to guess about it or use trial and error. Error
messages are an important part of your Web order form design. Customers
only encounter error messages when something has gone wrong, so put extra
effort into preventing angst by giving complete and clear explanations. Nothing is so simple it cannot be misunderstood.

What can an electronic shopping cart do for you? It can:

- Keep track of multiple visitors over multiple pages.

- Build a list of items purchased.

- Add prices so your customer can see a running total as he or she buys.

- Calculate taxes and shipping costs.

- Let your customer order from the same page that describes and shows the item, resulting in increased sales.

- Track attributes, such as colors, sizes, styles, and weights.

- Allow customers to change their minds (and let you monitor those changes).

- Simplify filling out your order form.

Good Web catalog software should automatically build a shopping cart for your site if you want one. If you need software to add a shopping cart to your site, choose from several shopping cart programs and services. Some are services, which you can use no matter what computer operating system you have. Some are products that run only on specific operating systems. Several are written in Perl, the same language in which CGI scripts are written. These are usually written for the Unix operating system, but theoretically, anything written in Perl can be easily modified to run on Windows, Macs, and other operating systems. Theoretically. Objects in mirror may be closer than they appear, so check with an experienced programmer first. Shopping carts can be complex, and modifying one is not for the faint of heart.

Free shopping carts:

- S-Mart Shopping Cart (Perl) is a good basic cart: **www.rcinet.com/ ~brobison/scripts**

- MiniVend (Perl) is complex to install, but as feature-rich as most commercial shopping carts. An amazing bargain: **www.iac.net/~mikeh/mvend.html**

- PerlShop (ad-supported service) gives you easy-to-install basic functionality in exchange for putting ad banners on your catalog pages: **www. arpanet.com/perlshop**

Available as either a free ad-supported service or adless $30 per month service:

- Internet Shopping Cart Server: **www.webisland.com/cart**

Commercial shopping carts:

- Rent-A-Cart (service) charges $20 per month: **www.rent-a-cart.com**

- CyberCart IP Pro (Unix, NT): **www.lobo.net/~rtweb**

- EZ Shopper (Unix, NT): **www.ahg.com/listcgi.htm**

- Internet AutoCart (perl): **www.autocart.com/Autocart/autocart.html**

- WebCart (Unix, NT): **www.staff.net/webcart.html**

- WWWOrder (perl): **www.virtualcenter.com/scripts2/WWWOrder.html**

Designing your Web site to generate sales

The World Wide Web is not just a catalog with a mouse. Some of the old rules you've learned about selling apply here, but you have new rules to learn as well. It's like the difference between a store manager and a cataloger. They may both sell the same toaster, but they will display, merchandise, and price that toaster in different ways.

The basic rules of sales still apply. Know your customers, especially what your customers want and how they act. Know whether your customers are businesses, consumers, or both. Business-to-business sales and consumer sales are as different on the Net as they are elsewhere, so you need differently designed and written Web pages for each of them. Know your competitors. The old advice "shop your competition" certainly holds true on the Web. You should buy from—or at least visit—your competitors' Web sites before you plan your own.

You also need to view your Web site as a part of your overall sales process and to discover where you can best use the Internet to strengthen and quicken your sales order cycle. If you divide your sales cycle into eight steps, examining each step can help you evaluate how you can best apply the Internet to that step. Your Web site can play a part in most or all of these eight steps:

1. Generate sales leads and customer inquiries.
2. Respond to leads and inquiries by providing information.
3. Receive order information and pass it on to fulfillment and accounting.
4. Provide purchase acknowledgements to customers.
5. Answer questions about orders that were placed.
6. Solve delivery delays and other problems.
7. Issue invoices and process payments.
8. Generate add-on sales and repeat purchases.

First, if you aim to generate sales, design your entire Web site to get your visitor onto your order page. This doesn't mean "be pushy and obnoxious." Being blatant turns off your upscale and young Net customers. Make it easy to find your order page. Put links to it (*understandably-named* links; give your prospects a clue) on all your pages, especially on your home page. Use good design, compelling copy, and effective salesmanship to motivate your customer to *want* to go to your order page.

Remember that on the Net, you cannot *annoy* your customer into buying. You must give them reasons to want to select your site and your order page. It is much easier to leave your Web site than it is to leave a retail store. Your Web advertisement must compete for attention with all the other resources on the Net. Why would anyone stick around to read your advertisement when they can click and leave?

From your customer's point of view, your Web site is a *buying* experience, not a selling experience. Look at your site through your customer's eyes. The strength of the Net is in marketing directly to your customers. To leverage that power, you must understand how your buyers commit. You must understand what stages your customers pass through on their way to making a decision to buy. You must discover the questions your customers ask at each stage. Answer *all* the questions and in the *right order*. Give your customers all the information they need to decide to buy. On the Net, your cost difference between providing one page of information and one hundred is trivial.

Measure the effectiveness of your site not by how cool it looks but by how many sales it generates. Don't get swamped with what David Ogilvy called "artdirectoritis," the disease of letting art and design upstage your product.

Remember that the Web lets you customize what you present to each prospect. You can show different artwork, different copy, and even different products and prices to each person. You might use this flexibility to present your current sales and pricing policies, or you might come up with new ones—possibly even new products. Instead of forcing customers to purchase an entire book, publisher Harcourt Brace and Company's Web site lets online customers purchase a complete book or just the chapters they need.

Ideas for Web sales: A quick tour

The giant trade show Comdex has used the Internet to accept online registrations at **www.comdex.com** since August 1994. The initial design of its Web site generated 500 to 750 registrations per week, which worked out to a two percent *conversion rate*, the percentage of registrants generated from each week's 25,000 to 37,000 visitors. Comdex registrants fill out an online form that is split into sequential pages, so you must complete each page correctly before you can get to the next page. Based on the initial response, the Comdex Webmaster discovered that Web visitors wanted to spend less time on an individual page and were impatient with Comdex's sales copy, preferring just hard facts. He redesigned the site to comply with this customer feedback. For Spring '95 Comdex, registrations jumped to 7,000 per week. The conversion rate surged as well, to a hefty 10 percent.

If you want your company brand to succeed, your Web site must reflect your distinct image. Image means *personality*. David Ogilvy pointed out that over time, brands with the most sharply defined personality are the most *profitable*. Every element in your Web site should be thought of as a contribution to your brand image. An example is the Ragu site, where everything exhudes the spirit of a zesty Italian mother, starting with its URL: **www.eat.com**. Graphics, typefaces, and copy all reinforce the feeling of a warm, caring, and fun-loving mamma who makes sure you eat well and don't catch cold. When you design your site, pay as much attention to detail as Ragu's crew does. Look at the hyperlinks. Instead of a boring link "To order T-shirt click here", Ragu gives you "Mamma Mia! That's a dandy shirt!" Even the copyright notice shows personality. The standard legal disclaimer is prefaced with "Mama's niece Ana, the lawyer, wrote this next part."

Saucony athletic shoes (**www.saucony.com**) made a less successful attempt to convey personality. Marathon runner George LeCours "hosts" this site. There are pictures of him throughout, and the copy is written as though LeCours wrote it. But the execution is somewhat hokey, keeping the site from reaching its full potential. Saucony makes good use of interactivity with an automatic product selector, in which the visitor specifies running shoe criteria and the Web site makes recommendations of the type of product best for that visitor. It also features an interactive dealer locator map. Click on the state you live in and a list of dealer locations pops up.

When building interactivity into your Web site, you need to make sure that the interactivity reinforces your selling proposition instead of distracting from it. Books That Work (**www.btw.com**) has interactive pages that nudge a prospect closer to buying. One is a paint calculator. Type in the sizes of a room's walls, and the Web server tells you how many gallons of paint you need to cover the walls. This directly demonstrates the usefulness of the products sold by Books That Work, multimedia that shows you how to do home and garden projects.

You can find other ways to put interactivity to work at your Web site by studying nonbusiness sites as well. For a quick lesson in interactivity (and a good idea generator), check out the National Budget Simulation at **http://garnet.berkeley.edu:3333/budget/budget.html**. It's a game in which you try to balance the federal budget by cutting spending in different categories and by eliminating tax loopholes. A simpler site tracks Fidelity Magellan's mutual fund performance at **http://edgar.stern.nyu.edu/fund_copy.html**.

Applying these kinds of interactivity in your own Web store can increase the effectiveness of your sales process. Interactivity can continue to build customer loyalty after the sale, when you use the Web for customer service and support. The next two chapters give you ways to do that.

More info

But first, here are two good sources of more Web store ideas and how to implement them—one's a Web site and the other's a book:

Hal Stiles' Point of Sale Page is a very good collection of links to information for people selling on the Web: **www.beachnet.com/~hstiles/post2.html**

Creating the Virtual Store, by Magdalena Yesil, (1997), Wiley, 364 pages. ISBN 0-471-16494-1. A thoughtful, clear, and thorough strategy guide to the business aspects of starting and running a store on the Web.

A $12 million per month online store

Digital Equipment Corporation uses the Internet more than most companies, especially for customer service and sales. Digital's online sales operation, Electronic Connection, sells more than $12 million online each month.

Before Electronic Connection, Digital did not provide a price list because its prices changed often. A printed list would quickly become out of date. On the Internet, Digital's prices are always up to date, and they are automatically calculated individually for each customer, including confidential special prices for top customers. Before Electronic Connection, customers had to call sales reps, answer questions, and then wait for the reps to go through many complicated steps to calculate prices. Now customers have all the information they need to make a purchasing decision. When Digital first introduced the service in a Telnet version in January 1994, it caused an immediate sales increase of $1 million per month.

To use Digital's Internet ordering service, customers enter a customer ID number. They fill in a form that considers the status of the company placing the order, the order's size, and special discounts to create a price quote good for sixty days. Customers can confirm an order based on a quote or create a new order from scratch. For each order placed, the customer receives online acknowledgment and a projected delivery date. Human assistance can be provided from Digital if an order grows complicated or if a customer has questions, but customers complete and send most orders entirely online. Instead of going to a sales rep, Internet-generated orders go directly to Digital's manufacturing departments, triggering an immediate build order. Customers can track the status of their orders on the Net whenever they wish. Deliveries are faster and more predictable. And since sales reps don't waste time on small, everyday orders, they can focus on building customer relationships, winning new customers, and planning complex sales—all situations where face-to-face salesmanship is still essential.

"It's a traditional catalog, only online," explained Steve Painter, Digital's electronic commerce marketing manager. "We will download as much information as we can to help them get through the purchasing process. A customer can even call up an existing price quote, change it, and use it to make an order. Resellers can place stocking orders, like 1,200 PCs, delivering 100 a month for one year. We try very, very hard to make it as easy and as fast for people to use as we can." The key to generating repeat business, said Painter, is to make your Web order pages as fast as you can. "Time seems to be the best measurement for people trying to do business online. Use only the graphics you need. Some sites get carried away with pictures, which make it take longer to place an order. Those art files go against you."

Digital's Web site practices what Painter preaches. Most pages at **www.digital.com** display flashy art, but to accelerate order-taking, Electronic Connection's pages at **www.digital.com/info/misc/electronic-connection.txt.html** have almost no art.

To move its high volume of transactions quickly, Electronic Connection runs on a 4-node VAX cluster with smaller machines hanging off as gateways, all outside a firewall and separated from Digital's internal network. Its Internet connection is carried on three T1 lines. Six hundred phone lines handle modem, fax, and voice calls. Additional leased lines directly connect Digital with its largest customers. Electronic Connection's staff of thirty includes 10 technical people.

The Internet brings customers from other countries, who also have different expectations. "Somebody has come in from just about every place in the world and opened an account," says Electronic Connection manager Ethel Hughey. Customers from overseas "are more formal. They usually always identify themselves and try to explain a problem in depth: 'I did this and this and this, and this happened.' Customers from the U.S., on the other hand, assume that I know them and say, 'I can't find this server. What's wrong?'"

"Price Lookups is the busiest module," Hughey says, because so many Internet prospects do price checks. "Order Status is used even more than the order process itself. They just keep checking on how their order is doing until it's delivered."

Digital also uses the Internet to reduce customer support costs. On its newsgroups, Digital's customers solve the problems of other customers. Sixteen of Digital's newsgroups have been ranked among the top 10 percent in readership of all 16,000 newsgroups. Its best-read group, **news:comp.sys.dec**, has 95,000 readers. The company is expanding its Net activities both to increase sales and to reduce costs. It implemented Activity-Based Cost Management (ABC), for "tracking expenses and tying them to tasks with the idea of driving costs down," explains Painter. It looks at, for example, "the cost of keying orders into a system, not the number of orders, not the number of line items. We home in on high-volume transactions and high-cost transactions."

For Digital, Internet sales grow weekly. More and more customers prefer ordering online, even though the company offers no incentive to do so. "No extra discounts, coffee cups, pens, or bonus premiums," says Painter.

For companies starting out on the Net, Painter recommends that you "start small. Start simple. Take your easiest product first, and your easiest customer set. Make that work extremely well. Then expand. That really works for us. It's a lot like any other business I've ever been in. The same things still apply. If you don't know who your customers are, you're not going to get much attention."

CHAPTER **19**

Customer Service

"On the Internet, the killer application is customer service."
—Eric Schmidt, President, Novell

One of the classic Internet success stories generated unexpected results. Some Federal Express marketing people thought it might be good to take something Fed Ex already used for customer service—its database of package-tracking information—and add an inexpensive Web face.

The marketing people wanted Web site visitors to look up shipments. Customers would see Fed Ex's step-by-step chronological record showing where each package went during every minute of its journey, detailing every truck, plane, and building the package passed through. The marketing people wanted to show this detailed record to differentiate Fed Ex from its competitors, who would be unable to produce such a step-by-step history.

The Web project cost $50,000 to build and another $50,000 to attract traffic. Then the marketing people turned their attention to other projects. They were surprised at a later meeting when an operations manager said, "That Web look-up is the best marketing project you have ever done."

According to someone who attended the meeting, the marketing manager looked at the operations manager and said, "It was." The operations manager revealed that the Web site saved Fed Ex $1.3 million per quarter in operating costs! How? When a customer didn't use the Web site, he or she would call Fed Ex's 800 phone number. That call is free for the customer, but Fed Ex pays for it. Adding equipment costs, salaries of customer service reps, and other expenses, the average cost for Fed Ex to answer a tracking call is $2.94. The company's profit margin per package is only $1.60, so each phone call causes a loss. But the cost of each Web page look-up is only *two cents*. The Web page reduced phone calls to the extent that Fed Ex actually needed fewer employees to answer phone calls and less office space to house them.

Besides reducing costs, the Web site succeeded as a marketing effort. Customers love it. Web site look-ups have grown to 35,000 per day. Fed Ex electronic commerce marketing manager Robert Hamilton said the Net is "one of the best customer relationship tools ever invented." (Don't overlook the fact that most Fed Ex customers are *businesses*, not consumers. This is a business-to-business success story.)

How does this apply to your own business? You're probably not in the shipping industry, but you have something in common with Fed Ex: customers. And many kinds of businesses (not all, as gurus proclaim) can use the Internet to cut customer service costs and at the same time increase customer satisfaction.

Author Theodore Levitt summed up business success with two thoughts. First, the purpose of any business is to create and keep a customer. Second, to do that, you must do those things that will make people want to buy from you.

The Internet can be one of the things that makes people want to buy from you. In the previous chapters of this book, I concentrated on new customers. In this chapter, I'll answer the question, "Now that I've got a customer, what can I do with him or her?"

In this chapter and the next, I talk about using the Net to improve sales order fulfillment, including post-sale service, like the Fed Ex story above. I cover how you can listen to your customers and learn from them, and ways you can provide personalized customer service. I talk about cheap, new ways to weld customers to your company, so they return to buy from you again.

What's that? You say that everything between your business and your customers is peachy keen? You don't need to improve? Good—that's the best time to upgrade. As John F. Kennedy said, "The time to repair the roof is when the sun is shining."

Use the Net to improve fulfillment

What is sales order fulfillment? It's what happens *after* a sale is made, but *before* the sale is completed from your customer's point of view. Fulfillment includes receiving order information and passing it to shipping and accounting, packing and shipping merchandise, answering questions about orders that have been placed, solving delivery problems and other problems, issuing bills, and processing payments. Order status is an extremely important part of fulfillment and an area where many businesses can use the Internet.

The Fed Ex story is about order status: Customers ask about orders they made that may not have been delivered. In the last chapter, Digital Equipment Corporation said order status was the most-used part of the company's Internet store. If you have a database of customer orders, link it to the Web. Database hook-ups are more expensive than a standard Web site, but order status lookups on the Web have been extremely successful for many companies.

Note that you do not have to wait for your customer to ask about an order. You can be proactive. If you have a customer's email address, you can arrange for your shipping system to automatically notify your customer when an order is shipped. The system can trigger an email message to your customer saying, "We shipped your order of 12 zygotes today. It went out via UPS and you should receive it by 3/3/98. If you do not receive it by then, please email me at george@service.yourco.com, or call me at 800-555-1212." Your email message should be from a person, and not from some bureaucratic "order department."

When a customer uses your Web site to look up data about an order, you know that he or she is interested in its ongoing status. When someone makes an inquiry on your Web site and the order is not yet shipped, your Web site can ask for your customer's email address, promising to send an email notification the same day that the order ships. If you send a partial order, you can send multiple notifications. It costs you nothing more to send extra email messages, especially those composed and sent by an automated system.

How to handle customer email

Welcome email. When your customer sends email to you, he or she saves you money and time. Email is cheaper than paying for phone calls, and because email takes less time per response, one rep can answer more emails per day than phone calls per day.

Quick response is the most important thing. Don't get elaborate. A brief reply that is quick reaps more rewards than a learned essay that takes time. Just use the email "Reply" feature to interject short responses in your customer's original message. If you get a puzzle that you can't solve, don't wait to reply. Send a quick acknowledgment saying you received the message, you can't answer it immediately, and you'll get back with an answer as soon as you can. This saves you from phone calls from angry customers asking, "Well? Didn't you get my email?"

Use form email letters. You will receive many email letters asking variations on common questions. Email makes it easy for you to answer these with friendly form letters. Form letters let you provide a swift response with facts that have been pre-checked for accuracy and text that has been proofread. Any good email software package will let you include a text file in the body of your message. For each of your common questions, create a standard reply and store it as a text file. You can personalize each form letter with a custom opening paragraph, quoting an excerpt from your customer's email message to show that your service rep read it. Form letters can be a big help with the international customers you get from the Net. You can translate form letters into the languages your customers use, so any of your people with minimal language abilities can reply.

Build a "greatest hits" collection. When people deal with customers, what eats up time is looking up information to answer questions. With email, you can build a library of questions and answers. Your customer service supervisor should receive copies of all inquiries emailed from customers and all answers emailed to them. This archive can be turned into text files of questions and answers. You can use these questions to build a FAQ for your customers. You can also use them to write standard boilerplate text to include in email replies to customers. Some businesses use the answers to build a printed reference manual for customer reps. Others use the questions and answers to create employee training materials.

Have a firefighting plan. I discussed this way back in Chapter 9, the one on email. You might return to the firefighting section there and apply it to your fulfillment staff.

Provide extra information. Remember, people on the Internet are knowledge junkies. They love information, the more detailed the better. One busy order desk manager told me that her secret is to *always* give a customer more facts than the customer asked for. Sometimes this is extra detail about the customer's order. Sometimes it is news. Sometimes facts about other products. The manager's primary goal is not sales, but to provide more information than the customer requested, thereby exceeding customer expectations. Customers respond with gratitude.

Planning and improving

Exceeding customer expectations is one goal of a successful fulfillment operation. Another is reducing unpleasant surprises to customers. To achieve these goals, you need to learn what your customers expect, to manage customer expectations, and to plan an operation to beat them.

A word of reassurance: Planning your Internet fulfillment and customer service is the same as planning any other fulfillment or service operation. The same business truths still apply. You will have problems, so allow "schedule pad" time to solve them. And don't announce an Internet-delivered customer service until *after* you have it up and tested.

A quick pointer: No matter how small your business is, have more than one printer linked to the computer you use for order processing. When you take orders from the Internet, if your printer stops, your cash flow stops with it.

One improvement to fulfillment that the Net makes easy is delivering post-sale information to your customer. If you have your customer's email address, it is inexpensive and easy to build a customized message addressing a customer's specific needs and to deliver the information via email. Your post-sales information might even be a product, delivered online. Conlin-Faber Travel sells travel on the Net, as do many other firms. What separates Conlin-Farber from the pack is that it adds value by using the Net to sell customized travel books. A customer fills out a Web form telling where he or she will visit and what topics interest them. Conlin-Faber assembles up-to-date facts covering just the destinations and interest of that one customer.

To know how your fulfillment meets customer expectations, you must measure your operations. You can apply your measurements to the yardstick of customer expectations—you must ask them to find out, there is no other way—and to industry benchmarks that tell you how well your competitors are doing. The next logical step is finding what kind of things you should measure.

Measure email messages. How many do you average per customer? Does one of your reps generate a higher average of complaints per sale? (Measuring complaints per rep is not always reliable. Other things being equal, your rep who handles the most sales *should* generate the most complaints.) How many email messages are processed per worker each day? Track your total customer email messages received per day; a sharp jump in this number is a flag, either indicating trouble or a marketing opportunity such as a hot new product. Track which employee responded to each customer message. Save each customer message and your response, filed by customer name.

To compare your business with other companies, look not only at companies in your specific industry, but also at direct marketers. Most Internet marketing is direct marketing, so benchmarks for direct marketers tell you *what kinds* of things you should measure in your business, and *what results* you should meet or exceed.

5 steps to customer service and support

The Internet gives you more feedback from your customers and delivers your communications to them. It lets you personalize information to meet an individual customer's needs. It speeds communication and gives your customers access to more people within your company.

All these attributes make the Internet—primarily email and the Web—valuable tools for inexpensively improving customer service and support. But the tools by themselves leave questions unanswered. What constitutes good Internet customer service? How can your business apply the Net to strengthen customer support?

I've identified five steps that companies use in providing Internet-based customer service and support. Not all companies apply all five steps. Many skip blissfully ahead and only implement Step 4, abandoning all others. But a company that implements all five steps builds a much stronger and more flexible customer service operation, one that delivers greater value to customers and yields more consistent results.

Step 1. Use the Net to let customers reach you more easily

Open the floodgates. You'll find out what your customers like, what they don't like, and what they need. On the Internet, your customers will tell you how to sell to them. If you don't think that's an advantage, you shouldn't be in business.

You'll have an easier time if you plan for an infrastructure to handle Internet customer communications. Who in your business will be responsible for answering customer email? Who will be the backup people? Which people will handle what kind of problem escalation?

From your customers' point of view, part of your communications structure will come from the *email addresses* you create. Customers expect to see some standard email addresses at every company: **info@yourco.com** for overall inquiries, **webmaster@yourco.com** for Web site questions, and so forth. For a list of these, see the sidebar "Addresses Your Business Needs" in Chapter 9.

An advantage of using a function-based address like **sales@yourco.com** as opposed to the name of a person in your sales department such as **j.caesar@sales.yourco.com** is that you can reconfigure your email software to send all correspondence for **sales** to one person or to make **sales** mail accessible to several people in your sales department. Additionally, it avoids vacation pileups.

If your business sells to *technical people*, watch out for a cultural bias of many programmers and technicians. They distrust (and often *loathe*) sales and marketing communications. You can avoid antagonizing these customers by using **service@yourco.com** or **support@yourco.com** instead of **marketing@yourco.com**. Don't create a marketing subdomain that stigmatizes your people, such as **s.holmes@marketing.yourco.com**; instead, try **s.holmes@service.yourco.com** or **s.holmes@support.yourco.com**. One company I know successfully uses the subdomain "help," as in **s.holmes@help.yourco.com** and the email address **help@yourco.com** for customer questions. Another alternative is **helpdesk@yourco.com**.

Tell your customers how to complain about problems, and explain your complaint resolution process. Even when you use the standard email addresses described above, your customers won't know how you want them to complain unless you tell them. This information should be on your Web site. If you print warranties or customer service instructions, include complaint resolution instructions. You might also include instructions for customers to submit suggestions to an email address such as **ideas@yourco.com**.

Remember that email and the Web are not the only communication options you can provide for your customers. You can use email discussion groups. Pegasus Software enrolls its customers in an email discussion group. Any customer anywhere in the world can ask a question on any aspect of Pegasus email software, and it will usually get answers from other Pegasus customers. This reduces the amount of support Pegasus must provide and creates a feeling of involvement among its customers that bonds them closely to its products. You can create your own Usenet newsgroups and use them for customer support. This is especially valuable for software firms and other high-tech companies. Digital Equipment Corporation and Silicon Graphics Inc. both report that their newsgroups save them support time (like Pegasus's email group, newsgroup customers help other customers) and provide insights into customer behavior that are valuable for marketing use.

The Internet is good for customer feedback, but not for solving your customers' most urgent problems. When your customer needs information right now, nothing replaces phone support. The Internet is not appropriate in situations requiring two-way problem diagnosis; it is not your best choice for situations when customer urgency is high. Use the Internet to reduce your customer service calls, but don't plan for it to replace them.

You can also use the Internet to conduct live two-way voice conversations, the equivalent of phone calls: "Click and speak to an attendant." You can build these Internet phone calls into your Web site as a way of providing live customer support. The first company to do this was Spanlink Communications (**www.spanlink.com**), maker of WebCall. You can visit its Web site, hear a demo, and talk with a live Spanlink representative. To provide live Internet phone customer support from your Web site, you must either place people on duty 24 hours to handle your calls, or assign someone to answer your Web site during designated hours and prominently plaster those hours all over your site. Using WebCall, your rep can see what displays on your site visitor's screen.

NetSpeak (**www.netspeak.com**) offers an array of different services for Internet telephone customer service. NetSpeak channels Internet calls into your regular phone lines, so Web site visitors calls can be managed by the same equipment and software that runs your existing call center.

AT&T offers its own version, Project iA, which uses regular telephone calls instead of Internet telephony. For a demo, go to its Web page at **www.att.com/easycommerce/projectia**. Type in your phone number on the page and your phone will ring within seconds. A live AT&T rep will answer your questions about Project iA. If your business provided this service, the calls would connect your representative with a visitor to your Web site while he or she was still online. Your rep could talk to the visitor and deliver new Web pages to him or her. Project iA costs $300 per month for your first 50 connected calls. Additional connections cost $2 each.

Some Internet phone software provides audio conferencing, so you can talk with many customers at once, and let customers talk with each other—kinda like a customer support party at your Web site. (Sounds fun. Where's my toga?)

You can also use live chat to provide customer support. America Online does an excellent job using online chat for support. During business hours, you can visit several support chat areas on AOL. Some provide support on specific topics. Some discuss any topic. Each "chat room" is hosted by an AOL support technician and contains several guests asking questions. You type your question and receive a live response from the technician, sometimes with helpful comments from the other attendees. You can choose from several brands of chat software if you want to add online support chat to your Web site.

Use the Net to provide as many alternatives as you can for your customers to reach you. Then tell your customers how to use those alternatives. The Internet is an ideal way to help customers navigate your internal organization and find people they need to reach. Let people know how and why they should reach your business, and who they should reach for different purposes.

The flip side of this coin is that you can let your customers tell *you* how to reach *them*. Silicon Graphics customer service Internet site includes updatable customer profiles. Customers can view the data Silicon Graphics stores about them and change it to keep Silicon Graphics up to date about their computers, people, email addresses, and other contact information.

With Internet customer service, it's important for you to set your customers' expectations at realistic levels. The Net will not solve every customer's woes, but it may prove helpful to some people in certain situations. Clearly define the situations in which your Internet support can help. Let customers know how you will use any data you ask for (not for resale). Tell them how you will answer questions and *how often* you will answer them. Customers get mad when they expect an answer in 15 minutes and you check for questions only once a day.

The slogan "Underpromise and overdeliver" applies to your Internet communications. Only promise response levels and results that you can exceed.

Step 2. Answer all complaints; acknowledge all compliments

This is basic, but you must make it explicit with all your staff. Every single customer email message must get answered. If you have a medium-to-large company, this can easily run into hundreds of messages per day. Fed Ex service reps, for example, answer about 700 email messages per day. Computer gaming company Catapult receives between 600 and 1,000 email messages on most days.

Even if your company only receives 30 messages a day from customers, you need to establish a standard way to respond to them. Assign ownership to one person with final responsibility for responding to customer inquiries. Set up procedures to ensure consistent, intelligent responses. Make sure no email is left unanswered.

Step 3. Track customer history

To leverage your support and service efforts, you must have a database of customer history. This database can be on 3×5 cards, a Macintosh, or a mainframe—it doesn't matter which. What matters is that it is continually updated and that it contains the type of information you need.

The next chapter goes into detail on this subject. The important point is to *have* your customer history database, to keep it continually *up to date*, and to be able to reach the information contained in it at *any time you want*. You can put your database to work on both of the following steps and on many other marketing and R&D activities.

Step 4. Add value with the Internet

The first step on this list asked you to create pathways for your customers to talk to you. With this step, it is your turn to talk back to them.

Once again, the Web hogs the spotlight in most magazine articles. The Web is effective, but it is not the only dish to serve your Internet guests. The Net gives you a smorgasbord. You can serve a variety of information and services so your guests can pick and choose.

One of the least expensive and most effective ways to provide service and support information is an email announcement list. With one email server, you can run several lists that send different information to different subscribers. For instance, keep your crude oil buyers on a separate announcement list from people who buy your dinosaur hand puppets. You can create distinct lists based on what languages customers speak, English, Swahili, or Teenage.

Besides costing less, an email announcement list offers another advantage over a Web site. The Web is not proactive; when you put news on your Web site, nobody will ever see it unless they hunt for it. Also, you have no control over timing on the Web. On the other hand, email announcements reach your customers when *you* want the information known. You have total control over when you send an email announcement.

One key to an email announcement list is to *ask* people to subscribe—don't add anyone to a list who hasn't specifically asked to join it. And provide information that your customers really want to hear, not press releases. Some companies' support lists are hugely popular. Microsoft's Windows 95 email announcement list has 750,000 subscribers.

As a step up from emailed announcements, you can use your same email list server to send longer information in the form of email newsletters. I vouch from experience that customers view email newsletters as extraordinarily effective improvements in customer support. Favorite sections include Q&A columns, customer profiles (not "I like your product because it's good" fluff, but lengthy, detailed pieces explaining real-life problems and their solutions), current support issues, and brief new product and service announcements.

Instead of sending one email newsletter to all the customers on your list, you can send each subscriber a custom-built, personalized newsletter. To do this, you'll need software that uses information in your customer history profiles to assemble each customer's newsletter from text files. Each file will contain data on one of your products, or news for customers of a particular type or from a specific location. With a targeted newsletter like this, each customer gets only what he or she can use. As an example, Catalina Marketing Corporation makes newsletters for pharmacists to distribute to their customers. Each customer receives a newsletter with contents based on his or her individual prescription purchases.

Telnet is another facet of the Net that some companies use for customer support. Several computer software companies and networking equipment suppliers use Telnet to log onto customers' computers and diagnose problems and performance issues. Using Telnet means that support technicians don't need to travel. Instead, they spot problems online and tell customers how to fix them. Customers prefer this approach because it's much faster than traditional support and costs less.

Of course, you can use the Web for service and support as well. Your Web pages for service and support will provide categories of information that are different from those you provide on sales-related Web pages. You can mix the two on one Web site, but keep their differences in mind. The key to sales is *persuasion*, encouraging a prospect to buy your offering; in contrast, the key to support is to *add value*. The person who wants customer support doesn't need to hear how great your product or service is. He or she already has it. Instead, this person needs to know how to *use* your product or service, how to *fix* it, or how to *find* some specific details.

To your customers, one of the most valuable services you can provide is to give them data that you already have, stuck inside your computer. You may think the systems that handle your sales order entry, inventory, invoicing, and accounts receivable are boring and not strategically important, but they become important when you use them to touch your customers. The success of Federal Express is only one of many such stories from the Internet. You can be a success story, too. Put a Web face on your support systems, and you give your customers up-to-the-minute information that is accurate and easy to reach. Your customers will perceive you as providing a much higher level of customer service.

Depending on your business, you might also give your customers a searchable "knowledge base" of maintenance and troubleshooting procedures. You can build this from the records of questions your support people answer, both on the Net and in the real world. Store them in a database with an Internet search engine and you're set. Microsoft's support knowledge base server contains 50,000 entries and answers more than 100,000 support requests every day.

Your Web site can also deliver support FAQs, service notes, online instruction manuals, and parts catalogs. Self-paced online training courses have been successful for several companies. Some companies like Motorola Semiconductor (**www.mot-sps.com/sps/General**) and Marshall Industries (**www. marshall.com**) put comprehensive information online about nearly all of their products. (If your customers are technical people, you might find usable ideas from the sites voted best engineering Web sites by the readers of *EE Times*: **http://techweb.cmp.com/eet/docs/f95/surf5.html**.)

Use your site to reduce customer support phone calls. If your Web site *generates* telephone questions from customers, you lose the cost savings.

To answer support questions, your customers might prefer Web pages with less flash than your sales pages. Intel's Web content design manager Tracey Erway reports that when Intel surveyed its clients about what they wanted, Intel was surprised by the results. Says Erway, "Customers told us, 'We'd like your site to be boring.' They wanted less than 40K per page, no colored backgrounds, and limited use of imagemaps." Intel customers wanted more information and many ways to reach it.

Some companies now make software specifically for Web sites that handle customer service and support. Vantive Corp. (**www.vantive.com**) and BateTech Software (**www.batetech.com**) have produced Web software for customer support services that track what individual customers request and use. Vantive's $25,000 VanWeb lets customers go to a Web page to fill out information requests, make suggestions, and report problems. It tracks the history of each individual request through to final resolution and builds a history database that customers and service reps can search for problem solutions. BateTech's Customer One costs $2,000, tracks individual requests, and provides ways for your staff and customers to look up information.

As you can see, the Internet gives you many choices of ways to add value for your customers: email, discussion groups, newsgroups, announcement lists, newsletters, Telnet, and the Web. When you've decided what types of Internet support you will provide, help your clients self-select what they need from your Net resources. Clearly define the purposes of each resource you provide, and back everything up by providing live contacts. When all else fails, your customers will want to communicate with your company's real human beings.

Step 5. Measure satisfaction and find areas to improve

Department store magnate John Wanamaker said, "When a customer enters my store, forget me. He is king."

Wanamaker had an advantage over Internet merchants. He could *see* his customers enter his store. He could walk up and talk to his clients. He could watch them buy. On the Internet, you can do that only by remote control. The bad news about the Internet is that in spite of all its interactive powers, you'll find it easy to drift out of touch with your customers and their needs unless your business makes a deliberate effort to keep in touch. You must measure your customers' satisfaction levels and find areas in which you can improve.

Don't design your Internet support projects in top-down style, presenting everything to your customers as a finished package, all tied up with a bow on top. Your customers should have a voice in your environment. Ask your customers how they want you to provide support and follow their lead.

Get candid and rapid feedback. Email is ideal for customer satisfaction surveys. When you gather information, one caveat: Don't upset your customers' sense of privacy. Your customer does not need to be a recluse in Montana to feel that privacy has been invaded. Ask for email addresses. Don't send unsolicited surveys. Be sensitive to which customers are offended by what sorts of information gathering. If a customer seems even slightly reluctant to give you certain data, back off. No one wants the Spanish Inquisition.

If you're careful, privacy invasion won't be a problem. You'll probably find customers eager to help you with their observations, which can be a big help in refining your own ideas to keep your Net support on target.

How do you measure the satisfaction of Web customers? Funny you should ask. That's the subject of the next chapter.

Targets for your Internet sales operation: Benchmarks, standards, and best practices

by William J. Spaide
Spaide, Kuipers & Company

Your operating and service requirements as an Internet marketer are quite similar to those of other direct marketers.

To better evaluate your own operating performance and to understand what separates industry leaders from also-rans, take notice of direct marketing operating benchmarks and best practices. These standards tell you what activities and costs are important for you to measure in your own business, and give you targets to meet or beat.

To this end, the following three tables present operating practices, cost standards and services standards that we have developed during our project work for more than 600 direct marketers over the last thirty years. The standards in these tables are best practices for a medium-sized direct marketing company (between $25 and $50 million).

Table A: Service Levels

Telephone Service

Activity	Standard
% Blocked Percentage of calls in which the caller receives a busy signal	0%
% Abandoned Percentage of accepted calls during which the caller disconnects before talking to a live operator	2-3%
Service Level Percentage of calls answered within a predetermined amount of time	80% in 20 seconds

Order Turnaround
In-house

Activity	Standard
The number of working days to process an order for in-stock merchandise from order receipt to shipment	2 days

Total (including delivery)

The number of working days to process an order for in-stock merchandise from order receipt to delivery to customer	7 days

% of Customer Inquiries to Orders
Number of customer inquiries, excluding returns, as a percentage of orders shipped

• Toll-free customer service phone number	25-30%
• Toll-paid customer service phone number	15-20%

Return Rate
Percentage of returns to total shipments

Staples/Gifts	5%
Fashion	17-24%
Business-to-Business	3%

Inventory Management (Initial Fill Ratio)
Percentage of in-stock items at time of original order

Staples/Gifts	90-95%
Fashion	75-80%
Business-to-Business	95-98%

Error Rate (Picking)

Percentage of picking errors to items picked	Less than 1%

Table B: Operating Costs

Activity	Standard
Average Wage Rate	
Average pay scale for production personnel within the various departments of the fulfillment operation	$6.50–$7.00
Cost per Order	
Direct Labor	
Direct labor costs per order, excluding fringe benefits and fulfillment management, for the following areas:	
Order Processing	
Mail and telephone order receipt, order processing, and customer service	$1.05
Distribution	
Receiving, quality control, storage and replenishment, picking, packing, shipping, and returns processing	<u>$0.90</u>
Total Direct Labor	
The sum of order processing and distribution labor costs	$1.95
Benefits	
Employee fringe benefits	$0.50
Shipping	
Costs associated with outbound shipments to customers, where this cost has *not* been offset by shipping and handling revenue	$2.50
Information Systems	
Total information systems costs shown as a cost per order	$0.80
Telephone	
Communications costs (including 800 numbers) per order	$0.60
Banking	
Credit card discount expenses, bank fees, bad debt, and customer adjustments	$0.75

(continued)

Table B: Operating Costs (*continued*)

Activity	Standard
Supplies and Other Variable Costs	
Packing supplies, printed forms, etc.	$0.83
Fixed Costs	
Fulfillment management costs, occupancy depreciation, equipment, service, and related overhead expenses	<u>$0.86</u>
Total Operating Costs	
The sum of all of the above costs	$8.79
% of Net Sales	
Total operating costs shown as a percentage of net sales	15%

Table C: Operating Practices

Part-time Workers (at peak):
50% of production workers during peak processing are part-time.

Toll-free Telephone Service: Provided for the following:
• Order-taking
• Customer service/support

Work Measurement:
The company has a formal work measurement system in place.

Bar-coding/Scanning:
The company uses bar-coding technology in its distribution function.

Materials Handling Automation:
The company has an extensive automated materials handling system.

Inbound Freight Consolidation:
The company has a program to consolidate shipments from its vendors.

(continued)

Table C: Operating Practices (*continued*)

Expedited Delivery:
The company provides next day and/or second day delivery
service to customers.

Labor Scheduling Process:
The company employs a system to project workload and
staffing needs on a daily basis.

---

*William J. Spaide is a partner in the firm of Spaide, Kuipers &
Company, which provides operations management and information
technology solutions to direct marketing companies. He can be reached
at **spaide@aol.com**.*

Increase Sales with Direct Web Marketing

"Simply looking at the number of hits that you get from each referring site is better than nothing, but incomplete—it's like your sales rep telling you she made 200 sales calls that day. Who cares? How many sales did she close?"

—Steve Podradchik, Marketwave

A wild-eyed cop bursts through the Emergency Room door and yells, "Hey, quick! There's a guy shot out here and he's dyin'!"

You are the doctor. What do you do?

Unless you want to kill the guy, your first step is to *examine your patient*. Is he breathing? Will convulsions block his throat? Is his blood loss life-threatening? Are his unconsciousness or convulsions caused by drugs? Until you know what's already in his bloodstream, you won't prescribe drugs.

As you work to save him, you'll monitor his respiration, pulse, blood pressure, temperature, and EEG changes so you know if your treatment helps or goes wrong.

Your patient is your Web site, and before you perform surgery on it, you'd better check its vital signs.

Who wants better Web results?

Everybody wants to improve their Web site. If your Web site hemorrhages money, you want to stop the bleeding and turn a profit. If your Web site makes money, you want to increase your profits, by cutting costs or increasing sales or both.

Don't stop there. You can also use your Web site as a test lab for your off-Web marketing. Controlled tests with Web site visitors can tell you what the best names are for your products, which prices are most profitable, and which offer pulls best. If you use it, your Web site gives you two marketing powers: the power to predict, and the power to improve.

When you combine the proven abilities of direct marketing with these Web-driven powers, the blend you create packs more punch than either of the two alone. I call the result direct Web marketing, the application of direct marketing techniques to Web technology.

In his classic book *Successful Direct Marketing Methods*, Bob Stone notes that a direct marketing piece "has three distinguishing marks: 1) a definite offer, 2) all the information necessary to make a decision, 3) a response device."

Any good marketing site provides all three of Stone's qualifiers. Great ones add one more: measurability. That's the first thing you need to do, because direct Web marketing is a three-step process: 1) measure, 2) predict, and 3) improve.

If responses can't be measured, if costs and income can't be calculated, it's not direct Web marketing. This holds true whether your Web site makes sales by itself or generates sales leads to be closed by sales reps. You must still measure Web-generated responses to know whether your site makes money or loses it.

If you run a Web site, even a simple home page, *you need numbers from it.* There are no ifs, ands, or buts here. If you don't track your traffic and measure your response, you might as well design your Web site by playing "Pin the Tail on the Donkey."

With the right numbers, your Web site can tell you how well it's working and point out directions to improve itself. Even if you have a zero budget and no technical know-how, you can use free products and services to generate valuable information.

Where do I get this valuable data?

The data you need for direct Web marketing will be assembled from multiple sources. Which sources depend on whether you run your Web site on your own computer or you rent space on a Web host's computer.

If you run your site on your own computer, gather data from:

1. **Traffic analysis software** works with your Web server software. Your Web server already logs your visitor traffic. Traffic analysis software works with these logs, and in some cases adds extra tracking capabilities that logs alone can't deliver. Free analysis programs exist for most servers, but don't give you as much insight as the software programs you pay for.

2. **Traffic analysis services** can be divided into two types. Some provide simple analysis. Others provide Web auditing. You only need the first kind if you do not have traffic analysis software. You only need a Web auditing service if you sell advertising on your site.

3. **Other systems** provide the business data that move you beyond mere traffic analysis. You'll need sales figures, costs of your Web site, costs of order fulfillment, and product costs. You'll probably need to get these from marketing and accounting systems. If you can't get them electronically, get them on paper. If you can't gather all the data I suggest, get as much as you can. A little data gives you more insight than no data at all.

If your site is located on a Web host's computer, gather data from:

1. **Your Web host** should provide traffic reports for your site. This service is worth paying extra for, if you get decent reports. You'll know what I mean by "decent" by the time you finish this chapter. If not, ask your host to let you run your own traffic analysis program.

2. **Traffic analysis services** fill two needs. First, if your provider won't give you any traffic analysis reports, some services provide simple reports. Second, if you sell significant levels of advertising on your site, you may need a Web auditing service to verify your traffic levels for advertisers. Most hosted Web sites don't need third party auditing.

3. **Other systems** are the same as "Other systems" described previously.

At the end of this chapter, I provide a list of available services and software programs. But before you dig into the details about those, you need to know what the good ones can do for you.

Who visits my Web site?

When the Web was new, everybody talked about how many *hits* or *accesses* busy Web sites received. Companies bragged about receiving 10,000 hits per week, or 50,000 accesses per month, or even a million hits per month. People batted those numbers around as if hits equalled newspaper readers or television viewers. Reality slowly settled in. We sobered up. Hits are misleading.

Let's say you have a home page with three graphics files on it. That's a total of four files, so if Jean Valjean visits it one time, that's four hits. On the same visit, Jean goes to another page with three more graphics generating four more hits, for a total of eight hits so far. Whoops! A glitch in the network. Jean presses the "Reload" button on that second page—four more hits. That totals 12 hits for one person visiting two pages. Error messages also generate hits, including "Error 404 - File Not Found" and the ever-popular "Access Denied." See how dramatically "hits" differ from "visitors".

A hit is generated by every request made to your Web server. It has no predictable relation to visitors or pages.

Instead, some people count *page requests*, the number of HTML pages visitors ask to receive from your Web server, not counting graphics. These are also called *page hits* or *page accesses.* Note that a request does not mean the page successfully displayed on your visitor's computer screen, which is called a *page transfer* (also called a *page download*). Even if you count only page accesses, Jean Valjean made three page accesses for one person visiting once. And his scenario was oversimplified. Page accesses by themselves aren't enough.

Fortunately, the cavalry is riding to the rescue. Before I bring in the guys on the white horses, though, we need to learn a little bit about Web site software and stretch your vocabulary.

What you can learn about visitors

If you have a site on the Web, you either are running your own Web server computer or are renting server space on a Web site host's computer someplace. In either case, your server generates *log files* that report on your visitor traffic. If your Web pages are on a host's computer, that host should give you traffic reports at least monthly. Most good ones report weekly. Some Web site hosts will let you FTP your log files to your own computer, where you can run reports from them. If you have your own Web server, your technical people can generate reports based on your logs.

All logs are not created equal. You have one of several log formats: common log format, extended common log format, combined log format, Open Market Inc.'s OMI extended log file format, or Microsoft's IIS log format. (You don't have to remember these, but the names may come in handy later.) The log format your server software uses determines what information appears in your traffic reports.

Web traffic reporting: The basics

Every time a visitor requests a file from your Web server (remember, a file can be a page, a graphic, an error message, or anything else your Web server provides), your software adds a line to your log files.

YOUR ACCESS LOG

The basic building block of Web traffic analysis is your access log. In the simplest log format it captures data like this:

```
hostname  identd  authuser  [date]  "request"  status  length
```

Hostname is the host computer that asked for this file. A host computer is not the same as the individual visitor's desktop computer; usually, a host is the big computer that connects several smaller computers to the Net. When a host computer asks your Web server for a file, the host can tell your Web server the host's name, but it doesn't have to. If the host doesn't provide the hostname, your log file records the host's *IP address*, a string of numbers and dots that gives the host's location on the Net.

Identd provides the visitor's identity, but only if the visitor's computer is set up to provide it and if your Web server asks for it. This is called *remote user identification*. It slows down your Web server horribly, so few Web sites use it.

Authuser gives the name a user provides to enter your site if your site requires a password to enter.

Date is the date and time of the request, in brackets.

Request tells what your visitor asks for, in quotation marks. It consists of an action in all caps followed by a file name and the version of HTTP used. The action is usually either GET, when your visitor asks for a Web page, or POST, when your visitor asks for a CGI script.

Status is not whether you drive a Rolls Royce, but what your Web server did in response to the visitor's request.

Length tells how many bytes of data your Web server sent in response to this request. If none were transferred, a dash prints instead of a number.

Here are four examples in the common log format:

```
mis.fedex.com - -        [10/Jun/1997:20:06:22 -0800]
  "POST /cgi-bin/stscript.pl HTTP/1.1" 200 9872
127.0.0.1 - -            [10/Jun/1997:20:06:37 -0800]
  "GET /index.htm HTTP/1.1" 304 -
greenjungle.com peter -  [10/Jun/1997:20:06:52 -0800]
  "GET /oops.htm HTTP/1.1" 404 -
usf.edu unknown -        [10/Jun/1997:20:07:19 -0800]
  "GET /oops.htm HTTP/1.1" 404 -
```

The first example shows a request from a host in the MIS department of FedEx (mis.fedex.com). Since your Web site does not use remote user identification and does not ask for a password, you have no names for either identd or authuser. Instead, you see two dashes. Next you see the date and time in brackets. Then, in quotes, **POST** (a request for a CGI script) followed by **cgi-bin** (the directory in your computer where the requested file lives) and **stscript.pl** (the name of the file). The status number **200** shows the file transferred successfully, and the final number **9872** tells you that the file was 9,872 bytes long. (If you know that your file **stscript.pl** is really 10,282 bytes long, the discrepancy in length warns you of a problem. This is called *abandonment*, when a visitor asks for a file from your Web site, but the complete file doesn't transfer to your visitor's browser. This often occurs when your visitor punches the "Stop" button to interrupt the transfer. Some people call this an **abort**. Note that your file can also fail to transfer because of a different reason, such as a software or network error.)

In the second example, you can't tell the requesting host's name. Instead, the log entry begins with the IP address **127.0.0.1**. The request in quotes tells you that the visitor asked your Web server to **GET** your Web page **index.htm**, but under status you see **304**, and the following dash indicates no bytes were sent. What goes on here? 304 stands for "Not Modified," which tells you that your visitor only wanted to see if your page had changed since his or her previous visit. It was the same, so nothing further happened. This warns you about *page caching*, which I discuss later.

The third example shows what happens when you turn on remote user identification. The second item is **peter**, the visitor's name. He requested your Web page **oops.htm**, and received an error 404, because you don't have a Web page with that file name.

The fourth example shows what you see if you turn on remote user identification and your visitor doesn't support it. Instead of a user name, you see the word **unknown**. This person also looked for **oops.htm**.

Based on this data from your access log, your most basic Web traffic reports should include:

- Daily traffic volume

- Hourly traffic volume (Most Web sites are busiest during office hours, but you never know; *Chemical Abstracts'* Web site gets so many visitors from Europe it is busiest at 4 a.m. EST.)

- Percentage of activity by top-level domain (Besides **.com**, **.edu**, and **.gov**, remember country codes like **.uk** and **.fr**. That's how *Chemical Abstracts* knows the early visitors are from Europe.)

- Percentage of activity by domain (Domains include company names such as **.citibank**, universities such as **.ucsf**, government agencies, and Internet access providers.)

- Your most-requested and least-requested files (Lets you know what areas of your site to expand. Warns you of problems. A file with zero requests may warn of a broken link.)

- Number of error messages and failed requests (Lets you know which files transferred successfully and which did not. Files with a low success rate have problems.)

All these numbers are useful, but an access log cannot track individual *visitors*. As the examples show, you can tell you have a visitor from a particular place, but you cannot tell *who* that visitor is. If your log had five lines of requests from mis.fedex.com, you don't know if your site had five FedEx visitors or one visitor five times. The same would be true of your visitor from usf.edu, or from 127.0.0.1, wherever that might be.

By itself, your access log cannot answer key questions, such as: How many separate *people* visited your site? How much time does an average visitor spend?

This basic access log information is worthwhile by itself. It gives you useful facts about each file request made on your site. But it grows more valuable when you combine its data with other key information.

YOUR REFERER LOG

After your common log (or its equivalent), the second-most important log report comes from your referer log. It produces data that looks like this:

```
http://search.yahoo.com/bin/search?p=investment+adviser -> /index.htm
```

This looks like gibberish, but it is actually extremely valuable. It tells you *where* your visitors come from and *why* people come to your site.

The example tells you this visitor came to you from Yahoo. It lists which page of Yahoo sent your visitor and, even better, gives you the actual *search terms* your visitor entered in Yahoo's search engine! In this case, the search terms are **investment** and **adviser**. The last item on the line tells you which page on your site the visitor requested.

Note that when a visitor comes to you by *typing* your URL instead of clicking on a link, your referer log is blank.

User agent log

Another log reports information in this format:

```
Browser name/version no. (platform; processor; other data) proxy data or other
```

This tells you what kind of browser people use to reach your site, and what computer operating system they use:

```
Mozilla/2.0 (Win 16;I)
```

Sometimes additional information is included. This example tells you that your visitor came via an AOL proxy server based on free CERN software:

```
Mozilla/2.0 (Compatible; AOL-IWENG 3.0; Win16)
   via proxy gateway CERN-HTTPD/3.0 libwww/2.17
```

The user agent log information can be useful if you want to present different Web pages to different browser users, such as frames only for visitors whose Web browsers can see them.

Apply the basics

You can apply these basic building blocks to give you two kinds of analysis: site performance and marketing effectiveness.

Reports based on these logs provide comparative indications about what parts of your site are most-used. You can use that insight to tweak your site. If a page with a new product draws low traffic, you need to do something to make the *links* to it more appealing. If no one goes from your product page to your order form, you need to change the product page itself.

Compare how many times a page was transferred versus how many times a graphic that appeared only on that page was transferred. The difference shows you how many visitors read your page but turned off your graphic. Most sites find that 20 to 30 percent of visitors turn off graphics. (Even on my own Web site, which has only a few small graphics files, 20 percent of my visitors never see them.) If your smaller graphics files transfer at a high rate, but large ones get abandoned, that's a clue. Your customers are voting with their "Stop" buttons that your larger graphics are too big.

You can use logs to measure responses to your advertisements. Create copies of your home page with slightly-different URLs. (This is the Web's version of the way advertisers use different 800 numbers to measure the responses of different advertisements.) If your home page is **www.yourco.com**, for instance, create **www.yourco.com/home1**, **www.yourco.com/home2**, **www.yourco.com/home3**, etc. For each one of your advertisements, banners, or press releases, use a different URL. You can count page transfers for each page's HTML file and get an idea of your advertisement's effectiveness. You don't need to change the rest of your site; when a visitor clicks on a link from your cloned home pages, the link will work the same as ever.

This gives you a start. But for stronger results, you need better information. At least get reports on unique visitors. Better yet, report on Web-generated sales. Insight Enterprises (**www.insight.com**) reports more than 56,000 page requests per day and more than $2 million in Web-generated sales. Which number do you think is more important to Insight's managers?

Beyond logs: A real live example

The best way to understand what more you can do is to see an example in action. Let's take a look at a real Web store that provides its actual traffic analysis reports—including actual sales figures—on the Web where you can study them.

The merchant is Movie Madness Merchandise, selling movie collectables at **www.moviemadness.com**. It is one of several Web businesses operated by a company called Netstores NW Inc. Fire up your Web browser and visit.

You'll find a large catalog of merchandise with secure online ordering. After you take a few minutes to familiarize yourself with the Movie Madness online store, go to **www.viaweb.com/vw/tesdriv.html**. (I'll wait right here.)

Click on the link for tracking tools. Movie Madness lets its online landlord Viaweb use the Movie Madness reports to demo Viaweb's traffic analysis capabilities.

From the menu of online reports, click on References. Note that you can sort the resulting report by number of visits, by quantity of orders, or (my favorite) by amount of income generated. For each referring URL, you can see the number of visits, a tiny graph showing visits over time, the number of orders (click on the number to go to the orders themselves), the total dollars of income generated from the referring URL, average income per visit, a link to the referring page itself, and a link called [details].

If you scroll to the bottom of the page, you will see that you can receive reports for different time spans: last 10 days, last 120 days, etc. Select the last 10 days and see what happens.

Find a referring URL that generated more than 10 sales, such as **www.yahoo.com**. Then click on the link [details] to the right of that line.

You now see what search terms people entered at that site to find Movie Madness. In addition to the name of the site and products like "movie memorabilia," you'll find search terms such as "star trek merchandise" and "fraiser." The search terms are all links; click on one to see the same page of search results a visitor saw before finding Movie Madness. If the Movie Madness marketers do the same, they can see how high Move Madness ranked in search engine results and review links compared to its competitors. Note that the report provides links to pages that generated sales as well as pages that didn't.

As a marketer, would you be able to apply similar information to increase sales at your site? Of course you would. This report shows that dozens of Movie Madness visitors find the site by entering "star trek merchandise." Do you think Movie Madness would attract more visitors by using that phrase in its page text and Meta tags? If you had a list of keywords and key phrases like this for your own site, you could use it to raise your site higher in search engine results. But there's more—we've only looked at one report.

Go back to the menu of reports and click on Click Trails. *Clicktrails* are the sequence of URLs chosen by a visitor as he or she moves through your site. On the Movie Madness clicktrails page, select a day and you can review all of the trails for that day, only trails of visitors who pressed the "Order" button, or just the trails of customers who bought something. A condensed version of one trail:

From	Altavista search for "Men In Black"
Jul 03 05:37:00	Men In Black
Jul 03 05:38:12	Movie Madness Merchandise Info Page
Jul 03:05:39:06	Men In Black Jay and Kay T-Shirt
Jul 03 05:39:52	Men In Black Jay and Kay T-Shirt into shopping basket
From	https://www1.viaweb.com/cgi-bin/wg-order?basket=37a7adfaeb51&unique=6826f4

Jul 03 05:43:23	<u>Men In Black Such A Human T-Shirt</u>
Jul 03 05:43:45	<u>Men In Black Such A Human T-Shirt</u> into shopping basket
Jul 03 05:48:38	Place order <u>moviemadness-2767</u>

This visitor (referred from the Alta Vista search engine) spent less than 12 minutes on the Movie Madness site and ordered two items. The times show you how long the visitor spent on individual pages. The odd long URL was created by the site's electronic shopping cart.

After you review a few clicktrails, go back to the report menu page. This time, select <u>Graphs</u>. You'll see a time graph. Scroll down to the bottom of the page. Notice how you can view graphs showing average number of pages viewed per customer, average number of orders per page view, average number of orders per customer, average *income* per page view, income per customer, and income per order. This kind of marketing analysis is only possible if you can track individual customers as they go through your site.

You can go back to the report menu page again and review <u>Hits</u> and <u>Reports</u>. The Viaweb reports give good examples of the kinds of information traffic analysis reports can provide. Some software provides more information than Viaweb's. Most software produces less, and most Web site managers never find out this much about their sites. How does Viaweb do it?

Beyond logs: CGI

It's a sad fact of life that your Web server can't keep track of who asks for what. It doesn't know if your files were downloaded by George Jetson or the pope. When visitors ask it for pages, it sends them out willy-nilly, never caring if twelve requests came from one person or not. Your server sees twelve requests and looks for an address twelve times before sending out your files. It never remembers, and so it never connects any request with any other request.

Using only your regular server software and HTML Web pages, you can't tell which of your files are sent more than once to the same person. But you can do all that and more if you add software programs—written in any of several computer programming languages—that follow a protocol called *CGI*, the Common Gateway Interface.

When your Web server uses a CGI program, it can track your customer's path as your customer moves through your site. You can tell where a visitor like

Jean Valjean went, how long he spent there, what buttons he pushed, and at what exit Jean left. *This is crucial information if you sell on the Net. Without it, you cannot build a running total of sales as a customer purchases your products. And you cannot link a customer's purchases with that customer's payment.* You also open the doors to a whole new world of measuring visitor activity.

You can track a unique visitor over one visit to your site, or across multiple visits if you store visitor history. To do this, you need some way to identify each visitor and keep track of him or her over the length of a session, and to separate his or her requests and responses from everyone else using your Web site at the time. You have two ways to do this: tokens and cookies.

A *token* is a code added to a page's URL which links that page to an individual visitor. It's like giving each presentation of your page its own serial number. If you just want to offer an electric shopping cart, tokens require your server to create custom Web pages on the fly for each visitor who browses your catalog and order pages. If you want to monitor sessions and visitors over your entire Web site, *all* of your pages need to be custom-created on demand.

That's a lot of work. Tokens add extra processing to your server, and extra work for your programmers and site administrators. Instead, you can have a cookie.

Have a cookie—it's good for you

We're not talking Nabisco here, we're talking Netscape. This cookie is a software cookie. They may not replace chocolate chips in your heart, but software cookies cause fewer cavities and leave fewer crumbs.

Cookies are featured in most Web browsers. Netscape Navigator and Microsoft's Internet Explorer both handle cookies. So does WebTV. Cookies provide distinction between different vistors without forcing the visitors to register or identify themselves in any way. In fact, cookies are completely invisible to Web visitors.

Netscape invented cookies. Its Web site describes a cookie as "a small piece of information which a Web server (via a CGI script) can store with a Web browser and later read back from that browser. This is useful for having the browser remember some specific information across several pages. For example, when you browse through a virtual shopping mall and add items to your shopping cart as you browse, a list of the items you've picked up is kept in your browser's cookie file so that you can pay for all your items at once when you've finished shopping."

What can you do with cookies on your Web site?

- Analyze traffic: Do you have 50 visitors, or one bozo hitting Reload 50 times?

- Store data temporarily between documents (shopping cart).

- Store data between frames and reloads.

- Award frequent visitor bonuses.

- Restrict downloads.

- Customize Web pages on a per-user basis.

- Help people navigate by showing them where they have been.

- Show returning visitors what you've added to your site since their last visit.

- Automate registration information and free your visitor from retyping a user ID.

- Change banner advertisements each time a visitor sees a page.

Your site can set up to 20 cookies in a visitor's browser. Most sites use at least two: one cookie to permanently identify the visitor, and a second to temporarily track the visitor's behavior during one visit.

Cookies do have some limitations. Most browsers support cookies, but not all of them. New browsers let visitors turn off cookies, so you can't count on using cookies for absolutely every visitor. Different brands of browsers store cookies in differently-named files, so cookies are lost when a person switches browsers. Multiple people using the same computer can use each others' cookies. Some proxy servers block cookies. When a person's cookie file fills up, the least recently-used cookie is dumped.

Another problem with cookies isn't technical, it's emotional. Some people fear cookies as a privacy invasion. This is exaggerated by reporters, who write about privacy but don't understand the Web. As a merchant, all you know about a cookie-using visitor is what he or she does on your own site. Fortunately, most people ignore the media sensationalism and use cookies.

David Carlick of Poppe Tyson Advertising observed, "The more a site knows about you, the happier you're going to be. If I go to a hotel, walk in the front door, and they say, 'Mr. Carlick, glad to have you back. I know you like a nonsmoking room with a window and we have a bottle of red wine waiting for you.' Is that invasion of privacy or is that service?"

There are security risks with cookies. They are unencrypted text. Never use them for passwords, credit card numbers, or other sensitive data. There is also a slight danger that cookies can be spoofed. This requires someone to know the names you have given your cookies, and setting up a server with a fake URL that mimics your own. If your competitor can lure your visitors to a counterfeit Web site, the competitor can read your cookies and change them. If this worries you, you can prevent it by first setting your server to always read the domain attribute of a cookie and ignore any domain that is not your own, and by adding a second cookie containing a checksum to insure your first cookie has not been changed.

Cookies are great. If you keep an eye on their limitations, cookies provide you with the easiest and least expensive way to track your customers and understand them.

For more on cookies, I recommend the excellent list of resources on Andy's cookie pages at **www.illuminatus.com/cookie**. For Andy's list of which Web servers support cookies, plus patches for server software bugs, read **www.illuminatus.com/cookie_pages/servers.html**.

Problems with Web traffic analysis

Let's look at some nuisances you'll want to avoid when measuring Web visits and tracking Web visitors. Most of these are technical advances whose repercussions decrease the accuracy of your reports.

Caching confusion. This happens when your Web page and its graphics are copied and stored on another computer. This is done by America Online, Prodigy, Microsoft Network, and some large corporations and universities because caching uses their computers more efficiently and because it gives their people much faster response times. If your Web site is popular enough to warrant caching, your visitor tracking can be off by hundreds or even thousands of visitors. If America Online copies your site once and that copy is accessed by five hundred AOL subscribers, your reports will show one visitor.

You have a couple of solutions. Microsoft Network will give you its hit counts for your site, but only if you lease a site on its network. Instead, you could make every page a dynamically generated page, as are pages that use tokens. You could update your pages constantly. Or you could set a Meta Pragma tag in your HTML code so that your page expires quickly, forcing the caches to reload. (Unfortunately, most servers that cache ignore this tag.) Caching is a problem mostly for Web sites with a high traffic volume, so you may not need to worry about caches at all.

Firewall blackouts. Your traffic reports may show many visits from what looks like one visitor from a large corporation or university. That visitor may actually be all your visitors from several locations of that institution, hidden behind a firewall. Most firewalls just give you the firewall address, and no specifics on your visitors. Cookies get around most firewalls. URL tokens get around all of them.

Geographic distortion. All traffic analysis reports that give you ZIP codes and cities for your visitors rely on matching visitor domains with a database of addresses for the organizations that have domain names. These usually give you a service provider's location or a corporate headquarters location, not the actual address of your visitor. If your reports show all visitors from **ibm.com** as coming from Armonk, New York, you know that's wrong. IBMers are all over the world, but your database can't figure out a way to report that.

Attack of the giant log files. Logs get huge. Microsoft generates 200 megabytes of log files every day! Yours won't be that big, but expect to buy big disks if you want to hold a couple of weeks of logs. Figure that one hit generates 100 bytes in common log format and 400 bytes in extended log format, plus supporting data. You're looking at about one megabyte of disk space for each 1,000 hits you generate.

The page counter fad. You can get free software to put a counter like the one shown in Figure 20.1 on your Web page. Counters show how many times a page has been downloaded. You have four reasons not to use page counters: 1) Counters can be spoofed to give you misleading results. Visit **www. cyberway.com.sg/~wildcat/terror.htm** for a sample. (Be prepared to wait a long time for the page to download.) 2) If your page is under-visited, your counter will make your visitors think you aren't a healthy company. No one likes to shop in an empty store. 3) If your site is busy, a counter tells your competitors, "Hey, this works! Rip off our idea!" 4) Counters make your page look amateurish.

Figure 20.1   *Avoid page counters like this.*

Employee distortion. I know of one company that thought it was doing great with its Web site. It was busy from day one. Then somebody spoiled the party by filtering visitors from the company's own domain name off the reports. The Web site was actually a ghost town. It looked busy because employees used it, but only a handful of prospects had ever visited.

What you measure you can improve

PC Flowers & Gifts president William Tobin says that computer buyers are much more demanding than catalog customers. He says that an unhappy customer can broadcast problems quickly on the Net, smearing your company's reputation overnight. As prevention, Tobin recommends you track *the percentage of your orders with errors*. Because PC Flowers & Gifts (**www.pcflowers.com**) measures its error rate, it was able to lower that rate. PC Flowers's error rate is now two-tenths of 1 percent. Do you know the error rate for your own company?

If you track errors, responses, sales, and profits, you can *improve* them. If you do not measure them, you will not know if attempted improvements help you or hurt. Edwards Deming, the American who turned around Ford and Xerox and whom the Japanese name responsible for their business success, based his entire strategy on the fact that if you don't measure results, you can't know whether you have improved anything or not. *Anything you can measure, you can improve.*

On your Web site, you can measure almost everything. Because changes are so fast and cheap to implement, you can test several alternatives and implement the winning versions right away. This kind of testing is both cheaper and more accurate than traditional market research. Market surveys and focus groups let your customers tell you how they *think* they will respond. Web testing tells you how they *do* respond. The Web is an ideal medium for improving your marketing prowess. It costs little to run a test, you can test under controlled conditions, and you can see results in a few *hours* if your site draws enough traffic. Most other kinds of market testing take weeks or months.

This astonishing speed lets you quickly adjust a test and run it again. Repeated tests and refinements that take months in traditional media can be done on the Web in a couple of days.

When you plan your tests, keep in mind these foundational truths of market testing:

- Test just one thing at a time. More than one muddies the water.

- The marketing for every product or service is built around a core offer. *The most important thing to test is your offer.*

- Make sure your test quantities are big enough to give you valid numbers.

- Test to avoid gray "maybe" answers and to provide "yes or no" answers.

- Don't test trivia. For example, when testing prices, don't test amounts that are almost the same.

The best kind: Split-run testing

Your Web site can do *split-run testing*. Create two separate Web pages, both completely identical except for one difference—perhaps a different promise in its headline or identical copy but different art. Your programmers can write a CGI script that will alternate and give every other visitor one of the two pages.

You can follow clicktrails (and maybe even sales) to measure the subsequent behavior of your visitors and compute how long the average visitor spends on page A and how long on page B (longer time indicates greater interest), where the visitors from A and B go next (a page that makes people leave your site is bad), and, most importantly, how many visitors to each page become buyers and the amount average A and B visitors spend. If enough people visit your site, you can implement a split-run test and have statistically valid results overnight. Then implement your winning page and look for the next thing you want to improve.

Make your first version your *control*, the standard to which you will compare new pages. When a new page tests higher than your control, make the high-scorer your new control. What to test? Copy. Headlines. Offers. Product names. Prices. Art. Premiums. Logo designs.

Sometimes actual profits are the exact opposite of what you'd predict. For instance, I know of one company that added the words "Free Gift" to its control; no other change was made. Rating profitability of its old control at 100, adding the words "Free Gift" dropped profitability to 51!

A more important factor than sales volume or gross profit per sale is to measure *profitability per time period*. Reducing your product price from $39 to $29 may produce a lower gross profit on an individual sale, but the lower price may increase the number of sales you make in a week so your profit per week goes up. Don't get burned trying to squeeze the last drop of blood out of each individual sale at the price of decreasing your total weekly profits. If your Web site attracts enough traffic, it might be feasible for you to measure profit per day or even profit per hour. The Web moves fast enough, and you can make changes quickly and easily enough, so profits per week becomes a valid form of measurement.

Traffic analysis products and services

The first companies to offer Web tracking products and services divided into two camps and attacked each other bitterly. Third-party services disparaged software packages, claiming that self-generated numbers weren't trustworthy unless audited by an independent third party. Software manufacturers derided the lack of Webmaster control over third-party reports, saying Webmasters want to run their own traffic reports.

When the dust settled, they discovered they were both right. There are two very different sets of needs for Web visitor reporting. Some businesses need only one, but many need both. You need a software program to measure and improve your Web site's results. You need an independent third-party service to verify your traffic to advertisers (but only if you sell a significant amount of advertising).

When shopping for a traffic analysis software program, the key question to ask is: "Can this software tell the difference between fifty visitors from microsoft.com and one visitor from microsoft.com hitting Reload fifty times?"

When I researched this software, I found that sales reps *always* said "Yes." To get the truth, you need to ask a tech support person how specifically their software determines unique visitors. To give you accurate reporting on clicktrails and visitor behavior, the software must identify unique visitors by using cookies or tokens, not IP addresses.

Also, ask which log formats a product supports. If your server uses Microsoft's IIS log format and the software reads only the common log format, this combination won't work for you even though your Web server and the software both run on Windows.

Commercial programs

Aria from Andromedia (**www.andromedia.com**) costs provides realtime, on-demand analysis of large Unix and Windows sites. It costs $7,000 to $50,000.

Bolero is a Mac product from Everyware (**www.everyware.com**) that is easy to use and costs $500 to $2,000. Windows and Unix versions will be available Real Soon Now.

Hit List Pro ($1,000) and **Hit List Enterprise** ($3,000) from Marketwave (**www.marketwave.com**) both provide good reporting, including referer log and keyword reports for Windows Web sites.

Insight from Accrue (**www.accrue.com**) actually implements its software at the router level, so it times data flow to the millisecond and can do low-level analyses that would otherwise be impossible. It is difficult to install and maintain. It requires its own Solaris computer, but can monitor Web sites running on any platform. Accrue leases its software for $8,000 to $200,000 per year including support.

Net.Analysis is made by Net.Genesis (**www.netgen.com**). This software package costs $6,500 for Unix and $2,500 for Windows. It provides very good reporting, including cookie-generated clicktrails. I/Pro distributes a product based on Net.Analysis.

SiteTrack from Group Cortex (**www.cortex.net**) uses cookies and tokens to record visitors, not hits. SiteTrack gives you good information on your visitors and what they do. It works with Netscape's Unix and Windows NT servers and costs $3,500. No extra programming is required and you don't need to change a line of your HTML pages. If a visitor's browser supports cookies, SiteTrack uses cookies. If not, it uses tokens. The Group Cortex Web site is an excellent example of fluff copy that takes up space without telling you anything useful, but don't let that blind you to the value of its product.

ThreadTrack from WebThreads (**www.webthreads.com**) uses tokens to report on clicktrails traffic. It does not require you to change Web pages or CGI scripts in any way. The $900 program runs on Unix and Windows. This one makes it easy for you to do split-run tests.

Usage Analyst is available only with Microsoft's Site Server (**www.backoffice .microsoft.com/products/features/UsageAnalyst/SiteServerE.asp**) and is one of the best traffic analysis programs. It tracks vistors' paths through your site, reports on time spent per page, and offers many other features.

Web Trends from e.g. Software (**www.egsoftware.com/webtrend.htm**) provides realtime analysis, but no reporting on clicktrails. It has problems handling log files over 100 megabytes in size. At $300, it's an inexpensive program for Windows.

Not recommended. Avoid paying for SurfReport from Bien Logic or Web Tracker from Cambridge Quality Management. They don't produce enough information to be worth your time.

Free programs

These are not as good as the traffic analysis programs you pay for, but you can't argue with the price.

Hit List Standard from Marketwave (**www.marketwave.com**) is the best free traffic analysis program I've seen for Windows.

Mkstats (**www.mkstats.com**) is a free Perl program written for Windows that provides some reporting (such as referer log reports) that Hit List Standard lacks.

Getstats (**www.eit.com/software/getstats/getstats.html**) is a free program for Unix, VMS, and Mac Web servers that supports common Web log format.

A service

Several services provide third-party traffic reporting, but they are aimed at the needs of advertisers and Web sites that advertise. You'll find them in the next chapter. The following service is not useful for that purpose. It is useful if your Web site is located on a Web host's computer and your host provides no traffic reporting.

Wishing (www.wishing.com) provides Web Audit and Web History services that small businesses can easily use. It reports on page accesses, not visitors. You just paste three lines of HTML code onto your Web page. An almost unnoticeable tiny icon will appear on your page. Web Audit costs $30 per month for a small account. Reports provide only standard information, but Web Audit is easy and inexpensive.

CHAPTER **21**

How to Buy and Sell Banners and Net Ads

"Nothing except the mint can make money without advertising."

—Thomas Macaulay

Cathay Pacific Airways reported that more than half of the registered visitors to its site at **www.cathay-usa.com** were generated by its banners on the InfoSeek site. The banner said "Click Here - Win 1,000,000 Miles." Of all InfoSeek visitors who saw the banner, 3.2 percent clicked on it to visit the Cathay Pacific site. Each day, between 500 and 1,000 visitors signed up to become Cathay Pacific "CyberTravelers." Several thousand of the Web site's visitors subsequently traveled to Asia on Cathay Pacific flights.

The Cathay Pacific story is one of hundreds that shows that businesses can generate Web site traffic and actual sales by paying for online advertisements. Since Tim O'Reilly and Dale Dougherty sold the first Web advertisements back in mid-1993, Internet advertising has mushroomed into a half-billion dollar industry. There is no end in sight.

This chapter assumes you want to do one of two things: buy Internet advertisements or sell them. (Or maybe both.) No part of the Net changes as quickly as its ad game, so I'll give you the basics and point you to places where you can catch the newest tricks of the trade.

Working vocabulary

Before you learn the lay of the land, you've got to know its lingo.

Reach, the quantity of your target market reached.

Frequency, how often you reach them.

Impression, a successful *banner* file transfer, as differentiated from a successful transfer of the page containing a banner. Some people call them **exposures**. It is assumed that if your banner transferred successfully, it was seen by the page visitor. The actual number of times your banner was seen may be higher due to caching.

Clickthrough, a click on a banner that causes a successful transfer of the advertiser's destination page.

Clickthrough rate, calculated by dividing the number of impressions (how many people *saw* a banner) by the number of clickthroughs (how many people actually *clicked* on that banner). Clickthrough rates are given as percentages. A one percent rate is typical. A ten percent clickthrough rate is outstanding.

CPM (cost per thousand), the standard way prices are quoted for online advertising. You can pay CPM prices for impressions or for clickthroughs. It is important to know the difference between impressions and clickthroughs and to be able to convert prices from one to the other. If you pay $20 CPM for impressions and your banner's clickthrough rate is three percent, you pay $600 CPM for clickthroughs (two cents per impression and sixty cents per click).

What can I charge? How much should I pay?

Want to see the most expensive real estate on earth? Go to **www.netscape.com/home/internet-search.html** and keep your eyeballs peeled for a box that says "Excite," so small my hand covers it. To rent that space for one year, Excite paid Netscape $5 million. Did you know pixels were so valuable?

Most businesses don't pay that much for Internet advertising. Digital Equipment Corporation pays $7,500 to $30,000 per month per banner on several Web sites with high traffic volumes. Russ Jones, Digital's Internet project manager, is not concerned with how many thousands of impressions a site offers. "How many times they *see* our traffic bar is irrelevant. What matters is how many times they click on it and go to our Web server. Our experience has been that people click about one percent of the time. So in the case of the Netscape Web server, where we were paying for a million impressions per month, we got about 1 percent—10,000 clicks—from that page to go to our Web site."

Your company may not be as big as Digital, but in general, if you plan to pay for banners and links, you can expect to cough up at least one to two thousand dollars a month. Sometimes, you can find a small, tightly-focused special interest Web site or online publication and pay just a few hundred dollars per month. But in general, buying Web ad space is no place for small fry or the faint of heart.

If you sell Web advertising, how much can you make? A rough rule of thumb is that your annual ad revenue can equal your number of page impressions per week. So if your Web site serves up 10,000 pages per week, you can charge $10,000 per year. You might be able to charge more if your audience is a big-spending, hard-to-reach group of people that exactly matches an advertiser's target market. In the same way, if you buy ads and want to reach an especially desirable group, you may have to pay more.

What you can pay for

If you put on your Advertiser hat, you'll see that Web sites that sell ads are one of two types: content sites, such as Pathfinder or ESPN SportZone, and search engines, like Yahoo. You'll buy advertising differently depending on whether you put your banner on a content site or on a search engine.

Content sites are easier. You'll pay to put your banner on a certain page. Depending on the site, you'll pay rent based on a time span (a week, a month, a year), on *impressions*, or on *clickthroughs*. This last alternative can be your best deal. In the previous Digital Equipment Corp. example, only one out of every hundred people who *saw* Digital's banner actually *clicked* on it. With clickthroughs, you pay only for people who actually visit your site.

Search engine sites offer more options. If you rent space for your banner on a search engine, you have the previous alternatives plus a fistful of extras. If you use search engines yourself, you may have noticed that when you search for a topic, your answer often comes with a banner advertising a product or company that relates to your topic. This is no accident. You can buy a search *category*, so every time someone asks for anything in your category, the answer will have your banner at the top. You can buy a search *word*, such as your company name or your product name or type. (No, you can't ask Vanna to buy a vowel.)

When Cathay Pacific put its banner on InfoSeek, it bought random placements plus the words "airline," "contest," "tour," "vacation," "weather," and "Cathay Pacific." Anyone who searched for any topic containing one of Cathay Pacific's words would see the airline's banner on their search results.

How much banners cost

Banners on Web sites are not cheap. If you want to compare costs with traditional media, you can sort of compare cost per thousand. (I'll come back to that "sort of" in a second.) Let's compare banners with other media. For print ads in business trade publications, CPMs run between $50 and $125. Figure on a $70 to $60 CPM for direct marketing. General interest magazines charge CPMs in the $30 to $60 range. Broadcast TV is a bargain at $5 to $10 CPM. Web content sites charge $10 to $100 (ouch!) for each thousand impressions. Search engines get $10 to $50 per CPM. That breaks down to five cents or less each time the search engine sends out your banner.

That's where CPM comparisons between print and online ads break down. Magazine CPMs are based on numbers of copies instead of impressions. Advertisers assume that every ad in the magazine is seen. On the Web, every ad, in fact, is seen—especially on sites that charge for only fully-delivered banners.

Fully-delivered? Magazine readers don't turn pages with their graphics turned off. All the estimates I've seen say that 20 to 30 percent of Web browser users surf with graphics turned off, or use their stop sign buttons to kill most banners before they ever display on their screens. (I do this myself.) Whether graphics are turned on or off, you can pay by the impression, but many of your banners die before anyone sees them. *This is why you need to negotiate Web advertising contracts to pay per* banner transferred *and not per page transferred or per banner requested.*

Another problem with impressions is that rookie advertisers often confuse impressions with people. Impressions just measure how many times a banner is exposed to a pair of eyeballs, not whether those eyeballs belong to different people. Here is where reach comes into play. A site may deliver 100,000 impressions per month, but if it attracts only 10,000 unique visitors per month, no matter how many banners you buy on that site, you still can only reach 10,000 people. When you plan to buy banners, calculate your CPM per 1,000 people reached when you can.

Larger advertisers often prefer to pay per clickthrough. Per clickthrough charges usually range 25 cents to $3 per click. Advertising sellers don't like being paid per clickthrough, because an the advertiser's banner generates little response if its design is lame. This puts the seller's compensation at the mercy of the buyer's creative skills, which is why sellers resist per clickthrough pricing except from advertisers who buy large amounts.

Clickthroughs beat the heck out of impressions, but they still aren't the best measurement of your banner's response. As the *Mercury News*'s guide to

Web advertising puts it, "If you're on the Web to interact with people, you should evaluate Web sites on their cost per order or cost per lead, not cost per thousand."

Henry Bertolon, president of computer retailer NECX agreed. He pointed out that Yahoo can cost more per impression than other search engines, but prospects from Yahoo are no more likely to purchase than prospects from less-expensive sites. Calculate your cost-per-lead and cost-per-sale when you pay for banners on the Web.

When buying banners, many sites allow you to choose to target your ads and deliver them only to viewers with a specific browser type/version, computer operating system, or domain (such as only harvard.edu). Per impression prices currently run about $10 CPM for untargeted banners, $20 for lightly-targeted.

If you sell advertising space, the more you target, the more you can charge. For instance, CuisineNet charges $30 to $40 CPM. To reach targeted visitors who have filled out a survey, C|Net charges $75 CPM. Sites that deliver customers to local businesses (where a customer will walk in a physical store) can get higher rates, up to $250-$500 CPM.

When buying Web ads, price isn't everything. I know one site that charges a high ad rate and has only 500 visitors total. At first glance, that sounds outrageous. How can anyone charge a lot for such a tiny potential audience? But if I told you the site was **www.advisorworks.com**, a members-only club where 500 top investment advisors (who manage billions in investment funds) exchange professional information and you sell investments, suddenly the price looks cheap. You can't reach these people otherwise. If someone quotes a high CPM or a steep monthly rate to you for advertising on a site, don't be put off. Look closely, because if the visitors are exactly who you need, a high price may be more profitable in the long run.

If you sell advertising on your site, you must be prepared to give a discounted rate to advertising agencies. They don't ask for a lower rate just to haggle. The standard agency discount is how agencies make their money; their clients pay full price, and the difference is the agencies' compensation. The lower rate paid by ad agencies is called the *net rate*, usually 15% off your *gross rate*.

Advertising on Search Engines

Buying banner space on search engines is a buyer's market. The large search sites deliver millions of pages each day, way more ad space than they can sell. Their prices are flexible. Minimum quantity is usually 100,000 impressions. You can buy three types of placement for your banners, with approximate per impression prices shown in Table 21.1. *General rotation* means that the search engine can place your banner on any vacant page it has. *Category rotation* costs more and means that you pick an overall category or categories of search terms; your banner will appear on all pages in those categories. *Search word* is the most expensive. You pick a specific word and your banner appears on the results pages of all searches for that word. The Cathay Pacific Airways' story is an excellent example of this technique, which usually generates a higher clickthrough rate and delivers visitors who are more likely to be receptive to your site.

If you like a last-minute bargain, you can negotiate for *remnant space*. At the end of the month, advertising sales reps feel pressure to make their quotas and are more willing to bargain. Leftover inventory goes cheap at the end of the month, usually half price or less. The more money you have to spend, the more bargaining leverage you have. Procter & Gamble bought a huge amount of remnant space on Yahoo for 5 cents per *clickthrough*. (Yahoo's regular prices work out to about four times as much.)

What results can you expect from advertising on search engines? Here are the numbers from an actual campaign. (Your mileage will vary.) Banner space was

Table 21.1	Per impression rates for advertising on search engines.		
	General rotation (untargeted)	**Category rotation (targeted)**	**Search word (targeted)**
Yahoo	$15-$20 CPM	$20-$50 CPM	$50-$60 CPM
Alta Vista	$25 CPM	$30-$50 CPM	$60 CPM
Excite	$24 CPM	$50 CPM	$65 CPM
Infoseek	$18-$26 CPM	$28-$45 CPM	$50 CPM
Lycos	$20-$30 CPM	$20-$45 CPM	$50 CPM
Hotbot	$20 CPM	n/a	$50 CPM

purchased for this campaign on three search engines: Excite, Lycos, and Yahoo. Using *the same banner art*, the clickthrough rate on the three engines was Excite 2.8 percent, Lycos 9 percent, and Yahoo 9 percent. Another variable is *guaranteed impressions* (the number of impressions you pay for) and *delivered impressions* (the number of impressions the search engines actually deliver). Like getting a baker's dozen when you pay for 12 doughnuts and get 13 for the same price, most sites that sell banner space throw in free impressions with the ones advertisers pay for. (Would-be Web ad sellers, take note.) Search engines have more unsold space and often give advertisers substantially more banner impressions then they pay for. In this campaign, Excite delivered one-and-a-half times as many banner impressions as it guaranteed. Lycos delivered twice as many, while Yahoo delivered an astounding four-and-a-half times as many! The final cost per clickthrough came to 35 cents for each visitor from Excite, 59 cents for each one from Lycos, and 61 cents from Yahoo.

Web page pirates

Somebody can make good money selling ads on your Web site, but it doesn't necessarily have to be you. Web page piracy is becoming common.

Here's the scam. Somebody copies your Web page, makes a minor change or two, puts it on their own site and charges for advertising on it. This happened to pages from my own site. It has happened three times to Mark Welch's excellent Web Banner Advertising page. (And Welch is an attorney! Who'd have enough gall to copy an attorney's page?) He now posts a warning on his page about Web page pirates. Other sites have been pirated as well.

Typically (but not always) Web page pirates are based outside the U.S., often in Israel or Russia. Copied pages are changed minimally; even typos are left intact. Graphics are copied as well as text.

If this happens to you, your best recourse is to find the offender's Web host and its Internet access provider. Threaten both repeatedly with legal action. (Threaten the access provider so it will cut the pirate's access to email.) Formal legal proceedings for copyright violation can take months or even years, so a threat will be more productive than the real thing.

Make your banner effective

The *Mercury News* reports clickthrough rates from 1 to 10 percent for the banners of its online advertisers. Here are a handful of quick tips to help you make sure your banner doesn't end up on the bottom of the response heap.

- First, ask for action: "Click here for easier income taxes" will draw more customers than "income tax services."

- A banner that uses curiosity will pull less visitors than one that promises a benefit.

- What's the single most compelling benefit for a visitor to enter your site? That's what should be on your banner.

- It should sell your *site*, not your company or your product.

- If you add something new to your site, say "new" on your banner.

- Contests and freebies do great on banners.

- Banners have short shelf lives. Several studies show that most of the people who will click on a given banner will do so the first time they see it. Some will click the second time. A small amount of people will click the third time, but after your banner's third exposure to a person, it rarely generates any significant response.

Remember that 20 to 30 percent of Web visitors surf with their graphics turned off. When they visit the page with your banner, Figure 21.1 is what they see on their screens.

To avoid this problem, make sure the page that displays your banner also includes an Alt tag with a text equivalent to the copy on your banner. Then, nongraphic visitors can read your Alt tag and click on it if it interests them.

For more banner design tips, visit Four Corners Effective Banners at **www.whitepalm.com/fourcorners**. This terrific site has sample banners with their actual clickthrough rates, more info on banner design than I've found anyplace else, and links to other sites with even more banner stuff. Check it out.

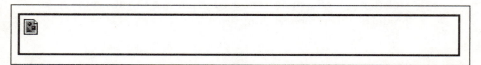

Figure 21.1 What 20 to 30 percent of people see instead of your banner ad.

Finally, your banners are wasted if you do not track your results to learn what flops and what works, as I discussed in the previous chapter.

Banner standards

To make life easier for both advertisers and the people who sell advertising space (should they be called advertisees?), standard sizes for banners have been agreed upon. Banner dimensions are given as being so many pixels wide by so many pixels high. (Photoshop and other graphics programs will tell you a graphics file size in pixels.) Banners are almost always either .gif or .jpg files.

The organization that established standard banner sizes is CASIE (Coalition for Advertising Supported Information and Entertainment, **www. commercepark.com/AAAA/casie/index.html**). CASIE's names and sizes are shown in Table 21.2.

A few holdouts still use nonstandard sizes, such as the Internet Link Exchange. This organization represents more than 100,000 small Web sites and uses 400w × 40h banners with its 40 × 40 logo grafted on the side, totaling 440w × 40h pixels.

To resize your banners to meet standard formats, visit the GIF Wizard Ad-O-Matic at **www.raspberryhill.com/gifwiz/adomatic.html**. This free service demonstrates the GIF Wizard software package.

Selling banner space

From the foregoing, you get the idea that selling banner space on your Web site is more complicated than it seems at first blush. First, you have to find advertisers to buy your space. Then, you must keep track of which banner appears where and when. "Banner A appears during next month, but only on my home page, and banner B paid for 1,500 impressions on my what's new and site map pages, plus 3,000 impressions scattered throughout the rest of

Table 21.2 Standard banner names and sizes from CASIE.

Full banner	468w x 60h	Button No. 1	120w x 90h
Full banner w/ vertical navigation bar	392w x 72h	Button No. 2	120w x 60h
Half banner	234w x 60h	Micro button	88w x 31h
Vertical banner	120w x 240h	Square button	125w x 125h

my site. Where do I put banners C through Z?" Delivery gets more complex when your advertisers want to target specific banners to specific visitors based on their behavior.

To do these things, you need to measure traffic and track visitors, as explained in the previous chapter. Traffic measurement for advertisements has its own unique twists, explained in a standard set of requirements for measuring Web site visitor traffic. It's called the CASIE Guiding Principles of Interactive Media Audience Measurement. You'll find the CASIE principles at **www.commercepark.com/AAAA/casie/gp/exec_summary.html**.

If your site is small and tightly focused, you can handle banner sales yourself. You can find advertisers by seeing who advertises on similar sites and by directly contacting companies that advertise to the type of people who visit your site. You can add your site to online advertising rate registries (you'll find a list of them at **www.markwelch.com/bannerad.htm**), places where advertisers go to find sites that take advertising. SRDS is probably the most important advertising rate registry. If your traffic level is sufficient, you can also find a Web sales representative who will hunt down advertisers for you.

Unless you sell advertising on only a handful of pages, planning which banners display when, where, and to whom quickly grows into a tangle of conflicting priorities. Choose between two ways of solving this problem: use banner management software or join an advertising network (or both).

Banner management software

Banner management software ranges from freebie scripts to the $20,000 AdServer software from NetGravity (**www.netgravity.com**), used by Yahoo, Pathfinder, and C|Net to manage their hundreds of thousands of ad spaces.

For a complete list of banner management software (annotated with interesting observations by Mark Welch), visit the Banner Ad Server Software page at **www.markwelch.com/ad_sw.htm**. Welch's list is extremely complete.

The only one I couldn't find on his page is Ken Jenks's CGI script (well, actually *three* scripts) that uses cookies to determine which GIF image to send to a visitor and to count clickthroughs. It's available at **www.o-a.com/archive/1996/November/0068.html**.

Advertising networks

An advertiser who needs thousands of banner impressions does not want to individually contact hundreds of Web site owners to haggle with each one. That's why banner advertising networks were born.

Each network represents many Web sites. Advertisers can deal with one network, or a few of them, and place advertising on many sites—one-stop shopping. The best networks are audited, so the advertiser feels reassured that results are reported accurately.

Web ad networks offer advantages to Web site owners as well. Networks handle advertising sales, so site owners don't need to hassle with selling. Most networks deliver banner art from their own centralized Web server, so site owners don't worry about juggling banners. Banner networks track delivery and report banner placements and results. They produce reports both for advertisers and site owners on banner results, revenue produced per page, etc. Theoretically, banner networks also handle billing and collections, so site owners get paid more reliably.

You have dozens of banner networks to choose between, from tiny to huge. Softbank Internet Marketing (**www.simweb.com**) only represents sites with 5,000,000 impressions per month or more. WebRep (**wwwebrep.com**) and DoubleClick (**www.doubleclick.com**) sell ads on Web sites that generate 1,000,000 impressions per month minimum.

If your site doesn't carry that much traffic, not to worry. There are banner networks to sell space for every size of Web site and to place banners in almost any language. Some don't pay you for the banners displayed on your site, but instead swap banner displays on your site for banner impressions on someone else's site. One of the largest such banner exchange networks is Link Exchange (**www.linkexchange.com**), which represents more than 100,000 Web sites.

There are drawbacks to banner networks. First, they cause a performance drag on your pages. Each page with a banner must wait to display while your visitor waits for the network's computer to process information from a cookie, and then waits some more for the network's Web server to send the banner art. Your page display times are at the mercy of the banner network's server. If it gets overloaded, your pages don't display at all.

The second problem with banner networks is that a lot of them are run by con artists who won't pay you as agreed and might not pay you at all. If somebody offers you an unbelievably good price for placing banners on your page, don't believe it. It's probably a scam.

For warnings about scams, and the most complete listing of banner networks and ad sales reps, visit Mark Welch's Web Site Banner Advertising page at **www.markwelch.com/bannerad.htm**. Second-best is the Ad Resource Directory at **www.adresource.com/silink2.htm**; in spite of being less complete than Welch's page, less up-to-date, and with all-glowing "reviews" written by the resources themselves, it is still quite useful.

Advertising audit services

The fast growth of paid banner advertisements on Web pages generated demand for a service that is common in the print and broadcast advertising worlds. It's called an *audit bureau*. Large advertisers want an impartial third party to verify your claimed traffic level. An audit bureau acts as an independent source to watch your traffic and report on it, sometimes giving you information you can't supply on your own, such as benchmarks to compare you with other sites.

The Web site owner pays to hire an audit bureau. You only need to hire an independent auditing bureau if you sell substantial amounts of advertising. Banner networks are audited themselves, so if you sell your banners through a network you don't need to hire an auditor as well. The most prominent auditors are:

- **I/Pro** (**www.ipro.com**) is the leading provider of independent auditing services. I/Pro's independent audit service, I/AUDIT, is conducted with Nielsen Marketing, the TV ratings people, and costs several thousand dollars. It is the preferred service for large advertisers.

- **NetCount** (**www.netcount.com**) offers AdCount to track advertising: banner exposures and clicks by hour and day, plus successful clickthroughs.

- Audit Bureau of Circulations at **www.accessabvs.com**

- BPA International at **www.bpai.com**

- Next Century Media (Cybermeasurement Index) can be found at **www. nextcenturymedia.com**.

Discrepancies between site logs and banner audits

When a banner network sells space on your Web site, you get paid based on the network's reports of how many banners were delivered to your site's visitors. Prepare for a shock—your banner network's audit log will claim fewer banners were served than the number of pages served according to your own site log. Discrepancies between HTML pages requested and banners served are often 10 percent to 50 percent. This hits you right in your pocketbook. Let's look at the main causes of this problem and what you can do.

Cause #1: Visitors browse with graphics turned off. I discussed this problem earlier in this chapter. You won't get paid for banners that don't display. Except for using as little graphics as possible on your pages, there is nothing you can do to get visitors to turn graphics on.

Cause #2: Impatient visitors, tired of waiting, kill graphics files in mid-transfer. Bad suggestion: DoubleClick asks you to use only image navigation, therefore "forcing" visitors to use graphics. First, you can't force Internet visitors to do anything. Second, image-only navigation is unreadable by spiders, which means your pages would be inaccessible to visitors from search engines. A better solution is to position banner tags above page content on your page, so the banner loads before your text displays. It also helps if you minimize graphics to reduce waiting time. Banner files should be less than 10,000 bytes in size. The smaller they are, the less time visitors must wait for them to display, and the more often you will get paid for a complete banner transfer.

Cause #3: Visitor's browsers cache banners. Web browser software stores graphics on visitors' computers. When a graphics file with an identical address is used twice, the software reuses the first copy of the file instead of reloading it from your network's server. To prevent caching, some networks (DoubleClick) let you use a slightly different banner URL each time a banner is presented. Others don't provide this service.

Cause #4: Proxy servers and sites cache banners. To improve performance, America Online copies the most-requested Web files and stores them on its computer. When an AOL user visits a popular Web site, AOL's computer retrieves the Web site's files from its computer, which is much faster than getting it from the Internet. Studies show that AOL users represent between four and ten percent of the traffic of many Web sites, and that AOL use is underreported due to caching. AOL isn't the only company that caches popular files. Most large corporations cache too. You can do little about this except to change your pages frequently and use slightly different URLs for banners, as mentioned previously.

Cause #5: Browser bugs do weird things. One version of Microsoft Explorer requested each HTML page twice for no particular reason, but each graphic file only once. Other browser eccentricities abound. You can do nothing about them.

Cause #6: Spiders request Web pages, but not graphics. Bad suggestion: DoubleClick suggests you block spiders! If you do, visitors from search engines won't be able to find your site and your traffic will drop. You *want* search engines to index your pages, so discrepancies caused by spiders are a good problem to have.

Cause #7: The Internet has bottlenecks. Sometimes files get stuck on the Net and aren't delivered. If this happens to your page text, a visitor may press his or her Reload button and try again. Few visitors care enough about a banner to press Reload to see what they are missing. Smaller banner file sizes (less than 10,000 bytes) reduce the odds of this happening.

Finding buyers and sellers

Before you sell Web banner space, I recommend visiting the Web Site Banner Advertising page at **www.markwelch.com/bannerad.htm** to find out about advertising networks, advertising rate registries, and related resources. Pay close attention to the warnings about scams.

Surprisingly, you'll find more resources on the Web for selling Net advertisements than for buying them. If your looking to buy Net advertising and want to avoid getting ripped off, note this important distinction: A media buyer is *not* a sales rep. A true media buyer is independent and works for you, the advertiser, to get the best media buys. On the Net, many companies call themselves "media buyers" and act as if they are media buyers, but they are actually sales reps interested only in selling you the sites they represent. For example, WebConnect (**www.webconnect.net**) poses as a media buyer but really represents its own list of 1,200 Web sites. Real Web media buyers include Alles Media Service (**www.cris.com/~Allmedia**) and Webster Group International (**www.wgi.com**). CMT Group Co-op (**www.cmtgroup.com**) is a Web media buying cooperative, but I'm not sure how effective it is. Ad Resource (**www.adresource.com**) has very good reports on Web and Net media buying.

Banner sellers and buyers both can take advantage of Adbot (**www.adbot.com**), which conducts auctions of unused advertising space.

Buyers and sellers can both profit from perusing directories of sites that sell advertising. Banner buyers can find places to advertise. Banner sellers can list their sites on the directories to bring more advertisers their way. Ad Central (**www.adcentral.com**) has a directory of about 250 Web sites that take ads. The Web Advertising Bureau directory at **www.wab.co.uk/wabdirectory.html** lists more non-U.S. sites, especially in Europe and Asia. Ad Juggler's Database of Available Ad Banner Space at **www.adjuggler.com/resources.shtml** mostly lists U.S. businesses. Vidya's Guide to Advertising on the Internet (**www.vidya.com/add-lib**) has a huge list (a 450 K file) of sites where you can promote your company for free. This goes beyond the usual links for Web pages. Vidya's directory includes places where you can promote products themselves. He also provides a so-so directory of purchasable ad space, where you can find places to buy banners or list your own space for sale.

Useful resources

If you're serious about Web advertising, join the Online-Ads email discussion list at **www.tenagra.com/online-ads**, or at least read through its archive of past messages. This is a wonderful place to keep in touch with new issues in online advertising and to get answers to your questions on the subject. A weekly supplement to the list called Digital Help provides a way for you to get statistics related to online promotion, to have someone review your site, to get opinions about Web advertising, and to post and find related job openings.

Sample banner sales contracts for you to review.

- www.o-a.com/archive/1996/November/0051.html

- www.digits.com/contract.html

- www.tale.com/sponsor/contract.rtf

- www.smartbiz.com/sbs/arts/cwa4.htm

CHAPTER **22**

Publicity Heaven

"It's almost like they built the Internet just for PR people."

—Rochelle Nemrow, Vice President, Press Access, Inc.

If I asked you, "What if you could design the ideal, dream vehicle for your PR?" your answer would be the same, whether your job title is public relations manager, media relations specialist, or publicist. You'd want this ideal PR vehicle to give you new places to reproduce your message. It'd better be fast, so you can create news releases and get them in people's hands in a couple of hours. Global reach would be nice, so you can spread your message worldwide. How 'bout a way to find people you can't find? And to reach people who won't return your phone calls. And a place to hang around with other PR people and swap ideas. And while you're dreaming, make it all cheaper than dirt.

The Internet can do all that and more. At a price, however. For publicists, the Internet creates much, much more work. The Net doesn't eliminate your existing workload. It adds new tasks, and it raises expectations among the people you reach.

Who can you reach on the Internet? Journalists *expect* you to be on the Net. You can reach industry and financial analysts—so your Internet PR directly affects your stock price. You can reach customers, investors, resellers, distributors, joint venture partners, suppliers, and probably a bunch of people I can't think of.

There are so many ways to publicize your business on the Internet, it is truly amazing. On the Net, your problem is not "How can I find one way to get the word out?" but "There are so many ways! Which do I choose first?"

And you have one other problem. It is life or death for you to understand Net culture. Every good marcom person knows that to win a customer, you can't expect the customer to learn your language. You must speak the customer's language. In the same way, you must learn the language and customs of the Internet. Since the Internet is interactive, if you push people's buttons on the Net, they push back—only harder. You won't make too many sales that way. Go out on the Net, and study it for a couple of weeks before you send out your first piece of electronic publicity.

What PR people do on the Net

"So I can use email to send press releases to everybody on the planet and post them to all of the newsgroups, right?" Not exactly. In fact, not at all. Most places on the Net consider press releases to be advertisements, and many newsgroups forbid any type of advertising or anything even close to it. Don't think you can send press releases to the general public on the Internet. Internet people view unasked-for press releases as intrusions and react with hostility. There are exceptions explained in Chapter 13, but expect to use the Internet to send press releases mostly to media contacts and to other people who ask for your releases.

So what do PR people do on the Internet? Mainly, four things: 1) Gather information. PR people are stereotyped as disseminators, but finding data is a big part of their job. 2) Spread information. 3) Communicate with press people (from both traditional media and new electronic ones). 4) Communicate with prospects and customers.

According to a 1997 survey of PR pros by Press Access, Inc. (**www. pressaccess.com**), 95 percent of press relations people surveyed have a Net connection, 65 percent of them provide PR information on their Web site, and 62 percent send news releases via email.

Press Access reported that the most common uses of the Net for publicity are (in order of greatest use) to email press releases and story pitches to editors; for research; to post PR info on the company's Web site; to monitor competitors; to track press coverage through online clipping services; to find editorial contacts and story opportunities; to read online publications, newsgroups, and email discussion groups; to disseminate news; to send files, software, and graphics; to monitor wire services; to monitor the stock market; and to create PR-oriented links to other Web sites.

For PR, you will use more than the Web. You'll also use email (especially email lists), newsgroups, FTP for sending pictures and graphics, and Internet Relay Chat (IRC) for typed press conferences and interviews. IRC is also a handy, free substitute for conference calls with people in other countries. Afterwards, you can print a record of your conference.

No matter how much you integrate the Internet with your publicity activities, it won't do everything. Somebody still has to take the editors to lunch.

Gathering information

The entire next chapter covers gathering information from the Net, including electronic clipping services and monitoring your competition. But people in public relations do specialized kinds of information collecting.

For instance, before you write a news release you can dig up background information to tie your release into a bigger picture. You might use Gopher to find data from university and government databases or FTP for info from archived documents. When you put your company information in context, the result is more and longer stories from your releases.

Most trade publications have Web sites, especially the ones covering the high-tech industry. They can be handy. Many include editorial calendars of topics for future stories, giving you advance notice of possibilities to plug your firm. (Unfortunately, Web-posted editorial calendars are not always kept up to date.) Some publications' Web sites include their mastheads, where you can find names and often email addresses of editors and reporters. You can page through archives of past articles to find a writer who covers your specific product area and would therefore be a likely prospect for your story pitches. Most industry and financial analysis companies have Web sites where you can find similar contact data, as do other organizations.

On the Net, you also have something else to find information from and about: ezines. Ezines are electronic periodicals that have no printed counterparts. You can use them as sources of information and you can place stories in them. Dominis.Com **www.dominis.com/Zines** lists both ezines and Web sites for printed magazines. Writers Write (**www.writerswrite.com**) has submission guidelines for more than 250 ezines looking for articles.

Press Access (**www.pressaccess.com**) lists ezines that cover business and high tech. This Web site also provides information about print publications. Press Access provides services for press relations pros, and its site provides links to high-tech publication Web sites, directions on how to get to publications' offices from the nearest airports (a clever idea), and every Monday, news of personnel and organizational changes in trade pubs.

Another service to help you gather information about publications is Technology News Tips at **www.gina.com**. It tells you which writers are looking for sources or information on technology topics, an ideal way to get coverage if your company markets high tech products.

Distributing your news on the Net

One of the most frustrating parts of the job is when you spend a lot of time creating a stupendous story idea just to pitch it to one of the media gatekeepers and get turned down. That's when angry PR people say, "Oh! If only I were the publisher!"

Well, guess what? You can be. As Tim O'Reilly, president of book publisher O'Reilly & Associates said, "On the Internet, *everyone* is a publisher."

You can publish your own PR newsletter if you want (see Chapter 13 to find out how), but your bread-and-butter publishing will still be sending out press releases. The nice thing about the Net is that if no print publication accepts your release, you can still give it exposure online.

The easiest way to send press releases electronically is to build a list of email addresses. You probably already have a contact database on Rolodex cards or stored in a database program. Start with that, add email addresses for each name, and build on it.

Important first step

This chapter assumes that you already add signature files on the bottom of your email messages. If you don't yet have a signature file, or you are not sure what one is, turn now to the section on sig files in Chapter 9. People who receive your news releases will not know how to reach you for more information unless you have a sig file.

Build your contact database

About half of all editors prefer receiving news releases by email, but some want snail mail, while others prefer fax. Not all editors want email. The way to generate the most coverage from your list is to survey the people on it and ask their preference. Some may ask for delivery by more than one method.

You'll have to indicate the preferred delivery method for each name on your list. As long as you are adding that data, you can add (or make space for) another item: alternate email address. Many editors have two or three email addresses. A person might have a public email address (the one given on magazine mastheads and at the ends of stories), a private email address (at work, but rarely given out), and a personal email address at home. Make space on your list to add all three for each name, just in case.

The Internet has created information overload, so your job is not to create *more* stuff, but more smartly-focused stuff. You won't want to send every release to every person on your list. Focus your efforts by finding out what subjects interest each name on your list, and target your news releases by interest. Grabbing all the email addresses you can and sending your release to them indiscriminately is spamming and will generate hate email instead of favorable coverage.

Where can you find appropriate email addresses? Often from the mastheads of publications themselves. Many list email addresses for editors and reporters. For links to the Web sites of 3,000 U.S. and Canadian magazines, visit **www.owt.com/dircon/mediajum.htm**. The best Web site to visit to get world-wide media email addresses is Email: Media **www.ping.at/gugerell/media**. A good, complete directory of U.K. contacts is the Media U.K. Internet Direc-tory at **www.mediauk.com/directory**. A quick way to get ahead is Paul Krupin's up-to-date and thorough *U.S All Media Email Directory,* which lists the email and postal mail addresses of more than 7,000 editors, writers, and executives with U.S. and Canadian print, radio, television, and syndicated media. You can order this useful directory in Microsoft Word format for $50, get a printed version for $50, or get it on Mac or PC disk as a ready-to-use database for $80 from Direct Contact Publishing at **www.owt.com/dircon**.

You can also ask for media names and addresses on your Web site. More on this in a bit.

Magazines with Web sites often include original material on their Web sites, so in addition to a publication's print editors you can add its Web editors to your list. One warning, though: Don't give a Web editor an advance story to hold unless you know that person really well. My experience is that Web editors don't hold a story; as soon as they get it in their hands, they release it.

Build different kinds of email lists for different purposes. You could have one for media contacts and another for resellers or distributors—whatever catego-ries you send printed releases to. You will also want to email news releases to sales representatives and other people *within* your company. Ask customers and prospects if they would like to receive your news via email. You may be surprised at how many will sign up.

But don't put customers' names on your press release list unless they *ask* to be. Along the same lines, it is a good idea not to offer your list to other businesses to use. Some people get upset when they receive email from an unfamiliar source, much more upset than they would get over receiving postal mail from a company they didn't know.

Once you assemble your email list or lists, it's time to write a news release.

Formatting email releases

Your email news releases will consist of three or four parts: a subject, an optional headline, the main body of your message, and a concluding signature, providing contact information.

Your subject sells your message

Your subject line is the most important part of your release. The subject line is what your addressee sees when he or she receives your incoming email message. *Your addressee will decide whether to open your emailed release or to trash it based almost solely on your subject.*

Imagine you're an editor or reporter who gets fifty or sixty email releases each day. Are you going to open each one and look at it? No way! You're going to scan the subjects, delete most of them, and open only the ones with the most appealing subjects.

So your job, when you write a release, is to create a compelling subject. Don't just type "Press Release" as your subject line. Give a concise summary of what your release is about. Don't write your subject in ALL CAPS; it makes you look like you're hawking a get-rich-quick scam. Most email software gives only a fixed amount of space to display a message's subject and cuts off what doesn't fit. Some software has room for forty characters and some for only twenty. So make your subject short, catchy, and put the most important words first.

You can put more information in your message's headline. A headline is quite different from your subject. The headline is the traditional journalistic head you put above the body of your release. Some people use headlines in email releases, some people don't. I have seen them work both ways.

KEEP YOUR BODY FIT

Screen real estate is limited, and many of the people who open your message (one publicist I know says way more than half) will never look beyond your first screenful of copy. Start immediately with your headline, and follow with a grabber, the most urgent, high-impact information your story contains. Since you want as much as possible on that first screen—the only part of your message that most of your readers will see—don't format your headline so it takes up several precious lines of first-screen real estate. Make it fit on as few lines as possible.

Keep your email release to 60 to 68 characters wide per line. Hit the return key to start each new line. This makes your body readable for people with email software that doesn't automatically wrap text.

Don't send attached files unless someone has previously asked for them. Many writers use software that has problems with attachments. Don't send a message that only directs a writer to your Web site. I get 5 or 6 announcements each week that say something like, "Important information—visit our new Web site to find out," and nothing else. I delete all of them. If you want a writer to go to your site, give at least a couple of paragraphs of background.

Editors can cut and paste directly out of your email news releases. This makes your quotes more important than in print releases. Write good dialog for your quotes. If you make a quote colorful, it gets cut and pasted more often, giving you more coverage.

Net publicists debate about how long your announcement body should be. Some people say your message should all fit on one or two screens of type. Some say it doesn't matter. Book publisher O'Reilly & Associates has had experience longer than almost any other company sending Internet press releases, and uses three to four screens. My experience is that announcement length should depend on the type of announcements you're sending, to whom you're sending them, and how often you're sending them.

This may sound obvious, but include only *useful* information. Cut out the company boilerplate. People view emailed messages as a more personal communication and resent fluff. If you send only to reporters who expect press releases, they expect longer material. For customers, prospects, and the general public, I'd keep announcements to two screens long, or three at the most. If you send rarely, your recipients won't mind longer messages as much. If you send two or more announcements a month, your messages will be better received when they fill three screens or less.

USE A SPECIAL SIGNATURE FILE

At the top of printed press release, you normally put contact information. At the top of an email press release, you don't.

On an email release, your contact information should be included in the signature file at the bottom. This should be the signature file of the marcom person who wrote the message. The important thing to provide is a *person* to reply to, not a *department*. For example, saying that your announcement is from marketing@yourco.com will not work. You need a human to whom recipients can respond, and that human's own email address and direct dial phone number. Make sure that person will be in the office on the days when your message goes out. Imagine if Joe Reporter were to call to warn you that your list server has gone berserk and emailed 27 copies of one message to him and probably everyone else on your list. Would it help business if Joe were to reach voicemail announcing his contact is on vacation and won't be back for two weeks?

Your non-publicity email signature files should give the URL of your company's home page. In contrast, the signature file of an email news release should give the Web address of the *press center section* of your site.

Sending email releases

In Steve O'Keefe's book *Publicity on the Internet*, he tells the story about sending his news release to 350 journalists. When he checked his email the next morning, "I had more than 50 messages. Most of them went something like this: 'You are a complete moron. Remove my name from your list immediately.' " O'Keefe had mistakenly put all 350 addresses in his message's "To:" field, sending everyone a 19-page message consisting of a 20-line news release buried beneath a 350-line header!

Don't make the same mistake. No reporter likes to see that he is one of hundreds on your list. Either use email list software so each message will go out with only one addressee's name in the "To:" field, or use the line on your email software labeled "Bcc:" to send your list. "Bcc" stands for "blind carbon copy," and sends a copy of your message to a person without adding the person's name to the header. If O'Keefe would have put all 350 names in his software's "Bcc:" field, his recipients would have received only his news release.

You'll find other tips on sending announcements to email lists in Chapter 13.

Mass email is easy for you to send, but it's impersonal and has less value than personalized email. You can turn this to your advantage when emailing releases to key editors. Break your email list into A list, people who you value more highly and know personally (at least slightly), and a B list. Send the As your press release prefaced by a short personal note and the Bs undifferentiated mass email. Your result will be enhanced relations with crucial editors and possibly more placements.

In addition to your own list, you can hire companies to distribute your release for you. The Global Internet News Agency (**www.gina.com**) offers a feature called Internet Wire that distributes your email news release worldwide to ezines and traditional media. Internet Wire costs $180 per release. Newstips at **www.newstips.com** emails one-paragraph high tech stories and contact information to 3,000 journalists for $350 per placement. Some distribution services specialize. Steve O'Keefe (**www.olympus.net/okeefe**) emails news releases about books. Eric Ward (**www.netpost.com**) emails notices about new Web sites.

Followup

After you send out your email releases, don't call editors and ask, "Did you receive my release?" That will only irritate them. If your message hasn't bounced back, assume an editor received it.

Editors will respond to your releases by emailing questions to you. When you reply to an editor, summarize the editor's original message. Otherwise, the editor (who may have responded to dozens of messages besides your own) won't remember what you are talking about. Don't copy the editor's *entire* message to you, just excerpt relevant chunks. A writer in a hurry won't appreciate digging through your reply to find needed info.

In addition to email news releases, make emailable versions of the other components of your press kit. A backgrounder about your company, lists of dealers, product information, price lists, executive bios, and other handouts will all be useful in electronic form. Your electronic press kit will need one other document that Internet users will expect. It is called a FAQ.

Create a FAQ

FAQ stands for "Frequently Asked Questions," and your FAQ document will be a list of them in question-and-answer format. Take a look at some of the FAQs on the Net to see how to format your own.

Your FAQ will be read online. People mostly read the first part of online documents and often don't make it all the way to the end. Put your journalism school classes to use by putting your most important information and most often-asked questions right up front. I recommend starting your FAQ with a brief (ten to twelve lines) summary of your FAQ's contents.

Update your FAQ information often—at least once a month. Twice a month is better. Highlight new material by putting *NEW* in front of it. A FAQ should not be a sales sheet, but a background piece about your company and your products. It should not be longer than the equivalent of five to seven pages of typewritten press release copy.

Once your FAQ is complete, make sure it is seen. Include your FAQ as a page on your Web site. You can also set up a mailbot server to automatically hand out your FAQ to anyone who sends email to **faq@yourco.com**.

Press center on your Web site

Many reporters look through 15 or more Web sites a day for info. More and more companies are taking advantage of this by creating a press center section on their Web site, a kind of electronic press kit. A virtual press center is cheap to create, and a good one will be appreciated by writers.

You'll find a good example on the Pointcast site at **www.pointcast.com**. First, Pointcast gives a list of PR contact people, clearly deliniating who is responsible for what, with an email address, phone, and fax for each. There is an archive of press releases, sorted by date. A catalog of small thumbnail images of Pointcast screen shots leads to downloadable full-size screen shots with clear instructions on how to copy them—an online photo archive. Another page lets writers sign up to be on Pointcast's email PR list.

From a writer's point of view, a much less successful Web press center is the one from Digital Equipment Corp. at **www.digital.com**. For this book, I needed to contact Digital's PR people. I searched through press releases at Digital's site, but none of them provided contact information. I spent about a quarter of an hour looking through the Digital site for any type of PR contact data at all. There was none—not a name, not a phone number, not an email address. Finally, I called the main switchboard for the entire corporation. After several phone calls, I reached a PR person who answered my original question. When I suggested that Digital might want to add PR contact information to its Web site, he replied, "Oh, no—we already have enough people contacting us now!" If Digital doesn't want people to contact it, why bother having a PR department at all?

The number one complaint journalists have about Web sites is lack of PR contact information. They want to see news releases, technical specs, pricing, product ship dates, and distribution and purchasing information. (Where can people buy your product? *Every* Web site should answer this question.) Competitive information and industry analyses are also welcomed, as are org charts and executive bios. Journalists get disgusted with overhype. They want substance, so stick with the facts.

Editors are in a hurry and are not patient. If you want your stuff read by people under deadline, use no graphics. Use animated graphics only to illustrate story points.

Your press center can also provide links to partners and other information sources that round out your story, add depth, and put it in context. Make sure all links have descriptions. As Rochelle Nemrow of Press Access put it, "Nothing is more annoying than having to go through five doors to get to the room you want," especially when you're pressed for time.

You can use an email autoresponder to provide email versions of releases and white papers. (Email is easier to cut and paste than Web copy.) Provide clear instructions: "If you would like an email copy of this release, email to news23@yourco.com." Some Web sites add a line at the top of news release pages saying, "Click here to download a Microsoft Word copy of this release," providing an easy-to-edit version for writers.

Herding editorial eyeballs

If you create a press center on your Web site, you must let editors know about it. Put its URL on the signature file at the bottom of your email news releases.

Plug it on your print releases, too. At the bottom of Lotus's printed press releases, it puts: "EDITOR'S NOTE: All Lotus news releases are available on the Internet, via the Lotus Development Corp. Home Page at **http://www.lotus.com**. The Lotus Home Page is an easy way to find information about Lotus and its business partners' products and services." You can do something similar.

Editors and reporters are heavy users of Internet search engines. Read Chapter 16, "How to Attract Visitors to Your Web Site." Use the tactics explained there, including page titles and Meta tags, to make your Web press center pages findable on search engines. Be sure to add Meta tags when you post news releases on your Web site, and *especially be sure to individually submit each press release page to the major search engines*.

Restricted access?

Should you use passwords to restrict access to your Web press center? An example of a company that does this is Chrysler. Its media relations site at **www.media.chrysler.com** requires journalists to provide their email address (for Chrysler's PR email list) and register to receive a password. In return, the journalist can use a search engine to access Chrysler's press releases and detailed product information.

Surveys of journalists claim that half of them will register for a site and half won't. I think willingness depends on the company more than the journalist. If you are a reporter covering Windows software and Microsoft requires you to register to get its press information, you'll register. The registration rate might not be as high for Don & Betty Benson's Software & Snowblowers.

If you choose password access for your Web press center, you've got to provide a lot of information in return, and promise journalists access or information not otherwise available. You'll have to do a sell job to persuade journalists to sign up, and let them know, "We won't sell or abuse your email address."

A compromise is to ask for a temporary log-in for one-time use: "Type your email address for semi-exclusive info." Or you can put press releases and other standard information outside the restricted area and use password access only for semi-confidential info. You can build your registration page so it acts as a confidentiality agreement. If you provide home phone numbers, put them in your restricted area, and store them in a database so evildoers can't copy them *en masse* and wreak havoc.

Talk to your government

Rush Limbaugh jokes about lobbyists, but somebody's got to represent your company's needs to government or you'd get legislated out of business. Skillful use of the Internet in lobbying has been frequent enough and dramatic enough that someone could write a whole book about it.

In February 1994, a last-minute amendment was tacked onto a major education bill in the U.S. House of Representatives. It required the government to license all parents nationwide who teach their children at home. This amendment had no strong opposition. It was expected to pass easily, so no major media covered it. More than one million American families now conduct home schooling, but they had to spread the news fast with no traditional media support. They sent messages to the **home-ed** and **home-ed-politics** email lists, and posted notices on the newsgroups **alt.education.alternative**, and **alt.education.home-school.christian**, **misc.education.home-school. christian**, and **misc.education.home-school.misc**. They reached 200,000 people in 72 hours through fax and telephone "trees." Opponents of the amendment used the Internet to spread the news and then used traditional methods to reach the representatives. They bombarded congressional offices with more than a million phone calls, faxes, and letters. Instead of passing easily, the amendment was defeated 424 to 1.

This ability to quickly reach large numbers of people who are strongly committed to an issue can be useful if legislation ever threatens your business. Businesses have used the Internet to conduct virtual Political Action Committees, holding all committee meetings online. Use of the Internet to disseminate information and organize has been applied hundreds of times in many countries, not just for national issues, but also for state and local issues as well.

If your company is concerned about legislation and regulations, Internet newsgroups and email lists can be valuable tools. You can use the Internet to track regulatory and legislative activities, and you can join with other businesses and individuals to make your views heard.

Providing Finger files

Finger is an Internet software program originally developed so people outside a company could find out information such as: who was logged onto the computer, what their Internet address was, and other information. Unfortunately, Finger became a major security risk. It is a favorite target of hackers and computer viruses.

Today, some businesses provide no Finger information at all. Others, however, use Finger to deliver marketing information. If the technical data so beloved by hackers is stripped from Finger, you can provide contact information, your order desk phone number, hours of business, and other information. For a simple example, Finger **info@clbooks.com**.

In most cases, the extra effort is probably not worth it. Finger is rarely used. It provides little interactivity compared with other Internet services you can provide. It is not essential for your company to provide a Finger server at all. If you do provide Finger information, make sure your technical people block all security holes. But don't spend a lot of money and time providing complicated Finger data. Most people will never see it.

A learning experience: The Pentium chip story

The pandemonium over Intel's Pentium chip cost the company millions of dollars and could have easily been prevented. The uproar started and grew on the Internet. A close look at this case demonstrates several important points about publicity on the Internet.

June 1994: Intel testers discover a division error in the Pentium chip. Intel managers decide that the error will not affect many people and do not inform anyone outside the company. This was Intel's first mistake. The company was right in that the division error could affect only a few customers, but not disclosing the information made Intel appear to hide a sinister secret. It sent the message to customers that Intel was not trustworthy. Disclosing the flaw upon discovery would have created only minor news, on the same low level as an automaker announcing a minor defect. (Today, Intel posts all known flaws on the Internet to avoid a recurrence of this problem.) Dr. Thomas R. Nicely, a professor of mathematics at Lynchburg College, Virginia, double-checks all his work by computing everything twice, on two different computers. The same month, he notices a small difference in the two results generated by the same equation on a 486 PC and on a Pentium-based computer. Dr. Nicely spends months successively eliminating possible causes such as PCI bus errors and compiler artifacts.

Wednesday, October 19: After exhaustive tests on several 486 and Pentium-based computers, Dr. Nicely is certain that the error is caused by the Pentium processor.

Monday, October 24: Dr. Nicely contacts Intel technical support. Intel's contact person duplicates the error and confirms it, but says that it was not reported before.

Sunday, October 30: After receiving no more information from Intel, Dr. Nicely sends an email message to a few people, announcing his discovery of a "bug" in Pentium processors. The speed at which events develop from that email message graphically illustrates the nature of public relations on the Internet. This is how PR works today. Businesses of all kinds, take note.

That same day, Andrew Schulman, author of *Unauthorized Windows 95*, receives Dr. Nicely's email.

Tuesday, November 1: Schulman forwards Dr. Nicely's message to Richard Smith, president of Phar Lap Software in Cambridge, Massachusetts. Phar Lap's customers write number-crunching software that could be affected by the Pentium flaw. Phar Lap programmers test and confirm the division error. Realizing the significance of the flaw, Smith immediately forwards Dr. Nicely's message to important Phar Lap customers, to Intel, and to people at compiler companies, including Microsoft, Borland, Metaware, and Watcom. He also posts the message to the Canopus forum of CompuServe with a note asking people to run Dr. Nicely's test and report results back to Smith. This is the first public disclosure of the flaw.

Wednesday, November 2: Smith receives about ten confirmations of the error from Canopus readers. Alex Wolfe, a reporter for *Electronic Engineering Times*, sees Smith's post on Canopus and starts research for a story. He forwards Dr. Nicely's message to several people, including Terje Mathisen of Norsk Hydro in Norway.

Thursday, November 3: Mathisen confirms the flaw and emails his findings back to reporter Wolfe. Mathisen goes to the Internet newsgroup **comp.sys.intel** and posts a message titled "Glaring FDIV Bug in Pentium!" Within 24 hours, hundreds of technical people all over the world know about the Pentium flaw. (Note that only two days have passed since Schulman forwarded Dr. Nicely's original message.) All hell breaks loose on the newsgroup.

Monday, November 7: Wolfe's article runs in *Electronic Engineering Times*, headlined INTEL FIXES A PENTIUM FPU GLITCH. In the story, Intel says it has corrected the glitch in subsequent runs of the chip, and Steve Smith of Intel dismisses the importance of the flaw, saying, "This doesn't even qualify as an errata (sic)." This is only the first print article about the flaw, but by this time there are hundreds of postings about it in CompuServe forums and Internet newsgroups. All research results are posted in public on the Net for the world to criticize and contribute to.

Wednesday, November 9: The ruckus spills out of the technical newsgroups and into business and investment newsgroups.

Tuesday, November 15: Tim Coe of Vitesse Semiconductors and Mike Carleton of USC announce on the Net that they have reverse-engineered the way the Pentium chip handles division and created a model that predicts when the chip is wrong. By this time, a furor has erupted on the Net. Intel still claims there is no problem. Intel's stock drops 1 $3/8$ points.

Tuesday, November 22: CNN's *Moneyline* program looks at the issue. Steve Smith of Intel says the Pentium processor's problem is minor.

Wednesday, November 23: MathWorks sends out a press release, MATHWORKS DEVELOPS FIX FOR THE INTEL PENTIUM FLOATING POINT PROCESSOR.

Thursday, November 24 (Thanksgiving holiday): The *New York Times* runs a story by John Markoff, CIRCUIT FLAW CAUSES PENTIUM CHIP TO MISCAL-CULATE, INTEL ADMITS. In the story, an Intel spokesman says the company is still sending out the flawed chips. A similar story by the Associated Press is printed by more than 200 newspapers and runs on radio and television news. Intel Applications Support Manager Ken Hendren posts a message on America Online and the Internet, revealing that Intel has no one providing customer support on the Internet. Intel seems unaware of the solidity of opinion on the Net about the Pentium processor's flaw. At this point, an offer by Intel to replace any flawed Pentium chips would have smoothed the waters. Instead, Intel makes an offer to replace a Pentium chip only after Intel has determined you used the chip in an application in which it would cause a problem. Intel customers are irate. The chip hits the fan.

Friday, November 25: This weekend, the Internet's humor newsgroups sprout Pentium jokes.

Sunday, November 27: A notice appears on the Internet newsgroup **comp.sys.intel**, from Intel's president, Dr. Andrew Grove, but bearing someone else's "return address".

Dr. Grove's posting has two problems.

- Since Grove's message was not posted from his own address, many readers assumed that it was a spoof—a forged message—and had been written by someone other than Grove.

- It should not have been released on the Internet first. There are some things you should not use the Internet to do. Put out standard press releases, yes. Distribute new product announcements, sure. But if your company lands in a jam in the *New York Times*, an email message is too commonplace, too everyday, and too trivial. There are times when a simple solution is best and times when only a bigger and more traditional approach will work. Intel tried to stop a rampaging rhino with a flyswatter. It should have called a press conference. Grove's email only fueled the flames.

Monday, November 28: Internet newsgroups are flooded with furious messages such as, "Having conclusively demonstrated themselves utterly unworthy of the public's trust, they still seem unable to comprehend what that means." No one from Intel responds to these posts.

November 29 - December 11: Intel receives thousands of messages and phone calls saying that Intel misses the point. Intel becomes a laughingstock on the Internet joke circuit:

> At Intel, quality is job 0.999999998.

> Know how the Republicans can cut taxes and pay the deficit at the same time?
> A: Their spreadsheet runs on a Pentium computer.

> We are Pentium of Borg. Resistance is futile. You will be approximated.

> The Intel version of *Casablanca:* "Round off the usual suspects."

> How many Pentium designers does it take to screw in a light bulb?
> A: .99995827903, but that's close enough for nontechnical people.

The situation degrades to a point past any logical response. People believe Intel does not stand behind its products. While the fury grows, Intel remains silent.

Monday, December 12: IBM issues a press release: IBM HALTS SHIPMENTS OF PENTIUM-BASED PCS. Intel counters with INTEL SAYS IBM SHIPMENT HALT IS UNWARRANTED. Internet analysts immediately demonstrate that IBM's claims are exaggerated, but at the same time, no one believes Intel.

Wednesday, December 14: Intel releases a white paper rationally explaining the situation. Too late. Intel's communications are jammed with tens of thousands of phone calls and email messages from worried and angry customers.

Friday, December 16: Intel stock closes at $59.50, down $3.25 for the week.

Monday, December 19: The *New York Times* prints a story by Laurie Flynn headlined ITNEL FACING A GENERAL FEAR OF ITS PENTIUM CHIP. It says that eight product liability lawsuits and two shareholder suits were filed against Intel. Flynn quotes Florida Deputy Attorney General Pete Antonacci: "They've got to stop acting like a rinky-dink two-person operation in a garage and start acting like the major corporation they are." About the same time, a *New York Times* story about the New Jersey Nets basketball team is headlined MENTALLY SPEAKING, NETS ARE PENTIUMS. Intel's lavishly promoted brand name has become an insult.

Tuesday, December 20: Intel finally apologizes and says it will replace all flawed Pentiums upon request. It sets aside a reserve of $420 million to cover costs. It hires hundreds of customer service employees to deal with customer requests. And it dedicates four fulltime employees to read Internet newsgroups and respond immediately to any postings about Intel or its products.

January 1995: Intel has received commitments to purchase all the Pentium chips it can manufacture through the end of 1995.

Lessons in Internet PR

What lessons can we learn from this story about public relations on the Internet? First, *respond to emailed complaints as quickly as possible*. Unless your company has people monitoring newsgroups, an incoming email message may be your first sign of a serious disturbance. When you receive an emailed complaint, ask yourself what would happen if hundreds of other people spread that complaint across the Net, as happened with Dr. Nicely's original message. Speed is extremely important in responding to any Internet crisis.

Another obvious lesson is that when you see hundreds of email messages and newsgroup postings that say you have a problem and you don't think you have a problem, think twice: You really do have a problem. You might not have a technical problem, but you have a PR problem. Intel said, "Pentium chips have a flaw, but it doesn't matter." Intel's customers said, "It does too matter." Intel responded "No, it doesn't," and even though Intel meant well, thousands of its customers on the Internet swore they saw Intel stick its virtual tongue out at them. In retrospect, it seems like a no-brainer, but Intel had the facts on its side and thought the facts mattered. They didn't. Your customers' illusions are more important than your reality. When you are absolutely sure you are right, you increase your likelihood of making a mistake. Ask any prosecuting attorney. The facts have very little to do with the outcome of a case—it's how the facts are couched and presented that sways your jury.

Unlike traditional news media, the Internet has no filtering process. Messages come quickly and from many sources. It is impossible for your media relations people to put a spin on Internet postings. That is why it is important for you to monitor what is being posted on the Net, and why you need to post proactive information. If Intel would have posted information about the Pentium flaw in June, it would have prevented almost everything that happened afterwards.

Another result of the lack of filters on the Internet is that newsgroups exaggerate. If someone posts exaggerated or angry newsgroup messages or sends flaming email about your business, you can employ the procedures Intel now uses. It has determined that even a large feeding frenzy is usually fueled by five or six instigators, or fewer. They are the people who are the most emotionally upset, who post most frequently, and who copy other people's messages to multiple newsgroups to "spread the word" of their point of view. First, you must identify these instigators. This is the vital thing. Who are the people who have a vendetta? Who feeds the flow? Send email to each person directly. Be conciliatory. Politely say that you realize the person has legitimate concerns. You think that this is a serious matter. Give the person your direct phone number and ask them to please call at his or her earliest convenience so you can clear this up immediately. The phone call is the key. When you get the person on the phone, he or she will be contrite. This is just human nature. It's easy to flame an intangible name or a company you don't know. Once you make human contact, however, it's easier to conduct a give-and-take discussion. Intel has used this tactic with repeated success.

If there is a continuing situation regarding your company and that situation is discussed repeatedly on the Net, don't just post one message and then go away for a week. Someone from your company will need to provide a continuing voice in the discussion, even if to just repeat your side of a story. The balance of postings in the Pentium story was easily more than a hundred postings by the public to every one posting by Intel.

Remember that *anything on the Net can be picked up by traditional media*. Had it not been for the fact that reporters now use the Internet as a news source, the minor flaw in Intel's chip would not have blown up in the media, which fostered the feeding frenzy. All the newsgroup postings in the world do not have the impact of a story in the *New York Times*.

And don't try to do *all* your public relations on the Net. Use the Internet as one ingredient in your mix, but not for everything. Some things—as Andy Grove's Internet message demonstrated—will have better results when done off the Net.

More info for the publicity-inclined

For inquiring minds who want to know, here are three Web resources and one book.

Public Relations Online Resources and Organizations (**www.webcom.com/ impulse/resource.html**) is the best Web directory I've found for links to PR resources.

The Public Relations Society of America (**www.prsa.org**) puts its entire *Red Book* online for free and its *Green Book* as well, plus links to local chapters, a resume posting service, and the latest PR salary survey.

Niehaus Ryan Group (**www.nrh.com/deepthoughts/deepthoughts.html**) provides essays on PR techniques, including a very good account of managing investor relations during the IPO process.

Publicity on the Internet by Steve O'Keefe (1996), Wiley, 400 pages. ISBN 0-471-16175-6. Full of true tales from the trenches, this is the best book on using the Net to generate publicity.

23

Competitive Intelligence and Market Research

"As a copywriter, what I want from the researchers is to be told what kind of advertising will make the cash register ring. A creative person who knows nothing about plus and minus factors, and refuses to learn, may sometimes luck into a successful campaign. A blind pig may sometimes find truffles, but it helps to know that they grow under oak trees."

—David Ogilvy, The Unpublished David Ogilvy

Near the end of Elvis Presley's career as a movie star, he finished every day at MGM Studios the same way. His chauffeur-driven limousine pulled up. Elvis got in the back seat with a bodyguard. A second bodyguard got in front with the driver. As his long car approached the studio gate, Elvis lay down on the car's floor. His bodyguards covered him with a throw rug so he couldn't be seen by the crowd of fans outside the gate. When Elvis was a couple of blocks away, his bodyguards uncovered him, and he sat up. The bodyguards did this every day, *but no fans waited at the gate*. None had for years. Nobody told Elvis, and he never knew.

Without market research, your marketing can be as out of touch as Elvis on the floor covered with a rug. Every successful company acquires competitive intelligence and does market research—whether it is formal or casual, logical or intuitive. On the Internet, your company still needs to answer the same questions as in its pre-wired days:

- How big are your markets? Are they growing or shrinking? What is your market share? Is it growing or shrinking? What other markets would work for you?

- Who are your competitors? How well are they doing? How do your best customers feel about them?

- How can you advertise and publicize more effectively? What characteristics do your most loyal clients share? Can you use this to pinpoint a common appeal to increase sales to your less-loyal customers?

- Who are your prospects? How can you tell a likely prospect from a hopeless one? What information does a prospect need to decide to buy? What is the most profitable way to reach your most likely prospects with that information? Would it be more profitable to change your pricing strategy? How can you speed up your sales cycle?

- Who are your customers? Out of all your customers, how can you spot your *most profitable* customers? How can you make your less profitable customers more profitable? How can you convert one-time buyers into repeat customers? What do your customers *really* think about your company and its offerings? What are the main reasons you lose customers? What are the main reasons you lose sales? What new products and services do your customers want?

Answers to these questions help you spot and heal wounds in your sales cycle and point to new ways to grow. The same numbers come in handy when you need to justify a project to your boss or buy advertising on the Web. To research these questions in the old days, you had to go to a library. On the Net, you rarely need to leave your desk. You get the same information—or better—in a fraction of the time and for pennies on the dollar.

On the Net, some strategic information comes from analyzing your company's own Internet activities. Your own Web site (as discussed in Chapter 20) and your email lists generate usage statistics that can reveal priceless information.

Email is easy to measure. How many names are in which of your email lists? What are your lists' growth rates per week? How many names cancel mailing list subscriptions each week? These numbers are all simple to track. Your technical people can write software to automatically report email list growth. Another mailing list question shouldn't be tracked weekly, but every time you do a mailing: What percentage of names from this mailing bounced back as undeliverable? If you see an upwards spike in this figure, look for a technical problem, either in-house or with your access provider.

But your own statistics won't expose the secrets of your competitors.

Competitive intelligence

Your first step in using the Internet to research your competition is to find and visit your competitors' Web sites. A good way to do this is to search Yahoo for your competitors' names. Do this even if you have already visited your competitors' sites; when you look up a competitor at Yahoo, note which Yahoo *category* your competitor is in. Then click on that category. You'll find other companies there and may discover new competitors you didn't know about.

In this chapter, I assume that you already know how to use Internet search engines and are familiar with the major ones. You might want to revisit Chapter 5 for a quick brush-up on these topics.

It won't hurt to visit a competitor's Web site weekly to keep up with its new developments. If your top competitor has a site, you can make it your home page so you check it automatically, every time you fire up your browser.

Your next step after investigating your competitor's site is to discover what other Web sites have links to it. For easy instructions, see the sidebar "Who Links to Your Pages?" in Chapter 16. Follow those links; maybe you can persuade those sites to point at your site instead.

If your competitor is important enough, you might want to look daily for new comments about it on newsgroups and Web sites. The easiest way to do this is to go to a meta search engine that searches many search engine databases at once. Good ones are **www.dogpile.com** and **www.highway61.com**. Search for your own company and product names as well as your competitor's names.

If your competitor is a publicly traded U.S. company, your next stop is the Securities and Exchange Commission at **www.sec.gov**. You can search its EDGAR database (and another database of non-EDGAR documents) for data on pub-licly-traded U.S. companies. If your competitor isn't publicly-traded, or not a U.S. firm, you must look at other sources. Several Web sites offer search varia-tions of the EDGAR database. One is at **http://edgar.stern.nyu.edu**. The most up-to-date and flexible version I've used is at **www.smart-edgar.com**. You can learn a lot about your competitor from EDGAR. For example, your competitor's IPO filing usually lists all companies your competitor sees as serious competi-tion. Executive compensation is reported, and you can often find Social Security numbers of officers and Taxpayer ID numbers of companies.

For information on both public and privately-held companies, Dun & Bradstreet at **www.dnb.com** (in U.K., **www.dunandbrad.co.uk**) is a reliable starting place. Its database contains profiles of 43 million companies in 200 countries; including sales figures and senior managers. A basic D&B Global Search costs $5, its Business Background Report goes for $20, and its detailed Supplier Evaluation Report costs $85. You can purchase these reports from the D&B Web site via credit card. If you subscribe to D&B, you can also get your competitor's credit report for about $30, which details a company's banking and payment history.

Spying on people

InfoSpace (**www.infospace.com**) has home addresses of 112 million people with listed phone numbers—probably yours. Go to InfoSpace's "White Pages" section, type in your name and see if InfoSpace gives your phone number and address. Click on your address and up pops a map of your neighborhood, with a red star marking your house. Click again for directions telling anyone how to find you. Scary, isn't it?

You've only just begun. If you know where on the Web to look, you can find all sorts of facts about people. Imagine knowing this information about your competitor's key people: their credit reports, political contributions, stock holdings, driving records, court records, real estate holdings, educational records, landlord-tenant disputes, and more. You can get a thorough understanding of a competitor's background: strengths, weaknesses, and hidden motives.

These personal details are available on the Net mostly for U.S. inhabitants, because the United States has much weaker privacy laws than most other countries. That will probably change in the near future, but in the meantime dozens of Net resources will provide you with eye-popping details about your competitors. Of course, the Net also provides your competitors with eye-popping details about you.

A good place to familiarize yourself with the Web's investigative power is the Stalker's Home Page (**www.glr.com/stalk.html**). This page is not really for stalkers, but is run by a privacy advocate dedicated to exposing Web sites' abuses of privacy, such as absent-minded universities that post the Social Security numbers of all their faculty and staff. (Once you have someone's Social Security number, you can find out almost anything about him or her.) Even without a Social Security number, you'll be surprised by what you can find. For instance, you can look up who in any ZIP code contributed to political campaigns: names, dates, amounts, and causes. I was surprised to find a modest neighbor of mine had donated tens of thousands of dollars to political organizations.

When you look for competitive intelligence on individual people, you'll have to use several sites. Rarely will one site deliver all the information you need. Try these:

- Information America (**www.infoam.com**) gives you an incredible amount of U.S.-only categories to research. Information America lets you find facts about companies, as well as individuals. It charges $10 to $105 per search.

- Cambridge Statistical Research (**http://kadima.com**) provides a good cheap nationwide name search for people tracing, providing current and past home addresses and listed and unlisted home phone numbers. Other searches are available at $1.25 to $3 per search.

- KnowX (**www.knowx.com**) has free searches and, for $7 each, many more on a wide variety of data, including personal assets, sales tax permits, and DBAs. Be patient, this is a very slow site.

- Deep Data (**www.deepdata.com**) provides a $20 Flake Index identifying people who've had legal problems, credit deliquencies, and criminal records.

- National Tenant Network (**www.ntnnet.com**) is a misnamed site. Designed for landlords, it tells you if a person has taken part in evictions or has had landlord-tenant disputes.

- Ameri.Com (**www.ameri.com**) does Department of Motor Vehicle record searches for 47 states and Sherlock people searches. Fees vary.

- Find a Friend (**www.findafriend.com**) provides nine different ways to search for a person.

If those aren't enough, you'll find bunches more at **www.yahoo.com/ Business_and_Economy/Companies/Information/Investigative_Services**.

Spying on companies

Do you know what your competitor is buying and selling, and to whom? TradeSmart gives you names and addresses of U.S. buyers who currently buy your competitor's products. Derived from a database of U.S. Customs manifest documents and updated daily, TradeSmart tells how much of a product was shipped, who shipped it, and who received it. You can search by company name or product category. TradeSmart charges $150 per month, or $50 for one-day's use, or $25 per report. It is part of the Trade Compass site at **www.tradecompass.com**.

Other useful company-watch sites:

- Hoover's Online (**www.hoovers.com**) provides free short profiles of 10,000 U.S. companies. For $10 per month, you can get lengthy profiles of 2,500 public companies, including balance sheets and income statements.

- The *Inc.* 500 database (**www.inc.com/500**) lets you search for information on the thousands of privately-held companies who have made *Inc.* magazine's top 500 list since 1983.

- National Trade Data Bank is part of the fee-based Stat-USA (**www.stat-usa.gov/stat-usa.html**) and has U.S. government-compiled data on thousands of U.S. and international companies. $150 per year, or $50 per quarter. For a users' comments on the National Trade Data Bank, visit **www.montague.com/scip/ntdb.html**.

- Business Information Services on the Internet (**www.dis.strath.ac.uk/business**) is an excellent annotated catalog by Sheila Webber (great last name!) of places to research businesses, especially European companies.

More on CI

People who work in competitive intelligence call it "CI" for short. These resources cover the field itself, providing how-to info:

- Fuld & Co. (**www.fuld.com**) provides a very good Internet Intelligence Index, and how-to info on CI under "Developing a CI Strategy."

- The Society of Competitive Intelligence Professionals at **www.scip.org** has info on the organization itself, plus links.

- The joint site for Thomas Investigative Publications and the National Association of Investigative Specialists (**www.pimall.com/nais/home.html**) includes links to subjects of interest to private investigators and articles on topics such as "Discovering and Recovering Digital Evidence."

- The Montague Institute (**www.montague.com**) has very good articles on competitive intelligence—especially on using the Internet for CI—and on market research, and useful directories of Internet resources on both topics.

Market research

Okay, now you know about your competitors. But what about an even more important group, your *customers?* If you want to understand your markets, the Internet is the place to be.

You can locate market information from governments, universities, corporations, industry associations, and data providers all over the planet. Topics range from census information and import-export statistics to advertising lineage and purchasing surveys.

You can monitor Usenet discussion groups on topics that affect your company. A good Usenet newsgroup is like watching a focus group on steroids. You don't have to guess how participants feel—you *know*. People in newsgroups are people with passions and problems.

You can conduct marketing surveys on the Net. You can search through thousands of online newspapers, magazines, and journals. You can capture demographic, statistical, and behavioral data from your company's own Internet traffic. You can do split-run tests of advertising concepts, package designs, and pricing ideas.

The most direct form of Internet marketing research is also the most simple: tally your email. Count incoming email messages from your customers. This is what happens when you send email to the President of the United States at **president@whitehouse.gov**. All incoming messages are logged and read. The subject or subjects of each message are noted, as well as any pro and con points of view. Every day the White House staff reviews reports of messages, which serve as an instant opinion survey.

If your company already conducts email correspondence with customers or prospects, it costs little for you to put a similar message tally operation into place. You can record the most basic statistic—the number of incoming customer messages per day—to reveal patterns and trends. Recording message *subjects* and preparing a simple daily report can reveal much more. Since email is such a quick response medium, this can be a surprisingly fast way to identify potential problems as well as indications of new opportunities.

In an interview in the February 1995 issue of *Micro Times*, CompuServe vice president Tim Oren told how quick customer reactions by email keep him informed. He said one advantage he has, "...being an old research guy now moved into the online business, is that if I want to try something out, I've got two million people out there, some portion of which will try it out and tell me real quickly if I have a winner on my hands or if I've got a problem. Instant test-tube. No need to guess. No need to run the focus groups."

That kind of instant interactive response is one factor that makes the Internet such a valuable tool for marketing research. You get insight—sometimes hard-hitting—into customer and prospect needs, and you get it quickly.

But that isn't the only kind of market information you'll need. Fortunately, the Internet is "Facts R Us." You'll find many places on the Net to find every other kind of market information. Some are free and some charge fees. Governments provide access to massive collections of data:

- FedStats (**www.fedstats.gov**) provides a central place to get U.S. government statistics. Of special usefulness in learning about markets are the Department of Commerce (**www.doc.gov**), Census Bureau (**www. census.gov**), and the Bureau of Labor Statistics (**www.bls.gov**).

- The government of Canada has a similar resource at Statistics Canada (**www.statcan.ca**), which provides information in both English and French.

- StateSearch (**www.nasire.org/ss/index**) is a searchable directory of 2,000 state government Web sites by subject and state.

The most useful spots for most market researchers are huge business and news services that charge for access to gigantic quantities of up-to-date information:

- Lexis-Nexis (**www.lexis-nexis.com**) provides data from thousands of sources, especially legal info. It includes access to Bloomberg Terminal financial data.

- Dialog (**www.dialog.com**) provides access to 400 databases, plus the full text of more than 1,100 newspapers and periodicals.

- DataStar (**www.rs.ch**) is a large European service that provides Web and Telnet access to many databases available nowhere else.

- *Financial Times* of London information services (**www.info.ft.com**) includes three separate offerings, FT Profile, FT Discovery, and FT McCarthy. They provide access to business info from thousands of sources worldwide.

- InfoMart (**www.infomart.ca**) lets you reach Canadian publications, Canadian criminal cases, and government databases.

Other business database services include Dow Jones (**http://bis.dowjones.com**), A Business Compass (**www.abcompass.com**), DataTimes (**www.datatimes.com**), Profound (**www.profound.com**), NewsNet (**www.newsnet.com**), I/Plus Direct (**www.investext.com**), and Questel-Orbit (**www.questel.orbit.com**).

How to conduct surveys

When you have more specific needs than databases or email tallies can satisfy, you can conduct marketing surveys over the Net. You can use email, newsgroups, and the Web.

Email surveys

Using email is the easiest way to conduct a survey on the Internet. It's also cheap and fast. The caveat here is to be careful, so you don't anger perfectly good customers and prospects. Strive for surveys without flames.

First, don't be intrusive with your email survey. Millions of people on the Internet pay for each message they receive or pay by incoming message length. These folks will not be happy to find an unexpected 10-page questionnaire from you.

Keep your survey short. You'll get the highest response rate with a one-screen (24 lines long) survey. A two-screen (48 lines) will do almost as well. Beyond that, response drops off sharply unless you offer incentives. You don't need to leave lots of blank space for replies. Your respondents can insert blank space themselves. Here's a simple example of formatting:

THE WRONG WAY

```
1. Was your Spade and Archer customer service representative:
   (chose one)
   A. Concerned and responsive
   B. Unconcerned and boring
   C. Hard-boiled

2. Please comment on the investigator(s) who handled your case.

3. What was(were) the name of your investigator(s).
```

That took seven lines. Here's how to do the same thing in four:

THE RIGHT WAY

```
1. Your Spade and Archer customer service rep was: (delete all but one)
   A. Concerned and responsive  B. Unconcerned and boring  C. Hard-boiled
2. Please comment on the investigator(s) who handled your case.
3. What was (were) the name of your investigator(s)?
```

What you will get back

```
>>
>> 1. Your Spade and Archer customer service rep was: (delete all but one)
>> C. Hard-boiled
>> 2. Please give any comments about the investigator(s) who handled your case?
   He wouldn't play the sap for me.
>> 3. What was (were) the name of your investigator(s)?
   Originally Mr. Archer. After Mr. Archer was shot, Mr. Spade handled my case.
>>
```

How do you get email addresses to use for a survey? If your company has its own email list, you can use it, but only if your survey covers the same topic that your email list addresses. Off-topic surveys make people mad and generate flames or responses with bogus answers instead of usable ones. If your company saves prospect and customer email addresses, you may be able to use those.

Don't use names from another company. People with no relationship to your firm will be hostile to unsolicited surveys from you. If another company offers its own list for your use, have the other company send your survey out from its Internet address under its own name, and structure the survey as if it were one from the other company. Don't rent email lists. They are useless for surveys.

Don't send your surveys out "cold calling." If people don't expect your survey, they won't answer it. This especially holds true for prospects, who may not even remember ever contacting your business. Instead, send a short prefatory message to your intended respondents and ask them if it's okay with them for you to email a short survey to them. Personalize this message—don't make it seem to come from an impersonal bureaucracy. Make it informal. When getting permission to survey someone, you want to be casual, even when asking someone in a country with an otherwise formal email style. Just keep it respectful. Say something like, "You contacted our company for information some time ago. I'd like to make sure that we sent you the right information and see what more we can do for you. May I ask you a few questions by email?" If you want to send a lengthy survey (a dozen or more questions), say "a survey" instead of "a few questions." No use calling a pickle a pig.

Sign your message with a *person's* name. Don't say this message comes from some cold-sounding and anonymous department. And if you market to programmers or technical people (and there are a lot of them on the Net), don't say that your survey comes from a marketing department or sales department, or even use the words "marketing" or "sales." Those are dirty words to technical people. In many companies, technical and marketing people are bitter enemies. Use "customer support" or "customer service" instead of the m-word.

Newsgroup surveys

Email surveys go to people who have had some kind of relationship with your company. There are times when you will want information from people with a strong interest in a specific topic, people who may have no interest in your company at all. You can do this by surveying the discussion groups known as Usenet newsgroups.

Of all the ways to conduct surveys on the Internet, newsgroups are by far the most potentially explosive. Mistakes here can generate hate mail and alienate prospects—not to mention ruining your survey. Do not attempt a newsgroup survey without reading this entire section carefully.

The first rule of newsgroup surveys is to pick your targets cautiously. Pretend you are walking in a minefield. Set your foot down in as few places as possible. Each newsgroup is completely different and runs by different rules. Don't judge a newsgroup by its name. Names will often mislead you.

For each newsgroup you select as a survey candidate, read about 100 messages or two weeks worth, whichever is a smaller number. You can probably read two weeks worth of messages in 45 to 90 minutes or so. This will give you a feel for the style and content of each potentially surveyable newsgroup.

Before you post a survey to a newsgroup, always look for its FAQ list— Frequently Asked Questions. A group's FAQ (pronounced "fak") will cover rules for posting—who can post and what can be posted. Most groups post their FAQs once or twice a month. There is an archive of FAQs for many groups at **www.cis.ohio-state.edu/hypertext/faq/usenet-faqs/html/ FAQ-List.html**.

The more closely your survey fits your audience, the less likely you are to receive bogus answers and angry replies. Restrict your survey to the appropriate interest groups for your survey's subject. Also note what geographical areas you want to cover. Most newsgroups are worldwide, but some are local to one area or country. For instance, newsgroups prefixed with "**au.**" are for Austin,

Texas, and "**ba.**" stands for the San Francisco Bay Area. All groups beginning with "**fj.**" are discussions in Japanese about Japan, and "**de.**" stands for Deutschland—Germany—meaning discussions are in German.

If you want to post to a worldwide group but want answers from only one geographic area, say so in your Subject line. Put "Only for AZ please" if you want responses only from Arizona.

When you have selected your final list of potential newsgroups to survey, cut it down to only the best groups. When you send the same message to many groups at once, it is called *cross-posting* and is considered bad netiquette. You might say, "So what? I pick my nose at the dinner table, so I certainly don't give a hoot about Internet manners." Yeah, but the Internet has an enforcer. A type of software program called a *cancelbot* patrols newsgroups and keeps them safe from scum like you. Present company excepted.

Cancelbots check how many newsgroups received a message. If a message is splattered across the newsgroup landscape like so many bugs across a windshield, cancelbots remove the bad messages and warn the offender. Companies have been kicked off not only for spamming identical messages, but also for misposting many slightly "customized" versions of the same message.

Next you need to consider how to *present* your newsgroup survey. You have alternatives based on whether you are looking for information, reactions, or quantifiable statistics.

If you just want a simple answer to a question or three, present your survey as a posted question from an individual person. End the Subject line of your message with a question mark: **Price of jeweled falcon?** All newsgroup messages asking questions should use a question mark. Posting a question from an individual in your company is also a good way to get a reaction to marketing ideas. "I want to know if anybody's had any experience with...", "Does anybody have any strong feelings about...", and "What would you think of..." are all good lead-ins for a short, informal question.

Within a couple of days of posting your question, you will have a few answers and possibly some reactions to your answers and to the topic of your question itself. Just sit back and watch the fur fly.

Your task is more complex when you want quantifiable statistical information. The problem with isolated questions—even if you ask a lot of them—is that you can't link the answers with other answers.

There is a problem with posting lengthy multiple-question surveys on a newsgroup. If you are successful in generating a response, no matter how carefully you instruct respondees to forward completed surveys to you instead of reposting to the group, many will miss your instructions and repost to the group. The group will become clogged with copies of your survey. People will be unhappy. Unpleasantness will ensue.

For complex surveys, you may find it more rewarding to post an invitation to participate. Respondees email you if they wish to join. To increase the response rate, your newsgroup posting can offer an incentive for participation.

Web surveys

If newsgroups are the trickiest way to conduct surveys on the Internet, the Web is the safest. On the Web, visitors come to you, so you don't have to worry about seeming intrusive.

The drawback to the Web is that you have to find a way to convince people to visit your site to take your survey. If your site is busy, handling thousands of visitors each week, no problem. Just pepper your Web site with invitations to visit your survey page. If your Web site traffic is low, be prepared. You will need to work to actively promote your survey location to generate enough traffic to make a survey worthwhile.

The Web's capability for creating fill-in-the-blank forms makes it easy to write and design Web surveys. Plus, you can blend your survey results with the statistical data your Web site captures for rich and detailed results.

Something to remember in Web surveys is that your survey can be generated on the fly according to your respondent's previous answers. If your respondent says "Yes" to the question "Do you invest in bonds?" the next page can be questions about bond investments. If your respondent says "No," the next page can be something completely different. You can custom-tailor Web surveys for each respondent.

Web survey products and services

- Research Connections (**www.researchconnections.com**) conducts Web surveys and—something unique—Web focus groups.

- CLT Research (**www.cltresearch.com**) offers Web survey software called The Opinionator.

- Mediamark Research (**www.mediamark.com**) sells I-Net, survey software that requires Mediamark to process the results for you.

- Applied Business Intelligence (**www.biztelligence.com**) sells BizTelligence for Windows, software that generates Web and email surveys. The Web surveys have built-in JavaScript error checking, which increases the accuracy of your responses. But what's really cool is that the software uses artificial intelligence to find hidden patterns in your results.

- Decisive Technology (**www.decisive.com**) sells Decisive for Windows, which generates Web and email surveys. It costs $800 to $10,000 for the version that generates both Web and email surveys, or between $500 to $2,500 for Feedback, a Web-only version.

- SmartChoice (**www.smartchoice.com**) makes SmartPoll, available as a Unix software program, for non-Unix companies as a standalone hardware/ software product, or as a service bureau offering. Prices start at $425 for one-time polling of 100 participants.

- Marketing Masters' product Survey Said for the Web (**www.surveysaid.com**) is a Windows program.

- WorqSmart (**www.wsmart.com**) produces Simply Surveys for Windows and the Mac to generate Web surveys, but one reader reported that his Webmaster was unable to get it to work.

Rules for Internet marketing surveys

Whether you conduct surveys using email, newsgroups, or the World Wide Web, these two rules hold true for all Internet marketing surveys:

1. *Only do consumer research with the agreement of the consumer.* Many Internet users have strong concerns about the use of their names and addresses, and about how their information will be used. Tell your potential respondents about the uses and implications of participating in

your survey. Be explicit. Let them know that their names and addresses will not be used for solicitation or sold to another vendor.

2. *Conduct surveys anonymously;* Internet surveys can be biased by a respondent's feelings about your company. For instance, a survey on Pentium microprocessors by someone whose Internet address ends with **intel.com** will pull different responses than the same survey by someone from **research.org**. This bias especially affects surveys done in your company's own Web site. Internet people respond more honestly than most, but it's harder to say negative things directly to someone. Being in someone's Web site is like visiting your kindly aunt's parlor. When she asks, "How do you like my cat?" most people will answer "It's very nice," even if it drools and has ringworm.

You can reduce the effects of that bias by conducting surveys in conjunction with a research company or an educational institute. Some of the most valuable Internet surveys are conducted by universities. Many are glad to work with private companies. For an example, visit the University of Michigan's Hermes survey of Web buyers: **www-personal.umich.edu/~sgupta/hermes**. On its Web page, Hermes openly invites businesses to participate and to suggest questions for future surveys.

News detectives

Ecola Newsstand (**www.ecola.com/news**) links to Web sites of more than 4,500 printed newspapers, business journals, and magazines that make their full text available in English. Most are free, some charge fees. While it's wonderful that Ecola Newsstand serves such a rich banquet of resources, it is impossible to fully digest so much news. Even if you cut Ecola's massive catalog down to the 60 or 70 business periodicals most useful to you, will you find time to read them?

Not a chance. To keep up with your competition and your markets, you need to stay on top of the news. But the Net is so rich in information resources that you will never even *find* them all, let alone read them. That's why it makes sense to have someone else search for important news for you, and pull only the stories you most need to see—like an electronic clipping service, only faster, cheaper, and smarter.

At first glance, Individual, Inc. (**www.individual.com**) seems to solve this problem. You choose what subjects you want Individual to cover from a list it provides. Individual's software combs stories each night from more than 400 English-language sources, and delivers your choices to you. Individual offers three news services: First! ($5,000 to $8,000 per company), Heads Up (headlines and summaries for $30 per month per person, plus $4 per complete article), and NewsPage (basic services free, premium services $4 per month; plus pay-per-view charges). On closer examination, Individual still doesn't solve the problem of sleuthing out exactly what you need and eliminating extraneous junk.

Individual's Achilles heel is that you receive stories based only on *its* list of topics, not on your own. Individual lets you choose which topics to deliver from a predefined list of hundreds. If your topic is not on that list, forget it. You cannot search for articles mentioning only your company's name, or your company president's name, or your competitor's name. When this book comes out, I will want its reviews delivered to me, but I can't search by my name or by my book's title, so Individual will be useless to me (and probably to you as well).

However, other services can give you what you need: the ability to search for *any* topics, names, or words that you wish. These companies act like news detectives, searching for clues you need and bringing back only the most relevant evidence.

Many such services exist on the Net. They differ in the sources they search, the ways you tell them your needs, the ways they present results, and the prices they charge. Some of the newer services use Web *push* technology to turn results into Web pages and deliver them to your Web browser, but unless the push technology lets you choose exactly what you want, its results may still be useless to you.

Here are some of the best news detectives on the Net:

- Reference.com (**www.reference.com**) searches 150,000 sources: newsgroups, email lists, and Web forums. You must register, but this valuable service is free. One caveat: its matches are loose, especially for multi-word topics, so you get some chaff with your wheat. Look for "Stored Email Queries" to set up a standing search which Reference.com will email to you.

- Newshound (**www.newshound.com**) searches 58 Knight-Ridder newspapers, plus Reuters, AP, Business Wire, PR Newswire, and the Kyodo News Service. NewsHound does not monitor Usenet newsgroups, and it does not search as many publications as Individual, Inc. But it not only searches articles, it also searches *classified advertisements*. NewsHound searches often—once an hour—and emails to you articles and advertisements that match your criteria. Or you can pick them up from its Web site. NewsHound charges $8 per month for up to five "hounds" (a hound is a standing search). You can modify your hounds based on how well what you receive meets your needs.

- MarkWatch (**www.markwatch.com**) is a specialized service. It looks for your product names and trademarks to see how people refer to your company and its offerings. For $900 per year, it searches Web sites, newsgroups, chat rooms, and email lists, plus 400 news providers, and reports on its findings. The MarkWatch service is good, even though its Web site is annoying.

- Cyberscan (**www.dnai.com/~cyberscan**) searches newsgroups and Web sites for your topics. Its prices vary.

- GINA, the Global Internet News Agency (**www.gina.com**) provides a service called WebClip that monitors newsgroups for $200 per month.

- eWatch (**www.ewatch.com**) monitors more than 33,000 newsgroups, 8,000 email lists (for $300 per month), plus forums on CompuServe, America Online, Prodigy, and Microsoft Network (for another $300 per month). Its WebAlert covers designated Web sites (for—you guessed it—$300 per month). For each service, you pay an additional $2 per clip (ouch!).

- Federal News Service (**www.fnsg.com**) provides access to same-day transcripts of briefings, press conferences, hearings, and speeches from the U.S. federal government. It also provides United Nations announcements and resolutions, and English translations of press conferences, statements, briefings, and interviews of Russian leaders. This is a free service if you just make searches and retrieve headlines; you must pay for the full text of stories. Or pay a monthly access charge for unlimited use.

- The *Federal Register* is available by 10 a.m. (EST) each day at **www. counterpoint.com** for a fee of $1,000 per year, searchable back to 1985.

For more news detectives, go to Yahoo and search for "personalized news."

CHAPTER 24

Purchasing, Logistics, and EDI

"Companies are not interested in building technology. They are interested in building their business."

—Jim Sha, CEO, Actra Business Systems

Any operation involving manufacturing, purchasing, warehousing, or transportation involves moving large amounts of information back and forth as quickly as possible. Anytime you move information, the Internet can be a useful tool. Saddam Hussein and the Iraqi army figured out the same thing. They used the Internet to support their command and control system during the Gulf War, much to the annoyance of the U.S. military.

Businesses also use the Internet for purchasing and logistics, often on a large scale. Larger companies are beginning to use the Internet for EDI (Electronic Data Interchange) to automatically move business data between their computers. Several industry associations and consortia are helping to speed the adaptation of the Internet to logistics needs and to make it accessible by smaller companies.

Steven Gage, President of CAMP, the Cleveland Advanced Manufacturing Program (**www.camp.org**), works on technology transfer for small and medium-sized companies. He believes the Internet is a big help in making manufacturers more competitive and in providing support to these and other companies. He points to TECnet (**www.mep.nist.gov/centers**), which provides government information, small business advice, and databases of used equipment for sale. Through it, manufacturers exchange information with each other and tap into technical discussion groups on the Internet. Subscribing companies pay only a small yearly fee to access TECnet.

At the forefront of the Internet and logistics is another organization, CommerceNet (**www.commerce.net**). A consortium of corporations, government agencies, and industry groups, CommerceNet spawned several working groups that focus on such issues as purchasing over the Internet and using the Net to integrate design and manufacturing.

One of the founding members of CommerceNet was AVEX Electronics (**www.avex.com**). AVEX helped define CommerceNet's strategic initiatives for shortening the time-to-market cycle for electronics manufacturers, by using such techniques as concurrent product development and electronic bidding.

"Access to knowledge from anyplace at any time—that's the goal," said Paul Kozlowski, AVEX president and CEO. "Any method to improve information flow is going to dominate in the coming decades. Electronic transactions for inventory, order placement, and engineering collaboration are going to be aggressively pursued by electronics companies."

"Doing business over the Internet has the potential to significantly improve the ramp-to-volume production process, all the way from conceptual design to full production," explained Mike Gordon, advanced systems manager for AVEX and a board member of EIDX, the Electronics Industry Data Exchange Association (**www.eidx.org**).

At some companies, engineers at different locations use the Net to view and edit new product designs at the same time. Engineers in quality, test, and other disciplines can collaborate in realtime. Customers of AVEX responded well to the idea of using the Net to send bills of material for competitive bidding.

In the long run, putting your inventory, delivery, and order tracking on the Net makes for more inventory turns, letting your company improve planning and reduce stock levels. From your customers' viewpoint, you will have faster and more flexible delivery. But in the short term, purchasing operations realize the most benefit from the Internet.

Purchasing and the Internet

The most frequently-used function of the Net for purchasing is as a humongous information resource. Buyers take advantage of hundreds of Buyer's Guides on the Net. Guides help you purchase everything from broadband telephone equipment (**www.broadband-guide.com**) to biotech products (**www. biosupplynet.com**). To find many more, visit your favorite Web search engine and look for "buyer's guide."

In addition to the Web, newsgroups are a big help for purchasers, from the largest companies to the smallest. In newsgroups, you'll find a lot of information about products (especially computer-related products), including the kind of insights you can only get from someone who has used a product first-hand. For instance, this example was posted on the **biz.comp.accounting** newsgroup in response to a small business purchaser asking about the difference between two accounting software programs, Simply Accounting and QuickBooks.

```
My personal opinion is to steer clear of Simply Accounting. I've worked
with the package a few times and my experiences have always been poor. As
far as QuickBooks is concerned, I do like this package. My clients that
use QuickBooks normally are satisfied with the package. A big limitation
to QuickBooks is it is very limited in the inventory area. If you have
inventory for sale, as opposed to offering only services, you might
consider MYOB from TeleWare...about as easy as QuickBooks but a little
more powerful.
```

You won't get that kind of evaluation from a sales rep worried about a commission.

Finding suppliers

Consider a purchasing agent who prepares a large RFP and sends it to prospective suppliers via email or lets them retrieve an electronic copy from a Web page. This approach saves printing costs, postage costs, and a great deal of time compared to the old hard-copy way of doing things.

The U.S. Agency for International Development procures goods and services costing $5.5 to $6 billion per year, and puts RFPs (written in governmentese, not English) for everything on its Web site at **www.info.usaid.gov**, where any company can bid on purchases. The agency reports that it significantly lowered costs in some cases and added many new vendors. USAID had never known about most of the new suppliers until they submitted bids.

General Electric reports similar results. GE makes more than $1 billion per year on Web-based purchases. GE does sourcing, bidding, and negotiating on the Net. It puts requests for quotes on its Trading Process Network (TPN) (**www.tpn.geis.com**), where any company with a Web browser can make a bid. 2,000 suppliers have visited its site and registered to bid on GE purchases. GE estimates its Web site has reduced prices by 10 to 20 percent, and says the costs of Web-based procurement operations are 30 percent lower. Web purchasing has reduced GE's requisitioning time for machine parts from seven days to two hours. GE now sells TPN to other companies so they can put RFQs on the Web.

Manufacturers aren't the only ones using the Web to locate suppliers. Womex (**www.womex.com**) helps retail buyers purchase merchandise for stores from 20,000 manufacturers in countries around the world. Buyers subscribe for

$50 a month. They find items on the Womex Web site by browsing through categories or by searching for keywords. The site presents the same product, marketing, and price information that buyers see on a paper product sheet. When a product looks good, buyers can reach manufacturers by email for samples or more information.

The Womex site specializes in the retail merchandise trade. Another similar service, Asian Sources Online (**www.asiansources.com**), serves more industries than Womex, but is geographically limited. Asian Sources gives buyers access to product and ordering information from 40,000 suppliers of retail merchandise, electronic components, and manufacturing supplies—all in Asia, but you probably guessed that. Asian Sources is free to buyers.

One of the best-known is Industry.Net (**www.industry.net**), which gained notoriety when it filed for bankruptcy (caused, in my opinion, by a top boss who bloated its staff to 250, including many overpaid execs). As I write this, Industry.Net is still in business and still extremely useful for buyers. Thousands of industrial suppliers provide catalog information and specifications for all kinds of industrial equipment, parts, and supplies. Products are viewable by product type, by manufacturer name, and by recency, so you can choose to review, for example, just the new machine tools introduced in the last six months.

Industry.Net's missteps boosted traffic for its competitors, including ProcureNet (**www.procurenet.com**), Manufacturing Marketplace (**www. manufacturing.net**), and specialty sites like PlasticsNet (**www. plasticsnet.com**).

The World Wide Web isn't the only part of the Internet purchasers use to locate new suppliers. Purchasers also use newsgroups and email lists. Condensed versions of RFPs posted on newsgroups reach a wide audience of prospective bidders. For example, I found a posting on **news:alt. business.import-export** from a purchaser looking for bidders to supply 1,000 PC clones. This newsgroup also includes for sale messages. It has offered Marlboro cigarettes in minimum lots of ten cargo containers, electrical capacitors, and 40,000 metric tons of metallurgical grade coke, apparently stuck on a loading dock in China and available for quick shipment at a bargain price.

An email buying-and-selling list called Trade-L is similar to that newsgroup, but more tightly managed. Trade-L is moderated. Neither spam nor multilevel marketing nonsense is allowed. If you purchase items in bulk—especially commodities—Trade-L can be a serious money saver for you. Visit its Web site at **www.scbbs.com/~tradewinds**. To subscribe to Trade-L, send an email message to **trade-l-request@intel-trade.com**. Make the "Subject:" of your message **SUBSCRIBE** and the body of your message just the single word **SUBSCRIBE**.

Cutting costs

Purchasers are always under pressure to reduce prices. The Net can be a cost cutter for both direct and indirect expenses, including reducing design work. PartNet (**www.part.net**), lets designers specify, find, and select parts from a collection of online parts catalogs, reducing design time by letting companies purchase existing parts instead of designing new ones.

A service called FAST Electronic Broker (**http://info.broker.isi.edu/1/fast**) uses the Internet to find new vendors and lower prices for purchasers. The Information Sciences Institute at the University of Southern California operates this nonprofit service. It costs nothing to join and charges no monthly or annual fees. It uses email and the World Wide Web to quickly disperse your requests for quotes and to send price quotes back to you quickly (as its name implies). You send your RFQ or RFP to FAST. It matches your needs with its huge database of vendors. Then it emails your RFQ to appropriate suppliers. You compare FAST's price quotes with any quotes you receive from other sources, adding an 8 percent surcharge to the FAST quotes (which is how FAST recoups its costs). You pay FAST only if you decide to order from one of its quotes. It is best for reducing prices on small quantity purchases.

GROUP DISCOUNTS

You can team up with other businesses to negotiate quantity discounts from a supplier, like the person who wanted to buy one car. He used newsgroups to find other people interested in the same car, then negotiated a low price from the dealer because of the quantity.

The same idea allows 3,000 local government agencies in Pennsylvania to get volume discounts on commodities. The agencies go to a secure Web site to buy from vendors under state master contracts for everything from food service to office supplies.

Similar cooperative organizations help businesses. The Brookstone chain estimates that RETEX, the Retail Technology Consortium, saved it $200 million and cut its credit authorization fees in half. Big savings like that explain why membership in RETEX (**www.retex.com**) jumped from 12 retailers to 1,500 in four years. RETEX is a nonprofit cooperative purchasing group, so retailers can gang up and buy high tech products and services for reduced prices. Member retailers get discounts on card processing, automation networks, teleconferencing, telecommunications audits, and other techie stuff.

Some Internet cost reduction solutions focus on very specific niche expenses. For example, RoweCom (**www.rowe.com**) offers a purchasing service called Subscribe to large corporate and academic libraries. Rowe handles ordering, renewing, and payments for subscriptions to serials, and reduces serials costs up to 8 percent per year. This can save tens or even hundreds of thousands of dollars annually for large organizations.

These nonprofit and for-profit cooperative Net organizations multiply like bunnies. The Internet makes them cheap to start and run, so if you can't find a purchasing co-op for the products your business uses, you can start your own.

OBI: Open Buying on the Internet

Open Buying on the Internet (OBI) gives purchasers a cheap, fast way of using Web catalogs to buy the high-volume, low-cost items that account for 80 percent of most companies' purchasing activities—what software company Ariba calls "operating resources," purchases that are neither raw materials for manufacturing nor products for resale. Examples are MRO materials and office supplies. The OBI standard was created by the nonprofit OBI Consortium, an offshoot of the Internet Purchasing Roundtable. It is supported by large corporations and high-tech companies including Netscape and Microsoft.

OBI uses the Web to help purchasing managers improve the way requisitioners throughout a company procure goods and services. It lets requisitioners buy from customer-specific Web catalogs, with prices, products, and services as negotiated for your firm, so someone buying one box of paper clips still gets your company-wide quantity discount.

How does OBI work? Say Kevin the supply clerk needs to buy a case of copy paper. Kevin fires up his Web browser, goes to his purchasing department's Web page, and searches for "paper" to find a list of approved paper suppliers. He clicks on a supplier's name to see prices and terms for that supplier. For each supplier, Kevin sees a custom-generated catalog, listing only the products and prices available to supply clerks in his company. This catalog is actually on the supplier's Web server, but Kevin doesn't know or care. After comparing terms from different vendors, Kevin picks Peter Piper's Pickled Papers, selects a type of paper (plain) and clicks on a "Create Order" button. A Web page appears with a partially filled-in purchase requisition. Kevin doesn't know that behind the scenes Peter Piper's Web server communicated with the Web server at Kevin's company, or that they verified each other's authenticity. He also doesn't know that his requisition is partially filled-in because his purchasing department supplied a requisitioner profile of Kevin. The shipping information is already entered, so Kevin enters his order quantity (one peck), his name, his employee number, and clicks on a "Place Order" button.

Kevin is done, but his purchasing department's computer isn't. It checks to make sure that Kevin is authorized to purchase this type of product and amount. The computer approves his OBI order information and passes it to Peter Piper's Pickled Papers, which picks a peck of plain paper, packs it, wraps it, and ships it.

That's a sample of a simple OBI purchase. OBI makes purchasing easy for requisitioners while letting purchasing managers minimize errors and maintain control. A purchasing department can create a list of preferred vendors and negotiate contractual relationships with them. Purchasers provide vendors with requisitioner profiles, approvals parameters, and tax status.

You must have a Web server to take part in OBI, because OBI Order Requests and OBI Orders are exchanged using secure Web servers. Your Web server must be able to authorize certain transaction types with a payment processing company.

More information on OBI is available from Supply Works at **www. supplyworks.com/obi/index.html** or the OBI Consortium at **www.obi.org**.

Software

The first OBI-enabled purchasing software is the Operating Resource Management System from Ariba (**www.ariba.com**), which costs $750,000 and up. It is completely written in Java, and so can run on any computer that has the horsepower to handle your transaction load. It includes a secure Web server, an adapter layer that interfaces with your existing systems, and applications for purchase and service requistions.

OrderXpert Buyer from Netscape subsidiary Actra (**www.actracorp.com**) will also cost several hundred thousand dollars. It will accept requisitions, consolidate purchase orders, and route proposed purchases to the proper parties for approvals. This OBI-enabled system will be available for Unix and Windows NT.

A forthcoming Internet-based purchasing system called OrderManager/Buyer from SpaceWorks (**www.spaceworks.com**) sounds promising, but SpaceWorks isn't sure whether it will support OBI or not. The SpaceWorks system will run on Unix and Windows NT.

A key advantage of OBI-enabled purchasing software is that you can buy from any other company that uses OBI software. With non-OBI purchasing software you must enable each vendor one at a time, and you have to alter your extranet security to let them in.

Unfortunately, the first OBI solutions are only for large companies. OBI software for small companies should be available in 1998.

More Net purchasing info

The National Association for Purchasing Management's branch in Silicon Valley has a site on the Net (**www.catalog.com/napmsv**) that provides more information on purchasing and the Internet. It includes an Internet-based course on purchasing fundamentals, articles on purchasing and EDI (Electronic Data Interchange), and links to dozens of other Web purchasing and procurement sites.

The parent NAPM also provides its own Web site for purchasers at **www.napm.org**. You'll find useful information, including the NAPM Semi-annual Economic Forecast, the monthly *NAPM Report on Business*, and articles from *Purchasing Today*.

Logistics and the Net

Cervecería y Maltería Quilmes S.A. brews Argentina's most popular beer, which it sells to distributors who transport beer by truck to thirsty South Americans. The brewer's distributors weren't happy. Their truckers had to drive hundreds of miles to the brewery and wait in a queue for their cargo. Sometimes drivers sat and waited for more than a day. To avoid such waits, the brewer's distributors spent an average of $2,600 apiece on phone calls each month, checking product and loading dock availability. Now the brewer puts truck loading schedules for more than 100 distributors on password-protected Web pages. The Web data is available on satellite links for about $140 per month, saving the distributors' money. Distributors can check their order status instantly on their Web page and receive billing information, so the brewer gets paid sooner.

Want another beer? Heineken (**www.heineken.com**) uses the Web to provide continually-updated data to its distributors from its home office in Amsterdam and from its distributors to the Heineken home office. Distributors enter their sales figures and orders on Heineken's Web site. Based on information from its Web site, Heineken reroutes shipments or adjusts production to fit changes in demand. In the dark, pre-Web era, distributors waited 10 to 12 weeks for their orders to be filled. Now Heineken fills orders the same week they are placed.

Both brewery stories show the difference that instant delivery of constantly-updated data can make on a logistics operation. The ability to obtain accurate demand and inventory information from multiple locations can create savings that ripple up and down a company's entire supply chain.

If you want to apply the Internet to your logistics, you must create your programming from scratch. Software providers are abysmally slow in creating standard packages to put logistics data online. An exception is the latest version of the R/3 inventory system from SAP AG (**www.sap-ag.de**), which runs over the Net.

Unfortunately for wholesalers and retailers, many manufacturers aren't using the Net to streamline wholesale distribution, but to eliminate it altogether.

Bypass surgery

Times are tough for retail stores that sell software. Egghead Software lost millions of dollars for several quarters in a row. Babbage's and Software Etc.

chains filed for bankruptcy. But more people buy software programs every day, and software manufacturers' sales are surging. What's going on here?

Manufacturers are stealing customers from retailers, that's what. Internet customers are buying products directly from manufacturers, bypassing distributors and retail stores. This trend is dramatic in the software industry, but many industries are in upheaval. Sluggish layers of intermediaries collapse as customers squeeze distribution channels to their most efficient point. After all, customers can buy wherever they want.

One example is a new approach in the famously inefficient book distribution business. AllBooks (**www.allbooks.com**) is a spin-off of Publishers Marketing Association, created by small publishers. AllBooks is a virtual distribution company, cutting out book distributors, giving better prices to retailers and higher profits for publishers. AllBooks sells to the trade (bookstore buyers and libraries), wholesale only. More than 200 small publishers make their products available nonexclusively on the AllBooks Web site. The site makes it easier for the small publishers to reach bookstore buyers and also makes it easier for bookstores to buy at one central location instead of 200 separate ones. Buyers place orders on the Web site. Orders go directly to publishers, which must fill and send orders within one business day. AllBooks charges publishers a 5 percent fee to cover expenses.

The Publishers Marketing Association's experiment with cutting out book distributors is successful enough so PMA has launched two more middleman-eliminators. The PMA Web site (**www.pma-online.com**) now includes an online remainders sale, cutting out remainder brokers, and a Foreign Rights Virtual Book Fair, with online buying and selling of foreign rights, cutting out rights brokers.

This elimination of middlemen is growing to affect wholesalers, brokers, and retailers in almost every industry. "Collapse the distribution chain. Cut out the middleman," advises Open Market president Shikar Ghosh. "What is going on now is a land grab."

Bypass is a threat, but it also means opportunity. The Net lets you communicate with and sell directly to your customers. You can take advantage of this directness or get taken advantage of. It's up to you.

Internet distribution

Companies in some industries go far beyond using the Net to improve distribution. They actually transport products across the Net. The range of products is limited. (Don't plan to shove your cow through computer cables.) But radio commercials, print job artwork, and software can be distributed worldwide, quickly and cheaply, through the Internet.

Software

Microsoft leads the way in software distribution. It has created a framework to establish standards for what it calls ESD, which stands for Electronic Software Distribution. (What will these companies do when they run out of three-letter combinations?)

Several companies have announced that they will support ESD, including companies which specialize in delivering software to cable television set-top boxes. ESD solves problems that FTP doesn't address: limiting distribution to authorized recipients, payments, and ensuring that software recipients have only the most-recent version of software.

Fifteen percent of packaged software is now sold through ESD. This is expected to rise to half of all packaged software within the next three years according to the Software Publishers Association.

For some companies, the figure is already higher that the current 15 percent. One software publisher says between 30 and 45 percent of its sales come through the Internet, including both ESD orders and sales that are filled by shipping physical disks. Almost half of this company's sales come from buyers outside the United States, but for ESD sales close to 70 percent are non-U.S. customers.

The people who buy software over the Net tend to be the *most frequent* software buyers. The SPA reports a study saying that 65 percent of them purchase software on the Net once a month. Frequent buying propels ESD's fast growth. One software company reported that revenues from ESD sales increased 55 percent in one quarter. Another said that ESD sales grew 100 percent each month.

Software vendors get help with ESD from companies such as NetSales (**www.netsales.net**) and Online Interactive (**www.online-interactive.com**). For more information on this topic, check out the Electronic Software Distribution Forum (**www.softletter.com/esd.htm**), the ESD subcommittee of the Software Publisher's Association, (**www.spa.org/sigs/internet/ESD.htm**), and the articles at **www.globetrotter.com/articles.htm**.

Print jobs

The old way of printing was print-and-distribute. You took your artwork to one printer, printed all your pieces there, and shipped them wherever you needed them. The new way is distribute-and-print. You zap your artwork over the Internet to the printers closest to the final destinations of your printed pieces. Your job gets to your printer more quickly, and you save freight charges and customs duties. And you don't worry about hassles from customs inspectors.

Many companies use the Internet to send files to their service bureaus for prepress work. Now printers around the world are getting into the act, linking with printers in other countries and supervising remote jobs for their local clients. For example, a worldwide organization called the International Printing Network let a client submit a color catalog to the client's local printer, George Litho (**www.george.com**) in San Francisco, and print it at InterOffset, a printer in Brussels, Belgium. Proofing can be a stumbling block in distribute-and-print; in this case, InterOffset sent a color proof by courier to George Litho for the client's approval.

International Printing Network reports that 15 to 20 percent of its gross sales are jobs transmitted online. Many are time-sensitive publications such as newsletters or financial information. The remaining jobs are large documents with hundreds of pages or color jobs with huge file sizes, which are too time-consuming to send over the Net unless you have a T1 line. Many International Printing Network printers maintain client companies' entire document databases, especially for clients in electronics, aerospace, high-tech, or heavy manufacturing. This ensures that all manuals, documentation, and other print jobs worldwide are produced from the most accurate and up-to-date files.

Another organization providing distribute-and-print abilities to your business is Worldwide Electronic Publishing Network. Abbreviated as WEPN (pronounced "weapon"), the organization focuses on printers providing jobs with a quick turnaround time. One client needed 300 copies of a 30-page document for a trade show. The job was submitted to a WEPN member in Washington D.C. by the client on her way to the airport. By the time she arrived in Hawaii, her job had been printed there, delivered, and was waiting for her at her convention hotel. WEPN's home page is **www.wepn.com**.

A third organization, Printers Link, also consists of printers that handle quick-turnaround jobs, including Xerox DocuTech and color-on-demand printing. Color-on-demand print jobs are four-color print jobs in limited quantities (usually 2,500 or fewer copies) that need to be delivered in one to three days. Color-on-demand jobs usually cost about $1 per copy more than conventional color printing. Printers Link is at **www.abcdprint.com/p-link/ p-link1.html**.

If your business could benefit from sending print jobs over the Internet, visit the Web site of PINC, Printing Industries of Northern California at (**www.pincnet.com**). In the Web site's online version of the book *Print Buyer's Guide,* you'll find an excellent checklist to use to prevent the "Oh, I forgot one thing" syndrome when you prepare or approve electronic art for print jobs.

Radio commercials

Digital Courier International, a subsidiary of BC Telecom, duplicates and distributes radio commercials electronically. An advertising agency can use a 56 Kbps or faster connection to send a radio spot once to DCI. DCI can zap the spot to hundreds of radio stations in less than an hour. Many major advertising agencies use DCI, which distributes to more than 75 percent of Canadian radio stations and a growing percentage of U.S. stations. DCI charges a one-time fee of $250 to set up an account with an agency or station and fees comparable to much-slower Federal Express for each commercial distributed. The agency saves duplication charges and lots of time.

Electronic Data Interchange

Electronic Data Interchange (EDI) is a term used to describe the process in which the paperwork for a transaction between two organizations goes directly from the computer of one into the computer of the other, bypassing the standard paper version. EDI is expected to grow at 24 to 29 percent a year, depending on which expert you quote.

About $45 billion in sales per year is conducted electronically, with about half of that handled in the U.S. EDI is also used for many kinds of non-sales transactions. Businesses, educational institutions, and government agencies use EDI to exchange invoices, purchase orders, insurance claims, tax returns, warranty registrations, warehouse orders, inventory reports, shipping notices, vehicle inspection reports, contract proposals, inventory transfers, debit and credit memos, customs declarations, delivery schedules, and many other kinds of transactions.

Benefits to EDI-using businesses include lower labor expenses, faster processing, better inventory control, greater accuracy, and closer relationships with customers and suppliers. Drawbacks to EDI are security risks and the huge amount of money and work required to get EDI started.

Most companies using EDI don't use the Internet, but are locked into proprietary vendors' systems on leased phone lines. These proprietary networks are called value-added networks, or VANs for short. Proprietary systems cost more and make it tough for you to switch to another vendor that costs less or offers you more features. John Katsaros, president of Collaborative Marketing (**www.collmktg.com/index.html**), surveyed VAN users and found that most are unhappy with their network provider, mentioning as reasons network downtime, lost transactions, and high expenses. Many of those companies are looking at switching to the Internet for handling their EDI transactions.

The pioneer in Internet EDI is the Lawrence Livermore National Laboratory. Since 1992, Livermore Laboratory has moved more than 3 million EDI transactions over the Internet, primarily for purchasing. The project has been highly successful. Lawrence Livermore Lab reports lower costs, better reliability, and better message tracking than a VAN provides for EDI.

In 1995, a second phase was added. Working with Bank of America, Lawrence Livermore actually *pays* its vendors over the Internet. Lawrence Livermore sends an EDI payment order over the Internet to the Bank of America in a Privacy Enhanced Mail message. The bank then transfers funds to the vendor's bank account via the Automated Clearing House. This system, the first totally automated production system doing financial EDI over the Internet, pays $300 million per year to more than 3,000 suppliers. For a study of this first project, set your Web browser to **http://haas.berkeley.edu/~citm**.

NASA and router manufacturer Cisco (**www.cisco.com**) followed in Lawrence Livermore's footsteps by implementing Internet EDI systems for themselves.

CommerceNet has an EDI Working Group. The group's charter is to define an architecture to link buyers, sellers, and service providers on the Net, and to enable the expansion of EDI in ways that make it affordable and practical for use by all types of organizations and individual people. The group is addressing concerns about reliability, scalability, ease of use, speed, and logging and auditing. CommerceNet is conducting pilot projects that let buyers browse multimedia catalogs that can generate EDI-formatted quotations and orders, solicit EDI-formatted bids, place EDI orders without browsing, and generate EDI-formatted invoices and payments. Sellers will be able to respond to bids, schedule production, and coordinate deliveries using Internet EDI.

About 85 percent of EDI transactions are between businesses, and 15 percent are between businesses and government agencies. The Clinton administration has done a tremendous amount to speed U.S. governmental EDI. It requires all federal agencies to make all purchases under $100,000 electronically (not necessarily through EDI—many are made through emailed purchase orders). This has created a bonanza for some businesses. MDT Corp. of Arnold, Maryland, started making EDI sales with the federal government in 1994, and business grew so fast that in less than a year a person had to be hired just to manage MDT's email traffic.

Can your business get in on this government business? Yes. A company called **Simplex** (**www.edi.com**) helps small companies do EDI with U.S. Government agencies. The only book on the subject is *Doing Business with the Government Using EDI* by Jan Zimmerman. (VNR, 1996, 200 pages) ISBN 044-202-1887. It's a dry read, but has some useful information.

Should my business do EDI?

First, EDI is not easy. You can't just drive to your local Egghead Software and buy "EDI in a Box" and pop it into your computer. Complicated technical details are involved. First, what computer software does your company have that you would need to move data into and out of? Even for purchasing transactions, one of the most common uses of EDI, you are looking at interacting with a lot of software programs. Your accounting software, your inventory software, and your purchasing software all have data that will need to be extracted, and other data will need to be input.

Sound like a lot of work? It gets worse. Then you need to go through the same routine for every company you do business with. Everybody uses different software. None of them format data the same way. Before we get into this deeper, you may have second thoughts, which would be wise.

EDI is not for every business. Not yet, anyway. Even with new software products that simplify EDI, it still takes a significant investment of time and technology to make EDI work. Your key to deciding whether or not to get involved should be your customers. Do you have several customers who want to conduct EDI transactions with you? Or maybe one large customer? If your customers make it worthwhile, take a closer look at EDI. If not, back off and wait for the technology to make it easier.

The need for EDI standards

Since there is little chance that the makers of accounting software and other business systems will wise up and implement a standardized way of formatting business data, several organizations have developed EDI standards. With such standards in place, a company translating outbound transactions can translate all of them into one format, instead of learning new formats for everyone it does business with. And the same benefit applies in reverse. A company translating incoming transactions needs to only work from one format instead of many. Less variety and less work.

This idea of an EDI standard format caught on quickly. Everyone thought a standard was a great idea. In fact, organizations thought the idea was so great that they created *two* sets of standards. Incompatible, of course. The American National Standards Institute created one with the catchy name of X12. It is used in the United States. The United Nations sponsored the Electronic Data Interchange for Administration, Commerce, and Transport format (EDIFACT). It is used in the rest of the world. Fortunately, software programs are available to convert one format to the other. The whole issue won't matter because X12 is being merged into EDIFACT, so there will be only one set of EDI standards.

EDI mapping software

Although EDI sounds great, you still need to get the information from your software programs into EDI format, and vice versa. This has been no small challenge. In the past, companies hired huge crews of custom programmers to slog out miles of code to move information into and out of EDI transactions. A typical EDI implementation project took more than a year of solid work, and one operating in six months was considered a miracle.

To meet these needs, mapping software was created. To use most mapping software programs, you extract data from your system and feed the files to the EDI mapper. It plucks out the data and arranges it in EDI format. Then you can send the formatted data via Internet Privacy-Enhanced Mail (PEM). When you receive an incoming EDI transaction via PEM, you decrypt it and feed it to your mapper. The mapper builds a file that you can feed to your business software programs.

You can choose from several mapping programs, ranging in price from $4,000 to $50,000: In my research, the best-rated are STX from Supply Tech (**www.supplytech.com**), Mercator from TSI International (**www.tsisoft.com**— Netscape resells the TSI program), and Visual EDI from EDI-Able. Zipper by Dakin Technology (**www.pcug.org.au/~daktec**) seems interesting. Premenos (**www.premenos.com**) markets two mappers, a general package called EDI/e and more specific software that links only with Computer Associates' manufacturing and distribution products.

Most mapping programs require your programmers to write *bridge programs* to extract data from, for example, your purchasing system, and to bring that data to your mapping software. A forthcoming product called Bridgeworks (**www.nocalshopper.com/bridgeworks.html**) will require no programming, and will be able to go from system to system finding the necessary data automatically, building a single EDI transaction or a relational database of several transactions when needed. Bridgeworks will make it possible to move data from one company's *applications* directly into another company's applications. This new software will decrease the technical phase of EDI implementation (which now takes 3 to18 months) to 2 or 3 weeks.

The Internet part of EDI

For EDI, the Internet plays two roles. It is both a delivery mechanism and a source of information. You probably expect the Net to provide a lot of info on EDI, as it does on every technically-related business subject. That the Net is a delivery mechanism for EDI also comes as no surprise. But there are other EDI delivery mechanisms, and to understand the Net's strong and weak points for EDI, you must first know a little bit about your alternatives.

EDI delivery pipelines

There are four different ways to send and receive business documents and transactions using EDI. Your company does not have to stick with only one alternative. You may use more than one. In fact, you may have a big customer force you to use its preferred EDI method, even when you have other options already in place.

Some people are fanatics about one EDI pipeline or another and will insist that their baby is the best one for all situations. Watch out for people like this. A delivery method has become their religion, and emotional considerations will blind them to your specific business needs. If your company goes with EDI, choose your connection method or methods based on the business considerations between you and the companies with which you will swap EDI messages. Don't get bamboozled into thinking that one type fits all.

Direct connection. You can swap EDI messages with your trading partner via two types of direct connection. 1) If your partner is a huge and crucial customer, you might lease a fulltime phone line connecting you and your partner 24 hours a day. 2) More commonly, you'll dial up your partner and connect directly via a modem.

Advantages: A direct connection is the most secure way to transmit an EDI transaction, and has no per-character or per-transaction charges, unlike an EDI VAN. A direct connection is also faster than a VAN connection, and gives you immediate proof that your transaction was received. Because direct connections are faster than VANs, they are widely used within the European automotive industry for just-in-time operations.

Disadvantages: Direct connections can be costly to set up, and time-consuming to manage. A direct connection links your business with only one other business at a time; other connections link you with many businesses. If your partner suffers a communications glitch, with a direct connection you must send your data over and over again until it gets through. Direct connections for EDI often require expensive software and custom programming.

In a discussion on the EDI-L email group about direct connections, David Bersch described a dialup connection to Wal-Mart, perceptively pointing out its disadvantages: "If I dialed into Wal-Mart more than 10 minutes after 8:00 a.m. EST, we would get busy signals, get dropped connections, and get no connection at least 50 percent of the time. It normally took 45 minutes to download, map out, import, and post our orders. But if we called Wal-Mart (after 8:10 a.m.), it could take up to three hours to complete the process, throwing our MRP for the day off." My recommendation is that you implement a direct connection only with a trading partner that is an important customer or supplier, one whose business with you represents both a large dollar volume and a large transaction volume.

Value-Added Network. A VAN is a company that runs its own proprietary network for shuttling EDI transactions between companies. VANs usually charge a small startup fee, monthly fees, and additional fees based on how many messages you send and how long they are. To conduct EDI with the federal government and with some large corporations, you must use a VAN or VANs that they specify.

Advantages: A VAN offers lower startup costs than other methods. Unlike a direct connection, a VAN connection lets you connect once to send and receive EDI transactions to and from many partners. A VAN usually supports different types of access methods. VAN accounts are slightly more secure than Internet EDI, slightly less secure than direct connections. A VAN guarantees EDI message delivery, but Internet software now does the same.

Disadvantages: Most VANs work on a store-and-retrieve principle; you send your EDI message to the VAN, and it sits there until your trading partner retrieves it. The time a message arrives is controlled by the recipient, not the sender. VANs cause a significant time lag between transmission and receipt. This makes a VAN slower than a direct connection or an Internet EDI transaction. VANs' per-character and per-transaction fees cause higher ongoing expenses than other EDI connections. You can only use a VAN to do business with other VAN-connected companies.

I recommend using a VAN for EDI if you need the guidance and support a VAN can provide, if you have the extra budget to pay the increase in cost of a VAN compared to the Internet, and if you will not send EDI transactions that are time-sensitive. Of course, I make that recommendation assuming that you have important customers who use a particular VAN. Sometimes a major customer will insist that you use a certain VAN. If your customers don't use VANs, neither should you.

Virtual Private Network over the Internet. To create a VPN, you configure your firewall to allow your trading partner to reach certain portions of your data via the Internet, and your trading partner configures its firewall to do the same for you.

Advantages: A VPN combines the advantages of a direct connection (speed, security) plus the lower setup and transmission costs of the Internet. The time a message arrives is controlled by the sender, making a VPN useful for time-sensitive EDI. VPNs are also flexible. You can use them as direct pipelines to remote offices, and because they're so cheap, as temporary connections for a short-term project. When you're done, throw your VPN away.

Disadvantages: Some businesses are justifiably uncomfortable with the idea of another company reaching behind their firewalls. Instead of having a VAN guard your security, your company must configure and maintain security on its own. Usually, you will want to set up a separate VPN configuration for each business partner, which adds maintenance work for your technical staff.

Use a VPN when you have important business partners that use the Internet and the technical staff to maintain your VPN connections and to keep an eagle eye on security.

Regular EDI transactions over the Internet. On the Internet, regular EDI transactions are encrypted and include a digital signature that proves that the EDI transaction is from the sender and that it has not been altered. They are sent through the Net just like any other email message or FTP file, and the receiving party acknowledges them with a return message, which also includes a digital signature.

Advantages: The Internet offers advantages of cost, and just as importantly, of reach. Using Internet email, buyers solicit bids and place orders with thousands of vendors, both vendors who use the Internet and other vendors who use traditional VANs. Internet EDI transactions are delivered almost instantly, much more quickly than VANs. The time a message arrives is controlled by the sender, making Internet EDI useful for time-sensitive transactions.

Disadvantages: You must install software to encrypt your transactions and create digital signatures. Out of all options except a direct connection, this one requires the most support time from your technical staff.

Some people view Internet EDI as more risky than alternatives for three factors. The first is perceived *insecurity*. Lack of security on the Internet is what drives businesses to use proprietary VANs. Now that Internet security software is available, this has become less of an issue. When proper security procedures are in place, Internet EDI *transactions* are as safe as VAN transactions, but the Net itself opens your company to other security breaches.

The second perceived factor is *unreliability*. No network will be 100 percent reliable. The critical factor here is not your connection method, but your communications software. Well-built communications software will not trust any network. After it sends a message, your software should expect to receive either an acknowledgment that your message was received intact at the other end, or that it was not. On any kind of network, when a message is delivered late or not delivered at all, your reliability is only as good as the software that warns you when something is not right.

The third factor is related to reliability. It is *lack of traceability*. When something goes wrong with an Internet message, how can you tell who is responsible? Traceability is not just an Internet problem. If you use a VAN for EDI, and your VAN connects to another VAN and loses your message, you will have a tough time finding out what happened.

Accountability on the Internet comes into question because people hold misconceptions about the way the Internet works. Using Internet software available today, you and your trading partner can set up your email so your EDI messages do not leave your computer until your system has contacted your trading partner's computer. Even then, your EDI message will not be deleted from your software's "outbound" file until your trading partner's computer has received your entire message and given your software notification that your message was received. You can still do this if you have a part-time dialup connection to the Net, by arranging with your access provider to hold your messages until receipt has been confirmed. With receipts in hand, you have a straightforward way to trace any problem to the exact step in the process in which it occurred.

With the advances in EDI software and the widespread use of the Internet, a variation of EDI called *New EDI* or *ad hoc EDI* has sprouted. Where traditional EDI is used only by business partners who have established relationships prior to implementing EDI, New EDI uses the greater flexibility and security now available to conduct EDI transactions on the fly. You can find out more about New EDI, and most other EDI topics, from the Net.

EDI info from the Net

The Internet is also a rich source of information about EDI and how to conduct it. If your company is interested in EDI, you can find a good explanation of how to start at "Getting Started with EDI," available at **www. catalog.com/napmsv/edi.htm**.

One of the best EDI resources anywhere is the EDI-L email discussion group. Top experts from around the world answer questions on EDI and argue boisterously about business and technical issues. If you want to find out the truth about EDI vendors and products, this is the place to go. The group is moderated, so there is no spam. It also provides good FAQs on EDI topics, including EDI and the Internet. To subscribe, email to **listserv@uccvma. ucop.edu** with a message saying nothing but **subscribe edi-l Yourfirstname Yourlastname**. You can also catch this discussion as a newsgroup: **news:bit.listserv.edi-l**.

An extremely helpful site to visit is the Electronic Commerce World Institute at **www.ecworld.org**. An EDI FAQ answers questions that small and medium-sized businesses have about EDI. You can read the entire book *A Road Map to EDI* by Stanley K. Ritchie at this Web site. It includes ten chapters and a glossary covering information from many sources. Ritchie tends to be a bit rosy-eyed in his view of EDI—for instance, his chapter on "Benefits and Limitations" is almost all benefits and few limitations. Still, he provides valuable information and lots of it. Another strength of Electronic Commerce World is its "Directory of EDI/EC Internet Resources," with many links to information and organizations to help you understand and implement EDI in your business. To get to this directory directly, go to **www.ecworld.org/ Resource_Center/Gateways/directory.html**.

The Electronic Commerce Resource Center at **www.ecrc.ctc.com** provides a different kind of information. This government-sponsored Web site is your key to free goverment assistance in implementing EDI in your business. ECRC's mission is to help "U.S. integrated civil-military industries," whatever that might mean, get started with EDI and electronic commerce. If you qualify, you can get free help from ECRC to plan and implement EDI.

The largest single source of EDI information on the Net is the Web site of Premenos (**www.premenos.com**). Go here for how-to information, EDI standards, contact information for EDI organizations, subscriptions to several email discussion groups covering EDI (including two on "New EDI"), and much more.

Internet EDI products and companies

Privacy-Enhanced Mail is used by some companies doing EDI on the Net. PEM provides end-to-end security, and it notifies you when your message is delivered. PEM EDI works over VAN networks as well as on the Internet. It can be used to carry any format of EDI.

MIME EDI provides a second way to handle EDI over the Internet. The EDI is encrypted and sent as a MIME email message. MIME EDI can carry EDI messages in any format. A third alternative EDI transport mechanism, less frequently used, applies FTP to shuttle encrypted transactions over the Internet.

Premenos is at the forefront of Internet EDI. Its $6,000 Templar system, available for both Unix and Windows, uses RSA public key cryptography and MIME email to send secure transactions across the Internet. Templar automatically confirms the receipt of an EDI transaction, showing the sender that the addressee received the transaction intact. A smaller version of Templar for businesses with low volumes of transactions costs $450. Note that Templar does not do EDI mapping, as described previously. You need to map your transactions before and after they move through Templar. Templar only handles the secure transport of EDI transactions and receipts. Any company looking at EDI should take a look at Premenos' Web site at **www.premenos.com**. There you'll find the largest collection of EDI information I've found anywhere on the Net, including links to many other organizations.

Actra Business Systems (**www.actracorp.com**) is a joint venture between Netscape and GE Information Services (GEIS). The idea is to put a familiar World Wide Web face on the clunky and difficult-to-use software that GEIS currently provides. Actra's ICXpert Internet EDI package takes business data from your existing software, converts it to EDI formats, and moves it across the Net to your trading partners. The system costs $25,000 and up and is available for Unix and Windows NT.

GEIS (**www.geis.com**) offers a service called GE InterBusiness. It uses SmartGate security software from V-One Corp. (**www.v-one.com**) that handles authentication. SmartGate identifies the individual person at the other end of an EDI transaction, not just the computer he or she uses. InterBusiness costs $99 per person plus a per-transaction fee. Software is available for Windows, Macs, and Unix.

Supply Tech makes a simple communications module for exchanging EDI over the Net. Details at **www.supplytech.com**.

JEDDI Corporation is a nonprofit consortium working to standardize Judicial Electronic Document and Data Interchange, a form of EDI for courts and the legal profession. JEDDI allows electronic filing of court documents and EDI payments of court fees. It will save millions of dollars in copying fees and storage costs. A Court Filing Markup Language (CFML) similar to HTML has been developed as part of JEDDI and is in use by some courts. More information is at **www.jeddi.org**.

Finally, I'll sort of recommend a book:

From EDI to Electronic Commerce: A Business Initiative by Phyllis Sokol ★★★ (1995), McGraw-Hill, 305 pages. ISBN 0-07-059512-7. This is both a rewarding and a frustrating book. It gives businesspeople realistic instructions on how to cost-justify and implement EDI. The author clearly knows her subject and delivers—in a wooden writing style—much valuable information. But, having worked only with value-added networks, she is biased toward them. Even though this book was published in 1995, the word "Internet" is not mentioned once. The author assumes transactions will be processed in batch mode, and shows little understanding of online transaction processing. Most infuriatingly, she discusses standards, but doesn't tell where to find them. She names EDI organizations, but doesn't tell how to contact them. She mentions publications like *EDI World*, but doesn't tell where to reach them. Minor quibbles are that the book is U.S.-centric with scant international information and is poorly indexed. On page 53, it states that bisynch protocols can go up to 9600 bits per second and asynchronous protocols handle up to 4800 bits per second. Those speeds are now considered horribly slow. In spite of its shortcomings, this is an important guidebook for any company considering EDI, and I do recommend it. Just keep its flaws in mind.

CHAPTER 25

118 Cheap or Free Business Resources on the Net

"It's not necessary to be able to understand everything to be able to use everything."

—Anthony Robbins

This chapter's collection of Web sites, newsgroups, electronic books, email discussion groups, newsletters, and programs gives you a taste of what your business can find on the Net.

Each item in this chapter was selected for its relevance for *businesses*. To clarify which items I found the most helpful, I've used a five-star rating system. Stars indicate *usefulness* and no other factor—not good design, not ease of use, not pretty pictures. I looked strictly for what would most benefit a business.

>★★★★★ Highest rating. Rarely given. Extremely valuable for most businesses or for most businesspeople.

>★★★★ A superior resource. One of the best of its kind. Very useful for many businesses or for many businesspeople.

>★★★ Recommended. Either somewhat useful for many businesses, or very useful for certain businesses or by people in certain positions.

>★★ Useful only for a small number of specialized businesses.

>★ A bit useful for a tiny number of businesses.

You'll find that I give many of the items listed in this chapter relatively high ratings (three stars or more). It's not that I am generous, it's just that I don't feel the need to waste dead trees on useless online sites—nor do I think it would be fair to you to include garbage just so the title of this chapter could read "200 Free or Cheap Business Resources" instead of "118."

The Internet changes constantly, so don't be surprised if you go to one of these sites and find something radically different from what I describe. Or you might find nothing at all. Addresses change; it's almost certain that some of these sites will move by the time you read this—some might even have dropped off the Net altogether.

Find lost sites with the URL-stripping trick

When you try an Internet address and it doesn't work, someone may have moved your destination to another spot, or given it a new name. Here's a search pro's trick that will often uncover such hidden resources. Imagine that you are looking for the Maltese falcon's Web page at: **www.detect.com/casefiles/ spade/falcon**

Instead, you get the "Error 404" message that tells you your file is not there. Just delete everything to the right of the last slash, so your URL looks like this: **www.detect.com/casefiles/spade**

You'll either get another Web page, a directory of files, or another "Error 404." If nothing looks like what you want, once again strip away everything to the right of the last slash: **www.detect.com/casefiles**

Maybe you'll find another file named **blackbird**. That might be your **falcon** file renamed. When I find a URL that won't work, URL-stripping will lead me to its replacement more than half the time.

If I've left out your favorite Net source for business information, or if you find a mistake, let me know about it. You can reach me by email at **vince@emery.com**. I will post all corrections, changes, and new discoveries on my home page, **www.emery.com**, for you to read. Think of it as your free update to this book.

Accounting and finance

The best accountants have a passion to organize information and make sure that it is right. So don't let this surprise you: Some of the best-organized and most useful resources on the Internet are accounting and finance resources.

Accountants and finance professionals from all over the world have pooled resources to create extremely valuable Web sites and email discussion groups. Any change in FASB standards, any new government regulation (at least, from governments of major countries), any new tax policy is communicated world-wide the same day it is issued.

Keep one thing in mind about these Web sites: In their quest for accuracy, these sites change. *A lot.* So when (not if) you look at a Web site from this chapter and you see something significantly different from what I describe, don't fret. Rejoice—you'll have found a resource that's been updated and improved.

AAccSys-L discussion group ★★★★ This moderately active email discussion group talks about *everything* having to do with accounting systems software and hardware. You will find questions, answers, and conference announcements. An archive of past messages is available at **www.csu.edu.au/anet/lists/ AACCSYS-L/index.html**. To subscribe, email to **listproc@scu.edu.au** with the message **Help me.**

Accounting Professional's Resource Center ★★★★ This site is run by Kent Information Systems (**www.kentis.com**). The folks at Kent help accounting and financial pros use computer technology, especially the Internet. You can sign up here for excellent email discussion groups on accounting topics, and read sample issues of Kent's newsletters. You'll also find Site Seeker, a quite good, well-organized directory of accounting and taxation resources on the Net.

Banking on the WWW ★★★★ This site (**www.wiso.gwdg.de/ifbg/ banking.html**) seems to have links to every bank on the Net, plus every site for bankers and a lot of resources and information useful for people in other businesses. In spite of its name, Banking on the WWW includes both Web and non-Web resources. Presented by the Institute of Finance and Banking at the University of Gottingen, most information here is available in your choice of English or German.

CA-Xchange ★★★★ The Canadian Institute of Chartered Accountants (**www.cax.org**) sponsors this gathering place for CAs and their friends. It provides closed email discussion lists and private newsgroups where professionals have access to and discussions with other top professionals in their fields. To join, you must be a Canadian CA, have an equivalent designation from another country, or be sponsored by a CA, and pay annual dues of $120 CDN for CICA members, or $150 CDN for others.

Chartered Accountants of Canada ★★★ You'll find two high points here. The first is an excellent and thoroughly-described list of Web sites dealing with the specialized field of **environmental accounting**, and with business and the environment in general. We're not talking just Canadian environmental resources, but stuff from the whole planet. The second high point is a selection of articles from *CAmagazine*. This site (**www.cica.ca**) also includes abstracts on forthcoming standards, accounting job openings, and you can read everything in your choice of English or French.

Commercial Finance Online ★★★★ Looking for money for your business? At this site you'll find a database of commercial banks, investment banks, financial consultants, and venture capitalists But wait, there's more! If you need financing, you can list your business finance solicitation or proposal in a searchable database. But wait, there's still more! This site also offers eight email discussion groups on professional finance topics: factoring, leasing, investing (including buying and selling businesses), import-export, mergers (including

M&As and LBOs), venture capitalism, trade opportunities, and asset-based lending. Discussions are delivered by email, but you need to visit this Web site (**www.cfonline.com**) to subscribe.

comp.app.spreadsheets newsgroup ★★★★ Whether you love your spreadsheet or hate it, this discussion newsgroup might help (**news:comp. apps.spreadsheets**). It is an active, high-volume group, with the latest bug reports and news, plus lots of questions and answers.

comp.os.ms-windows.apps.financial newsgroup ★★★★ This active discussion group (**news:comp.os.ms-windows.apps.financial**) on Windows software is only 5 percent spam, but it discusses personal finance software (Quicken, Quickbooks, Money, TurboTax) more than business accounting programs. It's still a good resource, with questions and answers, technical tips, bug reports, and user group meeting announcements.

CPA-MGMT-MRKTG email discussion group ★★★ This is a spam-free, moderated email discussion group on managing, marketing, and growing a CPA firm. In this group, questions from beginners generate some genuinely helpful answers from experienced vets. Subscriptions are restricted only to professionals in the field—neither students nor wannabees need apply. You need World Wide Web access to subscribe (**www.kentis.com/lists.html**).

CPENet ★★★ This nonprofit organization (**www.gnacademy.org:8001/ ~compass/**) presents dirt cheap courses to earn continuing education units for CPAs and other financial pros. Courses on accounting, auditing, management, taxation, fraud examination, etc. are delivered over the Net for $15 per CPE hour.

Double Entries **newsletter** ★★★★ If you want to know what's going on with the major accounting journals but you don't have time to read them all, read *Double Entries* instead. This short, chatty weekly newsletter gives good coverage of accounting news all over the English-speaking world, especially in the U.K., U.S., Australia, and Canada. Think of it as an electronic *Reader's Digest* for accountants. If you'd like to look at past issues, you'll find a handy archive on the Web at **www.csu.edu.au/anet/lists/ADBLE-L/index.html.** Subscribe by emailing to **listproc@scu.edu.au** with the message **subscribe ADble-L Yourfirstname Yourlastname**.

Ernst & Young Canada ★★★ Provides two good online books, *Doing Business in Canada* and *Managing Your Personal Taxes*, plus a quarterly newsletter for Canadian entrepreneurs and scads of information on Canadian taxes. Email your tax questions to E&Y; answers are posted weekly to a Q&A section (**www.eycan.com**).

Institute for Fiscal Studies ★★★ This British site (**www1.ifs.org.uk**) provides two interactive simulations on taxes. One lets you enter your own income and expenditures and see how proposed government budgets pinch your pocketbook. "Be Your Own Chancellor" puts you at the helm of the government. Change tax rates and structures, then see how your changes affect government revenues and sample families.

International Accounting Network (Anet) ★★★★★. This site seems to list *every* accounting resource on the Net. You and I know that Internet sites proliferate more quickly than tax hikes, so that's impossible. But the folks at Anet make a valiant effort. Some of the information here is low-quality, and some is for academics rather than businesspeople, but if you poke around you'll find things your business needs, plus useful stuff that you'd never even think about. **www.scu.edu.au/anet**. In the USA: **www.rutgers.edu/Accounting/anet/ANetHomePage.html.**

Kaplan's AuditNet Resource List (KARL) ★★★★★ This huge catalog of accounting, taxation, investment, and financial resources is not only frequently updated and understandably organized, but—even better—every resource is extensively and intelligently described by James M. Kaplan. KARL includes many, many resources both on the Internet (newsgroups, Web sites, email discussion groups, etc.) and off. You'll find pointers to hundreds of resources here—so many that you won't have time to look at all of them. Kaplan's site is a tremendously useful accomplishment (**http://users.aol.com/auditnet/karl.htm**).

Ormsby & Mackan ★★★ This site (**www.ormack.com**) offers monthly articles on taxes and accounting topics, and links to Canadian business resources.

Summa Project ★★★★ This vast, searchable directory of worldwide accounting resources is managed by the Institute of Chartered Accountants in England and Wales (**http://summa.cs.bham.ac.uk**). A good deal of the information here is not available elsewhere. You'll find lots of resources here, including the European mirror site of Anet.

Treasury Connection discussion group ★★★★ If you're a cash management pro, check out this discussion group on global treasury management. As a subscriber, you can post questions, answers, and comments by email. Every Friday, you'll receive a digest of all messages sent by subscribers over the past week, moderated and spam-free. You can subscribe either by email or on the World Wide Web, but either way you'll receive messages by email. Go to **www.nationsbank.com/corporate/treasury/connect.htm**, or email to **majordomo@www. nationsbank.com** with the message **subscribe treasury connection.**

Treasury Log ★★ Its name is in English, but this bi-monthly newsletter is in German (**www.go-public.com/TreasuryLog**). Each issue covers a different theme in cash management: "Treasury im Internet" (basic but good), "Treasury im Osteurops," "Cross-Border Cash Management," etc.

Finding a job

First, a word about Internet job-hunting strategy. When you read the descriptions of the resources in this section, you may say, "Gee, they all sound good. Which one should I use?"

You have just made a strategic error. You cannot try just one. Even the biggest Internet job finding resource is only used by some employers. You will need to use several of them, and you will need to use them repeatedly. Don't assume that one electronic resume that you post in one place will be read by the world.

You will need to tailor several versions of your resume to meet the needs of several different resources. Think of your resume as a continually evolving work of art, like a Michaelango sculpture or my godmother Connie's spaghetti sauce. You keep adding, removing, and rearranging ingredients until—voila!—you have a job. The only way to tell when your resume is finished is when you are hired.

Until then, keep your resume—and your job finding tactics—flexible. Remember, no matter how many rules people give you, there are many different approaches to every step in the job finding process. So stay loose, be creative, and see what steps you can discover that will get you a job and help you enjoy the process.

America's Job Bank ★★★★ A network links 1,800 employment offices across the U.S., gathering descriptions of about 100,000 positions. This is the largest pool of job opportunities anywhere on the planet. You'll find America's Job Bank (**www.ajb.dni.us**) a little tricky to use. Think of it as a competency test. If you pass, you get job opportunities and lots of them.

Career Resource Center ★★ This huge directory of Net resources for job hunters includes many resources that other directories don't catalog. Perhaps this is an advantage, but some resources in Career Resource Center (**www.careers.org**) have little connection with finding a job. This site doesn't put descriptions on the links it provides, so we'll never know *why* it listed these sites. (If I ever want a bad example to prove that descriptions make links more valuable, this is it.)

CareerPath ★★★★ The Internet is killing newspapers. Fortunately for job hunters, newspapers are striking back by putting all their help wanted ads on the Net. You'll find job opportunities here from ads in the *New York Times, Boston Globe, Los Angeles Times, Chicago Tribune, San Jose Mercury News,* and the *Washington Post (*www.careerpath.com**).

Catapult ★★★ We found the Riley Guide by far the best Internet directory for job hunters, but it's not the only good one. Catapult is a winner, too. It is not nearly as well-organized as the Riley Guide, not as complete, and without Margaret Riley's good descriptions, but the Catapult people found some goodies that Riley missed. See the Catapult directory of employment newsgroups (**www.jobweb.com/catapult/catapult.htm**).

IntelliMatch ★★★ IntelliMatch (**www.intellimatch.com**) combines two services, one for employers and the other for job seekers. It's a free resume bank service, and a good one. Although it matches resumes with job opportunities worldwide, 65 percent of the openings it fills are located in the San Francisco Bay Area.

JOBS-ACT job-finding email list ★★★★ Unlike most Internet job-finding services, this one is only for experienced pros in taxation, auditing, accounting, finance, and cash management. It is *not* for students. Subscribers receive job openings by email. (For an archive of past job openings, email to the same address below, but with the message: **ARCHIVE JOBS-ACT**). To subscribe, email to **jobs-act@execon.metronet.com** with the "Subject:" line **SUBSCRIBE** and for the body of your message **SUBSCRIBE** (Do NOT include your name).

Monster Board ★★★★ The Monster Board (**www.monster.com**) is one of the biggest and best job-finding spots on the Net. You can post your resume online. You can do a search of job opportunities posted to newsgroups. And you can use either a traditional search or a very good multiple-choice-based search to find even more job opportunities. If you use the multiple-choice search, remember to look under the "ANY" category as well as under your own country/state/city locale.

Occupational Outlook Handbook ★★★ This book, published yearly by the Department of Labor, provides detailed information on more than 300 occupations: what the work is like, training required, salary ranges, and future prospects. Go to **http://stats.bls.gov/ocohome.htm**.

Optimist email job list ★★ This list is run by a software design recruitment company that provides listings of available positions around the U.S., with special emphasis in the Silicon Valley and Multimedia Gulch areas of California. Email to **listserv@netcom.com** with the message **subscribe optimist-l**.

Riley Guide ★★★★★ If you want entertainment, go someplace else. But if you want a job, make the Riley Guide your first stop. You'll find no flash here, just the best guidance on two things: *How* to search the Internet for a job and *where* to search the Internet for a job. (You'll also find good instructions telling personnel managers how to use the Net to find new hires.) Margaret Riley, author of the book *PLA Guide to Internet Job Searching*, created this helpful site. It is a well-organized directory of hundreds of resources for job hunters. Riley describes each one and evaluates it so you understand its strengths and weaknesses. You'll know what to skip where to go, and what to do once you get there. Investing time with the Riley Guide at the beginning of your job search saves time and helps you avoid mistakes (**www.dbm.com/jobguide**).

Top 25 Electronics Recruiting Websites ★★★ If you're an electronics pro, check out this directory (**www.interbiznet.com/top25.html**). It shows which Web services electronics employers prefer to work with. It makes sense to look for work where employers look for employees, right? You'll find links to all 25 sites. They include staffing services, employment networks, matching services, and recruitment advertising sites.

Human resources management

You'll find an extremely active community of HR professionals on the Net, providing you with dozens of resources, covering many areas. Besides Web sites, I've provided places you can ask a question about where to find something and get informed answers from your HR peers worldwide.

Benefits Link ★★★★ Employee benefits: What kinds? How much? How do you put them in action? Go here to find answers, and to find software to help. You can take out a free subscription to *Benefits Link Newsletter* or read the archive of past issues. You'll also find job opportunities here, a directory of Net sites, and a library with hundreds of papers and publications (**www. benefitslink.com**).

Benefits-L ★★★★ This is a two-for-one deal: a good Web site at **www.mtsu.edu/~rlhannah/employee_benefits.html** and a very good email discussion group, both covering employee benefits. The Web site gives you a large directory of Internet resources dealing with employee benefits. Most have good descriptions, written by HR pros who actually use the resources they describe. The email discussion group is one of the best in the HR field, a great place to go for answers to your questions and to find news of the latest regulatory and tax aspects of benefits administration. To subscribe, send an email message to **listproc@frank.mtsu.edu** with the "Subject:" line of your message blank and the body of your message containing only the words **subscribe Benefits-L Yourfirstname Yourlastname**. If you'd like a discussion of Canadian benefits, follow the same instructions, but for "Benefits-L" type "Benefits-CA".

HR Management Resources on the Internet ★★★ Ray Lye put together this well-organized directory. He's carefully given each resource a good, short description. I was disappointed to find so few spots from the U.K. listed. Go to **www.nbs.ntu.ac.uk/staff/lyerj/hrm_link.htm** for more information.

HR Professional Gateway ★★★ Resourceful Eric Wilson of Portland, Oregon built this directory (**www.teleport.com/~erwilson**). He provides good short descriptions of each resource. Besides having the most complete directory of Portland, Oregon, HR information, Wilson provides good lists of HR Web sites, HR email discussion groups, and recuitment Web sites.

Just Management ★★★ *Just Management* (**www.fairmeasures.com/newsletter**) covers one topic: how human resources managers can reduce the possibility of lawsuits. Its articles are short, timely, and right on target. You can subscribe to the printed version for $24 per year, or read it online for free, and research back issues as well.

LaborWeb ★★★ The home of the AFL-CIO presents news, an Economics Research Library of issue papers, a boycotted products list, information on the "Stop the Pain!" ergonomics campaign, and a directory of union organizations on the Web. Go to **www.aflcio.org** for more information.

LHH Severance Study ★★★ Firing employees is an unpleasant but unavoidable part of managing people. You'll find dozens of Web pages about hiring, but this is the only one about firing. It gives you the results of a survey in which almost 3,000 companies explained their severance policies and procedures (**www.careerlhh.com/n_svstud.htm**).

Lists of Interest to HR Practitioners ★★★★ This is the most complete directory anywhere of email discussion groups for human resources management and related fields: nearly sixty of them in English and Spanish. If you want to talk with your peers worldwide and do it without leaving your desktop, visit this site. Besides obvious topics like benefits, training, career development, and reengineering, you'll find your peers eager to chat about less-publicized topics, such as conflict management. Go to **http://bcf.usc.edu/~thaase/speech/hrlists.html** for more information.

Relocation Journal **★★★** This online magazine helps employers relocate employees, both temporarily or permanently, in the U.S. or internationally. You'll find helpful articles, and one database on U.S. relocation destinations and another on international destinations (**www.relojournal.com/main.htm**).

Relocation Salary Calculator ★★ If your company moves a manager (or perhaps you) from Boise, Idaho, to the spudless streets of New York City, the manager will find that the old paycheck doesn't stretch as far in Manhattan. Your question is this: How much will your business need to pay that manager in New York City to equal the same standard of living back in Boise? Your answer is: Ask the Relocation Salary Calculator (**www.homefair.com/homefair/cmr/salcalc.html**).

School of Industrial and Labor Relations ★★ This Cornell University project acts as a repository of labor relations material. Its Web site appears impressive, but once you dig in, you'll discover it doesn't offer as much as you hoped. Still, you will find some good information at **www.ilr.cornell.edu**.

Social Security Information ★★★★ You know what you'll find here (**www.ssa.gov**). Forms, FAQs, forms, rules, and forms. Did I mention forms? Look for the Quick Reference Guide for Employers, which links you to seven online publications for employers and the self-employed. Also, check out the *SSA/IRS Reporter*, a helpful newsletter for employers.

Society for Human Resources Management ★★★★★ This is a supermarket of HR information (**www.shrm.org**). You want directories of HR resources on the Net? Choose from two. HR Cyberspace's Top 20 is Mike Frost's selection of the top 20 Web sites for HR pros. HR Links is a huge bunch o' links covering every area of HR. (To go directly to HR Links, try **www.shrm.org/docs/otherlnk.html**.) Want news about the field? SHRM produces *five* online publications. Not enough? More news sources are listed on the SHRM home page. Want a job? You'll find job opportunities for HR pros under Products and Sources. In Student Services, you'll find entry-level HR job opportunities. If you're new to the field or if you just hired your first employee and want to avoid legal hassles, read the SHRM FAQ. It is a good quick introduction, covering the basics of human resources management and warning you of the most important laws and regulations. Looking for HR vendors? Try the SHRM Buyer's Guide in the Products & Services section. If you're a member of SHRM, you'll find even more in a special members-only area.

Virtual Office for the HR Professional ★ Tom Cary said that "The ultimate test that I would like to propose for user friendliness is quite simple: If this system were a person, how long would it take before you punched it in the nose?" This Ernst & Young site (**www.idirect.com/hroffice**) has good information, but fails Cary's test. It is a triumph of graphics infestation over common sense. If you are a Canadian HR professional with a 56k or faster Internet connection, this site can be worth the hassle. Everyone else should back off.

Workplace Savings ★★ One of the most valuable benefits a U.S. company can offer employees is a workplace savings plan, usually a 401(k) or 403(b). Explaining plans to staffers is often the most difficult part of implementation. If you have employees who don't understand, plunk 'em in front of this Fidelity Investments site (**http://wps.fidelity.com**). They can read FAQs that explain savings plans, then use an interactive retirement planning worksheet to calculate how much to save.

The Internet as a business tool

If you use the Net as a central part of your business, resources here will be useful for you. You'll find how-to information, sources of software tools, and strategy guides from some of the top minds in the business of Net business.

Comprehensive Resource for Commerce on the Internet ★★★ If you want to receive online payments, and you have questions, go here for answers (**http://e-comm.internet.com**). You'll find an intelligently-assembled collection of links by Thomas Ho. Background on the subject and some how-to information, with some of the worst applications of frames I've ever seen.

Computer Operations, Audit, and Security Technology (COAST) ★★★★ This is the largest archive of computer security information and software on the planet (**www.cs.purdue.edu/coast/coast.html**). Most everything here is for technical people, but you will find some nontechnical information for the slightly-above-average businessperson, especially in the areas of Internet and Web security. You'll also find excellent coverage of secure financial transactions on the Net with credit cards and digital money.

Internet Cafe Guide ★★★ Want to pick up and send your email while you're on the road? There are now more than 1,000 cybercafes around the world where you can drop in and have a good meal seated at a computer on a T1 line. Cybercafes give you complete Net access, so you can get your email using Eudora, or by using Telnet to reach your Internet access provider. If you're not sure how, not to worry. Cybercafes have knowledgeable, helpful staff. Before you go on a trip, make virtual visits to the cybercafes in your destination city. Jot down addresses, phone numbers, and hours (some are open 24 hours), and you're set. You might want to check with your company's Internet administrator before you leave to get your personal IP address or remote login instructions and a password. Go to **www.netcafeguide.com/index.htm**.

Journal of Internet Banking and Commerce ★★★★ This good (and free) bimonthly online journal focuses on Net banking and electronic commerce in the U.S., U.K., and Australia. It presents articles by well-known people in this field. It doesn't give you how-to information, but news of evolving strategies and reports on what works. You can read *JIBC* on the Web, or subscribe to receive it via email (**www.arraydev.com/commerce/JIBC**).

Journal of Internet Purchasing A sister publication to the previous online journal, this free bimonthly online journal focuses on using the Net for purchasing. You can read *JIP* on the Web or subscribe via email (**www.arraydev.com/commerce/JIP**).

Matt's Script Archive ★★★★ A collection of free and public domain CGI and JavaScript scripts you can use on your Web site, including electronic shopping carts and other software for Net merchants. Before you use any of his programs, be sure to read Matt's FAQ first (**www.worldwidemart.com/scripts**).

Network Payments and Digital Cash ★★★★ An enormous collection of links on the subject. This site is overwhelming at first, but the helpful descriptions of links will give you your bearings (**http://ganges.cs.tcd.ie/mepeirce/project.html**).

Running an HTML Business ★★★ This email discussion group talks about the *business* aspects of running a Web site, not the technology. It covers how to word contracts, how to increase traffic, comparisons of different products. A fair amount of the messages are about job opportunities, with people looking to hire both permanent employees and freelancers. Email to **majordomo@daft.com** with the message **subscribe hwg-business youremail@youraddress.**

WebMaster Magazine ★★★★★ *WebMaster* is a business strategy publication, not a technical publication. Its online site has some—not all—that's written for the monthly print publication, plus a lot that appears only online, not in print. You'll find excellent articles here on using Internet and Intranet technology in almost every aspect of business. If you like what you see online, you can have more. Just fill out the online form for a free subscription to the printed *WebMaster Magazine* at **www.cio.com/WebMaster/wmhome.html**.

Web Week ★★★★★ *Web Week* is a very good magazine covering business use of the Internet (**www.webweek.com**). At its Web site, you can read all the articles in the printed version, and search an archive of back issues. For answers to questions on running a Web site, check "Ask Dr. Website." You'll find a section here of Web-related job opportunities. If you like what you see, subscribe. Fill out the online form, and get a subscription to the printed version of *Web Week*—for free!

WinZip ★★★★★ Does your business use the Internet and Microsoft Windows? Then you need WinZip. If the Net is important to your business, you'll get software from the Net. Ninety-nine percent of the Windows software you get will be *zipped*, compressed for faster downloading. You can tell because the file name ends in **.zip**. You'll need to unzip that software and put it where you need it on your computer, and this shareware program is the fastest, easiest way to do that. With WinZip, you can look inside a file *while it's still zipped up*, see what's inside it, and even read text files (like **readme.txt**) to see whether it's worth unzipping. Go to **www.winzip.com** for more information.

Marketing, advertising, and publicity

Marketing people pull many businesses onto the Internet, and especially onto the Web. You'll find hundreds of Net resources to help you market. Here are a few of the best, which will lead you to many more.

Ad Medium ★★★★ An archive of advertising shareware and freeware, plus lots of links to advertising resources at **http://uts.cc.utexas.edu/~tecas/**.

Advertising World ★★★★ The biggest list I could find of advertising resources on the Net—hundreds of sites carefully arranged in dozens of categories. Most links have short, helpful descriptions (**http://advweb.cocomm. utexas.edu/world**).

Communication Arts ★★★★ The inspirational magazine for designers, writers, and other advertising creative people presents an inspirational Web site, complete with online exhibits and rich databases of information and resources on several topics. Check out the directory of about 150 carefully-chosen Web resources with short descriptions at **www.commarts.com**.

DM News **Online Edition** ★★★★★ *DM News*, the weekly newspaper of direct marketing, brings you an online counterpart that's updated *daily*. This is not a newspaper for the creative side of advertising, but for people who handle the business side of direct marketing. If you think your business doesn't use direct marketing, think again. All customer loyalty programs are direct marketing. All telephone sales are direct marketing. And *all Internet marketing is direct marketing*. Look here for very good coverage of Internet marketing, direct mail, catalog sales, database marketing, home shopping, mailing lists, and the best coverage of international direct marketing you will find (**www.dmnews.com**).

HTMARCOM-High Tech Marketing Communications ★★★★ This moderated email discussion group covers every aspect of marketing for high-tech businesses. Look for "how-to" and "Where-can-I-find" information, plus many job opportunities. Email **htmarcom-request@wolfbayne.com** with the message **SUBSCRIBE HTMARCOM**.

iMarket ★★★ Register for free online market analyses of every four-digit SIC code and other resources for marketers at **www.imarketinc.com**.

internet-sales email discussion group ★★★★ This great group covers everything relating to the actual *sales* (as differentiated from mere marketing) of stuff online: credit card processing, international shipping, order form design on the Web, and many topics that won't cross your mind until you read about them at this site. Go to **www.mmgco.com/isales.html** for more information.

Marketing Lists on the Internet ★★★ A directory of more than fifty email discussion groups covering PR, advertising, market research, and related topics (**www.wolfbayne.com/lists**).

Marketing Tools ★★★★ If any high-tech tool can help you market your business, this good magazine will cover it. You can read the complete contents of each issue online, and use a built-in search engine to find information from back issues (**www.demographics.com/Publications/MT/index.htm**).

Media Central ★★★★ This site gives you information and news about the media, including a newsletter with an update on the newest Web resources for media and marketing pros. You'll find information here on the Web as a medium, and on cable TV, print media, catalogs, and other media (**www.mediacentral.com**).

MediaNet ★★★ Co-op advertising funds (sometimes called *trade allowances*) let you shift ad payments to your vendor. Trade promotion spending in 1995 was estimated to top $33 billion. This Web site helps you get your share (**www.medianet.com/index.html**).

Softpub email discussion group ★★★ This email discussion group discusses software marketing and packaging. Some good tips here for businesses new to this industry. Email to **softpub-request@toolz.atl.ga.us** with the message **subscribe softpub Yourfirstname Yourlastname**.

Web Marketing Today ★★★ Here's a triweekly newsletter for small businesses that market on the Web. Each issue is short, with good, basic information on

Web marketing. Read each issue on the Web site or subscribe here and have it delivered to you by email. You can also read articles from past issues at **www.wilsonweb.com/rfwilson/wmt.**

The Weekly Guerilla ★★★ Jay Conrad Levinson, author of *Guerilla Marketing* and *Guerilla Marketing Online,* presents an informative Web site for marketers, with new tips and techniques added weekly (**www.gmarketing.com**).

Small business and home office resources

As many people report, one of the great attractions of the Internet is that it helps level the playing field between small businesses and their larger competitors. The large number of entrepreneurs and small businesses on the Net has attracted a proportionate number of resources for small businesses, startups, and people who work at home.

alt.computer.consultants ★★ If your business consults about computers, software, or any aspect of computing, visit this newsgroup. Ignore the ads from headhunters and get-rich-quick garbage, and you'll find real consultants helping each other. Go to **news:alt.computer.consultants.**

Business Network International ★★★ Business Network International declares that its "sole purpose is to increase business through a structured system of giving referrals." In 1995, its referrals generated $105 million in business for BNI members in the U.S., Canada, and Europe. It obviously works. If your business depends on word-of-mouth referrals for sales, this organization (founded by author and businessman Ivan Misner) could be extremely valuable for you. There is no fee to attend meetings, but READ THE FAQ before you decide to join (**www.bninet.com**).

Consult-L email discussion group ★★★ Questions and answers about clients, billing, taxes, and other issues that affect consultants and independent contractors, especially freelance software programmers. To subscribe, email to **listserv@switchback.com.** Leave the "Subject:" line of your message blank, and make the body of your message **subscribe consult-l Yourfirstname Yourlastname.**

Edward Lowe Foundation ★★★★ This nonprofit organization supports entrepreneurship and provides valuable information. One of the best is a detailed report from Michigan State University describing what differentiates successful entrepreneurs from those who are not. Based on research into actual practices—what real entrepreneurs actually do—rather than theory, Michigan investigators found six "guiding principles" common to successful entrepreneurs. Those principles and the key actions derived from them are described in *Entrepreneurship and the Future of the American Free Enterprise System*, which you can read here. In spite of its title, the lessons it reveals are useful for businesspeople worldwide. At this site you'll also find dozens of directories, databases, and additional resources for entrepreneurs (**www.lowe.org**).

International Small Business Consortium ★★★ ISBC is a free database matching service for small businesses, providing free sales leads and purchasing information. The ISBC database locates and matches suppliers and buyers with its database. Members are suppliers, buyers, agents, and distributors from around the world. Go to **www.isbc.com** for more information.

Let's Talk Business Network ★★★★ Good resources for entrepreneurs, especially if your Web browser has Real Audio capabilities. You can hear interviews with top people in business explaining many topics. Short directories, good business articles, and other features round out the mix (**www.ltbn.com**).

misc.entrepreneurs.moderated newsgroup ★★★★ This active group is *moderated*, so ads are banned. All you'll find is information—and lots of it—on topics important to entrepreneurs and small businesses. Full of questions, answers, and advice, this newsgroup is an excellent resource (**news:misc. entrepreneurs.moderated**).

remote-work email discussion group ★★★ Telecommuting is still new enough that businesses don't quite have it down pat yet. This email discussion group helps smooth the edges, both by answering questions of teleworkers and by helping managers figure out how to plan and launch telecommuting programs. To subscribe, email to **remote-work-request@unify.com** with the message **subscribe remote-work**.

Small Business Administration ★★★★★ One of the biggest sources—if not *the* biggest source—of information for entrepreneurs and small businesspeople. Check out the **Shareware Library of Programs to Run a Business**, more than 500 shareware and freeware programs for businesses, each with a very short description. Software is sorted into groups for "Starting," "Financing," "Managing," "Marketing," and "Running Your Business."

Read the latest *Commerce Business Daily*—today's issue, searchable! Each issue gives you more than 100 sales leads from U.S. government and NATO agencies, arranged by product/service categories. *CBD* normally costs $200 a year to receive online, but you can get it free here. A section called **Financing Your Business** gives you sources for SBA loans, venture capital, surety bonds, *Directory of Small Business Lending Reported by Commercial Banks* (the complete book online), and loan application forms you can download and print. For these resources and many more, set your Web browser to **www. sbaonline.sba.gov**.

Small Business Advancement National Center ★★★★ This nonprofit educational organization is an excellent resource. You'll find hundreds of articles, industry profiles, and other publications available nowhere else. The "Bulletins" section contains the SBA Low-Documentation Loan Program, the SBA Greenline Revolving Line of Credit, and a directory of export hotline numbers. The "Proceedings" section provides hundreds of papers on every aspect of small business, most available here only. You'll find information on research, accounting, importing, exporting, and other topics. Use the search engine, or browse the stupefyingly-long directory of titles. Items in the growing "Publications" section range from terrific to outdated and obviously useless. A great find is the complete book *Exporting: A Practical Approach* by James Stewart. It's good, clearly-written and carefully-organized. No matter how small your business, you'll have an idea how to export when you finish *Exporting's* 20 chapters. Another gem is *Breaking into the Trade Game: Exporting.* If you're looking for financing, a good find is *Bankable Deals: A Question and Answer Guide to Trade Finance for U.S. Small Business.* When all else fails, try the "Information and Business Counseling Request Form," where staff from the Center will answer your questions (**www.sbaer.uca.edu/index.html**).

Telecommuting Resources Guide ★★★★ This book by Pacific Bell is a very good how-to guide both for teleworkers and for company managers. Appendices give you forms to evaluate a project, choose workers, choose managers, evaluate workers, schedule, analyze cost/benefit ratios, monitor security, and more. Go to **www.pacbell.com/products/business/general/telecommuting/ tcguide/index.html** for more information.

Telecommuting, Teleworking, & Alternative Officing ★★★★ Updated monthly, this rich Web site links to more information on telecommuting than any other spot on the Net. You'll find a good FAQ on telecommuting here, and links to many publications and newsletters (**www.gilgordon.com**).

Special interests

This is my potpourri department: useful business resources that don't exactly fit in one of my other sections. Enjoy!

American Productivity & Quality Center ★★★ How well does your company do compared to other companies in your industry? Is your customer satisfaction level higher or lower than your competitors? Does your company process and ship an order faster or slower than the average? Does it cost you more or less than than average to handle that order? Is your returns rate higher or lower? Is your cost per purchase order higher or lower? If you don't know the answers to these questions, your company could be a ship heading for the rocks and you won't know it until after you crash. What you don't measure, you can't control. The process of measuring activities in your business so you can compare your results with other firms is called *benchmarking*. Benchmarks let you set realistic goals for improvement, and measure your progress (or problems). The American Productivity and Quality Center gives you information on how to start benchmarking, case histories, and more (**www.apqc.org**).

Bionomics Institute ★★★ If you haven't yet heard of bionomics, this could be a turning point in your career. Traditional schools of economics are based on classical physics, the perception of the world as a predictable clockwork mechanism. Old-style economists think in terms of "the economy as a machine" and "the business as a machine." This is not realistic. I don't know of one single business that runs with the boring predictability of a machine, and I'll bet you don't, either. Bionomics rejects the clockwork theory. Instead, it bases economic principles on evolutionary biology. Bionomics sees the economy as an evolving ecosystem. Each business works to survive in its industry in the same way individual plants and animals work to survive in their surroundings. Visit this site to find out more. For a quick introduction, click on "What Is Bionomics?" on the home page. It will take you to "Bionomics 101" by Michael Rothschild. Go to **www.bionomics.org**.

Condition-Based Maintenance ★★ For people who monitor, diagnose, and maintain plant machinery, Johns Hopkins University presents a small directory of resources and a small library of online articles. The best part is that if you have a question on this subject, you can email an expert for information at **www.jhuapl.edu/aero/cbm**.

Craighead's Business Travel Library ★★★ Look up your destination country and find figures and facts about business travel—even suggested per diems for different cities (**www.craighead.com/intro/welcome.htm**).

Dual-Use Marketplace ★★★★ This oddly-named site is an unusual resource. It is a place where companies buy and sell new manufacturing technologies and new product ideas, a site where you can purchase and market licenses to use technologies, such as processes, software innovations, or equipment designs. Set your Web browser to **www.crimson.com/market**.

Europages ★★★ A directory of more than 150,000 companies in almost 30 European companies, plus European economics data. Available in English, French, German, Spanish, and Italian. Go to **www.europages.com**.

Gateway Japan ★★★★ This is an important site for anyone doing business with Japan (**www.gwjapan.com**). Much material here is available in English nowhere else, including Japanese government procurement announcements. You'll find more than 10,000 documents here, including books, directories, and links to other Japan resources with descriptions. The site is updated weekly. Some material is in Japanese, but Gateway Japan's unique search engine lets you search in *both languages*. You can enter a word in English, and find all mentions of it in both English and Japanese. You can enter a word in Japanese and do the same. Much information here is available for anyone, but membership (which is currently free) lets you reach much more.

Great Lakes Hay List ★ As an example of how almost every kind of business can use the Internet for buying and selling, here's an online hay market. Farmers advertise hay crops for sale and buyers post messages wanting to purchase hay. Email to **almanac@wisplan.uwex.edu**. Leave the "Subject:" line of your message blank, and for the body, type **send haylist catalog**.

History of Economic Thought ★★ This library of historic economics books gives you the complete text of famous works by 65 authors. (**http://socserv2.socsci.mcmaster.ca/~econ/ugcm/3ll3**) You can read *An Inquiry into the Nature and Causes of the Wealth of Nations* by Adam Smith, and the politically opposite works of Karl Marx. You'll also find Daniel Defoe's *Giving Alms no Charity* and *Employing the Poor*, Charles Babbage's *Economy of Machinery and Manufactures*, Vilfredo Pareto's *New Theories of Economics*, works by Toynbee, J.S. Mill, Hume, Hobbes, Malthus, and others. (Note: The last part of the URL is **/3LL3**, but with lower case els.)

International Business Resources on the WWW ★★★★ Michigan State University provides a large index of global business resources, with good descriptions explaining the value of each. You'll find overall information here, and you can also look up resources according to what country or region interests you at **http://ciber.bus.msu.edu/busres.htm**.

International Trade Network email list ★★★ Daily email on trade opportunities and import-export trends. Email to **majordomo@world.std.com** with the "Subject:" of your message **info intltrade**. Leave the body of your message blank.

Krislyn's Strictly Business Site ★★★ A well-chosen collection of links with information for businesspeople, covering almost every area of business. Links lack descriptions, but are usually rewarding (**www.krislyn.com/sites.html**).

Legal List Internet Desk Reference ★★★★★ The complete desk of this book by Erik J. Heels, an extraordinary comprehensive guide to legal resources online (**www.lcp.com**).

Michael Trick's Operations Research Page ★★★ Michael Trick, a professor at Carnegie Mellon University, created this directory with links to aspects of operations research. His helpful, short comments help you decide which resources will be most rewarding to explore. You'll find software, online journals, courses, job opportunities, leading experts in the field, papers, and other resources (**http://mat.gsia.cmu.edu**). Don't miss Trick's "Pick of the Week."

Multimedia Law Repositories and Related Links ★★★ Quick guide to Web sites with legal information about the multimedia and entertainment (**www. oikoumene.com/oikoumene/mmlinks.html**).

National Association of Female Executives ★★★★ One of the most helpful sites for businesswomen, with a good list of resources at **www.nafe.com**.

Offshore ★★★ A good electronic newsletter on offshore assets protection. It covers topics for businesspeople who have investments or operations outside their home country. Go to **www.euro.net/innovation/Offshore.html**.

Pointcast ★★★★ This free software, available in Windows and Mac versions, replaces your boring old screen saver with the latest financial news, stock quotes, and information. Pointcast is still a screen saver, but it's alive. It connects to the Net to bring you business news and financial indices. Set your Web browser to **www.pointcast.com**.

Public Domain Electronic Digest ★★ Twice a month, this newsletter gives you a short catalog of works from literature, the theater, and music that have passed into public domain, including descriptions. To subscribe, email to **nruggles@panix.com** with the "Subject:" line reading **subscribe PDED** and your message blank.

SoftInfo ★★★ A searchable database of information about more than 16,000 business software products (not shareware, but commercial products you can buy) for computers from PCs to mainframes (**www.info-partners.com/softinfo**).

Software Forum ★★★★ If you are in the software business, you may find the Software Forum the most profitable site on the Net. Originally called Software Entrepreneurs Forum, this nonprofit organization is devoted to the business side of the software game. It gives you access to resources no other place can match: insights from hundreds of experts who have built multimillion dollar software companies. No matter what your question, you'll get answers here from seasoned industry pros. At the Software Forum Web site, you can tap that huge reservoir of experience by joining an email discussion group or two. You have more than a dozen to choose from, categorized according to industry topics. Remember that the pros on these groups discuss business how-tos, not programming issues. You'll participate in discussions via email, but you must visit this Web site to subscribe. While you visit, poke around at some of this site's other offerings. You'll find news about software technology, computer and communications technology, business management, industry legal issues, finance, software marketing, and, of course, software sales. Set your Web browser to **www.softwareforum.org**.

Streamlining Procurement through Electronic Commerce ★★ This book presents the blueprint for the federal government to implement EDI and electronic commerce in its own purchasing departments. Useful if you sell to Uncle Sam, and for large corporations looking to purchase online. Go to **http://snad.ncsl.nist.gov/dartg/edi/arch.html** for more information.

Teaching Information Systems with Cases ★★★ This Web site is for Information Services managers, but don't let that scare you. What you have is its section on business case histories, which gives you a directory of "case repositories" all over the Web. You'll find links to several archives of case histories, especially about business use of the Internet (**http://ashley.ivey.uwo.ca/~isworld/iscases.html**).

Telephone Directories on the Web ★★★ This handy page lists all known telephone directories—both white pages and yellow pages—on the Web from everyplace in the world. Most are briefly described, so you get an idea whether a book has the information you need or not (**www.contractjobs.com/tel**).

Texas Marketplace ★★★ Now, Texas is a big state—they say it could use Rhode Island for a watch fob—so the Texas Department of Commerce built a Web site to match. Whether you want to plant your spread in Texas, or if you'd rather buy and sell to Texas wheeler-dealers, mosey on down to this Web site. It's free, but you must register to use the best parts. You'll find more than 30 business directories here! (I told you it was big.) The Texas Manufacturing Assistance Center is a very good directory of manufacturing resources on the Net, with clear descriptions of each. A directory called High-Tech Texas gives you a database of more than 2,000 companies in biotech, electronics, computing, optics, and telecommunications. *Hoover's Texas 500* is a database of the 500 largest companies headquartered in Texas. Market Exchange lets you buy and sell wholesale quantities—carloads and containerloads, mostly of commodities. You'll also find sales leads from Texas government bid requests and the U.S. Department of Commerce at **www.texas-one.org**.

Upside **★★★★** This is a great spot for managers and investors in high-tech companies. *Upside* is a monthly magazine that covers technology investing and venture capitalism. You'll find *all* of the feature stories and columns of the current issue of *Upside* on its Web site—even the cartoons. The insightful investigative reporting is excellent. And you'll find a searchable archive of back issues. And from this Net site, you can get a free subscription to the print version! You'll also find a directory of industry conferences, links to information for high-tech businesses, a short list of industry associations, stock prices for high-tech companies (live, but with a 15-minute delay), and a "Book of Lists" with financial and stock information on high-tech corporations. Set your Web browser to **www.upside.com**.

Washington Technology Online **★★★** A good resource for managers of high-tech companies in the Washington, D.C. area. Read online news and search databases of past articles and online resources. Sign up for email notices of news for high-tech businesses at **www.wtonline.com**.

Women's Web ★★★★ Includes the sites for the magazines *Working Woman* and *Working Mother*, with articles from the magazines, plus information and databases not included in the print versions (**www.womweb.com**).

World Postal Codes ★★★ Almost one-stop shopping for Postal code and ZIP code resources, plus other useful links from international direct mail expert Graham Rhind (**www.execulink.com/~louisew/postal-links.htm**).

ZIP Codes and Postal Codes ★★★ A few goodies that Mr. Rhind missed. The bar code fonts for Windows can help your business qualify for lower U.S. postal rates.
Canadian code anatomy: **www.westminster.ca/anatomy1.htm**
Czech Republic: **infox.eunet.cz/cgi-bin/gw_cis.pl/czinfo/psc_z/c**
European postal codes: **www.organik.uni-erlangen.de/info/LISTS/post_codes-europe.html**
Demographics for U.S. ZIP codes: **http://elca.org/re/zipnet.html**
U.S. ZIP code bar code fonts: **http://ancho.ucs.indiana/edu/FAQ/Windows/A6.5.5.html**
Yahoo's Postal Information: **www.yahoo.com/Reference/Postal_Information**

Improve your Web site

Here's one final resource, useful for any business with a Web site. If you'd like more resources, visit my site at **www.emery.com**.

Emery's Web Site Checklist ★★★★ This is a checklist you print out and use to improve your Web site. I first presented it at a lecture. Afterwards, one attendee said he used the checklist to evaluate his site, spent four days tweaking it, and increased his annual sales by a quarter of a million dollars. I can't promise the same for your site, but the checklist does catch missing details that can improve your response. There's no magic to it, just the accumulation of getting many small things right. It's divided into four sections, checking things that are important to your overall site, then things that are important for individual pages, your home page, and your sales order page. Set your Web browser to **www.emery.com/bizstuff/list.htm**.

Index